# THE POLITICS OF PLUNDER

## Books by Doug Bandow

*U.S. Aid to the Developing World: A Free Market Agenda* (editor, 1985)
*Unquestioned Allegiance* (1986)
*Protecting the Environment: A Free Market Strategy* (editor, 1986)
*Beyond Good Intentions: A Biblical View of Politics* (1988)
*Human Resources and Defense Manpower* (1989)

# THE POLITICS OF PLUNDER

## Misgovernment in Washington

**Doug Bandow**

**Transaction Publishers**
New Brunswick (U.S.A.) and London (U.K.)

Second printing 1990

Copyright © 1990 by Transaction Publishers.
New Brunswick, New Jersey 08903

Library of Congress Catalog Number: 89-5219
ISBN: 0-88738-309-2
Printed in the United States of America

Library of Congress Cataloging-in-Publication Data

Bandow, Doug.
    The politics of plunder : misgovernment in Washington / by Doug
Bandow.
        p.   cm.
    ISBN 0-88738-309-2
    1. Libertarianism—United States.   2. United States—Politics and
government.   I. Title.
JC599.U5B36   1990
320.5'12—dc20                                                    89-5219
                                                                    CIP

*For my loving family: the Bandows,*
*Wicals, Williamsons, and Mills*

# Contents

Acknowledgments                                                        xv
Introduction                                                           xix

**I.  Whose Life Is It Anyway?**                                        1

**Do Values Matter?**                                                   3
  1. When the Invaders Come                                   3
  2. The Next Hungarian Revolution                            5
  3. Remembering the Holocaust                                6
  4. Who Should Teach Values?                                 8

**Government by What Values?**                                         11
  5. America's 2 Different Constitutions                     11
  6. What Happened to the Concept of Theft?                  13
  7. Games Politicians Play                                  15
  8. Exploiting National Resources                          17
  9. Government as God                                       18
 10. A Little Tolerance, Please                                   20
 11. Just Another Sorry Attempt to Legislate Personal Views       22

**Does Freedom Matter?**                                              25
 12. The Right to Risk                                            25
 13. Uncle Sam as National Nanny                                  27
 14. A Fear of Ideas                                              29
 15. Economic Liberty and Democracy                              30
 16. The Real Story of Thanksgiving                               32
 17. Liberation Theology's False Prophets                        34
 18. God and Mammon                                               36

**II.  The Political Game**                                           41

**Sin City**                                                          43
 19. Let Washington-Bashing Continue                             43
 20. Hysteria Over PACmania                                      45
 21. Power Can Be Fun                                            48

**Do Elections Matter?**                                    57
22. America's House of Lords                                57
23. In Praise of the Nonvoter                              59
24. The Unnecessary Debates                                61
25. The Turkey Ballot                                      62

**Interest Group Heaven**                                  65
26. Preaching and Politics                                 65
27. Taking Evangelicals for a Ride in the Stars            67
28. Subverting Democracy                                   69
29. Celebrating Government                                 70
30. This Energy Lobby Can't Stop Crying Wolf               72
31. Robbing Banks—Legally                                  75
32. The Foreign Aid Network                                77
33. The Politics of Drought                                79
34. Businessmen as Born-Again Budget Cutters               81
35. Businessmen against Free Enterprise                    83
36. The Way Washington Works—But Shouldn't                 85
37. The Firing of Il Gucci                                 86
38. A Corporate Lobby Pulls Its Punches                    88

**One for All and All for One**                            93
39. One-Party System                                       93
40. Repudiating the Reagan Revolution                      95
41. The Reagan Counterrevolution                           97
42. Your Congress at Work                                 104
43. The Spending Problem in Profile                       107
44. Senator Establishment                                 110
45. Populism as Opportunism                               112
46. Senator Byrd's Pork Barrel Bid                        113
47. Al Gore's Dairy Sellout                               115
48. *Man of the House:* O'Neill's Destructive Legacy      117

**III.  The Federal Behemoth**                            123

**Deficits Forever**                                      125
49. The Budget Revolution That Wasn't                     125
50. We Need an Economic Bill of Rights                    133
51. Mandate a Balanced Budget                             135
52. Budgetary Chaos in Congress                           137
53. A Simple Solution to the Debt                         139
54. Balancing the Budget                                  141
55. 7 Spending Cuts Liberals Could Love                   143

**Endless Subsidies**                                           145
56. Uncle Sam's Free Lunch                                      145
57. Merchant Armada Sinks Oceans of Money                       147
58. Another Handout for Big Business                            150
59. Close Down the EDA                                          152
60. The SBA—Slash Business Assistance                           154
61. The Sack of Washington                                      156
62. The NASA White Elephant                                     158
63. Mass Transit Robbery                                        160
64. Subsidizing the Growth of Government                        162

**Farming for Dollars**                                         165
65. America's Permanent Dependent Class                         165
66. A Sweet Deal Gone Sour                                      174
67. The Sunflower Crisis                                        176
68. Uncle Sam's Legalized Larceny                               178
69. Subsidizing Rural America                                   180
70. Why 2 Billion Oranges Will Rot in the Fields                183

**Selling Off the State**                                       187
71. Privatizing Our Way to Savings                              187
72. Parochialism Reigns                                         189
73. Sell Amtrak                                                 190
74. Postal Service Doesn't Deserve Monopoly                     192

**Taxing Problems**                                             195
75. The Battle over Taxes                                       195
76. Repeal the Withholding Tax                                  197
77. Truth-in-Taxing                                             198

**The Regulatory Monster**                                      201
78. The Excesses of Big Government                              201
79. The Terrible Ten                                            204
80. Three Cheers for Airline Deregulation                       212
81. Federal Appliance Standards: Inefficient at Best            213
82. A Kinder, Gentler CAFE Standard                             215
83. Banking's Regulatory Crisis                                 217
84. Abolish the Federal Censorship Commission                   219
85. Drop the Cable Monopoly                                     221

**The Energy Uncrisis**                                         225
86. Keep Uncle Sam Out of the Energy Business                   225
87. Doomed Again                                                227
88. Deregulate Natural Gas                                      229

89. Let's Lease the Oceans                                      231
90. Congress's Nuclear Agenda                                   232

**Cleaning Up America**                                         235
91. The Clean Water Pork Barrel                                 235
92. Toxic Solutions to Toxic Problems                           237
93. Preserving America's Wilderness                             239
94. Sacred Cows Home on the Range                               241

**Free Trade is Fair Trade**                                    243
95. The Competitiveness Scam                                    243
96. Free the Japanese Autos                                     245
97. Drop the Steel Quotas                                       247
98. Kill the Textile Bill                                       249
99. No Protection for Semiconductors                            250
100. Casein for America                                         252
101. Is Dukakis Really as Dumb as He Sounds?                    254

**Market Manipulation**                                         257
102. Repeal the Antitrust Laws                                  257
103. Curbing Raiders is Bad for Business                        259
104. The LBO Bugaboo                                            261
105. Decriminalize Insider Trading                              263

IV. **Judging America**                                         265

**The Judicial Imperative**                                     267
106. Making Judges Accountable                                  267
107. Bork and Original Intent                                   274
108. Judicial Imperialism                                       276
109. Reaping the Judicial Whirlwind                             278
110. End Life Tenure for Judges                                 280

**The Lawyers' Game**                                           283
111. Save the Exclusionary Rule                                 283
112. The Nine Lives of the LSC                                  285
113. Lawyers v. Consumers: A Legal Monopoly?                    287

V. **The Helping Hand of Uncle Sam**                            293

**Jobless by Decree**                                           295
114. Destroying Jobs the Government Way                         295
115. Preserving the Freedom to Work at Home                     297
116. It's Time to Repeal Davis-Bacon                            299

117. Putting People Out of Work                                    300
118. Congress's Job-Killing Attack on Business                     302
119. Paying for the Eternal Free Lunch                             304
120. Child-Care Politics                                           306

**Whose Health?**                                                  309
121. A Failed Attempt at Political Blackmail                       309
122. The Duty to Die—and Pay                                       311
123. Dismantle the Doctors' Monopoly                               313

**Education for Sale**                                             315
124. The Money Illusion                                            315
125. Making Students Pay Their Fair Share                          317

**Homes for America**                                              321
126. How to Create a Housing Crisis: A Primer for
     Bureaucrats                                                   321
127. Challenging Rent Control                                      330
128. Sell Off Uncle Sam's Public Housing                          332

**The Consumer Protection Racket**                                 335
129. Consumer Fraud                                                335
130. Help Consumers Don't Need                                     337
131. Legalize Saccharin                                            339
132. Don't Ban Cigarette Ads                                       341

**Anti-Social Security**                                           345
133. Sun City for Social Security                                  345
134. The False Promise of Head Start                               351
135. Hands Across America—or in America's Pockets?                 353
136. The New Year: A Time to Give                                  355

**Civil Rights for Whom?**                                         357
137. New Directions for Black America                              357
138. Racial Quotas for Congress?                                   359
139. Reconsidering *Runyon*                                        360
140. The Fraudulent Civil Rights Act of 1987                       362
141. This Ruling Threatens the Rights of Women                     364
142. Comparable Worth is Worthless                                 365
143. The Gay Issue: Double-Edged Rights                            367

**Social Potpourri**                                               369
144. Should Society Condone Abortion as "Convenient"?              369
145. When to Resist?                                               371
146. Fighting the Porn Wars                                        373

147. RICO vs. Porn: Penalties More Shocking Than the
     Crime                                                    375
148. Is Death the Answer?                                     378
149. Gun Control: The Enduring Liberal Panacea               380
150. Refocus the Drug War                                     382
151. An Honorable CO in the War on Drugs                     383
152. Buying Culture                                           385
153. Moral Rights for Whom?                                   387
154. Sports Play in Fields of Government                     389


VI.  **The Global Playground**                               393

     **The Bipartisan Charade**                               395
155. "Outside of Politics"                                    395

     **When to Intervene?**                                   399
156. Using Force Abroad                                       399
157. The Legacy of Vietnam                                    401
158. Fewer Guns for Fewer Commitments                        403
159. What Next for NATO: Get the Superpowers Out of
     Europe!                                                  405
160. Cut Korea's Umbilical Cord                               413
161. Reagan's Senseless Persian Gulf War                     414
162. Break Relations with South Africa                       416

     **Leaving the Third World Alone**                        419
163. Forging a Policy of Benign Detachment                   419
164. Learning the Limits of Intervention                     421
165. Good Riddance to Mozambique's Machel                    423
166. Preparing for a New Jungle War?                          425
167. Good People, Bad Cause                                   426

     **The Terrorist Temptation**                             429
168. Reagan Takes on Libya—Sort Of                           429

     **Bombs Away**                                           433
169. Two Cheers for SDI                                       433
170. Ban Nuclear Tests                                        435

     **A Cold Draft**                                         437
171. Mercenary Morality                                      437
172. America Has No Need for a New Draft                     440
173. It's Time to Drop Draft Registration                   443

**War in Color**                                               447
174. Journalists at War                                        447

**Disunited Nations**                                          451
175. No Longer a Baby at Age 40                                451
176. The Dangerous Side of the UN                              453
177. America Turns Away the World of Refugees                  455
178. How Many Embassies Do We Need?                            458

**Foreign Aid or Hindrance?**                                  461
179. Cut Foreign Aid                                           461
180. Foreign Aid Prescriptions                                 463
181. The Marshall Plan Myth                                    469
182. The Foreign Aid Panacea                                   471
183. Starving the Third World                                  473
184. Mengistu's Policies Responsible for Famine                475
185. Aid Money That Just Buys Guns                             477
186. U.S. Aid is a Costly Disaster                             481
187. Subsidizing our Adversaries                               485
188. No More Aid for Mobuto                                    487

**Robbery at the International Development Banks**              489
189. Throwing Good Money after Debt                            489
190. Reagan's IDA Boondoggle                                   492
191. Banking's International "Black Hole"                       494

Index                                                          497

# Acknowledgments

There are many people who deserve thanks for helping to put together this collection. Most obvious are Irving Louis Horowitz and his colleagues at Transaction Publishers, for agreeing to take on the project, and Edward H. Crane, president of the Cato Institute, for making it a Cato book and backing my work since 1982. Other Cato staffers also warrant recognition: David Lampo and Kent Lytle helped bring this book to fruition; Sandra McCluskey and Julie Stewart have helped promote my efforts; Greg Taylor researched some of the topics that ended up on these pages; and David Boaz and Ted Galen Carpenter have given me the opportunity to write on a number of different subjects.

Moreover, Charlie Ohl and Nanette Wiser of Copley News Service have marketed my column for six years, whereas a number of editors—too many to name—at a variety of magazines and newspapers have run my articles and permitted me to reprint them here. Among those who have been particularly encouraging are Virginia Postrel at *Reason,* Tim Ferguson at *The Wall Street Journal,* Kyle Crichton at *The New York Times,* and Ken Grubbs at the *Orange County Register.*

Last but not least are members of my family who have stood behind me as I embarked on my seemingly quixotic quest to be a writer, policy analyst, political activist, and general troublemaker. Their love and support has helped me through the bad as well as the good times. I not only love them, but I like them too: my parents, Don and Donna Bandow, who have accepted my often idiosyncratic views with little protest; my sister, brother-in-law, and nephew, Shelly, Birkley, and David Wical, who prove there is more to life than politics; my uncle, aunt, and cousins, the Williamsons, who provide a little ideological balance within the family; and my other uncle and aunt, the Mills, who demonstrate how family ties can transcend geography.

The following publishers have generously given permission to reprint articles included in this work:

*The American Legion Magazine:*
   "The Excesses of Big Government" (April 1987).

*The American Spectator:*
   "Sun City for Social Security" (October 1985).
   "Foreign Aid Prescriptions" (September 1986).

*The Chicago Tribune:*
   "Mandate a Well-Balanced Budget" (April 1984).
   "A Simple Solution to the Debt" (June 11, 1985).
   "Let Washington-Bashing Continue" (January 20, 1987).

*City Paper:*
   "The Reagan Counter-Revolution" (June 6, 1986).

*Consumers' Research:*
   "Lawyers v. Consumers: A Legal Monopoly?" (June 1985).

*Human Events:*
   "Should Society Condone Abortion as 'Convenient?' " (December 3, 1977).
   "Mengistu's Policies Responsible for Famine" (April 12, 1986).
   " 'Man of the House': O'Neill's Destructive Legacy" (March 5, 1988).

*Inquiry:*
   "Consumer Fraud" (May 1983).
   "Save the Exclusionary Rule" (July 1983).
   "One-Party System" (August 1983).
   "Outside of Politics" (March–April 1984).

*Libertarian Review:*
   How to Create a Housing Crisis" (May 1980)

*The New Republic:*
   "Mercenary Morality" (October 19, 1987).

*The New York Times:*
   "Another Handout for Big Business" (August 21, 1983).
   "End Life Tenure for Judges" (September 6, 1986).
   "Break Relations with South Africa" (February 27, 1987).
   "It's Time to Drop Draft Registration" (July 23, 1987).
   "7 Spending Cuts Liberals Could Love" (December 1, 1987).
   "Curbing Raiders Is Bad for Business" (February 7, 1988).
   "Cut South Korea's Umbilical Cord" (March 31, 1988). Copyright © 1983/86/87/88 by the New York Times Company. Reprinted by permission.

*Policy Review:*
"The Terrible Ten" (Spring 1985).
"God & Mammon" (Spring 1986).
"America's Permanent Dependent Class" (Spring 1987).

*Reason:*
"The Budget Revolution That Wasn't" (May 1985). Reprinted, with permission, from the May 1985 issue of REASON magazine. Copyright © 1985 by the Reason Foundation, 2716 Ocean Park Blvd., Suite 1062, Santa Monica, CA 90405.
"Your Congress at Work" (April 1988). Reprinted, with permission, from the April 1988 issue of REASON magazine. Copyright © 1988 by the Reason Foundation, 2716 Ocean Park Blvd., Suite 1062, Santa Monica, CA 90405.
"What Next for NATO? Get the Superpowers Out of Europe!" (April 1989). Reprinted with permission, from the April 1989 issue of REASON magazine. Copyright © 1989 by the Reason Foundation, 2716 Ocean Park Blvd., Suite 1062, Santa Monica, CA 90405.

*Register:*
"Just Another Sorry Attempt to Legislate Personal Views" (March 10, 1983).
"The Dangerous Side of the UN" (May 18, 1983).
"US Aid Is a Costly Business Disaster" (March 13, 1988).
"Throwing Good Money after Debt" (November 20, 1988).

*USA Today:*
"Making Judges Accountable" (January 1988). Reprinted from USA TODAY MAGAZINE, January. Copyright 1988 by the Society for the Advancement of Education.

*The Wall Street Journal:*
"Subsidizing Rural America" May 9, 1984.
"The Spending Problem in Profile" (April 16, 1985).
"This Energy Lobby Can't Stop Crying Wolf" (October 8, 1985).
"A Corporate Lobby Pulls Its Punches" (July 23, 1986).
"Federal Alliance Standards: Inefficient at Best" (February 19, 1987).
"Businessmen as Born-Again Budget-Cutters" (November 19, 1987).
"Merchant Armada Sinks Oceans of Money" (September 12, 1988).
"Aid Money That Just Buys Guns" (June 14, 1988).
"RICO vs. Porn: Penalties More Shocking than the Crime" (December 30, 1988). Reprinted with permission of the Wall Street Journal © 1989 Dow Jones & Company, Inc.

*The Washington Post:*
   "The Gay Issue: Double Edged Rights" (May 23, 1979).
   "Games Politicians Play" (April 25, 1984).
   "Why 2 Billion Oranges Will Rot in the Fields" (August 9, 1985).
   "Preaching and Politics" (August 3, 1988).

All other articles courtesy of Copley News Service and *The Christian Science Monitor.*

# Introduction: The Way the World Works

> But whereas, at the time of the Versailles Treaty, most intelligent people believed that an enlarged state could increase the sum total of human happiness, by the 1980s the view was held by no one outside of a small, diminishing and dispirited band of zealots. The experiment had been tried in innumerable ways; and it had failed in nearly all of them. The state had proved itself an insatiable spender, an unrivalled waster. Indeed, in the twentieth century it had also proved itself the great killer of all time. . . .
>
> What was not clear was whether the fall from grace of the state would likewise discredit its agents, the activist politicians, whose phenomenal rise in numbers and authority was the most important human development of modern times. . . . At the democratic end of the spectrum, the political zealot offered New Deals, Great Societies and Welfare States; at the totalitarian end, cultural revolutions; always and everywhere, Plans. They marched across the decades and the hemispheres: mountebanks, charismatics, *exaltes,* secular saints, mass murderers, united by their belief that politics was the cure for human ills. . . . By the 1980s, the new ruling class was still, by and large, in charge; but no longer so confident. Most of them, whether alive or dead, were now execrated in their own homelands. Was it possible to hope that the "age of politics," like the "age of religion" before it, was now drawing to a close?[1]

As the century enters its ninetieth year, there is no more important political question. The most interesting struggles lie within the disintegrating Communist empire, as the rulers of the Soviet Union, China, Vietnam, and the Eastern European states grope for ways to forestall economic collapse without yielding too much political power. The progress so far, in terms of both economic and political liberalization, is dramatic but fragile. And in the end there is little that we—in the United States and, more broadly, the "free world"—can do other than wish those peoples well.

Yet even the West, despite its democratic and capitalistic heritage, still suffers from the deleterious consequences of this century's veritable deification of the state. And if the United States has never suffered from the sort of totalitarian rule that long characterized the Soviet Union, neither do we see the same level of popular reaction against past abuses. Indeed, though of late the expansion of government has slowed under a variety of more conservative leaders—Ronald Reagan in the United States, Margaret Thatcher, Helmut Kohl, and others abroad—the state has not shrunk. Whether the statist and collectivist waves have truly ebbed is yet to be seen.

Until they do, our freedom and prosperity will remain constantly at risk. For America's increased reliance on politics as the solution to every problem and alleged problem has turned envy into policy, stripped individuals and communities of their traditional social responsibilities, destroyed economic opportunities for the disadvantaged, promoted unjust foreign intervention, and undermined private moral and spiritual values. The solution to so pervasive a crisis will not come from a little tinkering here or there—whether a reduction in the rate of government spending, the devolution of one program or another from the federal to state governments, the creation of a few tax loopholes, or something equally modest.

Instead, what is required is a redefinition of the relationship of the individual to the state. The purpose of government should not be to rearrange economic and social relationships to fit the selfish preferences of influential minorities or even majorities. Not only is there no moral justification for systematic income redistribution, but the process inevitably breaks down, enriching not the poor but a ''new class'' of politicians, bureaucrats, lobbyists, and interest groups. Attempts to enforce ''social justice,'' an empty phrase that has been used to rationalize all manner of social engineering schemes, usually end up even more tyrannical, remolding private consensual conduct based on the whimsical desires of whoever happens to hold political power. Government involvement should require not only the presence of some pressing need that genuinely concerns the ''general welfare,'' a constitutional phrase that has been tortured to justify every new federal program but also a reasonable, indeed, compelling, expectation that public sector failure will not exceed the private sector shortcomings to be addressed.

This caution—based on a recognition of the fallibility of human beings, the inefficiency of human institutions, and people's tendency to abuse power—should also extend to government activities beyond the nation's shores. The justifications for intervention abroad are many: to promote development, protect American trade, defend allies, contain communism, spread democracy, and so on. Yet in practice U.S. policy has degenerated into a kind of crude realpolitik, whereby Washington subsidizes corrupt Third World dictatorships and wealthy industrialized states alike to maintain its influence. If isolationist Fortress America is not the best model today, neither is interventionist Pax Americana. The United States should encourage free economic and cultural interchange around the globe. But before it attempts to control events in other countries, Washington needs to consider what is just for foreign peoples; it also needs to make an honest assessment about what is actually in the interests of the American polity and not just the influential elites that directly benefit from such policies as foreign aid.

The result of this increased skepticism toward state action in all areas would be to move us back toward the limited governmental structure originally established more than 200 years ago by America's founders. Of course, it has become fashionable to deride their "simplistic" system, created as it was for a small, primarily agricultural, nation. Yet the problems of interest groups, concentrated political power, and government incompetence and injustice are eternal. Indeed, as society has grown more complex and the tools of coercion more deadly, the danger of misbegotten interference by government has grown even worse: That indeed, is probably the most important lesson of Stalin's collectivization, Hitler's Final Solution, Mao's Cultural Revolution, and even Roosevelt's milder New Deal, which swept away judicial protection of many individual rights, incarcerated more than 110,000 Japanese-Americans, closed the door to Jewish refugees fleeing Europe, surreptitiously moved the United States into war, raided the budget for political pork, cartelized American agriculture, and established a tradition of state economic control that impoverishes the nation to this day.

Is the age of politics drawing to a close? Yes, but only because statism has failed so badly in so many ways. This century has proved—in a far more costly manner than was imaginable before man demonstrated how destructive could be the power of modern technology in the hands of the all-powerful state—that politics does not offer the solution for the human condition. And though the ruling elites that once treated politics as religion have now abandoned their faiths, they are not yet prepared to yield power voluntarily. Thus if the first nine decades of this century have been devoted to the rise and fall of collectivist ideologies, the final one is likely to involve the fight to bring political systems around the globe into conformity with the new, freer intellectual paradigm. It is this struggle that this book is intended to address.

Part I reviews the big issues—man's relation to the state, the role of values, the purpose of constitutional government, and the religious basis of political and economic freedom. Though collectivism has held sway most of this century, it is the ideal of individual freedom and dignity that lies at the base of modern civilization. Against ancient statism rose Christianity, which marched across the Roman world preaching that people were made in the image of God and were individually responsible for their actions. Centuries later, the spread of classical liberalism encouraged a revolt against royal absolutism, mercantilism, and imperialism and helped enshrine the political sovereignty of the individual. A return today to the religious and philosophical values that provided the original foundation for the American republic would help this country secure a more prosperous and just future.

Part II examines how the American political process operates in practice. In sum, the game is rigged against the broad "national interest." Most performers in the political arena—legislators, bureaucrats, lobbyists—are driven by a desire to amass power, fame, and money. To them policy is important because it brings wealth and influence, not because it promotes prosperity or justice. A congressional district is now safer than a seat on the Soviet Communist Party Central Committee; most issues degenerate into interest group slugfests; and the theoretical differences between conservatives and liberals, Republicans and Democrats, and other groups usually dissolve in a bipartisan race to the federal trough.

Part III focuses on Uncle Sam as Sugar Daddy and malicious meddler. The federal budget is virtually unlimited, growing year by year and administration by administration. Virtually no interest group goes without some subsidy; the farmer's lobby is perhaps the greediest group of fiscal predators. The government conducts all manner of activities that would be better left to private enterprises. Uncle Sam uses the tax and regulatory systems for the same ends, whereas federal interference in the fields of energy, environment, international trade, and economic affairs has proved equally disastrous.

Part IV considers the activities of the federal government's least understood branch, the judiciary. The courts were originally intended to be bulwarks of liberty, to stand between the individual and the state. But since the New Deal, judges have become active participants in the socalled New Class, pushing to extend the reach of government. The legal game, like the political game, is also rigged, a monopoly controlled by the providers that stifles competition, hikes costs, and abrogates freedom of choice.

Part V grapples with the social issues, particularly the ways in which the government creates unemployment, reduces access to health care, undermines the educational system, creates a housing crisis, impoverishes consumers, promotes social insecurity, violates real civil rights, and tramples over any number of basic individual rights while claiming to be helping its citizens. It is in this area that the phrase, "I'm from the government and I'm here to help you," takes on special meaning.

Finally, Part VI examines America's global activities. U.S. foreign policy represents domestic policymaking writ large: bipartisan corruption, deleterious intervention, and endless subsidies. America's global alliance network forces it to risk the lives and wealth of its citizens to protect a score of populous and prosperous states. Meddling in the Third World has put the United States on the side of injustice by subsidizing a variety of tyrants who claim to be friends of Washington. And foreign aid, both bilateral and multilateral, has lived up to the old saw: It takes money from poor people in rich countries and gives it to rich people in poor countries.

All told, there is much to criticize and little to commend about the activities of the U.S. government at all levels. Alas, that is probably an inevitable consequence of the rise of statism. For the good intentions of those who have looked to politics for solutions to genuine—indeed, often overwhelming—social problems have been subverted by the actions of the many others determined to use the authority of government for their own ends. As state power increased, the potential for using the public sector for private enrichment also expanded, along with the willingness of people to take advantage of their newfound opportunities. The result is a process that corrupts most of its participants, whatever their original purpose in playing the game.

It wasn't supposed to be this way when the country was founded more than 200 years ago. And it doesn't have to be that way in the future. But the path back is not a smooth one. If this book in some way helps recapture the philosophical tradition that recognizes freedom to be the highest political ideal, it will have achieved its purpose.

## Notes

1. Paul Johnson, *Modern Times: The World from the Twenties to the Eighties* (New York: Harper & Row, 1983), pp. 727–728.

# I. Whose Life is it Anyway?

# Do Values Matter?

## 1. When the Invaders Come

*September 6, 1984*

"In our time," declare ads for the new movie, "Red Dawn," "no foreign army has ever occupied American soil. Until now."

The film opens with an airborne assault on a small Colorado town by Soviet and Cuban troops, part of a general invasion of the United States. A portly teacher lecturing on the tactics of Genghis Khan is the first victim as the high school is overrun, but several students flee to the mountains and eventually become highly effective guerrillas.

"Red Dawn" has predictably inflamed Washington's political wars, with hawks like former Secretary of State Alexander Haig attending its premiere, and reviewers for such publications as the Washington Post ridiculing it. Yet the movie, despite its implausible premise and occasional ideological excesses, is surprisingly good. Not only is it an engaging action film with some genuine passion, but it also makes us think, "What if?"

What if we were invaded? What if we faced a totalitarian government, whether imposed from abroad or established within? Who would resist, like the students in "Red Dawn"? And who would colaborate, like the town's mayor, who turns in his own son?

Thankfully, most Americans have never had to make such a wrenching decision. But this choice is all too real for many people throughout the world. Anyone growing up in the Soviet Union, for example, must either go along with the system or defy it. Those who choose the latter course pay the price. Aleksandr Solzhenitsyn was expelled from his native land; Andrei Sakharov was sent into internal exile. Unnamed millions more have simply disappeared into the Gulag—forever.

Not all conflicts of conscience are political, of course. The Roman Empire periodically persecuted Christians, in an attempt to stamp out the growing threat to the state religion of a deified emperor. Thousands of

3

believers chose death—from crucifixion, lions and beheading—rather than throw incense on a pagan altar.

That many people find transcendent values worth dying for is something that should make us proud; that so many more do not should give us pause. What leads a person to cross over the line from collaborator or acquiescer, to resister?

Forty years ago in Nazi Germany a group of generals and other military officers who stepped across that line were going on trial before the People's Court, charged with the attempted assassination of Adolf Hitler the month before, in the famous July 20 plot. Their effort failed, of course, as did numerous plots the previous year; as a result, some 200 of Germany's finest perished.

Col. Claus von Stauffenberg, who planted the bomb, was shot immediately after the coup d'etat collapsed. Adm. Wilhelm Canaris, head of military intelligence, who also passed information to the British, was hung. Gen. Erwin Rommel, Germany's celebrated "Desert Fox," committed suicide. Most of the conspirators were tortured; some were filmed as they were hung with piano wire, for the benefit of Hitler and his entourage.

Other genuine heroes emerged to oppose that barbaric regime. Noted theologian and pastor Dietrich Bonhoeffer attempted to assist British intelligence; he was arrested in 1942 and hung as the thousand-year Reich collapsed in April 1945.

Perhaps the most naive resisters of all were Hans and Sophie Scholl, university students in Munich, who set up a group called the White Rose. Their activities consisted almost solely of passing out leaflets. Nevertheless, they were quickly arrested and hung.

What all of these victims had in common—and the trait shared by the human sacrifices in China, Chile, Zaire, Romania and elsewhere today— was the willingness to, as the cliche goes, stand up and be counted at a time when it really mattered. They were willing to back up their beliefs with their lives.

If the dawn tomorrow were indeed Red, how would we react? Saul Friedlander, in his disturbing book, "Reflections on Nazism" (Harper & Row), observes that people around the world "have venerated oppressive, barbarous and terrorist power." There never seems to be a shortage of candidates struggling to rise to the top of systems steeped in blood, such as the Soviet Politburo. Would we have a similar surplus of oppressors, should the opportunity ever come?

Before he died four decades ago, July 20 plotter Count Peter Yorck wrote his wife: "I hope my death will be accepted . . . as an expiatory sacrifice . . . We want to kindle the torch of life; a sea of flames surrounds us."

May we all have his courage if the time ever comes that we need it.

## 2. The Next Hungarian Revolution

*February 22, 1989*

Thirty-three years after the ill-fated 1956 revolution, freedom seems to be forcing its way into the Hungarian system.

The government, beset by a host of economic problems, has legalized alternative political organizations and plans to hold multiparty elections next year; Hungary will then become the first East European state to countenance an independent opposition.

Moreover, the communist leadership has publicly split over the meaning of the ill-fated upheaval—one member of the ruling Politburo recently termed it a "popular uprising."

And in a dramatic break with past policy the regime has decided to rebury the disgraced leaders of the short-lived revolutionary government.

In the summer of 1956 a restive Hungarian population began pressing for reform. Silent resentment exploded into public anger with a huge demonstration on Oct. 23; the protesters demanded re-establishment of the rule of law, the end of collectivization and international neutrality.

Stalinist Matyas Rakosi's regime collapsed and party officials, desperate to stem the popular tide, turned to Imre Nagy, a reformer who had been deposed the previous year. He promised elections and announced Hungary's withdrawal from the Warsaw Pact.

But the U.S.S.R., unwilling to relinquish its grip, invaded on Nov. 4. Resistance in rural areas continued for weeks and an estimated 25,000 Hungarians died in their desperate bid for freedom.

Newly installed Soviet henchman Janos Kadar then wreaked vengeance on the survivors who had opposed Soviet-inspired totalitarian rule. Some 40,000 people were imprisoned while Nagy and upward of 3,000 others were executed; the killings went on through 1960, as the youngest rebels finally turned 18.

Nagy and many other revolutionaries were buried in an unmarked "potter's field." The government, determined to eradicate all evidence of the revolt, refused to disclose the grave locations to relatives.

However, the mothers of two executed students secretly watched the burial of their sons in Section 301 of a large Budapest cemetery. Mourners soon turned the area into an unofficial memorial.

For years Kadar's regime sought to discourage any remembrance of the victims, even bulldozing the grave mounds. It also punished anyone who spoke out about the revolt—for instance, Imre Mecs, a student revolutionary who served six years in prison, was fired from his state job after praising a fellow rebel at the man's funeral.

But Kadar was deposed last year and *glasnost* is now the watchword in the U.S.S.R. Under pressure from the victims' families, Communist Party leader Karoly Grosz recently agreed to rebury Nagy and four of his colleagues and allow erection of a monument.

Emboldened by this implicit acknowledgement that Nagy was not the counterrevolutionary of official description, the Committee for Historical Justice, made up of people who fought in and relatives of those who died in the struggle, is publicly demanding an accounting for and reburial of everyone who was executed.

Moreover, the writers' union weekly, *Life and Literature,* has run an article discussing Kadar's responsibility in the 1956 struggle.

The most serious attack on the official mythology, however, has been Politburo member Imre Pozsgay's description of the revolution as a "popular revolt." He earned an immediate rebuke from Grosz, but after a heated debate the party's Central Committee decided that the revolt, though ultimately subverted, was begun by "honest people" with good intentions.

Even this limited admission damages the Communist Party's claim to legitimacy. After all, the Communists initially came to power after World War II and regained authority after the 1956 revolution only with the help of the Red army; the continuing specter of Moscow's mailed fist helped sustain the regime in succeeding years. But now leading Hungarians are openly questioning the official justification for Soviet intervention.

Moreover, the Hungarian Communist Party is increasingly on its own. Not only is Stalin's rule being discredited in the U.S.S.R., but Moscow is starting to pull back its troops from East Europe and emphasize its allies' self-responsibility. Faced with a decaying economy, the Grosz regime is sitting atop a potential popular volcano.

The 1956 revolution demonstrated the price the Hungarian people were willing to pay for freedom: 25,000 dead, tens of thousands more wounded, perhaps 3,000 executed, 40,000 imprisoned and some 190,000 refugees.

And the saga will continue until the last Soviet tank leaves the country. That is not likely to happen soon, but Budapest's decision to rebury Nagy and four of his colleagues symbolizes the irreversible decay of communist rule.

Freedom is coming to Hungary.

## 3. Remembering the Holocaust

*April 11, 1985*

On the outskirts of one of the most fought-over cities in the world, Jerusalem, sits a memorial to some of the victims of the world's bloodiest war. Not an ordinary museum, Yad VaShem records no glorious victories, praises no valiant soldiers and inspires no patriotic fervor. Instead, it memorializes the millions consumed in World War II's Jewish Holocaust.

That war cost tens of millions of Gentiles their lives as well, of course. But even four decades after it ended, Adolf Hitler's massacre of the Jews retains a special horror, culminating thousands of years of religious intolerance, ethnic xenophobia and economic jealousy.

Yad VaShem is unimpressive on the outside, a low building set back from the omnipresent gift shop and parking spaces for tourist buses, but its contents reduce the most stoical of visitors to tears. Simply, but graphically, the museum chronicles the development of a calculated policy of official genocide, carried out with the acquiescence, if not approval, of an entire nation. That "Final Solution," which turned virtually every branch of the state—press, police, judiciary, prisons and military—into a tool of mass murder, continues to demonstrate what man is capable of doing to man.

Hitler spent years building on economic discontent and radical hatred before attaining the chancellorship in January 1933. "The Jews are our misfortune," proclaimed banners at Nazi Party rallies; Jews became the national scapegoats.

Jewish shops were boycotted and books by Jewish authors were burned. Jews were dismissed from government jobs and universities, the theater and the press. In 1935 the Nuremberg Laws officially reduced the status of Jews to that of "subjects," and forbade intermarriage between Jews and "Aryans."

For a while, the Nazis encouraged Jews to emigrate, and by the start of the war 60 percent of Germany's 500,000 Jewish residents had left. More would have fled had they had a place to go; some escaped the repression at home only to return when no other nation, including America, would grant them sanctuary.

All too reminiscent of the cold-blooded myopia of Western leaders then is the U.S. government's refusal to accept the thousands of El Salvadorans fleeing the civil war in their homeland. Prejudice and malice are limited to no nation or time.

But the persecution before the outbreak of war—and the photos of that period at Yad VaShem—is tame compared to what happened when German armies conquered most of Europe and much of the Soviet Union, placing millions more Jews under Nazi control. Jews then were increasingly confined in ghettos, interned in labor camps, denied access to food and tormented in every conceivable way.

By 1941 the slaughter began. In the occupied territories of the Soviet Union, the Einsatzgruppen began killing "hostile elements," including Jews. The Nazis' methods were simple but effective: The victims were rounded up, stripped and shot. The murderers were nothing if not meticulous; one of the most stunning photographs, displayed prominently in the museum, shows five women, including a child, standing arm-in-arm and dressed only in their underwear, calmly awaiting execution.

But firing squads alone could not implement the Final Solution. In early 1942, Nazi leaders met in Berlin to coordinate the work ahead—they estimated that 11 million Jews had to be eliminated from the territories either then under German control or soon to be acquired: 2,284,000 in Poland, 5,600 in Denmark, 330,000 in England, 3,000 in Portugal and so on.

German efficiency was turned loose with a vengeance, as a series of death camps were established. Auschwitz, Treblinka, Chelmno. The names will forever burn our souls. As many as 6 million Jews were killed in production-line fashion.

But it is all too easy to think of 6 million as only a statistic. Yad VaShem turns them into real people through wrenching photo after photo. Women and children being herded through streets. Young and old being loaded into boxcars. The official sorting of human beings between those to be gassed immediately and those to live a while longer. And mounds and mounds of gaunt corpses. The madness, the inhumanity, the senselessness is overwhelming.

There were a few individual heroes who helped Jews escape the Nazi' Hell on Earth, and trees are planted outside the museum to commemorate their courage. One of these is Raoul Wallenberg, who was recently honored at dinners across the United States.

A Swedish diplomat based in Budapest, Hungary, Wallenberg saved virtually half the city's Jewish population, only to disappear into the Gulag when the conquering Red Army entered Budapest in 1945. He fought one tyranny only to die at the hands of an even more murderous one.

Jerusalem is a wondrous city, the center of three religions, steeped in the most famous history of the world and bursting with the customs and cultures of different peoples. But few things in the city match the impact of Yad VaShem. For nowhere is there a more powerful demonstration of the danger of the state, the misuse of power and the cruelty of man.

# 4. Who Should Teach Values?

*April 22, 1987*

There is a growing consensus across the political spectrum that public schools should again promote traditional ethical standards.

"To be responsible citizens," observed columnist July Mann recently, children "need to be taught and have reinforced in schools such values as honesty, integrity, compassion, responsiblity, courtesy, respect for themselves and for others."

The campaign for "values" originated on the right, among religious parents concerned that their children were being fed a secularist, relativist philosophy. But even liberals now share many of the same concerns.

Washington, D.C., school superintendent Floretta McKenzie, for instance, admits to having made "a 180-degree turn" on the issue: "I don't think we can separate out the teaching of values from public education."

How effective the public schools, in contrast to family and church, can be in inculcating basic values is not clear. Nor is it obvious that we should trust the government to teach ethics, totalitarian states, of course, are only too happy to take charge of childrens' moral education.

But as long as public schools exist it is impossible to escape the issue: a "value-full" education is inevitable. The only question is what standards are taught.

Yet for all the theoretical agreement over the importance of values, far too many Americans, including teachers and other community leaders, do not live up to such high-minded principles. Which makes it difficult to pass values—good ones, at least—on to the young.

Among the most important moral standards that have been badly undermined are honesty and charity.

One recent Saturday, for instance, an automatic bank teller machine located in Georgetown, a fashionable neighborhood in the nation's capital, began dispensing $20 bills in place of $5 ones. Word of the machine's unintended generosity spread and a long line quickly developed at the machine.

"All the people were going through and trying to milk the machine," said the bartender at a nearby bar. Added a waitress, "everybody was saying, 'if we knew, we would have gone and taken some money'."

In short, scores of well-paid and well-connected people felt no compunction about stealing hundreds of dollars from a bank. How can we expect moral eunuchs like them to teach children anything of value?

Even many people who would never loot a malfunctioning money machine believe that theft achieved through the political process is different. Members of various interest groups, for instance, busily lobby Congress to pick their neighbors' pockets.

Farmers alone have forced the general population to spend $93.8 billion over the last six years to support their incomes. And many producers have reorganized their farms to evade the law's limit of $50,000 in subsidies per person; one Mississippi family formed 15 different corporations to collect

$1.2 million last year. The General Accounting Office figures this sort of organized theft from the body politic alone will hike federal spending by an additional $2.3 billion through 1989.

Just as many Americans have discarded honesty in their rush to grab a few extra bucks, so too have they forsaken the less fortunate.

According to the IRS, the average family with an adjusted gross income of $20,000 to $25,000 gives about $770 to charity—as little as three percent of its income. Families making between $30,000 and $50,000 give about $1,100, just 2.2 percent to 3.6 percent of their wages. Those earning more give away an equally small share of their incomes.

Nor have America's political leaders provided much of a role model. Ronald Reagan, despite his professed support for private philanthropy, gives less than four percent of his income to charity; Geraldine Ferraro, the 1984 Democratic vice-presidential candidate, regularly contributed barely .9 percent of her earnings to the less fortunate.

If politicians like these, as well as the voting public, are unwilling to make any personal sacrifice to help people in need, who is going to teach the importance of charity to the young?

Values undergird our society, which makes the transmission of basic moral principles to children so critical.

But before we embark on a new educational crusade, Americans need to take a long, hard look at themselves. Put bluntly, are they upholding the values they say they want taught in the schools? For until today's adults practice the principles they preach, they can't expect their children to take such standards seriously.

In contrast, once the lives of parents, ministers, educators and other community leaders truly reflect values like honesty and charity, children will learn them naturally—without the government's help.

# Government by What Values?

## 5. America's 2 Different Constitutions

*April 1, 1987*

This is the year of the Constitution, the 200th anniversary of the nation's basic governing framework. How well the system has worked—and whether it will survive another century—was the issue examined at a recent conference sponsored by Florida State University.

Among the more important topics covered was the Constitution's effectiveness during emergencies. For the nation's founders "intended their framework of freedom and government to endure through the ages, through storm as well as sunshine," observed Robert Higgs, a professor at Pennsylvania's Lafayette College.

Unfortunately, the Constitution's clear guarantees of rights to life, liberty and property have been consistently overridden by government during crises.

"The historical record is quite clear," said Higgs and there is no reason to expect the future to be any different.

Indeed, argues Higgs, there are really two constitutions—"the Normal Constitution, protective of private rights," and the "Crisis Constitution, hostile to private rights and friendly to the unchecked power of governmental officials." During emergencies the latter controls and as the number of crises have proliferated, so has the permanent power of the state.

The Crisis Constitution appeared during the Civil War when President Abraham Lincoln suspended habeas corpus, denying those detained by the federal government any recourse to the courts.

During the 20th century the Normal Constitution has been increasingly superceded. Before the start of World War I the federal government forestalled a national railroad strike by legislating a 25 percent wage hike.

This unconstitutional taking of property (from the employers) was nevertheless upheld by the Supreme Court. The court also validated

11

military conscription, even though the Constitution would likely never have been ratified had it authorized a draft.

The Crisis Constitution re-emerged during the Great Depression, the first non-war "emergency." The high court allowed states to halt mortgage foreclosures—which were "unambiguous impairments of the obligation of contract and therefore in clear violation of the U.S. Constitution," observes Higgs.

The Roosevelt administration nationalized private gold stocks and voided gold clauses in contracts. Roosevelt's action was illegal and he was prepared to disobey the Supreme Court if it ruled against him. But he needn't have worried: "contracts, however express, cannot fetter the constitutional authority of Congress," opined the justices.

During World War II the government exercised awesome power. Ten million men were drafted, 110,000 Japanese-Americans were pushed into concentration camps, economic production was controlled by the government, and consumer goods were rationed. Yet, complains Higgs, "the court found no reason to deny the government any of the many powers it was exercising at the expense of private rights."

During the Korean War the federal government reimposed many of its restrictions on commerce, wages and prices. The Supreme Court blocked President Harry Truman's attempted seizure of the steel industry primarily because he lacked legislative, rather than constitutional, authority to do so.

Price controls re-emerged under President Richard Nixon in peacetime; President Jimmy Carter voided Americans' court claims against Iran.

Even conservative Ronald Reagan has extended the Crisis Constitution by, for instance, banning travel to such nations as Cuba and Libya. Most recently he ordered all Americans out of Lebanon.

These steps are not only dubious on policy grounds, but also involve the exercise of state power far beyond that intended by the nation's founders. If America's fundamental governing document means anything at all, such federal overreaching should yield to the Constitution.

Yet—and this is probably the most disheartening aspect of Higgs' analysis—it may be unrealistic to expect any constitution to restrain government from acting irresponsibly during a crisis. As Aristotle rightly observed, "Those who carry arms can always determine the fate of the constitution."

The danger today, worries Higgs, is that "the Crisis Constitution will simply swallow up the Normal Constitution, depriving us at all times of the very rights the original Constitution was created to protect at all times."

Can anything be done to forestall this trend? At the very least the issue should be debated in this, the Constitution's anniversary year. For Higgs will be proved wrong only if the American people recapture the passion for liberty exhibited by the nation's founders two centuries ago.

## 6. What Happened to the Concept of Theft?

*March 9, 1988*

Congress was at its most natural—and its worst—last December, handing out generous slabs of pork to campaign supporters, developers, and a host of other favored interests.

Capitol Hill has drawn sharp criticism for using one mammoth Continuing Resolution to hide these sorts of appropriations and rightly so. Funding virtually the entire government in one bill both emasculates the president's veto power and undercuts Congress' accountability.

So furious was the uproar that in his State of the Union speech President Reagan pledged to send Congress a rescission package with the worst of the waste. But Office of Management and Budget Director James Miller now says that the administration will merely identify those measures that Reagan would like to see killed: "Essentially we are leaving it up to you," he told the Senate Appropriations Committee.

Unfortunately, the president is obviously not serious about controlling spending. For if he won't confront Congress over its profligacy, who will?

Indeed, the problem is more than procedural. For much of what Congress did in December would have been wrong—morally wrong—even had it passed individual appropriations bills. Congress' procedures are flawed, but its philosophy is worse. Put bluntly, lawmakers are stealing from the public.

Theft may seem like a strong word for what now routinely comes out of the legislative process. But that's only because we have abandoned any rigorous conception of individual rights and government responsibilities.

The public seizure of private resources should require a compelling justification. Yet most government transfers today are made to enrich one or another narrow interests. Uncle Sam has become an enforcer for greedy private groups that can't legally take other people's money directly.

Consider some of December's run-of-the-mill pork. Beekeepers successfully lobbied Congress to remove the $250,000 limit on individual loans; 15 honey producers will collect up to $6 million as a result. There is no public interest involved in making the rich richer: this is legalized theft.

Then there's the $2.6 million devoted to "develop fishery products." The modern-day highwaymen in this case were Alaskan fishermen, championed by Sen. Ted Stevens. His pork damages rather than promotes the "general welfare."

Residents of Kellogg, Idaho, will benefit from a $6.4 million federal subsidy for a Bavarian-style ski resort. No national interest is served by this expenditure, but Sen. James McClure, R-Idaho, is an influential legislator.

The Worcester Business Development Corp. and the city of Worcester will share $1 million to construct a biotechnology research park, courtesy Rep. Joseph Early, D-Mass. The grant may add a few jobs in Worcester, but what about the other communities across America that will lose jobs as their citizens underwrite Worcester?

But all of these—along with the $50,000 to study New Mexico wildflowers, $10 million to buy up sunflower oil, and many others—at least have some relationship to the United States. The same was not true of Sen. Daniel Inouye's short-lived $8 million grant to a private charity to build schools in France for North African Sephardic Jews.

There was no U.S. interest involved in building religious schools in Paris, ones that, notably, the French government had refused to construct. And unending public criticism, even ridicule, caused Inouye to ask Congress to rescind the funds. Yet did even one congressman question whether this expenditure was proper, whether it satisfied the Constitution's "general welfare" clause?

"It was a lousy $8 million," explained Rep. David Obey, D-Wis., a member of the budget conference committee. Similarly, Rep. William Lehman, D-Fla., explained, "Dan doesn't ask for much and when he has a small amount of the total package that seems to be important to him, you don't embarrass him."

But the $8 million—the "lousy $8 million," as Obey put it—was not Congress' money to give away. It belonged to working men and women across America. And it was wrong to take it from them with no overriding public interest at stake.

Members of Congress have a constitutional responsibility to reject improper appropriations, even if it means "embarrassing" a senior legislator.

Budget reform is essential: sensible lawmaking and electoral answerability are impossible so long as Congress routinely ignores statutory deadlines and flouts its own rules. But the more fundamental issue at stake is economic justice for those who pay Uncle Sam's bills.

Legislators need to rediscover the Eighth Commandment and its prohibition against theft. It is more important that Congress act morally than efficiently.

# 7. Games Politicians Play

*Government has no business promoting sports.*

*April 25, 1984*

The role of government seems to be constantly changing. Once government was to act as a night watchman, to protect life and liberty at home and abroad. Then it became a fiscal Santa Claus, to redistribute income and guarantee economic security. Now government has become a sports promoter: like the Roman Empire of old, the state is expected to provide entertainment for the masses.

Of course, the form of pleasure is different. In Rome it was circuses, chariot races and gladiators. In modern-day America, at least in Baltimore and Oakland, it is football.

The full-scale entry of government into the entertainment business has been sparked by the decisions of two football team owners to take their franchises elsewhere in search of better bucks. In 1982, Al Davis moved the Oakland Raiders to Los Angeles, and Oakland responded by asserting eminent domain over the Raiders to preserve the "social, cultural and psychological" identity of the city. Davis asked the California Supreme Court to toss out the case, but the court refused, saying that "times change," and "the acquisition and, indeed, the operation of a sports franchise may well be an appropriate municipal function." Davis and Oakland are still fighting it out in the courts.

Then earlier this year Baltimore Colts owner Robert Irsay spent months in a will-he/won't-he negotiation with Indianapolis, finally slipping away in the dark of night. Baltimore Mayor Donald Schaefer complained that Irsay had not notified him before he moved; in contrast to Oakland, which was prepared for Davis' move, Baltimore hadn't had quite enough time to ram an eminent domain amendment to the city charter through the legislature and governor's office.

But on the next day, while complaining that "it was sleazy to come in here and sneak out like they did," Schaefer signed city condemnation legislation that had zipped through the city council in just 25 minutes. Judges then issued an injunction against the team's move and a restraining order prohibiting the National Football League from transferring the Colts' "certificate of membership" or finalizing its schedule. In discussing a suit that could cost millions to fight and $40 million to pay for the Colts if the city wins, Schaefer says, "If I thought this was a frivolous suit we wouldn't be doing it."

Governments have always claimed the right to take private property for a "public use"; the property was almost always real estate and could be taken only to meet a compelling need. But courts have become increasingly willing to allow government to take intangible forms of property as well, whenever elected officials felt it would be convenient.

The attempt to condemn sports franchises further emasculates constitutional guarantees of private property rights. Oakland City Attorney David Self explained: "we got to thinking we can condemn land on which to build a stadium, the purpose of which is to provide a professional sports contest. You only need one more thing to have a contest, and that's a team. Why can't you condemn that, too?"

Local governments have built or refurbished more than 50 stadiums in the last 20 years, for a total cost of $6 billion. The reason municipalities force taxpayers—fans and non-fans alike—to underwrite the cost of big sports business is the same reason that a number of Brooklyn legislators are currently pushing for a taxpayer-supported stadium in Brooklyn: to revive the "borough's economy as well as its special identity and pride."

By the same token, New York City could build an oil refinery to get Texaco to come, or an airplane factory to lure Boeing, or an office building to snare Bank of London. It won't, however, and correctly so, for true economic revival can not be bought by the government's taxing local individuals and businesses to bribe potential migrants.

Thus the real issue is promoting an area's "identity and pride." But is this really any business of government? Oakland's David Self happily explained in 1982 that "we want the Raiders for a public benefit, not merely for private gain." But Robert Irsay told a reporter in Indianapolis, "It's not your ball team or our ball team; it's my family's ball team. I paid for it and worked for it." He's right. Why do a bunch of politicians have a higher claim to it?

In essentially expunging the Fifth Amendment's limitations on the taking of private property from the Constitution, we have unwittingly adopted legal tenets befitting a very different society. "All property is," as Nazi Party spokesman Ernst Huber explained in 1933, "common property. The owner is bound by the people and the Reich to the responsible management of his goods. His legal position is only justified when he satisfies this responsibility to the community."

Our government has traveled a long way from the role originally envisioned by the Founders. Ironically, in the state's transformation from night watchman to sports promoter, it is harkening back to an even more traditional duty. All that is lacking are the gladiators.

# 8. Exploiting National Resources

*December 1, 1983*

One of the hoariest of panaceas is making a comeback. New York Mayor Ed Koch and Ford Foundation president Franklin Thomas, for example, recently joined such people as past Secretary of War and State Elihu Root, the late sociologist Margaret Mead, and former congressman Pete McCloskey in proposing mandatory service for the young.

These would-be social organizers have two major goals. The first is to impose a number of values on the young. Koch speaks of creating a "spirit of altruism." Some talk of inculcating a sense of the "common good." And a century ago Edward Bellamy wrote of teaching the "habits of obedience, subordination, and devotion to duty."

The second goal of national-service proponents is to solve society's economic and social problems. For example, the Washington-based Potomac Institute has suggested that national service "could be an important alternative to unemployment, underemployment, or prolonged schooling." Others want to create a large pool of cheap labor to aid education, health services, parks, and even the arts.

The concern of such people over the values learned by the younger generation is understandable, and the desire to enrich the lives of other human beings laudable.

But universal national service is no solution. It won't work, and, indeed, in a free society it should not work.

Compulsory national service would be unlikely to purge the young of "selfishness," or any other disfavored value, since values are more effectively learned than imposed. Compassion cannot be coerced; service ceases to be service once it is involuntary.

The only value national service would teach would be that political might makes right: that those who control the political process can impose their values on everyone else.

Moreover, the cost of such a program would be enormous. The budget outlays alone would be in the tens of billions, and that expense would be dwarfed by the social cost of dislocating the career and educational plans of millions.

Nor would national service solve our problems. Social conscription of the young is no answer to selective youth unemployment. It would be more logical, though equally offensive, to draft all the unemployed, however old. Universal national service would not reduce the cost of providing social services, either; it would merely shift the burden onto America's youth. And forcing a young person who, for example, plans a career in geriatrics to spend two years cleaning bedpans is no bargain.

Even more flawed are the moral underpinnings of national service. Why does simply living create an obligation to spend years doing what someone else thinks is worthy? To the extent that individuals have an obligation to "do good," it is a personal, moral burden, and it should be up to the individual, not the state, to decide the form of service due.

And if service is owed to the government, why are only the young liable for the debt? Fifty-year-old bankers, lawyers, and politicians all benefit from living in the United States. They should be among the first people enrolled in any program.

Finally, what is service? The Potomac Institute says that national service should "help meet the real economic, social, and educational needs of the nation." But young people working in business, psychology, and teaching do precisely that. Such private employment also provides the wealth that people contribute to charity, use to provide for their dependents, and so on. Such private activity is "service" to society.

In fact, many national service proponents betray an Orwellian mind-set. In their lexicon servitude is liberty, and liberty servitude. Terrence Cullinan, for example, contends that: "The United States was founded on a doctrine of freedom for the individual. Yet this very doctrine is a compulsory one." Further, they believe that they have been anointed to decide the "public good," who owes service, and in what manner that debt is to be paid. Young people are simply fungible resources for use in "important" social projects.

Indeed, the Potomac Institute reported that: "International comparisons also fire some American imaginations. Millions of young people serve social needs in China as a routine part of growing up." Two members of its national service task force traveled to China, and returned "more determined than before to try to devise a democratic equivalent."

But there can be no democratic equivalent. In China, the state owns everyone; if our society is to be a free one, it must be built on the opposite premise. Any program of mandatory national service, no matter how well intentioned, would violate the principles and traditions of freedom upon which this nation was founded.

## 9. Government as God

*April 13, 1988*

There was a time when the First Amendment was thought to protect religion as well as speech. But government officials increasingly seem to think that it means protection from religion. At least, that's what the honorable City Council members of the nation's capital must believe.

The District of Columbia has long been noteworthy as the home of a parasitic federal bureaucracy, but the city government is not without its own accomplishments, including a particularly entertaining amalgam of venality and incompetence. And now D.C. can pride itself on forcing a Catholic institution to fund gay activist organizations.

In 1977 the district passed an ordinance forbidding discrimination on the basis of sexual orientation. Naturally no exemption was provided for religious institutions; in this city the government, not God, is considered to be the supreme arbiter of morality.

Located within the capital is Georgetown University, a Catholic school chartered directly by the Vatican. Georgetown takes its doctrine seriously and believes, as do all Bible-based Christian faiths, that homosexuality is wrong.

That doesn't make gays unique, of course: adultery, for instance, is also a sin. But there are as yet no adulterers' organizations demanding official recognition of their members' lifestyle.

There are gay groups, though, and they wanted Georgetown to provide them with office space, support services, funds, and access to school facilities. The university, not surprisingly, said no. For to subsidize homosexual organizations would be to support an orientation that violated fundamental Catholics tenets.

So the students, with the support of the D.C. "Human Rights Office"— which believes in protecting everyone's human rights except those of traditional Catholics—sued. And last fall the district's Court of Appeals ruled that Georgetown, while it needn't technically "recognize" the gay groups, had to grant them the same "tangible benefits" that it provided other organizations.

Georgetown decided not to appeal, settling the case on March 29. The school won't have to host gay religious ceremonies or meetings with a largely non-university audience, but Georgetown will still be forced to subsidize gay groups: "We've gotten everything we were looking for," exulted Laura Foggan, an attorney for the plaintiffs.

Moreover, Georgetown agreed to pay its opponents' legal fees, which are estimated to run between $600,000 and $900,000. It's bad enough that a religious school has to spend enormous sums of money to defend its right to follow church doctrine. But to require it to pay those who want to deprive it of its religious freedom is scandalous.

The point is, homosexuals have no right to force others to accept or support their lifestyle. Certainly government has no business discriminating against them: Anti-sodomy laws, for instance, are a vicious intrusion in the most intimate form of human conduct. And gays who pay taxes have as much right to government services and employment as anyone else.

But someone who decides to live openly as a homosexual should accept the disapproval of those around him. For many Americans still believe that there is a fundamental, unchangeable moral code by which men are to live.

Vindictive personal discrimination against gays, in contrast to disapproval of their conduct, is wrong—and even un-Christian, since Jesus commanded his followers, who are sinners like everyone else, to love their neighbors—but it is not a public matter. Using government to bludgeon homophobics into submission is even more intolerant than the original discrimination.

And gays certainly shouldn't expect to be subsidized by those who are offended by their lifestyle. Georgetown's homosexual students may reject biblical teachings, but no one forced them to go there. If they want to attend a university that recognizes their sexual preference, they should have enrolled somewhere else.

Indeed, to show up at a Catholic school and demand that it fund gay activist groups is, well, more than chutzpah. It is both selfish and spiteful, a calculated effort to trample someone else's fundamental beliefs for ideological purposes.

It's too bad that Georgetown decided not to appeal the case. For if the district can force the school to subsidize gay groups, what will be next? Office space for the campus atheists?

"We never intended to discriminate, or break the district law," says one Georgetown official. "We do reserve the right to be Catholic."

But the university's desires in that regard apparently don't matter. For the D.C. government believes that it, not God, is the city's highest moral authority.

## 10. A Little Tolerance, Please

*January 4, 1989*

With Christmas came the inevitable religious displays—and the equally predictable court cases.

The City of San Diego, for instance, hosted a private holiday exhibit that depicted Jesus along with Santa Claus; the San Diego chapter of the American Atheists responded with a lawsuit.

In 1987 the Jewish Community Recreation Center complained about the annual, life-size production. The city attorney recommended discontinuing the display, but a public outcry caused San Diego to again place it on public land.

The atheist group wants the courts to banish the exhibit for violating the First Amendment's "no establishment" clause. The law, however, is currently on the city's side: In 1983 the U.S. Supreme Court allowed a city-sponsored creche on private property.

But that ruling was recently attacked by several groups, including the National Council of Churches and the American Jewish Committee, which have asked the court to reconsider its earlier opinion and prohibit the display of nativity scenes and menorahs in public places.

Unfortunately, the last thing we need in this area is another lawsuit. If there is anything people should be tolerant of, it is other folks' religious beliefs.

In fact, the "no establishment" clause has been badly perverted as it has become a legal battleground over harmless religious symbols. The nation's founders intended to prevent the government from promoting one denomination or another—that is, from creating an American Church of England. But there is no evidence that men who resorted to prayer at the convention where they drafted the Constitution opposed non-denominational religious displays in public.

Indeed, the famous "wall of separation" language comes from a letter by Thomas Jefferson, not the Constitution. As well-reasoned as his opinion might be, it does not have the effect of law.

Nevertheless, the fact that the Constitution, properly interpreted, does not bar symbolic religious gestures by government does not mean that Christians, or members of any other faith, should use the state to promote their beliefs, however indirectly.

It isn't right to force Jews to fund a creche; it is understandable that an atheist may be offended at seeing a menorah in the local courthouse.

Moreover, there is something insulting about the very notion of the government promoting Christianity, a faith that is supposed to transcend city councils and public parks. It is particularly degrading when officials mix a nativity scene with Santa's sleigh. God doesn't need government's ham-handed, clumsy "help."

Thus, Christians should demonstrate the overarching tenet of their faith—love—by not forcing others to underwrite the public display of their faith. There is no shortage of churches and individuals willing to sponsor a creche; let them take responsibility for doing so.

At the same time, however, groups such as the American Atheists and the Society of Separationists should also show restraint. Though a depiction of Jesus' birth obviously has religious significance, it is also part of our cultural heritage. And where a creche is mixed with other traditional holiday symbols the message is primarily an affirmation of a shared culture rather than of serious religious beliefs.

In any case, where we are dealing with public places—parks, buildings, and the like—compromise is necessary to accommodate all sides. Since Christians and non-Christians alike "own" such property, they all have a right to help determine its use.

The problem is similar in schools. Religious families who can't afford to send their kids to private institutions are rightly frustrated by meaningless holiday pageants in which their kids sing "Frosty the Snowman." While children of other faiths should not be pressured to act out Christian themes, no one's interest is served when the public schools adopt the lowest, most vacuous, common denominator.

What is required, then, is a willingness to tolerate the views of others, so long as one's own fundamental beliefs are not violated. Whether or not a creche goes up in the local park simply should not become a divisive issue to Christians or non-Christians.

There is no more important freedom than the right to exercise one's personal faith. And that requires sharply constraining the power of government to promote any religion.

But many of the most emotional church/state controversies—the religious play in school, the nativity scene in the park—simply don't belong in court.

Though we hold many different beliefs, we have to live together. Which means that people of all faiths, or no faith, need to exhibit tolerance even when it seems inconvenient to do so.

## 11. Just Another Sorry Attempt to Legislate Personal Views

*March 10, 1983*

America's omnipresent guardians of the public morals have recently found a new menace to American society: video games. They are using zoning and many other weapons at their command to combat the games' spread.

Unfortunately, their crusade is merely another virulent form of America's age-old disease of intolerance. Once primarily confined to private acts of racial, ethnic, and social discrimination, intolerance has become widespread and institutionalized through public acts of economic as well as moral aggression.

Indeed, the use of government to impose some values and suppress others has become endemic to the American political system, perverting the role of government from that of protector of the rights of all to promoter of the whims of a few.

The most traditional example of this willingness to enact personal values is regulation of individual, consensual, moral conduct. Laws against fornication and adultery are still on the books in many states; many more prohibit voluntary homosexual relationships. Others ban pornography and prostitution.

None of these laws protects unwilling victims. Rather, they institutionalize as public law the particular religious and moral standards of arbitrary, ephemeral majorities—and vocal minorities. They set political norms to govern purely private, consensual conduct.

A similar form of intolerance is manifested against people whose social mores vary from that of the prevailing majority. Shifting majorities support prohibition of drugs and laetrile, but not alcohol and cigarettes. Such inconsistent restrictions are rationalized on the basis of health and safety.

However, adults, not government, are responsible for their own health and safety. The real reason behind the restrictions is an intense hatred of the different tastes of different people.

Similar assaults on freedom and diversity have been carried out by the new forces of censorship, who have successfully gotten television ads for cigarettes banned, and who unsuccessfully sought to ban television ads directed at children.

Intolerance, too, is the basis for the attack on video games. A school superintendent, whose job is to educate, not regulate, complains that lunch money "could be spent in the wrong direction." Parents, whose job is to care for their children, want to escape that responsibility by shutting down private businesses which they don't like.

Indeed, intolerance lies behind most regulation of economic matters. Few people give even a second thought to the propriety of enacting their own whims into law, coercing others to comply with their dictates. Examples include:

*Rent control.* Some tenants don't like market rents, so they use the political process to confiscate the property of property owners. Why should their coercive political judgment supersede the voluntary economic judgment of tenants and landlords? Even if rent control did not worsen housing shortages, which it does, using the political process to set rents is legalizing theft, an egregious abuse of democracy.

*Minimum wage.* Economic intolerance also manifests itself when some people vote that, irrespective of skill, experience or education, no one should receive below some arbitrary wage. Even if the minimum wage did not cause unemployment by pricing disadvantaged workers out of the marketplace, it would still be a usurpation of voluntary, private decision-making by majority whim.

*Protectionism.* Many groups don't like Americans buying quality, inexpensive products from abroad. They therefore use government to restrict or ban imports. Protectionism is a euphemism for exploitation; the rights of consumers and export industry workers are suppressed by a self-interested minority.

*Subsidies.* A final, ubiquitous aspect of economic intolerance is the refusal to accept responsibility for one's own livelihood. Uneconomic dairy farmers demand price supports; bankrupt cities and corporations beg for bailouts. The willingness forcibly to take from others to promote one's own economic interest displays venal disregard for the very values upon which this nation was founded.

Intolerance—moral, social and economic—is an unfortunate aspect of the American heritage. Americans should join classical economist Nassau Senior in detesting "paternal despotisms which try to supply their subjects with the self-regarding virtues, to make men by law sober, or frugal, or orthodox," and accept "that the main, almost sole, duty of government is to give protection."

Until they do, no person's freedom will be safe, because using political power to impose one's personal wishes on others is an abuse of democracy.

# Does Freedom Matter?

## 12. The Right to Risk

*May 1, 1986*

The procession of states passing mandatory seat belt laws continues to grow, with Maryland the 20th state, in addition to the District of Columbia, protecting people against their will. "The overriding reason here is public safety," declared one legislator before he voted to force motorists to buckle up.

The real issue, however, is something quite different. Not only has the response to seat belt laws been generally disappointing—in Illinois, New York and New Jersey, for instance, compliance rates have fallen sharply since the legislation was first passed—but seat belts have nothing to do with "public safety." Unlike brakes and brake lights, seat belts save the lives of their wearers and no one else.

Instead, the question is, should the government prevent people from taking risks? Or is the concept of individual freedom in this country broad enough to include the right to make arguably stupid decisions?

Admittedly, it's tempting to say government should double as public nanny. An estimated 10,000 lives would be saved nationally if everyone wore seat belts; the number of serious injuries would fall by as many as 327,000.

Testimony before the Maryland Legislature was especially impassioned: "You have the chance to save more lives in your career than I can," said one doctor, while another urged members opposing the bill to read future accident reports and "consider that you might have done something that might have prevented that."

But should government "do something" because it will save some people's lives, even if doing so contravenes basic individual rights? Life is full of risk-related choices similar to the decision to buckle up, and the government can't conceivably make all of them.

People would be safer driving big cars than small ones and taking commercial flights rather than going by general aviation. Hang-gliding may be exhilarating, but it certainly is more dangerous than, say, playing chess; smokers should chew gum instead. And so on.

By what standard does a legislature or regulatory bureaucracy decide what level of risk an individual may take? Which dangerous activities are labeled socially good?

Flying in a space shuttle, presumably so, but how about riding on a motorcycle? Or parachuting for sport?

Just as freedom of speech means little if only non-controversial communication is protected, the freedom to live should entail more than just conforming to some "safe" lifestyle preferred by the majority. Especially in a nation as diverse as ours, true liberty must include the opportunity to take chances that others will not.

But, reply seat-belt enforcers, the issue should be decided by the public because they pay the bill for "irresponsible" behavior. Medical bills, welfare services, even lost tax revenues, are all cited as justifications for making people protect themselves.

The argument, however, proves too much. For if indeed the government's potential financial stake entitles it to regulate people to ensure their continued health and productivity, then individuals have literally become the property of the state: freedom is a dead concept. Every decision—including such fundamental ones as what work to do, where to live, and whether to have children—has indirect effects on other people.

Indeed, just such a concern for the "public interest" has led to laws requiring motorcyclists to wear helmets and proposals to ban cigarettes. For the same reason, should not hang-gliding and rock-climbing be outlawed?

Why not assign a nutritionist to every family; doing so would promote health. Uncle Sam could even start making bed checks.

True, polls show that large majorities of people favor mandatory seat belt legislation even as most refuse to buckle up; the same is probably not true of national bed checks. But the consent of most drivers should not bind the rest. The proper level of risk-taking is not a matter of opinion polls or community standards.

Why not let those who want a roving seat belt Gestapo to remind them to hook up simply register at their local police station and display an appropriate sticker on their car. Then they, and not the rest of us, would have Big Brother as a passenger.

At times individual liberty seems to be a mere abstraction, especially when people's lives are at stake. But it is one of the principles that make life worth living, and therefore should be jealously guarded, even against seemingly minor incursions. For unless we have the opportunity to make mistakes—including not buckling up—we really have no freedom at all.

## 13. Uncle Sam as National Nanny

*November 23, 1988*

"It is a landmark victory for parents and children," said Peggy Charren, head of Action for Children's Television, after passage of legislation that would have regulated kids' TV programs.

Exulted Andrew Jay Schwartzman, executive director of the Media Access Project, Congress' paternalistic power grab would ensure that broadcasters "meet the needs of children."

Not that kids were asking for the government's help. The Federal Communications Commission once regulated kidvid, but dropped its restrictions four years ago without apparent effect. The FCC's reasoning was quite simple: the care of children is better entrusted to parents than to the state.

A number of liberal interest groups don't believe that families can manage by themselves, however. So they successfully lobbied Capitol Hill to overturn the FCC decision.

But Ronald Reagan—who has often been tarred as an enemy of the First Amendment—vetoed the attempt to turn Uncle Sam into Super Censor.

"The Constitution simply does not empower the federal government to oversee the programming decisions of broadcasters in the manner prescribed in this bill," he explained.

Unfortunately, Charren doesn't share Reagan's concern about freedom of speech, calling his action "ideological child abuse." And she will undoubtedly be back in January trying to turn Uncle Sam into a national nanny.

But Reagan was right to utilize his veto. For if Congress can ensure that TV is not sullied by undue "commercialization," why shouldn't it also protect, say, "traditional family" values? If an FCC badgered by Charren can restrict what stations broadcast, so can one responding to Jerry Falwell.

And if commercials are harmful to kids—who are subject to their parents' control—then ads presumably do far more damage to gullible adults. Shouldn't the FCC therefore limit commercials during regular programs?

Indeed, if Charren and her fellow activists can regulate what ads viewers see, why shouldn't they control the selection of programs? After all, if parents are not competent to care for their children, then they probably are not capable of running their own lives. Which means they need to be guided by Charren and her friends.

Limiting the number of ads would have been bad enough; far worse was the legislation's vague requirement that stations "serve the educational and information needs of children" or risk losing their licenses. For where the rules are unknown and unknowable, administrative discretion is virtually unlimited, allowing broadcasters to be punished for anything.

Anyway, what is the horrible problem that federal regulation was supposed to solve? That ads encourage kids to ask for particular toys or foods?

But lots of things, including the acquisition of a new plaything by a child's friend, gives rise to such desires. Parents have to "just say no" to a lot of requests—this is just one more.

Moreover, it is advertising that allows stations to carry kids' shows. If Congress pushes the number of commercials below a break-even level, stations will run adult fare instead.

The other complaint is that the quality of child's TV programming is bad. That may well be true, but who is better able to determine what is best for kids—parents, or some bureaucrats in Washington?

Indeed, Charren and the other enthusiasts of government control suffer from a severe case of arrogant elitism. They apparently consider cartoons to be frivolous, and presumably were horrified by the 1972 survey that found children preferred "Gilligan's Island" to "Sesame Street."

So they want to impose their exalted standards on everyone else. But an entirely proper purpose of TV is to entertain—to make children laugh.

And what if there really are no good shows on Saturday morning? (Actually, kids are more likely to watch evening programs with their folks; the "Cosby Show" is seen by more children than any other.) Parents can shut off the television and send their kids out to play.

If lots of people start doing that, the networks will have to adjust their programming. But if parents won't take responsibility for their own homes, they have no business complaining to Congress.

There was a time when it would have been unthinkable to ask the government to control what children watched. Parents recognized that they had the primary responsibility for bringing up their kids. But today Charren and others want to turn that duty over to the government.

Reagan's veto of the kidvid bill was the real "landmark victory for parents and children." TV stations should run the programs that viewers, not bureaucrats, want.

The last thing that we need is for Uncle Sam to act as the nation's nanny.

# 14. A Fear of Ideas

*September 20, 1984*

"Extremism in the defense of liberty is no vice," said Arizona Sen. Barry Goldwater at the Republican Convention, repeating the most famous line from his acceptance speech two decades ago. The Republican delegates applauded just like they did in 1964, but few of them seem to understand what defending liberty really means.

After all, it is the current Republican administration that is cracking down on private travel to Cuba. And it is the same administration that has denied visas to more than 800 foreigners because of their political views.

Travel to Cuba was first restricted in 1963, but President Jimmy Carter relaxed the regulations in 1977. The Reagan administration, however, decided that 40,000 Americans visiting Cuba every year posed a serious threat to our national security, and decreed that, with a few narrow exceptions, people couldn't spend any money to travel there. The ban survived a U.S. Supreme Court challenge on a 5–4 vote.

With its right to abrogate our rights affirmed on high, the administration is now busy threatening both the tourist industry and potential tourists; it recently subpoenaed a travel agency's records for the names of people who have visited or have received information about visiting Cuba. The penalty for violating the prohibition is as much as 10 years in prison and a $50,000 fine, though so far the administration has relied on administrative sanctions—barring a Texas travel agency, for example, from handling any more trips to Cuba.

The administration fears not only Americans visiting other lands; it also dreads foreigners coming to the United States.

Late last year, the State Department refused to grant a visa to Tomas Borge, a top Nicaraguan leader. The department has also denied entry to Hortensia Allende, widow of the deposed Chilean president; Nino Pasti, a retired Italian general who opposes the administration's deployment of missiles in Europe, and Ruben Zamora, an El Salvadoran guerrilla leader. The administration also twice blocked a trip by Roberto D'Aubuisson, the El Salvadoran rightist legislator, before finally approving a visa in late summer.

Even when the administration lets people into the country, it has prevented the public from hearing their views. Georgi Arbatov, head of the Soviet Institute of U.S. and Canadian Studies, was allowed to give a lecture tour, for example, but the State Department prohibited him from having "any contact with the media." Let him come as long as he's not heard.

The administration justifies its travel ban as keeping hard currency out of Cuba. But the amount of money involved is inconsequential, and most of it, if spent, would go to American or other firms that make the travel arrangements, not the Cubans.

The State Department blocked Borge's trip for a different reason, saying that it didn't want to give him a "propaganda platform." But since when is it the government's duty to protect the Council on Foreign Relations and Harvard University—places where Borge was going to speak—from being used as propaganda platforms?

More important, what about our rights to listen to the propaganda?

After all, through November we will have to put up with an enormous amount of propaganda from both Mr. Reagan and Walter Mondale. If we can sort through their self-serving mush, we can also see through the drivel spouted by authoritarians like Borge and Arbatov.

Admittedly, this administration is not the only one that has sacrificed our fundamental rights to make meaningless international points. Moreover, to really protect us, the law authorizing the travel and visa restrictions must be changed. But Ronald Reagan, more than any other recent president, has talked as if he believes "freedom" is more than just a crowd-pleasing noun to be randomly tossed into speeches. It's time he acted that way.

Indeed, preventing Americans from visiting that backward island prison known as Cuba is a sign of weakness, not strength. And denying us access to the views of foreigners with whom the administration disagrees is contemptuous of both our rights and intelligence. If the values of this society mean anything, it is that we should encourage, not discourage, the free flow of ideas.

In denying Borge the visa, Secretary of State George Shultz said that "as a general proposition I think we have to favor freedom of speech, but it can get abused by people who do not wish us well." He's wrong. Protection for freedom of speech matters most when the speaker and his opinions are unpopular; nor is the importance of our right to hear diminished when the speaker is from another land.

What we have to fear most in this world is not the lies of Tomas Borge or Georgi Arbatov, but the misguided efforts of Ronald Reagan to stop us from hearing them.

## 15. Economic Liberty and Democracy

*February 11, 1987*

Nearly a decade ago the Chinese Communist Party began a great experiment by loosening its death grip on the economy. Price controls were relaxed, agricultural collectives were abolished and foreign invest-ment was encouraged.

The result has been growing prosperity for the average Chinese citizen. But a potentially even more far-reaching consequence of the new economic freedom has been a swelling popular demand for political and civil liberty.

University students even staged large demonstrations in Peking and elsewhere for democracy—an event unprecedented for a communist state. Though the marches were suppressed and reformist party boss Hu Yau-bang was dumped, the government's response to the growing grass-roots movement was relatively mild.

Of course, the students still may never see democracy come to their country. After all, in 1957 Mao Tse-tung briefly encouraged dissent in his "let a hundred flowers bloom" campaign and then arrested all those who responded.

But that was two decades before the Chinese people started to enjoy the material fruits of economic liberty. It would be much harder today for the Chinese government to revert to hard-line Maoist policies.

And if the economic reforms continue, further political liberalization is likely. According to the latest ratings by Freedom House, a New York human rights organization, more than half of the world's 64 capitalist nations, those that rely primarily on the marketplace for industrial produc-tion and which do not maintain large government enterprises, are free. Another 23 are partly free; only eight are rated not free.

Mixed systems, where state involvement in the economy is much greater, tend to be less free. Of the 78 countries in this category, just 24 are free; 21 are not free.

Finally, 23 of 24 truly socialist states, including China, are not free. One, Hungary, is partly free.

So if political reform ever comes to China or the other totalitarian states, it probably will have to follow economic liberalization. Indeed, that is the case with Hungary, which has moved further than any other East Euro-pean state in allowing market-oriented innovations in its closely controlled economy.

One reason democracy and civil liberties rest on economic freedom is because private property is necessary for the exercise of the other rights. If you can't buy a printing press, typewriter or TV, for instance, you have no effective freedom of speech.

As a result of economic liberalization in China, ownership of small "Walkman" tape recorders is now widespread. Their original purpose was to record and play music, but students have begun dictating anti-govern-ment wall posters onto cassettes and circulating them.

In Taiwan, which has a per capita income several times that of the mainland—because the breakaway island nation has long had a generally free enterprise orientation—video recorders are more plentiful. Dissidents videotaped a recent confrontation between government and opposition forces and showed copies around the country of what was informally titled "The Ugly Cops."

For the same reason communist officials are concerned about the computer revolution. Solidarity activists in Poland used government facilities to print anti-government literature; the proliferation of personal units would make it virtually impossible for any state to control the flow of *Samzidat* materials.

Romania has gone so far as to ban use of typewriters by those it deems to be politically unreliable and to require other people to register their units. That nation, an economic basket case, never will advance without lifting such stultifying controls. But if it ever does so, dissent will grow.

Economic liberty does more than just guarantee access to the tools necessary for political and civil freedom, however. As the private sector grows in size the government's power automatically shrinks.

Widespread private ownership of economic resources allows the development of alternative centers of power, ranging from corporations and labor unions to think tanks and universities. In contrast, those who lose political struggles in one-party socialist states are consigned to oblivion, with nowhere to go.

The Communist Party will continue to stubbornly resist political change and may triumph in the end. But a decade of economic reform, with a perceptible movement toward capitalism, may have made the demand for democracy ineradicable and the continued expansion of personal freedom inevitable.

## 16. The Real Story of Thanksgiving

*November 19, 1986*

Every year at Thanksgiving millions of Americans eat a turkey dinner commemorating one of the nation's great historical myths.

After a particularly hard winter following the founding of the Plymouth Colony, goes the official story, the Pilgrims reaped a bumper harvest and celebrated with a thanksgiving feast in 1621. Yet, writes Richard Maybury for the Ludwig von Mises Institute, in reality "the harvest of 1621 was not bountiful, nor were the colonists hardworking or tenacious." In fact, the colony was near collapse.

William Bradford, the colony's governor, complained that the early

Americans shirked their farming duties and that the community suffered from "confusion and discontent." What little work was done was threatened by illicit scavengers. Wrote Bradford, "Much was stolen both by night and day, before it became scarce eatable."

While there were harvest-time celebrations in 1621 and 1622, the colonists were at best marking temporary sufficiency rather than permanent abundance.

Only the following year did the situation change. Observed Bradford: "Instead of famine now God gave them plenty, and the face of things was changed, to the rejoicing of the hearts of many."

Indeed, he added, "no general want or famine" afflicted the settlers in succeeding years. By 1624 the colony was exporting corn to its neighbors.

What happened was neither a spiritual revival nor a scientific breakthrough. Instead, the colonists implemented an economic revolution.

The early Americans started out, quite simply, as socialists. The colony, explained Bradford, required that "all profits and benefits that are got by trade, traffic, trucking, working, fishing, or any other means" be placed in the colony's common stock; by the same reasoning, all the settlers took "their meat, drink, apparel, and all provisions out of the common stock."

This misguided belief that altruism could feed a community was the reason the settlers were starving. In practice, those who contributed the most often received the least: wrote Bradford, "The strong, or man of parts, had no more in division of victuals and clothes, than he that was weak."

So the system naturally broke down.

"Young men that were most able and fit for labor and service," reported Bradford, objected to being forced to "spend their time and strength to work for other men's wives and children."

Successive poor harvests forced the colonists to rethink the economic structure of their community. Gov. Bradford abolished common ownership of property and allowed families to keep what they grew. Not surprisingly, food production sharply increased.

The Jamestown Colony had a similar experience. Established in 1607, the settlers suffered through several harsh winters and deadly famines.

Because individuals gained no direct benefit from working more, the majority of colonists lived off of the few who worked hard. Finally, after the colony was decimated by the winter of 1609–10, private ownership of land and crops was established.

The result was dramatic. Colony Secretary Ralph Hamor wrote in 1614 that previously "we reaped not so much corn from the labors of 30 men as three men have done for themselves now." The days of starvation were over: there was "plenty of food, which every man by his own industry may easily and doth procure," observed Hamor.

Unfortunately, people around the world still ignore the lessons of Plymouth and Jamestown. The great agricultural collectivization schemes of the Soviet Union, China, Tanzania and Ethiopia, for instance, have uniformly reduced harvests and caused mass starvation.

Yet China, at least, like the first American colonies centuries ago, has begun making food production a matter of individual responsibility. As a result, shortages have been replaced with plenty; exhortation and compulsion have proved to be less powerful motivators than the simple realization that one's future depends on one's own efforts.

Thanksgiving has evolved into a virtually meaningless custom. But the Plymouth Colony provides some important lessons for today.

The settlers reaped a bountiful harvest in 1623 not because they trusted in God and their destiny any more than in previous years; the critical difference was that they adopted a form of economic organization that held individuals accountable for their actions. So as we celebrate Thanksgiving with our families this year, we should reflect on the importance of the free market economic system in making such sharing possible.

## 17. Liberation Theology's False Prophets

*July 15, 1987*

Throughout history the Christian message has been distorted by a variety of worldly ideologies. The medieval church was used to buttress imperial power; bloody crusades were conducted under the banner of Christ. Today Christians on both right and left cite the Bible in their grab for worldly power.

One of the most distorted of the current heresies is "liberation theology." Popularized by Third World clerics like Catholic theologian Carlos Christo, known as Brother Betto, and Franciscan Friar Leonardo Boff, the doctrine defines the Christian Gospels in revolutionary terms, focusing on the overthrow, through violence, if necessary, of secular institutions.

Liberation theology is a seductive doctrine, given a world full of political repression and economic injustice. But the movement is a profoundly dangerous one, for liberation theologians, in their quest for a new moral order, have turned to a totalitarian political philosophy: Marxism.

Indeed, Boff and Betto recently organized a group of church officials to tour the Soviet Union for two weeks. Boff explains that he wanted to study the positive aspects of Soviet society that can be applied to Brazil; Betto says that "in socialist countries we need to show how Latin America has a pioneering role in the construction of future socialist societies with integration of Christians."

This fascination with communism—an atheistic movement responsible for tens of millions of deaths—is shared by some Americans on the religious left. The Maryknoll nuns, for instance, have been enthusiastic propagandists for Nicaragua's Sandinistas, who are growing increasingly repressive and unpopular.

Liberation theology is flawed in two important ways. The first is its perversion of scripture. For though Christ consistently spoke out against oppression, he made it clear that his mission was a spiritual one: "My kingdom is not of this world," he told Pilate before the crucifixion.

Of course, a Christian's faith must suffuse his life, including his attitudes and actions toward injustice. But the "liberation" taught by the Gospels is freedom from, not through, this world. Fighting to right flawed human institutions is merely incidental to forming a right relationship with God.

The second problem with liberation theology is that it misjudges the true sources of political and economic oppression. "In Latin America," declares Boff, "the big enemy is not Marxism, it is capitalism."

Boff could make such a naive statement only because he has lived under neither system. His country, Brazil, has suffered from political repression, but it has been at the hands of conservative military officers instead of leftist revolutionaries. Pope John Paul II, however, could provide Boff with some firsthand testimony about life in the shadow of the Soviet Union.

Boff's economic misconceptions are equally great. The gaps between rich and poor in Brazil are hideous, but they are not caused by the sort of competitive capitalism that exists in America. Instead, Brazil's economy is heavily mercantilistic, where private ownership is mixed with government control, leading to privilege and corruption.

That liberation theologians could turn to the totalitarian, impoverished socialist bloc shows how desperately radical change is needed in Latin America and throughout the Third World. The revolution needed, however, is not Marxism but democracy—and capitalism. For, writes Michael Novak, a scholar at the American Enterprise Institute who is sensitive to the problem of underdevelopment but also serious about Christ's message, "the heart of the capitalist idea is to begin at the bottom, by releasing the economic creativity of the poor."

Therefore, adds Novak in his thoughtful new book, *Will It Liberate?* published by the Paulist Press, "the whole structure of economic law in Latin America needs to be shaken at its foundations, and built on new pediments." Until such a capitalist revolution occurs, he concludes, "government officials continue to act as did the viceroys of the colonial period, restricting legal economic activities to their family and friends."

Boff and Betto are right to care passionately about Latin America's poor. But they should not let the material supersede the spiritual. "Seek first [God's] kingdom and his righteousness," Christ taught the multitudes. Even the end of poverty will mean little for people who are lost eternally.

In any case, all the latest pilgrims to Moscow will find is an even more idolatrous human ideology than the one they are trying to supplant. Liberation theology, unfortunately, will liberate no one.

# 18. God And Mammon

*The Creation of Wealth: A Christian's Case for Capitalism* by Brian Griffiths (Downers Grove, Illinois: Intervarsity Press, $5.95).

*The Good News of the Kingdom Coming: The Marriage of Evangelism and Social Responsibility,* by Andrew Kirk (Downers Grove, Illinois: Intervarsity Press, $5.95).

*Is Capitalism Christian? Toward a Christian Perspective on Economics,* Edited by Franky Schaeffer (Westchester, Illinois: Crossway Books, $9.95).

*Spring 1986*

It is now taken for granted that capitalism is a more efficient economic system than egalitarianism or socialism. But is it a more virtuous system? It is here the critics of market economics have focused their recent attacks. Naturally Christian theologians and Catholic bishops have been recruited as combatants, and the debate can get theologically esoteric. Nevertheless, it remains of interest to anyone with interest in policy, because policy necessarily has moral implications, and biblical teaching is valued for its moral insights by Christians and non-Christians alike. In recent months, a number of books have emerged equating Christian principles with either the free market or socialism.

Andrew Kirk, associate director of the London Institute for Contemporary Christianity, believes that traditional Western evangelicals are "perpetrating an unbiblical divorce between spiritual salvation and liberation from evil structures and systems in the world." The transcendental message of Christ's saving grace is, in Kirk's view, inextricably tied to Karl

Marx's economic program for worldly redemption: put bluntly, to be a Christian is also to be a socialist.

Kirk contends that "throughout the Old Testament, there are indications that the private accumulation of wealth was considered contrary to the terms of God's covenant with his people." But Kirk misconstrues the Scriptures, treating, for instance, condemnation of unjust enrichment as a stricture against making money. Moreover, the Promised Land of Israel was apportioned among individual families, not held or owned by the state to promote the general welfare. And Mosiac law, particularly the Eighth Commandment—"Thou shall not steal"—protected private property ownership.

Brian Griffiths, international economist and dean of the City University Business School in London, seeks to prove the opposite of Kirk's thesis, that the very nature of man—and his God-given stewardship over the earth—necessarily entails the production of wealth. "At heart the process of wealth creation stems from a fundamental human drive, the result of being created in the image of God."

For this reason, God explicitly promises to reward fecund economic management: "the plans of the diligent lead to profit" (Proverbs 21:5); and the barns for those who "honor the Lord" with their wealth "will be filling to overflowing" (Proverbs 3:9–10). Christ builds on this theme with his parables of the servants who multiplied their master's assets and were rewarded accordingly (Luke 19:11–26; Matthew 25:14–30).

Kirk also relies on the New Testament to argue that believers should possess little more than the daily necessities of life. But as Griffiths observes: "The ownership of goods, houses, and clothes is not a sin. Jesus had friends who owned such things and he stayed in their homes and went in their boats. In the various parables which dealt with profit and investment . . . there is never a suggestion that work, business, banking, or investment were of themselves wrong." Saint Paul writes that "the love of money is the root of all kinds of evil" (1 Timothy 6:10), not that money itself is bad.

In permitting the accumulation of wealth, Christian ethics establishes special responsibilities regarding its use. The primary principle—and the real lesson of the incident of the rich young man whom Jesus tells to "sell everything" he has (Mark 10:21), a passage Kirk relies on—is that loyalty to God must come before all else.

Believers are also to give freely to the needy. However, in contrast to Kirk's coercive government program to reduce income inequality, the Bible emphasizes voluntary individual action to alleviate suffering. There is no God-given right to a minimum salary of the sort Kirk proposes nor any biblical basis for treating wage differentials as immoral.

Indeed, God rewards people as He wishes, instead of "fairly" by human standards. Christ tells one parable where the landowner justified his decision to pay workers the same no matter how long they worked, stating that "Friend, I am not being unfair to you . . . Don't I have the right to do what I want with my own money?" (Matthew 20:12–15).

Kirk no doubt is disappointed that Christ did not stage a political or economic revolution. "My kingdom is not of this world," Jesus told Pilate during his trial (John 18:36). Kirk tries to explain away the clear meaning of these words, but to no avail. Jesus's entire ministry was a spiritual one: "Despite poverty around him and the oppression and injustice of the colonial situation in which he found himself, he rejects a secular interpretation of salvation," as Griffiths says of Christ.

The spiritual nature of God's kingdom is emphasized throughout the New Testament. "Our citizenship is in heaven," writes Paul (Philippians 3:18–20). Indeed the "struggle is not against flesh and blood, but against . . . the spiritual forces of evil in the heavenly realms" (Ephesians 6:11–12). The virtues cited in the beatitudes as worthy of divine reward are all spiritual—coercive redistribution of property is not among them.

The fact that Jesus never appealed to the secular authorities to help implement his kingdom should be no surprise, in light of the nature of government. For how does the state represent the values inherent to the kingdom of God? Governments do not love or forgive; public institutions are rarely humble or gentle. The state is a coercive institution whose power has frequently been used through history to trample on human freedom and dignity. Experience shows that the clergy too can be brutal and rapacious when it gains political power. Christians are better off trying to stop the government engine of injustice, rather than trying to become the newest engineers.

In any case, the sort of values exhibited by Christ—forgiveness, generosity, gentleness, compassion, humility, kindness, love—cannot be enforced by government. Jesus expected believers to exhibit these traits daily, not impose them on others; he commanded his followers to give to the poor, not to force their neighbors to give. Compulsory compassion is an oxymoron.

In short, "because the Kingdom of God depends for its very existence on an inward supernatural power, it is impossible to translate it into contemporary social, political, and economic institutions" writes Griffiths. "It was established by God, and its extension depended on the Holy Spirit."

Though Christian Scriptures provide no specific economic policy agenda, not all social systems are equally consistent with Christian values. It is in discussing this relationship that Kirk is weakest. For someone living in a free society, he has a remarkably caricatured view of capitalism and a naive opinion of socialism. Neither system "has begun to achieve what it has promised," writes Kirk, but at least "Marxism has exalted collective freedom—the freedom to enjoy a basically dignified life." Apparently Kirk is unaware of the low standard of living, lack of basic freedoms, and poor health care in the Marxist world; his approving reference to "African socialism," pioneered by Julius Nyerere of Tanzania, ignores the economic disaster which has overtaken that continent. And Kirk must be oblivious to the gulf that separates working and ruling classes in socialist nations, where political position determines economic status.

Brian Griffiths and Franky Schaeffer, unlike Kirk, disclaim any particular scriptural basis for their economic preferences. Schaeffer, for instance, simply argues that capitalism has proved to be the best economic system in terms of "preserving Christian and humane values." He proves his point by demonstrating both how market-oriented economies have delivered the greatest degree of material prosperity to all their people and how government has so often stood in the way of economic progress, especially in the Third World.

But an even more fundamental virtue of capitalism is its preservation of individual liberty. Kirk complains that capitalism "increases the freedom of some, but always and inevitably at the expense of others." In other words, a free enterprise system presupposes enforcement of the Eighth Commandment prohibition against theft. The reality is that liberty—political, civil, and religious—does not flourish where there is no strong private economic sector. "The very existence of a market economy," writes Griffiths, "is in itself an enormous restriction on the power of the state over people's lives."

The lack of coercion is why capitalism is the best economic system for imperfect human beings. No one has forced an official ethos, lifestyle, or occupation on Kirk; he would not have the same freedom in a state-controlled economy. The free enterprise system not only reduces the power of one person over another, but also promotes cooperation, despite the selfishness that pervades every society, because voluntary exchange generally rewards competitors who best meet the needs of other people—by offering the finest products and services at the lowest prices.

In socialist countries, by contrast, the economy is driven by coercion and managed through politics. With state power supreme, greed emerges in pernicious forms. Individuals not only pillage what others have created, but feel justified in doing so. An oppressor class emerges, wielding power and privilege in the name of "the people," while the people themselves live in the hope that they can find favor with, or better still join, this ruling elite. This is precisely the sort of envy enjoined by the 10th Commandment, "Thou shalt not covet thy neighbor's goods."

This is why Schaeffer is justified in concluding that "capitalism is no better or worse than the citizens who employ it as a system of commerce." It neither advances existing human virtues nor corrects ingrained personal vices; it merely reflects them. But "socialism is always worse as a system than the collective sum of its people." By divorcing effort from reward, stirring up covetousness and envy, and destroying the freedom that is a necessary precondition for virtue, it tears at the fabric of goodness that people are to establish with each other, and with their God.

# II. The Political Game

# Sin City

## 19. Let Washington-Bashing Continue

*January 20, 1987*

With a half dozen presidential candidates already on the campaign trail—and many more on the way—Washington is again a favorite issue. After all, attacks on entrenched interests and unresponsive bureaucrats in the nation's capital have long been a staple of American politics. George Wallace derided pointy-headed bureaucrats; Jimmy Carter ran as a political outsider. And Ronald Reagan's antigovernment rhetoric didn't change even after his election.

But voices are now being raised in defense of poor Uncle Sam. Harry Freeman, for instance, an executive vice president with American Express, has proposed that Reagan and all the 1988 presidential contenders "declare a moratorium on Washington-bashing." We've got to" rekindle the interest of private people in public service," Freeman says, and to do so we must "restore the luster of public service."

Indeed, Freeman is a founding board member of the Center for Excellence in Government. Formed in 1983, the center says its purpose is to serve "as an advocate for excellence in government." In an attempt to promote what it calls a "new vision of government management," the organization has been holding workshops, publishing reports and organizing conferences.

These efforts are undoubtedly well-intentioned. But do we really want excellence in government?

This may seem a strange question to ask. Mark Abramson, the center's executive director, simply contends that "whatever government does, it should do well." Yet this philosophy assumes that the state is a fundamentally progressive institution, one devoted to serving the "public good." Unfortunately, however, that view simply does not reflect reality.

Indeed, while Freeman attacks both Carter and Reagan for having been elected while "deriding government as part of the problem rather than

43

part of the solution," they were absolutely right—even though neither actually carried out his rhetoric. On issues ranging from trade to energy to agriculture to transportation, it is the government, at all levels, that has managed to create and exacerbate crises through inappropriate intervention. All too often the problem is the public sector.

Where that is the case, do we want government institutions to operate more efficiently? The federal bureaucracy created energy shortages through price controls and other ill-considered regulations; better-enforced regulations would only have made the crisis worse. Limits on textiles, semiconductor chips, sugar and other imports have sharply raised product prices. More effective execution of the law would cost consumers even more. And so on.

Of course, we probably would benefit if the criminal justice system ran more smoothly, defense procurement were handled more efficiently, and agency payments were made more accurately. But excellence was never really an issue when the government was a small institution dedicated to protecting liberty and maintaining the infrastructure necessary for a free society. Only when the size and scope of the federal government grew did it become cumbersome and inept.

In short, what should we expect but fraud and waste when Uncle Sam hands out checks to more than half the population? How can a monopoly like the U.S. Postal Service be expected to provide excellent service inexpensively? And why is anyone surprised by destroyed returns and erroneous property seizures as the IRS seeks to extract a quarter of people's incomes?

Thus, despite the efforts of Freeman, Abramson and others, today's government will never do its job well; "excellence in government" is an oxymoron.

More important, however, we shouldn't want a proficient public sector. Making the modern state—an institution that simultaneously responds to the most elitist, paternalistic whims of some groups as well as the basest, selfish desires of others—more efficient will reinforce the worst activities of government the most.

So let the Washington-bashing not only continue but also result in action. Though the winning candidate needn't appoint incompetents, neither should he act as if bringing "talented private people" into government, as Freeman urges, will solve anything. Indeed, given that government absorbs and redistributes wealth rather than creates it, we desperately need to keep the very best people out in the private sector where they can do the most good.

The implementation of policy cannot be separated from its basic soundness. We should first re-examine government programs, eliminating those which actually harm the public. Then we can worry about promoting excellence in government. For the definition of public service should be doing what is right, not doing anything well.

## 20.  Hysteria over PACmania

*February 10, 1988*

"Money is the mother's milk of politics," observed the late California state treasurer, Jesse Unruh, and that is no less true in the nation's capital than in the Golden State.

In 1986 candidates for the U.S. Senate spent $182 million. House candidates spent even more, $227 million, one-third of which came from PACs; 194 of the victors received more than half of their contributions from the money committees.

Good government groups like Common Cause are now demanding "reform," and Washington is going through another of its periodic moralistic fits. The Senate spent three months locked in a filibuster over the issue last year and Majority Leader Robert Byrd is planning to again push his legislation restricting the role of PACs and providing public financing for Senate elections. Some Democratic members of the House and Senate would go even further, having introduced a constitutional amendment to strip First Amendment protection from financial "speech."

There are sound objections to all of these proposals. Though incumbents tend to receive more PAC money, ratcheting down PAC contributions will hinder the odd challenger who can raise substantial amounts of cash; in that case, lower spending would enhance the incumbent's substantial built-in advantages. Indeed, the scare-mongering over candidates buying elections insults the intelligence of American voters.

In 1986 the 34 Republican Senate candidates collectively outspent their Democratic foes by $28 million; the Democrats still won 20 of the races. As for the supposed power of PACs, the 4,100 existing money committees represent virtually every interest known to man and are united only on the issue of the importance of their own existence, if that. While a certain amount of funding is necessary to run a credible campaign, "the bottom line," observes political strategist Edward Rollins, is "not how much you raise, but how you spend your money."

Public financing of congressional elections would be an even worse affront to the average American, who shouldn't have to pay for the campaigns of the gaggle of second-raters who now dominate Congress. Today, at least, the suffering soul in Peoria can turn off offensive TV commercials and vote against candidates who think they can buy votes. But public financing would make the electorate directly finance every obnoxious politico's ambitious bid for power.

Finally, tampering with the Constitution to take away this very important form of expression—which is why the Supreme Court voided restrictions on independent expenditures in *Buckley vs. Valeo*—would limit Americans' ability to influence their elected officials. Do newspaper editors and citizens' groups seriously want to isolate legislators from political pressure? Such an approach may appeal to incumbent congressmen, but anyone concerned about the appropriateness of the policy that emanates from Capitol Hill should think twice before attempting to turn Congress into an ivory tower.

More important, however, the attempt to reconfigure the political process ignores the fundamental reason that money intrudes into politics: today's virtually unlimited redistributive state. For interest groups are only willing to invest in candidates because they expect to reap a return come budget time. Restrict what government can do and the moneymen will lose interest.

Indeed, today's PACmania mirrors yesterday's hysteria over l'affaire Deaver. "Who is this man calling?" asked *Time* magazine and first-family-friend-turned-lobbyist Michael Deaver found himself called before congressional committees and eventually convicted of perjury. For a time political leaders and newspaper pundits gnashed their teeth over the dire threat to democracy, but interest in reform soon waned.

Last year, the Senate Judiciary Committee approved legislation to sharply restrict lobbying by former government officials, but the bill failed to come to a vote in the full Senate. While Deaver now awaits sentencing, the rest of Washington's "influence peddlers" remain in business—essentially unaffected by the moralistic tornado that briefly swept through K Street.

And if we're lucky, the enthusiasm for making the taxpayers fund the campaigns of everyone from Alan Cranston to Jesse Helms will dissipate in the same way, once pundits and politicians alike find some other issue about which to express their outrage. For the electoral money-men have always been and will always be with us, just like the "public affairs consultants" who use contacts, money or sheer chutzpah to open doors for individuals and interest groups seeking one favor or another from government.

In fact, the issue of election finance has been around for a century or more. Will Rogers once remarked, "Politics has got so expensive that it takes lots of money to even get beat with." The only difference between modes of election finance is who wields the most influence.

Up into the early 1970s the major electoral money brokers were the wealthy contributors who could almost single-handedly fund a campaign. With the post-Watergate reforms, the fund-raiser who can successfully squeeze lots of people for $1,000 contributions has become more important, as have the dreaded political action committees. So now that the PACs have gained some measure of perceived influence, the reformers want to again change the rules of the game, by further restricting PAC contributions or supplanting the committees entirely through taxpayer financing.

But doing so would not eliminate the influence of money on elections, nor would it prevent powerful interest groups from having disproportionate access on Capitol Hill. The political balance could shift: labor unions, which can mobilize unpaid volunteers, might find their power enhanced, while corporations would be reduced to sending letters to their shareholders. Nevertheless, those people with important organizational ties, economic resources, social prestige or fame would continue to "drown out" the voice of the average American voter.

Indeed, the attempt to restrict PACs, like the proposal to further regulate lobbying, treats symptoms rather than causes. For both lobbying and political contributions are unfortunate, but inevitable, aspects of democracy. After all, these attempts to influence policy simply are one means of petitioning the government on issues of concern; how can Congress start making fine distinctions between what kind of petitions are good and which are not?

Washington alone is the home of more than 3,700 associations, 3,300 PACs, 34 state offices and 20,000 registered lobbyists; many other groups operate from New York and elsewhere. All rely to some degree on connections developed through election contributions, volunteer labor, fund-raising and lobbying. Sanitizing this system simply is impossible.

True, new election rules might succeed in reducing the amount of cash involved, but they would not make the process more honest. Banning PACs would not turn elections into pristine debates over public policy decided solely on "merit"; doing so would only rearrange who most influences the outcome.

More important, the fundamental cause of labor unions, businesses and associations contributing millions to politicians is the fact that the federal government has enormous power to distribute favors through its vast regulatory apparatus and more than $1 trillion in spending every year.

As a result, special interests have an incentive to spend vast sums of money to gain a share of that pot of gold. And why shouldn't they, given the enormous potential that Congress has to enrich and destroy? Lobbyists and PACs together may have raised the price of access to obscene levels, but there's no reason to believe that they have corrupted the process. The system is inherently corrupt.

Said economist F.A. Hayek more than 40 years ago, "As the coercive power of the state will alone decide who is to have what, the only power worth having will be a share in the exercise of this directing power."

As long as the power and reach of the federal government expand, as they have even under President Reagan, the incentive to spend even more for influence will continue to grow.

Are congressional campaigns suffering from gross financial excess? Maybe so, but it is not the PACmen who are subverting democracy; instead, it is the political process that is creating, and defiling, the campaign fund-raisers. For as long as the federal government remains an endless cornucopia for the well-connected, interest groups will try to buy access.

If we really want to stop interest groups from buying policy, we have to reduce the value of the policy up for bid. There's no other way to purify politics or the politicians.

## 21.  Power Can Be Fun

*October 28, 1983*

The power of Washington's permanent government—the career establishment—is legendary. Perhaps more than anything else, it is the influence of these unelected bureaucrats that makes political change so difficult. However, a more subtle influence on national policy is the atmosphere of the capital, and the White House in particular. Having power is fun, but using it—running agencies, creating programs, just "doing things"—is truly exciting, bringing the sort of acclaim that most people crave.

From the moment the election returns are in and a candidate becomes the President-elect, he and his aides become the center of the political universe. This was as true for Ronald Reagan as for his predecessors, and he likes it. Communications Director David Gergen says Reagan "really enjoys the exercise of power." Gergen himself admits to being impressed with the grandeur and sweep of his office. Navy Secretary John Lehman has allowed that making money is not "one-tenth as much fun" as running the Navy. And a former aide to Franklin Delano Roosevelt, Jim Rowe, now 73 years old, says that "there are no better jobs in the world; I haven't done anything so important since."

Indeed, probably few former White House staffers or Assistant Secretaries would disagree with Rowe. Their attitude is a natural outgrowth of work in a government that reeks of perquisites, a city that uncritically grants prestige to government positions, and a system that glorifies and encourages state action. There are, after all, only a few who have been chosen to govern; who can reject this manifest destiny?

If nothing else, the mere trappings of office will convince you that you're a notch above everyone else. The President, for example, lives in a house run by 86 employees, which tourists wait hours in the rain to visit. There are limos, helicopters, and planes for travel, a barbershop for looks, a medical clinic for health, a movie theater, concerts, and parties for entertainment, and a bowling alley, tennis court, and gym for exercise.

The White House staff doesn't have it quite so good, but it nevertheless benefits from trickle-down status. My office, for example, when I was a Special Assistant to the President, was easily 300 square feet, with 15-foot ceilings, two balconies, a sofa, large chairs, a small refrigerator, and a fireplace. My dirty rug was replaced with a new one by the General Services Administration (GSA), even though I was satisfied with the cleaning job on my old one. Not bad for a 24-year-old a couple of years out of law school.

And my office wasn't even top of the line. You see, it was in the Old Executive Office Building (OEOB), the hulking granite structure next to the White House. Though this location is decidedly superior to the New Executive Office Building, which isn't even within the White House complex, it can't compare with the West Wing of the White House itself, in which the Oval Office and the Cabinet Room are lodged. Virtually every top aide works in the West Wing; the only exception early on was Lyn Nofziger, who voluntarily took a much more spacious office in the OEOB.

All sorts of paintings, watercolors, and presidential photos are available for White House aides. The White House art collection itself is at the disposal of the very top staff. Michael Deaver, for example, claimed a host of George Catlin paintings of the West; Ed Meese took a scene of the Civil War, and Martin Anderson a couple of paintings of Daniel Webster. I contented myself with about a dozen run-of-the-mill oils and watercolors, which admittedly wasn't bad for a single office.

The emphasis on office perks extends throughout the government. The GSA regulations are quite detailed: Big-shots get up to 750-square-foot offices, 50-square-foot kitchens with 300-square-foot dining areas, and 45-square-foot bathrooms. They are also entitled to wooden wastebaskets (rectangular metal ones go to mid-level people; round metal ones to peons), "executive" wood furniture (middies get "unitized" wood, while the underlings get metal), water carafes, dictionary stands, rugs, and so on.

But the White House is the place to be. Take your friends and relatives (and their friends and relatives) on tours of the Oval Office and Cabinet

Room. Show your less fortunate college classmates the Rose Garden. Or bring them to a welcoming ceremony for a foreign leader on the South Lawn.

Of course, virtually any White House staffer can do these things. If you're a bit more important you can get presidential matchbooks, cuff links, tie clips, stick pins, bracelets, glasses, and jelly-bean jars. If you're a little more important still, you can get tickets—free, of course—to the President's box at Kennedy Center. There you can enjoy watching the other patrons watch you as you enter the box.

For official business many White House aides can use official cars chauffeured by Army sergeants. I can't count the number of times I was greeted with "sir," had my door opened for me and the light turned on in back when I started reading. But we were the poor cousins compared to top Cabinet officials, who rate limousines. As one lobbyist declared to *The Washingtonian* magazine: "Do you expect Secretary Regan to pull up to the Treasury in a Pinto? This is a big-car town."

One's sense of self-worth is enhanced in other ways. High-ranking staffers can eat at the White House Mess, a fine, wood-paneled eatery a floor below the Oval Office. If a phone call comes in, the Mess staff immediately brings a telephone to your table. For the very highest aides— Deputy Assistants to the President and Assistants to the President (alas, I was but a Special Assistant)—a special Mess dining room is available. For staffers somewhat lower on the totem pole, there is an executive dining room in the OEOB.

Deputy Assistants and above can also use the gym in the OEOB; the masses of employees, who were able to use it under the Carter Administration, were shut out after (the story goes) a high-ranking aide returned from playing tennis to find his clothes tossed in the hall because it was then women's hours. So he quickly solved that problem by closing the gym, spending a few thousand dollars remodeling it, and reopening it to the elite. The right to use the White House tennis courts is even more closely guarded. The White House barbershop was formerly open to all, but is now restricted to the President and Vice President. Plans to add another hair-styling salon were scrubbed last year but only after congressional protests.

Other unique benefits of the White House include having photos taken with the President, and getting them, as well as certificates and letters signed by him, framed for your office walls. There are also a host of well-stocked parties to celebrate the Fourth of July, Christmas, and legislative victories (such as AWACS), and to honor departing staff members.

Perhaps the most fundamental divider between the average man and the Important People is the ID card, the magic piece of plastic that lets one walk or drive into the White House complex past all of the watching common folk. Ah, to strut past those dentists and teachers and laborers who will never do anything as important as you . . .

Indeed, the central importance of status and perks causes some of the bitterest internecine battles. Former Secretary of State Haig's celebrated anger about not being in the first helicopter during one leg of that trip in Europe was only the most publicized fight over the trappings of power. After all, the first decision a President has to make is not, Do we go to war? but, Who gets the corner office down the hall from the Oval Office?

This internal warfare often has made policy battles look mundane by comparison. Who gets to go on foreign trips? Who gets to take his staff on foreign trips? Who gets his staff into the White House Mess? Who gains White House passes, as opposed to the more restrictive OEOB ones, for his assistants? And who gets the beautiful models of historic American ships? (You think that last question unimportant? Think again. The Office of Administration received a pile of memos explaining the particular writers' desperate need for a model ship.)

As intoxicating as the perks is Washington's constant glorification of those who work in the White House. At times, everything seems to revolve around the White House. The *Washington Post,* for example, devoted a huge article to "The Right Table," which found, not surprisingly, that the best tables usually go to those with political power and connections—to White House aides, senators, and important lobbyists.

This attitude is symptomatic of the way Washington works. The *New York Times* reported on the chaos that attended one presidential news conference: the postponement of a college basketball game, the late arrivals to parties, and the setting up of TV sets at others. People just couldn't "miss a single beat from the White House drums." The head of the White House fellows program seemed to sum up the Washington experience when he spoke of the "sense of self-confidence that comes from hobnobbing with the high and mighty." There's nothing particularly wrong with wanting to hobnob with the high and mighty; frankly, I've enjoyed doing it. But the problem is that calling them high and mighty tends to make them believe that they really are high and mighty.

Even in my less than exalted position in government, I was treated far better than I had been before I entered the White House, and than I am now. For example, lots of people became unnaturally interested in what I thought. An official at one of Washington's many think tanks figured that a letter from me would help direct a study in the right direction. On the phone I found that secretaries who lazily asked me where I was calling from quickly got more interested after I intoned: "The White House."

Out of the blue I received a luncheon invitation from a prestigious graduate school; I was seated next to former Secretary of State Edmund Muskie. My junior college asked me to give a commencement speech. Some Republican groups asked me to speak and one gave me a Man of the Year award. Business groups asked me to speak on Administration policy, and one national convention had me on an issues panel. I was also paraded in front of a host of constituent groups by the White House's Office of Public Liaison—the visitors always seemed to leave satisfied that they had talked with "the White House." Even my letters were treasured. One student used a thank-you letter from me as a political credential; a California county supervisor released a congratulatory letter of mine to the press.

Lobbyists make it worse. (Where else but in Washington would a university—seriously—offer a degree program in lobbying?) One lobbyist worked frantically to set up an appointment between me and a natural gas pipeline company executive she was representing. The executive proceeded to tell me of his devotion to free enterprise, "but" (the most important word in most businessmen's vocabularies) he thought natural gas deregulation was unnecessary. I was less than supportive, but he and the lobbyist were both happy—they had spoken with "the White House." Another poor soul, who'd had trouble with the Department of Energy in the previous Administration, almost prostrated himself before me in an attempt to get me to bless his enterprise.

Once the Chamber of Commerce invited me over to an energy breakfast. One California utility company put on a lavish dinner for the Californians. Several oil companies took me out to lunch. Other lobbyists had extra tickets to political dinners. One even gave away Redskins football tickets.

Then there's the press. To reporters, you are the news. What you say—or write to a county commissioner—is important. It is no wonder that *U.S.A. Today* kicked off its inaugural issue with a gathering for virtually the entire power structure of Washington (which, unfortunately, I didn't get invited to since I'd left the White House). The best restaurants were the settings for lunches with Washington bureau chiefs and White House correspondents. Calls frequently came in on particular issues, and it was up to me what I did or didn't tell them. And when I visited my parents for the holidays, the local newspaper happily interviewed me.

In fact even foreigners recognized how important I was. A KGB agent from the Soviet Embassy took me to lunch during the transition, and called a few times afterward despite my refusal to return his calls, and sent me a Christmas card. And the State Department had me call several foreign embassies to impress them with how seriously the U.S. viewed one matter. They were, of course, duly impressed.

Great efforts are always made to greet the President in style on his return from trips abroad or around the country. Shortly after I left the White House last year a memo was circulated to all White House staff detailing the bus arrangements for staff and their guests, directions for those driving separately, and information on getting tickets for the arrival ceremony at Andrews Air Force Base.

Though ordinary White House staffers don't get welcome-home ceremonies, life isn't too hard. White House aides are often treated with even greater deference by other government officials than by outsiders. For example, when I was working on draft registration and military manpower issues, I had to approve some new Selective Service regulations. At the appointed hour I got in my government car and was driven across town to the Selective Service headquarters, where the Director met me in the lobby and escorted me to a conference room where the Deputy Director, Counsel, and a staff attorney were waiting. I dominated the meeting with my questions and concerns, left with the Director escorting me downstairs and offering to take me on a tour of the computer facilities whenever I liked, and got into my waiting car.

One time I called a senior Selective Service staffer but had to hang up before I was connected to him. He frantically called around until he located me, and apologized for our being cut off. Another time I called the then-Acting Director; his secretary brightened up considerably when she heard my name.

The treatment I received at the State Department was only slightly less ostentatious. During the incessant guerrilla warfare on the Administration's tough position against the Law of the Sea Treaty, I was frequently asked to attend meetings to set down the party line. I usually arrived, delivered my message in firm tones, and quickly departed. After one such session, I received several phone calls from representatives of the State Department and other departments asking me about my comments; it seems that one sentence I had rather innocently uttered had "really set off the meeting." They wanted me to find out if the White House was going off on some new tangent.

Later, to impress both our delegates from other departments and foreign delegates, I was asked to attend a couple of the Law of the Sea conferences. The State Department sent me first class, of course. I was exempt from routine delegation chores, and was able to push myself into meetings that representatives of regular agencies couldn't.

The Defense Department used the little things to emphasize the importance of White House staffers: A daily clipping service is circulated with little extras dropped in on a day's notice. The military people throughout the White House complex are polite, deferent, and full of "yes sirs." When the Pentagon put on an exercise simulating a future energy crisis, a full colonel came by to brief me, the participants were treated to lunch and a reception, and we all received several photos, courtesy of the taxpayers, to remember the sessions by.

Finally, most agencies firmly believe in the White House's right to know, if not the public's right to know. A friend of mine, who edited a political magazine, wanted a copy of the State Department's white paper on El Salvador. "Sorry," they said. "We're out." My assistant called them, and two copies were promptly sent over. Later on, one of the anti-draft-registration groups requested a copy of a Selective Service report. The response was the same: "We can't fine one." Oddly enough, they'd had no trouble previously finding a couple of copies for me.

Being treated so well tends to encourage you to treat other people like the inferiors they obviously are. One high official wanted to see me for five minutes at a particular time; I ended up leaving a meeting across town, spending 15 minutes driving to the White House, running in and out for an instruction that could have been handled by phone, and spending 15 minutes driving back across town. One middle-level staffer I knew was entrusted by his boss with a critical mission: to hand-carry a manuscript across town for another official to look at. And then there was the person who always had his secretary get me on the line before he'd get on, and always wanted me to come up to his office to meet. But perhaps most disturbing is the fact that what bugged me most was not that he did it, but that he did it to me, since I was higher in the hierarchy than he.

The perks, the way people treat you, the atmosphere—all of this would be funny were it not so important in shaping the attitudes of the people who shape national policy. The loss of perspective is understandable. Just think. Your work is important. What you think is important. You are important. And you become even more important by doing things. Time and again people, in complete seriousness, would justify their own empire-building as being "for the President." No stone should be left unturned "for the President." And most of them really believed it.

Perhaps our one satisfaction is the knowledge that every government official will be out one day. Hamilton Jordan, in his memoirs, relates Inauguration Day, 1981, when the Carters and their entourage were flown to Georgia. Suddenly Jordan had to figure out how to get forty miles away; "it had been years since I had to worry about such details." He had to hitch a ride with a friend. So, too, will every current White House aide have to worry about details one day.

Perhaps we should adopt the practice of the Romans so many centuries ago. They gave their Caesars returning from foreign victories a triumphal march along the Via Appia, just as we give our Presidents a parade down

Pennsylvania Avenue. But in Rome a slave continually whispered in the conqueror's ear, *Sic transit gloria mundi* ("All worldly glory is fleeting"). A former White House aide could serve in the same role today. In fact, I'd be happy to volunteer.

# Do Elections Matter?

## 22. America's House of Lords

*November 23, 1988*

In theory, the United States is a representative democracy. But Congress has essentially become a House of Lords, with competitive elections a thing of the past and members serving for life.

Only six of the 408 incumbents who defended their House seats this year lost, for a staggering 99 percent re-election rate. Just one incumbent who was not tainted by scandal fell.

Fifty-seven incumbents didn't even face an opponent while another 24 were opposed only by fringe candidates. And even most major party contests resulted in electoral massacres: all told, 370, or 85 percent, of the races were won by margins of 60 percent or more.

This was not the way the system was supposed to work. When the framers of the Constitution created the House of Representatives, they intended it to be the body most responsive to the voters.

And so it once was: In the second congressional election some 40 percent of incumbents were defeated. Between 1789 and 1896 at least half of the members were freshmen. The average congressional career in 1870 was less than four years; as late as 1920 the average was still less than seven. Henry Clay, who ended up as speaker of the House, served only six terms, or 12 years.

Today someone in his sixth term is lucky to chair a subcommittee. House Speaker Jim Wright was first elected in 1954, at the age of 31; it was 1987 before he claimed the top job.

Michigan's John Dingell chairs the Energy and Commerce Committee; he was 29 when he won a special election in 1955. Dan Rostenkowski of Illinois, who rules the Ways and Means Committee, was 30 when he was elected in 1958.

Not only do these men possess life and death power over bills on critical issues; they almost inevitably abuse their influence. One of the few

57

electoral casualties this year was Rhode Island's Fernand St. Germain, the chairman of the Banking Committee.

St. Germain, elected at age 32 in 1960, consistently worked to protect the securities industry from competition and to block attempts to deal with the savings and loan crisis. However, he lost only after he was caught accepting a stream of gifts from the companies he was aiding; even so, 44 percent of his constituents still voted for him.

The House's perpetual re-election machine also creates an ethic of greed and envy that erodes the very foundations of a liberal democracy. The unending pitch from legislators, Republicans as well as Democrats, is to keep them in power so that they can get more goodies for the district by robbing the general public.

Even the 54 Republican members of the "Reagan Revolution" class elected in 1980 changed their attitude toward government programs when they started thinking about getting re-elected.

Relates Thomas Hartnett, a former South Carolina congressman: "Who among us would want to go home having voted for cuts in veterans benefits, Medicare, student loans? . . . Who wants to be cut up by an opponent the next time around, when going along on all the various spending measures can ensure a long tenure in office?"

If congressional elections are to again become at least as competitive as the selection process for the Soviet Union's Communist Party Central Committee, we must cut down the built-in advantages of incumbency.

One is the $1.2 million for staff, which allows several district offices as well as a national one. The number of congressional staffers, many of whom do little else than promote the re-election of their bosses, has mushroomed in recent years.

Even worse is the franking privilege. House members sent out 758 million pieces of mail in 1986 for a cost of $96 million; the flood ebbed ever so slightly this year to just 600 million. Members have even developed sophisticated systems to target mailings to voters by their occupation and other factors.

These advantages are compounded by the tendency of interest groups to give almost entirely to incumbents, who, on average, outspend challengers by 4.3 to one. Those wanting favors from government simply bet on what is almost a sure thing: a legislator running for re-election.

Cutting down budgets, staffs and mailings is not enough, however. We should limit the number of terms that members of both the House and Senate can serve.

That is the only way to break up a permanent political class now devoted almost solely to maintaining its own power. Let a House member be barred from serving for more than three terms: a senator could fill two. Then there would always be a large number of legislators thinking of something other than getting re-elected.

Observes Hartnett: "It is time that we told (our representatives) that after a limited number of terms, we will give you a gold watch, a brass band, put you on a bus, send you home and let you live under the laws you passed while you were in Congress."

Which would be a lot fairer system than today's House of Lords.

## 23. In Praise of the Non-Voter

*November 2, 1988*

The presidential election is almost upon us and half or more of the potential voters may stay home on Nov. 8. Only 53.3 percent of eligible Americans voted in 1984, and the number is expected to be even lower this year.

As a result people have proposed everything from Election Day registration to automatically signing up citizens when they buy license plates. There are even some observers who support the Australia model, where voting is compulsory and refuseniks are fined.

But voting—that is, electing people who have enormous power over every aspect of our lives—is a serious responsibility. What is wrong with requiring people to engage in a little effort to register and vote?

In fact, the original electorate was limited to property owners in an attempt to ensure that voters had a real stake in the community. While such a restriction may be unrealistic today, it is not unreasonable to ask citizens to demonstrate some commitment to the polity before voting.

Nor is there any justification for placing a guilt trip on those who register but then decide not to vote. After all, if they really aren't concerned enough to wander down to the polls on Election Day, they shouldn't do so.

Indeed, the real function of voting is not to discharge some abstract civic duty, but to influence the election of a candidate and thereby affect government policy. If people don't care about the politicians or the issues, they are right not to vote.

One black activist has tied voting to racial solidarity, arguing that "whether we like or dislike candidates and their policies is less important than ensuring a massive black turnout at the polls. That way, blacks will have the political clout to demand concessions from the winner."

However, if people, whatever their color, really don't agree with any of the candidates, it doesn't matter much who is elected: none of them is likely to give much by way of concessions. And reflexive voting will only undermine a group's influence, since it will be taken for granted.

If, in contrast, enough people refuse to choose between equally bad alternatives parties will have to field better candidates to attract non-voters back to the polls.

In fact, the sad state of the public schools provides yet another reason not to dragoon people into voting. High school graduates these days have no idea where most foreign countries are; they have no sense of history and don't understand economics.

Even worse, they have been taught that our transfer society, in which interest groups use government power to reward private greed and envy, is a just system. Do we really want these people determining the fate of the nation? Until we produce a better educated electorate it's crazy to beg and bully people to vote.

Of course, this does not mean that democracy should be abandoned. The defects of a system in which a majority or an influential minority can use its influence to loot or repress everyone else is obvious; that's why we have all suffered so as the Constitution's limits on government power have been increasingly ignored.

However, there is no better system of governance. Monarchies and dictatorships offer even less freedom. As a result, we are stuck with the present, imperfect process.

But let's stop worrying about the number of Americans who show up at the polls. Though the United States now ranks No. 23 out of the 24 leading democracies in terms of the percentage of eligible citizens who vote, that number has varied widely over time, ranging from 43 percent in 1924 to 65 percent in 1960.

Anyway, the "right" number of voters is at most the number who actually go to the polls: Anyone not interested enough to vote obviously shouldn't do so. And, unfortunately, even some people who cast ballots haven't studied the issues, making the "right" number of voters even smaller.

It's too late to affect vote drives this election, but on Nov. 9 we should start planning some changes for 1990. The future goal should be to instill a civic ethic of not only voting, but also paying attention to issues and eschewing the use of the state to enrich oneself.

Registration should remain a requirement for voters, signifying the fact that casting a vote is serious business, unlike responding to an opinion poll. And the ubiquitous "public service" ads urging people to turn out on Election Day should instead ask them to vote only if they have given sufficient consideration to the issues to make a reasoned decision.

In the end, there is no better system than democracy and a democracy needs voters to function. But the democracy that gets the most voters is not necessarily the democracy that governs best.

## 24. The Unnecessary Debates

*October 5, 1988*

The American people have survived yet another election perennial, the presidential debate. After spending months sniping at each other from afar, George Bush and Michael Dukakis actually shared a platform together.

But the result was as much obfuscation as illumination. With fear of making a gaffe topmost in their minds, the candidates attempted to say as little as possible. Instead, their main goal was to project an attractive TV image to a largely disinterested electorate.

Yet in some quarters watching the debates has become a test of good citizenship. If you choose to ignore two low-quality political hacks trying to disguise their personal ambition with public-spirited rhetoric, you are considered to be basically unpatriotic.

The pressure on the networks is even greater. NBC, which paid hundreds of millions of dollars to televise the Olympics, a genuine news event that only occurs once every four years, was literally bludgeoned into carrying the debate along with everyone else.

But why? Anyone who wanted to see the debate could do so by simply switching to another channel. Why shouldn't people who preferred to watch the global sportsfest have that opportunity?

The fixation on debates makes no sense. In fact, presidential debates are a recent innovation, starting in 1960; the next one did not occur for another 16 years. And in 1980 the Carter and Reagan campaigns almost didn't reach agreement on their sole debate.

Unfortunately, there is no reason to believe that debates have caused voters to make better decisions. Richard Nixon was thought to have won his encounter with Jack Kennedy on substance, but the latter looked better on TV and picked up votes. Gerald Ford hurt himself with his comment about the lack of Soviet domination of Poland, but that was a meaningless flap.

In 1980 Reagan used his fabled charm to parry Carter's attacks, but the show demonstrated more Reagan's qualifications as a nice guy than as president. In 1984 the debates successively raised and then quashed the question of Reagan's age, but never reached the more critical issue of his almost non-existent management style.

And this year the first debate, at least, provided the same dearth of information about the candidates. Their sharp disagreements over a few specific policies obscure the fact that both would preside over an ever-expanding federal establishment. The only difference—but one not illuminated by the debate—is how fast the increase would be.

In fact, there is at least one sense in which today's debates are counterproductive. The Lincoln-Douglas debates featured prodigious minds arguing at length on serious issues. The current contests, in contrast, are carefully arranged events designed to highlight the one-liners and 30-second answers that make the lead on network news programs.

Moreover, in the aftermath of an avalanche of commentary on who won, what gaffes were committed, and which camp more fully met its goals, it is easy to lose sight of the substance altogether. Who would be the better president seems to be almost the last consideration.

The pitiful state of the American presidential debate is evidenced by the negotiations carried on by the Bush and Dukakis camps over such issues as the height of the lecterns. Even worse was the expectations game.

Bush's aides spent months pointing to Dukakis' earlier experience in moderating a TV debate show. Dukakis' staffers responded by citing Bush's experience in the 1984 vice presidential debate, "the only relevant experience," they said.

But who cares which candidate collected more points from debate coaches? What should be important is how the candidates would govern, not how they answer a few questions in a highly artificial setting.

The best thing for a serious voter to do is to tune out this sort of useless TV exercise. If you want to know who "won," just read the newspaper the next day. Any number of political analysts, campaign strategists, reporters, columnists and others will let you know their opinion.

If you are interested in substance, however, compare the records of two men who both have had long political careers. Look at the policies that they have advocated, the platforms of their respective parties, and the opinions of the people around them. If you can't make up your mind on the basis of their extensive public records, then, frankly, you shouldn't be voting. A 90-minute debate won't offer any new information.

It's too late now to cancel the final presidential and the vice presidential debates. But in 1992 we should drop these silly media extravaganzas and concentrate on getting the candidates to talk about substantive issues. Once they do that, then we can again worry about getting them in the same room to answer a few questions together.

## 25. The Turkey Ballot

*November 16, 1988*

One of the most depressing elections in years is finally over; unfortunately, someone won. It's regrettable that, when faced with two bad choices such as Bush and Dukakis, the American people couldn't reject both of them.

The solution is what Vermont activist John McClaughry has termed the "turkey ballot"—placing "none of the above" (NOTA) alongside the names of the candidates. Then the American people could say "thanks but no thanks" to all the contenders.

In fact, Nevada currently provides such a choice, and at least twice NOTA has won the most votes in primaries. The leading candidates still became their parties' nominees, but, not surprisingly, they lost in the general election.

Better, however, would be a system that applied to general elections as well as primaries, and that was more than symbolic. Let candidates for every office, from county dogcatcher to president, have to beat NOTA in addition to their fellow politicos.

The system could be quite simple. If NOTA triumphed at the polls, the leading candidate would not take office; instead, a second election would be held.

If NOTA again prevailed in a primary, no candidate would be fielded; the general election would feature whatever other contenders had won their respective parties' primaries.

If NOTA won a plurality in the general election, the state would schedule a new, special election. (Legislative seats could be left vacant, while executive offices, such as the governorship, could be filled temporarily by the outgoing incumbent.) Instead of holding new primaries, candidates would circulate petitions to get on the ballot. Another NOTA victory would cause the process to repeat.

A losing candidate with more chutzpah than common sense could run again. But one would hope that being voted a turkey by one's neighbors would have a sobering effect on even the most egotistical politician.

Indeed, successive humiliations by the electorate might become an effective way of driving some of the worst dregs out of the political system. Today, second-rate candidates get elected by beating third-rate opponents; with a NOTA system both the second-raters and the third-raters would lose.

Reforming the presidential system would be more complicated and would require a constitutional amendment. Nevertheless, the change would be worth the trouble.

Primaries could offer NOTA as an option, with uncommitted delegates chosen if NOTA garnered a plurality. The only restriction on the delegates would be that they could not vote for any candidate defeated by NOTA.

In the general election a NOTA victory in the electoral college would throw the contest into the House of Representatives. A NOTA popular vote override should also be added, forcing a new election, with a shortened campaign season, if NOTA beat all the contenders. Since it would be tough to hold a second election before the end of the incumbent president's term, he or she could remain in office as acting president until a winner was finally declared.

Perhaps the main problem with NOTA is that it would make the political process more unstable. There is an obvious advantage in having elections—especially for president—decided by a specific date.

However, it is more important to get thoughtful, qualified people elected to what are positions of enormous authority. Government should provide the framework necessary for a free society, not an endless soup kitchen for clamorous interest groups. If a few contests resulted in the defeat of both candidates—who so often treat elections, in the words of H.L. Mencken, as advanced auctions of stolen goods—we might see an improvement in the political debate.

Allowing voters to support NOTA would also give them the benefit of casting a ballot in which they could believe. No more would they be restricted to choosing the lesser of two evils.

Further, NOTA would provide a genuine option for non-voters who don't currently participate because they dislike the two main alternatives. Their protest against the political status quo could finally be registered at the polls.

This year is not the first election to feature two turkeys running for president. And it almost certainly won't be the last one to do so.

Unless we give the American people an opportunity to reject both major party nominees, that is. Then when candidates didn't offer thoughtful and principled leadership, we could tell them to try again until they got it right.

# Interest Group Heaven

## 26. Preaching and Politics

*August 3, 1988*

The presidential candidacies of the two ministers—Democrat Jesse Jackson and Republican Pat Robertson—may have failed, but clerical meddling in politics remains a constant. The Catholic bishops recently decided that the Strategic Defense Initiative was immoral; the General Assembly of the Presbyterian Church has voted to condemn nuclear deterrence. In July the Church of the Brethren adopted a resolution opposing covert military operations. Jerry Falwell, who says he has dropped out of politics, is nevertheless collecting signatures urging President Reagan to pardon Irangate defendant Oliver North. And the Virginia state convention of the United Methodists, which last year fought legislation creating a state lottery, has gone on record against parimutuel (racetrack) betting; the delegates even approved a plan for churches to take up a special offering to oppose the proposal.

In fact, religious lobbyists have battled each other over issues as diverse as contra aid and the Grove City civil rights bill during the past year. And come November the political firmament will be full of religious leaders making competing political endorsements.

This spectacle of clerics using the Gospel to promote their ideological preferences is not pretty. Three centuries ago those who desired to freely worship God crossed an ocean to found what became a new nation; today those who claim to follow God drag him into disputes over gambling.

The problem is not, however, simply the intertwining of religion and politics. It is not only proper but essential that people apply in the political arena the fundamental moral values they derive from their religious beliefs; a concern for human life rooted in the Bible deserves to be taken no less seriously than one based on the Humanist Manifesto. Indeed, if the atheistic totalitarian death states of this century have proved anything, it is that "the naked public square," in theologian Richard John Neuhaus' words, is a dangerous place.

But while the Bible—the most important sacred text in a nation where Christianity is the predominant religion—tells us a lot about right and wrong in dealing with God and our neighbors, it says much less about the role of the state. The covenant nation of ancient Israel may have been an ecclesiocracy, but it bears little resemblance to the society in which Jesus lived, let alone today's secular system. And Christ offered a blueprint for individual salvation, not a legislative agenda.

God's failure to provide a laundry list of divine public policies does not mean he is unconcerned about the human condition; the Bible is, for instance, full of general injunctions about one's duty to assist those in need. But man must rely on reason as well as revelation to determine the best means of achieving that or any other godly end. God equipped men with minds and, in the Epistle of James, offered to provide wisdom to those who ask for it. People should use their God-given abilities to decide the controversies of the day, instead of expecting to find a specific Bible verse on every issue.

Yet clerics on both the left and right continue to fall into the temptation of confusing God's general principles with their preferred policies. What is the scriptural objection to the Strategic Defense Initiative, for instance? The Bible calls men to be peacemakers, but it nowhere criticizes a space-based defensive missile system. While there are lots of practical questions about the viability and impact of SDI—issues that a prudent Christian must consider—one can as easily argue that SDI will promote peace as disrupt it.

Similarly, what Methodist doctrine does parimutuel betting transgress? There is nothing in the Bible to suggest that government should prevent people from wagering a few dollars on a horse race. Gambling may be a bad thing, but then the church's responsibility is to preach against it, not lobby for a government ban.

The religious right has similarly gone awry in its reliance on the state. Pornography and promiscuity, for instance, are condemned in the Bible as sinful. However, neither Christ nor the apostles turned to government to help them establish the Kingdom of Heaven. In fact, in his letter to the Corinthian church Paul did not even urge believers to dissociate from non-Christians who engaged in immoral behavior: "What business is it of mine to judge those outside the church?" he asked, "God will judge those outside."

The 1988 election may determine the nation's direction for years to come. But that doesn't justify clerics' jumping into the partisan fray, acting as if God is a Republican or a Democrat. For God's transcendent message is one of love, repentance and salvation, not conservatism, liberalism or any other secular ideology.

Christians and members of other faiths should be involved in civic affairs, and they shouldn't hesitate to act based on their religious convictions. They should not, however, confuse scriptural injunctions regarding peace and justice with any political party's platform.

## 27. Taking Evangelicals for a Ride in the Stars

*May 25, 1988*

As the Reagan administration tried to deal with the burgeoning Iran-Contra scandal in early 1987, the president "remained in the White House, isolated and remote," writes former Chief of Staff Donald Regan in his new book, *For the Record*. Paralysis ensued.

Why did the "Great Communicator" refuse to meet with the press or take his case to the people?

"The First Lady's Friend in San Francisco had predicted on the basis of astrology that harm would come to Reagan if he went out of the White House—or even, on certain days, outdoors," explains Regan. "All press conferences were also subject to the Friend's approval."

In fact, for seven years the highest elected official in the land has been adapting his schedule in response to the advice of someone who has concluded that the president's "sun is in the mid heaven. . . . His stars are very lucky for a country. And he has three planets in the sign of their exultation."

The first lady turned to astrologer Joan Quigley after the 1981 attempt on President Reagan's life. And despite the flood of criticism generated by the Regan book, Mrs. Reagan says that she intends to continue consulting with Quigley.

"It's a harmless thing," says the first lady's press secretary.

But there's nothing innocuous about the president ordering his life around what is essentially an occult practice. At best Reagan is making second-rate decisions based on nonsense. At worst he is submitting his life to what could be a pernicious, even evil, spiritual influence.

In fact, if the first lady wants to know what is wrong with conferring with an astrologer, she need only turn to the book that Reagan once said included the answers to every problem: the Bible. For God declared sorcery, divination and the interpretation of omens to be "detestable" and instructed his people not to listen to such predictions (Deuteronomy 18:9–10, 14).

But the astrology scandal may reflect more badly on the judgment of evangelical leaders who backed Reagan politically than on the president himself. For the "Religious Right" now has to explain why it so fervently backed someone who has not only proved unable—and largely uninterested—in implementing its political agenda, but who also allowed his official life to be shaped by anti-Christian practices.

Religious activists can certainly argue that Reagan remains superior to either Jimmy Carter or Walter Mondale on policy grounds. But the blind enthusiasm for Reagan exhibited by many Christian leaders is much harder to justify.

For instance, in 1980 Jerry Falwell declared that he would mobilize voters for Reagan "even if he has the devil running with him." Satan didn't end up on the ticket, but Falwell can hardly feel comfortable over who has been influencing Reagan.

In fact, the latest disclosures suggest that the president's frequent evocation of biblical values has largely been a show designed to win votes in the religious community. The president provided a little rhetoric and leading evangelicals fell into line behind him.

Not only have conservative clerics been used, they also have hurt their own cause by appearing to turn Christianity, with its transcendent message of a living God, into a political football. The debate has swirled around their personal predilections and failings rather than godly principles.

It's time for Christians to come up with a new, non-partisan political agenda. While they cannot walk away from the public arena—if biblical standards do not predominate, others will—believers need to recognize that the state is not a redemptive institution.

Moreover, Christians should not try to seize control of government in an attempt to "get theirs." Even in ancient Israel God prescribed justice for alien and Jew alike. And such a non-discriminatory standard is, if anything, more necessary in a secular society like our own, in which a majority of people do not follow Jesus.

Believers also should avoid setting political litmus tests. The Bible provides a lot of general principles for life; it does not speak specifically to the INF treaty, the B-1 bomber, or the minimum wage.

It's hard to take Ronald Reagan seriously any longer. For what other president has allowed his press conferences to be scheduled based on the conjunction of the planets?

But at least his flirtation with astrology can serve as a warning to Christians who have acted as if politics was another way to salvation. The evangelical community has been taken for a ride by an ambitious politician. It shouldn't let that happen a second time.

## 28. Subverting Democracy

*December 26, 1985*

With passage of the Gramm-Rudman bill, the administration and Congress may finally come under serious pressure to reduce the budget.

A good place to start cutting would be federal subsidies for partisan politics. For today, document George Mason University Professors James Bennett and Thomas DiLorenzo in their disturbing new book *Destroying Democracy*, there exists "a well-coordinated network of political activists" that has obtained hundreds of millions of dollars from government.

That so much money is wasted is tragedy enough. But that Americans are forced to subsidize lobbying by others for more federal spending is outrageous. As Thomas Jefferson observed two centuries ago, "To compel a man to furnish contributions of money for the propagation of opinions which he disbelieves is sinful and tyrannical."

It is technically illegal for public funds to go for partisan political purposes. However, with some 1,000 different federal grant, loan and contract programs, the potential for abuse is immense.

More important, write Bennett and DiLorenzo, "no real attempt has been made to enforce the law." The problem is really quite simple: Congressmen and bureaucrats benefit when the law is flouted.

The catalog of subsidized horrors is a long one. Indeed, hardly a leftist organization has failed to profit—handsomely—at taxpayer expense.

For instance, the Chicago-based Midwest Academy, a training center for leftist activists, collected nearly $600,000 from Uncle Sam. An affiliated group, the Citizens/Labor Energy Coalition, picked up almost $300,000 from the Department of Energy, VISTA and ACTION.

The Campaign for Economic Democracy, the Tom Hayden organization dedicated to promoting socialism under the guise of "economic democracy," benefited from more than a million dollars in grants made to related groups, including Communitas, the Center for New Corporate Priorities and the Laurel Springs Institute.

The national network of Ralph Nader "Public Interest Research Groups" was long on the federal dole, as well. And during the Carter administration the Federal Trade Commission unloaded cash on organizations ranging from the National Council of Senior Citizens to the Americans for Democratic Action, all of which were pushing for increased federal regulation.

At the same time, environmental groups such as the Sierra Club, Environmental Action and National Wildlife Federation were supping at the federal trough, courtesy of the Environmental Protection Agency and the Energy and Interior departments.

Millions of dollars have also gone to "welfare rights" organizations, which, naturally, spend much of their time lobbying for bigger welfare programs. The Coalition for Economic Justice, Community Nutrition Institute, Massachusetts Fair Share, Tenants Union Project and the National Council of Churches are just a few of the many winners in the federal grant sweepstakes.

Even large, broad-based national organizations have benefited from Uncle Sam's largess: examples include the League of Women Voters, the NAACP, the National Organization for Women, Planned Parenthood, PUSH, the Gray Panthers and the National Council of Senior Citizens.

More ludicrous still is the gift of hundreds of millions of dollars to labor unions. In fact, few unions have missed the public gravy train.

Finally, tens of millions worth of grants by the Legal Services Corporation to local legal aid groups have funded countless lawsuits against taxpayers, as "public interest" lawyers worked overtime to pick people's pockets.

Of course, no federal funds are officially earmarked for political advocacy. But, conclude Bennett and DiLorenzo, "vast sums of money are diverted from their intended purposes and are used to support political activities."

The Reagan administration has terminated many of the worst giveaways; however, some conservative groups have now snuck up to the federal trough. The U.S. Information Agency and the National Endowment for Humanities, in particular, have become slush funds for right-wing activitism.

Nevertheless, the vast majority of federal grants have gone to leftist organizations. And these recipients, warn Bennett and DiLorenzo, are "aggressively engaged in a concerted effort to undermine the foundations of private property and private enterprise."

As long as the federal government provides a trillion-dollar common pool open to all, interest groups will spend millions to grab a share of the spoils. However, there is no excuse for making taxpayers pay those who are lobbying hardest to loot the Treasury.

## 29. Celebrating Government

*August 9, 1984*

The City of San Francisco hosted two national conventions in recent weeks. Both showed us much of what is wrong with the United States, for both were self-serving celebrations of government.

Almost everyone is familiar with one of them, the Democratic Party convention. Who could fail to hear Mario Cuomo's absurd inclusion of Big Brother in the American family and Walter Mondale's one-sentence renunciation of a lifetime of catering to every person and group demanding the keys to the treasury.

Then there's the platform. Deliberately kept as non-specific as possible by Platform Committee Chairman and vice presidential nominee Geraldine Ferraro, the party document nevertheless invokes government to solve every ill imaginable. Whether the problem be the infrastructure, youth unemployment, the wetlands, the family farm or teen suicide, the Democrats think the state should spend more money, set up more commissions and hire more employees. Many more.

Ready to step in and organize these new employees is the American Federation of State, County and Municipal Employees, which held its convention a month before the Democrats. If the Democrats are the party of government, AFSCME is the union of government. Roughly 40 percent of AFSCME's million members work for states, and about a third for cities and counties. The remainder are employed by the federal government, school districts and the like.

AFSCME and the Democrats should have saved some time and money and held their conventions together. More than 100 delegates and alternates at the Democratic convention were members of AFSCME; the featured speaker at the AFSCME convention was Walter Mondale. And the policies endorsed by the union were indistinguishable from those embodied in the Democratic platform: let government do it!

Why does the union take this position? Because, Secretary-Treasurer William Lucy told the AFSCME convention, it is "a union that cares." And it would "continue to fight the right-wing movement to cripple government and cripple government services" and "the obscene unfairness of scrimping on child nutrition, education and care of the sick and the old."

Union President Gerald McEntee echoed the same theme. AFSCME, he said, "has led the way" in protecting "Medicare and Medicaid and social services against further cuts." The resolutions passed by the union, he proclaimed, "lay out an agenda for America; tax reform, adequate housing, economic renewal, civil rights and every other urgent social need."

Just who, you might ask, would man the new housing programs? Who would plan this economic renewal? Who would enforce new civil rights regulations? And who would provide the social services? Might it be AFSCME members?

Perish the thought, though, that the union might be acting in its own interest. Those who want to shrink government may be "greedy and self-centered," said McEntee, but certainly not AFSCME members. The union is just selflessly offering its "vision of America," one "based on compassion and common sense."

But it is precisely "compassion and common sense" that were manifestly absent in both San Francisco gatherings. Is it either compassionate or commonsensical to support more government housing programs when the ones we have now are prohibitively expensive, ghettoize poor people and enrich well-connected developers? Does it make sense to entrust housing to the federal government, which, through urban renewal and other programs, has actually destroyed a million more low-income homes than it has built?

Is it realistic—and fair to taxpayers—to expect federal spending for education and social services to continue ever upward, after growing 834 percent in real terms between 1962 and 1979? And does it demonstrate either compassion or common sense to ignore the financial catastrophe awaiting Medicare, which faces a cumulative deficit of as much as $400 billion by 1995?

AFSCME workers, McEntee declared, "understand the threat to public workers and public services and human dignity posed by Ronald Reagan." The Democrats understand, too; McEntee introduced Mondale to the union convention noting that he is "a public employee just like us and damn proud of it."

And that's precisely the problem. The party of government and the union of government are proud of their power over the rest of us. They understand that Mr. Reagan's minor effort to reduce federal spending—total real outlays will grow 15 percent under four years of President Reagan compared to 18 percent under Jimmy Carter—threatens their positions. So they offer torrents of rhetoric about need and greed, and beg us to overlook their record of repeated failures in recent decades.

Yes, AFSCME is "a union that cares." And the Democratic Party cares, too. But as the two conventions in San Francisco show, what they care about are themselves, not the people suffering from the programs they run or the taxes they support.

## 30.  This Energy Lobby Can't Stop Crying Wolf

*October 8, 1985*

Oil prices are down, but the Citizen/Labor Energy Coalition (CLEC)—supporters of which tried to storm the headquarters of the Natural Gas Supply Association in 1983—continues to act as the scourge of the energy industry. Despite declining public visibility and CLEC's inaccurate predictions of soaring energy prices, the coalition still has an "enormous impact on Capitol Hill," says Linda Stuntz, a staffer with the House Energy and Commerce Committee, "far more than it should."

CLEC was created in 1978 by representatives of about 60 different left-liberal organizations, and in 1982 absorbed Energy Action, a lobbying group funded largely by actor Paul Newman. Chosen to head CLEC was William Winpisinger, president of the International Association of Machinists and Aerospace Workers.

Though the oil companies are CLEC's favorite bogeymen, the ultimate target is business in general. Heather Booth, a CLEC co-founder, believes the coalition should help "destroy corporate control over our lives." In 1980, CLEC helped sponsor Big Business Day, which featured attacks on "corporate abuses" and support for "corporate democracy."

CLEC has developed an image of an underfinanced citizens' organization battling Big Oil, yet the organization is not Lilliputian; it now has upward of 300 affiliates, including labor unions, Jesse Jackson's Operation PUSH, the Gray Panthers and even religious organizations. And CLEC has expanded this vast network through door-to-door canvassing, raising millions of dollars over the years in the process. CLEC also has collected federal funds and even money from utilities opposed to natural-gas decontrol.

The group's strength, says one former Department of Energy official, is mostly a "grass-roots, obnoxious scare influence, the ability to get media attention." Not that CLEC itself is directly responsible for what Rep. Bob Whittaker (R., Kan.) calls the "bully-boy tactics" that have reportedly caused natural-gas industry officials to keep their phones unlisted and addresses secret. CLEC provides the intellectual leadership, while allied organizations, like National People's Action (NPA), with which CLEC co-sponsored an energy conference in 1981, supply the storm troopers to cow the opposition. It was the NPA, in the incident mentioned above, that nearly overran the Natural Gas Supply Association headquarters and that has used bus loads of demonstrators to intimidate opponents at work and at home.

CLEC has found patrons aplenty on Capitol Hill. CLEC assistant director Ed Rothschild says that Sen. Edward Kennedy (D., Mass.), Sen. Tom Harkin (D., Iowa), Sen. Paul Simon (D., Ill.) and even moderate Sen. Nancy Kassebaum (R., Kan.) are all supportive—at least on natural-gas decontrol. Former Democratic Rep. Toby Moffett, now a Connecticut gubernatorial candidate, is also a CLEC ally.

CLEC may be well-organized, and even well-received in many quarters, but its views are not fettered by accuracy. In 1981, for instance, CLEC predicted that President Reagan's oil deregulation would push prices to $70 a barrel by 1985. Today petroleum costs about $25 a barrel, less than when controls were lifted.

CLEC also expected decontrol of natural gas to be a disaster. In 1983 the coalition warned that deregulation would result in wellhead prices equivalent to $60 a barrel of oil, more than three times what industry analysts estimate they would be now even in a fully deregulated market (roughly half the gas is still controlled).

In 1981 CLEC forecast wellhead natural gas prices of $10 per thousand cubic feet (tcf) in 1985 with deregulation; in 1983 the group predicted that gas would cost $4.82 tcf in 1986. Yet the average price last year was only $2.63 tcf, and residential prices, instead of rising 20% due to partial decontrol this past January—as projected by CLEC—have fallen slightly.

This rather dismal record hasn't stopped CLEC from continuing to prophesy doom. In April the group warned that gasoline prices would jump 10 cents a gallon by July 4. However, prices increased only two cents a gallon during that period and have since dropped back down to lower than they were a year ago. (Factoring out higher gas taxes and inflation, gasoline costs a third less than it did four years ago, when CLEC predicted gasoline would hit $2 a gallon after decontrol.)

Mr. Rothschild contends that CLEC's record is no worse than anyone else's, industry and government included. He says his group's opposition to oil decontrol in early 1981, for example, was fueled by Exxon's projection of $50 a barrel for petroleum. Says Mr. Rothschild: It's "the problem of not knowing what we know now."

Has knowing what they know now caused CLEC's leaders to reassess their policy proposals? "In some respects the market is working," admits Mr. Rothschild, but he attributes much of the price decline to the 1981–82 recession. Moreover, he believes that "prices are still higher than they ought to be," and wants to encourage competition through divestiture, for example. However, there are already 10,000-plus energy firms; industry profits were only slightly above the economy-wide average during the energy crisis and now lag behind. If the oil companies are monopolizing the industry, they certainly aren't doing a very good job of it.

Is CLEC simply hostile to private ownership? After all, Mr. Winpisinger supports selective nationalization of private firms. Mr. Rothschild says no; the coalition is very "diverse, with avowed socialists and supporters of free-market competition."

Yet the "best example" he provides of a free-market member group is Tom Hayden's Campaign for Economic Democracy (CED), which supports ubiquitous government intervention in the economy.

Ironically, CLEC's animus to the energy industry has caused it to come out on the right side of some issues. CLEC strongly opposes an oil tariff. Mr. Rothschild has rightly ridiculed those energy-company executives who supported decontrol but now want the government to prop up prices on "national security" grounds.

With natural-gas decontrol off the front pages, CLEC has lost its key issue. But CLEC maintains its lobbying firepower in Washington and its local contacts are ready for action—particularly on utility issues. And many of its associated groups remain as busy as ever, having moved on to other issues like toxic waste.

CLEC proves that a little knowledge is a dangerous thing. With breathtaking studies, as erroneous as they are frightening, CLEC has generated considerable grass-roots support for policies that would only worsen the energy problem.

Energy is too important to be subject to the demands of groups like CLEC and its allies. Had they gotten their way the energy crisis might never have ended.

## 31.  Robbing Banks—Legally

*October 12, 1988*

Buried within legislation that is supposed to deregulate the banking industry is a provision that would strengthen the so-called Community Reinvestment Act, making banks even more vulnerable to blackmail by left-wing "community" organizations.

For this reason alone Congress should reject the "Depository Institutions Act of 1988," which has passed the House Banking Committee and is heading to the House floor.

In 1977 Congress enacted the CRA, directing federal regulators to consider a financial institution's "record of meeting the needs of . . . low- and moderate-income neighborhoods" in deciding whether to allow the bank or savings and loan to expand its operations. The law, as written, was unexceptional, since Congress rejected any credit allocation scheme and said that loans were still to be made "consistent with safe and sound (bank) operation."

However, misuse of the regulatory and legal process—often by government-funded legal aid attorneys—has allowed left-wing activists to turn the CRA into a blackmail tool. A variety of radical groups, including ACORN (Association of Community Organizations for Reform Now), have, in the name of the poor, shaken down financial institutions for an estimated $5 billion in loan concessions over the past decade.

Indeed, the CRA has taken on increased importance with the recent surge in interstate bank mergers. CRA challenges have jumped fivefold since 1984, denying consumers the full benefit of an increasingly competitive financial marketplace.

The strategy of ACORN and allied groups is to threaten to oppose efforts by banks and thrifts to buy or merge with other financial institutions. The left-wing activists prefer not to go to court, since their claims are usually without merit:

"Even if you file your CRA protest and pursue it, it is highly unlikely that the federal regulators will deny the bank's proposed merger as a result of your protest," admitted the Central Florida Legal Services in a memo to ACORN.

But the simple threat to file usually is enough to extort some blood money, since even a short delay can be extremely expensive for a bank.

"The only question is how much you get, not whether you get anything," observed Central Florida Legal Services.

For example, ACORN made its usual list of demands, including $100,000 for itself, to Hibernia Corp. of New Orleans. The bank refused and ACORN filed a protest, forcing Hibernia, despite a good record of community service, to undergo a raft of investigations and hearings by regulatory officials.

After spending tens of thousands of dollars Hibernia finally won approval of its application to buy another bank, but only after increasing lending in consultation with ACORN.

Exulted ACORN, "If a bank ever needed a reason to negotiate with ACORN instead of going to a full-scale war, then all it needs to do is look at the experience of Hibernia First National Bank."

ACORN and its allies usually demand money for the protesting organization, below-market interest rates on loans to businesses run by ACORN and its officers, low-interest loans, controlled by ACORN, in poor areas, minority hiring quotas, and cheap banking service for selected groups.

None of these is justified. Giving money to corporate blackmailers that are pushing up consumer costs obviously hurts the public. Incredibly, banks have been bludgeoned into contributing money not only for the radical groups' general operations, but also to host a publicity luncheon for one organization and to remodel the offices of another.

The low-interest loans and similar measures are supposed to redress bank discrimination against poor areas—through, for instance, "redlining." But the reason interest rates on loans to poor people are often higher is because the likelihood of default is greater. In fact, ACORN has tacitly conceded this point, attacking one company, Rainier Bank of Seattle, for operating "in the same way in all cases."

Unfortunately, banks and thrifts have routinely caved in to the radicals. Earlier this year San Francisco-based California First Bank agreed to spend $84 million in loans over two years to buy off its antagonists. Last year Riggs Bank in Washington, D.C., agreed to provide $40 million over five years in protection money. And the cases go on, year after year, all over the country.

No one wants to see poor neighborhoods left without credit, but banks and thrifts should not be pressured to make uneconomic loans. The flood tide of red ink that now threatens scores of savings and loans demonstrates how everyone suffers when financial institutions ignore the bottom line.

In any case, it is simply outrageous for the federal government to encourage what First Union Corp. Chairman Edward Crutchfield rightly calls "pure blackmail."

The CRA has created an extortion racket for ACORN and other left-wing groups. Congress should repeal the CRA, not strengthen it.

## 32.  The Foreign Aid Network

*June 24, 1987*

Proponents of foreign aid like to argue that their program has no lobby. International assistance is simply supposed to transcend politics.

Not that this self-serving myth should be taken seriously, of course. Despite their name, many Private Voluntary Organizations get most of their funds from the government—and lobby accordingly. U.S. manufacturers and farmers who want to sell more products abroad also press for increased foreign aid.

Moreover, the Agency for International Development spends millions annually to organize interest groups to defend its budget.

Direct lobbying with federal funds is illegal and AID has apparently observed the letter of the law. But the agency funds dozens of "educational" organizations that promote AID programs.

Much of the money comes from Biden-Pell grants, which were created by Congress, according to AID, to "facilitate public discussion, analysis and review of development issues" and to "extend and reinforce a constituency" for foreign aid.

The agency spent $2.7 million in 1986 to "educate" the public; Biden-Pell outlays are expected to run $2 million this year and as much as $2.7 in 1988.

Examples of questionable grants include the $179,400 given to the American Home Economics Association over the last two years. In a program expected to reach all 50,000 home economics teachers along with their 4.5 million students, the association is explaining "why countries such as the United States help Third World countries."

The Consortium for International Cooperation in Higher Education collected $245,577 last year. This group, according to AID, plans on targeting extension personnel around the country in an attempt "to enhance citizen understanding of the factors involved in world hunger and poverty and of the U.S. stake in international development." Including, no doubt, a thorough discussion of the need for more foreign aid.

The End Hunger Network has collected $879,283 in 1986 and 1987. This organization, concedes AID, is using taxpayer funds "to create support for programs aimed at combating poverty." Namely foreign assistance.

Generous grants to many other organizations—including E.A. Jaenke and Associates, the National Committee for World Food Day, and OEF International—look suspiciously like tax-paid endorsements of AID's programs. In no case has money gone to an organization dedicated to explaining how foreign aid is routinely misused by recipients, how it subsidizes perverse economic policies in Third World states, and how it enhances the power of often corrupt and repressive regimes.

Perhaps the most outrageous grant, however, is the $284,590 given to the Citizens Network for Foreign Affairs last year. In 1983 President Reagan's Commission on Security and Economic Assistance recommended that a coalition be created to, in AID's words, "work together toward building a broad base of support" for foreign aid.

Agency officials then helped organize and fund the group. And the Network, says Executive Director John Costello, plans on requesting another Biden-Pell grant next year.

The Network apparently has been careful not to transgress the technical prohibition against lobbying—"we are limiting our activities to public education," says Costello—but the group's purpose is clear. Observes one conservative AID staffer, the Network "is to inform the constituents of congressmen and senators for whom foreign aid is a potential issue."

Earlier this year the Network organized a conference on Capitol Hill to discuss international assistance. The conference location obviously was no accident.

Nor are the Network's publications shy about making the case for AID's programs. "Foreign Aid: Who Needs It?" asks one pamphlet. "We Do," it answers. The publication goes on to detail the amount of international assistance spent in individual states.

The problem is not that the Network, or any of the other Biden-Pell grantees, is doing anything illegal. Instead, the people at fault are the alleged fiscal conservatives in the Reagan administration—like outgoing

AID Administrator and Deputy Treasury Secretary designee M. Peter McPherson—who are spending the taxpayers' money to support their favored programs.

Of course, the misuse of federal money is hardly new. But it is one of the abuses that Reagan once pledged to curb. It's time he got serious about shutting down the leviathan's subsidized propaganda machine, starting with the Biden-Pell grant program.

## 33. The Politics of Drought

*July 6, 1988*

Will it never end? When harvests are bountiful, farmers ask the government to prop up their prices. And when a drought ruins their crops, they demand emergency assistance to prop up their incomes.

There's no doubt that months of dry weather compounded by above-average temperatures in June threaten to cause enormous hardship for many agricultural families. Plains states' harvests may be passable, but to the north farmers could lose half or more of their crops.

Tragic as the situation is, why should taxpayers be held responsible for the weather? Americans, whether by themselves or through local churches and other community associations, have a fundamental moral duty to help alleviate the suffering of their rural neighbors. That does not, however, mean that it is right for the government to seize taxpayers' money to give away.

Indeed, it's not as if Uncle Sam has not been generous to rural America. Since 1986 alone the government has paid farmers some $66 billion and spent billions more to fund research, subsidize exports, and underwrite home construction and community services. Probably no group in America has been more pampered by government than farmers.

And there are already a number of programs in place to deal with emergencies. The Farmers Home Administration, for instance, provides special disaster loans.

Moreover, the government subsidizes crop insurance to provide for an eventuality just like this summer's drought. Last year only 15 percent of farmers participated in the program, however: "Farmers are traditionally some of the biggest risk-takers in the country," explains John Gartside of the Federal Crop Insurance Corp.

That would be fine were farmers not now demanding that the taxpayers make up their losses. It's bad enough that Uncle Sam is willing to foot part of the farmers' insurance bill. But it's unconscionable for those who choose not to insure their harvests to then demand that the rest of us pick up the tab when the crops wither.

Of course, vote-minded politicians don't want to acknowledge the irresponsibility of their constituents. Instead, legislators are ready to rush in and create a host of new programs to respond to the drought.

One proposal is to forgive much of the $4.3 billion already paid out to farmers in subsidies for crops that will never be harvested. And some congressmen are even talking about guaranteeing farmers a minimum income—something no one else in America receives.

Unfortunately, these proposals merely illustrate how greed and envy are increasingly pervading public life. Workers demand tariffs to protect their jobs; lawyers use a licensing system to raise their fees.

Labor unions lobby for a uniform minimum wage and guaranteed rates on federal projects. Corporations expect export subsidies; failing companies demand handouts. Well-to-do families lobby Uncle Sam to pay for the care and education of their children. And farmers expect federal assistance at every step in their lives.

It is this constant attempt of people to use government to live off their neighbors that has caused federal spending to spiral ever further out of control, even under conservative Ronald Reagan. And until we start treating the taxpayer's interest in his money as a serious one the transfers to the politically influential will continue.

It may be too much to expect Congress not to take the politically expedient course of rushing in with federal money to bail out drought-stricken farmers. The human misery is real; the votes at stake are even harder for legislators to ignore.

But with federal deficits that remain ruinously high, congressmen have a responsibility to try to restrain their constituents' greed.

First, any relief package should spend no more than what the federal government will save in support payments—estimated to be about $5 billion—due to unusually low production and high market prices. Farmers already squeeze an obscene amount of money out of taxpayers; drought or not, that total should not be increased.

Second, assistance to individual farmers who failed to buy crop insurance should be strictly limited. Let Uncle Sam make sure that no one starves. But the taxpayers should not be expected to save the property of a businessmen who decided to gamble, and lost. The average home owner who doesn't insure his house can't get the government to build him a new one if the old dwelling burns down; farmers are no more entitled to federal protection.

If there is one constant in life, it is farmers lobbying for someone, anyone to subsidize them; the drought has merely made those demands more insistent. But it's time Congress lived up to its responsibility to the rest of us and said no.

## 34. Businessmen as Born-Again Budget-Cutters

*November 19, 1987*

Deficit reduction is in the air. Not only have Congress and the president's men sat down to arrange a fiscal compromise, but nearly 200 corporate executives, investment bankers, professionals and former public officials have signed newspaper ads pleading for federal frugality as part of what they call the Bipartisan Budget Appeal.

The group's organizer, Peter G. Peterson, a former secretary of commerce, has become the high priest of parsimony, receiving confession from a host of business and other civic leaders whose organizations have spent years cashing government checks. The executives' surprising repentance may have been triggered by their glimpse of the Wall Street version of hell—the stock market crash.

The fiscal penitents were far too modest to boast publicly about the financial sacrifices that they will have to make to fulfill their new faith. But their stories, which show the power of economic chaos to dramatically change individual lives, need to be told.

Perhaps the most dramatic born-again budget cutter is Chrysler's Lee Iacocca. His company, of course, required a massive federal loan guarantee to avert bankruptcy; Mr. Iacocca has also endorsed federal health insurance, a higher gasoline tax, more stringent fuel-economy regulations, tighter auto-import controls, and a government "industrial policy," all of which could improve his firm's earnings.

Another fiscal sinner who has repented of much is Dwayne Andreas, the head of Archer-Daniels-Midland. ADM received a $29.2 million subsidy for its gasohol operation last year alone; in the past, Mr. Andreas has lobbied such congressional friends as Senate Minority leader Robert Dole to impose draconian restrictions on alcohol fuel imports.

Then there are Budget Appeal supporters Frank Shrontz and T.A. Wilson, Boeing's president and chairman, respectively. Over the years, Boeing has benefited from so much subsidized credit through the Export-Import Bank that the agency has been informally called "Boeing's Bank"; before Messrs. Shrontz and Wilson's surprise conversions, Boeing consistently mobilized to oppose any proposal to cut Ex-Im funds. Other executives representing major Ex-Im Bank customers who have turned to the faith of fiscal responsibility include Douglas Danforth, chairman and

CEO of Westinghouse; W.F. Bueche, head of Allis-Chalmers; and Mr. Iacocca.

Yet another reformed budget-buster is Jay Pritzker, chairman of Hyatt. A half-dozen of his firm's hotels have been subsidized by Urban Development Action Grants, a federal slush fund for local building projects.

Equally moving has been the transformation of the many company executives whose firms once besieged the Synthetic Fuels Corporation for loans and price guarantees. Among the former fiscal pagans who now worship at the altar of the balanced budget are Fred Hartley of Unocal, Edward Donley of Air Products & Chemicals, Howard Allen of Southern California Edison, John Creedon of Metropolitan Life Insurance, John Hall of Ashland Oil, and Allen Murray of Mobil. In fact, the same John Hall who now publicly embraces fiscal responsibility was particularly outspoken in his advocacy of federal support for the synfuels industry.

Converts from companies that were double dippers—like Mr. Murray's Mobil—are especially important additions to the new budgetary faith. Mobil not only tried once to organize an industrywide synfuels consortium backed in part by federal funds, but one of its subsidiaries, Packaging Corp. of America, continues to buy subsidized federal timber. Other repentant Budget Appeal members whose firms "live off the fat of the land" for low-cost lumber are John Fery of Boise Cascade, Richard Madden of Potlatch, Philip Lippincott of Scott Paper, Burnell Roberts of Mead Corp., Brenton Halsey of James River Corp., and George Weyerhaeuser of Weyerhaeuser Co. How we should rejoice that so many who were once lost have now been found!

The evangelical budgetary fever sweeping corporate America has also captured James Pasman Jr., head of Kaiser Aluminum & Chemical, and Edwin Tuttle, Pennwalt's chairman and CEO. Both of their firms receive artificially cheap electricity from the federal Bonneville Power Administration.

More dramatic, though, is Stanley Pace's turn from budgetary iniquity. His firm, General Dynamics, finds its mother's milk in federal defense contracts, as does Ruben Mettler's TRW. Mortimer Zuckerman, editor in chief of U.S. News & World Report, J. Richard Munro, head of Time Inc., and Harold McGraw Jr., chairman of McGraw-Hill, all signed the Budget Appeal, atoning for years of postal subsidies. Similarly, guilt over the constant flood of federal research grants and student aid money may have caused fiscal sinners Howard Swearer, president of Brown University, and John McArthur, dean of the Harvard Business School, to kneel at the altar of budget restraint.

What could be more appropriate with the approach of Christmas than executives whose lobbyists once trod the corridors of Capitol Hill in search of government subsidies publicly renouncing their wicked ways? Indeed, who knows where these revivalist sentiments will stop? If the fiscal awakening spreads to members of Capitol Hill and the administration, we might even witness the Second Coming of the balanced budget.

## 35. Businessmen against Free Enterprise

*October 14, 1987*

One of the persistent myths of American government is that business is the last defender of the free market. Time and again, goes the story, an aroused citizenry had to drag reactionary businessmen into the 20th century by establishing new laws, agencies and regulations to protect the "public interest."

But, in fact, business has been ever-willing to sell out the market system. A century ago large manufacturing concerns constantly ran to Congress demanding high tariffs to protect them from foreign competition.

And businessmen, as much as citizen activists, backed the creation of early regulatory agencies like the Interstate Commerce Commission. The railroads, for example, favored the ICC as a means of squelching the fierce competition between different rail lines.

The New Deal spawned a flood of new government intrusions into the marketplace, many of which were supported by corporate America. Big business particularly loved the National Recovery Administration, which attempted to cartelize the economy.

In the years that followed, business was often first in line on Capitol Hill to receive public handouts. Firms were only too willing to support any subsidy or regulation if it promised them some competitive advantage, however transitory.

Unfortunately, the Reagan Revolution has changed nothing. In fact, the special pleading probably has gotten worse.

When Reagan first took office gasoline retailers opposed full decontrol of oil. Energy pipeline companies made the rounds of Washington to denounce proposals to lift natural gas price ceilings. Maritime interests lobbied furiously to maintain the prohibition on the export of Alaskan crude oil.

And now some of America's largest corporations are supporting a proposal by Sen. Edward Kennedy, D-Mass., to force employers to provide health insurance for their employees. The proposal is a horrible idea—it would cost billions while pre-empting the individualized employer/ employee bargaining over benefits that is the hallmark of a market economy. Kennedy is really attempting to push a costly national health insurance program through the legislative back door.

Yet American Airlines, Chrysler Corp., and several other large companies are backing the bill. Not that they are particularly worried about their employees; instead, they want to gain a competitive advantage over their lower-cost competitors.

American Airlines, for instance, is upset that Continental Airlines doesn't offer its employees insurance benefits quite as generous as its own. Rather than compete by increasing either its productivity or service quality, American Airlines is trying to force up its competitors' costs.

This is Chrysler's strategy as well. That company benefited from a multibillion bailout that was not available to its competitors, and its CEO, Lee Iacocca, has trooped to Washington time and again to wail for more federal aid.

Iacocca pressed for a huge gas tax to force consumers to buy his smaller cars; he lobbied for stricter fuel economy regulations to increase the costs facing Ford and General Motors. And now he wants to make his competitors pay higher health insurance premiums.

Similarly, following the recent earthquakes in California, a number of insurance companies began talking about the "need" for federal subsidies. Industry spokesmen said they would prepare draft legislation by the end of the year.

"We have to educate both the public and the Congress," said David Brummond, assistant general counsel for the National Association of Independent Insurers.

Business special pleading also permeates the ongoing battles over banking deregulation and restrictions on corporate takeovers.

The securities and insurance industries, for example, have spared no expense to prevent banks from gaining more freedom to enter new fields. And incumbent executives from all industries have busily lobbied Congress to halt hostile takeovers.

In all these cases, the businessmen give selfless reasons for supporting government regulation. Their real interest, of course, is hobbling their competitors.

America's economic future does not look bright: if the companies whose success has been made possible by the free market won't support the system, it's hard to imagine how our open economy can survive. But Chrysler, American Airlines and the rest of their ilk should realize that if the government eventually squeezes the last bit of entrepreneurship and freedom out of the U.S. economy, the firms that lobbied for special privileges, too, will die.

# 36. The Way Washington Works—But Shouldn't

*October 24, 1985*

Californian Mike Maynard spent his days in the military as a cook and hated the routine of breaking eggs. Not just one or two eggs, but dozens at a time.

So when Maynard became a civilian he solved the problem for cooks everywhere by inventing an egg-breaking machine, the "Egg King," that cracks up to 360 eggs a minute and automatically strains out the shells. Over the last five years restaurants, bakeries, hospitals, military chow halls, fast-food outlets, and hotels by the hundreds have purchased Maynard's device.

But not everyone is happy with what one egg distributor calls "the little monster." For the Egg King allows users to buy fresh eggs instead of having to pay premium prices for the frozen or dried egg mixture made from lower-grade eggs that producers otherwise couldn't sell.

So what to do? Get the government to put your competitor out of business, of course.

The United Egg Producers went to both the Department of Agriculture and the Food and Drug Administration earlier this year to ask for a federal ban on the machine. Neither agency had authority to outlaw use of the Egg King, and the FDA said it saw no need to do so, observing that with proper instruction of users "there will be little likelihood of this egg-breaking method resulting in adulterated egg products."

The FDA offered to take action if the egg producers could cite any hazardous "misuse of the machine," but the UEP admitted that it knew of no instances of illness caused by the machine since it went on sale nearly five years ago.

But the industry, proclaiming its selfless concern for Americans' health, hired a lobbyist and took the battle to Congress. On July 30, without hearings and after only perfunctory debate, the House Agriculture Committee stuck six lines—42 words in all—into the 525-page House version of the Farm Bill to put Maynard out of business.

It was more than a week before Maynard became aware of UEP's ploy, hired his own lobbyist, and eventually flew to Washington himself.

Nearly two months of political trench warfare then ensued. The UEP spread threats of doom, but restaurants, hotels and other Egg King users—who have their reputations at stake in the safety of their products—denounced the UEP's feigned consumer concern as being "without foundation."

Indeed, the Egg King has received widespread approval, from USDA's Meat and Poultry Division to state and county health departments to the Bakery Equipment Sanitation Standards Committee. California's Department of Health even concluded that the Egg King process "appears to be superior to the present hand method of cracking and straining of eggs."

But having the facts on his side almost wasn't enough for Maynard. The USDA, for example, flip-flopped five times in two years under UEP pressure, the last reversal coming overnight on Oct. 3 when, officials report, Agriculture Secretary John Block traded support for the Egg King ban to gain a few votes on another Farm Bill issue.

Despite the USDA's perfidy, Maynard, with the help of Rep. Robert Badham, the California Republican in whose district Maynard resides, won a narrow vote to remove the amendment before final House passage of the Farm Bill. But Maynard can't rest just yet: the issue now moves to the Senate, where UEP has pressed, so far unsuccessfully, for a similar provision.

And Maynard's apparent victory hasn't come cheap. He figures that it cost him more than $100,000 to hold off the UEP, a paltry sum for an industry trade association, perhaps, but a lot of money for a small business.

Says Maynard: "Never in my wildest fantasies did I think they would be able to legislate me out of business."

But they almost did.

Unfortunately, throughout the economy businesses are increasingly turning to politics to gain a profit. Over the last 10 years the number of Political Action Committees has jumped sevenfold, the majority of trade associations have shifted from New York to Washington, and the percentage of corporate CEO's regularly visiting the nation's capital has jumped from roughly 15 percent to 65 percent.

Maynard exhibits what is great about America's economic system, developing the proverbial "better mousetrap." We need to protect the Mike Maynards of America, rather than forcing them to spend tens of thousands of dollars to protect themselves from attacks by politically influential special interests.

The issue is moral as well as economic. For if we lose the basic right to make a living without having to obtain permission from our competitors and the government, we will lose the philosophical basis for our economic and political system.

## 37. The Firing of Il Gucci

*February 27, 1986*

The whole country seems abuzz: America's beloved master self-promoter, Lee Iacocca has been fired from an obscure government panel.

The facts of the controversy, including Iacocca's demand that other people resign in similar circumstances, have been lost in the symbolism surrounding Il Gucci. His firing, Iacocca modestly proclaims, "borders on the un-American."

Frankly, whether or not Iacocca faced a conflict of interest, he deserved to be dumped. Washington has enough loud, pompous windbags without him.

True, Il Gucci has passed himself off as a folk hero, selling millions of copies of his biography, topping the list of most admired business executives, and causing endless numbers of politicians to fawn over him. And Iacocca has been only too happy to oblige: "People are hungry for somebody to tell them something . . . people are hungry to be led."

But led where? Most observers consider Iacocca to be a sharp business manager and strategist.

Yet the moment he starts thinking about government policy, his mind turns to mush. He spouts utopian nostrums that would wreck the economy, passes off drivel as serious political advice, and postures as the leader who could save America—if only he were interested.

But what Lee Iacocca is really interested in is Lee Iacocca.

He worked his way up the Ford Motor Co. ladder, proving more than adept at corporate politics. In the late 1950s he attached himself to company president Robert McNamara and helped engineer the 1969 firing of another firm president, Bunkie Knudsen.

Anointed for the top job by Henry Ford II, Iacocca lasted nine years, before being fired himself. The clash of egos was just too intense.

Lured to Chrysler in November 1978 by a $1.5 million bonus, liberal stock options and a tidy $360,000 salary, Iacocca went to work to save a dying company. By mid-1979 the firm, despite his best efforts, was out of money and couldn't borrow. For anyone else, it would have been the end.

But not for Lee. After all, what American consumers wouldn't voluntarily put out in the showroom they could be forced to cough up by Uncle Sam. So to Washington Lee did go.

Iacocca bluffed and blustered his way past a gullible Congress, never letting the truth get in the way of a good deal. Chrysler would only lose $500 million in 1980 he promised; the company ran $1.7 billion in the red. The misrepresentations ran on.

In the end, an election-minded Congress folded, guaranteeing $1.5 billion in loans to the automaker.

Other firms—and small businesses in particular—were not so lucky. They ended up without credit and some of them undoubtedly failed as a result. But Il Gucci had made the government work for him. And it's a lesson he has not forgotten.

Do the Japanese produce a better, cheaper car? Slap a tariff on it!

Are American consumers turning to bigger cars, after Chrysler has downsized its auto line? Impose a 25-cent-a-gallon gasoline tax!

Have company health costs risen faster than planned? Call for national health insurance!

In short, is there a problem? Get the government to make someone else pay!

Even worse, Iacocca has turned into one of the nation's leading advocates of "industrial policy," Mussolini-style corporatism. Basically, Lee would use the federal Treasury to help his friends, letting the rest of us fend for ourselves.

Such fascist economic policies were fashionable in the 1930s, but have been discredited for decades. Il Gucci would do no better with them than did Il Duce.

Indeed, Iacocca calls America's lunatic agricultural subsidies a model for an industrial policy. And quotas on Japanese auto imports, the cornerstone of Iacocca's economic plan, cost American consumers almost $27 billion in the last two years alone.

In late December Iacocca generously laid out his program for America in a two-page spread in *Newsweek,* entitled "The Fine Art of Compromise." It was typical Iacocca blather.

We need "to regain the honorable old art of compromise." But Congress needs "the courage to say 'No' to special interest groups." Except, presumably, Chrysler.

People need to "stop building walls around their own pet positions." That is, other than Lee with his disastrous economic theories.

And everyone needs to make sacrifices, aside from those "who really need our help."

Can anyone really take the author of such tripe seriously?

"I'd like to be president for a year on appointment, but the Constitution doesn't allow it," says Lee.

We should be thankful for small favors. It's bad enough that we have to listen to Il Gucci pontificate. But we'd be really miserable if what he said mattered.

## 38.  A Corporate Lobby Pulls Its Punches

*July 23, 1986*

Earlier this year organizations ranging from the Chamber of Commerce to the liberal Citizens/Labor Energy Coalition joined to oppose an oil import fee. Notably absent from the coalition, however, was the Business Roundtable, perhaps the most visible representative of corporate America in Washington.

Individual members of the Roundtable have been involved in the effort, says Jack Blum, general counsel to the Independent Gasoline Marketers Council. "I guess [the Roundtable itself] chose its priorities differently."

The Roundtable did oppose the oil surcharge proposed by the Senate Budget Committee last summer, but not this time. Its failure to combat a policy it had to know was wrong, even fundamentally destructive economically, is symptomatic of problems with the Roundtable and corporate lobbying in Washington in general.

Formed in 1972, the New York-based Roundtable is an association of about 200 chief executive officers. It was a minor player on the Washington scene until the late 1970s, when it helped defeat such liberal initiatives as the Consumer Protection Agency and common situs picketing.

Yet the Roundtable's underlying philosophy is profoundly defeatist, emphasizing accommodation rather than opposition to government intervention. In this way, the Roundtable only too well represents the interests of its big-business members, many of whom look to government to protect them from competition and guarantee their profits.

**Search for Agreeable Middle**

The Roundtable's quest for compromise was particularly pronounced during the Carter years. Paul Weaver, a former Washington editor of Fortune magazine, says the Roundtable "spent most of its time avoiding challenges to Jimmy Carter. It is no surprise that its leadership, notably Irving Shapiro, was Jimmy Carter's favorite business lobbyist."

In fact, Mr. Shapiro, Roundtable chairman from 1976 to 1978, and a member until he retired as chief executive officer of DuPont in 1981, emphasized that "the art of government is to find compromises." Over the years the Roundtable's search for the agreeable middle has led the group largely to avoid controversial issues like the windfall-profits tax and Superfund, to support federal jobs and training programs, and to back federal wage and price guidelines. At the time of the Roundtable's endorsement of those guidelines, Mr. Shapiro said: "You just can't say that as a matter of conscience you won't cooperate in something so fundamental to the president's program."

Today, with the federal government largely in the hands of the more business-oriented Republicans, the Roundtable has maintained its accommodationist stance, often working against deregulatory initiatives. For instance, though the group proclaims itself opposed to "unwarranted intrusion by government into business affairs," it is fighting a Justice Department proposal effectively to junk Executive Order 11246, which establishes an affirmative-action program for federal contractors. (The Supreme Court's recent ruling upholding the constitutionality of state affirmative-action plans does not require creation of such programs in the private sector.) Business groups such as the Chamber of Commerce have called for elimination of quotalike goals and timetables, but the Roundtable's members, says James Keogh, a spokesman for the group, have developed such policies over the years and "have become accustomed to that process."

Indeed, there is another likely, but unstated, reason for the Roundtable's passivity: The large corporations it represents probably gain a competitive advantage from federal regulations such as affirmative action, which disproportionately burden smaller firms.

Another issue where the Roundtable has parted company with the Chamber of Commerce is over the restrictive immigration legislation now before Congress. The Roundtable is not opposing employer sanctions even though forcing business to act as an INS agent is both an affront to civil liberties and extraordinarily expensive.

Nor has the group been embarrassed about actively lobbying for new, self-serving, government regulation. For instance, the Roundtable likes mergers and therefore has routinely opposed anti-merger legislation. However, its members, incumbent managers all, apparently are not enthused about the possibility of someone taking over their companies. "Hostile takeovers initiated by raiders and conducted at a frenzied pace . . . lead to unacceptable abuses," warns the Roundtable newsletter. Andrew Stigler, head of a Roundtable task force on takeovers, testified before Congress urging new federal controls. The organization's Mr. Keogh denies that his organization is being inconsistent: It is simply "trying to bring some reason and care to the takeover process."

A similar attitude appears to govern the Roundtable's position on trade. International commerce is enormously important for big business, so the Roundtable understandably opposes trade sanctions and "continues to be anti-protectionist," says Mr. Keogh. However, the group has not weighed in against the destructive textile quota and surcharge bills before Congress. Moreover, the Roundtable wants not only to enforce "more aggressively" the laws governing "unfair" trade, but also to expand them; the Roundtable recently turned down a White House plea to help defeat the dangerous Democratic trade bill now moving through Congress. Such protectionism would hurt most U.S. businesses, but might help a few Roundtable members troubled by imports.

Indeed, it is in the trade area where former Fortune editor Weaver argues that the Roundtable has "shown its true colors." The organization has spent much of Mr. Reagan's presidency attacking the "overvalued dollar''; last fall the administration finally initiated action that has driven down the value of U.S. currency 30% and increased the price of imports for consumers. In essence, once the Roundtable saw deflation occurring under Mr. Reagan, it began working "for inflation and Carterism," says Mr. Weaver.

For different, but equally shortsighted, reasons, the Roundtable also has been a major proponent of raising taxes to reduce the deficit. For instance, in 1982 it "reluctantly," in Mr. Keogh's words, supported the largest peacetime tax increase ever. Not only was it the first group to capitulate when the Reagan administration began pressuring business leaders, but its support for the tax hike, says David Franasiak, director of federal affairs for Standard Oil Co., "basically immobilized the core of the business community."

Mr. Keogh admits that it "was a matter of great concern and disappointment" when Congress failed to fulfill promises made during the 1982 tax-hike debate that there would be three dollars of spending cuts for every one dollar in tax increases. But that didn't stop the Roundtable from urging a similar deficit-reduction package the following year, with a five-year $250 billion to $300 billion tax increase. And in late 1985 it formally urged another tax boost: "While we don't endorse any specific tax, we agree the time has come to consider a revenue increase."

But not just any tax hike. Earlier last year the Roundtable's policy committee criticized the administration's tax-reform proposal for increasing business taxes, and it opposes taxation of fringe benefits. At least the Roundtable knows what specific taxes it does not want raised.

Even more curiously, the Roundtable has promoted the snake-oil notion of "corporate responsibility." In 1981 the organization issued a detailed statement urging the corporation to become "a thoughtful institution which rises above the bottom line," giving "enlightened consideration to balancing the legitimate claims of all its constituents," and not just shareholders. After all, firm owners often are "most interested in near-term gain" while a broader view of corporate responsibility will "best serve" their interests. The corporate responsibility theme, which suggests that firms should be social reformers and philanthropic institutions, as well as economic producers, essentially concedes the principle of community control advanced by Ralph Nader and others.

Mr. Keogh disagrees, arguing that "if companies perform responsibly and consider the constituencies they need to deal with all of the time, that kind of performance will deter rather than encourage government regulation." Yet the strategy of preemptive surrender seems to be one that the Roundtable is all too fond of. Taxes, wage and price guidelines, Superfund—on all of these it has retreated before an aggressive public sector.

## Some Important Battles

The Roundtable has fought on the right side of some important policy battles. It helped de-fang the Humphrey-Hawkins Act, criticized government economic planning, and has consistently pushed federal spending cuts. The Roundtable also took a strong stand against the 1979 Chrysler bailout, though Chrysler's Lee Iacocca accused the organization of hypocrisy, observing that it had not taken a "similar position on federal loan guarantees to steel companies, to shipbuilders, to airlines, to farmers, and to the housing industry." Mr. Keogh responds that the Roundtable "simply hadn't taken a position till it became a major issue."

Finally, by bringing CEOs to Washington to meet directly with government officials and members of Congress, Mr. Weaver says, the Roundtable has made "a true contribution to the business lobby's techniques." Unfortunately, the Roundtable has used its clout as much against the market system as for it.

"I don't know that they're worse than anyone else," says Fred Smith, president of the Competitive Enterprise Institute, a Washington-based lobbying group. But the Roundtable could do so much better. If U.S. enterprise is to be kept reasonably free, the Roundtable and the executives it represents must learn to defend the market, not just the narrow interests of some businesses.

# One for All and All for One

## 39. One-Party System

*August 1983*

Paris has its spring clothing fashions, and Washington its summer political fashions. The latest political fad sweeping Washington is "bipartisanship."

It seems that whenever opposition arises to a proposal to expand government power, increase foreign intervention, or spend more taxpayers' money, the proposer reacts by praising the benefits of bipartisanship. It is, we are told, more important for people to join together and take action than to worry about what the action is.

The Democrats are suffering from a bad case of bipartisan fever as they avoid developing alternatives to the Reagan administration's military and foreign policies. Democratic analyst Ben Wattenberg, for example, decries opposition to Reagan's intervention in Central America and his massive military buildup, and urges Democrats to maintain a "healthy spirit of bipartisanship."

Perhaps the most embarrassing—and certainly the most dangerous recent example of bipartisan blather was the reaction to the President's Commission on Strategic Forces, or the Scowcroft Commission, which studied the MX missile. The commission essentially admitted that the justification for the MX—the so-called window of vulnerability—does not exist, but nevertheless recommended deploying the MX. Some commission members have admitted privately that their recommendations were purely political.

But Washington's MX-lovers did not read the report's fine print. The American Security Council, for example, took out full-page ads acclaiming the "bipartisan" commission's recommendations—without once discussing the supposed need for the missile. Instead, it told us that the Chamber of Commerce and AFL-CIO support the MX. That six Congresses have voted money for it. That four presidents have pushed it. And that "the

93

commission's recommendations have prompted a renewed spirit of bipartisan cooperation between the White House and Congress.'' Wow. Those are really convincing reasons to spend billions of dollars on a weapon that will not make us more secure.

Unfortunately, many congressional Democrats apparently share the Reagan administration's vision of a missile in every pot. For example, House Majority Whip Thomas Foley lobbied for the MX, supporting the administration out of a sense of—you guessed it—bipartisanship.

Then, Representative Les Aspin (D-Wis.) organized liberal votes for the MX. Aspin likes to posture as a critic of the military, and periodically sends out press releases attacking the Pentagon's waste of a few thousand dollars on perks for generals and such. But when it comes to billions wasted on unnecessary weapons programs, where does Aspin stand? With the yeas.

Aspin says that he voted for the MX in part because he was "convinced it would be a bad position for the Democrats to be against the Scowcroft Commission recommendations." After all, it was a "bipartisan commission, and lots of Democratic experts on defense said this was a good thing." Well, well. Why have Democratic congressmen elected across the country? Perhaps we should just appoint the requisite number of Democratic bipartisan experts to endorse whatever schemes the Republicans propose.

The debate on the MX missile is not the only area where many Democrats have been overcome with bipartisanship. For example, Senator Henry Jackson (D-Wash.) has proposed a National Bipartisan Commission on Central America. Wattenberg warns Democrats against sabotaging the administration's war in Central America, lest they lead America into a "Who lost Central America?" debate.

However, an even more successful bipartisan juggernaut occurred on a small matter of domestic policy—social security. The administration and Democratic congressional leadership joined together in bipartisan harmony to pass a $165 billion tax-increase plan that objective analysts admit may collapse in a few years. But newspapers hailed the "compromise," politicians patted themselves on the back, and Time's Hugh Sidey declared that the result proved "that our government dawdles, wastes, flubs, bumbles—but works."

In fact, what "works" is whatever triumphs in the Washington political game. The politicians are the contestants, the pundits the sports writers, the bureaucrats the home crowd. What interests them is not policies that are the best for people, but those that reelect the players, make the game exciting for the commentators, and enrich the spectators. Thus the enthusiasm for meaningless bipartisanship.

Occasionally public figures will tacitly admit this. White House Chief of Staff James Baker, for example, spoke at a recent political forum and began his standard rendition of the Reagan administration's accomplishments by reeling off its legislative victories. He was particularly pleased that these successes had enhanced the president's "leadership image." To Baker, accomplishment is judged by political victories and images, not policies and substance.

Baker then went on to declare that it is important that all presidents, Republican and Democrat, succeed. Apparently it matters not whether the particular president wants to nationalize the oil companies, double taxes, repeal the First Amendment, or involve us in a war. Washington's political game dictates that he should succeed.

But "bipartisanship" is worth nothing for its own sake—a bipartisan disaster is still a disaster. Should we feel better about more of our money being seized to build unnecessary weapons, underwrite military dictatorships, and bail out a governmental Ponzi scheme, just because the policies are bipartisan?

While the Reagan administration tunes up the war machine, the Democrats fiddle their bipartisan tune, desperate only to seize power again, nothing more. Their bipartisan duet may be a political success in Washington, but it's a flop for the American people.

## 40. Repudiating the Reagan Revolution

*February 1, 1989*

George Bush's accession to the presidency is being hailed as the triumph of political centrism. And with few ideologues staffing either the Cabinet or the White House, there is no "Bush Revolution" in the offing.

However, despite Bush's rhetorical moderation, he may turn out to have a greater political impact than Ronald Reagan. For despite candidate Reagan's ferocious attacks on Washington and its permanent establishment, President Reagan largely embraced the status quo. His eight years in office turned out to be the Reagan Interlude instead of the Reagan Revolution.

Indeed, Reagan did more than fall short of one goal or another: he left virtually no lasting imprint on policy. Whereas Reagan's professed model, Franklin Delano Roosevelt, still dominates the political debate 44 years after his death with his programs such as Social Security, most of Reagan's initiatives—his military buildup, for one—are even now being reversed.

Consider the dismal benchmarks of the Reagan record:

• Spending. Throughout his political career, Reagan assailed virtually every federal program. In 1980, candidate Reagan assured the Republican Party convention that he would "reduce the cost of government as a percentage of the gross national product."

Yet between 1980 and 1988, federal outlays climbed from $590.9 billion to $1,064.1 billion, a 25 percent increase after inflation. The annual real spending increase under Jimmy Carter, 3.6 percent, was only slightly higher than that under Reagan, 3.2 percent. Moreover, the federal government now takes 22.4 percent of the GNP, more than it did eight years ago; all Reagan has done is reduce the government's share from the modern record set by his administration in 1983.

• Bureaucracy. Not only is Uncle Sam spending more, but the executive branch has gone from 2,571,000 to 2,756,000 employees, a 7.2 percent jump—and more than five times as great as the increase under Carter. Moreover, after attacking the creation of the departments of Energy and Education, Reagan supported the establishment of a 14th department: Veterans Affairs.

• Taxes. Ronald Reagan's most important achievement may have been his initial tax cut, but federal revenue has nevertheless gone from $517.1 billion in 1980 to $909.0 billion last year; in real terms the government now collects 22.4 percent more.

The reason? Though Reagan's 1981 program cut collections by an estimated $1.488 trillion over eight years, bracket creep (as inflation subjected people to higher tax rates), Social Security tax hikes originally approved in 1977, and a half dozen Reagan-supported tax hikes together upped levies by $1.529 trillion over the same period.

• Regulation. The overall pace of federal rule-making slowed under Reagan, but his appointees continued to spew forth reams of new regulations. It was the Reagan administration, for instance, that played National Nanny with seat belt and air bag rules. The same administration, despite its free trade rhetoric, expanded restrictions on imports. And Reagan personally called his first Federal Communications Commission chairman, Mark Fowler, into the Oval Office to tell him to maintain controls over TV syndication.

Though the government continued to expand, for a time it appeared that Reagan had at least changed the political climate. Proposals for vast new social programs dried up in Congress; even liberal Democrats acknowledged that we lived in an era of limits.

Now, however, these implicit restraints have largely disappeared. If Congress remained reluctant to adopt major new spending initiatives, it was because of the Gramm-Rudman law, not Ronald Reagan. In fact, last year legislators passed, with Reagan's support, the multibillion dollar Medicare/catastrophic health insurance bill.

Most of the 1988 Democratic presidential candidates advocated expanding federal power. And Bush, Reagan's anointed successor, endorsed hiking the minimum wage, involving the federal government in day care, and spending more on education.

Neither Reagan's supporters nor his detractors should hold any illusions about his having fulfilled the mandate he carried into office. Candidate Reagan may have united the many disparate groups on the right, but President Reagan left their agenda largely unfinished.

Thus, in his own quiet, unassuming way, George Bush may do more than Reagan to slow our steady slide toward statism. statism. At least, it will be difficult for him to do much worse. For despite all of Ronald Reagan's stirring rhetorical attacks on government, it is larger, more expensive, and more meddlesome today than eight years ago.

## 41.  The Reagan Counterrevolution

*June 6, 1986*

On July 22, 1981, the cabinet council on natural resources and the environment met in the Roosevelt Room, across the hall from the Oval Office. What made this Wednesday meeting unusual was that Ronald Reagan was attending it; "the fellas," as Reagan likes to call his aides, had been unable to agree on an important issue and were forced to take the decision to him.

Council sessions normally elicited the attention of barely half a dozen cabinet officers or their deputies, but on this day the room was overflowing. Virtually every cabinet member was there: Housing's Pierce, Justice's Smith, Agriculture's Block, Treasury's Regan, Energy's Edwards, Transportation's Lewis, Defense's Weinberger. Also included were an assortment of other department officials and White House aides, including Ed Meese, Michael Deaver, and me.

With the exalted title of special assistant to the president, I was working for Martin Anderson, Reagan's first domestic policy adviser. I was able to attend the meeting because I was one of the staffers assigned to this particular cabinet council.

At stake was about $3.6 billion, hardly pocket change. Months before, Energy Secretary James Edwards—the South Carolina dentist who knew no more about energy the day he resigned than the day he was appointed— proposed federal loan guarantees and price supports for three synthetic fuels projects. The beneficiaries were to be Exxon, Amoco, Union Oil, and Tosco, but Edwards didn't care so long as the bill was going to the taxpayers and not him. Then Office of Management and Budget (OMB) Director David Stockman had refused to authorize the deals, as required by Congress. Edwards raged, Stockman dug in, and a reluctant president was forced to take sides.

The cabinet council meeting revealed the Reagan revolutionaries to be just a bunch of self-serving ideological eunuchs, a picture that emerges from Stockman's book, *The Triumph of Politics,* as well. The cabinet was united in its desire to cut government spending, so long as no politically popular programs had to be eliminated.

Edwards led off the meeting with a glowing description of the benefits of pouring billions into Big Oil's coffers. We would get $7 billion in value at minimal risk, he said; we would keep American dollars at home, create jobs, send a signal to OPEC, get the private sector involved, and do almost everything except cure the common cold. His colleagues happily joined in to support him. Weinberger—once dubbed "Cap the Knife" when he headed OMB—argued that the white elephant projects would reduce our energy vulnerability, Smith wished we had backed synfuels projects in the past, and Lewis thought subsidies could make up for federal energy taxes. Block felt the administration should be "doing something in this area," while Pierce outdid himself when he declared that "the time has come to act."

Among the cabinet, only Stockman opposed this high-priced corporate welfare program. He pointed to examples of unsubsidized private synfuels plants, the inefficiency of the proposed operations, the high cost of the fuels, and the heavy burden government borrowing was already placing on private credit markets. He warned of higher interest rates and asked for considerations of other firms that weren't asking for handouts. But all to no avail. Shortly after the meeting, Reagan decided to adopt the three white elephants—which later died as oil prices plunged.

This Reagan was the same Reagan who, in 1980, called federally-subsidized synfuels "energy fascism." It was the Reagan who had once called for voluntary Social Security, had over the years questioned virtually every federal program, and had promised to balance the budget by 1984. He was the right-wing revolutionary who had seemed ready to torch the very superstructure of the welfare state.

But as both Stockman and I found out in our own ways, Reagan the rhetorician used eloquent anti-government speeches to build one of the most committed constituencies in American politics. This bloc of voters regularly delivered him Republican gubernatorial and presidential nominations, and provided him with the base necessary to outpoll the Democrats.

And these people continue to adore him, wishing only that treacherous aides and obstructionist congressmen would "let Reagan be Reagan."

Reagan the office-holder, however, is something quite different. Writes Stockman, Reagan "was a consensus politician, not an ideologue. He had no business trying to make a revolution because it wasn't in his bones." Reagan certainly is a conservative, but he is a politician first, one concerned about winning victories on the Hill, earning plaudits from the pundits, and gaining honored status in the history books. Where policy comes into conflict with those other goals, as it almost always does, compromise is never far from Reagan's lips.

The lesson is a hard one to learn for those of us who committed ourselves to his "revolution." A few weeks ago the Reagan Revolution Reunion Committee awarded a half dozen medals of honor; the reception brought together several hundred Reagan loyalists who had helped their man win the presidency six years before. Much of the talk focused on Stockman and his apostasy. "The Reagan Revolution Lives!" was the rallying cry repeated by the attendees and by Attorney General Ed Meese, who bestowed the awards.

But what revolution is that? Reagan is now the big spender, proposing a budget of $1010.3 billion for next year, compared to the $994.2 billion approved by the House. Since 1980, when Reagan took office, federal outlays have jumped $389 billion, a 60 percent increase. The national government now takes a larger percentage of the GNP than it did under Jimmy Carter. In fact, during Reagan's first term, real spending, adjusted for inflation, rose almost as fast as it did during Carter's one term—15.5 percent compared to 13.5 percent. This is a revolution?

Stockman's book illustrates all too well why the Reagan administration never offered any hope of real, fundamental change. First, Reagan stocked his agencies and departments with the sort of Republican Party hacks who have populated Republican administrations from time immemorial. So naturally, when Stockman drafted what he calls the "blueprint for radical governance," he found his fellow Cabinet members to be, shall we say, less than enthusiastic.

For instance, Jim Edwards opposed decontrol of oil prices—a step repeatedly promised by Reagan, and which actually brought down prices. When Stockman went after the Export-Import Bank, commonly known as "Boeing's Bank" because of the billions it annually sends to the aircraft manufacturer, Commerce Secretary Baldridge leaped to the agency's defense. Alexander Haig organized a counter-offensive among interest groups, congressmen, and the media to block most of OMB's proposed cuts in foreign aid and State Department bureaucrats. Drew Lewis, the Transportation Secretary, "turned completely white when I first laid out my plans to scrap the local highway and transit subsidies," observes Stockman. Education, Health and Human Services, Housing, Justice, and every other department also resisted any proposal to trim any program, however slightly.

Stockman won most of the initial battles, primarily because he formed a Budget Working Group dominated by the few consistent anti-spenders in the administration. But over time, as new budgets were drawn up and Stockman lost the initiative, the resistance to his proposed cuts grew. By late 1982, Stockman writes, "the ridiculous was added to the picayune." Then-Secretary of Health and Human Services, Richard Schweiker, for instance, "submitted a 45-page appeal for restoration of 'devastating' OMB budget cuts, such as $1.5 million for his anti-smoking campaign."

Ironically, for the most part, officials like Schweiker didn't understand how ludicrously inconsistent their arguments were with the professed Reagan agenda. To administration officials, Adam Smith represented a sartorial style, not a political philosophy; at one natural resources cabinet council meeting a deputy cabinet secretary defended subsidies for the bloated maritime industry while wearing his Adam Smith tie. Former Agriculture Secretary Block created new food cartels by extending the system of federal marketing orders, while Reagan talked about freeing farmers from regulation. And after the administration came out for mandatory seat belt laws, a member of the vice president's deregulatory task force explained how the new initiative was fully consistent with the administration's program.

As Stockman's book makes painfully clear, cabinet members could succeed in continually padding their budgets and increasingly interfering in people's lives only because Reagan refused to take the political heat for saying no. At the end of 1982, for instance, Stockman relates how he created a multiple choice budget quiz for Reagan, allowing him to take any of three different degrees of cuts from every program. Reagan enjoyed taking the exam, but, says Stockman, the president "rarely chose to make a whack. They were mostly nicks. 'Yes,' he would say, 'we can't go that far.' Or, 'No, we better go for the moderate option or there will be a drumbeat from the opposition.' " The result was a five-year, $800 billion projected deficit.

The second problem was that even when Reagan agreed to a cut, it was virtually impossible to get it through Congress. And Republicans were among the biggest hogs at the public trough.

New committee chairmen in the Republican-controlled Senate, for instance, were not enthused about reducing the budgets under their control, whatever their rhetoric had been for years as members of the minority party. The Democratic House was even worse; having created a national dole for every interest group that could deliver at least three votes, the "party of the people" wanted to make sure that retirees, yacht owners, corporations, farmers, and everyone else continued to get theirs.

Even as the great budget victories of 1981, hailed as evidence that the Reagan tidal wave had hit the Hill, were less than they seemed at the time. The number-fudging on both sides was outrageous, as phantom cuts were used to make PR points, and votes for spending cuts were shamelessly sold for budget increases elsewhere. The conservative Democratic "Boll Weevils" wanted the sugar price support program; the liberal Republican "Gypsy Moths" wanted more money for Amtrak, Conrail, student loans, and a host of other giveaways.

Individual lawmakers, too, demanded concessions on program after program for their support for the overall package; as a result, the administration's supposed savings were eaten away daily. Reagan caved in on dairy price supports, the Economic Development Administration, water projects, as well as assorted feasibility studies, nurses' training grants, and virtually anything else that could be used to inch the administration forces closer to a majority. All in all, Stockman estimates that in just the few short weeks between House passage of the budget resolution and the reconciliation bill that was to implement the resolution, $10 billion in cuts were lost. Of course, Congress' refusal to say no continues to this day. Last month, the Republican Senate refused to kill a single program for next year.

The battle over military spending turned out to be even more ludicrous. Stockman agreed to a $1.46 trillion, five-year defense budget almost by accident. On the campaign stump, Reagan and his aides had variously urged between a five and nine percent real increase in outlays. In January, 1981, Stockman met with Weinberger and agreed to a seven percent increase—a compromise on the most profligate of Reagan's promises, but still a ridiculous growth rate. Even worse, the budget director was careless about the base year for the increase; Reagan had used Carter's 1980 military spending proposal when he promised a huge build-up, but Stockman accepted the Pentagon's proposal that they use Reagan's revised 1982 budget. "Instead of starting from a defense budget of $142 billion, we'd started with one of $222 billion," he writes, "and by raising that by seven percent—and compounding it over five years—we had ended up increasing the real growth rate of the United States defense budget by 10 percent per year . . . double what candidate Ronald Reagan had promised in his campaign budget plan."

When Stockman realized his mistake and tried to reopen the issue, he was bested by Weinberger, who didn't want to give up one dollar. Stockman proposed to reduce the five-year buildup to $1.33 trillion, a sizable expenditure by any measure; he got but $8 billion in savings. Weinberger even balked at accepting any cuts when inflation turned out to be only half what he and Stockman had originally figured. Only Congress stopped the Pentagon from collecting windfall on top of windfall.

Having found that the politicians in both the White House and Capitol Hill liked spending, Stockman turned ''responsible'' and began agitating for a tax increase. Reagan rewarded his efforts with four major ''revenue enhancements,'' starting with TEFRA in 1982, but finally grew stubborn and said no more. Stockman the accountant was shocked: ''What do you do when your president ignores all the palpable, relevant facts and wanders in circles?'' Stockman then worked with Congress and against the administration for a tax hike; finally, frustrated that his scheming failed, he quit. ''Politics had triumphed,'' he writes, ''first by blocking spending cuts and then by stopping revenue increases.''

Yet having understood so much, and fought so hard, Stockman comes to precisely the wrong conclusion. The fact that he—David Stockman—could not dismantle the welfare state has not demonstrated that special interest subsidies and rip-offs can never be ended. Reagan never put together the sort of massive, all-encompassing package of cuts that might have been worth a congressman risking his career over. More important, Reagan has only sparingly wielded his veto pen, despite numerous opportunities to block ridiculous expenditures.

Indeed, the tumultuous national referendum on everything in our half-trillion-dollar welfare state budget'' that Stockman writes of never was held. Yes, voters clearly want a lot of programs, particularly Social Security. But there is no evidence that the great unwashed masses would oust a congressman who voted against higher civil service pensions, nonsensical grant programs, and a host of other projects that benefit only a few narrow interests. In a democracy, activists tend to triumph over the inert majority unless the issue is important enough to interest the mass of people; Reagan never delivered the sort of radical assault on all federal spending, business subsidies, and military waste included, that just might have altered the political balance.

But even if Stockman is essentially correct—that the average lower-income person favors free Coast Guard inspections for yachts and giveaways to luxury hotel developers—that is still no reason for us to give up and bleed the taxpayers. To eliminate this year's deficit would require an average 60 percent increase in the personal income tax, for example. Such a step would devastate individual families as well as the overall economy. Moreover, following Stockman's advice to raise revenues would make even more permanent the lucrative federal dole for everyone who belongs to a group with a letterhead and a mailing list. Doing so, thereby ratifying the special interest looting that now occurs on a national scale by making it fiscally responsible, would be a rather high price to pay for making the national accounts balance.

Stockman's attitude is particularly peculiar since it is only the threat of $200 billion deficits, combined with the fear of credit dislocations and steadily increasing federal interest payments, that has caused Congress to trim spending around the edges (including defense). In short, Reagan's refusal to give Congress greater access to the national checkbook by hiking taxes—admittedly at the cost of a large deficit—has probably stopped spending from growing even faster. And for this we can be thankful.

Indeed, this may explain, more than anything else, Reagan's refusal to do what Stockman calls "a great act of statesmanship" and support repeal of the 1981 tax cut. Reagan has no interest in budget details, but he understands the concept of total surrender. If Reagan were to endorse a huge tax increase, not only would he be conceding that the most outrageous and wasteful federal pork barrel was a fixture of the American system, but he would be destroying what is probably his most important lasting legacy—halting the steady rise in the tax burden on Americans.

Not that his tax revolution is overwhelming. After accounting for Reagan's four tax increases, as well as tax hikes that were approved before Reagan took office, the net savings from his 1981 tax bill is about $5 per person a year. As a percentage of GNP, revenues have returned to about where they were in 1978, which is still higher than the historical average. But if Reagan were to accept Stockman's advice, taxes would actually rise during his administration; the last vestiges of the "Reagan Revolution" would then be swept away.

Stockman is neither the first nor the last presidential appointee who found that his leader had feet of clay; the former budget director may simply have earned more than anyone else for telling his tale. Moreover, *The Triumph of Politics* illuminates not insubstantial weaknesses—arrogance and disloyalty, for instance—in the storyteller, who was one of the most important architects of the "Reagan Revolution."

Nevertheless, Stockman's account remains a powerful indictment of a government that is used by everyone to live off his neighbor. And his angry message should cause us not to give up in the face of the hordes of would-be looters who roam the halls of Congress, but instead, to fight even harder to restrict a federal establishment run rampant. For even if the redistributionist state is beyond containing, there's still no reason to turn over our money without a fight.

# 42. Your Congress at Work

*April 1988*

There may have been a time in American history when members of Congress could not properly be presumed to be hoodlums who had merely gained legal sanction for their activities. Not likely, perhaps, but at least theoretically possible.

No longer, however. Before it left town last December, Congress voted to shut down two conservative newspapers, endorse the right of congressmen to fly their girl friends on federal planes, reward a senator's campaign supporter with an $8-million grant to the contributor's favorite charity, and distribute generous slabs of pork to universities, developers, municipalities, and other favored interests across the country. It was Congress at its most natural—and its worst—exhibiting a form of civic pornography that our democracy seems incapable of controlling.

America's finest no longer bother to approve an official budget and pass individual appropriations bills: Congress instead routinely ignores statutory deadlines and flouts its own rules, relying on one massive Continuing Resolution, or CR, to fund virtually the entire federal government. The CR is a pernicious creature, violating the constitutional balance by emasculating the president's veto power and allowing congressmen to escape public scrutiny by burying amendments in thousand-page bills.

However, in its rush to adjourn in 1987, Congress produced a masterpiece by even its own unenviable standards. Most unique was the legislators' vote to close two major newspapers that had criticized leading Democrats.

Congressional leaders first tried to use the CR to resurrect the "fairness doctrine" that empowers the Federal Communications Commission (FCC) to regulate the "fairness" of broadcasters' programming; President Reagan stymied their effort by threatening to veto the entire bill. However, the House and Senate conferees conjured up an even more noxious amendment that the administration was unaware of and that most members of Congress did not see before approving the CR.

The FCC prohibits "cross ownership" of a TV station and newspaper in the same market—one of many archaic broadcast regulations. The commission can, however, waive the rule, as it did temporarily for Rupert Murdoch, who owns the *New York Post* and *Boston Herald,* as well as a TV station in both cities. Murdoch had planned to apply for a permanent waiver.

But Sen. Edward Kennedy (D-Mass.), routinely assailed by the *Boston*

*Herald* as the "fat boy" and the "world's oldest juvenile delinquent," decided that it would be, in his words, "best for the nation and best for Boston" to silence Murdoch. So he enlisted Sen. Ernest Hollings (D-S.C.) to add language prohibiting any change in FCC rules or any extension of waivers—a provision that affects only Murdoch.

So unless New York's two senators are successful in their effort to reverse Hollings's amendment, Murdoch will have to either shut down the papers or hold a fire sale. If any good has come out of this shameful episode, it is that Congress's heavy-handedness has dramatically exposed the myth that broadcast regulation is not political and protects the public.

A racier bit of abuse involves federal transport for congressional girl friends. In February 1986 Rep. Charles Wilson (D-Tex.) arrived in Pakistan and asked the embassy to fly him and Annelise Ilschenko, a lobbyist, to another city. The Defense Intelligence Agency (DIA), in control of the planes, said no, since she was neither family nor staff.

Wilson told embassy officials he'd retaliate with budget cuts, and he tried, unsuccessfully, to reduce the DIA's funding later in 1986. He finally made good on his threats last winter, adding amendments to the CR eliminating the DIA's exemption from personnel cuts and cutting six of the agency's planes. (The conference committee eventually restored funding for four of them).

"It can't help but look like this kind of spoiled congressman with a bloated sense of self-importance trying to get back at someone for not flying his girlfriend around," Wilson acknowledges, but he refuses to defend his action. His staff says the congressman just wanted the DIA to receive a fair share of budget reductions—but his vendetta began in 1986.

Of course, it is hard to imagine a federal bureau that couldn't stand being cut. But we would be better off if Congress based spending levels on something other than personal spite.

But the CR is not really about budget reduction. Especially when you're a friend of and campaign contributor to a senator.

Zev Wilson is a board member of Ozar Hatorah, an organization concerned about North African Sephardic Jews. It has never been a favorite of the American Jewish community, so Wilson (Zev, not Charles) hit up his friend Sen. Daniel Inouye (D-Hawaii), to whose 1985 campaign he had contributed $1,000. Inouye then stuck into the CR, over State Department objections, an $8-million appropriation for—guess what?—Ozar Hatorah, to build refugee schools in France.

Why should American taxpayers fund such an enterprise? The preservation of the Sephardic Jewish "religion, language and culture" is a worthy cause, says Inouye: Wilson's political backing had nothing to do with the issue. Of course. (Under enormous public pressure, Inouye now says he "made an error" and will ask Congress to undo the dirty deed.)

The CR was loaded with this sort of pork. Let us count just a few of the ways taxpayers suffered so influential interest groups could enjoy life to the fullest.

• Beekeepers pressured Congress to lift a $250,000 limit on support loans. Rep. Silvio Conte (R-Mass.) estimates that 15 honey producers could gain $6 million.

• Conte, who fought the sweet deal for beekeepers, won a $60,000 grant for the Belgian Endive Research Center at the University of Massachusetts.

• Sunflower farmers' request for a new price support program was turned down—but Uncle Sam will buy $10 million worth of sunflower oil as a consolation.

• Sen. Lawton Chiles (D-Fla.), the Budget Committee chairman who regularly denounces the deficit, pushed through a $25-million research grant for . . . the University of Florida.

• The National Rural Electric Cooperative Association, believing that $53.1 billion in subsidies over the last 14 years was not enough, won approval of an amendment allowing local coops to refinance $2 billion in federally guaranteed loans, with no prepayment penalty.

• House Speaker Jim Wright (D-Tex.) inserted into the CR language directing the Federal Aviation Administration to give "high-priority consideration" to a new airport in Fort Worth—it just happens to be located in his district.

• Rep. Joseph Early (D-Mass.) successfully lobbied for an amendment forcing the Economic Development Administration (EDA), one of many federal slush funds, to provide $1 million for a high-tech research facility in Massachusetts.

• Sen. Lowell Weicker (R-Conn.) used the same tactic to subsidize a private research organization in his state.

• Oklahoma State University won a $250,000 EDA grant for an international trade center through the efforts of Rep. Wes Watkins (D-Okla.).

• Sen. John Stennis and Rep. Jamie Whitten, both Mississippi Democrats, arranged $3 million for the Institute of Technology Development in their state.

• The CR also included a $260,000 grant for cranberry research, $5 million for a Cleveland harbor project, $50,000 to study New Mexico wildflowers, and $97.3 million in grants to 10 different colleges for water quality research. And the list, unfortunately, goes on.

We are more than seven years into the Reagan revolution and nothing seems to have changed on Capitol Hill. Indeed, the stench may have gotten worse: who in 1981 would have predicted that liberal Democrats would eventually use the budget process to surreptitiously close down a critical newspaper?

Nor is there any reason to expect the situation to improve, whoever is elected president in November. Congress must abandon its parochial perspective, and that will not happen as long as voters expect their elected officials to bring home the bacon in the form of federal money. In short, we can look forward to a rerun of Congress's sorry budget show next December.

## 43. The Spending Problem in Profile

*April 16, 1985*

Four years ago, revolutionary fervor swept the capital. Not only had Ronald Reagan won the presidency, but the Republicans took control of the U.S. Senate. Conservatives committed to frugal government, like Sen. James McClure of Idaho, finally came to power. Sen. McClure, for one, became chairman of both the Energy and Natural Resources Committee and the Interior Subcommittee of the Appropriations Committee.

However, today, resistance to the Reagan administration's proposed budget cuts is being led by many of these same conservatives, including Sen. McClure. Uniformly regarded as bright, genial and sincere, Sen. McClure generally votes to cut overall federal spending—the National Taxpayers Union rates him among the more frugal senators, though his score fell sharply last year—and opposes a tax hike. But like so many other eloquent congressional proponents of fiscal responsibility, he does not believe budget-cutting begins at home.

Indeed, Randall Fitzgerald and Gerald Lipson, who were assigned by the Grace Commission to investigate congressional procurement practices, cite Sen. McClure in their book ''Pork Barrel'' as one of the worst ''perpetrators of the parochial imperative.'' Due in no small part to Sen. McClure's influence, for example, the Energy Department is the largest nonagricultural employer in Idaho.

Sen. McClure views federally subsidized power and water as basic rights. He has stymied efforts to both regularize and accelerate repayment of some $8.6 billion in Treasury debt by the six federal power-marketing administrations (PMAs) and pushed through a 1983 amendment blocking any White House ''studies relating to or leading to the possibility of changing . . . to a market-rate method of pricing'' by PMAs, which currently charge between one-third and one-half the market rate for electricity.

Why the aversion to making consumers pay their own way? In an interview, Sen. McClure said the Northwest already is suffering "tremendous price shocks." He also doesn't believe people should be charged a market price for public services: "We're the taxpayers. We ask our government to invest in things for us and it's done so we enjoy the benefits."

As for water projects, perhaps the most egregious form of federal pork, Sen. McClure has opposed efforts to make beneficiaries and localities pay more of the bill for dam safety, supported the boondoggle Tennessee-Tombigbee Waterway, and last fall supported adding $6 billion of new projects to the continuing resolution.

And when the Carter administration proposed to limit the eligibility of farmers for subsidized federal irrigation water, Sen. McClure denounced the plan as "part of the dogma of Marxism." Irrigation has "social value," he says.

Sen. McClure's energy record is, if anything, even more disappointing; he seems closer philosophically to his Democratic predecessor as energy committee chairman, the late Henry Jackson, than to Mr. Reagan.

Before becoming chairman, Sen. McClure cosponsored the legislation that provided massive federal energy-research assistance, and proposed an Energy Mobilization Board (which failed to pass). He has opposed some Department of Energy regulations, but sees "an ongoing need for a separate federal agency that will serve as a clear focal point for formulating national energy policy." He acknowledges that the department provides a forum for would-be regulators—"having the structure is an invitation to use it"—but figures that "we'll always have that pressure anyway" and intervention will occur only in an emergency.

Indeed, it is precisely this belief that underlies Sen. McClure's major legislative accomplishment, the Standby Petroleum Allocation Act (SPAA) of 1982. For despite lower Western demand for oil and the collapse of OPEC—which is selling less than half the crude it was just six years ago, and at 20% lower prices—and of price-fixing efforts by countries like Britain, Sen. McClure believes "the only question" about a future supply disruption "is where and when." The SPAA, a regulatory nightmare, would have put the government back in the business of deciding who got oil at what prices during a "crisis." Farmers, local governments, inefficient refiners and other special interests that did not want to pay higher prices for fuel could have gotten what they wanted through the political process. Reagan vetoed the bill, but Sen. McClure continues to press for standby allocation authority.

Unfortunately, this kind of federal meddling has caused energy shortages, long gasoline-station lines and rising prices in the past. In fact, Sen.

McClure admits that "there isn't any doubt that whenever the government gets involved it makes the problem worse." But since he thinks we won't be able to keep it from being involved, we should act now to "minimize the damage."

Despite his concern over the deficit, Sen. McClure does not expect to make large cuts in energy outlays, aside from reducing spending for the Strategic Petroleum Reserve. "We'll squeeze down as much as we can," he promises. But over the past four years he has used his Interior Subcommittee chairmanship to lard the budget of everything from the Energy Regulatory Administration to research on electric-hybrid vehicles. In fiscal year 1984 the Appropriations Committee approved nearly $500 million more for the department than the administration requested; spending this year also is higher almost across the board.

Even more expensive has been Sen. McClure's fixation with subsidies for synthetic fuels. Originally expected to hand out $88 billion to create a domestic synthetic-fuels industry, the SFC lost its first two presidents amid controversy, took three years to make its first award and has had to offer price guarantees as high as $95 a barrel to interest private companies. Thus, even if oil prices suddenly trebled, synfuels still would be no bargain. Yet Sen. McClure says that federal support for what increasingly looks like a white elephant is an "absolutely essential investment."

Nuclear power is another favorite of the senator's. He was a fervent supporter of the deceased Clinch River Breeder Reactor, a multibillion-dollar turkey. Here, as with synfuels, Sen. McClure sees the "public interest" involved: After three decades of development he believes nuclear power is still "so new and so untried" that the government must set parameters so utilities can measure the risks they face.

What prompts Sen. McClure to reject in practice what he supports in principle? One reason certainly is the "parochial imperative." A lot of energy research is conducted at the Idaho National Engineering laboratory, and the SPAA would have given farmers, an important Idaho constituency, preferential access to below-cost fuel in an emergency. The senator himself readily admits the importance of home-state pressures.

Idaho's senior senator exhibits the same loss of revolutionary fervor that seems to strike most politicians who spend years on the Potomac. The same person who once supported the "Liberty Amendment," which would repeal the income tax, successfully proposed to forgive millions in interest on federal loans to the John F. Kennedy Center for the Performing Arts, a gathering spot for the capital's elite. Sen. McClure says it was the "best way out of a bad deal." Since the center wasn't paying what it owed, the government sharply reduced its claim in exchange for a new promise to pay. If only most taxpayers could escape their debts so easily.

Sen. McClure illustrates the root cause of our trillion-dollar government. Decent and well-intentioned, he simply, as one exasperated White House official put it, "likes to subsidize all sorts of people." And until conservative leaders like him stop loading up the budget for their constituents, Washington's theatergoers and anyone else who claims to represent the "social interest," there will be no real budget cutting, let alone a revolution, in Washington.

## 44. Senator Establishment

*November 18, 1987*

Robert Dole, the Senate Republican leader, is now officially running for president. And his agenda is a simple one: to take power.

What he would do as president is less clear, but his record is not an encouraging one.

Dole has, for example, spared the taxpayers no expense in pandering to his farming constituency. He has spent his entire career supporting higher crop subsidies, increased food stamp spending, and larger commodity shipments abroad.

In fact, Dole, admits one of his staffers, invariably has "supported agricultural commodities" whether or not they were produced in Kansas. His approach of giving all farmers everything they want cost the taxpayers an incredible $26 billion last year and consumers another $7 billion.

Dole has naturally endorsed expansive crop export subsidies, even to the Soviet Union. He apparently sees no harm in strengthening America's prime adversary if doing so will buy a few votes back home.

Particularly sleazy have been Dole's endless efforts to enrich Archer-Daniels-Midland, the nation's largest agricultural processor. The firm has grown rich from a variety of federal subsidies for ethanol alcohol production and has, in turn, rewarded Dole with generous campaign assistance over the years.

Naturally, Dole hopes his slavish support for farmers—helping deliver something approaching $200 billion to them since he was first elected to Congress—will give him a victory in Iowa. Already a majority of the local Farm Bureau chairmen and many other agricultural leaders back him.

But farm subsidies are not the only boondoggle that Dole has promoted. He voted to bail out both Chrysler and New York City; he supported federal funding for the SST aircraft. Dole has also voted for an endless line of pork barrel projects, including the Clinch River nuclear breeder reactor.

More recently, Dole, who proposed catastrophic health insurance years ago, complained that health programs were "just another instance of how Congress puts spending on automatic pilot." But what did he do when a proposal to expand Medicaid came to a vote? He supported it.

Only once has Dole appeared to take budget-cutting seriously—in 1985, when he shepherded a plan to scrap 50 programs through the Senate. But Dole seemed to relish the politics rather than the substance; moreover, he has made no further efforts to seriously reduce spending.

Dole has, however, spent plenty of time lobbying for increased taxes, justifying his reputation as the tax collector for the welfare state.

His grandest moment came in 1982 when he helped push the Tax Responsibility and Fiscal Responsibility Act into law. TEFRA was a $227 billion grab bag of new and higher taxes, the largest tax hike in U.S. history.

In fact, Dole blithely ignored the Constitution to pass his tax increase. Article 1, Section 7 requires the House of Representatives to originate "all bills for raising revenues," but Dole and the Senate acted first.

Why? "The House didn't want to" act, explained Dole. So he simply steamrolled the nation's fundamental law.

This is what makes Dole's candidacy genuinely frightening. He is basing his campaign on competence, an ability to get things done—to be, in Dole's words, a "hands-on president." But the most important question is not could he do things well, but what would he do?

Aside from hiking taxes to pay for more welfare for farmers, there is no way to tell, for the word "principle" is not part of Dole's vocabulary. Says fellow Kansas Sen. Nancy Landon Kassebaum, "Bob waits to see which way the wind is blowing."

Which could mean, for instance, endorsing protectionist trade measures, which would cost Americans jobs. Dole professes to support open international markets, but in 1985 he felt the wind was blowing against free trade and voted to limit shoe and textile imports.

What would Dole's strong, take-charge foreign policy look like? Perhaps increasing export subsidies to the Soviets while simultaneously waging war on their client state, Nicaragua. After visiting Central America recently, he commented that "a little three-day invasion" of that country "wouldn't make anybody unhappy down there." What it would do to the young Americans who would be expected to fight and die he didn't say.

Were the nomination decided within the capital Beltway, Robert Dole would win hands down. But we can be thankful that the nation's founders did not leave the choice of president up to the politicians, bureaucrats and influence-peddlers who dominate Washington.

In fact, Dole's popularity with the capital's elite is itself a good reason to vote against him. For the Washington establishment remains the cause, not the solution, of most of our nation's problems. And Robert Dole is truly the establishment's candidate.

## 45. Populism as Opportunism

*January 21, 1987*

Newly elected House Speaker Jim Wright always has posed as a populist, even as he stoutly defended such big business boondoggles as the Synthetic Fuels Corp. But Wright now has outdone himself in purporting to speak for the little man while representing the establishment.

First, Wright engaged in his usual soak-the-rich demagoguery. He proposed "a stretch-out of tax cuts for the wealthy," delaying the reduction in the top rate from 38.5 percent to 28 percent next Jan. 1.

The fact that this would violate Congress' basic deal with the taxpayers—lower rates for fewer deductions—that got last year's tax bill passed obviously doesn't bother Wright. He's ready to start raising rates again.

Wright naturally argues that he is only trying to empty the pockets of the rich, but the term wealthy has lost all meaning if it includes those earning $54,000, where the 38.5 percent rate applies.

In any case, Wright's fixation on confiscating the earnings of the rich symbolizes how pervasively envy has infected our society. For why should higher income people be forced to pay a disproportionate share of their incomes in taxes?

The standard answer is that the wealthy can afford to pay more. But that is an argument for a flat tax, not progressive rates.

For example, if taxes were set at a uniform 15 percent, someone earning 10 times what his neighbor did would pay 10 times as much in taxes. That seems as fair as any tax system ever will be.

The progressive rate structure, in contrast, is tailor-made for demagogues. Money-hungry politicians can denounce the rich and finance programs for the interest groups with the most votes.

This happened after World War II, as Congress increased the top rate to an incredible 90 percent. The government taking 90 cents of every additional dollar earned was pure theft, but it satisfied a deep-seated popular animus against people who were financially successful.

And Speaker Wright is continuing in this disreputable, demagogic tradition. Even 28 percent is too high for a top rate; Congress should lower it further. Congressional leaders certainly shouldn't be considering breaking faith with the American people by pushing rates back up.

But Wright showed ignorance as well as opportunism when he went on to complain about "tax increases for poor people" hidden in President Reagan's 1988 budget, namely user fees.

For instance, the administration wants to increase the fee paid by home buyers whose mortgages are subsidized by the Federal Home Administration. "It's a tax," says Wright.

So too are administration proposals to have Medicare and Medicaid recipients pay a larger share of their doctor and hospital expenses, he argues. As well as proposed reductions in student loan benefits.

The basic point that Wright misses, of course, is that there is a very important difference between the government seizing taxpayers' earnings and reducing program benefits. Taxpayers have a moral right to their earnings; home buyers have no similar claim to subsidized mortgages.

Thus, the administration simply is trying to slow some of the special interest looting that occurs throughout government. And doing so hardly threatens poor people. As Office of Management and Budget spokesman Edwin Dale put it, "the buyer of a $90,000 house is not a poor person."

Indeed, for years the administration has proposed allowing the Coast Guard to charge for yacht inspections, but Congress consistently has blocked the plan. Presumably this is another of the "tax increases for poor people" that Wright opposes.

It is ironic that in this year, the 200th anniversary of the Constitution, the speaker of the House of Representatives does not understand that the nation's governing compact was drafted to contain the politics of envy. Unfortunately, over the years special interests have nevertheless managed to turn the government into one giant pork barrel, looting middle and upper income people and buying votes with the proceeds.

A true populism would recognize that the greatest threat to the average citizen is a government that breaks its commitments in a never-ending attempt to bleed more money out of the taxpayers. Such a populism would seek to bring down taxes for rich and poor alike and to curtail the federal government's endless stream of middle-class subsidies, which have caused the budget to run out of control.

But Jim Wright is not such a leader. Despite his rhetoric, he represents the governing elite, not the people. And his interest is in amassing power and votes, not in doing what is right.

## 46. Senator Byrd's Pork Barrel Bid

*May 4, 1988*

Senator Robert Byrd (D-W.Va.), the Democratic leader for more than a decade, says he's going to step down from that position next year. With the retirement of Mississippi's John Stennis, Byrd is in line to become chairman of the Senate Appropriations Committee, from which position, he says, he intends to "see that West Virginia receives the share for which it is eligible."

Put more bluntly, Senator Byrd doesn't believe that he has been able to bring home enough pork barrel projects to ensure his reelection. Though his colleagues profess to know of no request of his that was turned down—after all, no one wants to anger the Majority Leader—Byrd apparently thinks he can use the committee chairmanship to squeeze a few more dollars out of the taxpayers for his constituents.

Naturally, the home state folk are pleased with Byrd's maneuver. Indeed, no one seems happier than supposed proponents of fiscal responsibility like business. Says John Hurd, president of the West Virginia Chamber of Commerce, "we're very pleased with it. We're looking for help any place we can get it."

It is rare for a politician to offer naked greed as the reason for a career change. Sen. Byrd's candor is refreshing.

But that doesn't make his plans any more justifiable. The purpose of government should be to serve the broad public interest, not to enrich the supporters of the chairman of the Senate Appropriations Committee, whoever he may be.

In fact, Congress has no right under the Constitution—the legal framework that supposedly gives the federal government its power—to hand out local pork. Article 1, Section 8 authorizes Congress to collect taxes to provide for the "general welfare of the United States," not to subsidize influential interest groups.

Of course, we long ago moved away from the constitutional ideal. Last fall the Competitive Enterprise Institute, a Washington-based free market group, released its Pork Barrel and Subsidies (PBS) index. On average, House members voted against pork projects only 27 percent of the time, while Senators resisted the urge to steal from the national polity on just 30 percent of their votes.

Senator Byrd was one of 28 Democratic senators to score zero; 111 House members, primarily Democrats, also registered as perfect hogs. Among them were Budget Committee Chairman William Gray and Dan Rostenkowski, the Ways and Means Committee Chairman who presides over tax policy.

But the PBS is too abstract to bring the reality of pork barrel spending home to the average voter. Every American should be forced to read the 1,194-page Continuing Resolution and the 1,033-page Omnibus Reconciliation Act, the two bills which Congress passed last December to fund the government.

The legislation was loaded with special interest giveaways. In fact, legislators seemed to be more shameless than usual, enriching friends and punishing enemies on every page.

Fifteen of the nation's largest beekeepers received $6 million; sunflower growers collected $10 million in cash. The Oregon Historical Society gained $2 million.

Research grants flowed equally generously—$60,000 for Belgian endives, $50,000 for New Mexico wildflowers, $260,000 for cranberries, and $1.5 million for potatoes. Congress also selflessly offered to have the taxpayers pay to develop sonar catfish counters and cornstarch-based biodegradable plastic. Penn State University collected a handsome $285,000 to study milk consumption.

Congress also voted to prevent the administration from selling government planes that members like to use to fly around the country; House Speaker Jim Wright pushed through a $25 million airport for his friend, H. Ross Perot Jr. And legislators handed out wads of cash to such groups as the International Coffee Organization, the World Tourism Organization, the Woodrow Wilson International Center for Scholars, the Japan-United States Friendship Commission, and the Christopher Columbus Quincentenary Jubilee Commission.

Congress voted to build the usual roads which go nowhere in members' districts. An Idaho ski resort gained $6.4 million, courtesy of Sen. James McClure. And the Economic Development Administration was ordered to spend millions on projects that don't meet even its own lax criteria.

The glare of publicity on Congress' Christmas misbehavior embarrassed the legislators, but only momentarily. Indeed, Sen. Byrd's frank announcement that he is changing positions to increase his state's take suggests that, if anything, congressmen feel even less self-conscious today about looting the public to advance their re-election than they did five months ago. And while that may mean a few more dollars for the residents of West Virginia, it's bad news for the rest of us.

## 47. Al Gore's Dairy Sellout

*April 13, 1988*

If there has been one constant in the Democratic campaign for president, it's a willingness to pander to any interest group that controls more than three votes.

Richard Gephardt was the most vigorous practitioner of the "promise 'em anything" school of politics; Jesse Jackson and Michael Dukakis have not been far behind.

And now Sen. Al Gore of Tennessee, who originally positioned himself as a centrist Southerner, has joined the parade. In a desperate—and happily futile—attempt to generate votes in Wisconsin, Gore pledged to open the federal Treasury to the dairy lobby.

Barnstorming the state as "the only active farmer" in the race, Gore called for a 50 percent "phase-up" in federal milk supports. The goal, he said, was "to get family farm income back up to a level that farmers can survive on."

Wisconsin's 37,000 dairy producers undoubtedly would like to receive bigger government checks, but there is no conceivable justification for such an increase. Indeed, the only sensible policy would be to junk the entire system.

No program has raged further out of control under President Reagan than agriculture. In the last two years alone Uncle Sam has given farmers $49 billion.

And dairy subsidies have played no small role in this financial hemorrhage, running between $1.5 billion and $2.6 billion a year. So far this decade Uncle Sam has lavished some $14 billion on one of the greediest special interests to ever roam the corridors of Capitol Hill.

In fact, the program is ludicrous as well as expensive. To prop up prices the federal government has had to continually buy an ocean of milk—12.3 billion pounds worth in 1986.

Last year federal purchases fell to "only" 5.6 billion pounds because the government spent $1.1 billion to pay dairy farmers to go out of business. In this way Uncle Sam has enriched thousands of producers and even made 144 of them instant millionaires.

Individual checks ranged up to $10 million; Californian Joe Gonsalves, an $8 million winner, exulted that "it's almost like one of those lottery tickets." Except that the taxpayers were footing the bill.

And now along comes Al Gore with a proposal to give even more money to the dairymen.

Certainly these farmers are hard workers; many of them are struggling to stay in business. But that doesn't entitle them to a multibillion-dollar federal bailout, year after year.

Indeed, why is it more important to preserve the family dairy farm than the corner dry cleaner? Or the neighborhood pizza parlor?

The justification for the dairy dole offered by the National Milk Producers Federation is that the overall economy is "undergirded" by the agricultural sector. Thus, the only way the rest of us can prosper is to pump billions of dollars into rural America.

This self-serving analysis ignores the fact that the subsidies have to be extracted from everyone else before they can be paid to the milk producers. Needless to say, the average American would be better off if he got to keep his money instead of having it mailed off to Gore's favorite special interest.

Anyway, what industry doesn't "undergird" the economy? The dairy lobby's argument proves too much. If farmers deserve to be supported, so do autoworkers, oil companies, fitness club instructors and newspaper columnists.

The point is, virtually every business in the economy is dependent on other industries. These relationships are mutually beneficial and don't justify a host of new federal subsidy programs.

Having been able to amass only minuscule vote totals since Super Tuesday, Gore has begun to challenge Jesse Jackson's presidential qualifications. But Gore's willingness to pander to a lobby virtually unmatched in its venality—not that many years ago one producers' group tried to bribe the secretary of the Treasury to get his backing for higher price supports—raises questions about his own fitness for office.

For Gore, like the other Democrats, has unceasingly wailed about President Reagan's economic policies. But no president will be able to cut the deficit unless he evidences a willingness to "just say no" to the many clamorous interest groups, like dairy farmers, that believe the taxpayers owe them a living.

Indeed, the issue is fundamentally a moral one. The purpose of the government should be to promote the truly "general" welfare, but Gore, like most congressmen, apparently believes that the federal Treasury is just a lush cornucopia for campaign supporters. And that is the last perspective that we need to have represented at 1600 Pennsylvania Avenue.

## 48. Man of the House: O'Neill's Destructive Legacy

*March 5, 1988*

*Man of the House,* by Tip O'Neill with William Novak.

Only in America could someone who spent so many years denouncing "greed," "selfishness" and "meanness" cash in with as much vigor as has former House Speaker Tip O'Neill. O'Neill—who contends that Ronald Reagan's wealth has left him out of touch with average Americans— has been busy on the lecture circuit, earning up to $20,000 a pop. He's also appeared in ads for American Express and Hush Puppy shoes. And, of course, he's authored his autobiography. Actually, William Novak wrote the book, but no matter. It still provides a vivid portrait of someone who exemplifies the worst of Washington and our political system.

Not that O'Neill is not affable and sincere. He was, he writes in *Man of the House,* "a very sociable kid." He liked to play poker with other politicos—though not Richard Nixon, whom he considered to be a whiner. Using anecdote after anecdote, O'Neill assures the reader that he was a gregarious, warm-hearted fellow whose office door was always open and whose heart was always bleeding. And there's no reason to doubt him.

Nevertheless, O'Neill's legacy is not one that we should love. For he was consumed by politics. A rabid partisan, he acted as if the federal treasury were the Democrats' personal campaign fund with which to buy votes. Indeed, *Man of the House* unintentionally confirms what many of us always knew—that O'Neill never realized there was a national good that transcended the selfish special interest politics at which he excelled.

O'Neill began his "public service" in a state legislature dominated by Republicans. He naturally fumes about their blatant partisanship, but he learned his lesson well, ruthlessly suppressing the Republican minority.

Far more insidious, however, was O'Neill's willingness to twist every issue to fit his own partisan ends.

"All politics is local" O'Neill likes to say and his book is an unconscious paen to power politics, sleazy campaigning, pork-barrel budgeting, and the philosophy that nothing matters other than being re-elected. His advice to his successor, Jim Wright of Texas, was "to consider the party at all times," and that's certainly what O'Neill did. His book documents the former Speaker's willingness, again and again, to sacrifice the national interest to enhance his party's and his own influence.

Consider O'Neill's demagoguery on the Social Security issue. One of his proudest moments, he relates in his book, is when the Democrats "stood up to the President when he tried to cut Social Security." That may have been a nice vote-getter, but was it responsible or fair? The system has long been in trouble, facing a tidal wave of red ink early the next century. If Social Security survives, workers will have to pay payroll tax rates approaching 40 per cent. But O'Neill obviously never cared about Americans' retirement future; all he was interested in was votes.

In fact, when Rep. J. J. Pickle (D.-Tex.), then chairman of the House Ways and Means Subcommittee on Social Security, began working with the Administration in 1981 to try to forestall the threatened insolvency of Social Security, O'Neill demanded that Pickle let Reagan stand alone. In November 1982 the Democrats went on to demagogue the issue with great success.

In 1985, O'Neill behaved in the same irresponsible manner. The Senate Republicans pressed for a COLA freeze—hardly unfair for beneficiaries who are getting up to five times what they and their employers had contributed—but O'Neill balked, over the objections of many more centrist Democrats.

Again the only reason for O'Neill's action was political. Earlier that year he called high-income Social Security recipients "freeloaders," but he quickly retracted his statement (which, for some reason, he fails to mention in his book). O'Neill then pointed to the Senate Republicans' proposal, chortling, "I think we are going to have tremendous gains in the next election."

More cynical still has been O'Neill's tax-and-spend politics, where virtually every federal program was used to enhance the Democratic coalition. Yes, yes, he constantly tells us, all he ever wanted to do was help poor people. "With Ronald Reagan in the White House, somebody had to look out for those who were not so fortunate," he nobly relates in his autobiography: "That's where I came in."

But O'Neill was actually the ultimate proponent of "trickle-down" economics, apparently believing that by turning Uncle Sam into a fiscal Santa Claus who hands out billions in goodies to anyone who asks—so long as they pledged fealty to the Democratic party, of course—that the poor would benefit. Indeed, O'Neill embodied the phenomenon of interest group liberalism, which identifies anything that advances the Democratic voting bloc, to be in the national interest.

Whether it be more welfare benefits, business subsidies, or import tariffs, as long as a member of some interest group was for it, O'Neill would back it.

The Speaker comes by his myopic view of government naturally. His father, for instance, got a Boston city job through the patronage system. As a state representative, O'Neill would pass out "snow buttons" to constituents entitling them to shovel snow for the city; his book reeks of the almost religious belief that votes are properly bought with public funds.

Naturally, as a congressman, O'Neill shoveled vast amounts of federal loot into his district. During the 1970s, for instance, his office estimated that 41 per cent of the dollars that flowed into Boston were connected to some federal program.

Unfortunately, however, O'Neill's influence reached far beyond the confines of the 8th District of Massachusetts. He told one interviewer that he wanted to be remembered for helping "in the development of America," and he will—at least in terms of expanding the public sector. For O'Neill is an exponent of the view that government, not people, creates progress.

In 1981, O'Neill urged his colleagues to reject the Reagan Administration's attempt "to meat-ax the programs that have made America great."

And O'Neill was particularly frustrated that the middle class deserted the Democratic party after it had "made middle America."

In fact, despite O'Neill's attacks on Reagan for being ignorant and shallow, O'Neill's view of domestic policy was always limited to that of a local pol: Rep. David Obey (D.-Wis.) says O'Neill "never forgets the whole purpose of policy is to have a positive impact on human beings." Yet policies inevitably involve conflicting interests between different individuals.

Disproportionate Social Security payments may make retirees better off, but the taxes required to fund the system are grossly unfair to current workers. O'Neill worried only about those who were helped by government transfers; be never even considered the rights of those who were paying the bill.

But, of course, O'Neill's excuse was that he wanted to help the poor. On Harvard's commencement day in 1927, O'Neill "watched those privileged, confident Ivy League Yankees who had everything handed to them in life," he writes, and "someday, I vowed, I would work to make sure my own people could go to places like Harvard."

It might be possible to treat this argument seriously if O'Neill were the least bit discriminating in the federal programs that he supported. But the Speaker never met a federal outlay he didn't like, aside from a few weapons systems. Indeed, the programs that really go to the needy—food stamps, Aid to Families with Dependent Children, Medicaid, and other means-tested benefits—make up a very small portion of the budget.

In 1986, for instance, income and in-kind support programs ran roughly $55 billion, just 5.6 per cent of total outlays.

The biggest budget-busters are middle-class welfare programs, particularly Social Security, Medicare, and student loans, where rich and poor alike share in the loot.

Indeed, O'Neill, who, of course, uses his book to denounce congressional adversaries for supporting "the interest of big business," backed the Chrysler bail-out, the Synthetic Fuels Corp., which subsidized large oil companies, and the Export-Import Bank, which is informally known as "Boeing's Bank." These are the sort of needy beneficiaries upon whom O'Neill's caring government lavishes funds.

Many of the programs supported by O'Neill have gone far to ruin America. There's agricultural subsidies, for example. Last year the federal government spent $23 billion to satisfy one of the greediest interest groups in America; federal warehouses bulge with vast surpluses and farmers' produce continue to be overpriced on the world market, but the nation's legislators were primarily interested in buying a few more votes.

And who is most hurt by the federal government's intervention in the farm market? The poor, of course. No wonder O'Neill admits to a "limited" understanding of the system, even as he supported an ever-expanding federal role.

O'Neill won passage of most of President Carter's energy program, a mish-mash of controls and boondoggles that reduced energy production, encouraged imports, and extended Uncle Sam's reach to even setting the temperatures of office buildings. In fact, in *Man of the House* O'Neill is obviously bursting with pride over his role in passing the program, yet only when energy was left to the market, rather than micro-mismanaged by federal bureaucrats, did supplies increase and prices fall.

Then there's protectionism, one of the most destructive and regressive of economic policies, and one traditionally opposed by most liberals. But O'Neill supported everything from quotas on textiles to domestic content requirements for autos.

He liked to talk about saving jobs, but he ignored the effect of foreign retaliation as well as the job-killing impact of higher prices throughout the economy. Ironically—given O'Neill's professed concern for the poor—trade barriers weigh heaviest on the disadvantaged. Textile and shoe restrictions, for example, tend to raise the prices of the least expensive products the most.

The best that can be said, after reading *Man of the House,* is that O'Neill was genuinely unaware that there is any cost to government activism.

Before he left office, he complained that he took President Reagan at his word in 1986 when the President proposed that they work together to "fix" the budget process; yet, said O'Neill, after he requested "one little thing" for his district, a $2-million museum, "I'll be damned if he hadn't taken every bit" of the money out of the budget.

Obviously, in O'Neill's mind the problem with the deficit was too little pork barrel spending. But that should come as no surprise, since O'Neill's entire career was based on the "tax, tax, spend, spend, elect, elect" philosophy.

In his book O'Neill relates—with nary a word of regret—how members of both the Massachusetts state legislature and Congress illegally bypassed their respective budget processes to get projects for their districts.

Moreover, the agenda for the Democratic party, he said as he left office, is to keep saying that "you can't let the person with the calloused heart take away from them the rights that are there." The solution to the deficit, said O'Neill, is for people to "pay through the nose by taxation."

What about the basic right of taxpayers to keep their earnings? Why do dairy farmers, students, yacht owners, foreign politicians, corporate executives, and every other interest group in America have a higher claim to a person's earnings than the worker himself?

The creation of the acquisitive society, where everyone tries to use government to live off of everyone else, has damaged, perhaps irreparably, the fundamental values of self-reliance, independence and honesty that helped Americans build such a productive system.

After the disastrous Carter years, even O'Neill should have realized that his party's selfish fixation on redistributing the pie was reducing the resources available for everyone, poor included.

Higher taxes reduced the incentive to produce, work and invest; increased public spending diverted money away from productive private projects. And the realization that lobbying could be more profitable than manufacturing caused American business and labor to look to Washington, rather than themselves, to better their livelihood.

When O'Neill assumed the speakership he told the Congress: "Let us forget the frustrations of the past, and think of our unfulfilled potential." But virtually every policy he supported has made it more difficult for us to reach our potential.

Thomas P. O'Neill apparently never profited personally from his enormous political power. In fact, in *Man in the House* he expresses outrage when a constituent tried to pay him for helping with an immigration problem. Yet we would all be far better off if O'Neill had spent his time lining his own pocket rather than corrupting the entire political process. For a few thousand dollars in pay-offs would have been nothing compared to the billions in public funds squandered by O'Neill and his allies to advance their own narrow political interests.

"It's always nice to play a part in history," says O'Neill: "You're remembered when you do things like that." But it's far more important to act responsibly, whether or not one is lionized by one's peers. Unfortunately, this O'Neill has not done: partisanship, not compassion, was the hallmark of O'Neill's tenure in office.

He represents the multitude of unthinking public officials and political operatives who have turned the government into an engine of plunder, destroying the constitutional regime of limited government created two centuries ago. O'Neill is certainly not alone in having debased the American political system, but that, more than anything else, will be his legacy to the people of this great nation.

# III. The Federal Behemoth

# Deficits Forever

## 49. The Budget Revolution That Wasn't

*May 1985*

In Washington, the lengthy budget festivities are well under way. President Reagan is seeking essentially to freeze total federal spending next year at the 1985 level. He's come up with an attractive list of budget cuts—the Small Business Administration, the Export-Import Bank, food stamps, Urban Development Action Grants, the Economic Development Association, Amtrak, agricultural price supports, and the like. And this isn't all. In his inaugural address, Reagan pledged to "take further steps to permanently control government's power to tax and spend."

But we've heard all this before. Four years ago, Reagan promised an end to "waste, extravagance, abuse and outright fraud" in federal spending and pledged a balanced budget. Revolutionary fervor swept the capital. Meg Greenfield wrote in *Newsweek* that "you can mark down the first two weeks in February as the time when people all over this city—not just those ritually opposed to domestic budget cuts, but also those ritually and noisily in favor of them—looked at each other with disbelief and said, with shared alarm, 'My God, what if he isn't kidding?' " And Reagan wasn't, or so it seemed, when he targeted nearly 300 programs for total spending cuts of $49 billion just in fiscal year 1982 (October 1981 through September 1982).

But by the end of Reagan's first term, the old revolutionary fervor had come to naught. His zeal to cut the budget had disappeared. Last year, in fact, the government spent nearly *half again* as much in nominal dollars as it spent under President Carter in 1980. Washington gobbled up a quarter of the country's GNP (gross national product) in 1983, which is a peacetime record. And that percentage is not expected to drop back to its 1980 level before the end of Reagan's second term, if then.

It's interesting that despite all this, both Reagan and his most bitter political opponents claim that he has changed America's budget landscape

125

dramatically by cutting spending. Reagan himself issues proclamations about "near-revolutionary" budget austerity, while former Rep. Shirley Chisholm (D-N.Y.), for one, has charged that spending cuts have shredded the "social safety net." Both are wrong. The austerity has been largely imaginary, and domestic spending (which is what Chisholm tacitly equates with the "safety net") is actually *higher* now than before Ronald Reagan took his first oath of office.

## Measuring the Extravagance

In order to understand just what has happened so far under Reagan, it's useful to recall that budget savants use a special lexicon. Their technical terms include *nominal spending,* which means the face value of the federal budget, and *real spending,* which is the nominal amount adjusted for inflation. More important, though, is the political jargon. A "budget cut" is only rarely what most human beings would think of as a cut. Usually, "cutting the budget" means spending *more* money and only slowing the rate at which the budget is expanding.

With the proper terminology under our belts, we can turn to Reagan's record. There are many ways to assess that record, but it is most revealing to compare 1984 spending levels with:

• the budget in 1980, the year before Reagan took over;

• Jimmy Carter's proposed 1984 budget, which was drawn up before he left office in January 1981;

• the amount that Reagan's own Office of Management and Budget (OMB) says would have been spent last year if no cuts had been made;

• the 1984 budget that Reagan himself proposed during the 1980 campaign; and,

• the 1984 spending levels that he first proposed after taking office.

Let's look at them one by one.

The federal government spent $577 billion in 1980, Carter's last year in office. As huge as that amount is, it's still considerably less than the $842 billion in total outlays in 1984. Now, those are nominal figures—but even in real, inflation-adjusted terms, outlays grew an average of 3.4 percent annually during Reagan's first term of office, not much better than Jimmy Carter's 3.9 percent.

At the same time, Carter's record was substantially better in another important respect. The portion of the GNP absorbed by government increased in Reagan's first term by 1.6 percent, but under Carter, it edged up by only 0.2 percent.

So by the first measure, Reagan's record is not all that good. How about the second measure—Carter's lame-duck budget proposal for 1984? There are no laurels for Reagan there, either. In real spending, Reagan *exceeded* by 15.6 percent the spending that Carter had envisioned (although in fairness to Reagan, one should remember that Carter exceeded his other budget estimates).

Judged by the third standard, the Reagan record looks a bit better. The OMB has run an analysis—with the latest unemployment, inflation, and GNP forecasts—to project what spending would have been in 1984 by the "pre-1981 baseline." In other words, it calculated what the government would have spent under the Carter budget if neither the White House nor Congress had acted in any way to slow spending growth.

Without any of Reagan's budget initiatives, the OMB calculated that total spending would have been $51 billion higher in 1984. But in real terms, that success was less than dramatic: after accounting for inflation, Reagan reduced outlays from the pre-1981 baseline by only 0.4 percent. And even *that* figure is dubious, because it makes the unrealistic assumption that Carter in a second term would not have acted in any way to cut the growth of spending.

The fourth measure is one that Reagan devised for himself. In September 1980, Reagan unveiled his "Strategy for Economic Growth and Stability in the 1980s." He set as his goal "to bring about spending reductions of 10 percent by fiscal year 1984," which would result in expenditures of $760 billion. But when 1984 came along, he hadn't even come close. Spending for 1984 actually was more than $80 billion higher than Reagan's campaign target, a 10.8 percent overflow.

Reagan devised the fifth measure as well—this time, shortly after he entered the White House. In March 1981, Reagan sent Congress a package of budget cuts designed to reduce projected spending in 1984 by $81 billion. Two months later, he released proposals to reduce spending for Social Security an additional $11 billion through 1984. With the combined programs, Reagan's spending target for 1984 was $759 billion, a level slightly below his most optimistic 1980 campaign pledge. But the $842 billion spent by Uncle Sam last year was 10.9 percent about that 1981 goal. In real terms, the gap is bigger, since the 1981 proposals assumed more inflation in 1984 than actually occurred.

So, by four of the five measures, Reagan's budget-cutting policies have been a flop. And even by the only measure that makes him look good, the OMB projection, his record is not all that impressive.

## A Billion Here, a Billion There

Much of Reagan's difficulty in slowing, let alone controlling, federal spending derives from the way different components of the budget work, their relative sizes (see chart, p. 00), and how he treats them.

One component is interest payments on money the government has borrowed over the years in lieu of raising taxes or spending less. These payments make up about an eighth of the budget. They can be slashed only by retiring some of the national debt—but that requires other spending cuts or tax increases or both. Interest payments are increasing at an alarming pace. They've already doubled in nominal terms since 1980, when they were $52 billion, and the administration expects them to climb to $148 billion next year. The increase in real terms from 1980 to 1985 is 88.5 percent.

Another big component of the budget is military spending, which consumes more than a fourth of the budget. There's certainly no progress there. On the contrary, if there has been any consistent theme to the Reagan administration, it has been to increase defense outlays. Reagan has already increased nominal military spending from $134 billion in 1980 to $227 billion last year. Even in real terms, that hike is an enormous 35.3 percent.

Despite the size of those increases, they actually reflect only part of Reagan's real long-term impact on military spending. He has not only increased spending on the Pentagon today. He has locked in higher military spending for the foreseeable future by getting Congress to approve large increases in total "budget authority" for new weapons, which will be spent over a number of years. The Congressional Budget Office (CBO) reports that the portion of the military budget going to weapons procurement will climb from 26 percent in 1981 to 38 percent in 1987.

So, it will be increasingly difficult for future presidents or congresses to reduce outlays, since they would have to cancel ongoing projects to do so. In fact, OMB Director David Stockman confessed to *Fortune* magazine last year that "there is a certain inevitability to it all. The major systems have been launched, mission and policy objectives have been approved, the force structure of our armed forces has been raised, so there are not a lot of things that can give way."

There is also a category of federal programs considered "defense-related." There are nondefense programs that serve a military function, such as strategic stockpiles of resources such as oil and "foreign security assistance" (military aid). Reagan increased funding for these "national interest" programs, as OMB terms them, to $32 billion last year—24.8 percent more in real terms than in 1980.

Then there's social spending. When Reagan first announced his budget program, Sen. Howard Metzenbaum (D-Oh.) denounced it as "a perversion of justice" for the middle class. Metzenbaum need not have worried. The middle class is one of Reagan's biggest constituencies, so *its* welfare programs—particularly entitlement programs like Social Security, Medicare, and federal retirement benefits—were protected from big cuts as part of the "social safety net." Indeed, they weren't just protected from cuts. Spending for these programs *rose* from $185 billion in 1980 to $279 billion last year, for a jump of 17.3 percent in real terms.

While the middle class has faithfully supported Reagan, the beneficiaries of means-tested welfare programs (based on need) have never been a Reagan constituency. The administration has pushed harder to reduce federal spending for means-tested welfare programs, such as Aid to Families with Dependent Children and food stamps, than for entitlements benefiting the middle class. Nevertheless, means-tested welfare spending still climbed from $47 billion in 1980 to $65 billion last year, a 7.4 percent rise in real terms. The most Reagan has done is slow the rate of spending increase.

For some budget items, real spending under Reagan has declined. Examples include veterans benefits—but not because of Reagan's budget-cutting prowess. The number of veterans eligible for educational benefits was shrinking (spending on veterans has actually been declining since 1976).

There *are* victories for which Reagan can claim credit, chiefly in areas of discretionary spending. For example, after nearly quadrupling in real terms from 1962 to their peak in 1980, handouts to state and local governments and to private businesses have been cut by about half in real terms in four years. Even spending on "infrastructure"—the pork-barrel outlays for highways, water projects, and mass-transit systems that Congress loves—has been slashed substantially. And the "overhead" for government, which includes the administrative costs of regulating business, gathering statistics, collecting taxes, and so on, has been cut (even though IRS and law-enforcement spending has risen sharply).

Every success in budget cutting, however, is more than outweighed by a failure. Agriculture is one of the dismal tales. Spending on price supports and rural-development subsidies, for example, has increased from less than $9 billion in 1980 to more than $20 billion this year (in 1982, spending hit a record of almost $23 billion). And it is the really gargantuan categories of spending where Reagan's record has been less than stellar that make his successes look very paltry indeed.

*Culprits Galore*

Whose fault is it? There is, not surprisingly, enough blame for everyone.

The economy, which performed more poorly during Reagan's first term than the administration says it expected, is partly at fault. The recession increased unemployment-compensation payouts and outlays for farm-price supports. Meanwhile, higher interest rates and larger deficits pushed up interest costs.

But the economy can be used as a scapegoat only up to a point. After all, inflation was lower than expected. This *reduced* some outlays, particularly for indexed programs. At the most, the economy is responsible overall for pushing expenditures some $25 billion above Reagan's goal.

But that's only about a third of the $82-billion spending overflow. The other $57 billion of the 1984 "budget gap" is nothing but overspending, pure and simple. Who is most at fault there? Reagan says Congress, accusing it of turning down close to half of the domestic cuts that he requested for 1984, worth some $53 billion. Had those cuts been adopted, Reagan claims he would have nearly hit his target.

That may be true, but Congress made up for its extravagance on the domestic side by denying the Reagan administration some $20 billion in military and military-related outlay increases that it requested.

There's another flaw in Reagan's rhetoric. Not all cuts are created equal. To shift the blame to Congress, Reagan has lumped together all the program cuts he ever proposed—including those like the initial Social Security plan that had, in the words of one budget official, "a half-life of a week." Indeed, many of the Reagan cuts were proposed in one budget and subsequently dropped. Others, like reductions in Export-Import Bank funding, were explicitly reversed. And the administration did not fight equally hard even for the cuts it stood by.

And despite Reagan's claims, the difference between overall administration requests and congressional appropriations in the last three years has not been significant (see chart above). Indeed, the total congressional increase above Reagan's spending requests from 1982 to 1984 was only 0.6 percent of the total budget, and Congress appropriated $17 billion less for 1984 than he requested. They made a considerable cut in the proposed budget authority for the Pentagon, and they even shaved the administration's budget for some domestic agencies, such as the Department of Energy.

His budget-cutting reputation notwithstanding, Reagan made significant success almost impossible from the start of his administration by putting the major entitlement programs and the Pentagon essentially off-limits. Stockman now acknowledges that "our biggest failure was that we didn't create a much bigger and better package of spending cuts in the beginning. We should have gone after the big boulders—the social insurance programs. The rest of the budget is thousands of little pebbles."

It certainly didn't help matters that some of the administration's proposals involved phantom reductions. Stockman, for example, has confessed that "there was less there than met the eye" with the original spending cuts because the budget being reduced was artificially high. Two early "cuts" were downright fraudulent: spending for the Strategic Petroleum Reserve, which is now running about $2 billion annually, was simply placed off-budget, and Medicare payments were shifted back and forth between fiscal years 1981 and 1982.

This sort of budgeting with mirrors reappeared the following year, when Reagan pushed a tax hike through Congress on the strength of a promised three-year spending cut of some $284 billion. More than half that "savings" was simply a readjustment in arbitrary estimates of such things as interest rates. Some of the remaining reductions were equally dubious.

Moreover, Reagan did not propose all of the cuts he promised. The first-year budget program, for example, contained what Stockman called the "magic asterisk"—budget cuts to be identified in the future. But many never were. Partly as a result, Reagan's budget projections got progressively worse. His proposed budget for 1985, for example, has constantly escalated, going in nominal dollars from $844 billion in March 1981 to $959 billion in February 1985 (see chart on p. 00).

Reagan's cabinet officers and other agency heads are also among those responsible for the failure to curb spending. Many have consistently requested more than the official ceilings projected the previous year, let alone the levels first proposed in 1981. At the same time, the size of the cuts they have proposed to Congress has steadily fallen. The administration does not formally release internal agency requests, but some officials leak their department positions to build pressure from bureaucratic constituents and Congress. In December 1983, for example, the newsletter *Inside Energy* reported that "Energy Secretary Donald Hodel's credibility in budgetary matters appeared redeemed last week as DOE prevailed . . . to restore $800 million of the approximately $1.8 billion cut" from its 1985 budget by OMB.

This problem became so pronounced in the fall of 1983 that Reagan publicly ordered his cabinet members to revise their budgets to get them below the 1985 projections made the previous February. Presidential spokesman Larry Speakes called Reagan "stern and determined," but White House officials privately concede that virtually nothing came of the effort: the total budget request that went forward in 1984 was still higher than Reagan's 1983 estimates. Knowledgeable White House officials say that Reagan articulates the overall goal of cutting spending, but "item by item he caves in."

Even when Reagan restrains departments' budget requests, their officials often invite Congress to appropriate additional funds. In 1982, OMB was forced to instruct agency personnel to "refrain from giving opinions on how agencies might use more appropriations than the President requested,'' in order to help "strengthen discipline and support for the President's budget within the Executive Branch.''

And despite Reagan's denunciations of Congress's free-spending ways, he has vetoed *only five* money bills. (One of those actually appropriated less than Reagan wanted by slashing his proposed outlays for the military.) Reagan has wielded the veto as a threat, setting veto benchmarks above his proposals—but those targets must be too high, since Reagan seldom feels a need to veto anything. White House chief of staff and former Treasury secretary Donald Regan says that "Congress keeps slipping in, just over the edge, just taking a little bit, so there's nothing mammoth'' to veto. But if the administration doesn't veto those bills, Congress will keep "slipping in'' added spending, and total federal outlays will just keep on rising.

Another reason that the budget hasn't been tamed is conscious policy decisions by the administration. Reagan reversed himself on cutting both the Social Security minimum benefit, which he had earlier pushed Congress to eliminate, and the Export-Import Bank, which he had denounced in 1981 as "another major business subsidy.'' In 1983 he joined with Congress to enact a $5-billion pork-laden "jobs'' bill and to pass the $8-billion bailout of the International Monetary Fund (IMF). Moreover, the administration accepted roughly $1 billion in additional housing spending, some for a program that had been axed, to get the IMF legislation through the House.

*Low Taxes!*
*Big Spending!*

Ultimately, Reagan is a politician before a budget-cutter. In 1983 he denounced Congress for its profligate ways—then moments later in the same speech told the National Association of Home Builders that he was proposing an additional $5 billion for federal mortgage insurance on top of the $6 billion that had been approved six months earlier.

Which brings us back to the current season of budget-cutting. With his usual eloquence, Reagan used his inaugural speech in January to attack the federal behemoth—despite the fact that he had been in charge for four years. His newest budget includes meaningful cuts, but even before submitting it, Reagan made substantial progress almost impossible. Last year, for example, he vowed not to cut Social Security benefits "for anybody,'' and he assured senior citizens that he would "not betray'' them in an effort to cut spending. Yet Social Security and Medicare are two of the largest domestic programs.

So unless Reagan decides to do an about-face on defense (and so far, he has supported Defense Secretary Caspar Weinberger's intransigent demands for more money), the administration will continue to face a budget picture similar to that of 1981, with only a small portion of the budget open for cuts.

Indeed, the prospects are bleaker now than before. Since 1981, discretionary programs that can be cut without changing the law itself (unlike entitlement programs) have been reduced, many sharply; so Congress is unlikely to vote significant additional savings. Reagan once argued that cutting government spending "is like protecting your virtue: all you have to do is say no." But by the end of his second term, he probably will have made only modest adjustments in a few programs. Government, on the whole, will continue to grow.

In February 1981, Meg Greenfield wondered whether the administration's approach—"crashing through that layer of hypocrisy and that structure of legal payoffs that characterize our traditional budget building"—was "doomed." Despite Reagan's success in holding down spending in some areas, it appears that the answer to her question is yes.

As David Stockman observed three years after becoming the administration's resident wunderkind: "The budget system is not the problem. The problem is that this democracy is somewhat ambivalent about what it wants. It wants low taxes and substantial public spending." And until the public finally makes a choice, a genuine budget revolution—whether carried out by Reagan or someone else—seems unlikely.

## 50. We Need an Economic Bill of Rights

*February 16, 1984*

President Reagan is proposing that the federal government spend $925 billion next year, more than $16,000 for a family of four. Just two years ago he figured the federal budget wouldn't break the $900 billion level until 1987, but this most conservative of presidents has been unwilling to fight to control the growth of government.

In fact, despite persistent charges that the administration has gutted domestic programs, few have not grown. Last year farm price supports were up 61.7 percent from 1982; student financial aid jumped 47.9 percent. Health care payments increased 31 percent and low-income housing outlays rose 27.8 percent. Spending for Medicare was up 18.2 percent, Social Security 13.5 percent, Medicaid 9 percent, child nutrition programs 8.6 percent and food stamps 7.5 percent. If the administration has been unfair to anyone, it is the taxpayers, not the poor.

The problem is not that the budget is not controllable, but that the politicians will not control it. Policy is dominated by organized interest groups, represented by more than 1,000 lobbies and 15,000 lobbyists in the capital, fighting for what has become nearly a trillion-dollar pot of federal gold. They exert disproportionate pressure on the president and Congress because the issues that concern them—subsidies, tariffs, transfer payments and so on—affect them in a direct and major way. Thus, they have an economic incentive to organize and finance major lobbying efforts.

The general public, in contrast, is rarely galvanized by individual spending bills. Though people as a whole may be greatly affected, as individuals they are hurt by just a few cents or dollars; they therefore lack the incentive to organize. The result is a budget process that should be declared a national disaster.

Only a fundamental restructuring of the system can restore the sort of political balance envisioned by the founders of our nation. Economic rights—the freedom to keep one's earnings, own property, make contracts and to otherwise engage in cooperative economic interchange—are basic human rights that deserve constitutional protection from the depredations of government. There is a pragmatic reason to protect economic rights, as well. Government economic mismanagement through high taxes, spiraling spending and intrusive regulation has brought us vicious cycles of inflation, stagnation and unemployment. We will never fully enjoy our other liberties until we achieve stable economic growth.

One plan for constitutional protection of economic freedom has been offered by Martin Anderson, President Reagan's one-time chief domestic policy adviser. Anderson, now at the Hoover Institution, has proposed a five-part Economic Bill of Rights.

1. Balanced Federal Budget. Though the relationship between deficits, inflation and interest rates is not direct and automatic, in the long term deficits both increase inflationary pressures and push up interest rates, crowding out private investment.

2. Limited Federal Spending. Since one way to balance the budget is to raise taxes, the share of private wealth that may be appropriated by government should be limited. Though special interests would still have a disproportionate influence over the allocation of federal funds, the total spent would be limited.

3. Line Item Presidential Veto. Congress has been adroit at attaching the worst pork barrel spending schemes to legislation considered to be "essential," forcing presidents to accept higher spending than they wanted. The president should have the power, possessed by 43 governors, to veto any program, however small. It was this power that allowed

California Gov. George Deukmejian to cut $1 billion out of last year's California budget.

4. Gold Standard. As bad as Congress is, the Federal Reserve is often worse, acting as a legal counterfeiter to expand the money supply, causing rampant inflation. Tying the value of the dollar to gold would be one method of disciplining the monetary authorities.

5. A Prohibition on Wage and Price Controls. Limits on wages and prices do not restrain inflation; they just mask it, while creating bottlenecks and inefficiencies throughout the economy. Selective controls over specific goods like oil and natural gas have inflated demand, discouraged the development of additional supplies and cheaper alternatives and, in the end, cost consumers more.

Anderson's list isn't exhaustive. We also should require extraordinary majorities for Congress to approve spending and taxing measures, force periodic review and reauthorization of all government programs, from regulatory agencies to price supports, through "sunset" legislation, and prohibit Congress from engaging in the ludicrous sham of declaring billions in spending to be "off-budget."

The government will borrow nearly $200 billion this year, and almost as much next year. Neither the president not Congress has the will to stem this flow of red ink, nor the nearly trillion dollars in federal spending that is causing it.

Only fundamental changes—like a Bill of Rights for economic freedom—can prevent our economy from being swept away.

## 51. Mandate a Balanced Budget

*April 19, 1984*

In 1979 then-California Governor Jerry Brown confounded the nation by endorsing a constitutional amendment to balance the budget. Brown's support reflected more his far-flung political ambitions than any deep-held philosophical principles, but it nevertheless posed a dramatic challenge to the prevailing wisdom that the Constitution was no place to codify economic policy, and that a new constitutional convention would threaten our basic freedoms.

In the intervening five years pressure for such an amendment has continued to grow. Four out of every five Americans support it, and 32 states have petitioned Congress to call a constitutional convention. Only two more are needed, and balanced budget resolutions are now pending before legislatures in several states.

Despite the high-minded terms in which opposition to the balanced budget proposal is usually stated, something other than public-spiritedness motivates most critics. Indeed, it is unclear what they fear more: an amendment that might actually hold down spending, or the great unwashed public proposing fundamental reforms to the system.

That fundamental reforms are necessary is clear. We seem to have reached political gridlock, with $200 billion deficits and little incentive for Congress or the President to reduce them. For however much well-paid intellectuals like to prattle on about the American people being under-taxed, we face no shortage of taxes. In fact, President Reagan's much-heralded tax cuts of 1981 did little more than keep us even; according to the Federal Reserve Bank of Philadelphia, after bracket creep, multiple Social Security tax increases, the assorted tax hikes of 1982 and the gas tax increase, the total net reduction for all Americans from 1981 to 1988 will be just $77 billion, little more than $40 a person a year.

In contrast, spending has continued to climb. Reagan proposed a 1985 budget of $925 billion, two short years after he predicted we wouldn't hit that level until 1987. Real spending has increased 10 percent since Reagan took office, despite his pledge in the not too distant past to reduce it by 5.6 percent.

Concentrated pressure groups usually prevail against the diffuse body of taxpayers on any particular money measure, pushing total spending ever skyward. Without some sort of institutional limitation to force officials to say no, they will never have the political courage to protect the public's fiscal virginity. And this is the reality that is ignored by the argument that we should get this president to balance his budget before we consider a constitutional amendment.

Do we really want to enshrine economic philosophy in the Constitution? The question is bizarre on its face. The Constitution, despite recently tortured judicial interpretations, embodies an economic philosophy, one of private property rights and limited government. Thus, protecting the taxpayers from constant plundering by vote-seeking politicians is entirely consistent with its purpose and historical role. Indeed, the framers would not have been uncomfortable with a balanced budget amendment; Thomas Jefferson, for one, lamented that it was the one provision he regretted had not been included.

But a constitutional convention! However meritorious the amendment, would not a convention be unacceptably dangerous? After all, could it not run amok, sweeping away the Bill of Rights and wreaking havoc with the fundamental law of the land? Many scholars believe that a convention could be limited to the subject of a balanced budget. In any case, even a rampaging convention could only propose amendments; it could not impose them. Would 38 states agree to eliminate the Bill of Rights?

Such speculation is academic. Congress could end any prospect of a convention simply by passing a balanced budget amendment itself. In fact, it had just such an opportunity in 1982, but the House balked. If one, or even two more states join the convention bandwagon, let Tip O'Neill and his fellow spendthrifts vote out an amendment. How did people get the right to elect their Senators? It was not an act of charity by the Senators, who for more than a hundred years were chosen by state legislatures. Instead, enough states petitioned Congress to force a convention, causing Congress to vote out the 18th Amendment in 1912.

A constitutional amendment to balance the budget is no panacea, but people are kidding themselves if they think politicians will ever be fiscally responsible in the absence of strict constitutional limitations. It's time for some angry citizens to take charge; we should think of the balanced budget amendment as kind of a national Proposition 13. Unfortunately, there seems to be no other way to get Washington's attention.

## 52. Budgetary Chaos in Congress

*September 23, 1987*

Oct. 1 opens a new fiscal year, but Congress has yet to pass even one appropriations bill. The government probably won't close, but only because Capitol Hill is likely to approve a massive "continuing resolution" at the last minute.

Unfortunately, Congress' pathetic performance is as expensive as it is embarrassing. For election-minded legislators have routinely loaded up the CR, as the continuing resolution is called, with pork, daring President Reagan to veto the measure and shut down the government. A handful of cosmetic concessions has usually been enough to secure his signature.

Only serious budget reform can end this annual charade. In fact, the Senate voted to revamp the budget process earlier this year; House Republicans, too, have proposed major changes in congressional procedure.

The first problem involves the basic budget resolution. Since 1981, Congress has been an average of two months late in passing its initial budget; just once in the last 12 years has Congress met the legal deadline. One solution, suggested by Heritage Foundation analyst Stephen Moore, would be to switch to biennial budgets.

Even a Congress that is institutionally incapable of passing and implementing a budget in one year should be able to do so in double the time period. Outlays then would again be approved as part of individual appropriations bills, which are subject to much closer scrutiny than CRs.

Further, reforms would still be needed to enforce the budget resolution. Appropriations measures that exceed the numbers set by the budget resolution are theoretically barred from floor consideration, but the House has waived that rule nearly 500 times over the last decade; the Senate has used similar parliamentary stratagems to eviscerate special Gramm-Rudman limits on new spending bills. Thus, a super-majority of at least three-fifths should be required in both chambers to consider and pass any budget-busting legislation.

The role of CRs, too, needs to be changed. Last year's bill was 690 pages long; the sheer bulk of such measures often allows Congress to hide from the public bizarre expenditures, such as $200,000 paid in 1986 to reimburse the city of Frederick, Md., for a ransom it paid to Confederate forces in 1864.

At the very least, the CR should be divided into the equivalent of 13 appropriations bills for the purposes of a presidential veto. Better still would be to grant the president line-item veto authority for CRs, allowing him to kill individual expenditures.

Another fraudulent aspect of the budget process criticized by Moore is the fact that subsidized loan guarantees are ''off-budget'' and don't show up in the official statistics. Last year, in fact, Congress issued $160 billion in guarantees, a backdoor form of spending.

Though not all of the guarantees will have to be paid off, the cost—$8 billion in defaulted loans in 1986 alone—is rising. Were agencies required to purchase private reinsurance for their guarantees, a budget cost would automatically show up every year. Or guarantees could simply be counted the same as outlays, ending this disguised form of subsidy to favored interest groups.

Congress also regularly uses the budget process to create the fraudulent impression of budget ''cuts.'' The legislators ordered the Pentagon, for instance, to send out paychecks on Oct. 1, a day late, to shift a $3-billion outlay from Fiscal Year 1987 to Fiscal Year 1988. Congress should be barred from playing this trick in the future.

Finally, since presidents tend to be more cost-conscious than congresses—though the differences are generally small—the chief executive should be given greater influence in the budget process. A line-item veto, for example, would allow the president to block individual spending items now routinely added to legislation that presidents are loath to veto, such as CRs.

Moreover, the president needs new authority to kill programs even after

Capitol Hill has appropriated the money. In 1974 Congress terminated the president's power to "impound" funds and replaced it with the much weaker power to request a "rescission," which requires congressional approval. The president's authority should be strengthened by, for instance, requiring a congressional vote to block any cuts.

After six years of Ronald Reagan's presidency, total outlays continue to climb and the federal budget remains a cornucopia for the well-connected. Controlling Uncle Sam's wastrel habits will ultimately require the re-emergence of the political will to vote down and veto bloated spending measures. But until that commitment develops, reforming the budget process would be an important means of reducing somewhat the pressure for ever higher spending.

## 53. A Simple Solution to the Debt

*June 11, 1985*

It seems that everyone is concerned about the deficit. Nine-year-old Christopher Russell-Wood, a Maryland 4th grader, collected $216.01 from his classmates to help retire the national debt. He proposed that children across America send a portion of their allowances each week to Washington to make the government debt-free.

Indeed, last year some 2,500 people contributed nearly $400,000 for the same reason. This year's 1040 tax form advised filers that they could "just enclose in your tax return envelope a separate check made payable to 'Bureau of the Public Debt.' "

Unfortunately, with $1.57 trillion in federal debt outstanding at the end of 1984—and a projected increase to $1.84 trillion this year—it will take more than the contributions of schoolchildren to cover Uncle Sam's obligations. Indeed, with the deficit expected to be about $210 billion this year, and nearly as much in succeeding years, total public debt could double by the early 1990s.

No one is sure what the consequences of, say, a $3 trillion national debt would be, but few think the result would be positive. Pressure on interest rates would be tremendous, as the government borrowed hundreds of billions just to turn over expiring debt, and a significant amount of productive private investment would be discouraged. Perhaps more important, a spiraling debt would continually hike federal interest costs, locking in automatic spending increases in the future. Interest on the national debt more than doubled between 1980 and 1984, going from $74.8 billion to $153.8 billion; it is expected to run nearly $200 billion next year.

There is an obvious solution to the threat of more trillions in debt, of course: a series of balanced budgets, or even budget surpluses. But this would require some combination of tax increases and budget cuts, neither of which the political system seems ready to enact.

First, a tax hike, President Reagan says, would earn a veto; "make my day," he warns. As well he should. This year 19 percent of the gross national product is being collected by Uncle Sam—the 1981 tax cut just returned us to 1978 in terms of the proportion of private resources collected by the government.

Second, meaningful spending reductions may be impossible to achieve. During Reagan's first term, for instance, total outlays grew 13.5 percent in real terms, nearly as much as under Jimmy Carter. And even if Reagan and Congress finally agree on a compromise budget cut package in the range of $50 billion for next year, deficits will remain large and the total national debt will continue to grow.

Thus, the system seems paralyzed. Yet there is an answer, one that is both simple and effective. The government could repudiate the national debt.

Admittedly, the idea seems rather unorthodox—even shocking—at first. But Uncle Sam could just announce that he is not paying back the $1.57 trillion he owes, nor any more interest. In other words, the government could welsh.

Some holders of Treasury notes might file suit, of course, but that should pose no problem. The Supreme Court has shown a great willingness to ignore the clear meaning of the Constitution in reaching its preferred policy result; in this case, the majority probably would decline to second-guess public officials in their effort to find an "innovative" approach to solving our economic problems.

The benefits of repudiation would be overwhelming. At one stroke the mammoth debt hanging over the economy would be eliminated. No more concern over higher interest rates, reduced private investment, and so on.

The annual deficit problem would be solved as well. We are already well into the 1985 fiscal year, so even a timely abrogation of the government's liabilities couldn't stop payment of all the $180.3 in interest due this year. But in 1986 the government would save $199.4 billion, leaving it with a $20.9 billion surplus. The following year the positive balance would grow to $46.9 billion; in 1988 Uncle Sam would be $75 billion in the black.

Of course, if the government repudiated its debts, few people or institutions would purchase new federal securities. But that actually is another benefit. For what better way to ensure future balanced budgets than to make it impossible for Uncle Sam to ever borrow again? Fiscal responsibility would become a simple fact of life.

Not everyone would be happy with this solution, of course. A few churlish bondholders probably would complain; some conservative intellectuals might raise the hoary notion of sanctity of contract. But anyone foolish enough to trust the government deserves to end up with a portfolio of worthless federal bonds.

Unfortunately, the "structural" problem of $200 billion deficits is not likely to be solved without radical action. So if we want to stop the incoming tidal wave of red ink, what choice do we have other than an unconventional step like repudiating the national debt?

## 54. Balancing the Budget

*March 6, 1986*

During his State of the Union speech President Reagan turned to House Speaker Thomas P. "Tip" O'Neill and said: "The federal budget system is broken, it doesn't work. Before we leave this city, let's you and I work together to fix it."

O'Neill took the president at his word and proposed to . . . increase spending. The Speaker requested just "one little thing" for "the people of my district"—a $2 million Ironsides Museum. "But I'll be damned if he (President Reagan) hadn't taken every bit" of the money out of his proposed budget, complains O'Neill.

Everyone in Washington believes the federal budget process is a mess, but most of them, like O'Neill, think the problem is too little spending. If only we would start reviving old programs and creating new ones, then everything would be fine.

Indeed, though we may be entering the sixth year of the Reagan Revolution, the federal budget remains a veritable cornucopia for the well-connected. Farmers, retirees, welfare workers, college students, businessmen, artists and almost everyone else, including foreign dictators, still use the U.S. government to live off everyone else.

If the American people really want to keep more of their earnings, they have to rethink the very role of the state. Let the national government defend this country, provide for the basic needs of the helpless, and establish the infrastructure for a free society. And nothing more.

Then the billions in federal outlays would melt away. Not only would we balance the budget, we could do so at a much lower level.

For example, Mr. Reagan proposes to spend $282.2 billion on the military in 1987. More than half that is for NATO and tens of billions more go to Korea and Japan.

If the United States didn't subsidize its major allies—which are more populous and wealthy than their adversaries—it could dramatically cut the size of its conventional forces. A 50 percent reduction in those forces alone would save $64.3 billion in 1987.

International assistance also promotes unnecessary meddling abroad. Military aid often buttresses authoritarian regimes that deserve to fall; development assistance is notoriously wasteful and counterproductive. An easy 50 percent cut here would reduce outlays by $9.6 billion.

Social Security and Medicare will run $282.4 billion next year. These programs have never been self-insurance, despite the government's propaganda; cut off higher income recipients and save at least $55 billion.

Do the same with veterans benefits—we simply can't afford to subsidize the well-to-do any longer—and reduce spending by $5.3 billion or more.

Too much money, $118.4 billion, goes to overgenerous federal pensions and overlapping, even bizarre, welfare programs. Slash the federal bureaucracy and make sure the safety net catches only the truly needy, cutting out $23.7 billion in "income assistance."

A lot of programs make no sense at all. The administration is proposing to spend $4 billion on energy research next year, along with $1.4 billion in business subsidies and an incredible $19.5 billion on the farmers' dole.

Another $6.5 billion would pay for economic development programs that reallocate, rather than create, job growth; $9.2 billion would support what should be private space and scientific projects, and $1.7 billion would go for grants to states and localities., many of which are running budget surpluses. Kill all these boondoggles and save $42.3 billion.

Natural resource programs are expected to consume $12 billion in 1987; the federal government wastes barrels of cash on uneconomic water projects, subsidized grazing and timberland and general mismanagement. Surely $6 billion in savings is achievable by simply shrinking the size of the government's fiefdom.

Cutting subsidies for white elephant mass transit projects and highway construction could save at least $7.3 billion in requested transportation outlays. Getting the federal government out of education, ending subsidies to middle-class college students, and reducing social service projects to only the most basic ones would reduce spending by $21.4 billion or so in 1987.

Finally, health programs that do not serve the needy could be cut, saving $3.5 billion, while dropping counterproductive enforcement efforts against, for example, illegal immigrants would reduce spending another $2 billion.

The Bandow cuts total $240.4 billion, a reduction of 24 percent from President Reagan's proposed 1987 budget; the resulting $96.8 billion surplus could be used for a tax cut or a down payment on the national debt. Impossible, you say? Just stop expecting Uncle Sam to be an international Sugar Daddy.

The budget process does indeed need fixing, but neither liberals nor conservatives know where to start. Only by drastically redefining the role of government will we ever carry out a real budget revolution. And that doesn't include O'Neill's "one little project."

## 55. 7 Spending Cuts Liberals Could Love

*December 1, 1987*

Congress and the President recently cobbled together a dubious budget compromise to meet the Gramm-Rudman targets, but hardly anyone is satisfied with the package. If Congress ever intends to get serious about reducing the deficit, the Democrats need to stop reflexively defending every domestic program. Indeed, next time, Congressional Democrats should go on the offensive by proposing a package of domestic cuts.

They might start with the Export-Import Bank, a dole for big business and foreign dictators. Last year, the bank provided $6.1 billion in subsidized credits. Four companies alone—Boeing, McConnell Douglas, Westinghouse and General Electric—have historically accounted for roughly three-fourths of Ex-Im's subsidies. At the same time, unsavory foreign governments like Chile, Haiti, Ethiopia, Iraq, Rumania and Zaire have benefited from cheap credit.

The Bank naturally claims that it creates jobs by encouraging American exports, but in most cases it simply makes already "done deals" more profitable. Anyway, every dollar in credit provided to a favored business by Ex-Im is ultimately taken from another, since the supply of credit is limited.

Progressives who believe in equal treatment should also drain small business's subsidized trough. The Small Business Administration, like the Ex-Im Bank, makes and guarantees billions in loans every year. Almost 99 percent of small firms make it without S.B.A. subsidies, and an unknown number of businesses are stillborn because the S.B.A. has diverted credit to other companies.

The few companies that do benefit from the agency's support to do so largely because of their political clout. A $3 million agency grant and a $6 million loan figure in the Wedtech scandal; the agency has been accurately termed a "petty cash drawer" for politicians.

Even more bloated and wasteful is the farm program. Direct payments to farmers ran $25.8 billion in 1986 and around $23 billion in fiscal 1987. Yet, just 17 cents of every dollar goes to those farmers who are most in need. The subsidies for some firms are obscene: $29.2 million to Archer Daniels Midland for its gasohol business, $20 million to a California cotton farm, and $8 million to a single dairyman, Joe Gonsalves—to go out of business.

Progressives should also target the maritime industry's hefty subsidies. Its annual take ran $1.5 billion in 1986 and $1 billion this year. The tired pretext for this corporate welfare is national security—that we need our own merchant fleet, secure from wartime interruptions. But it would be better for the Pentagon to buy and mothball a few ships than to underwrite an entire inefficient industry. Patriotism is the last refuge not only of scoundrels but also of corporate executives trying to enhance profits.

Another program that should be on any liberal budget cutter's list is Urban Development Action Grants, a slush fund for local businessmen and politicians that has lavished nearly $5 billion on local building projects since 1977. Not surprisingly, big business has taken full advantage of Uncle Sam's open checkbook. As of 1985, General Motors had collected $50.3 million from five grants. Twelve Hilton hotels and six Hyatts were also underwritten by taxpayers.

Unfortunately, UDAG generates no meaningful public benefits, reshuffling rather than creating economic growth. In 1983 and 1984 for instance, New Jersey, New York City and Jersey City used $49 million in UDAG money to try to entice companies away from one another.

Nor is the progressive impulse reflected by Community Development Block Grants and the Economic Development Administration. Both programs subsidize many of the same business interests as does UDAG, and their benefits go disproportionately to the well-connected.

Numerous other programs deserve closer Democratic scrutiny. There is no principle of economic or social justice that warrants subsidizing every big businessman and local politico who asks for a hand out. It's time liberals took the lead in proposing domestic spending cuts.

# Endless Subsidies

## 56. Uncle Sam's Free Lunch

*November 21, 1985*

"If you've ever felt that you pay your taxes and get almost nothing back," runs the promotional blurb for Beryl Frank's "Encyclopedia of U.S. Government Benefits," "this is the book for you." And indeed it is.

Published by Dodd, Mead & Co., the encyclopedia spends 518 pages enlightening "the thousands of people missing out on important government benefits simply because" they "are not aware of them." Miss out on the federal cornucopia no longer.

Do you need aerial photographs of your land, perchance? Then check with the Department of Agriculture's Aerial Photography Field Office.

Or are you planning a flight abroad? Just call up the National Ocean Survey to get the necessary aeronautics charts.

Perhaps you want to develop a program for the elderly in your area, but don't want to pay for it. Then make a pitch to the Office of Human Development Services in the Department of Health and Human Services, which just loves to hand out money.

And if you're a farmer, you probably already know that you don't have to pay for quite a few things. Like research on plant and animal protection and production, processing and distribution of agricultural goods, and improved use of soil and water. Instead, the Agriculture Department's Agricultural Research Service is happy to pick up the tab.

Indeed, the section of the encyclopedia devoted to farm programs alone will keep any prospective federal leech busy. There are the crop price support programs, subsidies for soil and water conservation and natural disaster assistance payments. The Agriculture Department also underwrites home economics, nutrition programs, 4-H clubs and almost everything else known to man.

But we're not even through with the "a's" yet. The Federal Aviation Administration's Airport Improvement Program pays to upgrade local

145

airports; the Department of Labor runs a grant-laden apprenticeship and training program. And, of course, the National Endowment for the Arts distributes money right and left to favored "artists."

Now don't run to your typewriter yet—there are still 25 more letters of the alphabet to go through. The (American) Battle Monuments Commission, for instance, will let you know the best travel route to cemeteries and memorials.

Blind people are eligible for Supplemental Security Income payments from Social Security. Uncle Sam publishes a multitude of books and bulletins; subjects of interest include the daily weather map and "Treasures from the National Gallery of Art."

The Small Business Administration operates a multibillion-dollar slush fund for businessmen with connections. There's also the Minority Business Development Agency, a part of the Commerce Department, which provides all manner of technical and management assistance to private individuals and firms owned by people of the proper color.

All these wonderful federal benefits in only the first 48 pages of the encyclopedia. And the other 470 pages are just as full of opportunities to get someone else to pay your bills: child nutrition programs, college work study funding, subsidized crime insurance, Food Stamps, various forms of housing assistance, and a host of grants, loans, loan guarantees, and foreign investment protections for business.

All these programs, Frank assures the reader, are what make America great—"the services provided are in reality investments in the effectiveness and future of all its citizens." Why, everyone is entitled to a little help from his or her friends, right?

Indeed, Frank just bubbles over with enthusiasm: "The United States government is truly a government of the people, by the people, and for the people," and he hopes his book "will lead to a better understanding of your government and how it best works for you."

A "better understanding" of the government, however, will only cause one to realize how silly is the tiresome cliche, "a government of the people." Frank's "Encyclopedia of Government Benefits" demonstrates not only the responsiveness of democracy to the populace, but rather, the way in which concentrated economic interests use the government to try to live off everyone else.

"It pays to know your rights and how to claim them" says Frank.

But the more often we try to dine at Uncle Sam's expense, the greater becomes the tab we all have to pay.

Unfortunately, as long as people believe they can get the proverbial free lunch—whether in the form of cheap crop and crime insurance, subsidized loans for home construction and aircraft exports or grants for poets and major corporations—government spending will continue to spiral upward, and we will have fewer rights to our own earnings and lives to claim.

## 57. Merchant Armada Sinks Oceans of Money

*September 12, 1988*

The Sea-Land Corp., which has long opposed federal maritime subsidies, is working on a deal that will make the company, a subsidiary of CSX Corp., eligible for an estimated $48 million a year in public funds. "Sea-Land has gone from a strong position of government hands-off to government handout," observes Gerald Seifert, the general counsel for maritime policy of the House Committee on Merchant Marine and Fisheries.

That Sea-Land has been seduced by the ready availability of federal cash should come as no surprise. For this year the government is spending an estimated $224 million for so-called operating differential subsidies to underwrite high-cost American flag vessels; these outlays are expected to increase to $250 million in 1989.

Nor is this the full extent of the maritime dole. This year there's also $9 million on research and development and $77 million for state maritime academies, technical studies, and the like. Moreover, the Maritime Administration (Marad) expects to drop some $63 million on bad loans to shipping companies—down, however, from the $417 million of losses in 1987.

And until passage of the Omnibus Budget Reconciliation Act in 1981, the government provided construction differential subsidies to cover half the cost difference of building a ship in the U.S. and building one abroad. In 1980 the government spent $265 million on this program.

*Mortgage Guarantees*

Though construction differential subsidies have disappeared, the government is still responsible for $3.8 billion of mortgage guarantees for U.S.-built vessels. Moreover, Marad's direct-loan portfolio has jumped $249 million this year as a result of new credit advanced to financially strapped operators to forestall their default on the government's guarantees, as well as delinquencies that turned federal guarantees into direct loans.

So-called cargo preference laws provide an even more important, though largely hidden, subsidy. As of next year three-fourths of Food for Peace crops and grain sold under the Agriculture Department's export promotion program will have to be shipped on U.S.-flag carriers. In fact, all military equipment and three-fourths of other ocean cargo generated directly or indirectly by the government including oil for the Energy Department's Strategic Petroleum Reserve, weapons sold through the Pentagon's Foreign Military Sales program, and buses purchased with the help of the Urban Mass Transit Administration, must be hauled on American-flag vessels. Further, half the products subsidized by the Export-Import Bank must go in U.S. ships. These requirements cost the government as much as $500 million annually, though no one knows exactly how much.

Consumers as well as taxpayers pay to keep the merchant marine afloat. The Jones Act allows only U.S. companies to ply the cargo trade between American ports, which is why the maritime industry has fought so hard to block the export of Alaskan crude oil. There is a similar act for passenger vessels. Five years ago the Congressional Budget Office estimated that the Jones Act alone cost the economy $1.3 billion a year.

The Reagan White House has had some success in reducing maritime spending, killing the construction-differential-subsidies program and reducing direct outlays, which ran $652 million in 1980, to a decade-low $420 million last year. Unfortunately, however, these subsidies seem destined to increase. The administration has, for instance, proposed a $123 million increase (a 50% rise) in budget authority for ocean-shipping programs in fiscal 1989. Sea-Land's venture will reshuffle some existing payments but ultimately will hike total outlays by $13 million to $15 million annually. As more shippers default on their guaranteed loans, Marad expects its loan total to climb $90 million a year, exceeding $2.1 billion by 1991. The administration is even pushing a "reform" proposal that would lower the operating-differential-subsidies payment per ship but increase the number of vessels eligible for support, raising outlays next year about $25 million.

Moreover, Sen. John Breaux (D., La.), chairman of the Commerce Committee's Merchant Marine Subcommittee, has long supported new subsidy legislation and held hearings on maritime policy earlier this year. Finally, the Commission on Merchant Marine and Defense, a standing panel created by Congress and filled by the president, has recommended a wide-ranging program to "revitalize" the merchant marine, including expanded operating-differential-subsidies eligibility, procurement of civilian commercial ships in U.S. yards, new subsidies for American vessels engaged in the international trade, and expansion of the cargo preference acts.

The real concern of the maritime industry—unions and companies, liners and shipyards—is, of course, its financial well-being. U.S. seamen are the highest-paid mariners in the world, collecting twice the wages of Japanese crewmen and six times the money paid to Taiwanese seamen. American shipyard workers also make above-market wages, forcing companies to charge three times foreign rates. The only way such an uncompetitive industry can stay afloat is through generous government subsidies.

But the maritime industry is not so crass as to justify its dole on the basis of naked self-interest. Here, as in other areas, patriotism is the last refuge of the scoundrel. Federal maritime subsidies, it is routinely claimed, are a matter of national security.

It is true that the merchant marine would have an important role to play in a global war, but the past flood of subsidies—$7.2 billion in operating-differential-subsidies payments and $3.4 billion in construction-differential-subsidies payments since 1961 alone—has not prevented the number of U.S. flag carriers from dwindling. In fact, even with a variety of cargo preference laws the American-flag share of total U.S. ocean commerce has fallen from 30% in 1936, when Congress began directly underwriting the U.S. civilian fleet, to about 4%. Nothing short of massive new federal expenditures could overcome cost differentials that range up to sixfold.

Indeed, subsidies make the domestic industry even less competitive by encouraging waste. Operating-differential-subsidies payments, for instance, cover $4 out of every $5 paid to U.S. crewmen; operators feel little pressure to hold down costs. The old construction subsidies resulted in the same perverse incentives for American shipyards.

Anyway, there are other ways to meet legitimate security needs. Instead of trying to keep hopelessly costly companies in operation, the government should concentrate on buying—cheaply, in foreign markets—ships for its Military Sealift Command and National Defense Reserve Fleet. Instead of enriching seamen now serving on commercial boats, the government should intensify its use of the U.S. Merchant Marine Academy and the Merchant Marine Reserve and U.S. Naval Reserve to create a small cadre of trained merchantmen to be available in an emergency.

*Alliance Partners Should Help*

Finally, to supplement that force, the Pentagon should place the primary burden for providing merchant vessels in war on America's alliance partners. The U.S. has built a 600-ship Navy capable of guarding convoys; let economic powerhouses such as Japan provide the commercial fleet necessary for America to defend them.

The federal government spends far too much to underwrite one of this nation's least competitive industries. Marad should reject Sea-Land's efforts to get on the federal dole, but that is not enough; Congress should begin dismantling the subsidy program and looking for other ways to ensure U.S. security. It's time Uncle Sam stopped enriching private business and labor interests in the name of defense.

## 58. Another Handout for Big Business

*August 21, 1983*

Despite his call for budget austerity, President Reagan has proposed to expand the authority of the Export-Import Bank—increasing its ability both to lend and to guarantee loans by $4.7 billion. And many in Congress want even more subsidized financing for foreign purchasers of American goods.

This generosity comes after the Administration unsuccessfully sought, as part of its 1981 spending-reduction package, to cut the bank's direct lending authority by nearly a third—to $3.7 billion from $5.4 billion.

But the Ex-Im Bank, as it is called, has proven remarkably resilient in resisting budgetary curbs because of its broad, nonpartisan support. Congress never accepted all of President Reagan's proposed cuts, and the Administration was soon prompted to flip-flop its position as a result of mounting pressure from Republican Senators, such as John Heinz of Pennsylvania, Republican-leaning business organizations, including the Chamber of Commerce and the National Association of Manufacturers, and Democratic presidential contenders like Alan Cranston and Walter Mondale.

The bank is a classic example of corporate welfare: Roughly 70 percent of its loans enrich seven large corporations. The four biggest beneficiaries of the bank are Boeing, Westinghouse, General Electric and McDonnell Douglas; the outstanding loans for their sales total nearly $17 billion. The products subsidized by the bank are primarily manufactured goods, such as planes, nuclear and conventional power plants and telecommunications equipment.

Moreover, the Ex-Im Bank has effectively subsidized repressive regimes of all stripes around the world. The bank was originally established to facilitate trade with the Soviet Union. Angola, South Korea, Indonesia and the Philippines are among its customers. In 1981 the Ex-Im Bank even arranged $120.7 million in subsidized credit for Rumania to buy steam-turbine generators from General Electric.

Bank supporters argue that it creates "jobs." Every billion dollars in exports results in 40,000 jobs, claims T. A. Wilson, Boeing's chairman. So the way to get more jobs is simple—encourage exports by underwriting loans to foreign buyers.

But no one knows how many exports that Ex-Im Bank loans and loan guarantees actually create. The bank subsidizes about 60 percent of all export sales of American airliners, even though many of our aircraft have no comparable competition. In addition, credit terms are not the most important factor in determining sales. A study by the International Trade Commission found that American airline companies ranked financing only eighth in importance among 12 factors in making their purchasing decisions. Fuel efficiency, passenger capacity, price, range, availability, technology and quality were all considered more important.

The bank claims that nearly three-fourths of bank-supported deals would not have occurred without its subsidies. But it is impossible to gauge accurately what really clinched any particular deal. And, afterward everyone has an interest in overrating the value of Ex-Im financing; bank staff, American exporters and foreign buyers all want the program to continue whatever its actual impact. Rachel McCulloch, a University of Wisconsin economist, argues that the bank's 75 percent estimate is "impossible to believe." She thinks 7 percent is far more likely.

Admittedly, some jobs with some companies are "created." However, if subsidizing financing for exports creates jobs, then why not underwrite the cost of the products as well? Or just have the federal Government buy the goods and give them away?

The reason is, as the saying goes, "There ain't no such thing as a free lunch." First, Ex-Im loans have occasionally financed direct rivals of American companies; Pan American World Airways once attacked the bank for financing aircraft purchased by its foreign competitors. Britain's Laker Airways, for one, used $147 million in Ex-Im loans and loan guarantees to build its cut-rate operation.

Perhaps more important, loans and loan guarantees take money and credit away from most companies throughout the economy and give them to a few politically favored ones, namely those that sell to foreign buyers with Ex-Im financing. Economist Herbert M. Kaufman of the University of Arizona, for example, estimates that every $1 billion in loan guarantees crowds out between $736 million and $1.32 billion of private investment. Only last week, the bank initially approved $2 billion in loan guarantees to Brazil and Mexico.

The losers for the most part are invisible: small businesses that don't start up because of high credit costs, established businesses that don't expand because of tight money, and companies that fail when their banks say no. The result is thousands of lost jobs. By directly re-allocating credit from some businesses to others, the Ex-Im Bank indirectly shifts jobs from some companies to others.

Not surprisingly, then, independent analysts have sharply criticized the bank. The Congressional Budget Office has concluded that "the United States as a whole must lose from the program." John Boyd, a senior economist for the Federal Reserve Bank of Minneapolis, estimates that the cost of the Ex-Im Bank, in terms of the forgone return on the taxpayers' investment, has exceeded its benefits by between $200 million and $650 million a year since 1976.

Some supporters argue that Ex-Im financing is necessary to force the Europeans and Japanese to drop their export-subsidy programs. Unfortunately, trade wars more often escalate than abate: The head of France's largest airlines manufacturer, Aérospatiale group, has used the increase in Ex-Im Bank financing of American aircraft companies to demonstrate "the need for a more coherent financing mechanism" for French companies.

In fact, export subsidies are an American invention, dating from the bank's creation in 1934. The great expansion of foreign subsidy programs came only in the 70's, as the Europeans first developed commercial aircraft to challenge seriously the heavily subsidized American models. And even if other nations eventually drop their subsidies, American jobs at home will have been destroyed in the export wars the meantime.

Once the Ex-Im Bank boasted that it had never lost money on a bad deal; now $845.8 million in delinquent loans have piled up—and more accumulate every day. William Draper, president of the Ex-Im Bank, admits that it will lose some $700 million this fiscal year alone between bad loans that were written off and below-cost loans—loans made at interest rates below the bank's cost of borrowing. It is time to cut the bank off. Subsidizing Boeing and Westinghouse while other businesses fail by the thousands is not only inefficient, it is also grossly unfair.

## 59.  Close Down the EDA

*February 17, 1988*

Some government departments theoretically perform a worthwhile function. The Pentagon, for instance, is supposed to protect America from foreign aggression.

But other agencies serve no purpose other than to transfer wealth to influential interest groups. One such bureaucracy is the Economic Development Administration.

The EDA originally was created to promote growth in depressed areas around the country, but over the years legislators have turned it into a political slush fund to buy votes. Indeed, virtually no legislative district is not eligible for EDA money: Congress treats areas containing 80 percent of the population as depressed.

And when Capitol Hill finds even these almost meaningless standards to be too restrictive—as it does year after year—it simply waives them, directing EDA to fund specific projects. Last December, for instance, Congress included in its mammoth Continuing Resolution nearly $7 million in add-ons for 1988 opposed by the administration.

None of these projects met the EDA's criteria for need. In fact, two of the grant recipients never even officially applied to the EDA; they went directly to their legislators instead.

December's pork included $3 million for the Institute of Technology-Development in Jackson, Miss., approved at the behest of Senate Appropriations Committee Chairman John Stennis and his House counterpart, Jamie Whitten, both from Mississippi. The money, which comes on top of $4 million received by the institute in 1987, $6 million in 1986 and $7 million in 1984, will go for salaries, consulting fees and the like.

Congress also voted to give $2.5 million to the University of Bridgeport, in Bridgeport, Conn., to help construct the Connecticut Technology Institute. Bridgeport, with below-average unemployment and a per capita income 60 percent above the national average, may not be a typical depressed area, but Sen. Lowell Weicker, R-Conn., is a pork-barrel politico with substantial influence.

There was also $1 million for the city of Worcester, Mass., and the Worcester Business Development Corp. to create a biotechnology research park. The region's unemployment rate is 2.9 percent, but, explains Rep. Joseph Early, D-Mass., the project will help mitigate some pockets of poverty near the facility. However, the park's private developers previously balked at an EDA proposal to release the grant if 80 percent of the non-technical jobs went to lower-income residents.

Lastly, Congress approved $250,000 for the Center for International Trade Development at Oklahoma State University—on top of another $250,000 last year. This project, like the others, has nothing to do with alleviating poverty.

In fact, since 1984 Congress has added more than $108 million in pet projects to the EDA budget. Boston University alone collected $19 million in 1984, while Dartmouth College, the Oregon Health Science University Hospital, and a Columbia, S.C., railroad won lesser amounts in the 1985 EDA sweepstakes.

In 1986 the lucky EDA beneficiaries were the Fort Worth Stockyards and South Carolina's Lexington County. Finally, the Fort Worth Stockyards was a repeat winner in 1987, along with the Portland Museum of Science and Industry and Sumter County, Ala.

Indeed, there may be no better example of the sort of rancid pork that Congress distributes through the EDA than the Fort Worth grants. The city, located in House Speaker Jim Wright's district, received some $9 million from the EDA between 1974 and 1985.

That abundant largess was not enough, however, and the city, with a below-average unemployment rate, decided that it wanted to buy the property left by departing meat packers—at someone else's expense, of course. The result, courtesy Rep. Wright, was $11.8 million more in congressionally mandated EDA grants in 1986 and 1987, which Fort Worth has yet to decide how to spend.

At the same time, Wright was conveniently collecting more than $30,000 in loans and dividends from an investment firm co-owned with a developer involved in the stockyards project and staying at that same businessman's Fort Worth condominium. (Wright, naturally, has denied any impropriety.)

Even if Congress didn't treat the EDA as its own petty cash drawer, the program would still be a waste: more than 40 percent of the EDA's loans are in default. And one of its more "successful" projects, a 1983 emergency employment program, spent an incredible $20,000 a month for every job created.

The administration has waged a tenacious battle against the EDA, cutting its outlays from $1 billion in 1980 to $341 million last year. But that's still far too much wasted money. It's time that Congress looked beyond its parochial interests and closed down the agency.

## 60. The SBA—Slash Business Assistance

*January 23, 1986*

Faced with the need to cut federal spending by as much as $50 billion to meet the 1987 deficit limit established by the Gramm-Rudman bill, President Reagan has vowed that "no program will get a free ride." If so, one federal agency that deserves budget oblivion is the Small Business Administration.

A multibillion-dollar slush fund for Washington-wise operators, the SBA reallocates, rather than creates, economic growth, shifting credit to favored companies. The vast majority of corner groceries get along just fine without a helping hand from the taxpayers; the roughly $14 billion in outstanding loans benefited a mere .5 percent of America's small firms.

And so much money poured out on so few recipients has achieved no public purpose. Six of every $10 provided by the SBA have gone to companies in the retail, wholesale and service sectors—which are full of profitable, non-subsidized enterprises.

Indeed, the SBA's loan portfolio is a "What's What" of silly, unnecessary investments. Bars, liquor stores, golf courses, country clubs and pool halls have all tapped the SBA till. Advertising agents, lawyers, and even stockbrokers have also done well by Uncle Sam.

Had this money been at least honestly spent, the agency would be no worse than many other federal programs. But the SBA has become an easy mark for just about every rip-off artist around.

Consider the $65,000 loan to the owner of Show World, a Times Square business with live sex acts, nude shows and erotic paraphernalia.

The SBA also loaned and guaranteed loans worth $185,000 for the wife of a Boston pornography distributor to open a restaurant.

Then there's the firm that was part-owner in a gold mine in El Salvador and ran a homosexual Turkish bath in Milwaukee. To the SBA that was worth a $3.4 million loan—which was, unfortunately, lost when the business went belly-up.

But so what else is new? One of the Nixon White House plumbers collected $529,000 in SBA-guaranteed loans for use as investment in minority-owned firms—and spent the money on yachts, political contributions, entertainment and travel.

Burt Reynolds, Paul Newman and Norman Lear, along with more than 50 other celebrities, received $14 million in SBA assistance for an investment company with property in Beverly Hills and on New York's Park Avenue. Their firm, at least, has yet to collapse; roughly a quarter of the investment companies backed by the SBA since 1958 have ended up in liquidation, costing the taxpayers some $80 million.

The number of SBA horror stories are endless. "Virginia Man Pleads Guilty to Fraud," runs one newspaper headline: the founder of a minority business investment firm diverted $106,000 in SBA funds to his own use.

"Paint Firm's Default Revealed" declares another article title. A Chicago paint manufacturer went under, leaving $427,993 in SBA loans unpaid.

"D.C. Official Accused of Loan Fraud" tops one story. It seems that a high official in the District of Columbia city government hid personal assets after defaulting on a $123,000 SBA loan for a laundry and dry-cleaning business.

Ready for more?

"Brown Pleads Guilty" ran a recent headline. Need you ask what Brown pleaded guilty to? Defrauding the government in gaining a $213,750 SBA loan guarantee.

"New York Man Indicted in $1.6 Million Fraud" reports *The New York Times*. The victim, of course, was the SBA.

A used-car dealer tried to dispose of his assets after his firm became insolvent to avoid repaying $250,000 in SBA loans. The all-too-familiar refrain: "Dealer Accused of Trying to Bilk SBA."

And Chicago wouldn't be Chicago if it weren't for stories like this one: "3 Chicagoans Probed in U.S. Fraud Plot." No penny-ante schemer, a Chicago surety bond company linked to organized crime defrauded the SBA out of millions.

In fact, losses in this particular program approach $200 million nationally.

Articles detailing waste, fraud and abuse in the SBA go on and on. Everything from $33,000 loaned to a New York record store that never sold a single record to $18.6 million in loans to a New York small business investment company that, as usual, defaulted on its obligations.

The way to really help small business would be to eliminate the many ludicrous federal spending scams like the SBA. The agency draws capital away from deserving—and creditworthy—firms, subsidizing precisely those businesses most likely to fail.

The SBA's been with us for 23 years, and that's 23 years too long. But if Gramm-Rudman works, this federal wastrel may finally have no place to hide.

## 61.  The Sack of Washington

*March 27, 1986*

The budget-cutting barbarians have descended on the nation's capital, laying waste to America's historical and cultural patrimony. Unless Congress comes to its senses, civilization itself may come to an end.

Or so the librarian of Congress, Daniel J. Boorstin, would have us believe.

The hideous threat to America's future comes from Gramm-Rudman, which is requiring a 5.3 percent cut in the library's 1986 budget.

"This is not just another budget year," Boorstin told a House Appropriations subcommittee. With only a measly $220.3 million to spend, the library's situation "is serious, it is even dangerous, and could become tragic for our nation, Congress and the whole world of learning."

To Boorstin, even a small reduction in staff and acquisitions is inconceivable: "The only analogy I can think of," he says, "is the burning of the ancient Library of Alexandria in Egypt." The consequences of the cuts are "disastrous," he warns, and the damage "to a considerable extent will be irreparable."

Indeed, Boorstin has become the leading practitioner of the so-called

Washington Monument syndrome, that is, responding to proposed budget cuts by threatening to sacrifice the most politically sensitive of sacred cows. And his attempt to generate piercing screams from library patrons by reducing the facility's hours of operations has been immensely successful.

Protesting the library cutbacks has become the latest cause celebre in Washington. Demonstrators have refused to leave the library at closing time; promises attorney Russell Mokhiber, if the old hours are not restored, "We will escalate our activities to secure the library for the people."

The real issue, of course, is for which people? The Library of Congress, like the Kennedy Center and so much else in Washington, serves the nation's elite. Yet it is everyone else—the people outside the capital beltway—who pay the bill.

Of course, the country could easily afford to spend the full $238.5 million on the library; that's just a dollar a person, barely a blip in the federal budget at .023 percent of total outlays. And it's hard to get too upset with the government promoting the "cause of knowledge," as Boorstin puts it, handing on to future generations "the fully stocked, properly organized treasure of wisdom of the past."

But Gramm-Rudman is necessary because Congress has consistently refused to cut off even the most acquisitive of special interests. If Boorstin's wailing succeeds, every federal agency will begin demanding special protection lest the budgetary Huns torch another last, best protector of Western civilization.

Anyway, are no cuts in library services really possible without threatening America's future? Closing the reading room on Sundays seems like a small sacrifice to make for the taxpayers in Des Moines, San Diego and around the country.

In fact, despite Boorstin's outraged protests, every bit of knowledge is not priceless. He argues that "historians will look with amazement and incredulity at a nation that once could afford to build grand structures bearing the names of Thomas Jefferson, John Adams and James Madison . . . yet decided it could no longer afford to acquire as effectively and abundantly as possible, the current sources of knowledge."

As "abundantly as possible"—does that mean irrespective of the cost? Are Americans' earnings just an endless pool of cash to pay for every "worthy" project that someone proposes?

Indeed, if Boorstin really believes that the library will "be disintegrated in a decade and destroyed in two decades," that is, "unless the fiscal policy toward the library is repaired and reversed," he should propose charging those who benefit most from its operation—the users—for its services.

Moreover, let Boorstin appeal to lovers of knowledge everywhere to contribute to the library. The institution began with donations from Thomas Jefferson's personal library; if the threat to the library is as grave as Boorstin says it is, surely America's intelligentsia, including Mokhiber and his fellow protestors, will be happy to chip in to save the facility.

It's never easy to cut the budget, especially when the heads of the agencies are as eloquent as Daniel Boorstin. Which is precisely why Congress felt forced to pass the Gramm-Rudman bill.

So if our legislators give in to Boorstin's well-orchestrated scare campaign, yet another attempt to bring federal spending under control will founder. And if we waste this opportunity to rein in the federal behemoth, then the real barbarians—the budget-busters and fiscal wastrels—will destroy far more than the Library of Congress.

## 62. The NASA White Elephant

*October 12, 1988*

After 32 months of frustration, American astronauts have again demonstrated the reach of U.S. technology and will.

It's all very exciting—but also enormously wasteful. Every shuttle launch burns another big hole in the taxpayers' collective pocket.

Though the shuttle project has been grounded since the tragic Challenger accident in January 1986, NASA has been spending money freely—$9.1 billion this year, with even more, $11 billion, budgeted for 1989. The agency was therefore desperate for a successful flight to justify its labors.

While Christa McAuliffe's needless death has caused NASA to abandon some of the embarrassing theatrics of its earlier shots—a senator, congressman and teacher in space, for instance—good PR was still a priority.

NASA officials were shameless: the launch "was a great day for America," said Forrest McCartney, director of the Kennedy Space Center, greatly enhancing "America's prestige throughout the world."

Boosted by the success of the Discovery flight, NASA hopes to make seven shuttle launches in 1989 and 10 in 1990. The program will produce nothing more than a set of pretty TV visuals, but NASA bureaucrats don't care: after all, it's not their money.

Unfortunately, the agency not only wants more shuttle flights, which have already cost some $40 billion, but also a space station, the price tag for which seems to increase daily.

NASA now projects a final cost of $18 billion, but the estimate of $25 billion to $30 billion from the National Research Council seems more realistic. And who knows what the expense will be once the politicians finish their work on the project.

Despite their professed concerns over the deficit, both Republican George Bush and Democrat Michael Dukakis have endorsed not only the space station, but also the $500 million a year Mission to Planet Earth, involving the study of earth from space. In fact, NASA officials say spending will have to double over the next decade just to fund programs now on the books.

Then there is Mars. NASA officials dream of undertaking a manned landing on the red planet, which would cost $300 billion or more. And while Dukakis has so far avoided committing himself on this voyage to the stars, Bush has spoken favorably about it.

Instead of bankrupting the taxpayers to fulfill the childhood fantasies of space enthusiasts, it's time to recognize that manned space flight makes no sense, other than to build public support for an ever-increasing NASA budget. Twenty-six shuttle flights have provided no lasting benefits in return for the $40 billion spent; they are but an expensive ego trip for government officials.

NASA has used the shuttles to project a few satellites and conduct some experiments. But it would be hard to design a more expensive way to launch satellites than the shuttle:

"The illusion of cost-effectiveness is gone forever," says Dr. John Logsdon, director of the Space Policy Institute at George Washington University.

Even many scientists who back further space research advocate reliance on machines.

The space station and Mars expedition would be boondoggles as well. NASA feels inferior because the Soviets have a space station and the United States does not, but that hardly justifies creating another financial black hole.

And a Mars journey, just like the trips to the moon, would achieve nothing of value. If there is something that needs to be learned about other planets, unmanned probes can do the job just fine.

In fact, there is no need for a civilian space program. The Air Force can shoot aloft spy satellites and firms such as General Dynamics and McDonnell Douglas can launch commercial communications satellites.

Moreover, military research and development activities could be coordinated by the Pentagon. In this way defense-oriented space costs would be honestly traded off against other military expenditures.

As for the futurists who wax eloquent over the potential of space-based commercial production, scientific research and the like, they can finance private companies to explore the heavens. A number of firms are, for instance, interested in developing drug production facilities in the weightless environment in space; if the idea has merit they, not the taxpayers, should pursue it.

NASA is a feel-good agency, a program that it seems almost unpatriotic to oppose. And supporters of space exploration speak eloquently about fulfilling man's "dreams" and "destiny."

But there's no public purpose in spending untold billions on what is, in truth, a dole for the aerospace industry. Instead, the people who most want to explore the Final Frontier should spend their own money to do so.

## 63. Mass Transit Robbery

*April 15, 1987*

When Congress overrode Ronald Reagan's veto of the $88 billion highway bill, it did more than slow the president's political comeback. Congress also threw more good money after bad into the nation's mass transit sinkhole.

The legislation was loaded with all sorts of pork, but the cost of the 150 or so highway "demonstration projects" was dwarfed by the $18 billion allocated to public transit. While the administration sought to confine project spending to gasoline tax revenues, Congress voted instead to dip into general revenues to the tune of $11.6 billion.

Roughly $1 billion is going for "discretionary programs." Reagan proposed putting that money into a formula grant program, but Congress decided to keep its slush fund from which it can hand out cash to construction interests back home.

If anything, though, the specific projects funded by the other $17 billion are even worse.

Miami's system, for example, will receive more federal support, even though local residents now refer to it as "Metrofail." The $1 billion system—80 percent of which was paid for by the federal government—was supposed to carry 202,000 people a day. The average daily ridership is now 33,000; the annual deficit is $100 million a year, or $3,000 per rider.

Even more ludicrous is Los Angeles' proposed subway, for which Congress allocated $870 million, with more to come in the future.

Local planners have yet to decide on a route or to file an environmental impact statement. Moreover, the system's costs keep escalating: even Los Angeles transit officials have raised their estimate from $3.3 billion to $4.2 billion and outside analysts expect the actual cost to run far greater.

At the same time, the latest ridership estimate of 337,000 to 354,000 is ludicrously unrealistic. That is more than treble Chicago's riders per mile and roughly equal the usage rate in New York. Yet the population density of Los Angeles is barely one-fourth that of Manhattan.

Ironically, metro funding primarily subsidizes the well-to-do. A 1983 study found that 77 percent of federal operating subsidies go to the non-poor; in Washington, D.C. the income redistribution effects are particularly perverse. One-fifth of metrorail's riders earn more than $75,000 annually and three-fourths of them have incomes exceeding $25,000 a year.

The federal program, which underwrites both capital and operating expenditures, has also put private sector companies out of business. In San Diego, for instance, a profitable private bus line was destroyed by a new light rail system built largely with federal money and operated with a large annual subsidy.

Of the $8 billion in federal monies so far spent to underwrite local transit operations after construction, the Urban Mass Transit Authority figures that barely $1 billion was used to improve service. Roughly $2 billion went to enrich powerful municipal transit unions: Rep. Tom DeLay, R-Texas, points out that city bus drivers make 26 percent more than their private counterparts and government mechanics do 47 percent better.

Another $1.5 billion in federal dollars went to subsidize lower productivity in public systems. Incredibly, federal law prevents localities that receive mass transit funds from pressing their workers for improved performance.

Finally, $1 billion in federal funds kept fares artificially low, primarily benefiting the middle class.

All told, federal subsidies have encouraged municipalities to build the most wretchedly inefficient systems imaginable. We'd all be best off if the government got out of the mass transit business altogether.

Even if Congress is unprepared to turn off the financial spigot, it could still initiate some far-reaching reforms. Heritage Foundation analyst Stephen Moore, for instance, proposes changing federal rules to encourage the contracting out of transportation services, to tie grants to system efficiency, and to allow transit workers to share in productivity gains.

Moreover, taxis—which already carry more passengers daily than all other forms of urban transportation—should take on an even greater role through elimination of entry barriers in cities such as New York. Taxis are more responsive to consumer needs than mass transit systems, better serve poor communities, and are ultimately cheaper.

After 20 years and $40 billion in federal outlays, the evidence is overwhelming: public mass transit systems are wasteful boondoggles that primarily benefit a few middle-class businessmen and bureaucrats. Yet Congress seems not to have noticed. Ignorance may be bliss, but in this case it could send us all to the poorhouse.

## 64. Subsidizing the Growth of Government

*January 9, 1986*

"A silent revolution is under way in American government due to the nation's federal budget deficit," worries outgoing Virginia Gov. Charles Robb.

"By the end of the century, if not before," the federal government may "be responsible for national defense, the national debt, Social Security, income maintenance programs and little else."

The transformation of the U.S. federal system—triggered by Reagan administration cuts in grants to state and local governments—will only accelerate as the Gramm-Rudman Act forces automatic cutbacks in the more than $100 billion worth of intergovernmental transfers. States and counties, in particular, will become responsible for an ever greater share of public services.

The shift of power away from the national government is all to the good. Not only has the flood of subsidies turned states and localities into federal vassals, but it has encouraged the needless growth of government spending.

For "free" federal money has distorted the decision-making calculus of local officials, who no longer need raise the revenue necessary to cover the cost of their activities. Instead, Uncle Sam has paid other governments to undertake projects whose price exceeds any conceivable benefits.

Indeed, Clemson University economist Richard McKenzie figures that "by design, federal aid has been an important positive force behind the growth in state and local tax collections over the past two decades."

Many programs require cost-sharing by grant recipients, and local "tax effort" often determines the size of the federal check received. Federal aid also forces states and localities to "gold-plate" projects; sewage plant construction grants, for instance, are notorious for mandating the purchase of unnecessarily sophisticated equipment.

Finally, governments, like people, tend to spend money more carefully if it is their own. A case in point is New Jersey, which reduced costs by shifting children from state to private day-care centers—after federal aid was cut in 1982.

"We should have done this before" admitted Ted Allen, with the state

Department of Human Services. But why bother, as long as Uncle Sam is paying the bill?

Perhaps the best evidence of the fact that intergovernmental aid has artificially expanded public spending is the failure of most states to make up federal cutbacks. The bulk of state and local governments studied by Princeton University's Urban and Regional Research Center, for example, believed it worthwhile to restore less than 10 percent of lost federal funds.

Said Ohio's budget director, "We've cut discretionary programs: those things that are nice to have but that people don't need to eat."

Several federal programs are particularly efficient in promoting local profligacy. Urban Development Action Grants, for one, is an urban slush fund that has wasted some $4 billion since the program was created in 1977.

Projects are theoretically eligible only if they would not have gone forward without federal subsidies—that is, their benefits are not worth their costs. Grants have gone to luxury hotels, resorts, and convention centers, reallocating, rather than creating, economic development.

Mass transit subsidies are an even greater boondoggle, promoting systems that cities and states would never construct on their own. Uncle Sam covers 75 percent of capital construction costs and much of the annual operating expenses.

Consider Miami's new light rail line, opened in 1984. Daily ridership was supposed to top 200,000 last year, but barely 10,000 people a day climbed aboard. Both city and state will slowly bleed to death financially despite federal aid.

The federal highway program is another culprit. It is, allows one Reagan budget official, a "classic example" of a program that encourages wasteful spending.

Perhaps the wackiest proposal of all—recently killed in federal court—was Westway, a $15,000-an-inch superhighway for Manhattan. Only Uncle Sam's willingness to cover 90 percent of the bill caused the city and state to pursue a project with an official price tag of $2.25 billion when a simple freeway could be constructed for as little as $53 million.

Of course, the waste is not always in the billions. In 1983 the town of East Hampton, a wealthy Long Island resort community, decided to upgrade its local airport, with the federal government covering 90 percent of the cost.

Said town board member Randall Parsons: "The type of expenses involved would be unpalatable to local taxpayers."

Even in normal times we shouldn't subsidize such local profligacy, but doing so certainly makes no sense in today's fiscal climate. It's time for Uncle Sam to drop his role as intergovernmental sugar daddy.

# Farming for Dollars

## 65. America's Permanent Dependent Class

*Spring 1987*

It was to be the new gilded age of laissez-faire and limited government, but the "Reagan Revolution" died long before the Iran affair was revealed. Nowhere has Ronald Reagan failed more conspicuously than in his attempt to control federal spending: government outlays have jumped $424.6 billion since he was elected, an astounding 71 percent increase.

And no program has been mismanaged more disastrously than the farmers' welfare system. Direct payments to farmers ran $25.8 billion last year, a 545 percent jump over 1981. No sector of the federal budget has grown more.

Nor is that all the money received by rural America. In 1986, the federal government spent another $3.8 billion on crop research, soil conservation, and similar programs. Sugar quotas, peanut quotas, and citrus marketing orders provide billions more dollars to producers through higher prices instead of higher taxes.

At the same time, Uncle Sam has proved to be an incredible bungler as Farmer-In-Chief. Despite direct subsidies of $93.8 billion so far during Reagan's tenure—and at least $21.3 billion more this year—rural America is in disastrous shape.

For instance, the Farm Credit System, a cooperative rural network of 400 banks and associates, recently announced a $1.9 billion loss for 1986, on top of $2.7 billion in red ink the previous year. With farm bankruptcies continuing and almost one-fourth of the System's lending portfolio already foreclosed or impaired, a federal bail-out seems only a matter of time.

Despite several billion in export subsidies—$5 billion in short-term credit, $666 million in crop surpluses, and $500 million in longer-term credit a year—the American farmers' share of international food markets continues to shrink. Last year, food export earnings were down 60.5 percent from 1981. With China having passed the U.S. as a cotton exporter, Thailand now shipping more than twice the volume of rice as America, and Australia threatening the U.S. lead in wheat exports, few observers believe 1987 will be any better.

Finally, there's the simple human hardship of the 2,100 farmers who go out of business every week. Many borrowed heavily to purchase additional land and expand; since then export markets have shrunk, prices have fallen, and land values have plummeted. At least 178,000 of the 670,000 commercial farms are heavily in debt.

For many of the 29 percent of the farmers who own 83 percent of the agricultural debt, the burden has become overwhelming. Two-thirds of them owe more in interest than they earn from their crops. For many, bankruptcy has been the only option.

*Bizarre Hybrid*

Federal outlays are up, the Farm Credit System is tottering, exports are way down, and farms are failing. Something is obviously wrong. "How can so many farmers to broke if we're spending all this money to help them survive?" asks Senator Patrick Leahy (D-Vermont), chairman of the Senate Agriculture Committee. Unfortunately, it's all too easy to do when the federal government takes charge.

The "farm crisis" is a permanent part of American history. "When the going is good for" the farmer, H.L. Mencken wrote 60 years ago, "he robs the rest of us up to the extreme of our endurance; when the going is bad he comes bawling for help out of the public till."

The basic foundations of Uncle Sam's stint a Farmer-in-Chief are production restrictions and price supports. In fact, the federal government began with a variant of the sort of "supply management" program now being advocated by Senator Tom Harkin (D-Iowa) and Representative Richard Gephardt (D-Missouri). The 1933 Agricultural Adjustment Act set acreage limits for specific crops and paid farmers to reduce the amount of land they planted, in an attempt to push up producer prices. Cash subsidies, principally through "nonrecourse" loans, which allow farmers to forfeit their crops if loan rates exceed market prices, were originally only of secondary importance.

However, farmers continually lobbied to push up support levels—usually pegged to a mythical "parity" figure determined by the ratio of prices and costs in the years immediately preceding World War I—in effect, preferring a cash welfare program to a cartel. Large surpluses naturally resulted. As federal stockpiles increased, the government increasingly attempted to limit what farmers could produce. The Agricultural Act of 1956, for instance, established an "acreage reserve" which paid farmers to let their land lie fallow or to convert it to a particular "conservation" purpose.

But surpluses have persisted as farmers became both more efficient technically and more adept at manipulating federal programs. Frustrated Presidents and Congresses have then responded by tinkering with the support system, turning it into a bizarre hybrid of price props, acreage limits, import restrictions, and export subsidies. The only constant has been the increase in federal spending and the number of Agriculture Department (USDA) bureaucrats per farm—up tenfold since 1929, even as the percentage of the population living on farms has fallen by more than 90 percent.

The five-year bill that President Reagan ultimately signed in December 1985 did include some very modest future reductions in price supports. Then Senate Agriculture Committee Chairman Jesse Helms called the legislation "the beginning of a slow, but decisive, transition to market-oriented farm policy."

Barely two months later, however, agricultural consultant John Schnitt-ker observed that "you can't keep track" of federal farm spending because "it's mounting so fast." In early 1985, Congress has approved a budget resolution setting a three-year $34.5 billion limit on agricultural subsidies. The final Farm Bill, however, was expected to run $50 billion over the same period. But outlays were almost $26 billion last year alone; the Agriculture Department now expects farm spending from 1986 to 1988 to hit at least $70 billion.

The American people are also taking a hit as consumers as well as taxpayers. The milk, peanut, and sugar programs alone hike retail prices by $7 billion a year, estimates Ellen Haas, executive director of Public Voice for Food and Health Policy. The 1985 Farm Bill instituted new production cut-backs; milk, for instance, is expected to eventually cost an extra 10 percent.

Finally, the number of fat federal pay-offs to the rich only seem to increase after passage of the legislation. Archer Daniels Midland, a multi-billion dollar agricultural processing firm, collected $29.2 million last year to underwrite its gasohol business. One cotton farm took in $20 million. California dairyman Joe Gonsalves will soon receive about $8 million to go out of business; "It's almost like one of those lottery tickets," he says. Crown Prince Hans Adam of Liechtenstein and International Paper Co., partners in the Farms of Texas Co., split federal subsidies of $2.2 million in 1986 for growing rice and other crops. Indeed, last year the largest 4,760 North Dakota farmers together collected more than $1 billion, about $211,000 per farm; Nebraska's biggest 8,260 farmers took home $1.7 billion in federal subsidies, about $200,000 each.

Unfortunately, it is hard to imagine a system that is not permanently biased toward richer, bigger farms. For so long as payments are determined by production, the largest farmers will receive the most money. According to a Joint Economic Committee report released last year, farms with sales in excess of $500,000 annually received 44.2 percent of federal payments; operations with receipts between $250,000 and $500,000 took in another 27 percent. As a result, barely 17 cents of every dollar in federal support goes to those farmers in greatest need.

If nothing else, the 1985 Farm Bill proves that incremental changes will not solve the crisis that is overwhelming rural America and the U.S. budget. For the current programs are such a contradictory, inefficient mishmash that no amount of fine-tuning can put American agriculture on a sound footing or limit taxpayers' liabilities.

### Dairy: Milking the Public

Perhaps the most abusive subsidy system is that which enriches America's dairy farmers, whose political clout is legendary. The federal government averages $2 billion a year—the actual figure has ranged between $1.5 billion and $2.6 billion during Reagan's tenure—to buy carlots of milk, butter, and cheese at legislated levels. The current federal support price is $11.60 per hundredweight, about two dollars above the market-clearing level.

Of course, as long as the government offers to buy any amount of dairy products at above-market prices, it will be overwhelmed by sellers. Last year, for instance, the federal government purchased 12.3 billion pounds of milk equivalent; in 1985 Uncle Sam bought 16 billion pounds worth. The result has been warehouses full of cheese, butter, and nonfat dry milk. In 1985, it cost Uncle Sam another $234 million just to process, transport, and store the surplus.

Lowering price supports is the obvious way to stop dairymen from producing mountains of unwanted milk; Congress instead created a multibillion dollar "termination" program in 1985 to pay dairymen to go out of business.

Thus, after spending more than $14 billion so far this decade to encourage dairymen to produce as much as they want, the government is now forcing taxpayers to contribute $1.1 billion, along with $700 million in producer assessments, to convince those same farmers to retire. The individual "termination" checks range up to $10 million; all told, 144 dairymen are receiving more than $1 million each to quit their farms.

Ironically, this expensive slaughter of more than one million cows has had a devastating impact on the cattle industry. Beef prices fell 10 percent as soon as the termination program began the middle of last year; the value of producers' cattle inventories dropped by an estimated $2 billion. Complains John Ross, executive vice president of the California Cattlemen's Association, "We got kicked right in the teeth." The beef industry is one of the few agricultural sectors that receives no direct federal support.

### Grains: PIKing Our Pockets

Though no more ludicrous than the price props for dairy products, the subsidy system for grain is more complex and more expensive. In 1985, for instance, wheat subsidies alone ran $1.95 billion, more than nine times the cost in 1980.

Three forms of supports operate side-by-side. First, farmers receive "deficiency payments" to cover the difference between the price they receive from selling part of their crops and the "target price" set by the government.

Second, USDA lends money to farmers at a specific "loan rate" and takes their crops as collateral. If, as is usually the case, market prices remain below loan levels—late last year a bushel of corn was selling at $1.75 but had a loan value of $1.84—the farmer abandons his produce and keeps the money. Thus, the federal government regularly accumulates a hefty stockpile of non-dairy crops. Last December, 2.7 billion bushels of wheat, 10.3 billion bushels of corn, and 325 million bushels of oats and barley languished in federal storage.

Third, to help reduce these huge surpluses, Congress has created a "diversion" program. To qualify for cash supports, farmers must take a certain percentage of their land out of production—at least 20 percent for wheat farmers and a minimum of 15 percent for feed grain producers. The 1985 law also authorized USDA to initiate a paid diversion program on top of these minimums.

So last year, right before the congressional elections, the administration announced the government would pay feed grain farmers to cut their acreage another 15 percent. On average, producers are receiving $2 a bushel not to grow anything; Mark Ritchie, an analyst with the Minnesota Department of Agriculture, expects the program to cost between $2 billion and $2.5 billion. Not surprisingly, farmers, who can earn more from idling their land than from planting it, like the program.

Also last year, the government issued about $2 billion worth of "generic payment-in-kind certificates" in place of cash subsidies, in an attempt to further cut production. Farmers could redeem their PIK certificates for crops (from the federal surplus), use the certificates to pay off their government loans, or sell the certificates.

But farmers and grain dealers soon discovered how to manipulate the certificates, which eventually sold for up to 40 percent above their face value. Until last October, when USDA finally changed the program's terms, farmers could take certificates issued in regions where crop prices were high, buy cheaper grain elsewhere, put it under federal loan, and then pay off the loans at a highly discounted rate. Farmers and grain firms pocketed an extra 10, 20, 30, or more cents a bushel. The PIK scam cost taxpayers about $400 million.

Corn producers also benefit from two additional programs. Sugar import quotas have sharply hiked purchases of high-fructose corn syrup. Subsidies for gasohol—produced by mixing gasoline with ethanol alcohol from corn—also increase demand for the grain. Last year alone, USDA gave $53.8 million to gasohol producers, most of the funds going to a handful of large firms.

Uncle Sam enriches the nation's rice farmers in much the same way that he supports the incomes of wheat and corn farmers. The federal government establishes both a loan rate, roughly 85 percent of the five-year average market price, and a target price. Growers who want to collect these subsidies must reduce their acreage by 35 percent; the government also pays rice farmers to cut their planting further.

The rice program is a relatively new one, dating from only 1976. But it has quickly become one of the most expensive agricultural boondoggles, with costs jumping from just $2 million in 1981 to $1 billion in 1986. The loan system guarantees huge federal surpluses—145,540,000 hundred-weight of rough rice as of last December.

The case of rice illustrates how federal subsidies have undercut the competitiveness of U.S. agriculture. In 1981, Congress upped the rice loan rate on the assumption that world prices would continue to rise. They did not, so farmers chose to forfeit their crops and pocket the federal loans rather than accept lower prices abroad. The result was the virtually unprecedented increase in federal spending and surplus stockpiles.

Nonrecourse loans and deficiency payments are used to subsidize cotton growers as well. Cotton producers must set aside a quarter of their acreage to be eligible for federal payments. If domestic price support levels make U.S. crops uncompetitive internationally, USDA has authority to lower the repayment level necessary to redeem collateral crops. Thus, farmers can pocket part of the loan and still sell their crops; rice growers, too, can exercise this option.

Outlays for cotton growers have also run wildly out of control. In 1980, expenditures were $172 million; five years later Uncle Sam spent $1.1

billion on the program. Cotton stockpiles, like those for most other crops, are bulging. Moreover, the cotton farmers are still not satisfied with Uncle Sam's generosity; they are lobbying for import quotas.

*Sugar's Daddy*

If anything illustrates farmers' disproportionate political influence, it is the existence of $100 million in subsidies for the nation's 2,100 professional beekeepers. Though the Senate voted to kill the loan program in 1985, the House insisted on retaining it.

Honey price supports cause the same problems as do other subsidy programs. Taxpayer costs have skyrocketed, going from approximately $3 million in 1980 to $100 million in 1985; consumers pay roughly 23 cents a pound more than they should for honey. The government had 113 million pounds of surplus honey on hand last December.

Another sweet subsidy for farmers is provided by the sugar program, though its deleterious impact is largely disguised. Congress killed sugar price supports in 1974, but the Reagan Administration revived them in 1981 as part of an ugly political deal for the votes of several southern Democratic congressmen.

The price supports, in the form of nonrecourse loans, are only rarely used, however, for Congress imposed import quotas which raise domestic prices above the loan levels. World prices have fluctuated between three cents and eight cents a pound; the loan rate is 18 cents and domestic prices run about 21 cents.

Thus, while the program's budget costs are relatively small—the government ended up with 400 million pounds of surplus sugar last year, which it sold abroad at a loss of about $56 million—the consumer cost is horrendous, as much as $3 billion in higher prices, all to benefit just 12,000 domestic growers. To maintain the program at no budget cost has required the government to steadily tighten the quotas. Foreign sugar shipments ran about 4.8 million tons in 1981, but will be restricted to barely one million tons this year.

Not surprisingly, sugar demand has fallen as prices have risen. Most soft drink manufacturers, for instance, have shifted to high-fructose corn syrup. As a result, the sugar refining industry is suffering a depression: a half dozen plants have closed, many are operating at reduced capacity, and thousands of employees have been thrown out of work.

Wool price supports run about $100 million annually. Soybean growers are eligible for nonrecourse loans. In 1985 the Senate even voted to subsidize sunflower production—the scheme, rejected by the House, would have paid farmers two cents a pound or $35 an acre, whichever was higher.

Peanut and tobacco producers are eligible for loans, but they operate under domestic allotment and quota systems which restrict the supply to push up prices. Similarly, "marketing orders" are used to control the proportion of oranges, lemons, and other specialty crops that may be sold fresh domestically. Consumers, instead of taxpayers, bear most of these programs' costs.

Finally, USDA spends billions of dollars to benefit all farmers generally. Export promotion, credit assistance, crop research, disaster relief, rural development, and soil conservation all serve as fig leaves to justify huge financial transfers to the agricultural community. The 1985 Farm Bill, for instance, established a Conservation Reserve program whose ostensible purpose is to protect the quality of land. In essence, however, the Conservation Reserve is but another "diversion" program, with the government paying farmers to cut their acreage.

A system this complex has provided politicians with an unending opportunity to tinker at the margins. In January 1982, the administration inaugurated its first Payment-In-Kind program, which was to substitute crop surpluses for direct cash payments. The largest diversion program ever undertaken, PIK was a disaster: production fell only slightly; the government had to buy crops in some regions to meet its commitments; prices rose, making U.S. exports less competitive; sales of agricultural supplies plummeted. A program expected to cost $2.9 billion ended up costing several times more.

Some Republicans are now promoting "marketing loans," which allow farmers to redeem their crops from federal warehouses by paying as little as half of the amount of the loan they received from the government. They can then sell their crops on the open markets. The proposal would help encourage U.S. crop exports, but would still require taxpayers to make up the potentially significant difference between the market price and loan rates.

Senator Rudy Boschwitz (R-Minnesota) has proposed that farmers' payments be "decoupled" from their production. Doing so would reduce crop surpluses, but what criteria would then be used to distribute Uncle Sam's largesse? If anything, Boschwitz's proposal points out how unjustifiable any farm program is: why do people who happen to grow food have an automatic claim on billions of dollars from their fellow citizens?

## The Collectivist Solution

On the Democratic side, Senator Harkin wants the government to take a larger role in American agriculture, "managing" supply to fit demand, rather along the Soviet collectivist model. Under Harkin's proposal, farmers would vote on whether the government should control production. If they agreed—and Harkin would cut back their subsidies if they didn't—USDA would set crop quotas and issue marketing certificates. No domestic food company could buy from anyone without a certificate, effectively forcing every American farmer to join the government-enforced cartel and barring any imported food.

Consumer prices would jump as much as $20 billion annually; farm exports would vanish. With lower crop production, rural employment would fall by an estimated 130,000. Moreover, Harkin's proposal would extend state power beyond anything previously imagined in this country. Millions of farmers would face economic ruin if they refused to join the agricultural cartel or jail if they violated the government's dictates. Big Brother would be the dominant member of rural families.

The only serious alternative to the Harkin approach is to make farmers, like everyone else in America, operate in a free market. Tens of thousands of farmers would go out of business as a consequence, but those who survived would be financially stronger and the U.S. would once again be competitive internationally. Most important, American taxpayers and consumers would no longer be forced to spend billions to keep small numbers of beekeepers and dairymen in their chosen livelihood. Price supports, deficiency payments, nonrecourse loans, quotas, allotments, and the myriad other rural subsidies should all be ended—completely and immediately.

Of course, even some advocates of less federal regulation propose a transition between state-controlled and market-directed agriculture. Republicans on the Joint Economic Committee, for instance, argue that "apart from compassion to those in need and fairness in allowing time to adapt to change, there is the fact that producers of price-supported commodities have been encouraged to ignore market signals." However, it is hard to have much sympathy for those who have lobbied so hard for the very subsidies that have distorted their behavior. It is, frankly, time to consider the interests of taxpayers and consumers first.

A quick aid cutoff, of course, is politically inconceivable. Probably the best hope is a modified version of the proposal offered by Republican presidential hopeful Pete du Pont, who would decouple aid from production and phase out crop supports over a five-year period, cutting payments 20 percent a year. Du Pont's program could be improved by immediately lowering the maximum payment per farmer from $50,000 to $10,000, as has been proposed by the Reagan Administration, and by closing loopholes that allow beneficiaries to subdivide their operations. Such subsidy restrictions also should be imposed on cotton and rice producers, who are currently exempt.

*America's Permanent Dependent Class*

However much we may cherish the tradition "family farm," there is no reason to force other Americans to keep farms afloat any more than to save any other uneconomic family business, whether dry cleaners or corner drug stores. Just 8 percent of America's full-time farmers produce two-thirds of the nation's food; there is no public interest in subsidizing the many small operations which contribute virtually nothing to the nation's food supply and which generate no net income, even after counting federal subsidies.

Half of U.S. farmers today receive no direct government aid. Livestock operators, poultry farmers, and producers of many fruits, vegetables, and specialty crops operate profitably without federal handouts. Some traditionally subsidized, but struggling, farmers in America's heartland have been prospering by diversifying their crops, avoiding debt, and improving their management skills. Thus, even many small U.S. farmers—who are the most productive in the world—would survive an aid cutoff through selective expansion, careful operations, and increasing non-food income sources.

Government subsidies have become a way of life for too many rural Americans, creating a permanent dependent class. However painful it may be to make those farmers stand on their own, we must do so. The country can no longer afford to continue spending tens of billions of dollars to pay for food that rots in government warehouses. More fundamentally, allowing farmers, whose average net income in 1982 was $25,618, to force taxpayers, with average earnings of $27,391, to pay billions in subsidies is simply legalizing theft. It's time that the congressional majority representing the 97.7 percent of us not working on farms finally told the nation's most insatiable lobby "no."

## 66. A Sweet Deal Gone Sour

*February 24, 1988*

In his State of the Union speech President Reagan promised to propose rescissions for the scores of special interest measures included in Congress' 2,100-page omnibus budget bill passed last December. And the Office of Management and Budget is now working on what it has informally termed the "Pork Project."

There is no end of expensive rip-offs that deserve to be included in Reagan's package: one list of abuses issued by the Heritage Foundation runs 10 pages long.

House Speaker Jim Wright's $25 million airport, Sen. James McClure's $6.4 million Bavarian-style ski resort, Rep. Tom Bevill's $7.4 million for federal executive jets, Sen. Ted Stevens' $2.6 million for commercial fishermen, and Sen. Quentin Burdick's $10 million for sunflower growers are just the tip of the proverbial iceberg.

However, it is hard to come up with a sleazier action than Congress' elimination of the $250,000 limit on loans to beekeepers. This measure—pushed by Democratic Sens. John Melcher of Montana and David Pryor of Arkansas—could give as much as $6 million to the 15 largest honey producers in America.

Beekeepers first got on the federal dole in 1949 and, like so many of their farming counterparts, have demonstrated an uncanny knack for looting the Treasury. Though the program was once fairly cheap—in 1980 Uncle Sam spent about $3 million to support honey producers—just four years later the nation's 2,000 commercial beekeepers collected more than $90 million.

Between 1984 and 1987 they received another $333 million from the government. Outlays this year are expected to run $60 million to $70 million. And many individual beekeepers have grown rich off Uncle Sam, with some annual payments topping $1 million.

Critics of the program, led by Rep. Silvio Conte, R-Mass., have spent years trying to kill it. Finally, early last year they succeeded in restricting individual loans to $250,000—which is still five times the limit for other commodities.

But the American Honey Producers Association went looking for a few legislators to lend the rich a helping hand and found Melcher and Pryor. The result was a provision in the Budget Reconciliation Act, ostensibly designed to reduce spending, dropping the loan limit. Which means bee-keepers can again become millionaires at taxpayer expense.

The honey price support program, like the many other agricultural subsidies, makes no sense. For years the beekeepers received a "non-recourse" loan for their honey; when market prices fell below the loan level, producers simply forfeited their crops to the government and kept the proceeds.

As a result, the government became the world's largest beekeeper. At the start of last year Uncle Sam was storing 60.8 million pounds in surplus honey.

Indeed, beekeepers were essentially in business for one customer alone: the government. In 1985 producers placed 102 million pounds of honey under federal loan; Uncle Sam ended up with 98 million pounds.

So ludicrous was this system that Congress decided to try what are called marketing loans. Beekeepers can now pay off their Congress loans, issued at the inflated support price, at the lower market price and take back their honey to sell privately. The government loses as much money as before but it doesn't get stuck with as many barrels of surplus honey.

As a result, in 1986 Uncle Sam ended up owning "only" 36 million pounds out of the 178 million pounds of honey put under loan. Today the federal honey stock is down to about 7 million pounds.

However, the move from non-recourse to marketing loans has only made the program slightly less irrational, not justifiable. For the beekeepers' dole still serves no national interest.

Of course, ending the program would result in an industry shakeout. But keeping domestic producers afloat is an enormous waste: we all lose when the tens of millions in subsidies are drawn out of the economy every year. Moreover, beekeepers have no more moral right than dry cleaners or political columnists to force the taxpayers to keep them in business.

Congress may be unwilling to kill any program, no matter how wasteful, in an election year, but it has no excuse for not reinstating the loan limit. Can even the average farmer believe Uncle Sam is obligated to make rich beekeepers ever richer?

President Reagan should include the honey loan limit in his pork package and Congress should admit its error. For while the beekeepers' raid on the Treasury is not the most expensive bit of pork approved by Congress last December, it may be the most rancid one.

## 67. The Sunflower Crisis

*December 9, 1987*

Direct federal payments to farmers ran $25.8 billion in 1986, a 545 percent increase over 1981. All told, farmers have collected $117 billion under conservative Ronald Reagan.

A lot of farmers have become millionaires at taxpayer expense: in 1986 one California cotton farm collected $20 million while dairyman Joe Gonsalves was paid $8 million to go out of business. Even the crown prince of Liechtenstein has benefited from American taxpayers' largess.

Obviously something is very wrong with the system. Most people probably recognize the problem is too much government spending. But not Sen. Quentin Burdick, D-N.D.

Burdick, the chairman of the Appropriations Subcommittee for Agriculture, is more concerned that some of his rural constituents are not on the federal gravy train. Naturally, he wants to rectify this grave injustice.

Until now sunflower growers have struggled along without government support. But, contends Burdick, Europe is now subsidizing its sunflower growers. And unless the government intervenes to prop up domestic prices, he warns, "further reductions in sunflower acreage are expected to force the closing of crushing plants that depend on sunflowers for their principal source of supply."

No one wants to see the domestic sunflower industry disappear, of course. And no one wants to see more suffering in rural America. But we simply can't afford any more farm programs.

Uncle Sam's attempt to play farmer-in-chief has been an unmitigated disaster: the taxpayers have been looted, small farmers have continued to go under, large operators have grown rich, and U.S. exporters have become uncompetitive. Indeed, every new program causes new problems, leading to more government intervention and even more problems.

For example, price supports encouraged farmers to produce more; the resulting surpluses caused the government to mandate production reductions and to pay farmers to go out of business. Higher subsidies priced American crops out of the world market. The government responded by hiking export subsidies.

In fact, Uncle Sam has spoiled every food that he has touched. Milk, rice, wheat, corn, peanuts, cotton, tobacco, soybeans, sugar, wool and honey are all subsidized by the government; surpluses, consumer prices and taxpayer costs continue to run out of control.

Of course, sunflower growers understandably complain that they are at a disadvantage since other edible oil producers, such as soybean farmers, are underwritten by the government. In fact, warns Burdick, without a federal program sunflower producers may simply switch to other, subsidized crops.

But we no longer can afford to let misbegotten intervention justify more misbegotten intervention. Programs need to be dropped, not added.

True, Burdick emphasizes that he is only proposing a one-year program costing just $18 million. As such, he contends, it is a good investment: "Its benefits will flow far beyond just our sunflower growers to our seed companies, storage elevators, railroads and retailers."

The senator, however, knows that the program is unlikely to disappear after one year or stay limited to $18 million. Once the checks begin to flow, sunflower producers will fight tenaciously to maintain their place at the federal trough.

Moreover, Burdick's economics is bad. Every farm program is said to bolster other rural industries and the overall economy. But where does he think the $18 million for his constituents will come from? Some Arab sheikh? The pope?

The point is, the government would have to extract $18 million—along with its usual bureaucratic handling fee—from the private sector to pay the sunflower growers. Any benefit for North Dakota would be more than offset by losses elsewhere in the country. In short, agricultural subsidies are a zero-sum game in which most of us lose.

Nevertheless, intones Burdick, "the costs of an out-of-control fiscal policy must not be borne by the one sector that has seen so much damage in the 1980s." But no area of the budget is more responsible for "an out-of-control fiscal policy" than farm spending. Indeed, fiscal restraint is simply unattainable without cutting crop subsidies.

Anyway, reducing spending doesn't mean sacrificing rural America. For most of Uncle Sam's unending agricultural handouts have gone to the larger operators who have the most influence on Capitol Hill, not small family farmers: in 1986 4,760 farmers in Burdick's home state collected more than $1 billion, about $211,000 each.

For too long America has paid farmers tens of billions of dollars annually to produce food that rots in government warehouses. Starting with Sen. Burdick's sunflower growers, Congress needs to tell the nation's most insatiable lobby no.

## 68. Uncle Sam's Legalized Larceny

*March 18, 1987*

It was to be the gilded age of laissez-faire and limited government, but the "Reagan Revolution" died long before the Iranamok affair. And nowhere has Ronald Reagan failed more conspicuously than in controlling the budget.

Spending has jumped 72 percent since Reagan was elected. Even after adjusting for inflation the federal government has grown by one-fifth.

No program has expanded faster than the farmers' welfare system. Direct payments to farmers ran $4 billion in 1981 and $25.8 billion last year, a jump of 545 percent.

Nor is that all the money received by rural America. The federal government spent another $3.8 billion last year for crop research, soil conservation and similar programs. In almost every way federal agricultural policy has become more intrusive and expensive under Ronald Reagan.

Unfortunately, Uncle Sam as Farmer-in-Chief has proved to be a gross bungler as well as a wastrel. The Farm Credit System is near collapse, agricultural exports continue to drop, and 110,000 farmers are leaving their land annually.

And some farmers are getting very rich. The largest 4 percent of farms—with an average net worth ranging from $330,000 to $2.7 million—collect almost half of all subsidies. Farmers with sales exceeding $100,000 receive more than 10 times as much federal aid as do smaller operators.

One of the most outrageous examples of corporate welfare is the gasohol subsidy program.

Gasohol—a fuel source combining alcohol and gasoline—makes no sense economically. It survives only because of politics.

For instance, gasohol is exempt from the federal gas tax, a $480 million implicit subsidy last year alone. Congress also has imposed on imported gasohol a tariff of 60 cents per gallon, plus 3 percent of the product's value.

Moreover, gasohol producers have received surplus supplies of corn, from which grain alcohol is extracted. Says Michael Fumento, a Washington attorney, "The total subsidies are impossible to quantify . . . but the minimum figure is approximately 90 cents per gallon of grain alcohol."

Nevertheless, by last year the gasohol industry was ready to fold. Even the Agriculture Department's Office of Energy concluded that gasohol production "cannot be justified on economic grounds" and could not long survive.

But gasohol manufacturers, led by the multibillion-dollar firm, Archer Daniels Midland, lobbied hard for more government support. ADM alone has spent more than $500,000 in campaign contributions since 1979 to ensure its Washington influence; Reagan, Senate minority leader Robert Dole, and former House Speaker Tip O'Neill all picked up thousands of dollars each from ADM to help advance their political ambitions.

So last May, Agriculture Secretary Richard Lyng announced a new giveaway program to "permit the industry to survive"—two days after meeting with ADM chairman Dwayne Andrews. And since then ADM has collected $29.23 million, the largest subsidy for a single firm from any agriculture program.

Nor is ADM the only corporation that has busily looted the public purse. Indiana's New Energy Co. received $4.9 million, Pekin Energy Co., partially owned by Texaco, collected $4.8 million, and South Point Ethanol, half owned by Ashland Oil, picked up $4 million. Other big gainers included A.E. Staley Manufacturing Co., which pocketed $3 million, and Kentucky Agricultural Energy Corp., partially owned by Chevron, which received $1.8 million.

Secretary Lyng justifies the millions in corporate food stamps as a method of "saving jobs." But Fumento figures the cost of this latest subsidy alone to be $30,000 to $40,000 per employee. Far more jobs would have resulted if the taxpayers' $53.8 million had been privately invested elsewhere.

It's time Congress and the administration went back to first principles. Article 1, Section 8 of the Constitution limits the taxing power to provide for the "general welfare." But gasohol subsidies—and the rest of the farm programs—are legalized larceny, with a narrow interest group using government power to enrich itself at public expense.

Indeed, unless everyone, from voters to congressmen to presidents, starts taking the nation's fundamental document seriously, our republic will continue to degenerate into a giveaway state, with an ever-shrinking economic pie to divide. Eventually even the special interests will run out of people to rob.

It's not yet too late to reverse this trend. But unless Congress and the administration start cutting welfare for the greedy—and the farmers' dole is a good place to start—it soon may be.

# 69. Subsidizing Rural America

*May 9, 1984*

Reducing the deficit is the watchword in Congress these days, but interest in slashing the necessary $180 billion in spending, as well as cutting the $88.5 billion the government will lend or guarantee in loans this year, usually wanes when there's an opportunity to act. And act Congress could to reduce the billions paid to rural interest groups.

For example, in March the House ignored White House opposition and voted to forgive a $7.9 billion federal loan to the Rural Electrification Administration and to expand interest subsidies to rural electric cooperatives, for a total cost of $21 billion. The legislation, which is now before Sen. Paula Hawkins's Subcommittee on Agricultural Credit and Rural Electrification, received bipartisan backing, many so-called fiscal conservatives included.

The Congressional Budget Office estimates that the REA's loans will run some $4 billion annually in coming years. Since the agency will be spending more than it is collecting in loan repayments, it will soon be out of money, and therefore unable to make loans and loan guarantees at 2% and 5% interest rates. This threat to the rural co-ops' source of cheap loans led the National Rural Electric Cooperative Association to push the bailout.

The REA was founded in 1935 to bring electricity to rural America. It financed electric co-ops and even conducted traveling road shows to promote the use of electricity, prepared wiring and plumbing plans, and lent farmers the money to purchase and install appliances. Today it is as busy as ever, even though 99% of farms have electricity.

*No Rest for the Politician*

Of course, neither Congress nor the REA was content to stop with the electrification of America. In 1949, the REA was authorized to make loans and loan guarantees for rural telephone service; 13 years ago, Congress set up a Rural Telephone Bank within REA to make additional loans. Currently, 95% of farms have telephones, yet the REA is, all told, extending $560 million in new phone loans and guarantees this fiscal year.

But far be it for politicians to rest when even one fundamental need is unmet. In 1979, President Carter announced a series of steps intended to "overcome isolation in rural areas through modern communications technology," and REA Community Antenna Television loans were born. In the program's first year, 1980, $34 million in loans and $24 million in loan guarantees were extended to rural cooperatives for cable-television service.

Almost as important a duty for the REA as advancing new services has been subsidizing the costs of existing services. The price of electricity, for example, has been held down despite the higher cost of serving rural areas. Both the General Accounting Office and the Office of Management and Budget have found that customers serviced by REA co-ops pay less than unsubsidized utility customers; OMB puts the differential between 8% and 12%. (The REA maintains that 55% of the co-ops actually charge higher rates, and 45% lower rates.)

More than 30 million people benefit from REA-subsidized services—a powerful political constituency. But the REA is not the federal government's only subsidy for rural America. The Tennessee Valley Authority was established in 1933 to control flooding and promote navigation in the Tennessee Valley. Once it dammed the Tennessee River, however, it became an electrical utility and gained a new mission. The TVA has become a nearly $6 billion conglomerate involved in all forms of power generation and now differs little from any commercial utility.

That is, except in its electricity rates. Despite recent price increases, the agency's bills are still only about 60% of the national average. TVA consumers pay less than half what most Frost Belt consumers do, and only a third what New York City customers pay.

The TVA is able to provide cheap electricity because of its access to cheap federal loans. Direct federal support, aside from general research funding—$125 million this year—ended in the 1950s. But the TVA has been able to borrow regularly at several percentage points below market interest rates. It will get $200 million more in loans this year, leaving almost $2 billion in loans outstanding. (The TVA has other cost advantages from being a government agency, such as exemption from local property taxes.)

Cheap power has built the TVA its own constituency. It serves 2.7 million consumers in seven states and employs 50,000 people. Such political power has kept congressmen supportive and punished candidates who questioned the appropriateness of a federal utility.

The Agriculture Department also is, not surprisingly, full of programs to promote rural development—such as the Rural Clean Water Program, which started out as a "two-year experimental" program in 1980 to fight water pollution in rural areas. A minor $5.7 million blip in the federal budget last year, its costs have more than tripled since 1981.

Far bigger is the Farmers Home Administration, which made more than $6 billion in loans last year, and has more than $51 billion in loans outstanding. The generosity of the FmHA is expected to increase more than 25% this year, with new loans hitting $7.8 billion.

The mainstays of the FmHA are the rural housing insurance fund, which makes low-interest loans and loan guarantees for rural home purchases, rentals and repairs, and the agricultural credit insurance fund, which makes loans for farm enlargement and operation, soil and water conservation, watershed protection, economic emergency assistance and disaster relief. But there are more than a dozen other, smaller functions of the FmHA, each attending to an aspect of day-to-day life (housing, fire protection) that most other Americans are content to handle locally or on their own.

The administration went after the FmHA's budget in 1981, since 5% and 7% 40-year loans were being offered with no down payment required. Moreover, since Congress continually expanded the program without limiting borrowers' eligibility, many program beneficiaries were capable of getting credit elsewhere. As a result of the administration's stance, the growth in the FmHA has slowed, but total loans outstanding continue to mount, and will hit some $55 billion this year.

However, even these billions of dollars are not enough to satisfy many rural politicians. In the reauthorization for the Small Business Administration, which passed as part of the recent Omnibus Reconciliation Bill, Congress made farmers eligible for emergency disaster loans at even lower interest rates than those charged by the FmHA. Farmers who could find private sources of credit, for example, would have to pay 13¾% on FmHA loans, but only 8% on comparable SBA ones.

*'Really an Emotional Thing'*

Unfortunately, the lesson of the government's rural-subsidy programs is that politicians will always be finding new "needs" and interest groups will always be demanding more special treatment. Whatever justification the REA, for example, might once have had in spreading basic services has been replaced with the duty of keeping rural electric rates low. Why residents in rural areas believe they are entitled to force everyone else to cover one of the higher costs of rural living is hard to fathom.

But not so hard to understand is the reason even avowed fiscal conservatives enthusiastically support rural-subsidy programs. As OMB Director David Stockman once observed, there are "no real conservatives" in Congress; they all like to give speeches criticizing the deficit, and then vote to increase spending. Rep. Newt Gingrich (R., Ga.), for one, recently attacked "the strong effort by establishment politicians of both parties to avoid tackling any specific tough issues which might threaten their reelection"—about the same time that he voted for the rural-cooperative bill because "in my area it is really an emotional thing." He also is a friend of the FmHA.

Rep. Gingrich is a prime exponent of a supposedly new vision for America called the "conservative opportunity society." But periodically he and some fellow "conservatives" seem most interested in guaranteeing opportunities for their favorite special interests. Perhaps a more honest name would be the conservative opportunist society.

## 70.  Why 2 Billion Oranges Will Rot in the Fields

*August 9, 1985*

The PR firm of Hill & Knowlton recently picked up a difficult assignment—to whitewash the annual waste of millions of tons of food. Representing an industry group backed by Sunkist and other major citrus growers, Hill & Knowlton is trying to convince consumers that it is in their interest for the Department of Agriculture to keep more than 2 billion Valencia oranges out of their hands this year. Hill & Knowlton's task, observes Washington attorney Jim Moody, is rather like "being the PR firm for OPEC."

Marketing orders, which control production of everything from oranges to lemons to raisins, began as part of an economy-wide attempt to prop up prices during the New Deal. Most of the other federal cartel-setting schemes disappeared along with the Great Depression, but marketing orders lived on despite the end of what Congress termed an "acute economic emergency."

The primary purpose of the regulations is to improve grower earnings by pushing prices up to "parity" levels, based on the farmers' profit margin during the golden days of American agriculture, 1910 to 1914. Since the parity price usually exceeds the market price, USDA has an almost permanent excuse to regulate.

However, early this year the price of navel oranges rose to $9.55 per carton, more than $2 above parity, due in part to record-breaking freezes in Florida. After persistent prodding by some independent growers and the Capital Legal Foundation, a Washington-based free-market public interest law firm, USDA suspended the "prorate" volume restrictions on navel oranges.

For the first time in decades oranges were traded in a competitive market. Within a month the price of a carton of oranges fell nearly one-fifth; Karen Darling, acting assistant secretary for marketing and inspection services, calls the deregulation experience "terrific."

Lifting prorate helped U.S. consumers the most, reducing prices and providing them with an extra 150 or so million navel oranges to eat fresh. Moreover, independent growers who were willing to work for sales earned more; for example, Carl Pescosolido, a longtime opponent of the Sunkist-led cartel, says his profits were up 10 percent.

Of course, producers more comfortable lobbying for government restrictions than marketing oranges were not happy about being forced to compete. Sunkist president Russell Hanlin complains that deregulation prevented the cooperative—with navel orange revenues running $40 million ahead of 1984 without prorate—from squeezing even more out of its customers.

The success of the brief free market in oranges has encouraged organizations such as Citizens for a Sound Economy and the newly formed Agriculture for Market Oriented Policies, composed of independent growers, to press for the elimination of all controls. However, reform will not come easy: Hanlin, for one, recently told his members that "we must take a hard line" in support of marketing orders.

And Sunkist has the political muscle to back up its rhetoric. The co-op's Washington lobbyists, representing a heavily Republican constituency from California, have used their White House connections to squelch previous attempts to deregulate citrus production. The growers' influence extends to Capitol Hill too. Policies that force farmers to let mountains of oranges spoil are supported by a Who's Who of congressional liberals, including Alan Cranston, Henry Waxman, Barbara Mikulski, Morris Udall, Louis Stokes, Tony Coelho, Ron Dellums and Leon Panetta—who once wrote the administration that he was "gravely concerned" over inadequate spending for food assistance.

Sunkist is currently focusing on ensuring that the administration retains prorate on Valencia oranges, which are now in season. Earlier this year the Valencia Orange Administrative Committee, ever concerned about the welfare of the growers who control the committee, recommended a prorate level of 44 percent, which was approved by USDA. Thus, farmers have an "equitable marketing opportunity," as the committee terms it, to sell but 44 percent of their produce fresh to American consumers.

Why did USDA effectively nationalize half the nation's Valencia crop after concluding that deregulation of navel oranges worked so well? A department spokesman says that USDA's decision was "based on economics."

But there is no economic rationale for keeping 2 billion oranges off the fresh market. Instead, the administration is just kowtowing to California agribusiness. Until conservative free-market enthusiasts and liberal champions of the consumer place their professed principles before the votes of agribusiness, food will continue to rot in the fields.

# Selling Off the State

## 71. Privatizing Our Way to Savings

*August 15, 1985*

It took six months, but Congress finally adopted a budget, voting to reduce expected outlays of $1,023.1 billion next year by $55.5 billion, barely 5 percent. However, since some of the cuts involve funny numbers and the Budget Resolution doesn't mandate necessary program changes, the real savings will be far less.

Yet official Washington remains paralyzed. Political leaders call social spending "uncontrollable" and watch helplessly as federal interest payments escalate. Many have simply conceded defeat and are calling for tax increases to satisfy Uncle Sam's spending addiction.

There are ways to reduce spending, however, such as privatizing government functions—that is, spinning them off to the private sector. While Congress has been positively hostile to this approach, passing 21 laws since 1977 to prevent administrations from even studying privatization options, the British government has enthusiastically embraced the practice, divesting nationalized companies almost by the week, increasing access to private health care as an alternative to National Health Insurance, and selling off nearly 20 percent of the nation's public housing stock, 1 million units, to tenants.

Though there are far fewer state enterprises on the side of the Atlantic, the federal government currently provides some 11,000 different services in competition with private companies. Dropping these activities would benefit us all.

For example, privatization would both give consumers a choice and expose important services to competition. Moreover, unlike annual efforts to cut spending, privatization is permanent: "It needs to be done only once," observes analyst Madsen Pirie in "Dismantling the State," a report for the Dallas-based National Center for Policy Analysis.

A limited program of contracting out, for an estimated three-year savings

187

of $30 billion, was proposed by the Grace Commission—and recently publicized through a series of studies by the grass-roots Washington lobbying organization, Citizens for a Sound Economy.

Targets for divestiture include Uncle Sam's five Power Marketing Authorities, a network of 123 hydroelectric dams and 622 substations, which provide cheap electricity to a few lucky consumers. PMAs have not been repaying the initial federal investment or charging enough to cover operating costs.

The Pentagon runs a system of large retail grocery stores, called commissaries, for military personnel. The system is badly managed and costs taxpayers more than it benefits servicemen. Commissaries on bases in the United States could be closed and military pay increased; simply contracting out management of the system would save money.

Roughly $9 billion, one-third of the Veterans Administration budget, goes to pay for veterans' health care at 172 often obsolete medical and psychiatric facilities. Here, too, construction and management could be contracted out, though abolishing the separate VA system and instead providing veterans with health insurance for private care would cut outlays more.

Uncle Sam runs his own transportation system, owning two airports in northern Virginia—National and Dulles—as well as a fleet of a half million cars and trucks. The airports and many of the vehicles could be sold off, and private leasing considered in place of federal car ownership.

But the administration and Congress could move well beyond the Grace Commission's proposals. Stuart Butler, director of domestic studies for the Heritage Foundation, has offered an extensive privatization agenda in a new book published by Universe Books, "Privatizing Federal Spending."

Butler proposes that the federal government follow Britain's example, selling off a substantial share of its housing stock, as well as putting much of its land holdings on the auction block. He also would simply give away, perhaps to its employees, the money-losing Amtrak train service, and privatize the grossly inefficient Postal Service, along with the air traffic controllers.

The government could transfer many human services to the private sector as well through use of tax credits and vouchers, and by eliminating state barriers to private action. Finally, Butler would use expanded individual retirement accounts to reduce reliance on Social Security—a system unlikely to survive this century unchanged—for retirement income.

The House and Senate spent half a year debating budgets that differed from each other by just a few billion dollars. If Congress devoted half as much time to reviewing innovative proposals to reduce outlays, like a thorough privatization campaign involving everything from autos to Social Security, the flood of red ink could be slowed to a trickle.

## 72. Parochialism Reigns

*June 18, 1986*

For the past three years it has been illegal for the executive branch to study charging market rates for electricity generated by the federal government. Politicians such as Sen. James McClure of Idaho like having the taxpayers pay their constituents' electric bills.

Now the Senate has voted to go one step further—it would bar any expenditures to study privatizing the five federal power marketing administrations. Since the House was slightly more generous, setting a $400,000 limit on research that could save the taxpayers billions of dollars, the measure must go to conference.

Congress's false frugality is neither surprising nor unusual. For legislators who treat the federal budget as a private pork barrel don't want the administration to even think about limiting their power.

Ironically, the Senate would block systematic study of an area where the initial federal involvement was accidental.

Congress passed the 1902 Reclamation Act to make the desert bloom, inaugurating an orgy of dam construction in the West. One by-product was power generation, so in four years later Congress authorized the Interior Department to sell electricity; providing irrigation water remained the department's primary role, however.

Then along came the Great Depression, and the Roosevelt administration's grandiose plans to try to spend the country into prosperity. In 1933 Congress established the Tennessee Valley Authority (TVA) to develop the Tennessee River region; four years later the Bonneville Power Administration (BPA) was created to generate and sell electricity throughout the Pacific Northwest.

In succeeding years four more power marketing administrations (PMAs) were developed. As of 1984 the five PMAs and the TVA together ran 174 plants and produced 9.5 percent of the nation's electricity.

Given the fact that federal power has access to relatively inexpensive hydro sources, one would think that the PMAs would have paid back the taxpayers for their investment. But Uncle Sam is a softie when it comes to doling out cash.

Overall, the PMAs have repaid less than 20 percent of the total $15.6 billion federal investment; Bonneville has paid back but 8 percent of its initial funding. Indeed, between 1970 and 1984 BPA made one repayment of $126 million while borrowing an extra $5.3 billion. Last year BPA paid $226 million but collected another $394 million from Uncle Sam.

Naturally, the lucky consumers of federal power are getting a sweet deal. According to Heritage Foundation analyst Milton Copulos, PMA electricity prices run roughly one-third less than that for private electricity. The deal received by Bonneville customers is nothing short of extraordinary: BPA charges only 30 percent of the national average for its power.

There's no conceivable justification for Uncle Sam's electric pork barrel, so the administration proposed selling the five PMAs, with the deal to take effect in 1988; in the meantime the power administrations would be required to make serious debt repayments. (The TVA was not covered because of earlier Reagan promises.)

The administration estimates its proposal would save $13 billion from 1988 to 1991 alone. All told, the government could raise as much as $62 billion by selling the five PMAs, and $100 billion if the TVA were also auctioned off.

But those fine senators who wax so eloquent over the dangers of the deficit don't want their constituents to have to start paying the same electricity rates as the rest of us. Washington's Daniel Evans, for instance, called the administration plan "a ludicrous proposal that ought not to go anywhere and will not go anywhere."

And Oregon's Mark Hatfield self-righteously deplored wasting money on a privatization study—before voting for legislation to forgive up to $24 billion in interest on federal loans to the Rural Electrification Administration, another taxpayer rip-off, over the next three decades. The only reason that anyone could consider writing a report on selling the PMAs to be improvident, of course, is that the denizens of Capitol Hill are unlikely to approve such a proposal, no matter how sensible it is.

On the losing end of a 73 to 25 vote to bar any privatization research, one administration official complains that "we took on one of the most powerful lobbies in the country, public power, and did a half-assed job." But at least they tried.

The real villains are senators who don't even want the administration to study a proposal that would save billions. Despite huge deficits and the Gramm-Rudman Act, parochialism and pork-barreling still dominate Capitol Hill.

## 73. Sell Amtrak

*September 28, 1988*

The air is full of budget-balancing rhetoric this election year, but few politicians are willing to offend even one interest group by supporting specific spending cuts. As a result, sacred cows abound.

Consider Amtrak, which has bled taxpayers white for 17 expensive years.

In 1970 private passenger railroads were lobbying for federal subsidies to cover their losses while the industry's labor unions were pushing for outright nationalization. Congress compromised by creating Amtrak, a nominally for-profit corporation owned by the Department of Transportation.

Congress originally endowed Amtrak with $40 million, expecting the system to become profitable within two years. But Amtrak's red ink persisted, leading Congress to pour more money into the system, year after year. In 1988 alone Amtrak is collecting some $625 million in federal assistance; all told, Uncle Sam has spent more than $13 billion on the rail system and is expected to provide it with another $7 billion over the next decade.

This flood of aid has allowed Amtrak to add employees—its staff increased from 1,500 in 1971 to 18,800 last year—even though its passenger load has fallen since 1979. In fact, despite receiving billions in taxpayers' funds Amtrak's share of intercity passenger-miles has dropped one-fourth, from a dismal original .4 percent in 1971.

The Ford administration tried to cut Amtrak's losses, but the railway responded by threatening to abandon trains in the districts of legislative leaders. So Congress increased aid levels.

Then the Carter administration proposed dropping a number of money-losing Amtrak routes.

Observed Secretary of Transportation—now Sen.—Brock Adams, "We can no longer afford to provide disproportionately large and continually increasing amounts of federal funds for a passenger transportation system that is used by less than one-half of 1 percent of the intercity traveling public."

Congress, however, appropriated even more money for Amtrak.

Finally, the Reagan administration targeted Amtrak and succeeded in cutting subsidies to roughly half of their 1980 levels. As a result, Amtrak has been forced to improve its performance by taking tough steps to reduce maintenance and labor costs. In 1981 the railway covered only 48.5 percent of its expenses with its own revenues; as of last year Amtrak was accounting for 64 percent of its costs.

At the same time, however, the system's total number of passenger-miles increased only slightly, even in the crowded Northeast Corridor. In short, though Amtrak has become less inefficient, it remains a boondoggle benefiting very few people. Indeed, in many cases it would be cheaper for the federal government to buy passengers a plane ticket than to continue subsidizing their Amtrak trips.

Congress and the next administration should undertake a systematic overhaul of Amtrak, first reducing its losses and then selling off the railway.

Amtrak could, for instance, further improve its operations by taking new steps to reduce maintenance costs, dropping reservations for routes that never fill, placing employees under Social Security rather than the railroad retirement system, and contracting out food service operations. The Washington-based Citizens for a Sound Economy (CSE) estimates that these and other measures would save $267.2 million.

Amtrak could also divest some of its assets, reducing operating expenses and raising revenue. Many individual stations, for instance, could be sold, with Amtrak leasing back a portion of the space. Similarly, Amtrak could unload its Northeast Corridor track, leasing the right to use it from the new owners.

As Amtrak's losses fell it would become more attractive to potential buyers. Then the government could market its Amtrak stock, placing the railroad in private hands.

In more heavily populated areas, such as the Northeast Corridor, a private Amtrak could prosper. Other, underused routes would have no right to force taxpayers to fund their trips. Indeed, airplanes were invented to handle just the sort of cross-country trips that Amtrak is so poorly equipped to provide.

The obstacles to cutting the federal budget deficit are political, not intellectual. Privatizing Amtrak is one of literally hundreds of measures that would trim federal spending. It's time that the candidates who so fervently proclaimed their fealty to a balanced budget backed up their rhetoric with a little substance.

## 74. Postal Service Doesn't Deserve Monopoly

*July 2, 1986*

Fed up with the U.S. postal system's high prices and poor service, many businesses have been transporting foreign-bound letters overseas and then mailing them. Alas, it turns out that this practice is illegal.

At first the Postal Service threatened lawsuits to protect its monopoly. But now its board of governors has decided to change its regulations to legalize international remail services.

Board Chairman John McKean explained that the Postal Service wants to "preserve the benefits of desirable competition." Though Congress entrusted the service with a monopoly, he said, that "monopoly was not intended to protect us from having to face up to our own shortcomings."

The remail issue is relatively minor. If the Postal Service truly wants to preserve competition in the interest of consumers, it should suspend enforcement of the Private Express Statutes, which bar private firms from carrying first-class mail. Better yet, this monopoly should be repealed by Congress.

Take the case of Harold O'Brien, the owner of House & Senate Delivery Service. Even as the Postal Service prepares to allow overseas remailing, it is trying to shut down O'Brien's firm, which delivers messages to members of Congress for as little as 5 cents an ounce. Handling mail twice as fast as one-fourth the cost has gained favor with lobbyists and others who want to communicate quickly with lawmakers.

The firm was launched nearly four years ago, but until last November the Postal Service contended itself with writing O'Brien threatening letters. Then the service filed suit in federal court and warned firms using H & S that they could be fined and required to reimburse the Postal Service for lost postage.

O'Brien, who taunted the Post Office to sue him, remains unrepentant: "I intend to go on until they throw me in jail." He doesn't think that a jury will convict him; after all, he says, "everybody has horror stories about the post office."

Capital Legal Foundation, a free-market public-interest firm, is representing O'Brien. But his legal defense is a shaky one. Today the only exception to the Postal Service's first-class monopoly is extremely urgent mail, normally costing at least $3 a letter. In recent years the Postal Service has shut down private posts in Kansas and New York, while congressional proposals to decriminalize private mail delivery—the latest introduced by Rep. Philip M. Crane (R-Ill.)—have gone nowhere.

There is no excuse for continuing the federal postal monopoly. Mail delivery is 10% slower than in 1969, yet stamp prices have risen 50% over the last five years alone and may soon be upped again.

At the same time, there is no doubt that private firms could do a better job delivering the mail. U.S. government agencies already routinely turn to United Parcel Service to send out packages; over Christmas the Postal Service paid Federal Express to carry first-class mail over specific routes. Rural mail delivery is now contracted out to 4,800 private carriers, at a saving of up to two-thirds. And 50 billion pieces of regular mail a year are pre-sorted by private firms before they are mailed.

The only serious argument against allowing competition with the Postal Service is that private firms would "skim the cream," leaving the quasi-governmental body with the expensive, difficult routes. But UPS delivers to the continental 48 states at a standard rate; moreover, rural deliveries account for but 4% of the Postal Service's revenue. Anyway, why should urban dwellers, who pay more for everything from housing to food, have to subsidize rural residents?

The real "cream-skimmers" are Postal Service management and employees—"the highest paid semi-skilled workers in the world," observes John Crutcher, a postal rate commissioner—who use the monopoly to protect their artificially high wages. They, not the public, are the beneficiaries of the Private Express Statutes.

John McKean deserves much praise for admitting that his agency is not serving consumers well. But while he's right that blocking competition from remail services does not "enhance the welfare of our customers and the nation," neither does suppressing competition elsewhere. It's time the government stopped suing people for providing better service for less.

# Taxing Problems

## 75. The Battle over Taxes

*July 22, 1987*

The voters may have repudiated Walter Mondale's call for higher taxes in November 1984, but the Democrats won't give up on the idea.

The House Ways and Means Committee has come up with a list of 200 possible tax hikes and both houses of Congress have endorsed a budget plan that calls for $65 billion in new revenues over the next three years.

The administration, so far at least, is refusing to go along with the scheme. But the Democrats have tried to buy the president's support by offering $7 billion in additional defense outlays next year.

"The president is going to be forced into cooperating whether he wants to or not," says Senate Budget Committee member James Exon.

The plan has been put forward under the guise of deficit reduction, of course, but the extra revenue would instead be used to expand the federal special interest cornucopia. For whatever budget restraint Congress may have felt over the past six years has unfortunately ended, with expensive new proposals bursting forth almost daily from Capitol Hill.

In fact, a recent study by Republican staff members to the Joint Economic Committee has documented how the deficit has risen as a percentage of the gross national product over the last two decades even as the average tax rate has increased. For every dollar in new revenues, spending rose by an average of $1.58.

The evidence is also quite clear that inadequate tax receipts are not the cause of today's deficit. Budget numbers may be boring, but in this case they bear repeating again and again.

In 1980 the federal government spent $73.8 billion more than it took in: revenues ran $517.1 billion. Seven years later receipts had climbed 63 percent, to about $842 billion. But the red ink tide was running $173 billion.

Why did the deficit increase so sharply? Out-of-control spending. Since 1980 federal outlays have leaped 72 percent, or $425 billion.

And without any serious program cuts—Congress reduced projected outlays of about $1.066 trillion by a measly $11 billion—rising expenditures will keep the 1988 deficit near this year's levels even though Uncle Sam will collect an additional $75 billion, or 8.9 percent, next year without a formal tax increase.

In fact, while it is hard to find a Democrat who does not blame the deficit on Reagan's "huge" tax cuts, Reagan has barely kept people's tax bills from increasing. The original tax package reduced projected revenues by $1.488 trillion between 1981 and 1989. But inflation-induced bracket creep, before indexing kicked in, and Social Security tax hikes enacted in 1977 wiped out $937 billion of the cut. Four subsequent tax hikes, all supported by the administration, increased revenues by another $539 billion, leaving the actual nine-year tax reduction a paltry $12 billion, or about $5 a person a year.

As a result, Reagan has simply pushed the proportion of the GNP taken by taxes back to where it was when Jimmy Carter became president. In 1977, the deficit ran $53.6 billion, or 2.7 percent of GNP, the difference between spending at 21.1 percent and revenues at 18.4 percent.

In contrast, the deficit last year was $220.7 billion, an extraordinary 5.3 percent of GNP. The problem was not revenues, which took 18.5 percent of GNP, more than during the early Carter years and a higher average share than in the 1960s and 1970s. Unfortunately, expenditures, despite the stewardship of conservative Ronald Reagan, accounted for 23.8 percent of GNP.

Thus, the real deficit problem is the many would-be tax increasers in Congress, who simply have grown used to spending ever more every year, irrespective projected revenues. Under the guise of fiscal responsibility they want the American people to pay for Congress's profligacy once again.

If Ronald Reagan has not yet lost the will to govern, he must continue to refuse to be "forced into cooperating" with a Congress that wants to raise taxes. Instead, he should veto as many spending bills as necessary to slash the deficit. Though he lost the fight over highway spending—the billions in pork proved irresistible to Republicans and Democrats alike—he should be able to forge a blocking third plus one in most cases.

And the programs are there to cut. To save tens of billions Congress need only stop kowtowing to the self-serving lobbies that roam Capitol Hill's corridors.

Despite more than six years of the Reagan presidency the government takes a larger share of the GNP in taxes than it did when Jimmy Carter was inaugurated. The most important legacy that Reagan could leave us would be convincing Congress that enough is enough.

# 76. Repeal the Withholding Tax

*April 22, 1987*

Another April 15 has come and gone and about 100 million Americans have filed their 1040s. Some were able to use the short form; many had to fill out a dozen or more pages. But virtually all taxpayers had a large chunk of their income "withheld" by the government during the preceding year.

Withholding was adopted by Congress in 1943, 30 years after the income tax itself was established. No longer would Americans have to desperately scrape up the entire tribute demanded by Washington on April 15; instead, their ever-helpful Uncle Sam would simply deduct the money every week.

But withholding has done more than simplify the tax collection process. It has also encouraged the growth of government by effectively masking the true cost of public spending.

Indeed, about three-fourths of Americans suffer from the refund illusion. That is, they feel richer when they get a little of their own money back after allowing the government to take out more than they actually owe.

Of course, over-withholding—approximately 20 percent more is deducted annually than is due—provides Uncle Sam with an interest free loan. Which means that the effective tax rates are higher than the advertised ones for most Americans.

Yet people perceive their tax burden to be lighter. No matter how bad the bottom line on their 1040, most Americans receive a spring bonus. The refund may be their own money, but it still seems like a windfall gain, a lottery check or something similar.

Withholding does more than just create the refund illusion, however. By spreading payment over an entire year, it reduces the pain caused by federal taxation, which in turn lowers the visibility of the political process and its outrageous consequences.

This year the government will collect roughly $364 billion from the individual income tax, about $3,640 per filer, and another $273 billion, or $2,730 per person, through the Social Security payroll tax. Yet the average American doesn't know that the government is taking $6,370 of his income—he only sees a small weekly debit figure on his pay stub, and even that money doesn't seem like his since he never gets his hands on it.

In contrast, if every American had to send in a few thousand dollars on April 15, they would be very aware of the cost of government. They might even become angry enough to demand that Congress kill some of the outrageous transfer programs which are routinely approved when the generally inattentive public isn't looking.

Eliminating withholding would also kill the growing chorus for a tax increase. California's Rep. Vic Fazio, for instance, a Democratic member of the House Budget Committee, advocates higher federal levies; he recently wrote of "Congress' record of fiscal restraint," arguing that "slower economic growth and huge tax cuts have caused us to outspend our income."

It is no wonder that federal spending is so far out of control if assumptions like these underly the congressional budget process. Fazio says that Congress has cut domestic programs by $300 billion since 1981; domestic outlays have actually climbed from $508.4 billion six years ago to an estimated $718.7 billion this year.

What about those "huge tax cuts" he complains of? In 1981 Uncle Sam took in $599.3 billion. This year the total is likely to be about $842.4 billion. In fact, Ronald Reagan's 1981 tax cut has been almost wholly counterbalanced by previously legislated Social Security rate hikes and four subsequent tax increases.

Any honest review of the numbers proves that the deficit is due almost entirely to irresponsible spending. The recent deficit low was $40.2 billion in 1979; this year Uncle Sam's red ink is expected to exceed $173 billion.

Over the same period, tax revenues jumped $379.1 billion, or 81.8 percent. That hefty increase was not enough for Rep. Fazio and his colleagues, however. Outlays more than doubled, increasing $512.1 billion.

In fact, spending that accounted for 20.5 percent of the GNP in 1979 now takes 22.4 percent of the nation's production. At the same time, revenues have fallen barely .2 percent of the GNP and are expected to move above the 1979 level next year.

Taxes and spending are both too high; yet meaningful cuts seem unlikely, with Congress and the administration caught in a budget gridlock.

One way to force reform, however, would be to repeal withholding. Let's again make the size of the federal tax bite painfully obvious to all Americans. Then we might see Congress balance the budget—through spending cuts, not tax increases—very quickly.

## 77. Truth-in-Taxing

*April 17, 1986*

With the passage of the Truth-in-Taxing law last year, the IRS has had to draft new booklets and forms that tell taxpayers what the agency really means. The documents, as yet officially unreleased, should be read by every taxpayer.

*From the Commissioner:*

Here is the information you need to prepare Form 1040 and related schedules. If you think you actually understand this stuff, however, you should start over, because you've obviously made a mistake.

You may be able to file one of our shorter forms. Check "Which Form to File" on page 3 for the form which allows you the fewest deductions.

There have been a number of changes to the forms this year, which are listed on page 2. But just wait till Congress passes its "tax reform" bill: you ain't seen nothin' yet!

Be sure to include your entire income, for we're just dying to use the thumb screws we purchased last year. And remember, every extra dollar you keep for yourself puts an IRS agent's job in jeopardy.

Many people find that rounding off numbers makes calculations easier. Rounding is easy, too. Just round up to the nearest hundred dollars on income and down on deductions.

If you have any suggestions for improving the forms, please write us. We always enjoy a good laugh around the office and could use a few extra names to audit.

Finally, last year some refunds were delayed later than usual—actually, if we'd had our way, you'd never have gotten them. We regret the controversy, and believe that we have solved the problem—you won't see any of our employees talking to the media this year.

Finally, we are continuing to make every effort to improve the level of service to the public. (Not that you believe this line any more than we do, but we feel compelled to say it.)

*Important Tax Law Changes:*

Exemption for Children of Divorced or Separated Parents: Congress got tired of letting you deadbeats shelter some income with this one, so just forget it.

Deductions for Charitable Contributions: The lobbyists got to the legislators here—we plan on auditing everyone responsible—so you can deduct half your contributions if you don't itemize.

Business Use of Vehicles: Beginning in 1985, you must answer several questions if you claim a deduction for use of an auto. Like, is the write-off this year worth the harassment we'll give you for the next 30 years?

*Important Reminders:*

Social Security Benefits May Be Taxable: So you thought you already paid taxes for this program? Sucker!

Do You Want More or Less Income Tax Withheld in 1986? If you know what's good for you, you don't have to read any further. Lest you feel tempted to reduce the amount withheld, see Publication 47, "The Tale of the Greedy Taxpayer Who Was Audited Every Year for the Rest of His Life."

Telephone Service for Tax Refund Information: Don't call us, we'll call you.

*How To Use This Instruction Booklet:*

Who Must File: Everyone. We don't go for any of this tear-jerker stuff about you being disabled and earning no income.

When to File: On Jan. 1, if you owe us money. April 15, or never, whichever is later, if you're due a refund.

Exemptions: We don't care what the law says. We're tired of people thinking they should be able to cheat us out of money just because they have a kid or take care of an elderly relative.

Income: If you think you have some income you don't have to report, we invite you to stop by any IRS office and read Publication 48, "What We Do to Taxpayers with a Bad Attitude."

IRS Will Figure Your Tax and Some of Your Credits: If you want us to, we will figure your taxes for you. (Please, please let us figure your taxes!) If you paid too much, we will spend your refund for you. If you did not pay enough, we will bill you. Oh, will we bill you.

*1040 U.S. Individual Income Tax Return:*

Line 1, Income: How much did you earn? (The new form gets right to the point.)

Line 2, Adjustments to Income: How much are you trying to cheat us out of? (We don't plan on letting you actually take any of these, so you'd save us all a lot of time by just filling out the short form.)

Line 3, Deductions and Credits: How many times a week do you expect us to believe you went to church?

Line 4, Tax Computation: Double the amount in line 1, subtract lines 2 and 3, or $2.79, whichever is less, and multiply by 149 percent. This yields the tax owed.

Line 5, Payments: Whatever was withheld doesn't count. So stop whining and just send us the amount shown on line 4.

Line 6, Have a Nice Day: Or else we will audit you.

Sincerely, Roscoe L. Egger Jr.
Commissioner of Internal Revenue.

# The Regulatory Monster

## 78. The Excesses of Big Government

*April 1987*

When will our government stop acting as if every problem can be solved by a new law? During the past decade or so, 130 new regulatory laws have been enacted, each in some way controlling or limiting the actions of U.S. citizens.

Between 1974 and 1978—the so-called golden age of regulation—Congress enacted 25 major new regulatory initiatives, ranging from the Toxic Substances Control Act, the Energy Policy and Conservation Act, to the Fair Marketing Practices Act. This flood of legislation is more responsible than anything else for the nit-picking regulations that sap our nation's economic strength and erode our personal freedoms.

In 1985, there were 55 different federal agencies, employing 77,500 people, that were issuing mandates for the population to follow. The budget cost of this regulatory apparatus alone ran $7 billion, but the cost of compliance—in effect, government's hidden tax on business and consumers alike—ran 20 times as much. And even this figure understated the true regulatory bill, since counterproductive federal rules had reduced America's productivity growth and international competitiveness. Murray Weidenbaum, director of Washington University's Center for the Study of American Business, explained that the basic functioning of the business system had been harmed, especially "in the pace of innovation, the ability to finance growth, and ultimately the firm's capability to perform its central role of producing goods and services for the consumer."

Finally, big government's "helpful" hand had badly eroded the fundamental value upon which our republic is based: individual liberty. Who can forget the infamous auto interlock system that prevented drivers from starting their cars unless their seat belts were hooked? Although Congress repealed than standard after a widespread public outcry, today's car remains almost as much a design of Uncle Sam as the automakers Quite simply, the marketplace has lost its freedom to produce what Americans want to buy.

In fact, there is virtually no limit to the reach of government or the harm it causes. Restriction regulations inhibit business research and development, particularly in the pharmaceutical industry. The years and expense—as much as $300 million—required to prove to the Federal Drug Administration that a product is not only safe, but also effective, have reduced drug innovation and raised prices. Indeed, by delaying the introduction of important new drugs, said Dale Gieringer of Stanford University's Decisions and Ethics Center, "it's quite possible that the FDA bureaucracy could be killing three to four times as many people as it saves."

Federal regulation also has a dramatic impact on the cost of manufacturing. Air pollution controls alone ran $25.4 billion in 1984. While we all want a clean environment, the federal government has chosen the most inefficient form of regulation possible by dictating the specific technology that must be adopted by literally hundreds of thousands of different firms.

A new product cannot be sold without complying with myriad government rules. The Federal Trade Commission oversees advertising; Congress has set requirements for warranties. The FDA, Consumer Product Safety Commission, and Department of Agriculture all are involved in regulating labels.

Among the most extensive federal controls are personnel hiring and benefits. Companies are subject to rules issued by the Department of Labor, Department of Health and Human Services, National Labor Relations Board, Occupational Safety and Health Review Commission, Treasury Department and Equal Employment Opportunity Commission. A business with a pension program must file a variety of forms with the Labor Department, IRS, Pension Benefit Guarantee Corporation and plan participants. "Not surprisingly," said Jim Hansen of Dow Chemical, "any company will tell you its fastest-growing department is its legal department, and its legal department is dealing mainly in regulatory matters."

Unfortunately, an inordinate number of regulations are simultaneously expensive and senseless. A North Carolina construction firm had to provide a portable toilet even though a nearby service station allowed the workers to use its facilities. A steel company had to install a costly scrubber to reduce iron oxide dust; the heavy motor that ran the scrubber left the air dirtier than before. One Massachusetts supermarket was told to put in a nonskid floor by the Occupational Safety and Health Administration, then was ordered by the Department of Agriculture to replace it with a tile floor.

Then there was the 12-year-old from Alabama who built a tree house with windows and a shingled roof. He escaped the notice of the federal authorities, but not the city, which ordered him to destroy the house—or move the tree—because the structure was "fit for human habitation" and less than 20 feet from the street.

It was such cases that helped rouse public opinion against intrusive government and propelled the current administration into the White House. For a time it looked as if the administration was prepared to roll back the regulatory tide: It dismantled the Council on Wage and Price Stability, decontrolled oil and gave the Office of Management and Budget review authority over proposed regulations.

But the administration's program soon bogged down. Moreover, virtually all of its limited reforms could be reversed by the next President since few statutory changes were made. The President himself began issuing new federal mandates such as ordering automakers to install airbags and expanding agricultural marketing orders that cause farmers to let fresh fruit rot in the groves.

What is the answer? The American people have to pressure their elected representatives to consider the public's interest before that of Washington bureaucrats and interest groups. Reforming the regulatory process requires action by every branch of government. For example:

• Government officials must look for less-expensive, more market-related, approaches to dealing with environmental and safety issues. For instance, instead of empowering the EPA to dictate the form of technology that must be used to limit air emissions, Congress should set overall pollution levels and allow business to meet them in the most efficient manner possible. Studies by private research firms such as MathTech, and federal agencies such as the Government Accounting Office estimate that we could achieve current levels of environmental protection for as little as 10 percent of today's cost.

• The executive branch must consider costs as well as benefits before imposing burdensome rules. A decade ago the EPA ordered grain elevator firms to prevent grain dust from escaping into the air; unfortunately, concentrated grain dust is extremely dangerous, so the number of explosions in grain elevators increased more than 50 percent.

• The courts must stop making up law under the guise of interpretation. In recent decades judges have used their power to extend government's regulatory reach in an attempt to reorder society. Such "judicial activism," as it is called, has been expensive and undemocratic.

People are understandably concerned about their health and safety. But elected officials must realize that regulation is not the answer to every problem, and that even where some government action is desired, it can generally be carried out in a less-expensive and heavy-handed manner. It would be only fitting if, in 1987, the Bicentennial of the U.S. Constitution, the American people demanded that government return to the more limited role that it originally was intended to fulfill.

# 79. The Terrible Ten

*Spring 1987*

Ronald Reagan, in his first term, failed to carry out one of his most important promises: freeing America of unnecessary regulation. Upon taking office in 1981, President Reagan did end oil price controls, eliminate the Council on Wage and Price Stability, and freeze hundreds of "midnight" regulations proposed by the Carter Administration. But the Reagan team soon lost enthusiasm for cutting back federal jurisdiction. The Presidential Task Force on Regulatory Relief was disbanded; regulatory oversight by the Office of Management and Budget (OMB) was increasingly circumvented. And despite the election of the most deregulatory Congress in years in 1980, President Reagan did virtually nothing to tear out the statutory roots of regulation. What little he did accomplish can be reversed by the stroke of a new president's pen.

But a select few regulations belong at the top of any hit list. What follows are the 10 worst regulations that remain to be repealed. Some are so harmful that no one but the particular interest enriched will defend them. Others don't benefit even the groups in whose name they are issued.

## 1. Marketing Orders

At a time when hunger and malnutrition stalk the Third World, marketing orders imposed by the U.S. Department of Agriculture (USDA) require the destruction of tens of millions of cartons of food. In 1983, more oranges were destroyed by USDA dictates than by the unusually harsh winter freezes in Texas and Florida.

Marketing orders are an anachronistic outgrowth of Depression-era legislation intended to stabilize and raise the incomes of farmers by establishing cartels. The orders control the production and sale of $5 billion worth of specialty crops, including lemons, walnuts, hops, raisins, and oranges; limits are set by industry boards and enforced by the USDA. In 1983, orange growers were allowed to sell only 60 percent of their harvest. Lemon producers had to let rot—or sell as by-products, the economic equivalent of destruction—three-fourths of their crops.

By restricting sales, marketing orders obviously hurt poor consumers the most, since they can least afford inflated food prices. But the rules don't even help many farmers. Independent farmers almost always lose money because the USDA restricts the percentage of the total crop, not the total number of a fruit sold. Thus, many growers try to "earn" the right to sell one more orange by increasing total production. Their incomes may rise some in the short term, but as production climbs in succeeding years, ever tighter controls become necessary to hold up incomes.

Indeed, a 1981 USDA study found that marketing orders do not reduce price fluctuations; later surveys by the OMB in 1982 reached the same conclusion. By hindering futures trading and forward contracts, the production restrictions block the natural market mechanisms for reducing price instability.

*2. Draft Registration*

Three years ago, President Reagan reneged on his promise to rescind draft registration, one of President Carter's symbolic responses to the Soviet invasion of Afghanistan. President Reagan wanted to make a symbolic response to the imposition of martial law in Poland. However, since he has lifted most of the sanctions he originally imposed against the Polish regime and is prepared to allow Poland into the International Monetary Fund, he should remove this sanction against Americans.

Peacetime draft registration has no practical value. The Administration claim that eight weeks would be saved during mobilization is simply wrong, as a 1981 internal Administration study showed. Even if the United States didn't register young men until war was declared, the draft could be accelerated by other measures, such as using more sophisticated sorting and processing techniques. For peacetime registration to save eight weeks, organizing a draft would have to take seven days longer than in 1940, and almost as long as in 1917, despite decades of technological improvements.

Ironically, registration may even, in then-candidate Reagan's words, "decrease our military preparedness, by making people think we have solved our defense problems—when we have not." Eighteen-year-olds require training before becoming soldiers, so peacetime registration would not affect the flow of troops until four months after a mobilization. More critical to our nation's security is the status of the Reserves, who are supposed to be prepared for immediate action. Registration only diverts attention from improving their readiness.

*3. Homework Prohibition*

In December, the Department of Labor terminated its 42 year-old ban on home-knitting; it is now legal to employ people at home to knit sweaters and hats.

However, the federal prohibition, imposed under authority of the 1942 Fair Labor Standards Act, still applies to homework involving jewelry, women's apparel, handkerchiefs, gloves and mittens, buttons and buckles, and embroidery. The AFL-CIO, the Service Employees International Union, and the National Organization of Working Women, all want to extend the ban to telecommuting, where people perform computer and word processing tasks at home.

The homework regulation is ostensibly intended to prevent exploitation of workers, but the real beneficiary has been organized labor, particularly the International Ladies Garment Workers Union (ILGWU), which kept the Labor Department tied up in court for years on the home-knitting issue. The union fears competition from workers who will accept less pay because of the advantages of working at home; Max Zimny, the ILGWU's general counsel, said that home-knitters, many of whom are retirees and handicapped with few employment alternatives, "should find some other way to occupy themselves."

All the homework prohibitions should be repealed; people usually work at home because they want to. Commutes can be avoided and flexible hours kept; women, in particular, like homework because they can simultaneously pursue a career and raise a family. When the federal government ordered Virginia Gray, who supplements her retired husband's $400 Social Security check by knitting sweaters at home, out of business, she said: "Tell them to do their work down in Washington and leave us alone."

### 4. Mandatory Coal Scrubbers

Everyone believes in protecting the environment, which makes environmental regulation a favorite method to disguise measures designed to enrich particular special interests. A particularly expensive example of this practice involves the 1979 Environmental Protection Agency (EPA) regulations requiring all new coal-burning electric plants to install "coal scrubbers" to reduce sulfur emissions.

In 1971, the EPA set limits on the amount of sulfur dioxide per million BTUs of energy that could be released. Coal scrubbers do the job, but they are horrendously expensive—running as much as one-fifth of the total cost of a new plant. So utilities began meeting the EPA standards by burning low-sulfur coal (mostly from the West), and making other adjustments in their fuel generation processes.

However, the United Mine Workers, whose members dominate the high-sulfur, eastern coal fields, joined with environmentalist groups to lobby Congress to amend the Clean Air Act in 1977 to require all new utilities to use "technological" means (for practical purposes, coal scrubbers) to cut their emissions. Two years later, the EPA issued its implementing regulations.

The Congressional Budget Office (CBO) estimates that the scrubber rule costs Americans at least $3.4 billion a year. Assuming 4,500 jobs on net are "saved," which is unlikely, the CBO figures that taxpayers and consumers are spending $740,000 annually to preserve one coal miner's job—more than 24 times what the average miner earns. Paul Portney, a senior fellow at Resources for the Future, pointed out in *Regulation* magazine that unemployed manufacturing workers have been retrained and relocated for under $3,000 each. Even if we had to give every unemployed miner an executive-level pension and a home in the Bahamas, it would be worth it to dump the scubber rule.

## 5. Airbags

Next to sobriety, seatbelts are the easiest and most cost-effective way of reducing deaths and injuries from traffic accidents. In 1967, the Transportation Department ordered that seatbelts be installed in cars. But drivers and passengers refused to use them, so the regulators ordered the installation of passive restraints: airbags and automatic seatbelts. The Carter Administration decreed their installation in all autos by 1984, but the newly inaugurated Reagan Administration rescinded the rule in 1981. Ordered by the Supreme Court to reconsider its decision, the Transportation Department, under the new leadership of Elizabeth Dole, flip-flopped and mandated the use of airbags, unless a sufficient number of states passed laws requiring motorists to wear seatbelts.

The airbag rule will cost consumers dearly: Mercedes-Benz currently charges $875 for the airbag option, and replacing the system after it inflates runs even more. Storage and disposal of airbags, which contain volatile, explosive chemicals, will be difficult.

Requiring installation of airbags will do little to decrease the nation's highway death toll. The Transportation Department now admits that its previous effectiveness estimates were greatly inflated. Moreover, airbags only protect front seat riders in head-on collisions, which account for only 20 percent of all accidents. To the extent that airbags make people who normally use seatbelts complacent, causing drivers to leave their belts unfastened, airbags may actually make the driving population less safe.

## 6. Sugar Quotas

To pass its budget package in June 1981, the Reagan Administration needed every vote it could get in Congress, including those of Louisiana

Democrat John Breaux and a handful of his southern colleagues. In return for their yeas, President Reagan set the domestic price of sugar at nearly 22 cents a pound, three times the market level, and imposed quotas on foreign imports to prop up that artificial price.

The reimposition of one of the few trade barriers that had expired is costing American consumers some $3 billion annually—about $215,000 for every one of America's 14,000 sugar producers. Before joining the Administration, OMB Director David Stockman called the sugar price supports a "bailout for speculative interests that have gone sour."

Quotas are a particularly perverse form of trade barrier, because they cost consumers far more than they benefit domestic producers. Much of the difference goes instead to foreign growers who are still allowed to sell in the United States, but at higher prices. It would be more efficient to simply put sugar growers on the dole, though why they deserve subsidies more than sugar consumers is a mystery.

## 7. The Delaney Clause

While one part of the government works to keep low-cost sugar out of the country, another agency wants to keep low-calorie substitutes for sugar off the market. The congressional moratorium on the Food and Drug Administration's attempt to ban the artificial sweetener saccharin runs out early this year, and the battle over yet another extension is already brewing on Capitol Hill.

The Food and Drug Administration (FDA) first moved against saccharin in 1977 after studies—based on consumption of the equivalent of 750 cans of diet soda daily—found that the sweetener caused bladder cancer in rats. The agency's action was not uniquely perverse, but instead was mandated by the Delaney Clause, passed by Congress in 1959, which bars as a food additive any substance found to cause cancer in animals, at whatever dosage.

The clause has been grossly abused. The FDA is on the verge of admitting that it blundered in proscribing the use of cyclamates in 1970; an internal cancer assessment committee recently concluded that the original animal tests were badly flawed. Indeed, a U.S. Claims Court judge recently ruled that the FDA "continually misrepresented" the findings of scientists on the issue at the time.

Moreover, the relationship between carcinogens for animals and those for humans is wholly speculative; even different species of animals tolerate different substances differently. Penicillin, for example, kills hamsters and guinea pigs, but no other mammals, including humans. Of the hundreds of chemicals and food additives that cause cancer in animals, only ten are known to be carcinogenic for humans as well. And one, arsenic, causes cancer in humans but not in animals.

Ironically, if the Delaney Clause was applied to natural matter, hundreds of carcinogens would have to be banned—among them, as Edith Efron points out in her brilliant book, *The Apocalyptics,* sunlight, lemons, saliva, and testosterone. The Delaney Clause should be repealed, and the FDA told to deal only with genuine threats to the public's safety.

## 8. Bilingual Education

In its 1974 decision, *Lau v. Nichols,* the Supreme Court ruled that San Francisco schools had violated the civil rights laws by not providing some form of special instruction for Chinese-speaking students. The Court left local school districts to decide what kind of programs to adopt—whether English as a second language or bilingual teaching, for example—and acknowledged that English comprehension was the most important goal. However, the Office of Civil Rights proceeded to negotiate more than 400 "voluntary" agreements, under threat of a total cutoff of federal funds, in which schools committed to teach children in separate native language classes. Even under President Reagan, the Education Department has continued to force bilingualism on schools across America; the educational establishment seems bent, one commentator has observed, on creating "the only school system in the world where kids can become illiterate in two languages."

The policy of the Office of Civil Rights is entirely a bureaucratic invention: bilingual education is required by neither statute nor court decision. But former Education Secretary Terrel Bell and his closest aides were strong supporters of native language instruction for non-English-speaking students.

Mr. Bell's successor, William J. Bennett, has the opportunity to move America away from this form of educational apartheid. The policy is expensive—in addition to the regulatory program, the federal government spends some $140 million annually to promote bilingual education—and also counterproductive, making it more difficult for students to enter the American mainstream. One can only imagine the chaos that would have ensued had Uncle Sam opposed the use of English to teach the immigrant tides of the late 19th and early 20th centuries.

## 9. Federal Contracts Compliance Program

In 1965, President Lyndon Johnson promulgated Executive Order 11246, creating what Cornell professor Jeremy Rabkin says is "in some sense the institutionalization of a racial allocation system in employment." The order set quotas and affirmative action hiring requirements for the 300,000 businesses and other institutions that have contracts with the federal government. The program, involving every department and agency and enforced by the Labor Department's Office of Federal Contracts Compliance Programs, is the federal government's most extensive race-conscious program.

The system is bad for the same reasons that any quota program is bad: it bases individual success on membership in a group, not on personal achievement. Those excluded lose benefits that are rightfully theirs. Those included, even if qualified, may never be recognized as having succeeded for any reason other than their race or ethnic background.

The federal rules are also complex and expensive. Hiring goals and timetables are unrealistic; accurate surveys of numbers of minority workers are unavailable. The paperwork mandated is legion, and the specific requirements are constantly changing.

In fact, there is no evidence that the program has done any particular good for minorities—studies show that the average gap between the incomes of blacks and whites is smallest in industries that do the least business with the federal government—and we will never achieve a truly color-blind society until the government bars all forms of racial bias.

In early 1982, the Labor Department did propose to modify the regulations, but only to reduce the administrative burden on business. The White House then shelved the changes, due to the upcoming congressional elections. Now that President Reagan has been overwhelmingly reelected, he should demonstrate that he believes what he said in 1980: "increasing discrimination against some people in order to reduce it against others does not end discrimination."

## 10. Due Diligence

Ten percent of all American coal comes from federal land; that figure may reach as high as 25 percent five years from now. Uncle Sam's extensive land holdings, six times the size of France, also provide some 14 percent of all domestically produced oil and double that proportion of natural gas.

Not only does the government own the land; it controls the pace of development. The 1920 Mineral Leasing Act sought to combat the perceived evils of speculation by requiring companies to act with due "diligence" in developing their leases. If a firm failed to begin production within 10 years for coal and 5 or 10 years for natural gas and petroleum, it was to forfeit the lease. The requirement was essentially unenforced until

1976, when Congress passed the Federal Coal Leasing Amendments Act, setting an absolute 10-year deadline for coal leases.

The basic rationale of the due diligence requirement is faulty, for speculation serves a socially valuable function by saving resources for use in the future when they will be more valuable. Not only do private entrepreneurs profit from conserving resources, but the process promotes both supply and price stability.

Ironically, since lessees must "use it or lose it," the regulation encourages overutilization of federal lands. Coal firms respond to the provision by engaging in other forms of inefficient behavior, such as stockpiling coal mined on the federal lands in question and reducing production elsewhere. As for oil companies, the requirement reduces the incentive to explore areas where petroleum extraction is not likely to be economic for years. One Department of Energy study estimated that the cost of the rule applied to coal alone was $200 million annually.

The regulation should be abolished outright, but at the very least Congress could make it less onerous by, for example, allowing a company to pay advance royalties instead of losing the lease, at the end of the due diligence time period.

## Stemming the Tide

This list is but a starting point for deregulation. The Fairness Doctrine of the Federal Communications Commission stifles rather than promotes the discussion of important public issues; it deserves repeal. The Davis-Bacon Act sets artificially high wages on federal construction projects—it was passed during the Great Depression to keep cheaper black labor unemployed—and should be junked. The statutory requirement that books sold in the United States be printed here, the 55 m.p.h. speed limit, and restrictions on entry in the trucking industry are others that should be targeted for quick elimination in President Reagan's new term.

If the Administration doesn't take the initiative this year, when its political leverage is likely to be greatest, the regulatory reform movement may end, in the words of Robert Crandall of Brookings Institution, "as a kind of Henry George Society—meeting once a year to dream about what might have been." Let us hope that four years from now former Federal Trade Commissioner Michael Pertschuk will not be able to repeat what he said two years ago of this Administration: it is "the gang that couldn't deregulate straight."

## 80. Three Cheers for Airline Deregulation

*October 28, 1987*

As stories of delays and overbookings proliferate, some indignant souls are demanding re-regulation of the nation's airlines. The House has voted to have the Department of Transportation effectively set airline schedules; Senate Majority Leader Robert Byrd has pronounced himself to be embarrassed by his vote a decade ago to end federal controls.

Yet re-regulation would return us to the days of high fares and limited service—without addressing today's problems. Observes Cliff Winston, a senior fellow at the Brookings Institution, "It is hard to see how government regulation will be able to solve problems that are often the result of continued government intervention."

In fact, airline deregulation has been an enormous success, a fact that Congress should ponder before it again puts the government in charge of air travel. Decontrol has cut fares, improved service and promoted airline efficiency. At the same time, flying is now safer than it was before deregulation.

• Fares. There is essentially no disagreement that airline deregulation has cut prices. The General Accounting Office, for instance, estimates that the average charge per mile fell 6 percent between 1978 and 1984. And fares are roughly 40 percent below what they would have been under continued regulation. All told, the annual savings for consumers is between $11 billion and $12 billion.

• Service. As fares have fallen, more Americans have been able to fly. There were 278 million passengers in 1978; a record 450 million will take to the air this year.

In fact, virtually everyone in the country can now afford to fly. In this way deregulation has been of particular benefit to those of only modest means.

Along with increased access to the air has come more choice in what airlines to fly and when to travel. Overall, there are more seats, departure times and nonstop flights available; more people are also able to complete a trip on a single airline.

It is true that some smaller communities have lost flights, though commuter airlines often have made up the difference. Moreover, most of these towns are within driving distance of a larger airport.

A more serious criticism in recent months, however, is that the number of delays is increasing. Yet despite Congress' reflexive response to have the government run the airlines, it is federal mismanagement of the existing regulatory system that is largely to blame for growing air bottlenecks.

For example, under pressure from the Federal Aviation Administration, airports generally charge airplanes ranging from small prop crafts to large commercial liners the same, irrespective of when they take off or land. Differential fees would shift smaller commuter and corporate jets to less valuable flight times; charging more for peak periods would also reduce regular commercial travel at the busiest times, thereby cutting delays.

Moreover, the political nature of the FAA has hindered airport expansion. "Rather than trying to install new technology first at overloaded airports such as Chicago and Atlanta," recently editorialized *The Wall Street Journal,* "the politically sensitive FAA must divvy up its scarce resources evenly across the country so as not to offend the parochial interest of Congress." A private air traffic control system, in contrast, would be able to upgrade the most important facilities first, and to charge the carriers accordingly.

• Safety. A popular perception seems to be that deregulation has made air travel more dangerous. Yet the likelihood of death from flying actually has fallen: the fatality rate per 100,000 departures was .1 in 1978 but only .071 in 1985.

Last year was even safer, one of the safest on record. Not a single medium-size or large U.S. airliner crashed; the fatal accident rate for smaller commuter airlines was the lowest ever.

Consider other measures of safety. Fatalities per billion passenger-miles, which peaked in 1974, well before deregulation, were 1.6 in 1979, but almost zero in 1986. Another measurement is the fatality rate per flying hour—down by half since 1978.

The number of "near misses" is up, but that rise largely matches the increase in air travel. Moreover, the recent upsurge in reported near misses may be due in part to a new monitoring system implemented by the FAA in 1985.

If there is a crisis in the airline industry today, it is due to too much federal meddling, not too little. Airline deregulation has saved consumers billions of dollars while preserving the safety of this most convenient form of travel. Congress should be debating making the system more, not less, responsive to the marketplace.

## 81. Federal Appliance Standards: Inefficient at Best

*February 19, 1987*

During the 1970s, hysteria over the energy crisis led to the worst federal meddling imaginable: price ceilings, allocation systems, synfuels subsidies, windfall profits taxes, and even thermostat controls. Most of these counterproductive forays into the energy business were abandoned long ago as politicians discovered that a free economy naturally adjusts to price and supply changes. But the Senate has now passed and the House is considering one of the worst energy-saving ideas ever proposed: appliance standards.

In 1978 Congress ordered the Department of Energy to set efficiency levels for 13 appliances. The Carter administration, always ready to spend $100 to save a dime or two in oil, was happy to oblige, but in 1981 newly elected Ronald Reagan blocked the proposal. Instead, in 1982 he issued a "no standards" standard, leaving buyers free to decide the efficiency of the products they purchased.

The National Resource Defense Council filed suit, and the courts eventually ordered DOE to reconsider its rule. The "save energy" lobby also pressed Congress to force the department to act.

These groups were, ironically, joined by the Association of Home Appliance Manufacturers. For after DOE issued its "no standards" regulation, a number of states acted to protect Americans from the danger of inexpensive, less-efficient refrigerators. So manufacturers decided to support a uniform national system, however unjustified the specific standard, to eliminate having to meet varied standards for different states.

As a result, Congress passed the National Appliance Energy Conservation Act last session. President Reagan pocket-vetoed the bill but now, facing a likely veto override, says he will sign a slightly amended version of this legislation. The legislation is a bad deal for everyone except DOE bureaucrats.

• *Consumers.* Federal law already requires manufacturers to affix energy-usage labels to their products, but regulation advocates argue that consumers would benefit even more from appliance standards. The American Council for an Energy-Efficient Economy, for instance, claims the bill would save people $28 billion through the year 2000. The organization's figures merely prove that if you torture statistics long enough they will confess to anything, however. The council, for instance, unrealistically assumes that higher efficiency wouldn't cause any increase in appliance usage.

Anyway, nothing stops people from buying highly energy-efficient appliances today. One out of five of the most common type of air conditioners and more than one quarter of all gas furnaces now on the market meet the bill's standards. Consumers can choose from some 300 kinds of heat pumps whose energy efficiency exceeds the proposed levels. Indeed, according to DOE, the energy efficiency of refrigerators has increased 48% since the onset of the "energy crisis"; central air conditioners are 27%

more efficient. The "save energy" activists simply don't like the choices that people are making.

Restricting consumer choice in this way would naturally hit the poor and elderly hardest. For these groups—the former because of lack of funds, the latter because of age—generally prefer not to spend hundreds of dollars more for an extra-efficient furnace, for instance, when they can instead turn down the thermostat a bit and wear a sweater.

Similarly, high-efficiency appliances are of little value to consumers who use the products only sparingly, such as Floridians who purchase furnaces. Forcing them to spend a lot on more-efficient products to save a little on energy bills could make sense only to a congressman.

• *Utilities.* The power companies are supporting appliance controls to ease their future investment planning. Will they next lobby for a federal "lights out" law to save energy? Anyway, only about a quarter of energy demand is due to appliance consumption. Peak-load pricing is the logical means to reduce the need for new capacity. Some utilities are experimenting with other innovative means, such as paying consumers to shut off appliances during peak periods.

More important, appliance regulation may not actually lower energy consumption. First, pushing up product prices will cause consumers to hold onto their older, less-efficient models longer. Second, while the average consumer might not open the door of a more-efficient fridge more often, he probably would set his thermostat lower in the summer and higher in the winter if his air conditioner and furnace use less energy; he also might drop plans to purchase an insulation jacket for his water heater. Consumers have proved that prices matter—whether they go down or up.

• *The appliance industry.* Manufacturers have a legitimate concern over conflicting state standards. But the solution is federal pre-emption to eliminate barriers to interstate commerce, not federal controls.

The House should say no to a refrigerator police. Energy efficiency isn't the same as cost efficiency. More important, individual consumers, rather than congressmen and DOE bureaucrats, are best able to assess the appropriateness of investing money in more-efficient refrigerators and furnaces. Indeed, that is what a free society and market economy are all about.

## 82. A Kinder, Gentler CAFE Standard

*March 1, 1989*

As vice president, George Bush headed the Reagan administration's regulatory reform task force. Yet his Transportation Secretary Samuel Skinner is threatening to increase the federal burden on automakers.

At issue is the Corporate Average Fuel Economy, or CAFE, standard, which requires automakers to achieve an arbitrary average gas mileage for all the cars they sell. Passed during the "energy crisis" more than a decade ago, the law has proved to be deadly as well as economically costly.

CAFE, presently set at 26.5 miles per gallon, was established to save energy. Congress decided to force manufacturers to produce more fuel-efficient autos in order to cut gas consumption.

Consumers, however, refused to cooperate. In the early years, when energy prices were high, buyers preferred smaller cars. But as gas prices dropped people again began purchasing big "gas-guzzlers."

And who can blame them? Energy is not an absolute value; instead, it has to be balanced against a number of other factors, such as roominess, comfort and safety. And who is best able to make that trade-off: Washington bureaucrats or individual consumers? The question answers itself.

Since buyers didn't want the vehicles Uncle Sam was telling manufacturers to sell, as the CAFE standard rose from its initial level of 19 mpg the automakers had to either dump small cars on the market at a loss or curtail production of larger, more profitable models. This not only cost U.S. firms money; it also caused them to lose ground to the Japanese, who sold few big cars and were therefore largely unaffected by CAFE.

What has been the practical impact of the federal fuel standard? The Commerce Department estimated in 1985 that a 1.5 mpg increase in CAFE would cut domestic car sales by 750,000 and destroy 110,000 jobs. Last year the Federal Trade Commission figured a one-mpg increase would put 130,000 people in the auto industry out of work. All told, the FTC estimates that CAFE has so far cost an incredible $4 for every gallon of gas saved.

If the economic argument against CAFE was not persuasive enough, there also is the minor issue of lives. Big autos are safer than small ones: you are, for example, four times as likely to survive a two-car collision in a 4,000-pound car than a 2,000-pound one.

Therefore, a federal policy that pushes consumers into compacts is going to kill people. The only question is, how many?

A California engineering firm, Fatality Analysis Associates, has estimated the added yearly death toll at 500. Another researcher, Lester Lave, concluded in 1981 that CAFE killed an extra 1,400 people annually.

Then last year Robert Crandall of the Brookings Institution and John Graham of Harvard released a comprehensive study which concluded that CAFE had reduced the average auto weight by 500 pounds, thereby upping traffic fatalities by 14 percent to 27 percent. That means an extra 2,200 to 3,900 bodies littering the highways and between 11,000 and 19,500 more people injured every year.

Oddly enough, the Reagan administration, despite its professed commitment to deregulation, refused to consider the evidence of CAFE's deadly effects in deciding at what level to set the fuel-economy standard. This has prompted a lawsuit from the Washington-based Competitive Enterprise Institute, whose president, Fred Smith, complained that the government "has no business concealing the program's human toll from the public."

Equally callous have been supposed consumer groups that back CAFE, irrespective of its deadly effects. Were the industry to advocate a rule decreasing auto safety, consumer activists would be manning the barricades in opposition; when the regulation instead burdens the automakers, they apparently don't care how many people die.

CAFE is now in the hands of President Bush, who is formally committed not only to promoting continued economic growth and improved competitiveness, but also to creating a "kinder, gentler nation." Since CAFE fails on all three grounds—putting people out of work and burdening the automakers don't help achieve the first two objectives, while killing hundreds or thousands of people annually seems unkind at best—he would seem to have little choice but to support repeal of the regulations.

Why, then, is Transportation Secretary Skinner considering raising CAFE from 26.5 mpg to 27.5 mpg?

"We've gotten very sloppy in addressing the problem of energy conservation," he says.

But does he—and the president whom he supposedly serves—really believe we should spend $4 to save a gallon of gasoline? And how many unnecessary deaths does he believe that gallon is worth?

CAFE never made sense, but at least in 1975, when Congress originally passed the law, no one was aware of how many lives were at stake. Today there is no excuse for keeping this deadly anachronism on the books.

## 83. Banking's Regulatory Crisis

*May 29, 1986*

Banking officials fear they may be facing a crisis worse than the collapse of Continental Illinois two years ago, which resulted in a multibillion-dollar federal bailout. For the failure of farmers and oilmen throughout the Midwest and Southwest has put hundreds of banks at risk.

The Federal Deposit Insurance Corp. has placed 449 farm banks on its problem list, up from 370 last year; the Farm Credit System, a $66 billion cooperative lending network, lost $2.7 billion in 1985 and has nearly $6 billion in non-accruing loans, many of which simply will have to be written off.

Energy banks are suffering as well, with oil prices less than half what they were last year. The FDIC estimates that 563 banks have more than a quarter of their capital—$61 billion worth—tied up in energy loans. The number of problem institutions exceeds 100 and the FDIC warns that a "sizable increase" in failures is likely.

The problems facing the farm and energy banks demonstrate the sensitivity of many of the nation's 14,400 financial institutions to regional economic upheavals. The inability to local banks to diversify—both in terms of services and geography—and thus spread their risks has left them virtually helpless in the face of economic forces beyond their control.

The roots of today's crisis run back a half century and more. The Glass-Steagall Act and other Depression-era laws prohibit banks from dealing in securities or developing other than traditional "banking" services.

Perhaps more important, eight states, Texas and Kansas included, still prohibit any full-service branches, while another 18 allow only limited branching (within a single county, for example).

Compounding state branching prohibitions are barriers to interstate banking. The 1927 McFadden Act prohibits banking across state lines, except as authorized by individual states, and only 24 do so.

Thus, many local institutions are unable to tie into a multistate network that could carry them through difficult times.

All these regulatory constraints make banks heavily reliant on their local communities—with dire effects. In Texas, where "oil is the tail that wags the whole economy," in the words of Bernard Weinstein of Southern Methodist University, banks naturally become "oil patch" institutions.

Similarly, agriculture dominates local commerce in Iowa and elsewhere in the Farm Belt. But the farm bank problem is compounded by the existence of the Farm Credit System, a collection of land, credit and cooperative banks designed to lend solely to farmers.

More than 40 percent of the bank failures since 1970 have come in just a few states where branching is prohibited. And half of the 129 banks that failed last year were heavily reliant on farm loans; William Carner, a Missouri bank consultant, predicts that as many as 125 farm banks alone could go under in 1986.

The number of oil patch bank failures will be dwarfed by the looming farm debacle, but the energy banks are larger so their collapse may prove more expensive. FDIC Chairman William Seidman admits that his agency has a list of Southwest state banks that it would like to have sold or merged immediately.

How will this painful adjustment process be resolved? The FCS, with $3.5 billion in red ink expected this year, is searching for a federal bailout. But the Treasury should not be used to keep dying enterprises afloat.

Better in the short term would be for Congress to relax its strictures against interstate banking. In 1982 out-of-state banks were given limited authority to acquire institutions that had failed; the provision, twice extended temporarily, expires in July.

The administration and the three major banking regulatory agencies have proposed relaxing the rules to allow mergers with banks with as little as $250 million in assets, and to permit the acquisition of entire banking holding companies, as well as individual institutions, before they have formally folded. Some state regulators and local bankers are opposing the proposal, but there is no reason to allow costly bank failures when out-of-state institutions are willing to cover the losses.

Finally, Congress needs to permanently override state geographic protectionism and expand commercial bank powers to include underwriting municipal bonds, securities and commercial paper, investing in real estate and offering brokerage and insurance services.

Diversification—which has been coming slowly as technological and economic changes have overwhelmed antiquated legal prohibitions—may not save the banks that are failing today. But remedying the regulatory mistakes made a half century ago would reduce the number of banks that will close tomorrow.

## 84.  Abolish the Federal Censorship Commission

*May 31, 1984*

Congressman Mario Biaggi, a Democrat from New York, doesn't have a sense of humor. When the New York Metropolitan Opera decided to update the Verdi opera "Rigoletto" from Renaissance Italy to the Little Italy section of New York City in the 1950s, Biaggi protested that the production was offensive to Italian-Americans.

The Met eventually dropped such phrases as "a hotel in New York under control of the Mafia" from its promotional materials and withdrew the opera's libretto from the Lincoln Center bookstore. This, however, did not satisfy Biaggi, who initiated a congressional investigation of the Met and the Virginia Opera Association, which produced the new version earlier this year.

Biaggi's zany attempt to censor a harmless opera shows how quixotic self-important government officials can become. Far more serious, however, is his quest to censor the airwaves.

Biaggi wants to take away the licenses of TV stations if they portray ethnic groups, such as Italians, in a demeaning fashion. To monitor the broadcasters, he would establish an Office of Ethnic Affairs in the Federal Communications Commission, moving the FCC one step closer to becoming the Federal Censorship Commission.

Unfortunately, congressmen with no sense of humor are not the only people out to control what other Americans hear and see. The U.S. Catholic Conference has endorsed legislation to require all TV stations to run an hour of educational programming for children on weekdays. (The law would not, apparently, require children to watch the programs.)

A conference official testified that "a balance must be struck between the clear public interest needs of children . . . over against the freedom of speech arguments of broadcasters." Of course, what he really meant was that the stations weren't serving what he thought were the needs of children; the kids certainly weren't marching on Washington demanding more educational TV.

This, unfortunately, is the battle that has been going on most of this century. Which should prevail: the desires of elitists who think they know what's best for others, or the First Amendment rights of broadcasters?

Government first got into the broadcast business in 1912, when Congress authorized the secretary of commerce to hand out radio licenses. The department gave out licenses to all comers, resulting in overlapping frequencies and chaotic interference. Just as the courts began resolving the problem by creating the equivalent of property rights over broadcast channels, Congress nationalized the airwaves; the FCC was later established, in 1934, to regulate what had become public property.

The result of that regulation has been to make both radio and television as uninteresting as possible. For example, for years radio stations felt compelled to run "public service" programs—those interminable shows with unknown junior college professors talking about issues of interest only to themselves—on Sunday mornings. Thankfully, the FCC has freed the industry, and the listeners, of this burden.

Radio and TV stations often avoid controversy because of the Fairness Doctrine, which requires them to cover "both sides" of topics. Private groups have used the doctrine not to expand debate, but, instead, to scare stations into not covering issues.

In the early 1960s, for instance, the Democratic National Committee invoked the doctrine against stations that ran conservative critics of Presidents Kennedy and Johnson. Stations either dropped the commentators, or had to give the Democrats—who could well afford to pay—free time.

The equal time rule ensures that Americans who suffer through coverage of, or commercials by, one political candidate have to do so for every candidate in the race, including the Vegetarian Party candidate. As a result, broadcasters avoid staging debates—or running a candidate's old movies—so they don't have to give "equal" coverage to everyone else.

Mark Fowler, the current FCC chairman, has proposed to do away with most of these rules. Predictably, he's stirred up a hornet's nest of opposition from liberals, like Ralph Nader, who believe that the airwaves—like most other property—should belong to the government. But conservatives, like ERA opponent Phyllis Schlafly, also want to keep the FCC in business to bash liberal broadcasters.

However, in a time when there are six times as many radio and TV stations as daily newspapers in the United States—some 9,400 radio and 1,150 TV stations compared to 1,740 newspapers—the "airwave scarcity" argument for government regulation has lost all meaning. And where the technology exists to further extend broadcast spectrum use and to create definable property rights in frequencies that could be protected in court, there isn't even any need for the FCC to allocate channels.

Both the right and left use the FCC to muzzle a form of the press that should be free. We should get rid of it before the Mario Biaggis of the world decide we need a Federal Newspaper Commission, as well.

## 85.  Drop the Cable Monopoly

*June 25, 1986*

Some 25 million households across America have cable TV, but the majority of residents in the nation's capital are only viewing an endless political soap opera.

The District of Columbia City Council spent most of last summer wrangling with the local cable firm over their contract; in the Maryland suburbs a different company faces loss of its franchise after halting construction because, it says, its agreement is "commercially impracticable."

The problems facing the Washington area have recurred nationwide. But just changing firms will solve nothing if local governments continue to prohibit competition. The real problem is the use of the monopoly franchise.

Between 1979 and 1983 cable companies engaged in a frenzied bidding war for new markets. Municipalities, sensing a veritable pot of gold from controlling access, set all manner of ridiculous requirements: special channels for government and local interests, programming subsidies for favored groups, and wiring schedules based on politics rather than economics.

These sorts of terms, though justified as being in the "public interest," are really just expensive private giveaways. In Maryland's Montgomery County, for instance, the added cost of underwriting local programming alone could run $90 million over the life of the contract.

Companies generally went along with such exorbitant demands—estimated to account for fully 22 percent of cable's costs—because the firms figured they could use their monopoly position to wring sufficient revenues out of viewers. But the economic picture has gone sour, and cities as diverse as Milwaukee, Dallas, New York, and Denver have had to renegotiate their franchise agreements.

It's time localities dropped the franchise system entirely, allowing any firm to set up shop. For the argument that cable is a "natural monopoly" is just an excuse for giving local officials power to hand out favors at consumer expense.

If a specific market really can handle only one firm, there is no need to limit entry. Economists Bruce Owen and Peter Greenhalgh point out that where a firm "is responsive and efficient in its pricing and service quality then there will be little incentive for competitors to enter, and no need for an exclusionary franchise policy."

Are controls nevertheless needed to protect consumers from being gouged? To the contrary: because franchise agreements are structured to benefit interest groups and government officials, regulation inflates costs. The accounting firm of Ernst & Whinney estimates the regulatory premium for cable to be as much as $5.60 a month.

Anyway, there are no physical obstacles to more than one firm serving a particular area. In a federal district court case involving Boulder, Colo., for example, the judge concluded that "there can be competition in the marketplace, with the choice of price and service left to the consumers."

Cable companies compete head to head in Slidell, La.; Lehigh Valley, Pa.; Presque Isle, Maine; Mobile, Ala., and more than 30 other cities. The rivalry between two firms in Phoenix, Ariz. resulted in speedy wiring of the city, as companies gained subscribers by offering individual consumers, not local politicos, the best deal.

Says one observer, what distinguished Phoenix "from the run-of-the-mill cable war is that this contest was fought with trenchers and sweat, not flip charts, slide shows, and cocktail parties for community bigwigs."

Freedom for cable has even become a constitutional issue. In early June the Supreme Court ruled that cable TV services "plainly implicate First Amendment interests."

In the case, which was sent back to the district court for trial, the court of appeals blocked the city's plan to award a monopoly franchise. Doing so, said the court, was similar "to allowing the government discretion to grant a permit for the operation of newspaper vending machines only to the newspaper that the government believes 'best' serves the community.''

Observes Washington attorney Clint Bolick, ''Somehow cable television has slipped past the free enterprise bulwarks that have provided unique protection to communications media throughout American history.''

But the obvious failure of cable regulation, in the capital and around the country, gives us an opportunity to start afresh.

An open cable TV market would give consumers more of the service they actually want for a lower price. An even better reason to scrap the cable monopoly, however, is to limit the power of local government over an increasingly important form of communication. For no conceivable ''public interest'' can justify this breach of the First Amendment.

# The Energy Uncrisis

## 86. Keep Uncle Sam out of the Energy Business

*December 14, 1988*

Oil is a consumer's market, with prices having fallen roughly one-third over the past year. The continuing decline in energy costs is one reason the United States has continued to prosper economically.

So when the Organization of Petroleum Exporting Countries announced its latest agreement to cut sales and raise prices, the doomsayers made their usual appearance. America is becoming dangerously dependent on foreign oil, they warned, and the only remedy is a stiff tax on gasoline (or oil). Some even proposed subsidizing domestic producers.

But if the experience of the last decade has demonstrated anything, it is that the free market works. Throughout the 1970s the energy industry was entrapped in a web of price controls and regulations that encouraged imports and discouraged domestic production: a price explosion, gas lines and chaos in Washington ensued.

President Reagan, however, removed price controls and dismantled much of the federal regulatory empire. The result was lower prices, abundant supplies and the collapse of OPEC.

The energy cartel exercised its greatest control over the oil market in 1973, when it accounted for 56 percent of global petroleum output. As late as 1977 it still supplied more than half of the world's oil.

But OPEC has since lost much of its petroleum power. Between 1973 and 1986 OPEC production fell 41 percent. OPEC's share of international output went from 56 percent to 33 percent over the same period, and is even lower today.

The cartel's exports to the United States followed the same pattern, dropping from 74.7 percent to 41 percent of American imports between 1973 and 1986. Last year OPEC accounted for 51.4 percent of U.S. imports, but the number of barrels it shipped to this country remains fully 30 percent below 1977 levels.

And prices have collapsed. A barrel of oil cost an average of $31.77 in 1981 but only $12.66 in 1986. Adjusted for inflation that represents a fall of more than 60 percent. So even if OPEC succeeds in bumping up prices from the $10 to $12 level to $15, the cost will still be less than half what it was at the beginning of the decade.

The reason that OPEC has lost its grasp on the oil market is twofold. The first is that consumers have become more energy-efficient. Higher oil and gas prices caused people to insulate their homes, buy smaller cars and generally use less energy.

The second is the growth in non-OPEC producers. China has more than doubled its output since 1973. The Soviet Union has upped production by 40 percent. Mexico has quintupled output and Britain, which had negligible exports in 1973, now pumps roughly 2.3 million barrels a day.

In fact, OPEC's inability to dominate the market any longer was underscored by Norway's announcement, less than a week after OPEC adopted its new plan, that it planned to up production by 20 percent to 25 percent this coming year. Mexico, which also does not belong to the cartel, has vowed to follow OPEC's lead and cut its sales, but the heavily indebted Latin American state is unlikely to make more than token reductions, since it needs oil revenue to pay its bills.

Even OPEC members have an incentive to cheat. Iran, for one, is dissatisfied with the fact that its enemy Iraq has an equivalent quota; other countries will try to gain revenue by pumping a little extra oil while hoping their fellow members follow the agreement.

Moreover, as prices rise, additional U.S. production will come on line, putting downward pressure on prices. Old domestic wells cost a lot to run and are the first to shut down when market prices fall, but they still help dampen OPEC price hikes.

Though the OPEC accord provides no cause for the federal government to impose new taxes or controls, that doesn't mean there is nothing it can do to improve America's position as an oil consumer.

For instance, the Heritage Foundation's "Mandate for Leadership III" project recommends reviewing a half-dozen tax policies that currently discourage domestic exploration and production.

Moreover, the federal government should allow carefully controlled drilling in the outer-continental shelf and in the Arctic National Wildlife Refuge. Environmental groups, such as the Audubon Society, permit production in their animal reserves; similar dual use could be made of public lands. In fact, one small portion of the federal refuge, 1.5 million acres of the 19-million-acre tract, alone is thought to possess an oil field that may rival that of Alaska's Prudhoe Bay.

The Reagan administration has succeeded brilliantly in its management of energy matters by not managing. The incoming Bush administration should follow the same hands-off policy: instead of interfering, the government need only continue to stay out of the way. If it does so, OPEC will remain helpless in the face of the power of the marketplace.

## 87. Doomed Again

*November 15, 1984*

Something terrible is happening. Oil prices are falling.

Good news, you think? Lower oil prices, pundits caution, might make us complacent and eventually subject to OPEC's whims again. Unless, energy officials warn, consumers further conserve. And unless, politicians say, the government continues to subsidize uneconomic synthetic fuels projects.

Of course, a decade ago, something terrible also was happening. The Organization of Petroleum Exporting Countries embargoed oil to the United States, and in less than three months nearly quadrupled the price of petroleum.

Bad news? Of course, but we could muddle through, pundits cautioned, if the government adopted an energy policy. If, energy officials warned, consumers further conserved. And if, politicians said, the government subsidized uneconomic synthetic fuels projects.

Oil prices go up and doom approaches; oil prices go down and doom approaches. Energy, it seems, is a field that attracts the people Charles Maurice and Charles Smithson call the "doom merchants" in their excellent book, *The Doomsday Myth* (The Hoover Institution).

The doom merchants have a long and illustrious heritage dating back to Thomas Malthus, an 18th century British economist who contended that widespread famine and mass starvation were inevitable. Malthus was, of course, wrong, but that hasn't stopped others from updating his predictions.

For example, Paul Ehrlich warned of mass famines in the 1970s killing one-fifth or more of the planet's population in his 1968 book, "The Population Bomb." In 1972 the Club of Rome published perhaps the most famous doomsday report, "The Limits to Growth," which foresaw a world headed for disaster without "deliberate checks on growth."

And in 1980, the U.S. government produced "The Global 2000 Report," which concluded that "if present trends continue, the world in 2000 will be more crowded, more polluted, less stable ecologically and more vulnerable to disruption. . . ."

Indeed, doomsday books have themselves become a high-growth industry. Smithson and Maurice offer their own prediction of doom, calculating that if present trends continue, "in the year 2000 there will exist over 14 million doomsday books."

Luckily, the authors take disaster forecasts somewhat less seriously than do most doom merchants, who rely on the same sort of current trend extrapolations. The critical point so often overlooked by the modern Cassandras is that current trends never continue indefinitely.

As Smithson and Maurice explain, conditions always change because "markets work to eliminate shortages." If resources become more scarce, their prices increase (in the absence of government price controls). As a result, consumers reduce their demand and switch to substitutes, and producers search for new supplies and develop new technologies.

There are numerous examples where the market has eliminated potential crisis. A temporarily successful rubber cartel in the 1920s led to private research into synthetics; the first artificial rubber hit the market in 1931, a decade before the U.S. government financed large-scale synthetic rubber production because of World War II.

Moreover, around the turn of the century the United States faced a timber crisis; in 1905 President Theodore Roosevelt warned that "if the present rate of timber consumption is allowed to continue . . . a timber famine in the future is inevitable." But as wood became more expensive, railroad companies and other timber consumers used it more efficiently and substituted other materials for it. By 1922 the emergency had passed.

In these and many other cases the government, if it acted at all, usually made things worse—as it did during the energy crisis of the 1970s. And in the future consumers and producers will solve predicted catastrophes, like the worsening water shortage, unless the government prevents them from doing so.

Indeed, perverse state intervention is the only real danger we face. The economic vitality of the Roman Empire was destroyed by the sort of economic policies we see advocated by many people today: wage and price controls, restrictions on the movement of capital and government direction of the economy.

"Doomsday could arrive," Smithson and Maurice allow, but only "if we invite our own destruction by restricting the ability of the marketplace to function."

In recent years Americans have been inundated with frightening forecasts from a variety of doom merchants. But such projections of natural holocausts are a dime a dozen. It's time that the professional doomsayers admitted what the rest of us intuitively know to be true—that lower oil prices are good news, for example.

As Deputy Energy Secretary Danny Boggs recently told the American Association for the Advancement of Science, we're all better off with the results of the investments of our ancestors; "electronics, polio vaccine, medical technologies and everything else we have, rather than more billions of tons and barrels of oil that we didn't know how to use."

There are, indeed, few higher tributes to the practical, if not moral, virtues of a free society than the long-term progress consistently achieved and the predicted crises constantly avoided.

## 88. Deregulate Natural Gas

*October 22, 1986*

Perhaps Ronald Reagan's greatest success has been his victory in the energy war. But the economy still is suffering from legislation passed eight years ago by Congress—the Natural Gas Policy Act. While oil has been deregulated and prices consequently have plummeted, roughly half of all natural gas remains covered by incredibly complex federal price ceilings.

The reversal of a decade worth of price hikes by the Organization of Petroleum Exporting Countries provides Congress with a convenient opportunity to end the last vestiges of the government's ill-considered intervention in the energy market. Decontrolling natural gas would both increase the economy's efficiency and lower energy prices.

Natural gas first was regulated in 1954, but the consequences of doing so did not become truly disastrous until the oil crisis of the 1970s, especially during the Carter years of misguided regulation and misdirected demagoguery.

During the long, cold winter of 1976–1977 northern demand for natural gas jumped, but supplies were limited by federal price ceilings that took effect once the commodity crossed state lines. Schools and factories closed, workers were laid off and consumers shivered, while natural gas remained plentiful in Texas and other producing states, where federal controls did not apply.

Congress first passed emergency legislation to allow the sale of intrastate gas in the interstate market. And then, after one of its most bitter debates ever, Congress approved the Natural Gas Policy Act.

The NGPA applied federal price controls to all gas and made regulation permanent on "old gas," supplies discovered before passage of the bill. So-called new gas was covered by a bewildering array of regulatory categories through Jan. 1, 1985, when those limits expired.

Also in 1978 Congress passed the Fuel Use Act, which prohibited large utilities and factories from using natural gas. Normally consumers adjust their consumption as the product's price rises and falls; since Congress was holding the cost of natural gas artificially low, however, too many people wanted to use too little supply. So instead of lifting controls, Congress tried to legislate away some of the demand.

There is no way that such a regulatory scheme could operate without inflicting enormous harm on the economy. By limiting prices, Congress simultaneously reduced the incentive to increase production and stimulated demand.

Arbitrarily deciding who could and could not use natural gas guaranteed some politically fortunate consumers a cheap energy source, while forcing others, particularly large businesses, to use higher cost, alternative fuels. Holding down total demand also reduced pipeline volume, increasing the per-customer transportation charge.

And the perverse nature of the federal controls eventually forced up prices. For very low ceilings discouraged companies from increasing production of inexpensive "old" gas; instead, firms developed high-cost reserves of "new" gas, the price of which was unregulated.

Thus, partial decontrol in 1985 actually pushed down natural gas prices, contrary to consumerists' fears of a price "spike." Full deregulation, especially with the current abundance of cheap oil, would further reduce prices and rationalize a market that has been distorted by more than 30 years of federal control.

Unfortunately, while the Federal Energy Regulatory Commission has labored mightily to deregulate by administrative ruling, it has done almost all that it can: only Congress can repeal the law itself.

And the only way to get Capitol Hill to act is for the administration to propose legislation and make it a priority, akin to tax reform. All controls over both supply and demand should be eliminated simultaneously; deregulation should be immediate and total.

While such a program would stir up opposition on the left—from the Citizens-Labor Energy Coalition, the Nader groups, and the reflexive neo-socialists in Congress—"the emptiness of the arguments of those who warned of the dangers of decontrol is obvious," observes Heritage Foundation analyst Milton Copulos. For experience has shown federal energy regulation to bring price increases, supply shortages and economywide inefficiencies. Surely none of these is in the consumers' interest.

America has come a long way in six years, with a generally free energy market that is providing abundant supplies at low prices. But natural gas remains the great exception, the last bastion of perverse federal regulation. It is time Congress freed natural gas producers and consumers alike.

# 89. Let's Lease the Oceans

*August 2, 1984*

Barely five years ago we were suffering through the last of the great Energy Crisis. Prices were rising, gas lines were forming and President Carter was announcing yet another inscrutable government program destined to make us worse off.

But shortly thereafter, President Reagan dismantled much of the Carter scarcity machine—price controls, temperature restrictions, gas allocations, ad infinitum. Instead of moaning about selfish consumption, he focused on increasing energy production. One of his most important accomplishments was to grant exploration leases for 50 percent more acres of federal Outer Continental Shelf land—7.7 million acres—in 15 months than Carter did in four years.

Even so, the United States has leased barely 3 percent of the available offshore lands, roughly 30 million acres out of a total 966 million. In contrast, the United Kingdom has leased twice as much and Canada an incredible 30 times as much.

Though OCS leasing by the federal government has lagged far behind that of other countries, domestic offshore production still provides a significant boon for U.S. consumers; last year some 11 percent of oil and a quarter of natural gas produced in the United States came from federal OCS lands. And this amount could grow sharply: the federal Minerals Management Service estimates that some 43.5 billion barrels of oil and 230.6 trillion cubic feet of natural gas likely are available offshore at today's prices, more than double our current total proved reserves.

In fact, it was to dramatically increase domestic energy production that Congress amended the Outer Continental Shelf Lands Act in 1978 to "promote the swift, orderly and efficient exploration of our almost untapped domestic oil and gas resources."

But never count on Congress to be consistent. Soon thereafter it slapped a moratorium on the leasing of 700,000 acres offshore, and it expanded the moratorium to a total of 36 million acres for fiscal year 1983. It then added an additional 17 million acres this year.

Each of these moratoria has been "temporary"; each has been attached to the Interior Department appropriations bill. Now a number of coastal congressmen, fearful of the "blight" of oil rigs, are trying to extend the leasing ban yet again. In fact, a House Appropriations subcommittee voted to bar leases of some OCS land off Alaska, as well as the acres off the coasts of California, New England and Florida currently under the moratorium; the full committee wisely refused to go along. The issue is now up to the full House and the Senate.

Though nearly 900 million other unexplored acres are available for leasing, the areas placed off-limits are among the most promising, and involve almost half of the land that the Minerals Management Service has been considering offering for lease. The Interior Department figures that the 53 million acres now under congressional guard may contain as much as 1.35 billion barrels of oil and the natural gas equivalent of nearly a billion barrels of oil.

In fact, the prohibition on leasing is particularly myopic because it prevents us from making an intelligent trade-off between environmental protection and energy production, since it prevents us from knowing how much energy is out there.

In any case, the balance should not be hard to strike. Thirty years of exploration have led to no environmental damage. Even wide-scale production from some 30,000 offshore wells drilled since 1954 has resulted in only one major oil spill, in Santa Barbara, Calif., in 1969. And that accident apparently caused no permanent ecological damage. Nor has oil production hindered tourism and fishing.

Indeed, even environmentalists recognize that energy development and conservation can be entirely compatible. The National Audubon Society, for instance, allows oil and natural gas drilling on its 27,000-acre Paul J. Rainey Wildlife Sanctuary in Louisiana, which is the winter home of as many as one-third of North America's snow geese. The society has found that it can run the refuge to both protect the geese's habitat and produce energy.

At today's consumption rates and prices we need to locate some 8 million barrels of petroleum a day just to keep domestic reserves constant. If we are serious about doing so, we must turn to the millions of acres offshore, which are believed to contain more than half of America's remaining oil.

But getting serious means dropping the ban on leasing activities now. For even after new fields are found it takes up to 11 years to get them into operation—and as much as 15 years in more difficult and hostile environments. Thus, if we want adequate energy supplies in the next century, we need to be finding and developing them today.

## 90. Congress's Nuclear Agenda

*January 28, 1987*

One of the most important items of unfinished business left by Congress when it adjourned last fall was renewal of the Price-Anderson Act, which limits industry liability in the event of a nuclear accident. The legislation died in the cross-fire between environmental and industry lobbyists.

The Price-Anderson Act, originally passed in 1957, caps the industry pay-out at a maximum of $665 million, no matter how disastrous a reactor meltdown. (The utilities have to buy $160 million worth of insurance and are liable for an additional $5 million per plant if there is an accident.)

Such a settlement—the amount of which would be reduced by expenses like the industry's attorney's fees—would run far short in any serious mishap. The Soviet accident at Chernobyl, for instance, is estimated to have caused $2.5 billion in property damage.

And the General Accounting Office figures the property loss from a serious meltdown in the United States could exceed $15 billion. The human cost, with thousands of dead and injured, would run even higher.

Not only does Price-Anderson limit the libility of nuclear operators; it completely exempts nuclear designers and suppliers from any liability, even for criminal negligence.

Industry representatives justify their subsidy on the grounds that the federal government has limited the liability of other industries, including airlines and maritime. But, observes a report prepared by a coalition including the Environmental Policy Institute, the protection afforded the nuclear industry "is unprecedented in any other American law."

In no other industry are companies covered for gross negligence or, like nuclear suppliers, exempted from all liability. Moreover, limits on personal injury awards are set on a per-person basis, rather than in aggregate.

The industry then contends that nuclear power is a special case and could not operate without the liability cap. But there is no Price-Anderson Act for potentially dangerous facilities like hydroelectric dams or petrochemical plants.

Anyway, if nuclear power really can't exist without the liability cap, then the plants should close. No energy source should be developed unless its benefits exceed its costs, including accident risks. And the Price-Anderson Act hides, rather than eliminates, an important cost of fission energy.

There is reason to doubt the hard-luck stories of utility executives, however. In 1983 the Nuclear Regulatory Commission urged Congress to force nuclear power firms to self-insure; the NRC concluded that the industry could easily afford an annual $10 million deferred premium, which would have been less than 2 percent of average utility costs.

Moreover, the utilities currently buy roughly $1 billion worth of accident insurance to protect their own property. Firms pay an average of $5 million a year on premiums—in contrast to $400,000 for coverage under Price-Anderson—and commit themselves to contribute up to $40 million in the event of an accident. The comparable deferred payment under Price-Anderson is just $5 million.

Would it be too much to ask the industry to spend as much to protect the property of others as it spends to cover itself? The Environmental Policy Institute estimates that this would make as much as $20 billion in liability insurance available.

Of course, Price-Anderson is not the only federal subsidy for the nuclear power industry. The government has underwritten nuclear research, waste disposal and fuel-enrichment processes. Complains one Heritage Foundation report, the Reagan administration "gives the appearance of being for a free market in all things conventional, but virtually socialist on nuclear power."

And these subsidies should be killed as well. But it is Price-Anderson that has provided the biggest windfall for the nuclear power industry. And it is the most unfair subsidy of all, limiting as it does the ability of potential victims to seek compensation for their injuries.

As Congress ends the subsidies, it also should reform the regulatory climate facing the nuclear industry. U.S. rules are far more complex than those of nations like France, but do not necessarily result in safer plants. As a result, it takes years longer and costs millions more than it should to construct nuclear facilities. Only by removing both the government's helpful and harmful hands will we know whether nuclear power is economical and worth the risk.

Last fall Congress seemed prepared to extend Price-Anderson, though with a higher liability cap. But it's time fission energy survived in the marketplace on its own, just like any other fuel. Congress has twice extended the act since 1957; this year it should let the law expire.

# Cleaning Up America

## 91. The Clean Water Pork Barrel

*November 26, 1986*

Despite the flood of bad laws emanating from Congress before the November election, President Reagan blocked only one from taking effect, the Clean Water Act. Environmentalists, of course, were outraged; the incoming Democratic congressional leadership says it may simply repass the same measure.

Yet despite the fuss, Mr. Reagan was right to veto the legislation. For the bill, which provided $18 billion in local sewage treatment grants, was a pork barrel designed to win votes, not clean up water.

Congress first took an interest in the issue in 1899, when it voted to prohibit discharges into navigable waterways without a permit. But the landmark water legislation, the Clean Water Act, was passed only 14 years ago.

The long-range goal of that law was "to restore and maintain" the "integrity of the nation's waters" by eliminating all discharges. The legislation imposed strict technology-specific standards on industry and subsidized local treatment plants.

Water quality in the United States has improved as a result, but the cost has been enormous: between 1972 and 1984, estimates Paul Tramontozzi, with the Center for the Study of American Business, water pollution abatement activities ran $205.3 billion.

Unfortunately, observes Tramontozzi, Congress's basic strategy—of heavy regulation and large-scale subsidies—"has constituted a poor investment." For we could be getting far better environmental protection at far less cost.

The national goal of "zero discharges" in waterways allows no trade-off between health risk, which may be low, and cost, even though the marginal expense of eliminating smaller and smaller amounts of pollutants rises exponentially. A 1983 study of waste treatment processes found that it cost 22 cents a pound to remove 90 percent of one form of pollutant, "Biochemical Oxygen Demand." The price of cleaning the final 3 percent was $5.44 a pound.

Moreover, the sewage treatment subsidy program—the reason President Reagan vetoed the latest bill—is badly flawed. For instance, the grants focus on construction costs, inducing localities to build needlessly expensive plants that often are difficult to maintain; the General Accounting Office has found that more than half the facilities operate inefficiently because managers spend too little on maintenance.

Many of the plants have not even addressed real pollution needs. A 1981 *Washington Post* study concluded that "there is no evidence that the $30 billion grants program [now up to $44 billion] has helped measurably" to improve water quality.

And funding government expenditures for "end of the pipe treatment" discourages private polluters from adopting less expensive process changes that would reduce total emissions and reclaim higher quality waste products. This problem is exacerbated by mandatory technology controls, which both force firms to adopt specific, inefficient forms of pollution abatement equipment and essentially set a floor as well as a ceiling on plant discharges.

Indeed, the technology standards—a bureaucratic nightmare involving more than 60,000 individual polluters—are grossly inefficient. This form of detailed regulation does not take into account the ability of the individual business to cut its emissions, which varies widely.

Thus, major revisions are needed in the law before Congress reauthorizes the Clean Water Act again.

First, Congress should drop the grant program. The federal government is running a huge deficit; it doesn't have $18 billion to hand out for often unnecessary, always gold-plated local projects.

Second, the federal government needs to drop its "command and control" regulatory approach, whereby it specifies the clean-up technologies to be used by firms. Instead, the government needs to rely on overall output-oriented emission regulations.

That is, the government should decide the level of water cleanliness that it wants—after conducting a sensible cost-benefit analysis—and have business meet those standards by whatever means are most efficient. Such a market-oriented system could involve an effluent fee, essentially a tax on each additional unit of emissions. Or the government could auction off permits to pollute up to the total level of allowable emissions.

Both systems would force firms to internalize all the costs of production. In this way, businesses would have a continuing incentive to cut their emissions and firms that could most cost-effectively reduce pollution would automatically cut their discharges the most.

If the Democrats want to show that they deserve to govern, they need to eschew the political temptation of simply re-enacting this year's bill. We can better protect the environment at less cost, but to do so Congress must set aside pork barrel politics.

## 92. Toxic Solutions to Toxic Problems

*November 7, 1985*

Congress is preparing to turn yet another environmental issue into a self-serving pork barrel. Intended to clean up hazardous waste dumps across the United States, the new super-"Superfund" would actually impede environmental protection while creating a multibillion-dollar boondoggle financed by a dangerous new tax.

Toxic waste has become the latest environmental cause celebre. As well-publicized waste dumps like New York's Love Canal panicked the public, Congress responded with the $1.6 billion Superfund in 1980.

Now up for reauthorization, Superfund was supposed to be used to clean up dangerous "orphan sites," where the dumpers either could not be found or were insolvent. Unfortunately, however, the government has been more interested in spending money than in protecting people.

Indeed, we really do not even know how serious the problem of toxic waste is—barely 6 percent of cancer is thought to be the result of all environmental causes, compared to 35 percent linked to diet alone, for instance.

Probably the most serious threat posed by chemical dumps is water contamination. But, says Washington analyst James Bovard, "as a result of the Superfund's 'act now, understand later' mandate, we know little more about groundwater pollution today than in 1980."

In fact, Superfund actually has made waste cleanup more difficult by unjustifiably expanding liability for site cleanup beyond the traditional legal grounds of fault and causation. As a result, litigation has exploded; legal expenses eventually may exceed cleanup costs.

And, according to an analysis by the Washington, D.C.-based Competitive Enterprise Institute: "The failure to correctly and clearly apply traditional and well-understood legal principles to the problem . . . may well perversely encourage more pollution by providing less-effective legal sanctions over those who are, in fact, polluters."

Moreover, the revenue mechanism, a special tax on the petrochemical and oil companies, gives culpable parties no incentive to be more careful. The companies paying to clean up waste sites are not the ones primarily responsible for creating the hazards; in fact, says Milton Copulos of the Heritage Foundation, chemical firms have "been among those leading the effort to reduce hazardous waste generation."

Finally, the Superfund has become the ultimate political "free good." Uncle Sam picks up 90 percent of the tab, with states covering the remaining 10 percent. Localities—which traditionally have handled problems like contaminated water supplies—therefore are demanding comprehensive cleanup projects, irrespective of the health threat or cost involved.

Unfortunately, the proposals now before Congress would make Superfund even worse. Some legislators and interest groups want to expand the eligible sites to include almost any disposal area, regardless of the safety threat. Others, warns Copulos, are pushing to "impose stringent, unrealistic deadlines for site cleanups" and create "a vast new entitlements program under the guise of 'victim compensation.' "

The pending legislation would also cost up to $13.5 billion—eight times current outlays. And some environmentalists speak of eventually spending $40 billion.

To finance the expanded Superfund, Congress is preparing to impose a Value Added Tax on manufacturers. This tax also would hit polluter and non-polluter alike, giving companies no reason to improve their waste-disposal techniques.

It would also be the first VAT in America, and would provide Congress with an entirely new vehicle to increase tax revenues. For the VAT, essentially a national sales tax, is a hidden tax which could be hiked with relative ease; VAT rates in Europe have mushroomed.

Countering the threat posed by toxic waste sites around the country is a price we must pay for living in a technological age. However, Congress should reshape Superfund to meet the goal of environmental protection—rather than pork barrel politics.

Most important, the program should emphasize research to determine the magnitude of the problem facing us. Remedial efforts should be based on the fundamental principle that the polluter pays.

Legal liability rules also should be changed to encourage the re-emergence of private hazardous insurance. And any cleanup program should be narrowly focused on truly hazardous disposal sites: We cannot afford a vast new federal dole.

The renewal of Superfund is fast becoming an environmental as well as fiscal disaster. President Reagan should make good on his threat to veto the bills now working their way through Congress. Only responsible executive leadership will stop Superfund from becoming Superfiasco.

# 93. Preserving America's Wilderness

*October 17, 1985*

It is still early autumn, yet the first snows have fallen on nearby hillsides and distant peaks alike in southeastern Montana.

Much of this scenic land is part of Uncle Sam's 82-million-acre wilderness system, on which no commercial development, construction or use of motorized vehicles or equipment is allowed. Yet federal protection is proving neither certain nor cheap.

First, wilderness preservation depends on a sympathetic Congress. But political majorities are ephemeral, ever subject to changing crises and voters' whims.

And the wilderness system, no matter how sacred it seems today, is not exempt from such political pressures. Developers and environmentalists have clashed over access to such preserves as Glacier Peak Wilderness in Washington, and many other federal areas where mining and energy interests either possess pre-wilderness development rights or would like to operate.

Moreover, pressure to open up the wilderness would increase in any future energy or minerals crisis. The government already has "undesignated" wilderness land in one instance.

Nor is business the only wilderness antagonist. Off-road vehicle enthusiasts, for instance, and hunters often want to use "their" land in ways that conflict with environmental goals.

The fact that resource development may be worthwhile illustrates the major cost of federal wilderness lands: the lost opportunity to extract the underlying wealth.

The bulk of the wilderness is most valuable as it is, undeveloped, but there are some important exceptions. The Forest Service, for instance, has found prospective wilderness areas with important energy and mineral potential or even proven deposits.

Unfortunately, the political process does badly in accommodating both wilderness preservation and resource development; where neither environmentalists nor business owns the land, neither gains any benefit from recognizing the interest of the other. Therefore the environmental lobby pushes to lock up the land while developers press for uncontrolled access.

Yet we can have our cake and eat it, too, so to speak. For example, one firm, Energy Fuels Nuclear Inc., successfully negotiated with environmentalists and Congress to exempt from wilderness protection those areas with high-grade uranium deposits in Arizona.

EFN's effort took seven years, however: the company would have been better off if the land had been owned by a private party, like the Audubon Society.

For the national Audubon Society allows limited oil production in its Louisiana Rainey Reserve. As owner of the animal and bird sanctuary, the society had to balance the opportunity for financial gain—and thus an improved ability to protect wildlife elsewhere—against the potential for environmental harm.

The Michigan Audubon Society faced a similar situation with its Bernard W. Baker Sanctuary, and chose to permit drilling, as well. But the resident sandhill cranes remain undisturbed, since Michigan Petroleum uses advanced technologies to reduce noise and contain drilling fluids.

The Audubon Society experiences demonstrate an alternative to federal control that would simultaneously ensure the permanent protection of wilderness lands and adequate consideration of the opportunity cost of development: privatization. The federal system simply could be sold off. Or, lest people fear that large developers would snap up all 82 million acres—unlikely since most wilderness has limited value to profit-making businesses—Uncle Sam could give wilderness lands to well-established environmental groups.

A less radical reform, which would maintain public ownership of wilderness areas while making its managers accountable for any development potential, has been proposed by Richard Stroup and John Baden of the Montana-based Political Economy Research Center. They would establish a wilderness endowment board to manage wilderness lands.

Board members, appointed by the president and confirmed by the Senate, would be empowered to sell development rights and trade acreage, if doing so would help advance wilderness values. The board would not be subject to the normal political pressures that bedevil the Forest Service and the Interior Department, though Congress still could undesignate wilderness land.

America's wilderness remains at the center of a never-ending political struggle.

John Oakes, former senior editor of *The New York Times,* complains that the national preserves are under assault from "real estate promoters, mining operators, big-game guides and hunters."

Now—when there is no impending resource crisis or legislative deadline—is the time to consider how to preserve the nation's pristine lands while allowing valuable development to proceed. Either privatization or a Wilderness Endowment Board would provide better protection at lower cost in the years ahead.

# 94. Sacred Cows Home on the Range

*June 27, 1985*

The chances of really cutting the federal budget seem to be shrinking daily. And no small share of the blame rests with Westerners, who are supposed to be the quintessential Americans: self-reliant, suspicious of Washington and dedicated to free enterprise and private property. The problem is they are—except when the federal government is helping them.

For that reason, a region that gave Mr. Reagan 60 percent of its presidential votes is leading the opposition to many of his budget-cutting initiatives.

Sens. Mark Hatfield, James McClure and Robert Packwood, for example, Republicans and committee chairmen all, have been busy fighting proposals to trim subsidized power, timber sales, mineral leases, farming, rural development, parks and grazing land.

Shouldn't Westerners give up a little of their federal largess when their fellow countrymen are losing money for programs like Amtrak, Urban Development Action Grants and revenue sharing?

"We've got to work on the deficit," admits Maxine Albers, a Republican county commissioner from Colorado, "but we find ourselves in the same position as everybody else—cut, but cut somebody else's program."

Among the most fervent critics of President Reagan's budget cutting is Idaho's McClure. The chairman of the Energy and Natural Resources Committee, McClure spares no opportunity to attack federal spending. But when it comes to programs that benefit his state, he instead reserves his attacks for the "OMB ideology" behind the administration's proposed cuts.

Indeed, McClure and fellow "conservative" Sen. Malcolm Wallop of Wyoming have joined with Reps. Morris Udall of Arizona and John Seiberling of Ohio, both liberal Democrats, in developing legislation to hold down grazing fees for public lands.

The federal government currently owns half of the West, and more of states such as Idaho. Much of that land—307 million acres worth—currently is leased out to cattlemen for $1.35 a month per animal. The fees actually have fallen in recent years even though a new federal study estimates the average market rate for grazing leases to be between $6.53 and $6.87 a month. Leases on better quality land run as much as $10 a month per animal.

Moreover, as range fees have declined—raising only $23 million last year—federal range management expenses have increased. Including the costs of surveys and other such services that are required when the government leases land, Department of Interior economist Robert Nelson estimates that the government spends between $100 million and $200 million annually to administer its rangeland.

Artifically low grazing fees also have indirectly reduced the land's quality. In 1976, for example, the Interior Department admitted that 83 percent of the public rangeland was in "less than satisfactory condition." The problem, point out Daniel and Nancy Ferguson in their angry book, *Sacred Cows at the Public Trough* (Maverick Publications), "is that the ridiculously low cost of public forage invites overgrazing and makes profitable the grazing of degraded public lands that could not support grazing in a free-market economy."

Thus, the administration, in an attempt to both cut costs and enhance environmental protection, has proposed examination of several alternative pricing structures. But stockmen—who have cultivated an image of independence "roaming the range"—view the attempt to make them pay a fair market price for their forage as un-American. Cheap rangeland, it seems, is an entitlement just like Social Security.

Indeed, it is precisely this attitude that derailed the administration's modest land privatization program. The Interior Department identified some 4.4 million acres of public land—less than 1 percent of the total 700 million acres of federal holdings—as suitable for sale. But McClure effectively blocked the administration's efforts.

He "just shut us down," says one Office of Management and Budget official.

Why? McClure is quite candid about wanting the taxpayers to continue underwriting Westerners' use of federal land. In Idaho, he points out, you can hunt almost anywhere for free, while in a state like Maryland you have to pay to use private property.

"I rather like the difference in favor of public access," he allows. "So do most of the people who live in my state."

Unfortunately, everyone likes having someone else pay his way. In fact, this is why we have a federal program for every interest group. Westerners don't like having to fund Food Stamps and subsidize Amtrak, but when it comes to grazing their cattle or hunting. . . .

We live in an acquisitive society, in which almost everyone, conservative as well as liberal, seems to believe that someone—anyone—owes him a living. And though ideological opposites like James McClure and Morris Udall disagree on many issues, they do agree on one thing: the importance of protecting programs that benefit their constituents.

One by one, the sacred cows are escaping the Reagan Revolution roundup. Unfortunately, they seem to have found a perfectly comfortable home on the range out West.

# Free Trade Is Fair Trade

## 95. The Competitiveness Scam

*March 4, 1987*

Politicians like Congressman Richard Gephardt of Missouri, the first announced Democratic presidential candidate, are fond of promising to make America competitive again. But all they are doing is presenting their familiar protectionist nostrums in attractive new packaging.

Their rush to protect domestic manufacturers from foreign competition will further impoverish consumers. For trade barriers are already costing U.S. citizens $65 billion a year, five times as much as in 1975.

Because of import restrictions, sugar runs several times the world price and autos cost one-third more than they should. The prices of rubber boots, sweaters, jeans, gloves, heavy motorcycles, purses, teddy bears, pickup trucks, clock radios, steel, machine tools and lumber also have been grossly inflated by trade restraints.

Yet all this "protection" has not made American producers more competitive. The government has limited foreign steel shipments since 1968, but one-third of the domestic industry's capacity is obsolescent and its labor pay scales are excessive.

In fact, import barriers, though hiking short-term profits, reduce the pressure on firms to make fundamental reforms. Argues Merrill Lynch analyst Charles Bradford, "An industry is always weaker after protection."

But the ugly reality of American protectionism has been lost in the hysteria over the trade deficit. Senators Lloyd Bentsen, D-Texas, and John Danforth, R-Missouri, recently introduced legislation that would mandate retaliation against foreign nations and give greater assistance to domestic industries. Even worse is Gephardt's bill, which would impose quotas and hike tariffs, threatening to trigger a full-blown trade war.

Unfortunately, most labor unions and many companies are supporting this counterproductive strategy. Lane Kirkland, president of the AFL-

CIO, hails Gephardt's brutal attack on international commerce as "a constructive beginning to overcome the trade crisis."

And Anthony Harrigan, president of the U.S. Business and Industrial Council, argues that we must "take whatever steps are needed to safeguard our industries," including imposing new trade restraints. Other business organizations, such as the National Association of Manufacturers, also have climbed on the protectionist bandwagon.

Yet despite all the political hand-wringing, the economy has proved to be remarkably resilient, creating 12 million new jobs over the last five years.

Senator Bentsen, for one, concedes this increased employment—during a period in which we were supposed to be "deindustrializing"—but argues that the jobs have been primarily low-paying service work. He's wrong, however: *Newsweek*'s economics writer Robert Samuelson calls that notion "economic fiction."

In fact, the high/low pay work mix has remained essentially unchanged for a decade or more. And though one-fifth of the workers who lost their jobs in factory closures between 1979 and 1984 ended up in jobs paying at least 20 percent less than before, one-third of the displaced workers found new work paying an extra 20 percent or more.

But if Congress wants American firms to keep producing new jobs, it needs to resist proposals to encumber business with restrictions on plant closings, requirements to provide parental leave, and so on. Europe, for instance, has limited firms' ability to fire workers. Instead of saving employment, this legislation has discouraged new job creation; that continent's unemployment rate has jumped from 2 percent to 11 percent since 1970.

Defensive measures are not enough, however. For the economy to grow even faster in the future, existing government regulations on workers and employers alike must be lifted.

Ed Hudgins of the Heritage Foundation points to federal labor laws that raise business costs and antitrust rules that discourage research cooperation as two areas needing reform. Further, he proposes that the government reduce the cost of capital by cutting corporate tax rates and ending the double taxation of dividends (which are now taxed as part of corporate profits and again when paid out to shareholders).

Most important, the federal government needs to reduce its share of the nation's economic resources by cutting spending and taxes. For despite Reagan's rhetoric, under his administration, government outlays have grown as a percentage of gross national product and tax revenues are up substantially.

Competitiveness has become the new economic battle-cry, but legislation introduced by ambitious politicoes like Gephardt and Bentsen would do far more harm than good. For true competitiveness will only come by freeing up the international marketplace, not closing it down.

## 96. Free the Japanese Autos

*January 13, 1988*

Seven years ago newly inaugurated Ronald Reagan abandoned his previous support for free trade and restricted Japanese auto imports. He called the limits temporary and "voluntary"—after threatening to legislate quotas if Japan did not comply.

Detroit said it merely wanted a little time in which to become more competitive. General Motors' president asked for just two or three years' breathing space; then, he promised, U.S. auto firms would battle the Japanese head-to-head. Chrysler's Lee Iacocca, too, proclaimed that all his company needed to succeed was a brief respite from foreign competition.

However, in 1983 the carmakers took a new tack. They lobbied the administration to retain import restraints until the Japanese established auto plants in the United States.

Two years later Ford and the United Auto Workers (UAW) made another demand: Japan had to hike the yen's value. The quotas could not be dropped, they argued, until Japanese imports were made more expensive and the price of American exports fell.

It is now 1988. American automakers have been insulated from vigorous foreign competition for nearly seven years. Japanese companies have been producing cars in the United States since 1982.

And the dollar has fallen to record lows. In fact, the yen is 50 percent more valuable now than it was in 1985; the cost of Japanese cars has jumped 20 percent over the same period.

But what does Ford President Donald Petersen want Uncle Sam to do? Slash Japanese imports—now 2.3 million cars a year—by more than one-fourth.

Petersen argues that such a cut is justified because many of the Japanese autos now produced in the United States use Japanese parts. But Ford's greed is matched only by its hypocrisy: all of the domestic American manufacturers also use foreign parts.

In any case, Petersen's proposal is based purely on naked self-interest. The American car manufacturers never intended to use the import restraints to become more competitive; even Rep. Richard Gephardt, the

Democratic presidential candidate who is pushing for a trade war to gain a few votes, acknowledges that Japan still makes the finest autos: "All the best-rated cars were Japanese. All the worst-rated cars were American."

Instead of using the extra time and money to improve its products, Detroit raised its prices at every opportunity, raking in hefty profits and handing out generous executive bonuses.

In 1980 the average new car cost $7,574. Last year its price was 80 percent higher: $13,520. As a share of family income, autos now cost 25 percent more.

Indeed, the International Monetary Fund estimates that the first three years of auto restraints alone cost American consumers $17 billion. Yet Petersen wants to wring even more out of consumers.

The UAW, of course, argues that import limits, despite their high cost, are necessary to protect jobs. In fact, the union has supported everything from quotas to the draconian domestic content bill, which would have required cars sold in America to be built here, in an effort to inflate the already generous wages paid to its members.

However, Reagan's quotas cost U.S. consumers nearly $160,000 a year for every auto industry job saved. We would be better off simply paying displaced workers their old wages.

And the belief that import quotas save even one job overall is a pernicious illusion. For making people spend more on high-priced U.S. cars leaves them with less money to buy other—American—goods and services.

The result is lower employment elsewhere in the economy. A Wharton Econometrics study estimated that if everyone who bought a foreign car between 1981 and 1985 instead had purchased a more expensive domestic model, the United States actually would have lost 4,000 jobs.

Ford Motor Co. is sitting on $9 billion in cash; it, not the larger General Motors, is America's most profitable automaker. Yet Donald Petersen isn't satisfied: he wants the government to guarantee even higher earnings for his company.

In contrast, GM, with bulging inventories and stagnant sales, has just announced that it is taking the one, simple step that will substantially boost its sales—a price cut. However, it is doing so only because of its deteriorating market share, down nearly one-fifth over a year ago. Until now GM had remained more committed to squeezing every last dollar out of buyers than in rebuilding its competitive position.

The Reagan administration should live up to its free market rhetoric and stop kowtowing to industry pressure, dropping the "voluntary" limits on Japanese autos. It's time that America's carmakers earned money the old-fashioned way: by producing a superior product that satisfies consumers.

## 97. Drop the Steel Quotas

*March 9, 1989*

Caterpillar Inc., a major manufacturer of heavy construction equipment, is one of America's leading exporters. But it is also one of many domestic firms that are losing business to foreign concerns because U.S. restrictions on steel imports have sharply boosted production costs.

The Reagan administration imposed the "Voluntary Restraint Agreements" (VRAs), as the steel quotas are termed in today's Orwellian newspeak, five years ago. The restrictions expire in September, but the steel industry has already begun lobbying to extend them.

And the manufacturers' influence with the Bush administration is showing. Commerce Secretary Robert Mosbacher recently said, "I think the question is not whether we will, but how long should we" continue protecting the industry.

The import quotas were originally intended to be temporary, an emergency measure to allow the struggling steel makers to retool. And the industry has dramatically streamlined its operations—running at 96 percent of capacity last year, compared to just 70 percent in 1985.

The steel makers also have benefited from the fall in the dollar. As a result, reports the Stern Group, U.S. prices are competitive internationally for the first time in two decades. Indeed, the industry, which collected $2 billion in profits last year, now boasts that it can produce steel cheaper than Japan, West Germany and South Korea.

Why, then, are the steel makers afraid to compete in the marketplace?

The industry argues that some foreign firms are underwritten by their governments, but it's not clear that such support is as great as the U.S. producers would have us believe. Moreover, American firms have received their own subsidies over the years—millions in loans and loan guarantees.

Anyway, Uncle Sam shouldn't be expected to protect business from every vagary in the international marketplace. The mere fact that the trading world is unfair doesn't mean that consumers should be stuck with the bill.

And the cost of protecting some of America's biggest corporations has been high. The Stern Group estimates that steel prices have increased an average of 15 percent since 1986; the costs of some specialty products, such as stainless steel, have jumped 30 percent to 40 percent. As a result, steel buyers had to spend an extra $6.5 billion last year alone.

Moreover, shortages of some products have developed because foreign manufacturers are barred from shipping additional supplies. All told, "The VRAs have contributed to steep price increases, lengthening lead times and sharply reduced tonnages," says Andrew Sharkey, president of the Steel Service Center Institute.

Unfortunately, price increases for steel, a basic commodity, ripple throughout the economy, raising the cost of everything from tools to washing machines. And not only do consumers pay more, but rising prices reduce the demand for steel-intensive products, putting employees in such industries as autos, machinery and metal manufacturers, who outnumber those in the steel industry more than 25-to-one, out of work. The Center for the Study of American Business estimates that the VRAs saved about 17,000 steel industry jobs but destroyed 52,400 jobs in steel-consuming industries.

Perhaps the greatest irony, however, is that steel quotas, intended to improve America's standing internationally, make many U.S. firms less competitive. Some companies are losing domestic market share to lower-cost importers.

Davis Walker Corp., for instance, says that it has had to pay 10 percent to 15 percent more than its foreign competitors for steel, allowing them to undercut its prices for hangers, mattress box springs and other products. As a result, the firm has lost business and laid off workers.

Moreover, U.S. manufacturers, which accounted for 61 percent of U.S. exports in 1986, are losing sales overseas. In some industries steel accounts for 20 percent or more of costs, so even small hikes in prices and minor disruptions in supply put U.S. firms at a serious competitive disadvantage.

"We had the opportunity to pick up business overseas, but we couldn't get enough (steel)," says Richard Walsh, an executive vice president at Mondie Forge Co.

In fact, the U.S. government's intermittent protection of the steel industry over the last 20 years is one of the main reasons domestic manufacturers lost ground during the 1970s. Continuing this misguided policy will prevent America's industrial sector from ever fully recovering.

Everyone wants a healthy steel industry. But we shouldn't sacrifice the well-being of the rest of the economy to guarantee the profits for a few businesses with disproportionate political clout.

Instead, it's time to deregulate the steel market and drop the import quotas. During the campaign President Bush resisted the Democrats' protectionist demagoguery. He should now put his free trade rhetoric into effect.

# 98. Kill the Textile Bill

*September 21, 1988*

The clothing trade is one of the most protected industries in America. Tariffs average 18 percent and there are 1,500 different textile and apparel quotas.

As a result, industry profits were up 8.6 percent last year, on top of a staggering 67 percent jump in 1986. Earnings for the second quarter of 1988 rose 61 percent over the same period last year.

Employment in the apparel industry has increased since 1985. Moreover, between 1982 and 1987 textile stock prices jumped 838 percent—not bad for an industry that claims it's about to go under.

Unfortunately, consumers have not fared as well as producers.

William Kline of the Institute for International Economics estimates that textile import restrictions cost about $20 billion annually—$238 per household. Poor families, who devote a larger portion of their incomes to necessities such as clothes, are the hardest hit; about 3.6 percent of their limited incomes goes to enrich the apparel industry.

And consumers will have to ante up even more—another $80 to $120 per household—if the textile legislation just passed by Congress becomes law. The bill, which President Reagan has vowed to veto, would further limit clothing imports.

"This is about the survival of the textile industry," pontificated South Carolina Sen. Ernest Hollings, even as U.S. exports were rising 22 percent over last year.

But consumers would not be the only victims of new import restraints. As prices rose, sales would fall, putting retail workers in the unemployment line.

The International Business and Economic Research Corp. warns that in excess of 52,000 sales and related jobs would be destroyed by the textile bill—more than the number of factory workers whose positions would be "protected."

Moreover, if Washington keeps out foreign clothes, American exporters will be excluded in turn. One European official, for instance, warns that the Common Market nations would be "obliged" to retaliate if the textile bill becomes law.

Among the most vulnerable industries is agriculture. Some 85 percent of U.S. farm shipments go to the 40 countries that would be harmed most by the textile bill. These countries will not stand idly by if Washington destroys their domestic textile industries. In fact, when the United States restricted $50 million worth of Chinese textile imports in 1983, that country canceled $699 million in planned wheat purchases.

But farmers are not the only people whose livelihoods depend on exports. Today some 5.5 million jobs are tied to merchandise sales abroad.

Anyway, Congress' rush to protect the textile industry, occurring so soon after its passage of the omnibus trade bill, when legislators proclaimed themselves to be "shocked, shocked" over foreign trade barriers, is the grossest form of hypocrisy.

The United States shelters roughly 35 percent of its manufactured goods from foreign competition, up from just 8 percent in 1975. With restrictions on everything from cars to semiconductor chips to mushrooms to clothespins, the United States is more protectionist than Japan.

And Charles Oliver of the Washington-based Citizens for a Sound Economy Foundation figures this melange of trade barriers cost the economy some $65 billion in 1986 alone. Textile quotas and tariffs were the most expensive, followed by limits on imports of steel, dairy products and sugar. Cars, personal computers, peanuts and a host of other goods also cost more because of tariffs and other trade restrictions.

Moreover, these costs ripple through the economy, making other domestic manufacturers less competitive internationally. Automakers have to pay more for steel; computer manufacturers must spend more on semiconductor chips. And so on.

The problem of protectionism ultimately comes down to the imbalance between visible benefits and invisible costs. Textile workers in South Carolina know when Sen. Hollings votes to cut imports. But the workers at a small clothing retailer that fails because of higher apparel costs aren't aware when Sen. Hollings votes to put them out of work.

Congress seems to have declared war on the global economy, first passing the recent trade bill, signed by President Reagan, and now voting to impose new restrictions on textile imports. This is economic royalism at its worst, ripping off poor people to provide bigger dividends for shareholders and bonuses for executives.

It is also stupid. The United States became the most prosperous nation on earth by promoting and participating in an open international trading system. But Congress now risks igniting the sort of devastating trade war that greatly exacerbated the Great Depression. Then everyone—including U.S. textile workers—will lose.

## 99. No Protection for Semiconductors

*August 3, 1988*

These are boom times for the semiconductor chip industry. Sales around the world are expected to be up 30 percent this year.

But U.S. firms—with profits of $1.5 billion last year, more than double the $633 million earned in 1986—are pleading poverty. Two years ago the Reagan administration imposed on Japan a pact setting minimum prices and restricting competition for U.S. firms. That agreement collapsed in June, however, and American manufacturers are now demanding a new round of government protection.

In fact, Irwin Federman, chairman of the Semiconductor Industry Association, argues that America must "repel" Japan's semiconductor "attack." He wants $350 million in tariffs and $100 million in federal research subsidies.

More government intervention is the last thing that either U.S. consumers or chip producers need, however. For instance, the 1986 accord as much as quadrupled prices, harming domestic industries that buy chips. American computer makers lost sales, profits, and jobs—between 7,000 and 11,000, according to a new study by economist Arthur Denzau, with Washington University's Center for the Study of American Business.

The protectionist pact has also slowed the introduction of U.S.-made hardware and software. Author George Gilder cites as examples delays in the development of new Apple, Sun Microsystem, Hewlett-Packard and Compaq products. As a result, Japanese firms threaten to make serious inroads in a market heretofore controlled by U.S. manufacturers.

And, as is usually the case with protectionist measures, average consumers have had to pay more. Computer prices have been falling for years, but the drop has markedly slowed. In fact, in May Sun Microsystems imposed an unprecedented surcharge on its add-on memory package.

But the companies that have been "protected" have nevertheless continued to lose ground to the Japanese, which should come as no surprise. During the late 1970s and early 1980s they let their R&D outlays fall to 6 percent to 7 percent of sales, half that of Japanese firms; the Japanese have also been spending more on plant and equipment. Yet federal protection, by reducing the competitive pressure on American companies, has encouraged them to invest less.

Not that all domestic firms are in trouble. Hundreds of smaller U.S. chip makers are prospering, dominating specialized markets, such as EE-PROMs. In fact, over the last five years some 100 entrepreneurial chip firms have started up.

U.S. manufacturers also continue to rule the microprocessor market, which ranks second in importance to Japanese-dominated DRAM production. In fact, Japan's biggest chip maker, NEC, is using U.S.-made Intel chips in the personal computers that it exports.

Moreover, the Japanese lead in DRAM chips could be quickly eroded by lower-cost competitors in South Korea or elsewhere. To break into the microprocessor market, in contrast, the Japanese would have to either achieve a marked technological breakthrough or develop the ability to run existing software supported by American chips without infringing the patents of U.S. firms, neither of which is likely.

Anyway, the fastest growing chip market in the future is likely to be for customized chips, designed to meet the needs of specific businesses and products. And Japan's ability to mass produce DRAMs will not carry over into this area.

Ironically, writes Gilder, through the 1986 pact "the United States bailed out Japan's semiconductor industry at precisely the time when Japan's own information sector industrial policies are in disarray."

Despite intensive Japanese attempts to dominate the computer industry the U.S. lead in software has actually been growing; American production is five times that of Japan. U.S. dominance of the hardware trade has slipped some, but America still makes two-thirds more computers than Japan.

And though Japan has made substantial gains in the chip market, U.S. firms collectively outproduce the Japanese. IBM remains the world's largest manufacturer of DRAMs; Intel is the fastest growing big firm. The 1986 agreement actually helped turn around a Japanese industry that lost some $4 billion during the mid-1980s due to overproduction.

If Uncle Sam gives in to industry pressure for new protectionist measures, it may end up ensuring eventual Japanese dominance of the entire information market.

Warns Denzau, "We are sacrificing the future to regain the past."

Everyone, including America's semiconductor chip manufacturers, will ultimately prosper only in a free and open market.

## 100. Casein for America

*October 15, 1986*

No session of Congress seems to end without an attempt to limit imports of casein, a milk protein. And this year has been no different; a proposed amendment to the Omnibus Trade Bill, as well as several separate measures, would restrict the availability of casein.

Casein is used both in manufactured products and foods. Glue, cosmetics, and pharmaceuticals rely on one form; the edible version goes into frozen pizza, infant formula, cake mixes, potato chips and host of other products.

All told, more than 50 million households—almost everyone—use casein-based goods.

Unfortunately, the fact that casein is not only well-nigh indispensable, but also freely traded on the world market, just seems to enrage domestic milk producers. For the dairy lobby, not satisfied with its more than $2 billion in annual subsidies, wants to eliminate all potential competition.

America had a thriving casein industry before 1949, when Congress voted to create a price support program for dairymen—where the government pays inflated prices for surplus milk and cheese. But then the more than 600 casein plants went out of business, as dairymen found they could make more money selling their milk to Uncle Sam than by producing casein. Ever since then the United States has had to import the protein.

Embarrassed by a dairy surplus measured in the billions of pounds, domestic producers blame casein for driving their products off the market. But between 1975 and 1984 casein imports represented only 1/10th of 1 percent of total U.S. milk production. The only reason there is so large a cheese and milk surplus in federal warehouses is because the government pays farmers above-market prices to produce ever more.

Were this not the case Uncle Sam would not have embarked on a multibillion program to pay dairymen to go out of business. Some lucky producers are becoming millionaires simply by selling off their cows.

And even the Agriculture Department (USDA)—which runs the milk price support program—has admitted time and again that casein is not the cause of the dairy surplus. A report earlier this year found that there was "no logical basis" for tying the two issues together; casein import levels were unrelated to federal surplus dairy purchases.

The International Trade Commission has reached similar conclusions. Not only does the ITC reiterate the lack of a connection between casein imports and federal surpluses, but it reports that dairy products "are not considered by most of the end users of the imports to be a primary or technically viable substitute for casein in many of its current uses."

Unfortunately, the dairymen, perhaps the greediest lobby in a city full of insatiable interest groups, don't care about the facts. While banning casein wouldn't measurably increase the demand for milk, doing so would eliminate any possibility of competition and would give them a major political victory, which is important for an industry that depends on Washington for a generous welfare program.

While a casein ban might not make dairy farmers richer, it certainly would make consumers poorer. A March 1986 USDA study, for instance, estimated that a 50 percent tariff would hike casein prices from 96 cents a pound last year to $1.44 per pound; that would take about $66 million out of Americans' pockets.

Even worse is the proposed 50 percent quota, based on a multi-year average: casein imports would drop from 229 million to 88 million pounds and prices would jump at least $180 million. Indeed, some industry groups figure quotas would triple casein prices and cost consumers as much as $350 million.

Limiting casein imports would have another pernicious effect—pushing products off supermarket shelves entirely. Warns USDA, trade restrictions would price some casein-based goods out of the market. As a result, concluded the department's study, "consumers would have fewer . . . products available to them."

Finally, slapping controls on imported casein would undercut attempts to open up foreign markets for American goods. Today casein is an important symbol of international commerce because it is freely traded; shutting out imports could cause countries like New Zealand, Australia and Ireland to retaliate. And if they did, American workers, as well as consumers, would pay dearly to satisfy the avarice of the dairy lobby.

In years past the administration has managed to defeat efforts to ban casein by promising to conduct yet another study. This time Congress should simply say no—permanently.

## 101. Is Dukakis Really as Dumb as He Sounds?

*October 19, 1988*

Dan Quayle has said a lot of stupid things, but he never claimed to be a genius.

Michael Dukakis, however—Mr. Competence—doesn't have that excuse. Yet his recent attack on foreign ownership in the United States was far dumber than anything Quayle has said.

Appearing at a factory owned by an Italian firm, Dukakis denounced Quayle for arguing that Americans should be "happy" that foreigners were willing to invest in the United States.

"Maybe the Republican ticket wants our children to work for foreign owners, pay rent to foreign owners and owe their future to foreign owners, but that's not the kind of future Lloyd Bentsen and I want for America," said the Democratic nominee.

Oh really? Would Dukakis prefer that U.S. workers receive an unemployment check from Uncle Sam instead of a paycheck from a foreigner?

But Dukakis is not alone in his fear of foreign investment. The Moral Majority, which apparently sees no difference between building new factories and blowing up old ones, headlined an article in a recent issue of its newsletter: "It's Cheaper to Buy Us than to Bomb Us."

Though Dukakis delivered his speech at an Italian factory, it is the specter of little yellow people that apparently raises the most hackles. Yet Japan's investment in America only ranks third, after that of Britain and the Netherlands; European direct investment in the United States is more than five times as great as that of Japan.

Moreover, though Japanese investment in America has grown sharply since 1980, the bulk of Japan's spending in the United States, 60.3 percent of it last year, has been on Treasury bills. This gives Japan no control over any American firm.

Anyway, the current value of U.S. investment abroad gently exceeds foreign holdings in this country. And last year the net inflow of direct foreign investment was a paltry $3 billion, a mere blip for a nation with a gross national product of $4.5 trillion.

Because American firms still invest hundreds of billions overseas every year, Washington has steadfastly opposed attempts by other nations to slow the expansion of U.S. enterprises. Indeed, to limit foreign investment here would not only be hypocritical; it would also be extremely foolish.

IBM and Exxon alone invest in more than 100 nations. Foreign retaliation in response to U.S. restrictions could cripple their and other American firms' operations. In short, if we want to play in a global marketplace, we have to let others play.

Nevertheless, the scaremongering continues, not only by Dukakis, but also a bevy of congressmen who have proposed numerous restrictions on foreign investment. Mind you, these are legislators who just a few years ago voted to require Japanese automakers to produce their cars in America.

Most critics, such as Martin and Susan Tolchin, a newspaper reporter and university professor, respectively, attack foreign investment in apocalyptic terms. Foreign investors, say the Tolchins, are "threatening to engulf America and undermine its ability to control its own fate and to defend its position as a premier industrial power."

But many opponents have much more mundane—and selfish—concerns. Consumerist Ralph Nader, for instance, has attacked 'foreign takeovers" of office buildings because rents have risen in the nation's capital. The mayor of Honolulu, Frank Fasi, wants to stop the Japanese from buying big homes in that city's luxury neighborhoods.

Anyway, even the Tolchins, authors of *Buying into America,* recently published by Times Books, acknowledge that similar fears about U.S. investment were voiced in Europe two decades ago. But those countries now welcome American firms.

And part of the "problem"—though foreign investment really doesn't deserve to be called that—is caused by U.S. regulations. Foreign banks, for instance, have greater freedom to operate in some states than do domestic institutions.

The basic question that Americans need to ask each other about foreign investment is quite simple. Are we better or worse off because other people find the United States to be an attractive place in which to invest?

To ask the question is to answer it. Foreign owners provide capital to expand American firms and retool U.S. factories; some $80 billion a year of their money also goes as pay to 3 million Americans. In fact, between 1975 and 1985 wages at foreign affiliates of U.S. companies increased four and a half times as fast as the overall average.

Where national security is genuinely involved—say a Soviet-controlled entity trying to buy a defense contractor—the matter can be handled under current law. But in the main Americans should welcome, not shun, foreign investment.

So the next time Michael Dukakis takes to the stump to warn that foreigners are buying up America, he should be more honest in describing the kind of country he really wants: insular, uncompetitive and unproductive. Foreign investment is one case where there are lots of winners and virtually no losers.

# Market Manipulation

## 102. Repeal the Antitrust Laws

*December 28, 1983*

The Reagan administration can't make up its mind about the antitrust laws.

Its outgoing antitrust chief, William Baxter, has supported softening restrictions on mergers, joint research and development projects, and manufacturers setting retail prices for their products. But at the same time, Baxter, apparently with visions of FBI sting operations dancing in his head, suggested banning all conversations between corporate chief executives unless they were taped, with the tapes sent to him.

The threat to use police state tactics to enforce the antitrust tactics to enforce the antitrust laws, along with the inexcusable waste of cases like the 15-year, 104,000-transcript-pages-long IBM case should cause us to reassess the antitrust laws. Tinkering with them is not enough; instead, the antitrust laws should be abolished.

The most important reason is moral. People should have the right to make voluntary arrangements with their own property. The fact that higher prices may result—as a practical matter, private price-fixing agreements are virtually impossible to maintain without government support—does not justify abrogating fundamental property rights. Such basic human rights should count as much as theoretical economic efficiency. Indeed, only businessmen have their rights so restricted. Instead of enforcing "free competition" in the labor marketplace, for instance, the government encourages workers to unionize.

Moreover, the antitrust laws require individuals to follow competitive norms routinely violated by government. The original purpose of the Interstate Commerce Commission was to fix railroad rates, pre-empting the Sherman Antitrust Act, which had been used to strike down railroad cartel pricing agreements. And when the Aluminum Co. of America was sued for alleged antitrust violations in 1945, the government was imposing tariffs on imported aluminum, which restricted foreign competition.

Indeed, the government routinely uses tariffs, quotas and entry restrictions to create cartels and raise prices at the behest of special interests. Government, not private monopolies, is the greatest threat to competition: we should keep its hands out of the economy altogether.

Antitrust laws also often prohibit socially valuable conduct and punish economically efficient behavior. For instance, in the IBM case, the government attacked IBM's competitive practices of discounting and introducing new product lines.

Similarly, in the ALCOA case, ALCOA was found to have illegally monopolized aluminum production by—literally—embracing new opportunities, anticipating and supplying new demand and having an efficient organization. ALCOA could have escaped liability under the court's ruling only by reducing its output, raising its prices and refusing to satisfy new demand. Such conduct would have benefited no one, least of all consumers.

In fact, some antitrust laws are affirmatively anti-competitive. The Robinson-Patman Act prohibits "price discrimination," severely limiting price cutting. And envious auto competitors have urged the government to block the GM-Toyota joint venture on antitrust grounds.

Finally, the antitrust laws are too imprecise to give people fair warning of potential liability. Under Section One of the Sherman Act, violations occur if the conduct is "unreasonable." This transparently simple term encompasses every form of economic activity, the market effects of which frequently cannot be accurately predicted in advance nor understood afterward. To determine whether conduct is "unreasonable," the courts carry out full-scale—and frequently flawed—economic inquiries into industry market structures, and compare the results with often jumbled legal precedents. There are few clear rules.

Even where the courts have attempted to provide some certainty by, for example, declaring practices such as price fixing and group boycotts to be "per se" unreasonable, ambiguity persists. Merely labeling the offense per se only shifts the unclarity one step further back: the question then is what constitutes group boycotts.

The law under Section Two of the act, which strikes at those who "monopolize" or "attempt to monopolize" also is confusing. There are two separate and conflicting lines of court authority on what constitutes "monopolizing."

The Sherman Act and its companion measures don't belong in a free society. They violate people's economic rights and often reduce, rather than increase, competition. Those who fear that repeal would leave a world monopolized by a few big corporations should consider the divestiture movement of recent years caused by a force more powerful than the U.S. government—the need to make a profit in a free marketplace.

And those who care about protecting civil liberties should heed Adam Smith's admonition that no law to prevent price fixing "could be executed, or would be consistent with liberty and justice."

Let's ban the antitrust laws, not businessmen's conversations.

## 103. Curbing Raiders Is Bad for Business

*February 7, 1988*

Congressional action to preserve a free market is now more necessary than ever, since Delaware, the nation's second-smallest state, adopted legislation to sharply restrict contested mergers. The measure, signed by Delaware's Governor last week, will affect companies around the country.

Last April the United States Supreme Court upheld Indiana's anti-takeover law. As hometown companies in other states became takeover targets, legislatures raced to protect incumbent management. All told, 29 states have enacted laws limiting shareholder rights.

Nevertheless, these measures, though effective in a majority of states, covered only a small minority of the nation's largest businesses. More than half of the Fortune 500 are incorporated in Delaware, which until late last year had refused to join the anti-takeover stampede.

However, corporate chief executives placed unremitting pressure on state officials to restrict takeovers; "I've seen the Business Roundtable's stretch limousines circling the Delaware state house," complained corporate raider T. Boone Pickens. The result was passage of the legislation, which would require management approval for most mergers, dooming unfriendly bids. Until now just 20 percent of business capital in America was insulated from the takeover market; Delaware's decision to outlaw most hostile takeovers freezes roughly 80 percent of corporate America under current management.

Of course, the assault on stock owners' freedoms is not confined to state governments. Some business leaders are urging Congress, too, to consider legislation that would either tilt securities laws further toward incumbent managers or use the tax code to penalize mergers. However, these proposals—which are being debated in a national forum in the face of serious opposition—would only make hostile takeovers more difficult to accomplish. The Delaware measure, which originated with the private lawyers who make up the state bar's corporate law section, essentially exempts half of American business from the operation of the market.

Granting businessmen de facto life tenure in this way threatens to short-circuit a process that helps insure an efficient and competitive economy. Hostile takeovers, despite the negative connotations of the phrase, are good for the economy. Quite simply, the existence of a market for corporate control allows anyone who thinks he could do a better job of running a company to buy it.

Not surprisingly, executives who lose their munificent salaries and perks have a different view of hostile mergers. They contend that takeover specialists pillage helpless companies for the sake of short-term profits. But manufacturing productivity has been growing and business investment is up, despite increasing takeover activity. Moreover, contrary to the conventional wisdom, takeover targets tend to spend less than average on their research and development programs.

Some critics complain that takeovers generate paper profits rather than real economic improvements. But a raider can justify the premium he pays for his shares only by making the company more productive. And he usually succeeds: on average, takeovers increase company values 8.4 percent. If the buyer fails to do so, the public is no worse off, since the original shareholders gained what he lost. Nor is there any net reduction in investment capital, unless the sellers burn their proceeds from the deal.

Moreover, shareholders are undisputed beneficiaries of a vigorous market for corporate ownership. Prof. Michael Jensen of the University of Rochester estimates that tender offers increase target stock prices by an average of 30 percent. In 1984 and 1985 alone, takeover battles generated $75 billion in premiums for stock owners—an average of more than $1,500 a person. Even unsuccessful raids make stock owners richer.

In contrast, government protection for incumbent management drives down stock prices. In 1986 New Jersey placed temporary restrictions on takeovers; prices for 87 affected companies fell by 11.3 percent. A Securities and Exchange Commission survey found that stock prices for 74 companies with headquarters in Ohio declined an average of 3.2 percent, for a $1.5 billion loss, after the state passed restrictive legislation. And the Federal Trade Commission estimates that New York's anti-takeover rules, reduced equity values by 1 percent, costing stock owners $1.2 billion.

For this reason, stockholders—the real owners of a company—in contrast to managers pleading for government protection—recognize the importance of allowing a vibrant market for corporate control. Institutional investors, in particular, have vigorously opposed proposals for company "poison pill" defenses to discourage tender offers.

Delaware state legislators undoubtedly understood the importance of the issue, but they apparently feared an exodus of companies in search of protection elsewhere; the corporate franchise tax is the state's second-largest source of revenue. And for this reason the state violated its duty to help preserve a vibrant, free national economy.

The only solution now is Federal pre-emption of state anti-takeover laws. But if Congress allows states like Delaware to continue placing the imperative of parochial politics before national economic good sense, then we will all lose.

## 104.  The LBO Bugaboo

*January 4, 1989*

Congress rarely misses an opportunity to interfere in the economy, and leveraged buy-outs, or LBOs, may be this session's major target.

LBOs, where the management typically borrows money to buy the company and take it private, have become the latest symbol of business greed and excess. The $25 billion fight over RJR Nabisco capped a string of LBOs involving such corporate behemoths as Kraft, Beatrice and Safeway.

Some critics of LBOs have turned apocalyptic.

"What is being done threatens the very basis of our capitalist system," says John Creedon, president of Metropolitan Life Insurance Co.

Others make it a moral issue: Economist Robert Solow charges, "There's something sick about a society where you can get filthy rich doing this sort of deal."

But why? True, we're naturally jealous of people who appear to make money effortlessly. And there is a soap opera quality to the big takeover battles. That doesn't mean LBOs are bad, however.

Takeovers create a market for corporate control. That is, they allow outsiders to oust incumbent managers who are more interested in personal aggrandizement than firm efficiency.

Many LBOs add a slightly different twist: They turn the incumbent executives into owners. Today most corporations are run by men and women who have very little stake in their own companies. A LBO gives the managers a much greater incentive to succeed.

Should LBOs nevertheless be restricted? One concern is that increased corporate debt could leave firms vulnerable in a recession. Even Federal Reserve Chairman Alan Greenspan has warned banks about lending for LBOs.

However, LBOs are responsible for only a very small share of overall business borrowing. Moreover, not only is the growth of debt of non-financial enterprises slower now than a decade ago, but the ratio of corporate debt to equity has fallen sharply—from 109 percent in 1974 to 75 percent today.

Banks obviously need to exercise caution in arranging individual loans, but there is no evidence that they have been thoughtlessly risking their money on LBOs.

Institutions such as Manufacturers Hanover have strict standards for backing LBOs and have racked up few LBO-related losses as a result.

LBOs also have been attacked for diverting capital through meaningless paper-shuffling. But the deals actually create new wealth: RJR's shareholders received roughly twice what their shares were worth before the LBO. Unless they burn the proceeds, which seems unlikely, they will have more to invest in other companies.

Another charge is that LBOs promote monopolistic economic power. House Speaker Jim Wright, for instance, argues, "The intensification and concentration of economic wealth into the hands of fewer and fewer have begun to erode the broad base of the American economy."

But LBOs are as likely to reverse economic concentration as promote it. Indeed, many deals are based on spinning off assets to other operators; the RJR LBO essentially reverses the 1985 RJR-Nabisco merger.

Moreover, many employees—average working stiffs—have bought their companies through LBOs. In 1984 workers purchased Oregon Steel Mills through an employee stock ownership plan. Roughly 1,500 companies have been taken over in this manner.

Another question is the fiduciary duty of corporate managers trying to buy their firms on the cheap. RJR's executives expected to reap a tenfold return under their LBO proposal. The answer to this problem, however, is for company directors to hold a fair auction, as in RJR's case, where the firm sold for 50 percent more than the initial bid.

Lastly, LBO critics charge that the deals are "subsidized" by the taxpayers because the interest on the debt used to finance the purchase is deductible. But the real problem is the double taxation of dividends, which cannot be deducted by the firm as a business expense but which are taxed when received by investors. This encourages companies to rely more on debt than on equity (stock).

In fact, much of the criticism of subsidies simply masks a desire to rake in more cash. House Ways and Means Committee Chairman Dan Rostenkowski allows that "if there's revenue there, that's a place to get it."

There's no doubt that greed is one reason well-paid executives propose billion-dollar deals. But what right do politicians, who devote virtually every waking hour trying to buy votes, have to denounce greedy businessmen?

Anyway, LBOs offer an instance where some people's greed makes the rest of us better off. Though not every LBO will work, most will turn out well.

Congress should ignore the latest public hysteria and leave LBOs alone.

## 105. Decriminalize Insider Trading

*January 18, 1989*

U.S. Attorney Rudolph Giuliani has gained another notch in his belt, a $650 million settlement with the investment banking firm Drexel Burnham Lambert.

But his corporate crusade is misdirected: despite the assumption that insider trading is the white-collar equivalent of murder, most insider deals neither wrong individuals nor destabilize markets.

Nevertheless, late last year Congress doubled the maximum jail term and quintupled the top fine for insider traders. The purpose, said Rep. Matthew Rinaldo, R-N.J., was to "send a clear signal . . . that insider trading will not be tolerated."

However, Congress didn't bother to clarify the definition of insider trading, to give investors fair warning as to what constitutes illegal conduct. Legislators were too interested in scoring political points to bother.

Traditionally the law was thought to prohibit only "insiders," such as firm executives, from using privileged information to make a profit. But the Securities and Exchange Commission has increasingly prosecuted outsiders who have no relationship with the companies involved.

For instance, in 1984 the SEC sued University of Oklahoma football coach Barry Switzer because he had traded stock based on a conversation that he overheard at a track meet. Yet Switzer had committed no wrong: He was lucky, but no more so than a buyer who decided to purchase shares based on his horoscope.

Of course, those who sold probably were upset that they unloaded their stock, but they had wanted to sell and got the price they demanded. And the market as a whole benefited from Switzer's trading, which helped nudge the share value up to its true market level, providing a more gradual rise in prices.

Though Switzer ultimately prevailed in court, former *Wall Street Journal* reporter R. Foster Winans was not so fortunate. Winans wrote what was essentially a gossip column on the stock market; he was convicted for disclosing the articles' contents the day before they appeared to a broker who sometimes traded on the information.

Winans violated the *Journal's* code of ethics and was justifiably fired.

But he had no fiduciary duty to any of the firms involved and his friend's dealings involved information that had been "Heard on the Street," the title of the column.

The SEC has since begun prosecuting arbitragers, further extending the law's reach.

Even in cases involving obvious misdeeds—such as Dennis Levine's sale of proprietary information from his work at Drexel to Ivan Boesky— the real problem is not "insider trading" but a breach of fiduciary responsibility. Boesky and Levine didn't rob sellers even as they made millions from their insider deals. Everyone who sold his shares did so willingly.

Instead, Levine's wrong was to improperly disclose firm secrets, violating Drexel's fiduciary duty to its clients and sullying the company's reputation. Drexel had an obvious civil cause of action against Levine for violating the terms of his employment; Drexel's clients also had a right to collect damages from both Levine and the firm if their acquisition costs were raised.

But the only conceivable criminal case against Levine and Boesky—but not Drexel's much-publicized Michael Milken, who appears at most guilty of technical violations of the securities laws—should have been one akin to industrial espionage, and even that would be difficult to justify, since Levine misused information that he was given, rather than stealing secrets to which he was not privy.

Of course, the SEC claims that insider trading prosecutions are necessary to protect the "integrity" of the market. But there is no such thing as a "level playing field" for the stock market.

A broker in New York is almost certainly going to know more about business trends than a retiree in Peoria. And it is simply impossible to control every potential insider: corporate executives and directors, investment bankers, lawyers, lenders, secretaries, printers, arbitragers, friends and relatives, and so on.

Anyway, we are all better off the faster share prices reach their correct levels. Otherwise, millions of people will be making incorrect and costly investment decisions based on inaccurate prices. In fact, stock markets in nations with either non-existent or ill-enforced insider trading laws, such as Hong Kong, New Zealand, France and Japan function fine.

Of course, allowing people with legal access to proprietary information to make millions seems "unfair." Abstract moralism is a poor basis for criminalizing conduct, however.

While those who profit from insider information may be greedy, they don't belong in prison unless they have committed theft or fraud. The latest crackdown against insider trading may be good politics, but it is bad economics and bad law.

# IV. Judging America

# The Judicial Imperative

## 106. Making Judges Accountable

The names William Rehnquist and Antonin Scalia strike terror in the hearts of liberals across America. Both men are intelligent, articulate, and committed; both are also among the most conservative members of the Federal bench. Also, because the two Supreme Court justices are relatively young, they probably will influence the direction of American jurisprudence well into the next century.

Yet, it is those on the left, who most doggedly have opposed President Reagan's high court nominees, who also have guaranteed Rehnquist's and Scalia's lasting influence by championing the independence of judges. Judicial appointment is for life; Congress has removed fewer than a half-dozen Federal jurists in history through the cumbersome impeachment process. While the courts will bend to persistent political pressure over time, enduring judicial landmarks—including desegregation, school prayer, and abortion—have withstood bitter attacks by the other branches of government and the public. Thus, with Reagan likely to fill roughly half the Federal bench before he leaves office, liberals may increasingly regret the fact that judges have well-nigh absolute power for their entire lives.

The judiciary was intended to play a key role in the original constitutional scheme. Its most literal function is to adjudicate private, as well as public, disputes. However, where judges intervene in public conflicts, their overriding duty is to protect the individual from the state. The other branches also were to respect personal liberty, but the framers feared the influence of "factions" and runaway majorities on Congress and the President. The courts were to provide the final defense of freedom—to be, in James Madison's words, "an impenetrable bulwark against every assumption of power in the legislative or executive." Life tenure and the difficulty in removing judges were supposed to shield judicial decision-making from hostile popular or legislative majorities, allowing judges to place fundamental constitutional liberties beyond the government's reach.

However, over time, the judiciary has lost sight of its proper constitutional role. The framers intended the Constitution to protect economic liberty; "governmnent is instituted to protect property of every sort," wrote Madison. For nearly 150 years, from 1790 to 1937, the Federal courts regularly struck down coercive legislative enactments. With the advent of the New Deal, the Supreme Court stood against many of the now-discredited legislative initiatives of the Roosevelt Administration, such as industry-wide price-fixing and Federal control of agricultural production.

Ironically, the Court's protection of individual rights caused the political left to attack judicial independence and to press for greater political control over the courts. Under pressure from the Democrats, who then dominated the executive and legislative branches, the judiciary finally abandoned, in the famous "switch in time that saved nine," its role of protecting economic freedom from the expansive state. Observes law professor Robert McCloskey, "it is hard to think of another instance where the Court so thoroughly and quickly demolished a constitutional doctrine of such far-reaching significance."

In succeeding years, the Supreme Court, though protective of civil liberty, consistently trampled over property rights while engaging in what University of California at Berkley political scientist Martin Shapiro describes as "a consistent and comprehensive constitutionalization of the New Deal's fundamental vision of social justice." The judiciary became an active policy-making branch, expanding the size and reach of the public sector by taking the initiative where elected officials—and the electorate—refused to act.

Indeed, the judiciary consciously has substituted an ideology of egalitarian social justice, enforced by an ever-expanding Federal establishment, for the limited government/individual freedom framework created by the nation's founders. The negative rights of protection against government have given way to positive rights of access to government benefits—in effect, the right to use government against other citizens.

The most egregious example of judicial overreaching was the invalidation of state abortion laws in *Roe v. Wade* by the Supreme Court in 1973. The Court created, out of whole-cloth, a constitutional right to an abortion from the Fourteenth Amendment, which was approved by states with restrictive abortion statutes in force. The Warren Court also moved a long way, observes Shapiro, "toward creating constitutional rights to at least minimum levels of subsistence, housing, and education and to the administrative fairness and legal services that would ensure access to welfare state services."

As judges engaged in ever-broader forms of social engineering and forced taxpayers to fund faddish new social policies, conservatives attacked "government by judiciary" and proposed bringing the courts under the control of majoritarian institutions. However, the political left—which had once led the fight for democracy and "self-government"—was all too happy to achieve in the courtroom what it could not win in the voting booth. So, liberals have gamely defended the icon of "judicial independence," resisting any restriction on judicial authority.

Now, however, conservatives are appointing the Federal judges, and it is jurists on the right who increasingly will be disregarding progressive values as they exercise their enormous, essentially unreviewable, authority.

*The need for judicial accountability*

Since neither conservative nor liberal judges can be trusted to fulfill their constitutional role of protecting all forms of liberty, we should make judges answerable for their decisions. While preserving the independence of the judiciary deserves a high priority, so does protecting the integrity of our market economic and democratic political system. Today, at least, our system of checks and balances is out of equilibrium. Executive and legislative abuses are constrained both by popular will and judicial review; judicial excess, however, is restricted by little other than the sense of propriety on the part of the judges themselves. The constitutional scheme simply does not envision any branch or level of government exercising unaccountable power.

The key to reversing judicial policymaking, without destroying the courts in the process, is to adopt a package of reforms that changes the reward structure facing judges and restricts their power, but does not eliminate the degree of independence necessary for them successfully to meet their constitutional responsibility of protecting individual liberty. In short, judges must remain insulated from direct majoritarian pressures, but be ultimately accountable to the other branches of government and the people.

The Reagan Administration has been relying on the appointment process to transform the Federal bench. Unfortunately, however, Reagan's appointees seem to have as distorted an understanding of their constitutional role as do sitting liberal jurists. Conservative judges may draw back from inventing new rights from constitutional provisions where none were intended, but the right seems likely to expunge from the nation's fundamental law all protections for economic liberty even more quickly. For example, in *Hawaii v. Midkiff* (1984), the Supreme Court upheld a blatantly unconstitutional state seizure of private property, effectively excising from the Constitution the Public Use clause, which limits the power of eminent domain; the Court's opinion was written by Reagan appointee Sandra Day O'Connor.

So, it is critical that institutional reforms be adopted to curb judicial power as well. Some proposals that have been made in the past—giving Congress the right to overrule court decisions and making judges stand for election, for instance—would dangerously undermine the judicial branch, making it impossible for the courts to place basic constitutional rights beyond the reach of elected officials and the public. Still, narrower restrictions on the judiciary would help restore balance to the governmental system.

For example, constitutional limitations on the power of government necessarily would limit the ability of judges to intervene promiscuously and improperly in both economic and political affairs. Such measures could be broad in scope; for example, an economic "Bill of Rights" would restore vitality to the Constitution's explicit restrictions on Federal regulation of the marketplace, whether by Congress or the courts. A new, more restrictive "general welfare" clause would reverse the judiciary's willingness in recent years to redistribute resources to clamorous interest groups that were unable to achieve their goals through the political process.

Narrower institutional changes would be valuable as well. A number of federal constitutional amendments, including the very important Fourteenth, were introduced and passed with the purpose of overruling particular judicial decisions. In recent years, many proposals have been made to stop busing, one of the more egregious examples of improper judicial activism; specific amendments should be considered to restore meaning to such important constitutional provisions as the Public Use, Contracts, and Interstate Commerce clauses, which the courts have eviscerated in their rush to validate the expansion of state power.

As important as such changes would be, they are difficult to implement; since 1789, some 10,000 constitutional amendments have been proposed in Congress, but only 33 have been submitted to the states and just 26 of those were ratified. Moreover, passage of no single amendment would remedy more than a few judicial abuses, which range widely, from abortion to eminent domain; trying to respond to judicial misinterpretation on a case-by-case basis is not enough, for that would leave the initiative for major policy shifts with the judiciary. Courts still would provide the easier means to force social change or income redistribution on an unwilling citizenry, and judges would pay no penalty for consciously disregarding the nation's fundamental law, even if a ruling occasionally was overruled.

Therefore, the over-all exercise of judicial power must be reshaped. We should adjust the basic institutions to make the third and supposedly least dangerous branch accountable for its actions. One means of doing so would be to streamline judicial disciplinary procedures. Doing so would help safeguard the public both from judges who proved to be incompetent or intemperate and those who abused their power.

Today, the House may impeach and the Senate remove federal jurists, but the process is cumbersome and rarely used; over two centuries, only six judges have been removed, while another eight have resigned rather than face a Congressional trial. Moreover, impeachment generally is thought to be reserved for criminal or corrupt conduct; the Constitution's reference to "good behavior" may simply be horatory. In contrast, most states have independent commissions or boards to review judicial conduct. The state grounds for discipline are generally broader, including various kinds of misconduct or disability, and it is significantly easier to remove errant state jurists than federal ones.

Therefore, Congress should be given greater power to punish judges who act improperly. First, the grounds for impeachment could be extended to include persistent abuse of power by judges who usurp the authority of other branches or fail to implement clear constitutional guarantees.

Second, an entirely new disciplinary process could be created, such as the Joint Committee of Judicial Conduct proposed by the late Sen. John East or an independent body. Grounds for punishment could include "judicial malpractice" on substantive issues, and the sanctions could range from removal to several less stringent measures, such as suspension.

Though giving Congress greater authority over judges would create some risks to the basic independence of the bench, so long as the new disciplinary procedure remained substantially more restrictive than the usual Congressional committee process, judges would have little to fear from precipitous legislative retaliation for politically unpopular decisions. In 1964, Congress did increase the salaries of Supreme Court justices by substantially less than those of other Federal judges to demonstrate its anger over recent Court rulings, but those same politicians steadfastly refused to treat seriously proposals to impeach liberal jurists Earl Warren and William Douglas, or to strip the Federal courts of jurisdiction over controversial issues, which would only take a majority vote.

Another way to increase judicial accountability would be to limit judges' terms. By making judges answerable to the Congress and the President, this step also would reduce the need for new disciplinary procedures. Indeed, ending life tenure for Federal judges very well may be the easiest way to trim judicial authority without destroying the institution in the process. Today, only three states—Massachusetts, New Hampshire, and Rhode Island—provide for lifetime judicial appointments; the rest set terms ranging between four and 12 years.

A similar system should be instituted at the federal level. Judges could be appointed for, say, 10 years; reappointment and reconfirmation would be necessary for the jurist to remain in office. (There are all sorts of variants at the state level; in Vermont, for instance, judges, once chosen by the governor, are able to serve additional six-year terms so long as the legislature does not affirmatively vote against them.) Such a system hardly would be an extreme change. Today, members of most independent regulatory bodies, such as the Federal Trade Commission and Federal Communications Commission, are chosen for set terms.

This system would guarantee significant autonomy. Judicial terms would extend well past the normal presidential or Congressional term and Congress still could not overrule court decisions, but a judge who consistently had exceeded his authority, or who had exhibited a severely restrictive view of the Constitution's guarantees, could be refused reappointment or reconfirmation, allowing his removal without the trauma of an impeachment trial.

Ending life tenure does not favor any particular ideological viewpoint—it simply assures some accountability to other government institutions. Had succeeding Congresses and presidents been able to adjust the composition of the bench during the 1960's, Earl Warren's tenure as Chief Justice might have been cut short. However, had Warren Burger been limited to 10 years service when he was appointed in 1969, Jimmy Carter, rather than Ronald Reagan, would have chosen Burger's successor.

*Making judges answerable*

Finally, periodically requiring judges to gain public approval would make jurists ultimately answerable to the very people they are supposed to be protecting. Fifteen states use some variant of the "Missouri Plan," under which judges are appointed by the governor, legislature, or judicial commission, and later subjected to a retention vote by the electorate. In California, for instance, supreme court and appellate judges must receive a majority yes vote to remain in office; the state of Illinois requires a 60% affirmative vote.

More than half the states go even further, requiring at least some of their judges to run in contested elections. In several—such as Alabama, New Mexico, and Texas—the races are partisan; others, like Kentucky and North Dakota, rely on nonpartisan contests. Moreover, several states, including California and New York, require trial judges to run for office, while subjecting appellate judges to retention votes or reappointment proceedings, respectively.

Making Federal judgeships elected posts seriously would undermine the judicial institution. Although incumbent state judges regularly are returned to office, an election, especially a partisan race, turns a judge into just another politician, forcing him to raise money, seek support from interest groups, cater to party officials, and campaign for votes. Clearly, the electoral process does affect judicial decision-making; at a symposium organized by the conservative Federalist Society, some California trial judges frankly discussed how an upcoming election affected trial assignments and the release of opinions. Thus, turning the full political pressures of democracy loose on judges through contested elections would threaten that most important role of the judiciary—the protection of individual liberties from majority abuse.

Retention contests, in contrast, make judges equally accountable, but sharply reduce the politicization of the judiciary. Although the 1986 campaign over the retention of a majority of the members of the California Supreme Court proved to be an especially nasty one, that court is a special case, having given a distinctively partisan flavor to rulings ranging from the death penalty to reapportionment to tax cuts. Also, until 1986, no justice had ever been rejected by the electorate.

Indeed, if anything, the California experience proves the value of the retention vote system. Gubernatorial appointment and 12-year terms provide state supreme court justices with substantial independence; even when they face the electorate, most judges hold their positions without controversy. However, where judicial excesses have been particularly egregious, the voters ultimately do have an opportunity to respond. "There is," argues California journalist Mickey Kaus, "nothing inherently dangerous or scary about asking the people, once every six years or so, to vote yes or no on judges."

In a very real sense, we do face a "judicial crisis." Conservatives are right in arguing that the courts have improperly usurped power. Many judges effectively are rewriting the Constitution to replace the right to protect one's property with the right to seize another's wealth. However, judges also are failing to intervene to uphold genuine guarantees of individual liberty, even where authorized to do so by the nation's governing document.

Thus, in reforming the judiciary, it is not enough to reduce judges' power, for that would leave Americans even more subject to abusive majorities. Instead, it is necessary to change the judicial institution so that it better protects all of the values enshrined by the founders.

To do so, court reforms must be severe enough to circumscribe judges intent on remaking society; jurists must lose both the institutional incentive and authority to overreach their intended role. After all, "it is axiomatic that all wielders of power, judges included, ever thirst for more," observes

Harvard law professor Raoul Berger, which is, of course, why the Constitution establishes a government of three separate branches. The courts are to be independent, not divine.

Still, the controls over the courts must not be so stringent as to destroy judicial autonomy. Judges must be free from improper interference by other institutions and popular majorities, since unrestrained majoritarianism, both legislative and popular, would be far more dangerous than continued judicial activism.

Creating the best synthesis of accountability with independence will take some care. Judges should not be directly responsible to majorities, whether in Congress or the polling place. Thus, jurists should not be made to run for office in contested elections, nor should their decisions be reversible by a simple Congressional vote. For the same reason, Congress should not use its power over court jurisdiction to bar judges from deciding controversial issues; the problem is inappropriate jurisprudence, not jurisdiction.

Nevertheless, the judicial branch, no less than the legislative and executive, should be answerable for its conduct. The power of the courts can be reduced by constitutional changes that will limit the authority of all branches of government. Moreover, judges should be removable by the legislature and public for cause, including political abuse of their positions. Streamlining the disciplinary procedure for errant jurists, appointing judges for a set term, rather than for life, and requiring periodic popular approval for judges to retain their positions would all create an invaluable degree of accountability for the judicial branch. These steps, in contrast to the more severe restrictions proposed by many conservatives, would limit activist abuses without eliminating court autonomy. Judges still would be sufficiently insulated from majoritarian pressures to protect the constitutional rights of unpopular individuals and groups.

Today, civil libertarians are having nightmares about the Rehnquist Supreme Court in the year 2010. If federal judges were no longer answerable only to God, those bad dreams might disappear.

# 107. Bork and Original Intent

*October 28, 1987*

The Senate battle over Robert Bork, though cloaked with the rhetoric of high philosophical principle, was really just another political brawl over control of the federal judiciary. Nevertheless, the issue of constitutional interpretation, and Judge Bork's professed support for a jurisprudence of "original intent," were what roused his opponents to such a frenzy.

Yet, in their rush to arms, both liberals and conservatives ignored a glaring inconsistency in Bork's philosophy of "intentionalism:" his opposition to judicial intervention even when necessary to enforce constitutional provisions as intended by the framers. In practice, Bork believes more in judicial restraint than in "original intent."

This bias against judicial action, in contrast to the sort of liberal "activism" that extends the Constitution beyond its intended scope, shows itself most clearly in many conservatives' acceptance of pervasive government encroachments on property rights. The left may have killed the Constitution's guarantees for economic liberties, but the right has helped write the obituary.

The "original intent" of the nation's founders, however, was to protect economic freedom. "Government is instituted to protect property of every sort," wrote James Madison, and the judiciary was to be "an impenetrable bulwark against every assumption of power in the legislative or executive."

For nearly 150 years the Supreme Court fulfilled its constitutional role by striking down intrusive legislative enactments. Federal judges relied on explicit provisions, such as the Public Use, Commerce, and Contracts clauses, as well as more general doctrines grounded in natural rights and Substantive Due Process. One of the reasons it took so long for the federal government to become a compliant tool of avaricious special-interest groups was because judges stood as a "bulwark" against coercive state power.

Only when faced with Franklin Roosevelt's "court-packing" scheme did the Supreme Court abandon economic freedom. The Supreme Court's attempt to protect these minority rights was simply overwhelmed by majoritarian pressures.

Once control of the judiciary was in their hands, liberals became supportive of judicial activism—except in the economic field. Conservatives, too, abandoned economic liberty, though they advocated the interpretive doctrine of "intentionalism."

Yet many conservative jurists, like Robert Bork, have given short shrift to the founders' original intent where it conflicts with their preference for judicial passivity. Bork, for instance, recently acknowledged that judges may have acted improperly in not actively protecting economic liberties. "But that is not my concern," he added.

In fact, it was President Reagan's first Supreme Court nominee, Sandra Day O'Connor, who authored the 1984 opinion in *Hawaii Housing Authority vs. Midkiff* that effectively abrogated the Fifth Amendment's restrictions on the taking of private property. A legislature's use of eminent domain, ruled the court, need only be "rationally related to a conceivable public purpose,'' a non-standard that would have shocked those who framed and approved the Constitution.

Given changed American attitudes toward government, it would not be easy for judges to rehabilitate constitutional provisions that have lain dormant for a half century. But the Supreme Court need not begin by striking down the New Deal. Last term, for instance, the Supreme Court stiffened the constitutional requirement that the government compensate people for regulating their land; these cases provide the foundation for expanded protection of economic liberty in the future. Unfortunately, fervent advocates of judicial restraint, like Bork, would be unlikely to help restore this much needed constitutional balance.

Of course, this does not mean that liberals like Justice William Brennan, who essentially believe that judges should follow their *zeitgeist* in interpreting the Constitution, are closer to the truth than Bork. Brennan's philosophy turns the courts into yet another forum for interest group politics and strips certainty of enforcement from all constitutional rights.

In contrast, a doctrine of "original intent"—one that takes into account the philosophy of the nation's founders and the principles they intended the Constitution to advance—provides a far more coherent and defensible interpretive framework.

Thus, the collapse of the Bork candidacy is as much an opportunity as a defeat for the administration. For if President Reagan now chooses as Bork's replacement a nominee who really believes in the "original intent" philosophy that Bork only symbolized, we will move a large step closer to developing a jurisprudence of individual rights that is genuinely grounded in the Constitution.

# 108.  Judicial Imperialism

*October 21, 1987*

Robert Bork may have lost his fight to sit on the Supreme Court, but the issues raised by his nomination remain as important as ever. Indeed, a federal judge in Missouri has just provided another example of the sort of judicial imperialism criticized by Bork.

For years District Court Judge Russell Clark has attempted to run the Kansas City schools. Though the system was no longer segregated by law, Clark wanted to entice white suburbanites to send their children to decaying municipal schools through millions of dollars in new programs and improvements.

Local voters—black as well as white—consistently said no to higher taxes, however, voting down four separate tax hikes in the last 15 months.

So Clark has simply ordered the district to nearly double its property tax rate and to impose a 1.5 percent income tax on those who work in the district. "A majority has no right to deny others the constitutional guarantees to which they are entitled."

But Clark is obviously not interpreting the U.S. Constitution. That document requires non-discrimination in education, not fancy new "magnet schools." In fact, the local parents—who are the guardians of the children in whose interest the judge purports to be acting—decided to exercise their constitutional rights by refusing to pour more of their limited paychecks into a system that many observers believe has been badly mismanaged.

Particularly outrageous is Judge Clark's attempt to tax people who don't live in the district. There was "an abundance of evidence," he said, that many people lived in the suburbs to escape the inner-city schools. Therefore, he concluded, "it would be equitable to involve those people in a plan to help defray the district's desegregation expenses."

Since when does a family's decision to move away from violent, dirty, unsafe schools require it to subsidize those schools? Especially when that family already is paying taxes to support its children's current school.

The judge, of course, says he weighed the respective constitutional rights of the taxpayers and students, and concluded "that the balance is clearly in favor of the students who are helpless without the aid of this court."

He is engaging in mere sophistry, however. The fact that inner-city voters won't spend more on their children's schools violates no provision of the Constitution. Indeed, money alone cannot solve the enormous social problems that surround such schools.

In contrast, the taxpayers have a basic right to their incomes; the Constitution contains several explicit guarantees of citizens' economic liberties. Said founder James Madison, "Government is instituted to protect property of every sort."

And people are to lose control over their incomes only when their elected representatives—who are accountable to the voters—follow a specific legal procedure to increase taxes. The legislative process may be badly flawed, but it is still fairer than a court proceeding in which taxpayers are not even represented.

The original purpose of the judiciary was to act as a "bulwark" against the expansion of state power, to protect individuals from government. But since the New Deal, most judges have worked to extend the reach of the public sector.

Yet even as jurists literally seized control of school systems, prisons, public housing projects, mental institutions and sewers, few attempted to set tax rates. The New Jersey Supreme Court went so far as to threaten to shut down the state's schools unless the Legislature passed an income tax to equalize spending between districts, but even those activist judges didn't claim the right to impose taxes by judicial fiat.

Judge Clark, however, wants to go where no judge has gone before. His order, exulted Arthur Benson, the plaintiffs' attorney, was "a very creative and exciting thing to do."

However, the Constitution does not authorize judges to do "creative and exciting" things with other people's money. State officials plan on appealing Judge Clark's decision; the Court of Appeals should swiftly overturn his order.

If not, this sort of judicial overreaching could encourage direct disobedience of the courts. "Judge Clark has decided to raise taxes," the local authorities could say in effect: "Let him collect them."

In the past governments occasionally have resisted judicial dictates and the consequences have not been pretty. Yet acquiescing to Clark's order would also set a dangerous precedent. For the decision represents, in the words of University of Chicago law professor Michael McConnell, "a breathtaking expansion of judicial power."

America is not a perfect place. But the Constitution does not authorize judges to roam widely, imposing their peculiar vision of social justice on the rest of us. Despite some important flaws in Robert Bork's philosophy, he, at least, recognizes that there must be some limits on judicial power.

## 109. Reaping the Judicial Whirlwind

*November 11, 1987*

The back benches of liberal America emptied as one interest group after another joined in opposing Robert Bork's nomination to the Supreme Court. Labor unions, the American Civil Liberties Union, environmental organizations, and even groups like the National Mental Health Association entered the fray.

None of them ever really addressed Bork's judicial philosophy; instead, their prime criterion for opposing him was naked self-interest. Durwood Zaelke of the Sierra Club Legal Defense Fund, for instance, frankly admitted that his group feared that a Justice Bork would be hostile to its lawsuits.

Conservative organizations, too, got involved in that nomination fight, but they generally backed Bork because they supported his "original intent" jurisprudence, not because they expected him to rule in their favor in specific cases. Indeed, interests like business did nothing to aid a nominee who was attacked for being allegedly pro-business.

There was good reason to be concerned over Bork's willingness to defer to popular majorities, for the "original intent" of the Constitution's framers was to limit government power, including that of the legislature. Bork's stance, however, was an understandable, if unfortunate, overreaction to liberal judicial activism, which has turned the courts into avid promoters of ever-expanding state power.

The proper role of the judiciary is a serious issue which warrants a serious national debate. But liberal groups, which traditionally have advocated judicial independence, transformed the Bork nomination into a vicious political slugfest. Their willingness to loose majoritarian forces against Bork—and the threat of People for the American Way, Sen. Edward Kennedy, and other left-leaning activists to mount a similar campaign against Reagan's next nominee—ultimately could undermine the judiciary's ability to enforce the Constitution.

Indeed, while liberal opponents of Bork won that battle, having sown the wind they eventually may reap the whirlwind. For if the left may block nominees for opposing its pet causes, then the right is entitled to set its own litmus test for federal judges.

Let a future Democratic president nominate a bright, high-profile liberal to the Supreme Court. There was a time when such a candidate would have been approved with only token opposition. In 1979, for example, Jimmy Carter appointed left-wing Rep. Abner Mikva to the federal appellate court; Sens. Kennedy and Joseph Biden, among others, successfully defended Mikva against charges that he was too much a liberal partisan to be a judge.

Kennedy and Biden continued to profess their support for judicial independence after abortion opponents challenged President Reagan's first high court nominee, Sandra Day O'Connor.

"Single-issue politics has no place" in the confirmation process, intoned Kennedy. Senators should not apply a "a philosophical litmus test," argued Biden.

But with the flip-flop of Kennedy and Biden and the virulent interest group campaign against Bork, the past consensus over the generally respectful handling of judicial nominations has probably been irrevocably shattered. If a President Dukakis were to nominate Judge Mikva or a similar activist liberal to fill a Supreme Court vacancy, right-to-life groups would have ample precedent to rally against him.

Businessmen and property owners could attack the nominee's pro-regulation bias. Opponents also could vilify him for favoring racial quotas and forced busing and for consistently supporting expensive, anti-demo-cratic social engineering schemes.

In fact, Richard Viguerie, the conservative direct-mail promoter, has already given us a taste of the rhetoric to come.

"Liberals," Viguerie wrote after the Bork nomination faltered, "want a Supreme Court that will guarantee 'gay' rights . . . allow teenagers to have abortions without their parents' knowledge or consent . . . set rapists and murderers free on technicalities . . . and mandate racist and sexist 'affirmative action' quotas."

Given the success Viguerie and other conservatives have had with negative campaigns in the past, they could very well defeat Mikva or other leading liberal high court nominees.

Certainly senators should consider a candidate's judicial philosophy before voting on him. But if the Constitution is to effectively protect any rights, approval of Supreme Court appointments cannot be based on how nominees are expected to vote in particular cases. Choosing judges in that way would subject them to the very public pressures from which the Constitution seeks to insulate them.

Yet that is precisely what left-leaning interest groups have done in killing the Bork nomination, a precedent the right is not likely to forget. In which case liberal judicial nominees, too, may end up victims of single-issue judicial politics.

## 110.  End Life Tenure for Judges

*September 6, 1986*

The names William Rehnquist and Antonin Scalia strike terror in the hearts of liberals across America. Because Supreme Court justices are appointed for life, both men will probably affect the direction of our jurisprudence well into the next century.

Yet it is those on the left, who have most doggedly opposed President Reagan's High Court appointments, who have also guaranteed Justice Rehnquist's and Judge Scalia's influence by championing the indepen-dence of judges. And with the President likely to fill roughly half the Federal bench before he leaves office, liberals may increasingly regret the fact that judges have well-nigh absolute power for their entire lives.

The judiciary was intended to play a key role in the original constitu-tional scheme: James Madison said that the courts were to be "an impenetrable bulwark against every assumption of power in the legislative or executive." Life tenure was supposed to shield judicial decision-making from hostile popular or legislative majorities, allowing judges to place fundamental constitutional liberties beyond the Government's reach.

However, under pressure from the Democrats who dominated the executive and legislative branches during the Great Depression, the judiciary abandoned its role of protecting economic freedom from an expansive state. In succeeding years, the Supreme Court took a leading role in implementing the social vision of the New Deal. The judiciary became an active policy-making branch, expanding the size and reach of the public sector by taking the initiative where elected officials refused to act.

As judges created "rights" out of constitutional whole cloth and demanded that taxpayers fund faddish social policies, conservatives attacked "government by judiciary" and proposed bringing the courts under the control of majoritarian institutions. The left, happy to achieve in the courtroom what it could not win in the voting booth, defended the icon of "judicial independence," resisting any restriction on judicial authority. But now conservatives are appointing Federal judges. And it is jurists on the right who wield enormous, largely unreviewable authority.

Since neither conservative nor liberal judges can be trusted to fulfill their constitutional role of protecting all forms of liberty, we should make judges more accountable for their decisions. Executive and legislative abuses are constrained by popular will and judicial review; judicial excess is restricted by little other than judges' own sense of propriety.

The easiest way to trim judicial authority without destroying the institution in the process would be to end life tenure for Federal judges. Today, only three states—Massachusetts, New Hampshire and Rhode Island—provide for lifetime judicial appointments; the rest set terms ranging between four and 12 years.

A 10 year term for Federal jurists would guarantee significant court autonomy: judicial terms would extend well past the normal Presidential or Congressional term and Congress still could not overrule court decisions. But a judge who had consistently exceeded his authority, or who had exhibited a severely restrictive view of the Constitution, could be refused reappointment or reconfirmation, allowing his removal without the trauma of an impeachment trial.

Ending life tenure does not favor any particular ideological viewpoint; it simply assures some accountability to other Government institutions. Had succeeding Congresses and Presidents been able to adjust the composition of the bench during the 1960's, Earl Warren's tenure as Chief Justice might have been cut short. But had Chief Justice Warren Burger been limited to 10 years' service when he was appointed in 1969, Jimmy Carter rather than Ronald Reagan would have chosen his successor.

Making judges serve a set term would guarantee both the accountability and the independence of the Federal bench. The judicial branch, no less than the legislature, and executive, should be answerable for its conduct. The courts are to be independent, not divine.

Yet judges would still be sufficiently insulated from political pressures to protect the constitutional rights of unpopular individuals or groups. Some who want to limit the power of the courts suggest that we make judges stand for election or strip them of jurisdiction over controversial issues. Limiting judicial terms would be a far more effective way to achieve the same goal, for it would curb activist abuses without eliminating court autonomy.

Today, civil libertarians are having nightmares about the Rehnquist court in the year 2010. But if Federal judges were no longer appointed for life, those bad dreams might disappear with a new President and Congress 10 years from now.

# The Lawyers' Game

## 111. Save the Exclusionary Rule

*July 1983*

Back in 1911, federal marshals heard that one Fremont Weeks was selling lottery tickets by mail; they promptly broke down his door and took everything they could find. He was convicted, but the Supreme Court, appalled at the blatant disregard of the Fourth Amendment's guarantee against "unreasonable searches and seizures" by law-enforcement officials, overturned his conviction in 1914 and barred federal courts from using illegally seized evidence. Justice William Day wrote that "the tendency of those who execute the criminal laws of the country to obtain conviction by means of unlawful seizures . . . should find no sanction in the judgments of the courts." Thus was the origin of the exclusionary rule—eventually extended to the states in 1961 in *Mapp* v. *Ohio*—by which the Court gave substance to an amendment then in danger of becoming a dead letter, ignored and unenforced.

But today the rule has come under increasingly sharp attack from police officers, prosecutors, and politicians, and the Supreme Court is taking another look at it in the pending case of *Illinois* v. *Gates*. In an unusual move, the Supreme Court ordered a second set of hearings in the case and raised the issue of modifying the exclusionary rule, particularly in cases where the officers believe in good faith that their search was legal.

The principal argument made by opponents of the rule is that it frees the guilty. The Bureau of Justice Statistics and the federal National Institute of Justice say that up to 55,000 serious criminal cases, including as much as a third of all drug cases, have to be dropped each year because of the rule. Moreover, in cases that do go to trial, the conviction rate is lower where evidence has been suppressed because of the rule.

But raising the specter of prisons across America being emptied by the exclusionary rule is just scaremongering. A General Accounting Office study found that only 0.4 percent of federal cases were not prosecuted because of problems with illegal searches, and only 1.3 percent of those that went to trial lacked some evidence because of the rule (half of the defendants in these cases were convicted anyway). Between 1976 and 1979, only 4.8 percent of the cases in California rejected by prosecutors were rejected because of the exclusionary rule; that was just 0.78 percent of all California felony cases. And according to Ira Glasser, executive director of the American Civil Liberties Union, only sixteen of 2857 cases in 1980, seven of 2277 in 1981, and one of 2621 in 1982 were dismissed because of the exclusionary rule in one Midwest jurisdiction. Indeed, the politicians and law-enforcement officials are simply pandering to the public perception that criminals are being set free: *New York Times* columnist Tom Wicker reports that a member of President Reagan's Task Force on Violent Crime told him that the rule had to be changed not because it prevented many criminals from going to jail, but because people thought that it did.

Few violent crimes are involved in such cases; a recent Heritage Foundation study acknowledged that "the incidence of suppression of evidence in murder cases is low. It is far more common in cases involving weapons, gambling, and narcotics violators"—in other words, cases that should not have been brought to trial, because no one had been wronged.

And what of the few violent criminals who do go free because illegal evidence against them is thrown out of court? They do not go free because "the constable blundered," for there would have been no evidence to convict the defendant had not the constable blundered in the first place. In virtually every case, the evidence was collected only because the constitutional rules were broken.

The exclusionary rule performs two particularly valuable functions. The first is to deter unconstitutional police conduct. Even the Justice Department, in its *Gates* Supreme Court brief, admits that *Mapp* helped end "palpably egregious police misconduct" and encouraged state police to request warrants and become more professional. The Heritage Foundation study concluded that the "rule probably can have a limited, long-range deterrent influence," adding that the rule would be much more effective if supplemented by "measures to educate and discipline law-enforcement officers."

Unfortunately, these supplementary measures would be jeopardized if the rule falls. The good-faith exception, for example, would place a premium on ignorance; police could better claim an "honest mistake" if they had less sophisticated training and reduced coordination with prosecutors in search and seizure matters.

Moreover, the good-faith exception, by allowing court use of evidence if the officer used a warrant later found to be invalid, would effectively immunize the warrant process from review. Magistrates could routinely issue warrants even if they lacked probable cause, because they'd know that any evidence gathered could still be used in court.

Some have suggested deterring lawless prosecutorial conduct by allowing illegally obtained evidence in court only if the relevant police department had promoted compliance with the Fourth Amendment through training and disciplinary measures. Others suggest that people whose rights have been violated be allowed to sue for damages.

But training and disciplinary programs are more likely to be established with an effective exclusionary rule that provides a meaningful sanction. Merely admonishing, or even enjoining, police departments to establish such programs would likely fail, for program effectiveness and seriousness would be virtually impossible to monitor, and inadequate measures would be accepted to avoid letting "the guilty go free." Damage suits, on the other hand, would be entirely appropriate—but criminal defendants would have virtually no chance of convincing a jury to award them compensation.

The second purpose of the rule—indeed, the original basis for it—is to help protect peoples' right to privacy. Justice Joseph P. Bradley wrote that "the essence" of an illegal search "is the invasion of [a person's] indefeasible right of personal security, personal liberty, and private property." It would be inconsistent to provide constitutional protection against certain searches and seizures because they violate fundamental individual rights, but then to allow the fruit of such illegal actions to be used against a defendant.

However the Supreme Court rules in *Gates*, the fight over the exclusionary rule is likely to continue. But the rule remains as important today as it was seventy years ago. Appeals Court Judge Malcolm Wilkey complains that simply modifying the rule would not be enough; to stop the guilty from going free, he says, police would continue to lie about what they did and judges would continue to "be inclined to 'believe' the officer, even if [they] well know from all the surrounding circumstances that the officer is lying." That an appellate judge is willing to acknowledge the existence—today—of widespread contempt for fundamental individual rights among judges as well as police officers underscores the need to strengthen, not weaken, our constitutional safeguards. And that includes the exclusionary rule.

## 112.  The Nine Lives of the LSC

*July 30, 1986*

One of the most enduring bureaucratic institutions in the nation's capital is the Legal Services Corp. Despite persistent efforts by the Reagan administration to kill the corporation, the LSC survives, spending more than $300 million a year.

The LSC originally was intended to provide legal assistance for the poor and spent only $71 million in 1975. Barely three years later its outlays had more than doubled, and then doubled again by 1980, to $320 million.

With the vast expansion in budget came a concomitant change in purpose: the LSC became a fount of leftist political activism, using the courts to force the sort of wealth redistribution that even a spendthrift Congress was unwilling to legislate.

Federal funds were used to oppose a tax cut initiative in California in 1980; that same year LSC training manuals urged attorneys who collected public moneys to ally themselves with "the Democratic coalition." Once Ronald Reagan took office, LSC officials organized a "survival campaign" for the social programs targeted for elimination by the new administration.

And LSC activists, who profited so handsomely at taxpayer expense, were successful in preserving their agency.

President Reagan has been able to cut the budget slightly—outlays this year are running $312 million—and his appointees have eliminated the corporation's most outrageous partisan political activities. Yet congressional opposition to even the most minor reforms has been strong.

Surprisingly, one of the most persistent protectors of the LSC bureaucracy is Sen. Warren Rudman, a New Hampshire Republican.

For instance, earlier this year the LSC proposed regulations to restrict lobbying by groups receiving grants from the corporation. Rudman, chairman of the Commerce, Justice, State and the Judiciary subcommittee, disapproved the change.

Late last year the LSC tried to implement record-keeping requirements for publicly funded attorneys; Rudman and other members of Congress blocked this attempt to increase the accountability of grantees. Similarly, Rudman and Ernest Hollings, the ranking subcommittee Democrat, denied a LSC request to reprogram money to computerize the operations of grantees, to improve the corporation's oversight capabilities.

Attempts to save money have met with scarcely more success. The LSC tried to close four regional offices, which duplicate work carried out in the corporation's District of Columbia headquarters.

However, Rudman and Hollings blocked the proposal; their letter of June 9 explained that "the committee has received objections from a majority of the senators from the affected states." It seems a half million dollars in taxpayer funds is of no matter when politicians want pork for their constituents.

Finally, the LSC proposed to cut "National Support" grants by 10 percent, Regional Training grants by 21.6 percent, and Migrant Component grants by 21.6 percent. The House and Senate, however, refused to countenance such changes, even though, LSC officials complain, these funds underwrite more left activism than poor people's services.

Congress should do away with the LSC, for a federalized network including the district headquarters, regional offices and numerous partisan grantees, is not the best way to meet the legal needs of the poor.

Even had LSC attorneys in the past not been more interested in using poor people for political gain than in helping them, with 600,000 attorneys in the United States, organized into countless city, county and state bar associations, there is virtually unlimited potential for expanded private pro bono activity.

Indeed, tearing down the monopoly barriers to the legal profession that attorneys have erected in an attempt to protect their earnings would allow more of the people most likely to handle the cases of lower income people to become attorneys. For the current system mostly penalizes those people who, however qualified, are unable, for educational or financial reasons, to meet the stringent requirements set by many states.

Anyway, closing down the LSC would not prevent states and localities from subsidizing legal services for the poor. In fact, the administration has proposed spending $2.7 billion next year in social services block grants, part of which could be used by the levels of government closest to indigent people to create non-partisan programs to meet high-priority legal needs.

In any case, Congress should give LSC officials greater latitude to economize on funds and discourage political activism. Congressional micromanagement of the sort practiced by Rudman and his colleagues, while the norm for Washington, helps no one, including the poor people supposedly served by the LSC.

# 113. Lawyers v. Consumers
# A Legal Monopoly?

*June 1985*

The legal marketplace is one of the most tightly regulated in America, and one over which consumers have virtually no control. Rules regarding attorneys are invariably set by legal organizations; the effect is a professional cartel, which has reduced consumer choice and pushed up fees.

In recent years, however, some of the restrictions on who can become a lawyer and what attorneys can do once in practice have been relaxed. Price-cutting, advertising, improved service and increased client responsiveness are now being seen at all levels of the profession. A visible symbol of this change is the large numbers of TV commercials that have been appearing in behalf of lawyers and legal clinics. The result has been to increase competition among legal practitioners, giving consumers a wider array of options and bringing down the cost of legal services.

The American Bar Association's Commission on Advertising, for example, found "evidence throughout the country that professional advertising has in many instances reduced the total cost to the consumer of legal services for routine matters." The American Legal Clinic Association estimates that prices have fallen about a third in the past decade, and in 1984 the Federal Trade Commission released a study showing lawyers' fees for wills, uncontested divorces and other routine services to be between 5 percent and 13 percent lower in states that allowed greater freedom to advertise.

These changes, however, have affected only marginal aspects of the situation. Numerous features of the legal system limiting competition and consumer options still remain in place. To begin with, anyone performing certain legal services who does not possess a bar card can be prosecuted for the "unauthorized practice of law" (UPL). For example, bank officers often cannot put together trusts; accountants must steer clear of some tax matters; labor consultants dare not give advice on legal questions; real estate agents cannot handle some aspects of property transactions; paralegals are prohibited from putting their names on pleadings; and legal secretaries are just supposed to type. No matter how knowledgeable the other professional or para-professional, no matter how qualified they are to perform a particular duty, the work is off-limits to them.

The UPL standard is a patchwork across the United States; what functions non-lawyers can perform varies widely from state to state. But everyone, from state bar officials to academic investigators, agrees on the effect of UPL on consumers: to increase legal costs.

An example of a bar-initiated UPL suit is the case of Rosemary Furman of Jacksonville, Florida. Furman has spent virtually her entire career in the law. A legal secretary and court stenographer for 22 years, she had been helping clients with simple, noncontroversial legal matters—name changes, uncontested divorces, bankruptcy protection, wills, adoptions, and the like—for the past dozen years. Furman didn't appear in court. Instead, she procured the necessary forms and helped people fill them out.

Furman's clients were happy; they received expert assistance for only $50, a fraction of the cost of a regular attorney. But local lawyers were not pleased. So, in 1977, a complaint for the unauthorized practice of law was filed against Furman.

The result was preordained. State bar officials didn't prove any harm to consumers, but they didn't have to—Furman was doing prohibited lawyers' work. She could type up the legal papers, the court declared, but she could not point out errors to her customers—many of whom were ill-educated—or answer their questions. Furman found this an odd position to take if one is concerned about consumers: "I had been correcting the mistakes of lawyers and judges all my professional life, and now I was told I could not do the same for illiterate people."

So Furman continued to advise her clients, and she soon was hauled into court again, held in contempt, and sentenced to jail. Though granted clemency by Florida Governor Robert Graham and the state cabinet, Furman had to close her office and now faces nearly $8,000 in legal fees. But she remains unrepentant. "Why," Furman asks, "should anyone be forced to pay expensive professional fees to someone who accomplishes no more than what a reasonably competent secretary could do?"

Furman's fight has had some results. Last year, for example, the Florida Supreme Court finally allowed trial court clerks to distribute divorce forms to the public. A group of Furman's clients also filed a class action lawsuit against the state bar and the Florida Supreme Court, which oversees the bar, to try to establish the public's right of court access without a lawyer.

Furman's case is one of several which have been fought out in recent years, testing the right of non-lawyers to provide some aspects of legal service. In this connection, many law firms recognize the value of professionals in other fields. For years virtually every large law firm has employed dozens of paralegals to handle legal matters for which an attorney's expertise is unnecessary. Now firms are increasingly bringing lobbyists, physicians, accountants, economists, public relations experts and other professionals on staff.

But what is good for law firms should be good for law consumers, and so far it hasn't been. In perhaps the most exhaustive study of the UPL issue yet conducted, Stanford law professor Deborah Rhodes says that "at every level of enforcement, the consumer's need for protection has been proclaimed rather than proven." She concludes that the present treatment of UPL is "inconsistent, incoherent, and, from a policy perspective, indefensible." She therefore urges that the sort of services provided by Furman and others like her—form preparation and oral advice—be completely deregulated.

*Restrictions on Supply*

The lawyer's monopoly also is enforced through tight controls on access to the profession. The organized bar, for instance, regulates law schools to limit both their number and their total output. Today almost all states require attorneys to graduate from a law school accredited by the American Bar Association (ABA) or a particular state bar association; only California allows graduates of unaccredited schools to sit for the bar exam.

These standards usually are justified as necessary to protect the public, but the demand for such regulation has always come from lawyers, not consumers. Moreover, many of the regulations do little to guarantee the quality of either schools or graduates. Instead, the often lengthy approval process has deterred the establishment of new schools and restricted the number of graduates from existing schools.

And, of course, once they graduate, prospective attorneys must then pass the bar exam, which varies widely by state as far as the subjects covered, the test's difficulty and grading practices. Indeed, a half dozen states allow graduates of state law schools to join the bar without taking the same exam that prospective attorneys from even the most prestigious institutions in the nation are expected to pass. And by contrast, 18 states require attorneys from out of state, who have already passed one or more bar exams, to sit for another one.

The bar exam has come under increasing scrutiny. Last year, for example, seven people who flunked the California bar exam sued the state bar's Committee of Bar Examiners after it was revealed that, for the first time ever, officials raised the passing score above 70 percent, flunking nearly one in eight of the July 1983 examinees who otherwise would have passed.

The bar claims the change was a "technical" one intended to maintain the same difficulty of the exam. Yet, as the former Deputy Director of Operations for the Justice Department's antitrust division, Richard J. Favretto, has pointed out, "lawyers write, administer, and grade bar examinations. [One should be] suspicious of any system in which those in the market determine who can enter."

*Restrictions on Competition*

Finally, the legal monopoly is consummated by restrictions on competition between established lawyers, the most serious of which used to be blatant price-fixing. Some states once treated fee reductions as a breach of an attorney's ethical duties. One local bar association in New Jersey "disapproved" competitive bidding for business; a New York bar group warned its members that cutting fees encouraged clients "whose main consideration is to acquire maximum services at the minimum price."

Fee-setting disappeared only a decade ago, when the U.S. Supreme Court held that the practice was a "classic illustration of price-fixing" and therefore illegal under the Sherman Antitrust Act. The court suit that struck down minimum fees was filed by a consumer, Lewis Goldfarb, who went to 19 different attorneys in Fairfax, Virginia, none of whom would charge less than the rates fixed by the county association's fee schedule.

It took two more years to tear down another rule that held up legal prices—the prohibition on advertising. Though attorneys, including Abraham Lincoln, had advertised throughout the 1800s, in 1908 the ABA formally banned advertising in its model guidelines, a standard subsequently adopted by most state bar associations. Like fee-cutting, advertising in violation of bar association rules was considered unethical and could serve as grounds for an official reprimand, suspension or even disbarment.

The fight for the consumers' right to know was led by two lawyers. In 1976, John Bates and Van O'Steen, the owners of a small Arizona legal clinic that specialized in simple, uncontested cases, decided to test the law by running an ad offering "legal services at very reasonable fees." The ad violated state bar rules, and disciplinary proceedings were instituted against them. Bates and O'Steen carried their fight to the U.S. Supreme Court, which, in 1977, ruled that lawyers had a constitutional right to advertise their services. Justice Harry Blackmun wrote for the 5–4 majority that "commercial speech serves to inform the public of the availability, nature, and prices of products and services, and thus performs an indispensable role in the allocation of resources in a free enterprise system." Further, he concluded, "the listener's interest is substantial: the consumer's concern for the free flow of commercial speech often may be far keener than his concern for urgent political dialogue."

The organized bar remains hostile to the concept of advertising, however. Many state bars and the ABA still attempt to limit advertising. Last year's revised ABA model ethical rules, for example, prohibit lawyers from, among other things, using client endorsements and testimonials and stating their areas of specialty. J. Paul McGrath, head of the Justice Department's antitrust division, wrote to the state chief justices of each of the 40 states then considering adopting the ABA rules. In his letter, he stated that the "overly broad" rules "would restrict the flow of useful information from attorneys to consumers of legal services.

Finally, ethical rules traditionally have barred attorneys from "soliciting"—that is, recommending that consumers hire them. This issue, too, went to the U.S. Supreme Court, with the justices observing that "in-person solicitation serves much the same function as the ad in Bates." But the court declined to grant solicitation the same degree of constitutional protection as advertising, so the vast majority of state bar associations continue to prohibit most forms of solicitation, including by direct mail. The ABA model rules prohibit or discourage all oral and most written advances to potential clients.

However, these barriers also are breaking down, though more slowly than restrictions on advertising. The Justice Department, for example, has been forcefully advocating that states "permit all solicitation and advertising except the kinds that are false, misleading, undignified or champertous." And some state courts are starting to agree: late last year New York State's highest court tossed out a prohibition on the use of direct mail as violating a lawyer's First and Fourteenth Amendment rights.

The slow but steady collapse of the legal monopoly is good news for consumers. Prosecutions for the unauthorized practice of law are coming under increasing scrutiny; the efficacy of law school regulation and bar exams is being increasingly questioned. Set fee schedules are a thing of the past, and price and service information is being increasingly transmitted through advertising and solicitation.

Deregulation does not mean that no consumers will get hurt by unethical or incompetent lawyers. But a more freely competitive market, which Favretto has called a "benign form of regulation," will better protect consumers. Private groups can get more involved in recommending attorneys to their members and offering pre-paid legal plans; consumer groups and local law enforcement officials can monitor fraud and misrepresentation, as they do for other businessmen and professionals. Serious instances of incompetence, which occur even today, can be combatted through malpractice lawsuits.

We live in a litigious society, but the provision of legal services needn't be as expensive nor as mysterious as in the past. If consumer activists and legal reformers have their way, people's access to the law will continue to increase.

# V. The Helping Hand of Uncle Sam

# Jobless by Decree

## 114. Destroying Jobs the Government Way

*May 30, 1985*

For 45 years Joseph Falk has made a living as a street vendor in the nation's capital. The 79-year-old Falk hasn't gotten rich—last year he made about $2,700—but he's not on welfare either. However, Falk no longer can sell his pens and air fresheners to District of Columbia cabdrivers, courtesy of Mayor Marion Barry.

The district government has just implemented a batch of new regulations, reducing the number of vending licenses issued, requiring vendors to post a $500 bond, barring sale of manufactured items and limiting the areas where vendors can peddle their wares.

Every vendor, including Falk, who plied his trade from a box, also must buy a stand or cart. And not just any cart. Hand trucks must be made of pressure-treated wood, have wheels 32 inches in diameter, and be "stained and varnished" or painted with a "predominant" color and one or more "accent" colors. Lest the vendor have trouble matching different hues, the regulations specify use of "the Grumbacher Color Computer (color wheel) manufacturer No. B420."

What great social purpose does the municipal color scheme achieve? The Barry administration says the rules are necessary to protect consumers and "reorder the balance between street vendors and stores."

Consumers, however, didn't complain about their ability to walk down the street and pick up an umbrella in the midst of a sudden summer thunderstorm. Instead, the opposition to vendors came from those staunch defenders of free enterprise, local businessmen. The manager of a women's apparel store, for instance, complained that the vendors "destroyed our accessory business." But no more, she now exults.

Unfortunately, Washington is not the only city where the street's self-employed are denied their right to earn a living. New York City cracked down two years ago on what Mayor Ed Koch denounced as a "hydra-headed" menace. After the city issued 25,000 summonses and confiscated merchandise 20,000 times, Koch declared that "we have them on the run."

The district's move toward economic totalitarianism illustrates merely one more way in which the government consciously puts people out of work. Vendors are not alone in being licensed; taxicab "medallions," which give the owner the right to drive a cab, cost $60,000 each in New York City. Needless to say, the Big Apple has fewer taxis per citizen and fewer minorities driving cabs than do cities without a taxi monopoly.

Moreover, hundreds of professions and occupations, from haircutting to TV repair to law, cannot be entered without obtaining the approval of some industry group after enduring years of irrelevant training and passing arcane tests. Though the stated justification for such rules is consumer protection, occupational licensure always is imposed at the behest of existing practitioners.

The federal government also routinely puts people out of work. The minimum wage, for example, effectively prevents employers from hiring people who are unable to produce $3.35 worth of goods or services an hour. This law destroys hundreds of thousands of jobs, and hurts most the least educated and least skilled.

Another job-killing federal regulation is the Davis-Bacon Act. Passed in 1931, the law requires contractors on federally funded construction projects to pay workers the "prevailing wage," normally the higher union scale. The legislation was passed to put blacks out of work; Democratic Congressman Algood of Alabama, for instance, explained to his colleagues the need to remedy the threat posed by "cheap colored labor" to "white labor throughout the country." Davis-Bacon still takes jobs away from non-union workers.

Washington's Mayor Barry and his counterparts across the nation speak eloquently of the crisis of unemployment, the human cost of joblessness. Yet their own policies help consign millions across the nation to a future without hope.

About the time that the new street vending regulations were going into effect in Washington, the local Democratic Party held a reception at the luxurious Hyatt Regency Hotel on Capitol Hill. Street vendors, many of them members of the city's black underclass, protested outside as denizens of the city's black elite drove up in chauffeured limousines. But the Democratic heavies didn't seem to notice; after all, they have it made.

Yet vendors should have the same right to try to work their way out of poverty as did Marshall Field, B. Altmann, Richard Sears and J. C. Penney, all who began their entrepreneurial lives on city streets. Of course, many sidewalk merchants, like Joseph Falk, earn just enough to avoid starving. But they, too, are living the "American dream" of self-employment.

The imperious guardians of public order across the United States should respect the right of people, whether curbside vendors, black teenagers or non-union construction workers, to earn money and self-respect without interference.

## 115. Preserving the Freedom to Work at Home

*November 3, 1986*

The International Ladies' Garment Workers' Union (ILGWU) has declared war. Its opponent is the US Department of Labor, which recently proposed a rules change that, says union president Jay Mazur, "gives the green light to the thousands of sweatshop operators throughout this country who exploit our most vulnerable workers."

How is the Reagan administration supposedly returning the United States to the manufacturing dark ages? By allowing people to work in their homes if they choose.

In 1943 the Federal government banned "industrial homework" for seven products: knitted outerwear, gloves, women's apparel, buttons and buckles, jewelry, embroidery, and handkerchiefs. The restriction, the department said, was intended to help enforce the Fair Labor Standards Act; but the regulations were adopted largely to reduce competition with unionized companies and make it easier for the union to organize.

In succeeding years the Labor Department has busily enforced the rules. In 1979, for instance, the government cited several Vermont companies that purchased sweaters and outerwear knitted at home; roughly 1,000 people, many of them retirees working to supplement social security, lost their livelihood.

The newly elected Reagan administration moved to lift the home-knitting ban. After a three-year court battle people gained the right to knit at home, but the six other trades remained outside the law.

So earlier this year the department began arresting employers in North Carolina; the government shut down the Tom Thumb Glove Company, for instance, putting 85 people out of work. The administration finally decided to exempt all home workers as long as the employer filed with the Labor Department and paid the minimum wage. The final rule may yet be changed and faces a likely court challenge from the union; nevertheless, people should soon be free to work at home if they desire.

This reform is long overdue. For too long the government has sacrificed jobs for ILGWU's selfish economic interests. Mr. Mazur may say he cares about the "most vulnerable workers," but his real concern is his members, who fear home-based competition. The union just wants to keep people out of work to jack up its members' wages.

The growth of homework has created important new employment opportunities, allowing people to design the work environment that best meets their individual needs: women seeking to combine motherhood with a job, the disabled who can't commute, and anyone who prefers to set his own schedule. Indeed, homework is uniquely an employee's choice, so it is not surprising that the workers supposedly being exploited don't want the government's "protection."

The union campaign against homework strikes hardest at those who have the fewest job options outside the home. Said retiree Virginia Gray when the Labor Department stopped her from knitting, "Tell them to do their work down in Washington and leave us alone. Our knitting's our living."

The homework ban has ominous implications as telecommuting—using a computer and telephone to link a work station with an office—becomes more popular. There may be as many as 1 million telecommuters today, and the Center for Futures Research at the University of Southern California expects that number to hit 5 million within a decade.

But organized labor is, if anything, more frightened of the "electronic cottage" than of home knitters. The Service Employees International Union, National Organization of Working Women, and AFL-CIO have all called for bans on computer homework. Said ILGWU past president Sol Chaikin, "We cannot afford to wait for a new history of exploitation, wage and hour violations, child abuse, and loss of office and factory jobs." But no labor leader has yet presented any evidence of mistreated telecommuters.

The question of homework comes down to personal freedom. Why should the federal government prescribe where people can and cannot work? What right does a bureaucracy have to set the proper life style for employees?

When the home knitters were fighting for their right to work, Max Zimny, the union's general counsel, said the women "should find some other way to occupy themselves." But it is Mr. Zimny and his colleagues who should be doing something, anything else, rather than trying to keep people unemployed. It's time the federal government left the home workers alone and treated this country as if it really were the "land of the free."

# 116. It's Time to Repeal Davis-Bacon

*June 12, 1986*

Texas Sen. Phil Gramm, fresh from stampeding the federal establishment by co-authoring the budget-balancing law that bears his name, is taking on yet another sacred cow: the Davis-Bacon Act.

Davis-Bacon was passed in 1931 and requires contractors on government projects costing more than $2,000 to pay their workers "prevailing" wages—normally union scale. The legislation, a multibillion-dollar windfall for construction unions, was passed for the express purpose of keeping "cheap colored labor" from competing for jobs held by whites.

Gramm has proposed raising the law's threshold to $1 million for military construction. Last year there were 17,246 defense "contract actions," worth $7.2 billion, covered by Davis-Bacon; freeing the bulk of these would save an estimated half billion dollars over the next five years.

Naturally, Robert Georgine, president of the AFL-CIO's building and construction trades department, opposes the amendment. It would "emasculate" the law, he complains.

In fact, there are few laws that more deserve emasculation. Davis-Bacon is a foolish attempt to set a minimum wage for highly skilled construction employees; it props up union scales while keeping less experienced, disadvantaged workers unemployed.

All told, the Congressional Budget Office estimates that the law hikes federal costs by $1 billion per year. Indeed, Davis-Bacon probably imposes millions more in hidden costs by discouraging many contractors from even bidding on federal projects, thereby reducing competition.

Equally pernicious is the impact of Davis-Bacon on those people trying to break into the job market. Since the purpose of the law is to protect the earnings of the best-paid construction workers, it requires that even less skilled helpers and apprentices receive full journeymen's wages. Thus, firms with Davis-Bacon contracts tend to favor highly trained employees since the pay rate is the same.

The result is to remove yet another rung from the economic ladder of opportunity for new workers seeking job experience. Though someone with less education and training might be willing to work for less in an attempt to get ahead, Davis-Bacon says no.

And those who are hurt are disproportionately minorities. That is, the law works precisely as it was intended to.

Consider the Philadelphia project run by the House of Umoja, a neighborhood group. Umoja wanted to build housing for delinquent black youths; the first phase of the contract was publicly supported, so Davis-Bacon applied. The contractor used no local workers: they simply were not productive enough to earn union wages.

The second part of the project relied on private contributions, was not subject to federal wage fixing, and therefore cost 40 percent less. Equally important, the Ujoma Construction Co. provided most of the workers, who were largely local residents and ex-offenders.

But later construction was again supported by the federal government, thereby freezing out disadvantaged workers who desperately needed job opportunities. Complained construction director Thomas Massaro, it was a tragedy "for the proud and proven young men of the Umoja Construction Co. to sit by once again as outsiders earn big dollars on their block."

A law this pernicious should be eliminated entirely. Not only should Davis-Bacon be repealed, but congressmen who have supported it in the past should be permanently barred from ever wailing about the needs of the poor and disadvantaged.

Gramm would not go quite that far, he would merely exempt most military construction projects from the law. But President Reagan, who has studiously avoided the issue after promising construction unions in 1980 that he wouldn't push to repeal Davis-Bacon, now is not only supporting the Gramm proposal, but has also suggested raising the threshold on federal civilian projects to $100,000.

As usual, good ideas like Gramm's face a difficult fight. Last year the Senate approved a similar amendment, also authored by Gramm, by a 49-to-48 vote; the issue was then "traded away in conference with the House," says a Gramm staffer. However, he thinks the measure's prospects are now better, particularly given the administration's support.

Davis-Bacon is one of those issues where there is only one side. There's simply no justification for forcing taxpayers to subsidize the wages of the highest-skilled carpenters, electricians and steamfitters, while keeping minority youth and disadvantaged, inexperienced workers unemployed.

The construction unions have shown that they can take care of themselves. It's time Congress worried about the young men who work for the Umoja Construction Co., and the rest of us.

## 117. Putting People out of Work

*March 18, 1987*

Economic ignorance dies hard. Sen. Edward Kennedy, D-Mass., and Rep. Augustus Hawkins, D-Calif., have joined to introduce legislation that would hike the minimum wage by more than one-third, raising it from $3.35 to about $4.50.

Rep. Mario Biaggi, D-N.Y., would set the wage level even higher, at $5.05. And both bills would peg the minimum to half the average hourly wage rate in the future.

Some increase in the minimum wage seems likely to pass at least the House. Hawkins and Kennedy "feel so strongly about this," says one aide, that "I don't think they're going to compromise."

Such a hard-line stance undoubtedly pleases organized labor, a key Democratic constituency. For while union leaders like to talk about helping the working poor, they know that federal wage-fixing sets a floor under their members' earnings by knocking lower-paid workers out of the market.

The basic problem with the minimum wage is that it tells firms not to hire people who lack the education, training and skills necessary to produce at least the minimum level of goods or services.

Some companies hire workers with more experience; other firms simply leave marginal positions unfilled. And many businesses automate, replacing elevator operators and bank tellers, for example, with machines.

Moreover, points out Heritage Foundation analyst Bruce Bartlett, increases in the minimum wage have encouraged companies to lay off workers during recessions, since employees can't temporarily accept lower wages in order to save their jobs. Kennedy may never have faced such a dilemma, but many other Americans are not so lucky.

And millions of jobs are potentially at stake. Even the Minimum Wage Study Commission, a liberal-dominated panel, estimated that every 10 percent hike in the minimum wage reduced teenage employment by 1 percent, or 80,000 jobs. And many studies suggest the employment loss is even greater—2 percent or 3 percent for every 10 percent increase in the minimum level. That means Rep. Biaggi's bill could put as many as 1.2 million young people out of work.

Economists are not the only observers who recognize that a rising minimum wage hurts the most vulnerable members of society, especially poorly educated minority youth. So do many of the social workers who focus on teens. Indeed, the National Conference of Black Mayors supported an early Reagan initiative to create a sub-minimum wage for the young.

Federal wage-setting does more than just destroy jobs. For instance, employers forced to raise cash pay may drop or cut whatever fringe benefits they offer. Such a step could make all workers, and not just those employees officially covered by the minimum wage, worse off.

Even more fundamental is the moral issue of forcing employers to pay more. In effect, the minimum wage is a tax on companies that hire the disadvantaged and the young.

Such a policy obviously does not encourage firms to use more unskilled workers. Moreover, penalizing a select few businesses in an attempt to achieve what is presumably a general national goal is grossly unfair.

If the government wants to increase people's earnings, it should do so through a program for which everyone pays; this is, in fact, the purpose of the many existing federal welfare programs. Such an approach neither puts millions of poor people out of work—directly, at least—nor discriminates against firms that are hiring the workers who most need help.

So Congress should abolish, not raise, the minimum wage. Good intentions are not enough: experience has proved beyond any doubt that this law hurts potentially millions of poor people.

At the very least, Capitol Hill should reconsider the "Youth Employment Opportunity Wage" proposed by Reagan during his first term. That bill would have cut the minimum for teens to $2.50—and created anywhere between 250,000 and 430,000 jobs.

The tragedy of young people, especially ghetto teens, who can't find work, is ever present. And every year they go without a job they become less employable, never having gained the skills and responsibilities that come from even a low-paying job.

So before Congress acts, Kennedy and Hawkins and Biaggi should pause for a moment to consider the likely consequences of the legislation they so blithely support: thousands more young blacks out on the streets, without hope or an economic future. It is time for such avowed liberal humanitarians to choose between the wishes of big labor and the needs of the poorest of the poor.

## 118.  Congress's Job-Killing Attack on Business

*July 29, 1987*

Fifty years ago fringe benefits accounted for just 3 percent of employees' wages; they now represent more than a third of all compensation. Most of this increase occurred voluntarily, as businesses competed to hire and retain skilled employees.

Health and dental insurance, maternity leave, profit-sharing and similar benefits are not cheap—the food-distribution industry alone spends $6,163 per employee annually on fringe benefits. But now Congress is threatening to kill the Golden Goose of American business.

For years government has used its regulatory power to expand the reach of the public sector at business's expense. The minimum wage, for instance, requires a few labor-intensive employers to bear the cost of raising poor people's incomes. By 1985 mandated fringe benefits represented 10 percent of employees' salaries.

But the growth of the deficit—with its added pressure on federal spending—has increased Congress's desire to find new ways to stick business with the cost of federal programs. Last year Congress voted to require firms to maintain health insurance for fired employees and their families for up to three years, at a cost of $1.5 billion annually.

And now Sen. Ted Kennedy, D-Mass., long a frustrated proponent of national health insurance, is pushing legislation to force companies to provide health benefits for all employees, including part-time personnel. Kennedy estimates the bill's cost to be $20 billion, but that figure ignores the negative employment impact of such a huge, indirect tax hike on business—a million jobs lost, according to the Institute for Research on the Economics of Taxation. All told, IRET estimates that Kennedy's "free" benefit would cost about $100 billion.

Ironically, even many workers who keep their jobs would lose under the Kennedy bill. Anyone whose wage was above the legal minimum might find his earnings cut to pay for the health benefit. Even congressmen should understand that there ain't no such thing as a free lunch.

But the Kennedy bill is just the leading element of what Rep. Jack Kemp, R-N.Y., calls "the broadest, most sweeping and concerted attack on small business survival in memory."

Congress is considering legislation to force companies to provide 18 weeks of unpaid family leave, at a cost of $2.6 billion or more annually. Also under debate is a proposed increase in the minimum wage from $3.35 per hour to $4.65 by 1990. Such a jump would cost hundreds of thousands of disadvantaged workers their jobs and soak business for $4 billion to try to solve the societywide problem of poverty.

Despite administration opposition, Congress has voted to restrict the right of firms to close or move their factories. Such controls, by publicizing a company's problems, would make failure more likely and could discourage marginal operations from starting up.

Serious threats to business other than mandated benefits include comparable worth legislation, which would turn wage-setting over to the federal bureaucracy or the courts, protectionist trade legislation, and numerous tax hike proposals.

Kennedy's health insurance bill and the minimum wage hike alone would raise the cost of hiring a low-wage worker by as much as 62 percent. The inevitable result would be a large drop in employment.

Indeed, new federal regulations would be particularly harmful because their burden would fall disproportionately on smaller firms. Between 60 percent and 75 percent of workers without health insurance are self-employed or work for companies with fewer than 25 employees; smaller businesses would also have the most difficult time providing extended leave for employees.

Yet it is small business that has added 9 million jobs to the economy since 1981. On average, 70 percent of new jobs created every year are with small firms.

Unfortunately, one of every five new firms already folds within a year and those small businesses that survive don't run a profit for an average of 18 months. Costly new mandated benefits would prove fatal for many more enterprises, disabling the great American job machine.

It is America's market economy, with its open invitation for entrepreneurs—nearly 700,000 businesses were created last year—that has led to the sort of economic growth that is still the envy of the world. And as companies have prospered, they have naturally paid their employees more and provided them with better benefits.

But Congress's drive to pick up a few votes by mandating special benefits could backfire on all of us. For there is no free lunch: every American will end up paying for the bill Congress is trying to ignore.

## 119. Paying for the Eternal Free Lunch

*July 16, 1986*

The nation's capital is suffused with a belief in the never-ending free lunch, that all things good and wonderful can be costlessly provided by a simple vote of Congress. This has never been more evident than with the House Education and Labor Committee's passage of H.R. 4300, the Family and Medical Leave Act of 1986.

Co-sponsored by 98 congressmen, Republicans as well as Democrats, the bill would force firms to grant employees up to 18 weeks of unpaid "family leave" in the event of a birth, adoption or family illness. Medical leave of as much as 26 weeks would have to be made available if the worker himself got sick.

The company also would have to maintain health insurance during an employee's absence and provide a returning worker with comparable work. More ominously, the legislation creates a commission to study the possibility of granting employees paid leave.

There's nothing wrong with encouraging workers to stay home with their families, of course, but the fundamental question is: Who should pay? Going to work for a firm does not make it responsible for one's life; deciding to have a child does not entitle one to force the boss to help out.

Supporters of the bill proclaim it to be a pro-family adjustment to the realities of a world in which half of all women with small children work. Other advocates of liberal leave policies put the case in even more apocalyptic terms.

Stephen Webber, a board member of the United Mine Workers, testified before Congress that: "Employer policies can still devastate our children's well-being. When a company can force a nursing mother back to work, when a company can deny a father or mother a chance to bond as a family with their newborn . . . much has yet to be done."

Alas, Webber has lost sight of a simple, but enormously important, principle—individual responsibility. Ever since slavery was abolished, no firm in America can "force" a nursing mother to work. What companies can say is that if workers want to keep their jobs, they have to show up.

Is this harsh? No. It simply reflects the fact that the purpose of business is to produce goods and services for consumers, not to promote the "bonding" of parents and newborns.

The misguided notion that somehow employers should provide all sorts of services to their workers has led to legislation forcing companies to continue health insurance benefits for laid off employees and proposals to require corporate day-care facilities. As usual, politicians put their personal notions of justice into law and hand someone else the bill.

And it is not as if Americans are losing their jobs wholesale when they start families. Organized labor, which is backing H.R. 4300, already is perfectly free to bargain for liberal leave benefits. Indeed, that is the purpose of unions: to improve their members' compensation.

Nine out of 10 firms now grant maternity leave; 40 percent offer paternity leave. Moreover, roughly 40 percent of women have a right—by contract with their employer—to reclaim their jobs.

As the concept of family leave grows in importance, more workers are likely to demand liberal leave rights. But if they do so, it is only fair that they give up something in return.

For providing extended parental and medical leave is not costless; just as employees now trade off salary for pension plans and fringe benefits, so too should they bargain for extended leave rights. Labor doesn't deserve to get something for nothing through H.R. 4300.

Ironically, if the House bill were enacted, firms would probably start unilaterally lowering the value of the other benefits that they offer. Their only alternatives, as the cost of hiring workers rose, would be to raise prices or fire employees. (Such unfortunate possibilities probably have not occurred to Washington's believers in the eternal free lunch.)

Thus, though federally mandated leave might give workers more opportunity to be with their children, it would reduce employees' ability to
negotiate for the compensation they preferred most. Argues Virginia Lamp
of the U.S. Chamber of Commerce, "Employers and employees, not
Congress, can best design employee benefit packages."

There was a time when people who made voluntary choices, like
parenthood, were expected to bear the costs of their decisions. Today,
however, Congress seems determined to separate responsibility from action.

But our lawmakers have yet to find a way to eliminate the cost of
legislating their wildest whims. Instead, here, as always, Congress would
just make someone else pay the bill.

## 120. Child-Care Politics

*August 10, 1988*

If it really is darkest before the dawn, the presidential race is going to
get a lot worse before November 8. Most recently both Michael Dukakis
and George Bush have been trying to score political points off of children.

Democrat Dukakis has endorsed, in principle, a $2.5 billion measure
introduced by Sen. Christopher Dodd, D-Conn., and Rep. Dale Kildee, D-
Mich. The legislation, recently approved by the Senate Labor Committee,
would regulate and subsidize day-care centers across the nation.

Congressional Republicans have come up with their own, less expensive
measures. And Bush went before the National Federation of Business and
Professional Women's Clubs to unveil a $2.2 billion tax credit scheme. His
plan, which helps families rather than bureaucrats, is better than Dukakis'
approach but is still unnecessary.

After all, the federal government already provides some $7 billion
annually for day care through grants and tax credits. That's about 40
percent of all outlays on child care, private as well as public.

And neither Dukakis nor Bush has explained why the government has
to provide any subsidies at all for child care. Day care is the responsibility
of families, not the state. After all, the decision to have a child implies a
willingness to care for him or her.

The entrance of more women into the work force has made day care a
more important issue for many families, of course, but parents who both
work should be willing to pay for that service out of their extra wages.
Why should families where one parent decides to stay home with the kids
have to subsidize those which decide differently?

Day-care vouchers for poor families might be a useful adjunct to the welfare system, since the subsidy would help make them independent financially. But even then the government would be underwriting child care because it made policy sense, not because people were somehow "entitled" to it.

Anyway, there is no day-care emergency that requires solving. The Labor Department recently concluded that, despite some spot shortages, "there is not an across-the-board availability crisis of national proportions." In fact, the number of day-care spaces has increased nearly 10 percent annually for the last 25 years.

Between 1960 and 1986 the number of formal day-care centers jumped from 4,400 to 39,929; the number of kids served rose from 141,000 to 2.1 million. Even more children are cared for by an estimated 1.65 million unlicensed neighborhood providers and relatives.

And there would be more spaces available were it not for local restrictions that discourage informal neighborhood care. Many cities, for instance, refuse to allow a provider to look after children in a home judged safe to live in.

Some of the rules, detailed in a study by Heritage Foundation analyst Robert Rector, are inane. Texas requires the installation of stainless steel sinks; California once ordered a woman who cared for six children to build separate bathrooms for boys and girls before enrolling any additional kids. In different states, inspectors have variously regulated the attire of dolls, toddlers' "lesson plans," the direction that doors swing, and the height of outdoor fences.

The Dodd-Kildee bill would only worsen this regulatory morass by creating federal standards. In fact, one is entitled to suspect that supporters of the legislation are more interested in enriching the established child care industry than in helping poor parents care for their kids. For the new regulations, setting staff/child ratios, for instance, would benefit financially those who are lobbying hardest for the legislation—the "bureaucrats, planners, consultants, regulators, trainers, and state service providers," in Rector's words.

To be eligible for federal funds, states would have to apply the national standards to all providers, whether subsidized or not. The federal money would only go to a few selected institutions, however, those most able to play bureaucratic politics. Smaller enterprises, religious-affiliates, and neighborhood providers would be squeezed out by the bigger operators.

And despite all of the wailing about the plight of the poor, the emphasis on large, establishment centers reflects a bias toward the middle and upper classes. More than 80 percent of day-care users are two-earner families, whose median income is 50 percent higher than that of single-earner households; poor parents generally rely on family members and informal providers. Handing checks to well-to-do working mothers might be good politics, but it is not just policy.

Congress politicizes any issue that it touches, and day care is no exception. But there is no excuse for giving the federal government control of child care in the United States. Uncle Sam is not fit to become the nation's nanny.

# Whose Health?

## 121. A Failed Attempt at Political Blackmail

*June 22, 1988*

Congress has never been an institution prone to resist a special interest cause advanced by a sophisticated demagogue. So when the House voted down Rep. Claude Pepper's long-term health-care plan, it demonstrated rare political courage in the face of an unprecedented attempt at political blackmail.

Pepper, the 87-year-old self-anointed advocate of the elderly, has gained enormous influence by backing a host of new spending programs for senior citizens. He would loot the federal Treasury if doing so would buy him another vote or two.

Not surprisingly, the Florida congressman has long been a major stumbling block to any reform of Social Security, which is threatened with collapse early the next century as the huge baby boom generation retires. He cares not at all about the young; let someone suggest changing a system that taxes the poor most heavily while paying one-third of its benefits to the upper-middle class, and Rep. Pepper will become his demagogic worst.

The congressman was naturally in favor of a catastrophic health-care benefit as part of Medicare. And when the Reagan administration jumped on the bandwagon there was no stopping the proposal.

That legislation, newly approved by Congress, will cost $34 billion over the first five years and almost $60 billion annually by 2010. Most seniors will pay higher Medicare taxes to assist just 3 percent of the elderly. Numerous private options, including health-care IRAs, were available, but congressmen win votes by disbursing funds, not solving problems.

Even worse, however, was Pepper's proposal to create a major new "entitlement" for long-term health care. Like other similar social programs, costs were expected to quickly soar out of control: the Health Care Financing Administration predicted that benefits would run $63 billion over the first five years, $23 billion annually by 1993, and an incredible $89 billion a year by 2011.

The program was to be initially financed through a higher payroll tax, but as costs escalated other tax hikes would become necessary. These increased levies would cut the number of new jobs being created, making a poorer America and an increasingly unstable Medicare system.

Despite the popular horror stories, no new program is necessary to provide medical care at home; Medicare already covers that. Instead, Pepper wanted Uncle Sam to pay for cooking, cleaning, and other services—for everyone, no matter how well-off.

These activities are important, of course, but most of them are now handled by relatives and friends, as they should be. For the care of someone is first and foremost the responsibility of those closest to him; the taxpayers do not have an obligation to make costless every travail of life.

But Rep. Pepper was prepared to bankrupt the younger generations to take care of his constituency. So he played every dirty trick possible to ram his bill through Congress.

He first violated regular House procedure, working out a deal with Speaker Jim Wright to bypass the committee system and bring the bill directly to the floor. Yet if there is legislation that cries out for detailed hearings, the opportunity to offer amendments, and time for serious consideration, it is a new, multibillion-dollar entitlement program.

The Florida congressman also tried a little political demagogy. Though the fight against his bill was led by two Democratic committee chairmen, Dan Rostenkowski of Ways and Means and John Dingell of Commerce, Pepper held a news conference warning that "a lot of Republicans are going to get defeated if they vote against this bill."

The threat was not an idle one: Cheap political shots from the Democrats on Social Security have cost a number of Republicans their seats.

Finally, Pepper added a little emotional blackmail on the House floor. "This is a day I've waited and worked and, I might say, prayed for for 50 years."

In a choking voice, he added: "When you go home tonight and close your eyes to sleep and ask what did I do to lighten the burden of those who suffer, you can say you voted to help those who need help. It may not answer all the problems, but it will cool the brow of those who suffer and offer a little care."

But Rep. Pepper's moving rhetoric had nothing to do with reality. After all, his bill would have enriched a Rockefeller as much as a poor widow.

Instead, the congressman believes in power and votes; his compassionate tone merely masked a greedy, self-serving grab for political power.

The issue was not what had he waited 50 years to do. The question was: What was the right thing for Congress to do? And in this election year a majority of legislators surprisingly answered the question correctly. Come November voters should reward those members who refused to succumb to Rep. Pepper's attempted special interest blackmail.

## 122. The Duty to Die—and Pay

*April 12, 1984*

For someone twice elected governor of Colorado, Richard Lamm doesn't have much sense. Lamm recently told the Colorado Health Lawyers Association that the elderly have a "duty to die and get out of the way" to "let the other society, our kids, build a reasonable life." Lamm, who is 48, said that the terminally ill should not resort to high-technology medical treatment to artificially extend their lives.

Predictably, Lamm's remarks caused a furor. After all, who is Lamm to judge the quality of other people's lives? And how can we decide that the lives of the elderly are not worth saving? Moreover, when does someone have a "duty to die?" When he has five months left to live? Or five years? There is something just a little ominous in a government official—particularly the chief executive of a state—talking about people's "duty to die."

Yet Lamm has addressed, however maladroitly, a problem that may eventually wrench our society apart: Who should pay to preserve whose life? The average American lives 11 years longer today than he did 40 years ago, and the steady advance of technology and transplant capabilities continue to increase life expectancies.

The price of this added life, however, has not been cheap. In the last 20 years health care costs have soared from $27 billion to $247 billion, of which the federal government now pays more than 40 percent. And medical cost inflation shows no signs of abating.

Indeed, the solvency crisis that last year threatened to overwhelm Social Security (and which still does, despite last year's $165 billion tax increase) will hit Medicare within the decade. The trust fund is expected to run out of money by 1990, and accumulate a deficit of $250 billion by 1995. This fiscal disaster looms because our population is aging and living longer, and because the elderly are taking advantage of ever more expensive medical treatments.

Thus, unless we eventually say "no more," the taxpayers will be devoting 20 percent or more of their incomes just to providing health care to the elderly. We simply won't be able to afford to keep everyone alive as long as they want—fully one-third of Medicare expenditures are now spent on people who have less than a year to live.

The distinction that Lamm missed, however, is that no one has a duty to die. Anyone who wants to survive at all costs has a perfect right to do so. But that person does not have a right to force the rest of us to bankrupt ourselves to fund every process necessary to keep him or her alive. The quality of our lives must be considered as well as the quality of the life being extended.

A particularly pernicious danger posed by expanding federal medical programs is that they politicize more and more decisions over life and death instead of leaving them to patients and their doctors. In the socialized medical systems of Britain and Sweden, for example, the government controls the bulk of medical resources, and therefore the health destiny of most of the population. Both governments routinely make conscious decisions that some lives are not worth saving.

There is a tacit understanding in Sweden, for instance, that organ transplants and other expensive operations will not be performed on the elderly. Older patients in Britain are routinely passed over in favor of younger ones for treatment by the government. In fact, even the lives of some of the young are not considered worth saving by the health bureaucracy; Britons suffering from acute kidney disease rarely receive the necessary, but expensive, life-saving treatment. (Medicare covers kidney dialysis, and the program's costs soared more than six times in the first seven years.)

The twin problems of the value of life and who should pay to maintain it are not limited to the elderly. The administration's attempts to review the medical records of Baby Jane Doe, a baby born with severe birth defects, brings up the problem of the severely disabled young. Medical advances here, too, can extend life.

Should such lives, that are "not worth living" to most of us, be extended? And at what cost? It would be genocide for the government to decide that the severely handicapped must die. But it would be de facto slavery to force everyone to pay to maintain every life for as long as is medically possible.

The elderly, as well as the disabled young and middle-aged, do not have a duty to die and get out of the way. But neither do they have a right to force the rest of us to underwrite the preservation of their lives at any cost. The test of true compassion is not the expansiveness of government programs.

We may not like the way Gov. Lamm put it, but we can't ignore what he had to say. For the advance of medical technology, such a boon to everyone, requires us—sooner rather than later—to grapple with some of the most difficult of issues.

## 123. Dismantle the Doctors' Monopoly

*October 31, 1985*

The cost of health care has increased faster than the price of almost anything else in recent years: spending nationally has jumped from $27 billion to $247 billion between 1960 and 1980, alone. And without the adoption of major reforms, medical costs are expected to exceed $800 billion by 1990.

This steady increase has been blamed on everything from technological advances to soaring malpractice awards, causing all levels of government to assert greater control over the health-care industry. However, the root cause of medical hyperinflation is the lack of competition within the health-care industry, largely engineered by doctors' professional organizations like the American Medical Association.

For instance, the AMA, backed by state and local governments, has allocated health-care services between doctors and other professionals, like nurses, reserving the most important—and lucrative—tasks for physicians. At the same time, medical school regulation and other licensing requirements make it difficult to acquire an M.D.

To preserve their privileged position, doctors also have enlisted state agencies to put alternative medical practitioners, like midwives, out of business. Finally, in the name of protecting the public, the AMA has restricted competition within the profession, outlawing advertising, for instance, and even blocking the growth of proprietary hospitals, prepaid medical care and more competitive forms of health insurance.

The net result of the doctors' monopoly has been to increase costs and reduce choice for consumers, both of practitioners to serve them and facilities to use.

Ironically, for much of our history the health-care market was essentially unregulated. As of 1850, states were eliminating the few health licensing statutes that existed, and large numbers of people were entering medical practice.

Consumers benefitted from this influx, but doctors were less pleased with the popularity of their work. Physicians organized the AMA in 1847 and began lobbying to raise the drawbridge to the profession. One report submitted to the first AMA meeting deplored "the very large number of physicians"; it was "no wonder that the merest pittance in the way of remuneration is scantily doled out even to the most industrious in our ranks.''

In ensuing years the AMA secured passage of laws restricting entry into the profession and outlawing alternative medical practitioners. The doctors' lobby made little secret that its main focus was to eliminate competition: The new laws routinely exempted existing physicians from complying with the licensing requirements, for instance.

But the number of doctors continued to grow, so the AMA organized a new campaign. Based on the famous and flawed "Flexner Report," organized medicine took on the nation's medical schools, cutting their number almost in half in just 20 years. Finally, the terrible "oversupply" of doctors was no more.

Only now, decades later, has the number of medical schools and students been edging upward. As a result, we are seeing a refreshing outbreak of competition; in some cities doctors even advertise senior citizen discounts and house calls.

Nevertheless, the AMA continues to maintain a tight hold over the profession. And until that influence is broken, consumers will remain the victims of an economic cartel that operates in anything but the public interest.

Licensing could be abolished entirely, with incompetence and fraud punished through civil and criminal procedures. Insurance companies, hospitals and local, voluntary, medical societies could assist in policing the health-care profession: firms like General Motors have already begun evaluating care at institutions frequented by their employees.

Even if licensing is retained, other medical professionals like nurses should be given increased authority, the requirements for becoming an M.D. should be relaxed, and competition, both from alternative practitioners and within the profession, should be encouraged. In short, the health-care field should be cleared of obstacles imposed by the AMA and local medical societies—and enforced by state governments—that have no purpose other than to enhance the market position and financial status of doctors.

Progress has been slow but increasingly sure; for the first time in 140 years the direction of medical regulation itself shows signs of health. The most humane act that the long-standing partnership between government and the medical establishment could perform would be to stand aside and allow this trend to continue, further cutting health-care costs and increasing consumer freedom of choice.

# Education for Sale

## 124. The Money Illusion

*September 23, 1987*

If there is one thing that the Democratic presidential contenders believe American education needs, it is more money. In the words of Education Secretary William Bennett, they have a "cash-register mentality."

The Democrats uniformly oppose cuts in federal outlays for education. They all want higher salaries, more student aid, and more grants to schools. They seem to think there is nothing that cannot be solved with a little more money.

But schools are not being starved for cash. Education outlays from all levels of government are running $161 billion annually, hardly pocket change.

Indeed, only one country spends a larger percentage of its gross national product on education than the United States—Sweden. America devotes more of its GNP to schools, 6.7 percent, than does the U.S.S.R. (6.6 percent), Japan (5.7 percent), and the United Kingdom (5.5 percent). Other industrialized states, like France, Switzerland, and West Germany, lag even further behind the United States.

Are federal outlays inadequate? The Department of Education is spending roughly $20 billion this year, almost 50 percent more than it did under Jimmy Carter.

Anyway, there is no evidence that any of today's educational problems stem from inadequate outlays.

Last year, for instance, the National Assessment of Educational Progress concluded that children don't write very well. In response, the National Education Association naturally called for more teachers to reduce class sizes. But the pupil-teacher ratio was falling from 27 in 1955 to 18 today even as student performance declined.

More recently, the National Endowment for the Humanities reported the results of a survey of 17-year-olds. Fully two-thirds of students could not place the Civil War within a half-century of its occurrence. Nearly half had no idea when World War I took place and 39 percent didn't know when the Constitution was drafted.

Similar surveys have found an equally pervasive ignorance of geography. And a review of the performance of students from two dozen countries in math found that in most categories U.S. kids didn't even place in the top 10.

In none of these cases is more money the answer: schools have not been canceling history and math courses to cut outlays. Instead, the expensive government monopoly that now controls the education of America's children simply has no incentive to provide quality service.

In dramatic contrast—and providing perhaps the only bright spot in American education—is the success of private schools.

Roughly one out of every eight students today is educated privately; they routinely outperform their public-school counterparts. As a result, an incredible 49 percent of parents whose children now attend public schools say they would send their kids to a private school if they could afford to do so. Interestingly, non-whites, many of whose children are currently trapped in non-functional inner-city schools, are more desperate to escape the public educational system than are whites.

Indeed, the very fact that private schools continue to survive is evidence of their superiority. Observes Pete du Pont, the only presidential contender to propose serious educational reform: "The government provides education free of charge at public schools, and still people choose to pay thousands of dollars in tuition to send their children to private schools. It's the biggest case of predatory pricing in history, and still the government hasn't been able to drive its competition out of the marketplace."

The only way to save American education is to shift the entire system in the direction of private schools.

First, all parents—who now must finance public institutions even if they send their children to private schools—need to have a serious opportunity to send their children to private schools. This requires some combination of tuition tax credits and vouchers to ease families' financial burdens.

Second, failing public schools should be allowed to fail. Today parents have to pay for local public institutions no matter how poorly they perform; it is time parents were able to pull out not only their children but also their tax contributions from low-quality schools. Here, too, a voucher program would do the trick.

Federal grant aid, too, should be voucherized. Then schools would be forced to compete for students, with the good institutions expanding and the bad ones dying.

Education should be a major issue in 1988; the current system is turning out a class of strung-out ignoramuses. But proposals to spend more money, whether advanced by Democrats or Republicans, deserve a failing grade. The only hope for today's students is to force the public schools to compete by giving parents real freedom in deciding on their childrens' education.

## 125.  Making Students Pay Their Fair Share

*February 12, 1985*

As President Reagan's fiscal year 1986 budget was released, an instantaneous howl arose across Washington from interest groups and election-minded politicians. Inveterate pork-barreler Republican Sen. Mark Andrews of North Dakota, for example, said the budget had "enough horror to scare the pants off anybody."

Among those frightened are college students who look to Uncle Sam as their sugar daddy. For Mr. Reagan is threatening the mishmash of educational subsidies created by Congress over the past two decades.

The largest of these programs, Guaranteed Student Loans, gives an average of $2,306 to almost 3.7 million students. Pell Grants provide nearly $1,100 on average to roughly 2.6 million students. National Direct Student Loans, College Work Study programs and Supplemental Educational Opportunity grants also benefit millions of students.

At the same time, state aid has expanded; 7 percent of total college financial assistance now comes from state grants. Indeed, this has been the fastest growing form of aid, rising 27 percent between 1980 and 1984.

Student aid programs were originally justified as a way to promote national security. In the aftermath of the Soviet launch of Sputnik 1 in 1957, and the assumed threat to the American intellectual system, Congress passed the National Defense Education Act, first establishing student loans.

In 1959 outlays were still a minimal $31 million, but, as Detroit analyst David Stewart observes, college assistance programs were soon "transformed into electoral weapons," causing spending to climb steadily. The justification for such federal largess changed from national defense to welfare for the poor.

Immediately before the off-year elections in 1978, however, Congress turned student aid into a pork barrel for the middle class by dropping the GSL program's needs test. Two years later Congress increased the maximum loans available per student and created the Parent Loan Program.

Charles B. Saunders Jr., vice president for government relations of the

American Council on Education, said his organization wised up; "the more people eligible, the bigger the constituency for student aid."

Appalled by the regressive nature of this income transfer to the well-to-do, Mr. Reagan has worked steadily to cut it back. In 1981 the interest rate was raised; in 1982 a needs test was reimposed. A loan origination fee was implemented in 1983 and increased in 1984.

But Congress refused to go along with the administration's severest proposed cuts—the political constituency that Saunders spoke of proved to be powerful, indeed. Students and educators alike poured out their sob stories in Washington.

Virginia Smith, president of Vassar College, even blamed the federal government for luring her school into the loan business and then trying to reduce the taxpayers' burden: "It never occurred to us that someday they might be cut off precipitously. . . . We took on these tasks . . . with the assumption that the federal government would underwrite it. It seemed like the right thing to do."

Despite likely resistance from the very middle-class voters who formed the core of Mr. Reagan's electoral coalition, however, the administration is trying again. In an attempt to save $736 million, Mr. Reagan wants to limit each student to $4,000 maximum in subsidized federal aid, and to require him to contribute at least $800 to his education.

More significantly, Mr. Reagan would cut off grants, loans and subsidized jobs to students whose families earn more than $25,000, and terminate loan guarantees for those from families making in excess of $32,500. Finally, he would push the interest rate for guaranteed loans up to market levels.

Mr. Reagan's proposals represent a move toward genuine social justice. It is bad enough to force people, including young workers who choose not to go to college, to subsidize those who want a university degree, and who will end up earning more than the average taxpayer. But it is morally obscene to make the working poor underwrite the education of America's elite in the elitist of graduate and professional schools.

Indeed, the U.S. Census Bureau reports that nearly half of the students who depend on parental support come from families earning more than $25,000 annually. The reverse Robin Hood syndrome is particularly pronounced at the better schools: The University of Michigan, for instance, estimates that family incomes exceed $30,000 for four out of every five of its GSL applicants.

Moreover, nearly three decades of massive government student assistance effort has probably had the unintended side effect of increasing overall university costs and tuition levels. For universities, despite their non-profit status, have an institutional incentive to collect more money and grow larger; federal aid helps them do so. As Stewart observes, because of billions in taxpayer largess, "students, parents and college administrators don't have to face the real costs of education."

The taxpayers should no longer have to foot the bill for the college education of their neighbors' children. Instead, students should pay for their own B.A.'s, Ph.D.'s and J.D.'s; it's time they were taught that there is no such thing as a free lunch.

# Homes for America

## 126. How to Create a Housing Crisis:
## A Primer for Bureaucrats

*May 1980*

America is facing a new national crisis—the lack of adequate and affordable housing. Rising prices and shrinking supplies are creating volatile social dynamite that few politicians know how to defuse.

Between 1973 and 1979, the cost of the average home rose 107.1 percent, and, because of higher interest rates, mortgage payments increased a staggering 197.8 percent. The price surge in some areas, like Southern California, has been even worse. In contrast, the median family income has risen only 57.7 percent during the same period, and the Federal Home Loan Bank Board estimates that 85 percent of Americans cannot afford a home as first-time buyers.

New housing starts have fallen from roughly two million annually in 1977 and 1978 to 1.7 million in 1979 and a projected 1.2 million this year; apartment construction has fallen off 80 percent since 1965. And the Pacific Builders Conference estimates that because of past shortfalls, Californians will be without 500,000 needed homes by 1981.

The problem is perhaps best illustrated by New York City, where 374 people recently signed up for the prospective vacancy of an elderly woman tenant who lay dying. Within 15 minutes of her death, her apartment was rented.

Why must Americans fight for an apartment over the corpse of a deceased tenant? It is not the fault of private industry, which is ready and willing to build the needed housing. Rather, it is the fault of a government which refuses to allow the housing to be built. In fact, government regulation of land use and housing has become so pervasive that John McClaughry, President of the Institute for Liberty and Community, has described it as "the new feudalism," with the state merely replacing the monarchy as "a less personal but more permanent" ruler.

This system, while abrogating individual liberty, has also devastated the private housing market. A Housing and Urban Development Department (HUD) task force reported in 1978 that "Regulation by all levels of government is a major factor in increasing housing costs . . . and [t]he proliferation of government regulations, many of which are unduly burdensome, affects all areas. . . ." George Sternlieb, Director of Rutgers University's Urban Studies Center, estimates that this regulation adds roughly 20 percent to the cost of a home, an estimate supported by Sanford R. Goodkin, publisher of the Goodkin Report, and the National Association of Home Builders. The Pacific Coast Builders Conference estimates the cost to be slightly more—from 20 percent to 30 percent—of a home's price.

Regulation forces costs up in three distinct ways. Zoning—regulating the specific use of land—both decreases the supply of available land and increases the cost of building on that limited supply. HUD has concluded that "Land-use, environmental, no-growth and exclusionary zoning regulations have . . . constrained [the] land supply severely, particularly for low- and moderate-income housing." The American Bar Association (ABA) has found that 99.2 percent of the New York metro area's residentially zoned land bars apartments and mobile homes.

Moreover, as William M. Schenkel, real estate professor at the University of Georgia, points out, restrictive zoning forces families to buy new property and build larger homes than they need. The ABA, for instance, found that more than half of Connecticut's vacant land was zoned for a minimum of one or two acres; one particular municipal ordinance required an air conditioner, garbage disposal, master TV antenna, automatic washer and dryer, two off-street parking places, and eight square feet of swimming pool or tennis court per 100 square feet of living space.

Such regulations make the development of lower-income housing difficult, if not impossible; they embody a conflict between a privileged elite who want open space and high property values, and the rest who desire affordable housing. Examples of such conflicts abound. In Placentia, California, in 1978, Reese Development Corporation proposed building 84 four-plex units to be sold at $47,000 each. The planning commission wanted to lower the density, so Reese successively submitted plans for 61 townhouse units at $80,000 each, and 31 single-family homes at $115,000 each. Thus, the government planners decreased the housing supply by 63 percent while increasing its cost by 245 percent.

Costs are also forced upward by the government permit process and building codes, involving a myriad of agencies, inspectors, and rules. The average California developer must deal with the Environmental Protection Agency, HUD, 26 state agencies, the State Coastal Commission and its six regional commissions, the county, and at least one of any number of cities, school districts, and special districts. The regulations cover environmental impact statements; permits for plumbing, vents, and building; approval for sewer and water hook-ups; required solar heating mechanisms; and so on.

Such regulations, according to a 1979 Los Angeles Mayoral housing committee, make it "inordinately and unnecessarily difficult to build new housing. . . ." R. Barry McComic, president of AVCO Community Developers, Inc., estimates that because of such regulations, the national average for moving from raw land through the various levels of government is 15 months, and in California, two years. The Pacific Builders Conference similarly estimates that projects which once took six months now take two years. According to HUD, these extensive delays "exact a heavy cost in terms of overhead, inflation, reduction in the return on investment, and fees and charges. . . ." San Francisco developers and architects estimate that these delays caused by the sequential permit method alone add 10 percent to housing's cost.

Building codes—which specify the materials and techniques for construction—have also been harmful. HUD concluded that "Increased and excessive standards are a factor in escalating the costs of financing, land development, housing construction and rehabilitation, and the provision of supporting amenities, as well as occupancy costs." The variation among municipal codes makes mass production difficult, and the codes bar new materials and techniques, thereby freezing past technology into place. This may discourage some innovation, and has prevented the adoption of technological advances that most observers estimate could save 15 percent of construction costs; as far back as 1922, then Commerce Secretary Herbert Hoover complained that out-dated codes increased costs 10–20 percent.

The third way in which government increases the cost of new housing is by imposing what HUD terms "disproportionate" and "burdensome fees and impact taxes." Bernard J. Frieden, Urban Affairs Professor at MIT, confirms that many communities force developers—and ultimately consumers—to finance projects that benefit the entire community, such as a $27,000 bicycle path in Petaluma. George Peterson, of the Urban Institute, has estimated that these fees average $4,652 per dwelling. The Building Contractors Association reported in January, 1978 that in California, the fees amount to more than $8,000 for a $50,000 home, and $13,000 for an $80,000 home. Moreover, since the passage of Proposition 13 in June, 1978, Frieden found that California fees have increased by 26 percent, or up to $3,000; Goodkin estimates the increase to be as much as $4,000. Such increases led UCLA professor Fred Case to conclude that "higher fees are pricing moderate-income Californians out of the housing market."

However, most government officials not only seem blind to their role in creating the housing crisis, but, like Edward H. Lehnen, a Democratic Manhattan Assemblyman, believe "government . . . can only get more and more involved" in the housing market.

Government programs are not lacking. New York City offers tax abatement for new construction and rehabilitation. Los Angeles has created a Housing Authority to build, and to assist private developers in building, low-cost housing. California, through the California Housing Agency, floats bonds to provide money for lending institutions to lend at below market interest rates. California has also pioneered the concept of "inclusionary zoning"—forcing the developer and other consumers to provide low-cost housing. The city of Palo Alto, for instance, requires some developers to offer 10 percent of their units at roughly 40 percent of their cost to moderate-income families. And the State Coastal Commission requires builders to reserve 25 percent of their new homes for low- and middle-income buyers at reduced prices; it even recently ruled that a 300-room luxury hotel had to set aside 45 of its rooms at one-half the regular rate for the economically disadvantaged. The federal panoply of programs includes: buying mortgages and reselling them at below the market rate, subsidies to build low income housing, rent subsidies, insuring mortgages and subsidizing interest rates, rehabilitation subsidies, urban renewal, and public housing.

But the impact of such programs has generally been perverse. Urban renewal, for example, now discontinued, took land by eminent domain, cleared it, and then sold it to private developers. HUD estimated that by 1975, 612,850 housing units had been demolished, being replaced by only 265,161 private units, half of which were expensive luxury apartments. The result was nearly one-half million fewer homes for the economically disadvantaged.

In fact, 65 percent of the displaced residents were blacks or Hispanics, whose displacement made way for civic centers, office buildings, and luxury apartments, which, according to the Committee for Economic Development, were utilized by "upper-income, predominantly white families." Moreover, those residents forced to relocate had to pay more for their housing; a Boston study found that 30 percent of the displaced residents faced rent increases of up to 73 percent. Finally, it was estimated that half of the projects would have been built elsewhere anyway, without displacing anyone or spending any tax dollars.

Federal public housing for the poor, according to Stanford University economics professor Richard F. Muth, has segregated "the poor into separate ghettos, walling them off from the rest of the city," has had high turnover rates, and has suffered from extensive juvenile delinquency. Some projects have been so unappealing that even the poor have refused to live in them: the Providence Roger Williams Homes has a 40 percent vacancy rate; the St. Louis Pruitt-Igoe has had one of 80 percent (and has since closed down). Moreover, the cost of each unit averaged $80,000, their construction costs averaged 20 percent higher than similar private units, and they cost substantially more—ranging up to an additional $64 a month in Seattle for a one-bedroom unit—than private apartments.

In fact, taken together, by 1968, government programs had created a demolition deficit of over a million units (see Figure A)—a figure that has since increased, though the government does not know by how much.

In Michigan State University economist Richard Craswell's words: "Thus, while people have increasingly come to believe that private enterprise has got the cities into a mess that only the government can get them out of that same government has been destroying over a million low income units, . . . actively working to reduce the amount of housing available to the poor, driving up prices and pushing inhabitants into even worse housing."

Government has also furiously legislated to remedy supposed "abuses" of the market—and has, in the process, made things even worse. For example, the number of rental apartments being converted to condominiums and stock cooperatives has been doubling each year in California since 1976, and has risen nationally from 45,000 in 1977 to 145,000 in 1979. Josef S. Nobel, President of a Los Angeles conversion management firm, estimates that conversions only account for "barely one-half of one percent" of the rental supply, but cities such as Evanston, Illinois, Denver, Boston, Los Angeles, and San Francisco have frantically passed ordinances restricting conversions, requiring relocation assistance for tenants,

**FIGURE A**

| Program | Date | Demolitions | Construction |
|---|---|---|---|
| Urban Renewal | as of 1/1/68 | 404,000 | |
| Urban Highway Clearance | 1956–1968 | 330,000 | |
| Public Housing—Site Clearance | as of 12/68 | 177,000 | |
| Public Housing—Equivalent Eliminations | as of 12/68 | 143,000 | |
| Building Code Enforcement | 1960–1968 | 384,000 | |
| State Action | 1960–1968 | 208,000 | |
| Total Units Demolished | | 1,646,000 | |
| Public Housing | 1950–1968 | | 559,000 |
| Demolition Deficit | | 1,087,000 | |

and mandating special protection for the elderly, handicapped, disabled, and single parents. These measures further disrupt the housing market, since some people's only hope to purchase a home is a condominium. Moreover, they will ultimately exacerbate the rental crisis. For example, giving special protection to "disadvantaged" tenants makes them more expensive to the landlord, encouraging landlords to avoid renting to them whenever possible.

Further, though in the short-run such ordinances help prevent any additional decrease in the rental stock, in the long-run they virtually assure that there will be no increase, because they effectively lock owners into rental units forever. Destroying the landlords' flexibility will drive them away from the rental market altogether; they will build condominiums or office buildings instead.

Finally, government is increasingly legislating the "final solution"—rent control. Once confined to the Northeast and three Alaska cities, this housing blight has recently spread to over a dozen California communities, covering about half of California's ten million tenants. Rent control is a seductive panacea turned to by frustrated and ill-informed people intent on ignoring economic reality. People who would never think of controlling anyone else's wages, prices, or dividends think nothing of penalizing only landlords for our housing crisis.

In fact, landlords, most of whom start out with negative or zero cash flows, do not deserve such treatment. Between 1967 and 1979, the Consumer Price Index rose 107 percent and rents only 71 percent. As Bill Femske asked in a letter to the *Los Angeles Times* in 1979: "Do the City Council and the vocal renters think it is easy to run a building where this year gasoline has gone up 40 percent; electricity rates up 18 percent [by a city-controlled utility]; plumbing charges up 24 percent; natural gas 12 percent; maintenance charges a whopping 35 percent; and worst of all my insurance is up 300 percent from two years ago?" However, irrespective of rent control's moral implications, its practical effect is the euthanasia of the private rental market. Even Swedish socialist economist Assar Lindbeck admits that "In many cases rent control appears to be the most effective technique presently known to destroy a city—except for bombing."

In particular, rent control creates and intensifies housing shortages, thereby raising prices in the long-run. First, it discourages investment in the rental industry, keeping, according to Roger Starr, former head of New York City's Housing and Development administration, "the supply permanently inadequate." Numerous economic studies have demonstrated that as the profit incentive, or reward, for apartment construction falls— through rent control, for example—fewer apartments are constructed.

Investors will instead invest in alternative projects—single-family homes, condominiums, office buildings, motels, or even, according to Jeffrey Palmer of the Wharton School, interest bearing securities, or in alternative regions: the *San Diego Union* recently reported on a shift in investment from rent-controlled California cities to Denver. Moreover, the 1976 Massachusetts Harbridge House report and studies by Gruen Gruen and Associates and the Development Economic Group have all found that many thrift institutions and insurance companies refuse to make loans for rent-controlled construction.

In fact, in virtually every community with rent control the supply of rental housing has either held constant or fallen. Under rent control in Washington, D.C., the number of apartments has fallen from 199,100 to 175,900, and new construction has virtually ceased, despite a growing demand for apartments. In some Brooklyn neighborhoods, virtually no new housing has been constructed since 1935; in Manhattan, where rent control has been most strict, the rental supply contracted by 1,000 units between 1943 and 1967—elsewhere years of a national housing boom. A few decades ago, 70 percent of New York City's apartments were privately financed; now only 10 percent are. For the two years that rent control was in effect in Miami Beach, there was no new rental construction. In Boston, the Mayor's Committee on Rent Control concluded that rent control reduced the quantity of units available to low- and moderate-income people—a result also conceded by most observers in Cambridge, Massachusetts. Finally, rental construction is at an all-time low in California, with virtually all new construction being condominiums. In October, two USC researchers concluded that rent control had discouraged apartment construction in Santa Monica, Berkeley, and Davis, and more recently, the *Wall Street Journal* reported that rent control had worsened Los Angeles's "already critical rental housing shortage by driving off big builders and their money sources."

Rent control also restricts the housing supply by making some apartments unprofitable, encouraging their abandonment. This phenomenon is most pronounced in New York City, where some 20,000 rental owners went bankrupt between 1967 and 1970, and owners *annually* walk away from some 30,000 units because, official city reports admit, they cannot afford the upkeep. Abandonment also substantially increased in Lynn, Massachusetts, before rent control was repealed, and "walkaways" from marginally profitable properties are becoming increasingly common in Washington, D.C. Of course, as two USC researchers confirmed in California, rent control also speeds the conversion of existing rental units to condominiums and stock cooperatives, further worsening the initial rental shortage.

Another deleterious effect of rent control is to impair the maintenance and repair of apartments. It is difficult, if not impossible, for landlords to cover increasing costs of fuel, taxes, plumbing, carpets, etc., when their rents are controlled. And as Starr points out, when many minor problems are not repaired, they then may become major problems, ruining an apartment. Under rent control, Miami Beach apartments suffered widespread cutbacks in maintenance and services. The Gruen Gruen & Associates study of New Jersey found that rent control discourages repairs and keeps lenders from making improvement loans to landlords. In Los Angeles, managers admit that they are doing "nothing for renters now," and suppliers of carpets, furniture, and other items to landlords report that their business is off 30 to 70 percent since rent control was imposed in 1978. According to New York City reports, the difference between proper maintenance costs and the rents allowed landlords is almost $300 million. It is therefore no surprise that the city estimates the existence of 400,000 deteriorated units, and economist Richard Muth reports that New York City is the only major city for which the fraction of substandard dwellings failed to decline during the 1950s. The *Amsterdam News,* the city's largest black newspaper, even editorialized that "we in minority areas live in rat-infested buildings that resemble bombed-out war areas. And . . . this type of housing is rapidly increasing . . . solely because of rent control."

Rent control also encourages tenants to hold apartments as long as possible, slowing apartment turnover. This misallocates housing, since shrinking and growing families fail to move to more efficient quarters. It also impairs the mobility of tenants, controlling particularly newcomers, and the poor (who tend to move most often).

While controlling the poor, rent control frequently benefits the rich. Luxury apartments are often exempted, artificially skewing investment away from lower income units. Where such apartments are covered, the well-to-do, such as New York City's Mayor and the President of the American Stock Exchange, have their rents subsidized. In fact, the U.S. Senate Banking, Housing and Urban Affairs Committee concluded in 1977 that in New York City, "a small, privileged group of long-time residents, largely middle class" are rent control's prime beneficiaries.

Rent control, by lowering rental property values, also shifts the property tax burden to homeowners. The value of rental property has declined in this way in Cambridge, Massachusetts, rent-controlled New Jersey municipalities, Miami Beach, and New York City. In the first three years of rent control in Washington, D.C., the assessed value of apartments fell by 1 percent, while that for single family homes and condominiums almost doubled.

A more insidious effect of rent control is the encouragement of personal discrimination. The excess demand from the rent control created shortage must be rationed in some manner other than price; landlords are apt to choose professionals, whites, families without children, etc. UCLA economist Harold Demsetz found that the *Chicago Tribune* carried a higher percentage of racially discriminatory ads during World War II than before or after the war-time controls.

Finally, rent control results in the creation of yet another bureaucracy, subject to political patronage and corruption, and burdened by excessive costs and administrative delays. New York City spends millions of dollars annually on its rent control programs. The *Washington Post* has described the D.C. program as "an administrative nightmare," citing six month delays for *unopposed* rent increase applications.

Renters are rightly angry over high rents, but their anger should be directed not against those who provide rental housing, but against those who block it. Political myopia cannot overcome economic reality—more housing, not more regulation, is what is needed.

Many advocates of increased government intervention in the housing industry realize that their programs are failing, but consider this fact, in effect, beside the point. Martin Anderson, author of *The Federal Bulldozer,* has written that after talking with local community leaders about urban renewal, he found a "consistent theme running through their off-the-record statements. . . . They were not seriously concerned with the poor people living in the areas they had tentatively marked for renewal; they were not concerned with any personal gain; they were not even very concerned with getting a substantial amount of cash from the rest of the taxpayers via Washington. But they were concerned with *power.*" In fact, power—subject as it is to abuse and misuse—is what housing regulation is all about. Power to dispense grants of privilege to favored interests. Power to override individual rights. Power to shape growth as the elite believes best. And power to control the construction and allocation of housing in our society.

There is one positive alternative to the failed politics of power and control—the free market, the same free market that, between 1950 and 1968, created 32.4 million new homes while the government was destroying over a million. Indeed, Bernard Siegan, author of *Land Use Without Zoning,* argues that "the least fallible of city planners is the free market," pointing out that in the Texas cities of Houston, Pasadena, Wichita Falls, Laredo, and Baytown, which have no zoning, the market has separated uses and allocated land to its highest-valued use. If any errors are made, the market corrects them; zoning would only lock them in.

Private land use planning is supplemented in such cities by voluntary restrictive covenants, which assure property owners as to the future use of their property. Private civil court action—either for nuisance or trespass—helps deal with improper land uses. And arbitration can at times be substituted for reliance on the courts.

The National Commission on Neighborhoods has also suggested replacing traditional building codes with an essentially privatized system patterned after that in France, where builders are liable for structural defects. Builders normally buy insurance to protect against malpractice claims; insurance companies hire private investigators to check buildings; and mortgage lenders and property insurance carriers generally require warranty insurance before they will issue a mortgage or insurance.

Even within the current regulatory structure, private individuals are working to meet the housing crisis. For example, in San Francisco, Action for Better Elders (ABLE) is arranging house-sharing for senior citizens. Some lenders are now offering variable mortgage payments, to increase over the life of the mortgage as the person's income increases. And so on.

The housing crisis is a *manufactured* crisis, caused and promoted by a government that has systematically placed the power to control our housing destiny in the hands of arrogant elitists, both elected and appointed; sacrificed individual rights for the financial gain, aesthetic pleasure, and personal advancement of others; restricted the supply of land; created unconscionable delays in building; increased the costs of construction; discouraged innovation; regulated and ruined the rental market; and destroyed over a million homes.

City councils and their planning officials produce no housing. Nor do rent control or HUD administrators. Rather, builders produce housing. And if government officials are serious about solving the housing crisis, they will eliminate, not increase, government regulation of the housing market.

## 127. Challenging Rent Control

*September 17, 1986*

Rent control has long been one of the most destructive of panaceas, a popular urban disease that afflicts much of the nation. However, the Ninth Circuit Court of Appeals has just issued a landmark opinion, authored by recent Reagan appointee Alex Kozinski, that raises serious questions about the constitutionality of rent control.

Economists have long understood that restrictions on rents reduce the supply of apartments, cause landlords to abandon their property, and immobilize the poor. Even Swedish socialist Assar Lindbeck admits that "in many cases rent control appears to be the most effective technique presently known to destroy a city—except for bombing."

However, politicians in search of votes have preferred to ignore economic reality; leading journalists, artists, and even businessmen, too, have consistently supported the discredited policy of rent control. As New York journalist William Tucker details in an upcoming book, people ranging from Mayor Ed Koch to actress Mia Farrow enjoy subsidies, courtesy of an indentured landlord class.

Indeed, rent control is wrong not so much because it is stupid—and there is no more effective way to exacerbate a housing crisis than rent control—but because it is immoral. What right does the government have to single out landlords and arbitrarily confiscate their income?

Unfortunately, until now owners—the majority of whom tend to be middle-income people—have had nowhere to turn for help. More renters than landlords vote, so city councils and state legislatures routinely have rebuffed pleas for relief.

And the courts simply have walked away from the issue, despite the Constitution's explicit protection for economic liberty. At most, the wave of lawsuits involving rent control has forced cities to allow landlords a minimal return on their investment.

The city of Santa Monica, Calif., for example, was allowed to prevent owners from going out of business. So much for individual liberty.

But in a case brought against the city of Santa Barbara, Calif., the Court of Appeals has shown unusual sensitivity to the important rights involved.

Two years ago Santa Barbara enacted rent control for mobile home parks. Rent increases were strictly limited; landlords could evict renters only in narrow circumstances.

The owners of one park filed suit against the city, arguing that their property had been taken without compensation. The trial court dismissed the case, but the appellate judges ruled that the issues raised were serious enough to warrant a trial.

The challenge rests on a simple point: the government, by giving tenants a perpetual legal right to a lease at below market rents, has transferred a valuable property interest from landlords to renters. As a result, tenants effectively control the use of the property and collect a windfall profit—reflected in their mobile home's price—when they sell.

This property redistribution is arguably a "taking" under the Constitution. When the city transferred the right to determine who occupies the property from the landlord to the renter, it changed "the fundamental relationship between the parties," stated the Appeals Court.

Normal rent control ordinances only benefit tenants while they are renting, but in this case, observed the court, "landlords are left with the right to collect reduced rents while tenants have practically all other rights in the property they occupy. . . . This oversteps the boundaries of mere regulation and shades into permanent occupation of the property for which compensation is due."

The theoretical goal of the city ordinance, of course, was to alleviate a housing shortage—which normally would be considered adequate justification for use of eminent domain. But in this case, where the government is simply taking money from landlords and giving it to tenants, "there would be significant doubt whether these purposes are achieved, or could rationally be thought achievable, by means of the ordinance," stated the judges.

Finally, the city did not reimburse the park owners for their property loss, which could be another ground for voiding the ordinance. Thus, the appellate judges ordered the lower court to consider the issue of compensation as well.

Landlords in Santa Barbara are still a long way from getting justice; it will take a courageous trial judge to stand up to the greed of tenants and political opportunism of local officials.

But the decision by the Ninth Circuit may lead to a serious rethinking of the constitutionality of rent control. If so, Judge Kozinski and his colleagues will have earned the gratitude of poor renters as well as property owners.

## 128. Sell Off Uncle Sam's Public Housing

*June 11, 1985*

The Reagan administration is embarking on an experiment that could dramatically change how the government houses the poor.

Following the lead of Britain, the Department of Housing and Urban Development has inaugurated a small-scale project to sell public housing units to its lower-income tenants.

The Public Housing Home Ownership Demonstration program, announced HUD Secretary Sam Pierce in early June, will involve the sale of almost 2,000 units by some two dozen local housing authorities in such communities as Denver, Nashville, Tenn., Chicago, Baltimore, Los Angeles County and Washington, D.C.

Utilizing discounted prices and government mortgages, the program, Pierce said, will allow public housing residents to become home owners and give them a greater "opportunity to participate more fully in their communities and neighborhoods."

Administration officials, who had to overcome opposition from congressional Democrats, view the current effort as a test to determine the feasibility of a full-scale program involving many of the nation's 1.3 million units of public housing. If the experiment succeeds, it is "entirely possible," says Kenneth Bierne, a deputy assistant secretary at HUD, that the administration will "move forward" with an expanded effort.

Supporters of privatization point to the British experience, where roughly a half million homes have been sold since 1979. Stuart Butler, head of the Heritage Foundation's domestic studies program, says the key is to give individuals or cooperatives the right to purchase units even if local bureaucrats object.

Such an approach has been picked up by Rep. Jack Kemp, R-N.Y., one of the most thoughtful and innovative members of Congress. Kemp is supporting HUD's efforts, but he also has introduced legislation to initiate a national program. The logic of privatization, says Kemp aide Thomas Humbert, "is so compelling that we need to go beyond a couple thousand tenants."

Skeptics remain, of course. Some observers question whether people below the poverty line can afford to be home owners. However, the Congressional Research Service estimates that at least one-fifth of current tenants could afford to purchase their units at a discount. And that, Humbert explains, doesn't take into account any "dynamic behavior"— residents working more and pooling family resources. Anyway, tenants would not have to buy; they simply would have "an additional option," Humbert says.

Ironically, some usual supporters of privatization object to the program for a different reason. One White House official, for example, complains that putting units into the hands of public housing residents "bypasses the working stiff" who is unable to afford his own home. How is that fair, he asks.

The answer is that it isn't fair. But since the taxpayers already have been forced to pay for a bad deal—deteriorating housing that quarantines the poor—we would be better off selling the units. If nothing else, large-scale sales would help reduce federal outlays; Uncle Sam has spent more than $140 billion on housing programs since 1968.

Experience shows that privatization also would improve property upkeep and maintenance.

"If it was theirs," says Travis Dixon, a resident of the District of Columbia project Kenilworth Courts-Parkside, "they would care" about litter and the drug-pushers.

A major stumbling block to an expanded sales program is congressional pressure on the administration to replace any units taken "out of the low-income housing stock.'' Indeed, Humbert says that the fear of fewer public housing units is ''the big hang-up.''

But there's no reason to pour more money into a program that serves both tenants and taxpayers so poorly. Since the homes are being sold to their tenants, the poor still are being served, only more efficiently. More-over, a compromise suggested by Humbert might be to issue rental vouchers to replace any units sold, thus allowing other lower-income people to choose private housing instead of public projects.

In any case, privatization so clearly benefits the poor that he doesn't ''see how anyone can be against it.''

The tenant ownership project is an example of the sort of innovative new approaches to old problems that our nation desperately needs. Not only does it reduce federal spending, but also, as HUD Assistant Secretary June Koch says, it is a step away from ''paternalistic control of the poor'' and a step toward their achieving ''the American dream'' of home owner-ship.

The administration and Congress should move forward with a full-scale program as soon as possible.

# The Consumer Protection Racket

## 129. Consumer Fraud

Washington is full of people who make their living speaking out on behalf of other people without ever having been asked to. The most visible of these self-proclaimed spokesmen are "consumer advocates." The Reagan administration's recent proposal to deregulate natural gas prices has brought them out of the woodwork in droves and encouraged them to pontificate loudly about what America's consumers (that is, all of us) really want.

For years, the organized consumer groups have ably used the emotional appeal of "consumerism" to implement much of their agenda. (After all, who wants to be known as anticonsumer?) They've created and expanded all manner of government agencies, starting early with the Interstate Commerce Commission (ICC), the Food and Drug Administration (FDA), and the Federal Trade Commission (FTC). But the 1970s were the heyday of consumer politics. The Consumer Product Safety Commission (CPSC) was created, the FTC roamed far and wide (even earning the title "national nanny" from the *Washington Post*), and only a presidential veto stopped the creation of a Consumer Protection Agency.

Consumer politicos typically use their agencies to reshape the economy according to their personal views of "economic justice," often threatening fundamental freedoms in the process. The attempt of the FTC, for example, to ban TV ads directed at children would have infringed the First Amendment. Basic economic liberties are at stake, too, including the right of producers to sell goods and services, and the right of consumers to freedom of choice.

Cities, states, and federal agencies have placed a host of controls on products and services desired by consumers. Most states control the interest rates on loans and charge accounts. Many cities restrict the price and availability of housing through rent controls and building regulations. The federal government has controlled energy prices for three decades.

Such "proconsumer" restrictions are in reality nothing more than the

336 The Politics of Plunder

systematic scapegoating of those perceived to be "bad guys" (landlords, money lenders, oil producers). This form of "economic justice" actually means manipulating the political process to benefit one group of narrow interests at the expense of others.

The results of these machinations often are clearly antagonistic to the real interests of consumers. The classic example is the creation of the ICC before the turn of the century, ostensibly to protect farmers from rapacious railroads. Lo and behold, the railroads quickly took control of the commission through its appointees and used it to restrict competition and jack up prices. The truckers soon realized what a sweet deal this was and got themselves regulated by the ICC as well.

Even where the agencies haven't been captured by the industries they regulate, controls usually hurt consumers. Federal energy price controls have inevitably led to shortages and gas lines. Natural gas prices in the United States are now increasing 20 to 25 percent a year even as oil declines, because the federal controls are so bizarre.

But when the political consumerists want an emotional appeal to restrict consumers' freedom of choice, they talk about "safety." Power lawn mowers must have expensive "deadman's switches" to stop them in case the user relaxes his grip. Toys that a child could swallow must be banned. Cars must have airbags. Ad infinitum. The problem with most government-mandated product safety features is that many consumers don't want them. The professional consumerists don't care, of course: They want them, so everyone else must get them too. They view people as being too stupid and careless to make their own decisions properly, so self-appointed advocates have to make their decisions for them.

Unfortunately, consumerist "safety" programs are often unsafe for consumers. The FDA, for example, has kept lifesaving and health-enhancing drugs off the market. In 1977 the CPSC considered dictating the design of children's playgrounds, including requiring barriers on slides. However, it dropped the idea when someone pointed out that these barriers could become more dangerous than the slides because kids could use them as bannisters.

The failure of the organized "consumer movement" to reflect the general consumer interest doesn't mean that there is no need for a genuine consumer movement. If nothing else, consumers have a stake in a growing economy without inflation and artificially high interest rates. Thus they should fight high government spending and taxing, huge deficits, and rampant money mismanagement.

Another fundamental consumer issue is free trade. The threat to this economic freedom has probably never been greater. Consumers are also injured by agricultural programs which hold up prices and reduce supplies, and by licensing procedures for professionals, which restrict competition. Those interested in the welfare of consumers should focus on such areas where special-interest groups have eliminated normal market protections for consumers.

In fact, according to a Harris survey, only 21 percent of the American people want more regulation. However, the change of direction rests in the hands of consumers themselves, who have, we trust, more sense than their elected representatives. Here in Washington, City Council member H. R. Crawford has introduced a bill to require full-service gas stations to "render the kind of full service a motorist expects at a full-service pump— including fuel pumped in a prompt fashion, a clean windshield, oil and tire pressure checked, and access to a free public toilet." You see, consumer Crawford drove up to a full-service pump and was told to "pump it yourself." Then, indignity of indignities, he had to pay 25 cents to use the toilet. Most people, I think, would have had sense enough to drive off and never return. But not Crawford.

We don't need protection from gas station attendants who don't pump the gas. The people we do need protection from are the elitist spokesmen who feel helpless without the government stepping in.

## 130.  Help Consumers Don't Need

*August 5, 1987*

A House committee has voted to take credit cards away from 15 million Americans, giving new meaning to the gag line: "I'm from the government and I'm here to help you."

Not that Congress understands what it is doing. When the House Banking and Urban Affairs Committee voted to limit credit card interest rates—using a formula that would reduce the current average from 18 percent to about 14 percent—it thought it was doing consumers a favor. But the legislation would actually encourage banks to issue fewer cards and hike non-interest fees.

The number of Visa and MasterCard cards in circulation has risen 86 percent since 1980, to 186 million. Middle America has clearly decided that the convenience of plastic money is worth the cost.

Which is not surprising, since the credit card industry is highly competitive. The 12 biggest Visa/MasterCard issuers account for just one-third of the market. And these bank cards face competition from a host of specialty cards, like American Express, and retailer cards.

Competition is strong: cards for better customers, like American Express's Optima card, offer lower than average rates. Manufacturers Hanover cut its credit card interest rates to 17.8 percent, causing a 22 percent jump in business. An Albany, N.Y., credit union reduced its rate from 17.2 percent to 16.2 percent, increasing its business 50 percent.

Nevertheless, congressmen get re-elected by responding to constituent complaints and some cardholders want an even better deal. So Rep. Frank Annunzio, D-Ill., who chairs the Consumer Affairs subcommittee of the House Banking and Urban Affairs Committee, is leading the campaign to tie the allowable interest rate to the return on U.S. Treasury bills.

Annunzio thinks banks can make a profit by simply keeping cards out of the hands of deadbeats.

"If card issuers had been selective in handing out cards in the first place, they wouldn't need high rates now."

But as Michael Becker points out in a study for the free market advocacy group Citizens for a Sound Economy, banks cannot know in advance which customers will welsh. Instead, financial institutions hand out cards to those who meet some general criteria.

Thus, "if banks stop giving credit cards to anybody who might be a credit risk," warns Becker, "honest individuals earning modest incomes who lack credit records would be denied credit cards."

A lot of people could be hurt. Industry analyst Spencer Nilson estimates that 15 million people would lose their cards if Congress restricted interest rates. That is about one of every five current MasterCard/Visa cardholders.

Even for people who were still able to get cards, interest rate limits would be a bad deal. Today many consumers take advantage of the "grace period" in which to pay their balance without any interest charge.

Yet if Congress lowered interest rates by legislative fiat, many financial institutions would drop their grace periods. In fact, some banks have already voluntarily traded off lower interest rates for no grace period.

Even consumers who keep a running balance and now pay 18 percent or more in interest could lose from congressional rate-fixing. For banks would probably hike the annual fee to make up for their lost interest revenue. Becker, for instance, calculates that a bank could counteract lower interest rates for the average customer by raising its annual fee from $15 to $35.

Banks could employ a host of other stratagems to make up the lost interest as well. The billing cycle could be shortened; late fees could be raised. Financial institutions could also increase the amount they charge retailers, which would both hike product prices and make stores less willing to accept cards.

The actual experience in states with interest limits shows how costly regulation is. In Arkansas, for instance, lower income people are less likely to get cards than those in neighboring states. Card fees are also higher and the number of extra services provided are fewer.

Moreover, retailers who issue cards charge more for their merchandise. Major appliances cost 5 percent more in Arkansas than in surrounding states.

As usual, Congress is preparing to cause enormous economic damage in its attempt to solve a non-problem. Credit card consumers are not being gouged; they are receiving more than enough benefits to justify the amount they pay.

Anyway, rate ceilings would make most people worse off, denying millions of Americans access to bank cards and raising the fees paid by everyone else. Consumers don't need this kind of "helping hand" from government.

# 131. Legalize Saccharin

*April 25, 1985*

The ban on the artificial sweetener saccharin, imposed by the Food and Drug Administration in 1977, is about to expire, and Congress appears likely to extend for yet another three years its moratorium on the prohibition. Indeed, the FDA, bowing to the inevitable, says it does not oppose the legislation.

Actually, that's the least the FDA can do. When the government banned saccharin it left Americans with no effective sugar substitute until aspartame was introduced in 1981. For in 1969 the FDA proscribed the use of cyclamates, the only other widely used sugar substitute, for allegedly being a carcinogen.

The FDA poses as a self-interested defender of the helpless American public, but the facts reveal a far different record. For example, the FDA "continually misrepresented" the findings of scientists in 1977 when it banned cyclamates, according to U.S. Claims Court Judge Judith Ann Yannello.

Yannello, who recommended that the federal government compensate the now defunct California Canners and Growers Association to the tune of $8.2 million, ruled that "no one had found cyclamates to be carcinogenic." Yet the FDA "repeatedly reported that cyclamates had been found to have caused cancer," Yannello found.

And five years ago, when Abbot Laboratories petitioned for reapproval of cyclamates, the FDA refused. Though Abbot could point to a study that found only one rat in 520 to have developed bladder cancer (a form of tumor that occurs spontaneously) after consuming large amounts of the sweetener, America's official food protectors decided that Abbot would have to test 100,000 rats to demonstrate the safety of cyclamates with "reasonable certainty." Abbot declined; the cost of doing so could have hit $100 million.

But now, even the FDA is having some second thoughts. Spokesman Jim Greene says the agency is considering lifting the ban. For in 1982 the FDA's own cancer assessment committee reported that there was "no credible evidence showing that cyclamates cause cancer in animals."

No similar evidence of gross misconduct on the part of the FDA has turned up in the case of saccharin. But even if the tests do prove that rats, after consuming the equivalent of 750 cans of diet soft drinks a day, contracted cancer, there is no agreement on how relevant that result is for humans.

The point is crucial. For the Delaney Clause, passed by Congress in 1959, requires the FDA to ban products that, in whatever dosage, cause cancer in animals. It matters not whether the poor rats were fed the equivalent of one candy bar or 1 million candy bars a day. If cancer results, the substance comes off the shelves.

Yet, as noted author and commentator Edith Efron makes clear in her stunning book, "The Apocalyptics: Cancer and the Big Lie," published by Simon & Schuster, the American public has been consistently misled by the political and scientific establishment. And one of the most fraudulent tools used to "protect the public interest" is animal testing.

For of the hundreds of elements carcinogenic for animals in some quantity, only 10 are known to cause cancer in humans; one, arsenic, causes cancer in people but apparently not in animals. Indeed, different species sometimes tolerate substances differently.

Though it is easy to determine that something causes cancer, it is virtually impossible to demonstrate that a substance is not carcinogenic. You cannot, for example, conduct an experiment with people drinking 750 cans of diet drinks per day as you do with rats. As a result, the process is hopelessly skewed toward restricting Americans' freedom of choice.

This bias in the testing regime, Efron argues, complements the political bias of many of the scientists and regulators, who believe they should control what Americans eat and drink. Indeed, most of the experts asked by Efron to review the manuscript before its publication lauded the book— but refused to let their names be used. One of them said the problem was "your book will come out before I retire." Americans are supposed to obey the scientific priesthood; professional apostates apparently are dealt with severely.

The expiration of the congressional moratorium on the FDA's saccharin ban provides Congress with an opportunity to reconsider the basic regulatory structure. By setting aside the FDA's action for eight straight years, Congress clearly recognizes that the 1959 rules don't make sense. The Delaney Clause doesn't protect lives; instead, it protects the enormous power of a small clique of scientists and bureaucrats.

Congress should repeal the Delaney Clause. It's time to focus on protecting the public from genuine dangers, rather than letting people like Sidney Wolfe, head of Ralph Nader's Health Research Group, work to proscribe the use of products like artificial sweeteners, simply because, in his opinion, "Who needs them?"

## 132.  Don't Ban Cigarette Ads

*February 25, 1987*

The tobacco industry has "lots of money but also lots of problems" says one official. And one of those problems is legislation introduced by Rep. Mike Synar, D-Okla., that would prohibit virtually all tobacco advertising.

Synar's bill also would forbid cigarette firms from sponsoring sports events—such as Virginia Slims tennis tournaments. "The goal is to have a smoke-free society by the year 2000," says Synar aide Debbie Wesslund.

At the same time, a bipartisan group of senators is pushing to double cigarette taxes and eliminate the business tax deduction for tobacco ads. The surgeon general also has intensified his campaign against cigarette smoking.

It's tempting to join in these attacks. After all, some 350,000 people die every year from cigarette-related diseases; tobacco is the largest single cause of cancer. Even one industry spokesman privately admits that the only people who deny the health dangers of smoking are those who work for the Tobacco Institute.

Nevertheless, do we really want Uncle Sam to be a national nanny? If we are serious in calling America a "free society," then we have to protect people's liberty to make mistakes.

Since smoking does affect other people—whether so-called secondary smoke poses a health danger to non-smokers is a matter of heated, but inconclusive, debate—it is certainly reasonable for companies to limit where people can light up. But we should not get the government involved; the issue is best settled privately and informally, rather than in the political arena.

Far more objectionable, however, are the proposals by Synar and his colleagues to not so gently push 50 million Americans out of their deadly habit.

Hiking the tobacco tax, for instance, would allow the federal government to take more money out of Americans' pockets, as if 25 cents out of every dollar earned was not already enough. Moreover, we shouldn't want politicians and bureaucrats manipulating the tax system to discourage activities they simply don't like. Next will come a special tax on boxers' gloves, since that sport is so dangerous.

Preventing tax write-offs for cigarette ads is an even worse misuse of the tax system, for advertising is clearly a cost of doing business and as such should be deductible. If Congress wants to penalize the tobacco industry, it should do so openly.

Prohibiting cigarette companies from sponsoring athletic contests would let Uncle Sam regulate yet another area of American life. It simply isn't Washington's business who underwrites sports events.

Finally, there's the ban on advertising. (Synar's bill would allow companies to present price information, but no pictures of "beautiful people" puffing away.)

Those who argue that a ban would be constitutional are probably right, at least given the way the Supreme Court currently interprets the Constitution. Last year the Court upheld a partial prohibition on casino ads in Puerto Rico.

However, that decision is an unfortunate one. Dissented William Brennan: "I see no reason why commercial speech should be afforded less protection than other types of speech where, as here, the government seeks to . . . deprive consumers of accurate information concerning lawful activity."

Of course, some observers argue that pictures of healthy people using an unhealthy product is inherently deceptive. But every ad carries the surgeon general's warning.

Anyway, no one who values free speech should want the government to censor advertising on such dubious grounds. For restrictions on cigarette ads would only encourage federal officials to meddle even more elsewhere in the economy.

Indeed, there is no end to products that well-meaning paternalists might try to keep off the market—or at least off TV. Foods rich in cholesterol, sugar and salt, skateboards, hang gliders and even cars are all dangerous in varying degrees.

Yet the basic purpose of the First Amendment was to allow good and bad ideas to freely compete in an intellectual marketplace, rather than to empower government to choose a winner. When the Supreme Court started breaking down state barriers to advertising more than a decade ago, it concluded that "the free flow of commercial information is indisputable."

People shouldn't smoke. But in a free society individuals must make such basic decisions about their own lives.

The proper response to cigarette ads is not for the government to ban them. It's for private groups like the American Cancer Society to begin buying anti-smoking ads. Then the intellectual marketplace, rather than government, will determine whether America ever becomes a "smoke-free" society.

# Anti-Social Security

## 133. Sun City for Social Security

*October 1985*

Two years ago House Speaker Tip O'Neill and Rules Committee Chairman Claude Pepper, along with Senate Majority Leader Robert Dole and a herd of other congressional leaders, stood smiling at each other in the Rose Garden as President Reagan signed into law a $165 billion Social Security tax increase. With the Social Security system facing imminent insolvency, a bipartisan whirlwind had pushed through the recommendations of the National Commission on Social Security Reform in just three months. The legislation, Reagan said, "demonstrates for all time our nation's ironclad commitment to Social Security."

Washington's political establishment was supremely smug about having saved the system: House Ways and Means Committee Chairman Dan Rostenkowski modestly declared that "we have reason to be very proud of ourselves." The *Washington Post* enthused that the process was something to reflect upon "if you get discouraged from time to time about government's inability to deal with the hard problems."

In fact, the solution "for all time" is likely to last little longer than the bail-out legislation of 1977, which was to have safeguarded the financial soundness of Social Security through the year 2030. What was then the largest tax increase in American history—$227 billion worth—was also hailed as a bipartisan triumph. Alas, the year 2030 came some 47 years early, and we should not be surprised if "for all time" comes to an end sooner than expected as well. According to a report by the Committee for Economic Development, a New York-based organization composed of business executives, university presidents, and other civic leaders, if the economy performs even slightly less robustly than Congress assumed it would perform when it passed the 1983 legislation, the system may "be threatened again with insolvency before the end of this decade."

The prime architects of the "for all time" solution, of course, remain optimistic. Congressman Pepper's aides say that he is not concerned about another solvency crisis, and Senator Dole says that the trust fund reserves, though low, "should be sufficient to ensure that benefits are paid through the 1980s." OMB spokesman Ed Dale says that it would take a drastic worsening of the economy to get the system into trouble, particularly because of the automatic cut in the cost-of-living adjustment (COLA) if the trust fund reserves drop severely. As a result, he says, he doesn't "regard solvency as something to worry about."

On the other hand, Phil Moseley, an aide to Republican Congressman William Archer, says that another financial crisis remains a real possibility. Archer first raised this concern while serving on the Commission in 1983; the COLA provision, Moseley says, is not necessarily enough. And a knowledgeable Senate Finance Committee staffer, who asked not to be named, agrees, saying that in a bad enough recession even a COLA freeze won't save the system.

Others express doubts about the bipartisan remedy as well. Laurie Fiori of the American Association of Retired People says that at the time there was a "great deal of anxiety" at the AARP over whether the bailout package would be sufficient. The reserve margins are dangerously thin, she adds, and should the economy not perform, "we could be in the soup again."

Indeed, former White House aide Peter Ferrara, whose proposal for Social Security reform was rejected out of hand by the Administration last fall, points out that even the 1984 Annual Report of the Board of Trustees for Social Security acknowledges that another recession could wreck the system. And shortly after the 1983 measure was passed, Richard S. Foster, the system's deputy chief actuary, distributed a memorandum which declared:

> If actual growth is more rapid in 1983, but then restricted by another recession within the next few years, the trust funds would be in a worse financial position than indicated under the pessimistic assumptions. . . . Depletion of the . . . trust funds would be very likely under these conditions and could conceivably occur within a few years from now.

The reason the system could get in trouble for the third time in barely more than a decade is that the 1983 legislation was designed not to remedy the severe defects in the design of the system, but to save the political hides of the President and Congress. Social Security remains a pay-as-you-go program with an aging population, a potential fiscal disaster when the baby boom generation reaches retirement age.

Most insiders seem to hope that the system will scrape by through 1990, when scheduled higher tax rates are expected to build up a substantial surplus that will carry the system into the next century. "The nineties will be more comfortable," says one Administration official. Yet that comfort may last only a few years; A. Haeworth Robinson, a former chief actuary of the system, told Congress in 1983 that its proposals did "not even come close to resolving Social Security's financial problems—except those . . . for the next seven years. To resolve the longer range financial problems, the tax rate would have to rise considerably above its currently scheduled level."

Unfortunately, what politicians have yet to address is that as long as Social Security is not set up on an actuarially sound basis, it will remain vulnerable to economic and demographic changes. This uncertainty caused the Commission great difficulty even in estimating the magnitude of the problem in 1983; the cumulative deficit forecasts for 1990 ranged between $50 billion and $450 billion, causing Commission Chairman Alan Greenspan to declare:

> It's very easy to move this cumulative deficit by $100 billion, and so it's possible to get, you know, really very substantial numbers which I don't think we ought to as a commission try to close, and that's sort of why I would come out subscribing to the way Bob Beck [a fellow commissioner] puts it, that we sort of stipulate that the number is 150 to 200 billion dollars.

Even if the Commission made the best guess then possible when it chose to "sort of stipulate" the size of the deficit, reality may turn out to be far different, depending on the performance of the economy. For example, the Commission's recommendations were based on mildly "pessimistic" predictions of the inflation rate falling to 4 percent—forever. And the unemployment rate dropping to 5.5 percent, real wage growth increasing at one percent annually, and productivity climbing 1.9 percent—all forever. Yet just five years ago we had back-to-back years of double-digit inflation; unemployment hasn't been as low as 5.5 percent since 1973. Real wages have declined slightly over the past 15 years and fell 1.6 percent between 1978 and 1982 alone; productivity grew only 1.2 percent annually during the 1970s. Thus, if past experience is any indication, the system will continue to face deficits, not surpluses, and the red ink could become truly catastrophic; a drop in real wage rates alone could double the projected deficit.

The fertility- and death-rate projections underlying the 1983 bail-out are also suspect. The Commission predicted the fertility rate would climb in the future, even though it has fallen over the past two centuries. Richard Rahn, chief economist for the U.S. Chamber of Commerce, argues that as barriers to women entering the work force, particularly in high wage jobs, continue to be removed—thus increasing the "opportunity cost of women dropping out to have a child"—the birthrate will further decline. The Commission also assumed that the increase in life expectancy will slow down (Americans live an average of fourteen years longer than when Social Security was first enacted). But medical advances continue to accelerate.

Even if the Commission's assumptions hold up, the surplus that is to accumulate before the end of this century may not last long enough to fund benefits in the next century. Given the political nature of the system, and the pressure to increase benefits (pressure that caused Congress and President Nixon to approve a 20-percent benefit hike in 1972 and Reagan and Congress to waive the 3-percent COLA threshold in late 1983), any surplus probably will be spent. If nothing else, it might be used to bail out Medicare, which will face an estimated $250 billion cumulative deficit by 1995. In that case, the huge Social Security deficits projected by the Commission to occur in the next century will go unfunded that much sooner. The question, then, is not whether Social Security will go under— but when.

The only long-term solution to the crisis is to split the welfare and retirement aspects of Social Security. This is not a new idea; proposals to privatize Social Security's retirement function and to shift its welfare role to general assistance programs go back more than twenty years. Unfortunately, politicians foolish enough to use the words "Social Security" and "voluntary" in the same sentence—Barry Goldwater in 1964 and Ronald Reagan in 1976, in particular—were punished at the polls.

But that was before the proliferation of individual retirement accounts— IRAs—in this country, which has given new meaning to the term "voluntary." With the American public's general acceptance of IRAs, the opportunity now exists to sell a major reform plan to stem the red ink. For example, the young could be allowed to use expanded IRAs, or some other actuarially sound vehicle, to guarantee their retirement incomes, while a pay-as-you-go income transfer system, like welfare, was used to protect those unable to save for the future or to take care of themselves when they became elderly. Allowing the young to get out of Social Security, at least partially, would provide them a better return on their retirement investment while reducing the future obligations of the system.

One of the most realistic proposals along this line comes from Peter Ferrara, author of *Social Security: The Inherent Contradiction*. Ferrara would guarantee benefits to current retirees by issuing them a government bond, allaying fears that their retirement lifeline will be cut. Workers would be allowed to invest in a "Super IRA" and to take a credit against their income tax equivalent to 20 percent of their Social Security taxes paid; they could direct their employers to make a similar contribution, with the employer receiving the tax credit. The worker's future Social Security benefits would be reduced proportionally by his IRA investment. (Ferrara would also eventually allow an additional 10-percent credit for IRA contributions with which to purchase life insurance.)

The distinguishing feature of Ferrara's proposal—which is being promoted by such groups as Citizens for a Sound Economy and the Heritage Foundation—is that Social Security taxes would be left untouched, to forestall any public perception that the system was being tampered with. It is, in his view, far more salable politically than earlier proposals to phase out the system entirely.

It is not surprising that Social Security reform had no chance of going anywhere last election year. But in the future a plan relying on IRAs, like Ferrara's, to separate the retirement and welfare functions of Social Security at least partially, may become a serious option. Indeed, in one sense it is the Administration's only option: Unless Reagan plans to do nothing, thereby joining the usual gaggle of Social Security groupies and pollyannas in ignoring the system's slow slide over a financial cliff, the Ferrara plan is the only way around the President's pledge last year not to cut benefits or to raise taxes. (The much-discussed freeze on this year's COLA increase—which appears dead—would not ensure the long-term solvency of the system.)

As for Congress, which is, if anything, more reluctant than Reagan to target benefits, the plan offers a relatively painless solution to a very painful problem. Senator Dole said he supported the 1983 bail-out package because he was "not aware of any major financial proposal or alternative financing package that could have gained bipartisan support. The votes were just not there for enacting larger benefit reductions, larger tax increases, or general revenue financing." Ferrara's plan, because it would do none of these, would stand a good chance of being taken seriously.

But many roadblocks remain. The first is simply the sense that America's retirement lifeline is being severed; the AARP's Fiori says that there will always be a great deal of anxiety among beneficiaries to preserve the system, which creates "built-in resistance to change." One Administration official observed that there is a distinct split even between conservative intellectuals and conservative politicians, and that "among the latter there is no constituency for a radical transformation of Social Security."

Another problem is the deficit. A sympathetic White House aide, who asked not to be identified, says that if the IRA idea had been proposed in 1937, or even 1950, it would have been "terrific." But he doubts that any politician is willing to worry about making the system more sound in fifty years—which Ferrara's plan would do—when he has to worry about the revenue loss from the income tax credit next year. Similarly, OMB's Dale maintains that "anything that increases the budget deficit would have a couple strikes against it."

Nonetheless, Ferrara remains optimistic. His proposal would increase the overall budget deficit only by a relatively small amount, and only in the short-term. If the 20-percent retirement option were in effect this year, and people on average took advantage of half the permissible level (which is probably optimistic), the government would "lose" $14.5 billion. More important, by cutting Social Security payments in the long run, the plan would eventually reduce government spending.

Ferrara sees the "Super IRA" as the only reform package likely to appeal to the young of all ideological stripes. Workers now entering the system apparently harbor few illusions about the value of their forced "contributions"; one Administration official admits there is widespread skepticism among the young about whether they will ever receive any Social Security benefits. "There is evidence," he says, "that the young are worried and might be open" to such an idea.

Younger Americans, in other words, are realizing that they are the final losers in a fifty-year Ponzi scheme. The early investors—the elderly now on Social Security—are getting between 2.7 and five times as much as they and their employers contributed, plus interest. And, despite the widespread myth to the contrary, the recipients of this windfall are not poor; nearly one-third of all Social Security payments currently go to families with incomes above $30,000 a year.

By contrast, what will the young get back when they retire? Anthony Pellachio, the Deputy Assistant Secretary of Health and Human Services for Income Security, calculates that depending on the beneficiary's salary history, a 25-year-old male will lose between $9,780 and $80,175 (in current dollars), and a similarly situated female will at best gain $2,857 and could lose as much as $56,920. That's not much of a return on an average of $300,000 in forced contributions. What's more, for the young today to collect *anything,* coming generations could well have to contribute far more in taxes to Social Security than is currently planned—potentially 35 to 40 percent of their incomes—just to keep the system afloat.

Can this message be transmitted not only to the young, but to everyone concerned about generational fairness? Can we reform the system before it destroys us? Rahn, of the Chamber of Commerce, thinks a plan like Ferrara's is "probably too complex to explain simply in a political world," but that it may be adopted in an ad hoc fashion as IRAs are gradually expanded and Social Security benefit growth is slowed in real terms. Adds the AARP's Fiori, "Obviously, incremental changes in the program are easier to achieve than radical changes,'' and according to Susan Dower, formerly with the House Republican Conference, a "grassroots educational program'' could prepare the groundwork for such reform.

Ultimately, of course, prospects for genuine reform will depend on Ronald Reagan. Last year, before the campaign heated up, Reagan called the 1983 tax increase a "temporary fix,'' and warned the system may eventually confront a "day of reckoning.'' He concluded that "what we need to do is a revamping of the program,'' though "we must never pull the rug out from current beneficiaries.'' Now that he no longer has to worry about another election, he has the best opportunity yet to defuse an issue that has bedeviled him since he first suggested, two decades ago, that the system be made voluntary.

## 134. The False Promise of Head Start

*January 25, 1989*

Sacred cows roam the halls of Capitol Hill, and few social programs have garnered more bipartisan praise than Head Start, which aids preschoolers. Called the "Great Society jewel'' by liberals, Head Start has won from George Bush a promise to expand it.

Head Start, which now spends more than $1 billion annually, is intended to remedy social disadvantages that would otherwise hinder poor students' educational progress. The goal is as laudable as it is simple: to break the cycle of child poverty-educational failure-adult poverty.

Alas, what seems sensible in theory has not worked in practice. Before Head Start was established, a similar Indianapolis preschool program had been discredited; researchers found it did not increase student performance.

The Great Society was designed around dreams rather than facts, however. So Head Start not only was created, but continues to grow steadily even as evidence of its failure accumulates.

For instance, in a recent article in the Heritage Foundation's *Policy Review,* Enid Borden and Kate Walsh O'Beirne point to a 1968–69 study by the Westinghouse Learning Corp. and Ohio University, which found no long-term benefits from the program. These results called into question the very basis of Head Start. Nevertheless, the liberal *New Republic* responded by editorializing that it would be unfortunate "if congressional Scrooges were to use the study as an argument for junking the whole program.''

In 1976 Westinghouse's findings were supported by a professor at the

University of Maryland, Gilbert Austin, who concluded that any Head Start gains dissipated after a year or two. "We have learned that it is not enough just to create a preschool," he said at the time.

A later study claimed astounding results for compensatory assistance, but the services offered by the small Michigan program differed substantially from those provided by Head Start. Moreover, the sample was just 123 students; the chairman of the University of Michigan economics department warned that one should not put "an inordinate amount" of faith in the results.

And no other study has replicated the Michigan findings. Indeed, in 1985 CSR Inc. released an omnibus report, commissioned by the Department of Health and Human Services, that synthesized the results of more than 210 Head Start studies. Its conclusion? Though "children show significant immediate gains as a result of Head Start participation . . . by the end of the second year (of elementary school) there are no educationally meaningful differences."

Even the nutritional and medical aspects of the program yielded no long-term benefits, for health and nutritional practices in the home remained unchanged. In short, the temporary boost provided by Head Start cannot counteract a disadvantaged family environment.

The program's lack of success does not mean that we should accept as inevitable the many barriers facing poor youth. But genuine concern requires recognition of the failure of traditional panaceas. "We cannot afford to pretend that Head Start breaks" the cycle of poverty, warn Borden and O'Beirne.

Instead, we should set as our first priority a renewed emphasis on family and community values. Uncle Sam cannot provide a loving home life, nurture an interest in learning, and instill a sense of self-worth and hope; instead, these must develop through an individual's daily interaction with his family, friends, and neighbors.

As for policy, the primary initiative must come from the local level. For instance, elementary schools need to stop dumping poorer kids into classes for the "mentally retarded." The result is to lower everyone's expectations and virtually guarantee the children's failure. (In fact, one reason the Michigan preschool succeeded was its ability to reduce future mislabeling of its students.)

Second, local schools, aided by community associations, need to emphasize parental involvement in their kids' education. The Michigan project included weekly home visits with parents; the 1985 CSR study concluded that "children of parents who are highly involved in Head Start perform better on cognitive tests at year-end than children whose parents were less involved."

In both these cases there is little the federal government can do. Which means that Head Start will remain irrelevant in the long-run, "merely treating the symptoms of childhood poverty," in the words of Borden and O'Beirne.

We can no longer afford to keep sacred cows grazing at taxpayer expense, even one as highly regarded as Head Start. The good intentions behind the program simply are not enough to justify its continuation.

## 135. Hands Across America—or in America's Pockets?

*June 5, 1986*

Celebrity charity is in. Endorsed by every famous person imaginable, Hands Across America and its human chain drew 5 million people and raised an estimated $30 million.

If Hands' money goes to promote community self-help projects, then the silly gimmicks and self-serving corporate ads will not have offended us in vain. Hunger does exist in America and we should help those in need.

But there is a real danger that this latest publicity-fed campaign will promote expensive non-solutions to a non-crisis.

"The problems of hunger and homelessness in the United States are growing at a frightening pace," claim Hands' press releases. "There is widespread hunger and famine in America," says organizer Ken Kragen.

This would be terrible, if true, but it's not. For there is no evidence that tens of millions of Americans are going hungry: "the perception of widespread hunger is rooted in subjective, anecdotal impression, based on isolated and unrepresentative cases," says Heritage Foundation analyst Anna Kondratus.

Her conclusion is backed by a 1977 Health, Education and Welfare report that found "true malnutrition is virtually non-existent in this country." The isolated instances of hunger that do exist are caused primarily by ignorance.

Indeed, poor eating habits are not closely linked to poverty, but instead "are found in all income groups," concluded the HEW study. In 1980 the average caloric intake of low income people was 2,897, well above the recommended daily allowance. And food is becoming increasingly affordable—the percent of income spent on food has dropped steadily, from 20.2 percent in 1960 to 14.4 percent in 1985—the lowest ever.

But Hands' organizers and their allies seem undeterred by the facts, preferring to lobby Uncle Sam for more programs and spending.

The campaign has already given a grant to the Physicians' Task Force on Hunger in America, a left-leaning group that has tortured general economic statistics to manufacture claims of a hunger crisis. The organization has also blamed Reagan administration policies for increasing malnutrition, even though the organization's own figures show virtually no increase in hungry people between 1979 and last year.

Moreover, there is no reason to believe that spending billions more on food programs is the answer to anything.

Between 1955 and 1980, real federal outlays on nutrition jumped 30 times; yet, during the same period, average calories consumed by the poor fell. Indeed, lower income people without food stamps currently meet more RDA nutrient levels than those receiving federal food subsidies.

Anyway, it's not as if Uncle Sam has been idle. In 1970 there were 4.3 million people receiving food stamps; last year that number was 20.9 million. Some 1.5 million children received free school lunches in 1977, while 1.8 million do so today. And an additional 3 million kids are fed through the Women, Infants and Children program.

Even Mr. Reagan, despite his professed disdain for social spending, has approved steady increases for federal food programs. In 1981 outlays were $15.6 billion. This year they will run more than $19 billion, a 22 percent increase.

Indeed, despite Mr. Reagan's budget cuts, since 1978 the number of poor households receiving food stamps has increased and the inflation-adjusted benefits per family have grown sharply. Admits the Urban Institute, "The legislation of 1981–82 did not have as large an impact on recipients as previously thought."

Nevertheless, the activist groups think only of more taxpayer dollars. When President Reagan told a group of students that the only reason people went hungry today is that they don't know "where or how to get this help," Paul Del Ponte of the Food Research and Action Center called the statement "outlandish" and said Mr. Reagan had cut nutrition programs by $12 billion—a truly "outlandish" claim if there ever was one.

Then, when Mr. Reagan decided to join in the Hands' human chain, Sen. Tom Harkin, D-Iowa, complained that "those in this country who suffer from hunger deserve more from their president than a photo opportunity." Harkin, of course, cares so much about the hungry that he never rests in his efforts to use federal agricultural programs to jack up food prices for his farm constituents.

Those who participated in Hands Across America deserve credit for caring. But they should not be misled by the sophistry of the project's organizers.

There is no hunger crisis sweeping the nation. And the pockets of malnutrition that still exist are best met through community education and private efforts, not additional raids on the public Treasury.

## 136. The New Year: A Time to Give

*January 6, 1988*

Christmas is the one time of the year that almost everyone thinks about the less fortunate. Churches host special Christmas dinners; Salvation Army members solicit donations at street corners.

Groups collect toys for needy children. Shelters are opened for the homeless. And everyone revels in the movie Scrooge's conversion from skinflint to philanthropist.

But now that Christmas has passed the poor's need for generous assistance is, if anything, greater than ever. For the cold of winter is quickly replacing that warm holiday feeling.

Americans are a generous people. Despite recent changes in the tax law that make giving less remunerative, they apparently contributed more in 1987 than in the previous year.

Not even the stock market crash has markedly affected Americans' contributions. In fact, since 1962 market downturns have led to increased giving.

And people's response to specific hardship cases—victims of fires, for instance—remains extraordinary. When presented with an individual case of need, most people rush to help their fellow man.

Nevertheless, there is much more that we could do. We are a wealthy nation; our homes are filled with the latest technological gadgets that make an already easy life more comfortable. We act as if three TV sets, two cars and a VCR are our birthright.

In short, Americans give but few sacrifice. On average people contribute between 2 percent and 4 percent of their adjusted gross income to charity. That is, Americans give away just 2 to 4 pennies of every dollar they earn—after subtracting such extras as IRA contributions.

Unfortunately, top government officials provide no leadership in this area. In 1984 compassion became a campaign issue: Democratic vice-presidential nominee Geraldine Ferraro charged that Ronald Reagan was not "a good Christian" because of his administration's budget cuts.

Yet Ferraro personally contributed less than 1 percent of her income to charity. Giving by Vice President George Bush, Reagan and Democratic presidential nominee Walter Mondale—all of whom are wealthy—ranged between 3 percent and 4 percent.

But the moral failure of politicians provides no justification for the rest of us to shirk our responsibility to our disadvantaged neighbors.

"If anyone has material possessions and sees his brother in need but has no pity on him, how can the love of God be in him?" asked the Apostle John. (1 John 3:17)

Nor is the increased government welfare role cause for people to relax. Through the 1960s and 1970s federal welfare spending jumped 652 percent; outlays for education and other social programs climbed 834 percent.

Yet millions of Americans remain poor. And many of these people have become almost totally dependent on the federal government, locked into a sterile, unfeeling system.

Indeed, an entire generation is being destroyed in crime-ridden, inner-city ghettos. Federal money and programs have provided no solution to the most basic of human problems.

The only hope is for individual Americans to reach out to their less fortunate brethren. For only such personal contact, with the creation of role models, transmittal of moral values, and tailoring of aid to meet individual circumstances will help make the needy self-sufficient.

For example, smaller, private facilities have proved far better than large government institutions in assisting the homeless. In New York City Franciscan priests have created three St. Francis residences that offer shelter, food and psychiatric care.

"These people needed help, and it was clear that putting them in large shelters or impersonal hospitals was no solution," said Father John Felice. "For us, it was an act of simple human decency."

Father Felice's "act of simple human decency" needs to be emulated across America. Sen. Mark Hatfield, R-Ore., once estimated that if every church in the nation sponsored a welfare family the government's rolls would be empty. Civic and community associations could make a similar commitment.

And there are innumerable charitable efforts that deserve Americans' support. An increase in giving need not even be painful. Trimming our insatiable material appetites just a little would provide resources that could help feed and clothe those in need.

One of the most beautiful aspects of Christmas is the increased concern for the less fortunate. But that Christmas spirit would mean so much more if it were to persist throughout the year. Then we would be living a little bit more like the person whose birth we just celebrated.

# Civil Rights for Whom?

## 137. New Directions for Black America

*August 12, 1987*

Both the National Urban League and the NAACP held their annual conventions in July and political confrontation was in the air.

"We will fight" the nomination of Robert Bork to the Supreme Court "all the way," said Benjamin Hooks, executive director of the NAACP, "until hell freezes over, and then we'll skate across on the ice."

But there was also an unusual tentativeness at the two conclaves, a recognition that all answers to the problems of blacks will not come from government.

"The black community itself must assume responsibility for dealing with the problems of our communities," Urban League President John Jacob told his group.

Jacob still has a hopelessly naive view of the public sector's ability to do good—especially given our recurring experience with the reality of government programs. But at least he understands that poor blacks can't count on Uncle Sam to simply drop them into the economic mainstream.

For instance, Jacob and other black leaders are pushing to recreate the basic moral consensus that once existed in poor neighborhoods.

"Values like education, high expectations and hard work are what helped black Americans survive," said Jacob: "Undermining those values today is . . . acting as subversive agents for those who want black people to be poor and hopeless."

Changing a ghetto culture that actively discourages work, honesty and achievement will require rebuilding family structures. Legal reform— holding parents responsible for the actions of their children, for instance, as advocated by the NAACP—may prove to be part of the answer.

But of more lasting impact will be increased activity by voluntary community organizations, like churches, businesses and civic groups.

"We call upon the more fortunate segments of black America to enlist or re-enlist in this fight,'' said Hooks. ''If we are not prepared to work for our salvation, our race will be doomed.''

Even where the solutions are not obvious, black leaders are now talking about formerly forbidden topics. Black New York City Police Commissioner Benjamin Ward recently called the fact that most crime was committed by young black males ''our little secret.'' In response, City Councilman Wendell Foster, president of a coalition of black ministers, organized a commission to study the issue.

Also required is a change in government policies that actively discourage black independence. Just 5 percent of women on Aid to Families with Dependent Children work; in contrast, 60.4 percent of all female household heads are employed. Something is so obviously wrong with the existing system that even the NAACP endorsed the concept of ''workfare'' to make welfare beneficiaries work for their checks.

Unfortunately, though, civil rights organizations are still unwilling to break with the grand liberal coalition and to attack other government economic restraints that confine many blacks to the underclass. For instance, according to a Rand Corp. study last year, improved education has been the most important cause of black progress over the last 40 years.

Yet the public school system in inner cities no longer educates: nearly half of blacks between 21 and 25 are functionally illiterate. Poor blacks desperately need greater control over their educational futures—which means being able to send their children to quality private schools.

Thousands of black Baptists already sacrifice financially to send their children to Catholic schools in the nation's major cities. More would do so if they could use either vouchers or tuition tax credits to escape failing public institutions.

Another still untouchable issue for leading black organizations is economic protectionism benefiting organized labor. The minimum wage puts the most disadvantaged in society out of work; the Davis-Bacon Act, which requires payment of union wages on federally funded projects, protects unions from cheaper black labor. Licensing for everything from taxis to plumbers limits the economic opportunities available to the underclass.

Nevertheless, there is hope.

''Pervasive and persistent poverty has eroded but not destroyed the strong, deep value framework that for so long has sustained black people,'' concluded a remarkable report issued by the Joint Center for Political Studies earlier this year. That framework can be rebuilt.

Thus, while most black leaders still look to government for answers that aren't there, many finally recognize that poor blacks cannot wait for Uncle Sam. Only when the basic moral values that once undergirded black

America are resuscitated—and when the black community unites to break down economic barriers now created by government—will we see true equal opportunity for all.

## 138. Racial Quotas for Congress?

*March 30, 1988*

Rep. Peter Rodino, chairman of the House Judiciary Committee and a 40-year veteran of Congress, says he will retire in January. What makes the New Jersey congressman's decision noteworthy is that Rodino, a white who represents a largely black district, has been under pressure from black politicians to quit.

Says Newark Mayor James Sharpe, "The courts carved out the district more than a dozen years ago to elect a minority congressman, and it's time to get that done."

But the judiciary actually intervened to stop the state Legislature from drawing district lines to dilute blacks' voting strength, not to dictate the race of the candidate elected.

Even presidential candidate Jesse Jackson has gotten involved, campaigning for Rodino's black primary opponent in 1986: "In those districts that have a majority of blacks we should have black congresspeople."

Who is the "we" Jackson is referring to? Jackson doesn't live in Rodino's district. The voters who do live there, black as well as white, should elect the best candidate possible, someone who will honestly and competently represent them in Congress, irrespective of his race.

Do Jackson and his fellow thinkers really want a political quota system? If so, it would be the first step toward resegregating America. For if black majorities are entitled to black representatives, presumably white majorities have a right to white congressmen.

Which means that blacks would never have a chance to be elected in the vast majority of House districts. And that no black could ever sit in the U.S. Senate.

Indeed, why should political quotas be limited to race? How about religion? Predominantly Roman Catholic districts would get Catholic congressmen while Lutheran populations would get Lutheran representatives. And why shouldn't we distribute seats on the basis of sex and socioeconomic status?

The only obvious benefit to black voters of having a black congressman is to provide community leadership. In fact, Newark City Councilman Ralph Grant, the leading contender to replace Rodino, says that is precisely why he wants to be in Congress, "to serve as a role model for the young people I talk to on the Newark street corners."

But even if true—how many politicians reach for higher office to self-lessly give the young someone to look up to?—there are already no end of influential black politicians, including Newark's mayor. It is more important to develop successful black businessmen, social workers and parents for young people to imitate.

After all, the black political role models have not always been good. Former congressmen like Adam Clayton Powell and Charles Diggs gained national attention for their personal corruption, not their dedication to the poor.

Moreover, local self-help initiatives, rather than more government programs, offer the best hope for halting the frightening downward spiral into poverty, crime and dependency of many ghetto communities. Despairing people need enlightened leadership, which is not likely to come from a political hack who will be spending most of his time kowtowing to a partisan congressional majority in Washington.

Anyway, black America desperately needs greater integration with, not separation from, the rest of the country. Only when all people think in color-blind terms will blacks have full equality of opportunity.

And this applies to politics as well as everyday life. Los Angeles Mayor Tom Bradley almost won California's governorship in 1982. Had he run simply as a "black candidate," he would not have been taken seriously.

In fact, one is entitled to suspect that Jackson and other black politicians in search of de facto minority quotas are more interested in advancing their own careers than the interests of black voters. Rodino's district has had a black majority since 1972 and his constituents have had ample opportunity to replace him with a black.

Yet Rodino has consistently turned back black primary opponents with majorities ranging from 57 percent to 76 percent; he defeated Donald Payne, a Democratic Newark City councilman, with 60 percent in 1986. What Payne and other black politicos are really frustrated about is the willingness of local black residents to vote for a white candidate whom they believe to be more qualified.

Race relations in America are fragile enough without the nation's black political leadership pressing for a system of political segregation. Hopefully black voters in other districts will prove to be as discriminating as Rodino's constituents, choosing the best candidate available, even if he happens to be white.

## 139.  Reconsidering *Runyon*

*July 20, 1988*

The liberal interest groups are agog. The Supreme Court recently decided to hear an appeal in the employment discrimination case of *Patterson vs. McLean Credit Union.*

Though the lawsuit at issue is itself nothing special, in accepting the case the Supreme Court indicated that it might be willing to overrule an earlier civil rights decision, *Runyon vs. McCrary.*

In *Runyon* the Supreme Court used a Civil War-era statute to ban racial discrimination by a private school. That ruling since has been applied in more than 100 cases, involving all sorts of business transactions and different forms of discrimination, such as age and citizenship.

Of course, discrimination against blacks and other groups is odious. But *Runyon* suffers from one important defect: It was wrongly decided. The original statute, passed in 1866, was only intended to bar discrimination by state and local governments.

In fact, Justice John Paul Stevens even admitted that he was voting with the majority in *Runyon* to uphold social expectations, not the law.

"There is no doubt in my mind," Stevens wrote in his concurring opinion, that the Supreme Court's "construction of the statute would have amazed the legislators who voted for it. . . . Were we writing on a clean slate, I would therefore vote to reverse."

Nevertheless, the civil rights community—which long ago abandoned support for color-blind policies in favor of quotas and government coercion—has reacted with horror at the prospect of *Runyon* being reconsidered. Amicus, or "friend of the court," briefs have been filed by 119 House members, 66 senators, 112 liberal interest groups, and 47 state attorneys general, all urging the Supreme Court to leave *Runyon* unchanged.

What is significant, though, is the fact that few of *Runyon's* supporters are defending the case on the merits. Instead, they are relying on precedent, contending that the Supreme Court should leave settled law alone.

Yet "those who raise this argument," observes Michael Greve, a scholar with the Washington Legal Foundation, "never had much respect for precedent when it came to inventing ever-new judicial rights and remedies, no matter how flimsy their foundations."

Only now have the left-leaning enthusiasts of activist courts discovered the virtue of judicial restraint.

There is, of course, value in stable law. But bad stable law is still bad law. And *Runyon* is, despite its high-minded intent, bad law.

The 123-year-old statute upon which *Runyon* is based states that "all persons . . . shall have the same right in every state and territory to make and enforce contracts as is enjoyed by white citizens."

The law simply means that states cannot prevent blacks from making and enforcing contracts. It does not empower blacks, or anyone else, to force someone to enter into a contract with them.

And that was settled law for more than a century. In fact, the landmark

1964 Civil Rights Act, which barred discrimination in public accommodations, would never have been necessary had the earlier legislation applied.

However, an artful attorney concocted an appealing if erroneous argument and sold it to a court willing to ignore the law in order to achieve its ends. As a result, people may sue for damages if they believe someone has discriminated against them.

What basis is there for letting nine unelected judges make up the law?

Marc Stern, a staffer with the American Jewish Congress, argues "that the core notion that private segregation is not acceptable enjoys wide support" and that the civil rights groups' "task is to show that *Runyon* is not out of joint with society."

That is not the issue, however. The fact that discrimination is a moral evil opposed by the majority of Americans does not mean that judges should have the unreviewable power to penalize bigots. Judges are supposed to enforce the law, not create it out of whole cloth.

Indeed, since *Runyon* involved a statute rather than the Constitution, Congress could easily amend the law to cover private discrimination. If 66 senators really like *Runyon*, they should introduce legislation to make it the law, instead of relying on unelected judges to do their work for them.

If the Supreme Court is to be the guardian of our liberties, it must honestly interpret the law and not become the captive of any interest group, whether right or left. And that means making some difficult decisions, like overturning *Runyon*.

Then if Congress wanted to further regulate private behavior it could do so—but only after debating and voting on the issue. For no one's rights, including those of minorities, will ever be safe if elected politicians can continue hiding behind unaccountable judges.

## 140. The Fraudulent Civil Rights Act of 1987

*March 23, 1988*

One of a congressman's duties is to dream up euphemisms for truly wretched legislative proposals.

An illustration of this practice is "The Civil Rights Restoration Act of 1987," recently passed by both houses of Congress. Only a presidential veto stands between this bill and the freedom of countless Americans.

Over the years Congress has, in the name of civil rights, created a web of intricate regulations that apply to everyone but Capitol Hill. Unfortunately, the original concept of civil rights, which meant equal opportunity, has been steadily corrupted by political activists more intent on gaining power than achieving justice.

For example, the civil rights laws now allow people to essentially extort money from companies and schools by threatening lawsuits over imagined instances of discrimination. Federal regulations often use quotas, explicit or implicit, to reorder society. In fact, the enforcement bureaucracy has become more interested in numerical parity than justice.

Pennsylvania's Grove City College was one of the many victims of federal harassment. The school received no government aid but because its students benefited from federally guaranteed loans Uncle Sam asserted the right to regulate all of its activities. So Grove City, which had never been charged with discriminating against anyone, filed suit and in 1984 the Supreme Court ruled that the anti-discrimination clause applied only to the specific program receiving public assistance—in this case, the financial aid office—rather than the entire college.

By sharply restricting Uncle Sam's power to meddle, the decision actually advanced people's civil rights. The fact that a few students collected college loans no longer allowed Uncle Sam to, for instance, dictate how much the school had to spend on women's sports.

Naturally, an enormous hue and cry arose from the civil rights lobby, which had gotten used to running other people's lives, to "restore" the law. And the Reagan administration, afraid of appearing to be against "civil rights," backed legislation to reverse the decision in the area of education.

That wasn't good enough for legislators like Sen. Edward Kennedy, D-Mass., however, who saw an opportunity to extend the government's reach beyond just universities. So they proposed that the federal government essentially subject anyone who benefited in any way from any federal program to all of the civil rights regulations, no matter how unjust, wacky or costly.

The issue is not whether a federal contractor can, say, refuse to hire a black. What the Kennedy legislation would do—despite proponents' disingenuous assurances to the contrary—is allow the federal government to tell a corner grocery store that accepted Food Stamps to build access ramps for the handicapped and dictate policy to an entire state if just one agency collected a health grant.

A company could find itself subject to a new series of regulations if even one employee participated in a federal job training program. And federal regulators could descend on a church or even an entire denomination if just one of its activities, such as a summer camp, received federal support. Even a farmer who accepted a government check could find himself forced to modify buildings, file a raft of federal forms, and allow government inspectors onto his property.

What makes the bill so dangerous is that Congress and the courts would probably not be content to simply enforce existing law. Instead, they are likely to make up new and ever more extreme "rights" in the years ahead.

In fact, under the guise of "civil rights" alcoholics who fail to show up for work can now sue for damages if they are fired. Drug addicts, too, would like to be protected from "discrimination" for their "illness." Gay activists want the government to protect their "sexual preference." And the list goes on.

Unfortunately, the Kennedy bill would foist all sorts of special interest "rights" on churches, businesses and other private organizations across America.

Congress did pass an amendment declaring that Catholic hospitals could not be forced to perform abortions. But Civil Rights Commissioner William Allen warns that this stipulation could be voided by the Supreme Court, which would leave religious hospitals at the mercy of federal regulators.

The most important civil right for all individuals, black and white, male and female, is to be protected from an overreaching federal bureaucracy dominated by influential interest groups determined to impose their will on others. But the "Civil Rights Restoration Act" would vastly expand the power of government to intimidate and torment innocent citizens.

The legislation should not become law. If Congress really cares about the civil rights of all Americans, it will uphold the president's veto.

## 141. This Ruling Threatens the Rights of Women

*May 12, 1987*

The latest feminist victory against discrimination—the Supreme Court's ruling that the state of California can force the Rotary club to admit women—is a major blow against everyone's freedom.

The government may still allow small, independent clubs to set their own admission standards if, in the court's words, the group involves "the kind of intimate or private relation that warrants constitutional protection." But organizations like the Lions, Kiwanis, and Elks apparently have lost control over their memberships.

While forcibly opening up such clubs obviously benefits women, it vastly increases state interference with the most minute and personal of social and business relationships.

Indeed, in the name of nondiscrimination, governments have banned discounts for women during "ladies' nights" at bars and restaurants. A children's hair salon in Los Angeles was sued for charging girls, who tend to have longer hair, more than boys. Price breaks for women at a car wash have been ruled discriminatory and illegal. One male patron even sued a night club that barred men, but not women, from wearing shorts.

In none of these cases was the discrimination invidious. Irritating, perhaps. But nothing like the old Jim Crow rules that treated blacks as subhumans.

And while there's no logical reason for organizations like Rotary to exclude women, human relationships are not logical. Which is why freedom of association—a right protected by the First Amendment—is so important.

Indeed, there are women's-only organizations, like the Cosmopolitan and Colony clubs in New York and the Spa Lady chain of fitness centers. They, along with establishments that cater to homosexuals, are threatened by rules that ban all discrimination.

In a free society like ours, the government should stay out of interpersonal relations whenever possible. Social change may take longer as a result, but it will still occur.

In fact, the Rotary case arose after the local club in Duarte, Calif., decided to induct women to help counteract a declining membership. Three dozen Kiwanis clubs have also defied their international organization by admitting women. And many women's colleges have gone coed because of economic pressure.

This sort of voluntary movement toward non-discrimination is preferable to heavyhanded government regulation. Where innocuous discrimination persists, whether it be men's business clubs or ladies' discount nights, it should be accepted as inevitable in a pluralistic society.

A free people must tolerate intolerance, for the cost to liberty of trying to expunge every last vestige of discrimination from society is too high.

## 142. Comparable Worth Is Worthless

*October 29, 1986*

Often Congress acts most responsibly when it doesn't act. Which is what the Senate did in refusing to order a study of the federal civil service system to assess the "comparable worth" of each job.

Ohio's Rep. Mary Rose Oakar introduced legislation to create a nine-member "Commission on Compensation Equity" and hire a consultant to study federal job categories.

The consultant was to use points—based on education, responsibility and any other factor that struck his fancy—to rank various positions. He would then have determined whether the jobs primarily filled by women provided lower salaries than "comparable" male-dominated positions.

Finally, the Office of Personnel Management would have been required to implement any recommendations coming out of the study. Which probably would have entailed restructuring the civil service system so that consultants rather than the market process determined wage rates.

Oakar was able to steer her "anti-sex discrimination" bill through the House, but the Senate sensibly let her proposal die. Democrat Oakar, however, has vowed to keep trying, and Senate sponsor Daniel Evans, a mush-minded Republican who nevertheless should know better, warns that "we'll attach it to each critical bill that comes along" in 1987.

But the concept of comparable worth is simply crazy. It may not be "fair" that, say, a professional athlete makes more than a political columnist, but should the government declare them to be of equal value?

Indeed, more than two centuries ago Adam Smith posed the paradox of the fact that water, a necessity for life, is cheap, while diamonds, an attractive luxury, are very expensive. The critical difference is supply. Whatever the intrinsic "value" of a nurse's services compared to those of a truck driver, it is the interaction of both demand for and supply of the service that determines its price.

In practice comparable worth has proved to be a misleading pseudo-social science, one that enshrines as law the personal prejudices of the particular consultant conducting the study.

Of course, advocates of government wage-setting churn out reams of documents justifying their studies. Says Alvin Bellak, a partner in the Hay Management Consultants, "Job evaluation is a disciplined, objective process for rank-ordering jobs on an agreed compensable value scale."

But the actual experience of the 13 states that have tried to implement comparable worth in some degree has been anything but "objective." Richard Burr, an analyst with the Center for the Study of American Business, went to the trouble of studying existing state valuations and discovered widespread geographic discrimination.

It seems that in ranking a secretary, laundry worker and data entry operator, Iowa and Washington state rate the secretary highest, but disagree on the status of the other two. Minnesota thinks a secretary is the least valuable of the three positions; Vermont puts secretaries at No. 2.

Indeed, the states agree on almost nothing. Photographers are judged more than twice as valuable by Vermont than Iowa; Minnesota treats a nurse, social worker and chemist as equivalent positions, while Iowa rates the nurse 29 percent higher than the social worker, who in turn is considered 11 percent more valuable than the chemist.

In short, comparable worth, like beauty, is in the eye of the beholder.

Under such a policy wages are no longer set by the market—which signals what prospective purchasers of the service are willing to pay—but by the whims of bureaucrats and consultants.

Are women still discriminated against in the workplace? If so, it has nothing to do with the fact that a truck driver may make more than a nurse. Such wage differentials arise because of the way supply and demand for the particular service interact, not because of some male conspiracy.

True, on average women earn only two-thirds of what men do. But this aggregate number is meaningless: women work 9 percent fewer hours than their male counterparts, have less experience and education, and are more likely to interrupt their careers to bear a child.

Because these factors are changing, younger women are earning progressively more and closing the pay gap with men. And this process will continue over time—without federal wage regulation.

Comparable worth is a medieval concept, a "just price" for services. But if our society is to remain free, employment, and compensation, must remain a matter to be decided by employers and employees, not Rose Mary Oakar and her highly paid consultants.

## 143. The Gay Issue: Double-Edged Rights

*May 23, 1979*

The current debate over gay rights has obscured the real issue—the difference between two principles. One is discrimination by the state against homosexuals; the other is discrimination by private individuals against homosexuals—and state action to prevent such discrimination by individuals.

A clear example of the first kind of discrimination is the recently defeated Proposition 6 in California. The measure would have let local school boards dismiss (or refuse to hire) any employee who had engaged in homosexual activity likely to come to the attention of children. It might even have applied to people who were not homosexual themselves but who "advocated" homosexuality.

By making open homosexuality itself a basis for dismissal, the law would have institutionalized discrimination by the state against individuals because of a characteristic unrelated to their performance as teachers. Such a law would not have accounted for the individual characteristics of the particular teacher involved since, in any specific case, the homosexuality might not affect the students or the effectiveness of the teacher. Moreover, even if it did have such an effect, it might be more than balanced by an exemplary record of competence, compassion and experience.

This is akin to discrimination on grounds of any other personal decision, political, sexual or social. But unless the decision gets in the way of personal performance, individuals should not be penalized by the government for them. Moral and religious qualms about homosexuality do not give rise to a moral right to withhold government jobs, benefits or services because of them.

The worst form of such governmental discrimination has been criminal sanctions against homosexual acts between consenting adults. These laws are wrong for the same reasons Proposition 6 was wrong: They discriminate on the basis of an irrelevant personal decision. But criminal sanctions go further, punishing people directly for their personal choices, in an area where the government has no business being. Being fired from one's job is a severe, yet indirect, form of punishment, but it does not compare with the stigma, loss of liberty and disruption of one's life that result from criminal prosecution and imprisonment.

However, after having fought the coercive power of the state for years, homosexual-rights activists are now trying to marshal that same coercive power on their own behalf. At all levels of government they have been seeking legislative intervention to stop discrimination by private individuals against homosexuals.

The string of recently repealed homosexual-rights ordinances are examples of their activities. The ordinances generally ban discrimination by private individuals against homosexuals in employment, housing and accommodations; almost 40 cities across the nation have adopted similar measures.

The problem with these laws is that they violate the rights of homosexual-phobic people. For just as government action should not be used to discriminate against homosexuals, it should not be used to bludgeon people into accepting homosexuality in their private affairs. Private individuals should be free to associate with, rent to and do business with other individuals who make whatever voluntary decisions (whether sexual, social or political) they prefer. Though such discrimination may be silly, dumb and even immoral in someone else's eyes, that "someone else" has no right to interfere in these personal choices of individuals. Freedom includes the freedom to be wrong.

Homosexuals have the right to decide what sort of life they will lead. Once they've made that decision, they should not suffer discrimination by the state because of it. However, they must accept the consequences of their choice; they have no right to use the state to suppress people's negative response to their own lifestyle decisions. If homosexuals have the right to assert their own lifestyles, others have the right to run their own lives based on those same choices.

# Social Potpourri

## 144. Should Society Condone Abortion as 'Convenient'?

*December 3, 1977*

The Supreme Court has again thrust the provocative issue of abortion into contention, by ruling that taxpayers are not constitutionally required to finance abortions. Despite the anguished cries from pro-abortion groups, the court's ruling was correct— government funding of abortions is a policy decision for politicians, not a constitutional decision for judges.

This is therefore an appropriate time for a fresh look at the 1973 abortion decision, which has been rigorously criticized by constitutional scholars for its egregious usurpation of the legislative function. The court then effectively held, in the apt words of columnist Patrick Buchanan, that the unborn child was "the personal property of the mother—to be destroyed, disposed of, or kept, as she saw fit."

The fundamental issue remains the same—the convenience of the pregnant woman versus the existence and development of the life that she carries. This is the bottom line, at which point the balance must be made.

On the one side is the life of the unborn child. It is genetically complete from conception, and its heart is beating by 25 days. Electrical brain waves may be recorded as early as 43 days. All of the unborn child's body systems are present by eight weeks, and working by 11. By six weeks it will respond to some stimuli; by nine or 10 it can squint, swallow, and make a fist. And as the unborn child develops, it can respond to pain, cold, taste, light and signals.

Birth is, in fact, merely one incident in a continuing developmental process, which continues until death.

For example, tear ducts are not functional until after the first month of post-natal life. Changes in the circulatory system, and the separation of the atria of the heart into right and left chambers, take place after birth. The nervous system continues to develop structurally for at least a year

369

after birth. And other organs, such as the sex glands, take years to become functional.

An editorial, in favor of abortion, in the September 1970 issue of *California Medicine*—the official journal of the California Medical Association—recognized that the rhetoric surrounding abortion betrays "a curious avoidance of the scientific fact, which everyone knows, that human life begins at conception and is continuous, whether intra or extra-uterine, until death. The very considerable semantic gymnastics which are required to rationalize abortion as anything but the taking of human life would be ludicrous if not often put forth under socially impeccable auspices."

On the other side, a compelling justification certainly should be required to justify the destruction of human life. A number of different rationales have been advanced, but only the hardship and inconvenience of the pregnancy to the putative mother deserves consideration in the final balance.

Among those deserving little weight is the most pragmatic one; abortion, whether moral or immoral, should be legalized because women will otherwise get abortions from "backroom hacks." This argument dodges the moral issue altogether.

Should homicide be legalized? The aggressor may be killed by someone defending himself. Should burglary be legalized? The burglar may get bitten by a watchdog, shot by an irate victim, or be injured while escaping. The moral necessity for a law cannot depend on whether its violators suffer from its violation.

Another frequent argument is that the woman should be able to "control her own body." This is true enough, but the unborn child is not merely an appendage, tumor, cyst, or diseased organ. Rather, it is a genetically separate, unique, and developing human being. Abortion itself asserts control over another person's body—that of the unborn child.

The most insidious argument for the destruction of the unborn child is that abortion is necessary to prevent the birth of unwanted, and thus mistreated, children. The argument ignores the possibility of adoption, and the fact that the relationship between unwanted births and child abuse is unclear; in fact, there is evidence that children from wanted births suffer more abuse.

In any case, killing the unborn child runs against the human experience—most people want to live, at most any cost. How can we play God and decide, for someone else, that it is in their interest that we kill them, so they won't live an unfulfilling life? How many people would have preferred to have been aborted, in *their* own interest? Would you?

If this rationale is accepted, logic dictates that it be expanded; all of the arguments for killing unwanted unborn children also supports killing unwanted born children. The beginning of the "legal life" of a person could be set at some other arbitrary point, such as five days, five months, or five years. Then the child could be "evaluated," and painlessly "aborted" if it was found to be unwanted or otherwise inconvenient.

Thus again, we have a make-weight argument. We cannot seriously speak of killing the unborn child for its own sake; rather, we are killing it for the sake of the putative mother. The burden of pregnancy is the only valid consideration which should go into the balance.

This burden certainly can be a major inconvenience, but it must be weighed against the transcendent value of human life. Should society condone killing because it is convenient? Such an inconvenience would have to be monumental; only a threat to the mother's life satisfies this condition, and thus should force the unborn child to yield its life.

Society must realize the tenuous line that has been drawn: is there any rational reason to separate expendable and non-expendable life at birth? If you are not willing to kill a human being a minute after birth, then how about a minute before? And a minute before that? By denying the humanity of the unborn child, who is manifestly growing and living, we are denying it for all human beings.

Albert Schweitzer's admonition should not be unheeded—that "[i]f a man loses reverence for any part of life, he will lose reverence for all life." No more striking an example of this is possible than the doctor in Westminister, Calif., who attempted to abort a seven-month pregnancy, but failed. Shortly thereafter, the woman went into labor and gave birth; the doctor returned and allegedly strangled the child.

The result—the *same* person attempted to kill the *same* human life twice in the *same* day. Yet it was only illegal the second time. What sort of society draws such a tenuous and arbitrary line between killing and protecting the same human life, in the space of one day?

We face a continuing moral crisis, for, as Dr. Bernard N. Nathanson noted, after presiding over 60,000 deaths as the head of the largest abortion clinic in the world—the Center for Reproductive and Sexual Health in New York: "We must courageously face the fact, finally, that human life of a special sort is being taken." This arbitrary line between life that is valued, and that which is worthless, it not healthy for children, or other living things.

## 145. When to Resist?

*February 7, 1985*

As they have every year for the last 12, antiabortion demonstrators recently converged on the nation's capital to protest the Supreme Court's

1973 decision legalizing abortion. Speaking to the crowd by a loudspeaker hookup from the Oval Office, President Reagan promised to work to end "the national tragedy of abortion."

The issue has taken on a special urgency as bombings of abortion clinics spread across the nation, with 30 reported attacks since 1982. Supporters of abortion tried to make an issue of Mr. Reagan's delay in publicly denouncing the incidents; under pressure, he finally issued a statement, pledging to "do all in my power to assure that the guilty are brought to justice."

But should the bombers be "brought to justice"? Some abortion foes, including ministers, have refused to condemn the attacks, arguing that the resultant property damage is a small price to pay to stop a process that has killed 15 million unborn children since 1973.

Their argument is not without force. The issue of abortion is an intractable one, involving the balancing of two very important interests—the right to life of the potential person and the liberty of the putative mother.

But even most thoughtful skeptics acknowledge the uncomfortable similarity between abortion and infanticide and the lack of a meaningful physiological difference between the fetus before birth and the baby afterward.

So assume for the moment that you believe legalized abortion to be mass murder. Then why isn't the bombing of clinics justified?

Matthew John Goldsby, accused of attacking four different Florida abortion operations, said he believed his actions were worthwhile if he saved one life. And given his view of abortion, he's got a good point.

After all, isn't the use of force legitimate to protect fundamental interests and other people's lives? Imagine that we have entered the new scientific age, when clinics have been established to "improve" the gene pool by killing young children judged to be misfits.

Terrible, right? So a group organizes, becoming the philosophical heirs of the abolitionists of the 1800s. They help children escape, disrupt the operation of the killing facilities, harass officials involved in the eugenics process, and, eventually, start bombing the clinics. Are they justified?

Indeed, how about the abolitionists? Slavery was an abominable institution that lasted nearly a century after the United States won its independence.

Anti-slavery activists routinely broke state and federal laws to prevent the return of escaping slaves under the odious federal Fugitive Slave Act. The unbalanced John Brown even hoped to stir a slave insurrection by taking over Harper's Ferry. Was force a legitimate means to help slaves gain their freedom?

And today, some animal lovers have begun breaking the law and using the threat of violence to promote their goals. For example, animal rights activists across the nation have broken into laboratories to steal animals being used for research.

Moreover, someone claiming to be with the Animal Liberation Front recently phoned in a bomb threat to a San Diego department store that sells furs, as well as a hotel where a furriers' convention was being held. A spokesman for the People for Ethical Treatment of Animals said that her organization certainly "wouldn't do something like this," but, she added, "it might have to take something like this" to end the killing of animals for furs.

And that's the basic point. The pro-lifers and the animal-rights people, like the abolitionists more than a century before them, don't have the political power, nor the public support, to win within the democratic process. So a few of them are resorting to extralegal means to uphold what they believe to be transcendent moral principles.

If forcible resistance is ever justified, it certainly should be used only in defense of important interests—like life and basic liberties. Moreover, activities that jeopardize innocent lives, such as bombing public buildings, should be extremely difficult to countenance under any circumstances. Taking innocent life to save innocent life is not a moral judgment to be made by self-anointed elites.

Thus it is deceptively easy to condemn the abortion bombers out of hand. They are, after all, destroying property, threatening lives, and, in a sense, attacking the democratic process itself.

However, if the pro-lifers are right—that abortion cannot be morally justified—why shouldn't people come to the aid of the unborn, using force if necessary? Unless one is unwilling to ever sanction violent resistance to legalized tyranny, whether involving slaves in the pre-Civil War South, antiabortion activists in the United States today, or, say, the Jews in Nazi Germany, the question is a much more difficult one than most people seem to think.

## 146. Fighting the Porn Wars

*July 2, 1986*

Bob Guccione, the publisher of *Penthouse,* is upset. He's been running radio ads denouncing the threat of censorship.

Has Ed Meese shut down Guccione's magazine? Are local police arresting *Penthouse* subscribers? Is the death penalty being imposed for possession of pornography?

Well, no. Actually, what Bob, the great civil libertarian, is so upset about is that other people are exercising their First Amendment rights.

In recent months religious groups like the National Federation for Decency, local churches, and feminist organizations across the United States have been picketing retailers who sell "adult" magazines, writing letters to corporate officials, and organizing boycotts. As a result, firms like Rite Aid, Dart Drug, People's Drug, and Southland Corp., which owns 4,500 7-Eleven stores, have all stopped selling *Penthouse* and its competitors.

And the smut publishers are worried. Guccione alone acknowledges a loss of 15,000 outlets.

So Bob has taken to the airwaves—for the good of us all, of course. To protest "censorship," as he calls it, he wants you to buy *Penthouse,* or even *Playboy,* if you don't like his brand of porn.

Moreover, he wants everyone to write his or her congressmen. To what end is not clear—to press for federal legislation forcing retailers to sell *Penthouse,* perhaps? But clearly the important thing in Bob's view is to keep his magazine on sale and profitable.

Actually, the growing citizen fight against what is an $8 billion a year assault on the religious and moral values of most Americans is wondrous to behold.

Since 1982 the circulation and ad revenues for both *Penthouse* and *Playboy* have been falling; *Playboy* is even losing money this year. The declining fortunes of such "male sophisticate" publications is taking place without government prohibitions, federal prosecutions and official censorship.

And this is the way it should be. People who happily applauded lettuce boycotts to support Cesar Chavez shouldn't criticize churchgoers and feminists for protesting something that grossly offends their values.

Civil libertarians do have a valid complaint with the Attorney General's Commission on Pornography, which sent intimidating letters to retailers earlier this year. The commission also ignored the facts in trying hard to blame crime on pornography.

Rapists and child molesters may like porn, but that unsurprising correlation does not prove that pornography causes such crimes. Indeed, Washington writer Martin Morse Wooster reviewed the federal war on pornography in an article in *Reason* magazine earlier this year and found that no significant study has found any evidence linking smut and crime.

To say that porn does not cause crime does not mean that it is harmless, of course. Its growing availability and acceptance have probably accelerated the breakdown of traditional moral values. And feminists seem right in arguing the "adult" publications degrade women, at least in the minds of porn consumers.

However, the sale of sexually explicit materials is the price we pay for a free society, a necessary cost of allowing people to decide how to live their own lives.

After all, do we really want the government deciding what pictures are too dirty for people to look at? Would anyone be safe from hordes of obnoxious censors if localities could ban any materials that they wanted?

In fact, the most insidious form of pornography may be the softcore sex that now permeates so much of the entertainment world. For, as argues Ken Grubbs, an editor with the *Washington Times,* it is this material that reaches the most people, subtly tearing away at what have been fundamental moral tenets undergirding our society.

Yet empowering the government to ban modestly suggestive films and magazines, as well as nude statues in museums and who knows what else, would give it enormous power over our lives. That sort of authority would be simply inconsistent with the requirements of a free society.

So even the most ardent porn foes should keep the government out of the fight. For when we protect the right of merchants to sell dirty books and magazines, and to show pornographic films, we are really protecting the freedom of all of us to live without Big Brother peering over our shoulder.

But we should simultaneously applaud the efforts of community, religious and feminist groups to halt the obscene tide. For not only are they using the First Amendment, but they are using it to promote values that benefit us all.

# 147. RICO vs. Porn: Penalties More Shocking Than the Crime

*December 20, 1988*

RICO—the Racketeer Influenced and Corrupt Organizations Act—has come under increasing criticism, particularly from conservatives. Yet to date the right has been silent about the misapplication of this organized-crime-fighting tool to at least one kind of independent, if unsavory, business: shops that trade in sexually related materials.

A RICO conviction not only brands one as a racketeer and mobster, it also results in the forfeiture of all assets involved in the case. This makes the statute the atomic bomb of a prosecutor's arsenal, wreaking havoc far out of proportion to the "crime" committed, whether by Wedtech go-between E. Robert Wallach, investment bank Drexel Burnham Lambert—or the neighborhood supplier of pornography.

The first federal obscenity case resulted in the 1987 conviction, now on appeal, of Virginians Dennis and Barbara Pryba for selling six sex magazines and four videotapes, valued at $105.30. On top of the usual jail terms and fines, the judge ordered the seizure of the Prybas' three bookstores, worth $1 million, though most of their inventory was non-pornographic. Even the jurors were shocked at the latter penalty, telling *The American Lawyer* that the punishment did not fit the crime.

Yet this disproportionality is precisely why the government has chosen to use RICO against such merchants. Said Cynthia Christfield of the Justice Department, who assisted the local U.S. attorney's office in the Pryba prosecution, "We wanted to do RICOs to wipe out the business." RICO, explains Robert Showers, the former head of the department's National Obscenity Enforcement Unit, allows you "to take out the enterprise as a whole."

It is easy to sympathize with such an effort. Most pornography simply exploits women to satisfy men's lusts, and offends widely and deeply held religious values.

But a free society's existence is extremely tenuous without tolerance, even of people who like to look at dirty pictures. Which is why the Supreme Court has interpreted the First Amendment to protect sexually explicit materials that are not "obscene"—essentially lacking any real social value. For items that fall outside these bounds, lawmakers can and have set specific criminal penalties. Why, then, the resort to RICO, an unrelated, draconian statute, in simple obscenity cases?

In fact, doing so abuses the law. Although we now read some claims to the contrary, Congress's declared purpose in passing RICO was "to seek the eradication of organized crime in the United States." And the legislation was to do so primarily by protecting legitimate firms from mob violence, conducted under the cover of a multitentacled enterprise. While Congress recognized that some pornography operations may be tied to organized crime—in 1984 it added obscenity as a "predicate offense" under the act—it did not intend to treat anyone who showed a sex flick as a mobster. (Last session Congress added a forfeiture provision to the general obscenity law, but limited its impact to prevent the mass seizure of unrelated assets, as in the case of the Prybas.)

Most local "adult" establishments, especially stores like the Prybas' that handle primarily non-pornographic materials, are neither controlled by organized crime nor dedicated to muscling their way into other businesses. Thus, they shouldn't be prosecuted under a law that was not intended to penalize their conduct.

Moreover, there is the pesky First Amendment. Though the sale of legally obscene, in contrast to simply erotic, materials may be punished, it is not just another crime. The difference between constitutionally protected speech and legally proscribed speech is often a fine one; as a result, inexact punishment can easily hinder the exercise of First Amendment rights. Especially in cases like the Prybas, where the bulk of the business is in protected speech, there is a danger both in forcing store owners to weigh the legal liability of every item on their shelves and in confiscating their entire inventory if they are convicted of crossing the line.

Thus, where freedom of expression is involved, the government must more carefully tailor the punishment of prohibited conduct to avoid discouraging lawful activities. In fact, the Supreme Court has voided state laws that sought to close adult movie theaters and bookstores for having violated obscenity statutes. Explains Washington lawyer Robert Corn-Revere, who specializes in First Amendment cases, "Rounding up books or films presents constitutional issues that do not arise for other types of contraband traditionally associated with organized crime, such as gambling paraphernalia or liquor." Even the judge in the Prybas' case, T.S. Ellis, observed. "No matter how important the elimination of obscenity may be, the First Amendment cannot become a casualty." Yet that is what happened.

If the current legal test for obscenity were at all clear, the threat to free speech would not be as great. But the "I know it when I see it" approach is a poor standard by which to criminalize conduct, especially where the result may be the forfeiture of any asset, even a home, that was "derived" in some way from the proceeds of the illegal act. (The jury did not find all of the materials involved in the Pryba case to be obscene.)

And though the U.S. attorney general may not envision closing down a B. Dalton's or Crown Books because one arguably obscene book turned up on their shelves, a local prosecutor might be tempted to make an example for political gain. In fact, after Fort Lauderdale successfully used the Florida RICO law to put local adult bookstores out of business, city police began visiting family video shops warning them to "clean up their acts," without citing any particular films as obscene. Many of the operators dropped potentially questionable movies, but such a procedure would be an even worse nightmare for the average bookstore.

Maxwell Lillienstein, general counsel of the American Booksellers Association, worries that bookstores "can't possibly know all of the books they have," yet "most contemporary fiction today is sexually explicit." Just one successful RICO case could cause sellers to eschew any book with any possibility of being declared obscene by any jury in any small town.

The Supreme Court will soon have an opportunity to rule on the use of RICO against porn operators; it has agreed to hear a First Amendment challenge to an Indiana statute. If the court upholds the law, we are likely to see far more RICO obscenity prosecutions, not only in the 20 states that have RICO laws covering obscenity, but federal cases that lack legislative support.

A pornography-free society is a worthy end. But using RICO to wipe out everything touched by smut both undermines the rule of law and imposes a punishment disproportionate to the crime. Worst of all, it threatens the basic constitutional guarantee of free speech that undergirds the republic.

# 148. Is Death the Answer?

*May 6, 1987*

With its latest ruling on the death penalty, the Supreme Court has removed the last major legal challenge to capital punishment. Though some of the 1,900 people on death row will still get their sentences overturned on appeal, no constitutional barriers remain to block their execution.

In the recent McCleskey case, the high court upheld Georgia's death penalty even though killers of whites are far more likely to be sentenced to death than are those who murder blacks.

The crimes at issue varied somewhat—blacks were more likely than whites to be killed in domestic disputes instead of robberies—but the racial discrepancy was still huge. A black killing a black received the death penalty 1 percent of the time while 22 percent of blacks who murdered whites were sentenced to die.

But a majority of the justices concluded that evidence of general racial animus was not enough. A defendant, wrote Justice Lewis Powell, "must prove that the decision makers in his case acted with a discriminatory purpose."

And the court probably had no choice but to uphold the statute, despite the racist stain on the sentencing process. For there was no evidence that Warren McCleskey did not deserve his punishment: he gunned down a cop during a 1978 robbery.

Moreover, to throw out the death penalty on these grounds could require the court to dismantle the entire criminal justice system. For there are undoubtedly disparities in prison sentences based on defendants' racial and social backgrounds as well. Yet we can't stop punishing criminals because their sentences will be unequal.

Nevertheless, the death penalty should not be used promiscuously, despite the court's decision. The apparent reluctance of people to actually sanction killing by the state—roughly 700 people have been sentenced to death over the last three years but only 58 have been executed—stems naturally from the nature of the punishment.

Indeed, is death ever justified as a sentence? The issue is a gutwrenching one because it involves fallible human beings deciding whether or not to take the life of another.

In principle it is hard to criticize execution as a response to particularly barbarous crimes. Life is sacred, but not inviolate: indeed, the very sanctity of life may demand that the supreme penalty be exacted.

Of course, friends and relatives of the condemned often make teary appeals for mercy. But retribution, too, is an important principle of justice. In many cases, only a sentence of death can adequately affirm the victim's right to life.

Yet what about lives wrongly taken? Amnesty International estimates that at least 23 innocent people have been executed since 1900. That may not seem like many cases in 87 years and far more innocent people probably have been sentenced to prison. But death is permanent and irreversible, making the cost of even one mistake very high.

The danger in giving government the power to kill grows when courts are systematically biased against certain groups. Earlier this century in the South, for instance, blacks were victimized by a "justice" system built on racism.

The problem was far worse than judges and juries taking the victim's race into account when sentencing properly convicted murderers. Then the criminal justice system was so distorted that a whole class of people were liable to be unjustly convicted and killed.

The local establishment simply used the police power as yet another weapon with which to cow the minority. While those days are now over, the potential for abuse is always present.

Unfortunately, the much debated deterrent effect of capital punishment does not help settle the issue. Common sense suggests that the severity of the penalty affects criminal behavior, even though it is almost impossible to document any impact of capital punishment on murder rates. But certainty of conviction may be far more important than the potential sentence in deterring crime.

Anyway, the fundamental justification for killing killers should be retribution: quite simply, that they deserve it. Without that moral foundation, deterrence is irrelevant. Otherwise the state could execute an innocent man if officials thought doing so would help combat crime.

Thus, while the Supreme Court has cleared away the final broad legal obstacle to the death penalty, it has not made the basic decision about killing killers any easier.

Capital punishment may very well be constitutional and an appropriate punishment for an evil act. But is the possibility of mistake too high? Moreover, should we trust the state with people's lives? The high court's decision does not help us answer these questions.

## 149. Gun Control: The Enduring Liberal Panacea

*April 20, 1988*

Violent crime and murder rates are up in Baltimore, so the Maryland state Legislature has voted to outlaw the manufacture and sale of cheap Saturday Night Specials. A nine-member board will decide which firearms have legitimate uses; all others will be banned as of Jan. 1, 1990.

Baltimore's crime problems mirror those of Washington, D.C., which suffered 228 homicides last year, the highest number in more than a decade. Since the nation's capital already prohibits handgun sales, City Council Chairman Dave Clarke has asked Virginia and Maryland to pass similar laws.

Unfortunately, however, there is no reason to believe that Maryland will find relief from violent crime through its new law or that homicides would fall in the district if Virginia and Maryland outlawed firearms. Gun control is the ultimate liberal panacea, ideologically sacred but completely ineffective.

The most obvious problem is that legislative enactments are more effective at disarming honest, law-abiding citizens than criminals. In fact, six out of 10 of the district's homicides last year were related to drugs. Does anyone seriously believe that people who deal in illicit drugs won't always be able to buy a firearm, whatever the law says?

In fact, outlawing guns in a country in which people already own roughly 140 million firearms would be a prescription for massive civil disobedience. A Cambridge University study admits that "50 years of very strict controls on pistols has left a vast pool of illegal weapons" in Britain.

Nor will Maryland's more limited ban on Saturday Night Specials do any good. A 1985 National Institute of Justice survey found that roughly 70 percent of criminals had relied on larger, more expensive models. The state will be disarming poor ghetto residents, not murderers.

If gun control won't reduce combat between rival drug gangs, it might forestall some spontaneous killings among acquaintances. But police files are replete with murders committed by axes, knives and other weapons.

In fact, a University of Wisconsin study concluded, "Gun control laws have no individual or collective effect in reducing the rate of violent crime."

However, assume that a federal firearms ban would save a few lives. Would it be justified?

The slogan, "Guns don't kill people, people kill people," may be simplistic, but it is basically accurate. The one out of 400 gun owners who abuses his weapon should be punished, not the other law-abiding 399.

Indeed, cars kill 50,000 people a year: should they be outlawed? Alcohol is actually involved in more homicides than are pistols. The solution, of course, is to hold drunks accountable for their crimes, not to renew Prohibition.

Clarke naturally argues that "there is no urban beneficial purpose for a handgun," but it is hard to think of a more important value than self-defense. Prevention of violent crime may not be a high priority in upper-class neighborhoods that receive close police attention, but a personal firearm may be one's only real protection in a ghetto.

Of course, some victims get hurt despite their guns and there are vigilantes who abuse their right of self-defense. But the National Institute of Justice survey found that 40 percent of criminals had decided not to commit a crime at least once because they believed the would-be victim was armed; more than one-third said they had been "scared off, shot at, wounded or captured" by an armed private citizen.

In fact, 57 percent of those surveyed said that they were more fearful of meeting an armed victim than a cop. And this statistic is backed up by the work of law professor Don Kates, who has concluded that armed would-be victims have a higher success rate in thwarting crimes than do the police.

In contrast to proposals to outlaw gun ownership, current congressional concern over the development of plastic handguns that could escape detection at airports is understandable. But so far the issue has been hijacked by gun control advocates, who would use the issue to ban dozens of existing metal pistols as well as plastic ones. A better solution would be to simply require the use of enough metal ribbon or powder in weapons to ensure their detection.

The steady increase in homicides in cities like Washington, D.C., and Baltimore is yet another symptom of the tragic deterioration of urban America. But gun control is not the answer.

New restrictions on firearms sales would not reduce crime. More important, tighter controls would leave honest citizens less able to defend themselves. And a government that is unable to protect its people has no right to disarm them.

# 150. Refocus the Drug War

*June 8, 1988*

Young men are being gunned down on the streets of the nation's capital, and that city's Board of Education is considering a new strategy to combat drug abuse: school uniforms.

"My students are out there dealing" to earn money for expensive new clothes, complains Park View Elementary School principal Shirley Hayes.

Of course, student pushers can find lots of things other than clothes to buy. So increasingly desperate government officials are coming up with lots of far more draconian ideas.

The City of Los Angeles has inaugurated massive neighborhood crackdowns, sweeping up innocent and guilty alike. New York City Mayor Edward Koch has proposed strip-searching travelers at the border. Customs Commissioner William von Raab wants to shoot down suspected drug smugglers' planes. And Senate Minority Leader Robert Dole recommends executing pushers.

Cities like Washington, Los Angeles and Chicago are outfitting their cops with semiautomatic weapons, everyone wants to hire more law enforcement officers, and Congress has voted to divert the U.S. military to the drug war.

But none of these measures will do anything other than turn America into a police state. The drug war has been irretrievably lost.

Under President Reagan the federal government alone has spent $21.5 billion to control the drug trade. The result? The supply of cocaine, the latest drug of choice, has more than doubled since 1982.

Drug-related killings are rising even as the nation's overall murder rate falls. And increasing numbers of kids—1,658 last year in the nation's capital alone—are being arrested for drug offenses. Court systems are clogged and prisons are overflowing. More of the same enforcement measures is no longer a realistic option.

Why have drugs, like alcohol earlier this century, proved so difficult to control? Because the new prohibition has made selling drugs one of the world's most profitable enterprises, a criminal entrepreneur's dream.

Which is why gangs fight to control the drug market. And why pushers invade schools. And why drug overlords are able to terrorize and corrupt foreign governments almost at will.

The only way to make progress in the drug war is to sever the link between crime and the drug trade. And the only way to do that is to legalize adult drug use.

Doing so would cause the criminal drug empires to collapse overnight. For if drugs were legal, prices would fall and there would be no exorbitant profits to be made by the back-alley pusher, the urban gang and the Columbian kingpin. Lower drug costs would also make it unnecessary for the average addict to rob and steal to support his habit. For the same reason casual users wouldn't have to become pushers to earn drug money.

Moreover, kids would face fewer temptations since the drug trade would no longer be in the hands of criminals eager to ruin youngsters' lives for an extra buck. R.J. Reynolds, for instance, does not put tobacco pushers into elementary schools. Of course, many young people are able to get cigarettes and alcohol through older friends, but the problem is more manageable than illicit drug use. In particular, moving drug sales into the open would stop young abusers from being sucked into the criminal underground.

Though decriminalization has gained support from such establishment figures as Baltimore Mayor Kurt Schmoke, many people recoil in horror at the idea. But what possible justification is there for maintaining a policy that has manifestly failed?

True, drugs are dangerous—last year some 6,000 deaths were attributed to cocaine, heroin and marijuana. But roughly 320,000 people die annually from smoking cigarettes and alcohol abuse kills another 125,000. Which is the more serious problem? Anyway, while the death of a few adults who foolishly misuse drugs is tragic, the government's hopeless attempt to protect irresponsible people from themselves is having a far more ghastly, even catastrophic, impact on the rest of us.

Would adult legalization increase drug use? Perhaps, though drugs now appear to be readily available to anyone who really wants them—just drive slowly down any number of big city streets. And consumption of some drugs, such as marijuana, has actually been falling as users lose interest. In any case, it's time we gave up expecting Uncle Sam to act like Big Brother. Drug abuse should be treated as a social problem, such as alcoholism, rather than prosecuted as a crime.

Drug prohibition has failed. And ever harsher enforcement measures will not solve the problem. Let's stop trying to protect consenting adults from themselves. Then we can concentrate on saving our kids.

# 151. An Honorable CO in the War on Drugs

*July 6, 1988*

Yet again the U.S. government is proving that the war on drugs is as dangerous for non-combatants as for pushers.

When Eli Lilly & Co. politely informed the State Department that it would not sell the government its chemical tebuthiuron, marketed under the trade name of Spike, for use in foreign drug eradication efforts, Uncle Sam attacked Lilly.

"Whose war on drugs is this?" asked Ann Wrobleski, assistant secretary of state for narcotics. "Is corporate America not part of it?"

Wrobleski went on to threaten legal action to seize Lilly's patent: "We've got lawyers across the executive branch" studying possible options, she told an angry congressional committee.

Wrobleski also held a press conference to vilify the company for going "AWOL" in the war on drugs, trotting out an Agriculture Department scientist and the head of the Drug Enforcement Agency to criticize Lilly.

Wrobleski's frustration is understandable. After all, she heads up one of the least effective programs in government: the campaign to eliminate foreign drug production.

That means going into other nations to destroy their coca crops. But while the administration is officially committed to wiping out half of Latin America's coca plants by 1993, so far the effort, despite the cooperation of local officials, has eliminated only 3,500 acres out of more than 370,000 acres of coca.

Which is why Wrobleski wants to bomb several Andean nations with planeloads of Spike. Other defoliants have little effect on the deep-rooted coca plants, leaving hand-wielded machetes as the primary means of destroying poor peasants' coca fields.

But spike is not without its hazards. The Environmental Protection Agency, for instance, has concluded that more tests are necessary to determine the chemical's effect on groundwater supplies and has warned against the defoliant's use in water or wetlands. (Peru's coca-producing areas average more than 10 feet of rain a year.)

The environmental group Greenpeace supports Lilly's stand, contending that the chemical could have a "devastating impact" on the environment and local residents. Moreover, Greenpeace warns that no tests have been carried out on the long-term potential for "general chronic effects, cancer, birth defects and genetic damage."

The controversy has even caused Peru to back away from the aerial eradication program. Officials in that nation were not pleased to learn that the State Department was prepared to use a potentially dangerous chemical on their people.

Wrobleski and her administration colleagues say there's nothing to worry about, of course, but they don't live in the targeted areas. And the United States has consistently ignored the interests of the foreign nations involved.

In Peru, for instance, American insistence that the government destroy what is the peasant farmers' most valuable cash crop has increased support for the communist insurgency known as the "Shining Path." A U.S.-sponsored aerial assault that succeeded in not only destroying people's livelihood but also ruining their health could further destabilize Peru's fragile democracy.

Lilly's reluctance to aid Uncle Sam's foreign crusade does not stem only from an abstract concern about the health of foreign peasants. The company also reportedly fears the possibility of retaliation by drug over-lords against its 1,000 employees in Peru.

Wrobleski denounces this as "intimidation," but what's wrong with a company being concerned about the safety of its personnel? It's easy for Wrobleski, who lives in the comfortable environs of the nation's capital, to dismiss the danger to a Lilly worker living in Lima.

The drug war is hopeless—America is far too porous a land for the government to ever stem the flow of white powder and other illicit substances. The only answer is an increased public awareness of the dangers of drugs and greater self-control by those who now turn to illicit substances for fun.

In any case, Uncle Sam should stop browbeating foreign nations over their drug production. The problem is not that Peruvian peasants grow coca plants; the problem is that American professionals snort cocaine. Targeting foreign countries is a politically cheap way to avoid cracking down on the millions of average American users.

Lilly's willingness to stand up and declare that there is something more important than the drug war—like the lives of its workers and the health of foreign peasants—is an act of genuine moral courage. With the government pressing for increasingly arbitrary and draconian sanctions against even minor drug use, more people and firms need to declare themselves to be conscientious objectors in the war on drugs.

## 152. Buying Culture

*July 19, 1984*

The federal budget is the world's largest ocean, a vast pool of unowned resources constantly trolled by fishermen of all stripes. Among the most active fishermen are the artists, led by the 190-member Congressional Arts Caucus, now the largest on Capitol Hill.

The amount of money involved is small—this year the National Endowment for the Arts will spend some $145 million, not even two one-hundredths of a percent of total federal outlays. Yet the fight against President Reagan's proposed budget cuts seems to be a sacred moral crusade; Ohio Sen. Howard Metzenbaum calls administration officials "cultural Neanderthals."

There is probably no other cause as privileged as this one: no lives are being saved, children being fed or poor being clothed. Instead, an artistic and political elite is magnanimously using our money to direct the spiritual uplifting of the United States.

Patrick Hayes of the Washington Performing Arts Society says, "Our music makes adult audiences happy, makes the performing artists happy and brings the joy of music . . . to children. All this must continue."

Indeed.

To bring this happiness to the United States—after all, the Constitution says the government is supposed to make us happy, doesn't it?—caucus Chairman Rep. Thomas Downey, D-N.Y., wants the government "to encourage the arts in every conceivable way." Not only will we all luxuriate in the warm glow of opera across the nation, but "starving artists" will earn their keep and more.

Leontyne Price performed at the White House last year on her return from a grand vacation across Europe; she allowed that "if we could get funds from the government to maintain ourselves, that would really be the ultimate in showing how we are appreciated."

In fact, the duty of America's poor to subsidize their cultural betters is believed to be so obvious, so clear, so manifest that some artists seem irritated that they even have to ask for money. Price, for one, pouted that "we still have to take a tin cup, which I think we collectively resent."

Collective resentment over having to earn a living or not, it's time that these high-minded tax lushes asked the public to contribute the money voluntarily. For even if we believe that government-subsidized art ennobles people—and Milton Friedman has wondered how people's "tastes can be uplifted by TV programs they do not watch or books they do not read"— that is not the government's concern.

As historian Edward Banfield observes in his hard-hitting new book, "The Democratic Muse" (Basic Books), "The American regime exists for purposes that are not served by art, and the support of art is not among the powers that were given to the federal government."

Government art subsidies pose other problems. Federal bureaucrats, for example, all too often have underwritten junk, like obscene poems, and material of interest to only a favored few, like the feminist periodical Heresies, the Gay Sunshine Journal and studies of West African drumming techniques.

The NEA also gives the government an excuse to meddle in the arts.

The New York Metropolitan Opera and the Virginia Opera Association are both recipients of NEA grants and both recently performed a version of Verdi's "Rigoletto" updated for organized crime. Unfortunately, both found themselves the subject of a congressional investigation led by Rep. Mario Biaggi, D-N.Y., who charged the productions with being "patently offensive to the Italian-American community."

Really offensive, however, is the reverse Robin Hood effect of the government's cultural ventures. The immediate beneficiaries of the forced largess from autoworkers and supermarket clerks are the lucky people who get paid to pursue their chosen lifestyles as poets, museum curators and violinists. But even less needy are the predominantly upper- and upper-middle-class operagoers and museum aficionados who simply want someone else to help pay for their entertainment.

Dismantling the NEA would not end culture in the United States; all told, private contributions for art have increased more than tenfold from 1965 to $2.7 billion this year. And many organizations have successfully expanded their private financial bases since President Reagan's cutbacks by hiring fund-raisers, holding radio marathons and increasing admission prices. They just didn't have the incentive to do so before.

For too long a self-serving and privileged class has been living it up at our expense, spending the equivalent of the total income of some 14,500 Americans every year. They know the racket they are involved in, composer Milton Babbitt told a recent New York conference on the arts, "Public funds, private funds, steal it, send it!"

It's time the taxpayers sent them a bill instead of a check.

## 153. Moral Rights for Whom?

*December 14, 1988*

Before adjourning last October, Congress established a National Film Preservation Board to anoint certain movies as "culturally, historically or aesthetically significant"—labels will be required for colorized or edited versions of those films. And come January Rep. Richard Gephardt, D-Mo., and Rep. Edward Markey, D-Mass., will be pushing legislation to impose even more draconian controls on the art market.

Their proposals spring from the European concept of "moral rights"— under which a French judge recently blocked the TV broadcast of a colorized version of John Huston's "The Asphalt Jungle"—which seems appealing at first glance.

After all, who can be on the side of profiteering vandals who would, in

Hollywood producer George Lucas' words, "mutilate and destroy for future generations the subtle human truths and highest human feeling that talented individuals within our society have created."

However, this moving rhetoric masks a blatant attempt to strip consumers, viewers, collectors—everyone except the artist—of any influence over the development of American culture.

Markey, along with Sen. Edward Kennedy, D-Mass., who has sponsored companion Senate legislation, would treat as a copyright violation any "distortion" of an art work. You could buy a statue or painting, but you couldn't change it to suit your own taste.

An artist might even be able to sue you for the way you displayed the object. Tom Palmer, an analyst with the Competitive Enterprise Institute, reports that absurd cases abound in France. One artist was able to force a company, despite their contract to the contrary, to build a fountain that he had designed after it decided to abandon the project because of cost overruns.

Gephardt would stretch this bizarre "moral rights" concept even further by applying it to movies, banning the colorization of black-and-white films, for instance.

And his efforts have been endorsed by the likes of Lucas and colleague Steven Spielberg, who traveled to Washington earlier this year to testify before a Senate subcommittee. Spielberg, for one, argued that the "moral principle" at stake was "of greater importance to our national self-esteem than another buck on the bottom line."

However, what these celebrity lobbyists are interested in protecting is not artists' rights, but their personal prerogatives. Spielberg thinks permission from the director and screenwriter should be required for a company to change a film after it has been exhibited.

But what about the "moral rights" of actors and actresses, whose work is also integral to the creative process? And don't members of the technical crews have any rights?

Anyway, what gives any artist, whether the producer or the wardrobe consultant, a right to prevent a firm from altering a film that it paid for? The director could negotiate for veto rights over any subsequent changes. Or he could finance his own movies.

Instead, Hollywood's tinsel aristocrats are demanding special privileges at everyone else's expense. In fact, Spielberg's provision would be an open invitation to extortion: even a director or screenwriter who had no artistic objection to a studio changing a movie could demand a handsome fee for granting his assent. Whether color should be added to old movies is simply not an issue for Congress.

The Markey-Kennedy bill also would give artists 7 percent of the profit on any resale of their works. It is "a matter of simple justice," says Kennedy.

But what is fair about giving an established artist who voluntarily relinquished all rights to a painting years ago an enormous windfall? Nothing prevented him from asking for a royalty arrangement, akin to that received by authors.

Moreover, the artists who are clamoring loudest for a share of a collector's profits have been strangely silent about their willingness to share in any losses. Anyway, buyers who know they will lose 7 percent of any appreciation on a painting will offer less money for it initially, hurting new artists the most.

Despite the high-sounding rhetoric surrounding the concept of "moral rights," artists are no more public-spirited than anyone else. In fact, Spielberg is frank about his disdain for the great unwashed masses: "The creation of art is not a democratic process" and the public has no right "to participate in its creation."

Today American directors, painters, and other artists are free to negotiate whatever terms they want regarding the resale and alteration of their work. Federal "moral rights" legislation simply represents an unjust and selfish power grab by the nation's cultural elite.

By creating the National Film Preservation Board, Congress has already done more than it should; the government should stay out of the art business.

## 154. Sports Play in Fields of Government

*December 27, 1987*

The nation's founders conceived of government as a night watchman, to do little more than protect life, liberty and property. Then, with the New Deal, government became a fiscal Santa Claus, redistributing income. Now, government is becoming a sports promoter. Rather like the ancient Roman empire, many states and localities entertain their citizens, guaranteeing the show will go on.

Over the last 20 years governments have built or rebuilt 50 stadiums at a cost of $6 billion. There's the Pontiac Silverdome in Michigan, for example, and the Metrodome in Minneapolis. New Orleans boasts the Superdome—at an incredible cost of $163 million. According to an estimate by the Brookings Institution, U.S. taxpayers spend about $45 million each year to subsidize sports extravaganzas concocted by local officials. Yet more stadiums go up every year.

Consier microscopic Irwindale, a Los Angeles suburb, population 1,161. Irwindale plans to build a $115-million stadium to lure the professional football Raiders away from Los Angeles. Irwindale even gave the team's owner, Al Davis, a non-refundable $10 million "signing bonus" for agreeing to the deal.

Meanwhile, in Washington, Redskins' owner Jack Kent Cooke, reportedly worth close to $1 billion, is looking for a new, domed stadium—built with someone else's money. He thinks an arena on the order of $200 million would do. Local officials, despite some initial efforts to stand together, are preparing to engage in a bidding war involving various combinations of cash and tax preferences. One county chairman has already talked of a "public-private partnership" to finance a new stadium; Washington Mayor Marion S. Barry Jr., a Democrat, has proposed "a regional cooperative venture" among local governments. Sen. John W. Warner of Virginia, a Republican, is exploring the possibility of federal subsidies.

At the same time, Maryland Gov. William Donald Schaefer, a Democrat, is opening the state treasury to Baltimore Orioles' owner Edward Bennett Williams. At Schaefer's urging, the legislature approved a $201-million bond issue to fund two stadiums—one for the baseball Orioles and another for a professional football franchise, if one comes to town. Disgruntled taxpayers collected enough signatures to put the issue to a statewide vote but Schaefer used a legal technicality to throw the initiative off of the ballot.

Yet many sports moguls, having invested nothing in the arenas where their teams play, feel little community loyalty. Davis' Raiders have been hopscotching across California; Robert J. Irsay took his football Colts from Baltimore to Indianapolis. Other teams have threatened to leave unless local governments give them extensive financial concessions.

And government officials stretch rules as they desperately try to hold on to professional franchises. Either localities hike subsidies for millionaire owners of profitable clubs or governments try to go in the sports business themselves by seizing the teams. Oakland, for instance, waged an unsuccessful court battle for years to claim the Raiders by eminent domain. The city claimed the takeover was necessary to preserve its "social, cultural and psychological" identity.

David A. Self, an Oakland attorney who filed suit against Davis, explained: "We got to thinking we can condemn land on which to build a stadium, the purpose of which is to provide a professional sports contest. You only need one more thing to have a contest, and that's a team. Why can't you condemn that, too?"

Similarly, Baltimore—the city now planning two stadiums at taxpayer expense—attempted to block the Colts' 1984 move through eminent domain.

While courts have said that government can seize private property, that doesn't make it right: A team belongs to someone else and no serious public interest is advanced by government taking it.

Indeed, there are only two reasons for government to build a stadium: local employment and municipal ego. "You look at the prestige, you look at the jobs," says Maryland's Schaefer, "you look at the things it generates in a city."

But what economic benefits do massive complexes and professional sports actually generate? "The record has been very spotty," concedes Dennis M. Lafferty, executive director of the Greater Cleveland Domed Stadium Corp. Therefore, he adds, his organization makes no "grandiose claims." The record is uneven because money spent on sports facilities is diverted from other investments. A Case Western Reserve University study concluded that building a new stadium in Cleveland would merely "recirculate" local money.

A report by Chicago's Heartland Institute suggests, in fact, that municipal sports arenas may have a negative economic impact. Economist Robert Baade studied nine different regions and found that in seven cases the city's share of local income actually fell. "It may very well be that sports spending overall detracts more than its value from the city economy," he warns, concluding that "stadiums don't produce enough direct economic benefit to absorb debt incurred." Experience elsewhere backs up Baade's work. Jerome Ellig, an economist with the Washington-based Citizens for a Sound Economy, reports that New Orleans suffered slower job growth than surrounding communities as it built the Superdome.

But officials like to build public sports complexes for "prestige"—the satisfaction of having a pro team. Can this be a valid purpose of government—squeezing taxpayers so that the mayor can take visiting dignitaries to a ball game?

Does this mean that Cooke shouldn't have a facility with the extra 20,000 seats he desires, or Davis shouldn't have his stadium? Of course not. Let them build their own facilities. One-third of existing stadiums are privately owned, including the Los Angeles Forum, Maryland's Capital Centre and Miami's new Dolphins Stadium.

Indeed, the Dolphins' football complex provides a model for other cities. For years, owner Joe Robbie complained about the public stadium's condition but voters three times rejected bond proposals to pay for renovations. So Robbie decided to raise $100 million in private capital and build his facility. While he would have liked government to pick up the tab, he concluded that "this stadium is a monument to a free, competitive enterprise system and showed that anything government can do, we can do better."

Surely such monuments are also within the capabilities of Cooke, Davis and Williams. Such men would not be franchise owners were they not already successful businessmen.

They, like Robbie, could put together a project that banks and investors would find attractive. "With 20,000 people on the waiting list for season tickets and a city full of lobbyists looking for glamorous ways to entertain influential policy makers, surely the Redskins could work a similar deal," says Ellig.

If voters are smart, they will ensure that the private way becomes the wave of the future. Polls show that a majority of Maryland residents oppose Schaefer's twin stadiums, which is why he fought so hard to keep the issue off of the ballot. In November elections, citizens of San Francisco and New Jersey rejected proposals to build new public facilities; Oklahoma City and Cleveland residents voted down similar initiatives in the past.

Entertaining the masses may have been expected of ancient Rome, but Americans can amuse themselves quite nicely without government subsidizing the gladiators of today.

# VI. The Global Playground

# The Bipartisan Charade

## 155. "Outside of Politics"

*March/April 1984*

As criticism mounts against the Reagan administration's Lebanon policy, particularly its undeclared war on Syrian and Druze forces, we are hearing new calls for a bipartisan foreign policy. Secretary of State George Shultz, for one, has charged that Congress's debate, led by the Democrats, over withdrawing the marines "just totally took the rug out from under U.S. interests," strengthening our adversaries. He says Congress—and, by implication, Reagan's Democratic critics—should leave the question of using force abroad to the president.

In fact, for more than three decades there has been no more effective tactic to silence criticism of any administration's policies than to charge the critics with helping the enemy. When Republican Senator Robert Taft opposed NATO and foreign military aid after World War II, he was called a communist sympathizer. And now the Heritage Foundation warns that "a major effort to make sharp cuts" in military spending may encourage the Soviets to be "uncooperative."

The concept of a bipartisan foreign policy was developed at the close of World War II to forestall opposition to America's new role as world policeman. Throughout the 1920s and 1930s, so-called isolationists vigorously opposed American political and military involvement overseas. The internationalist establishment, led by the Roosevelt administration, was able to overcome the reluctance of the American people to join another European kill-fest only by taking incremental steps toward war, like providing destroyer escorts for British convoys and imposing an economic boycott on Japan.

Eloquent justifications for a bipartisan foreign policy rolled off the tongues of America's top statesmen. Dean Acheson, for example, claimed that "foreign policy has no lobby, no vested interest to support it, and no

395

constituents." Therefore, it must be developed "outside of politics." Otherwise, "no consistent foreign policy is possible."

Of course, the campaign for bipartisanship was organized by a very powerful constituency, one well represented by people like Dean Acheson and Republican Senator Arthur Vandenberg of Michigan. Vandenberg started his career as a leading isolationist, but after World War II he became a believer in America's world responsibilities. So strong was the bipartisan tide that by 1950 isolationism was widely regarded as extinct; the isolationist old right finally died in 1953, along with Robert Taft, then Senate majority leader.

The collapse of the honorable opposition to America's pervading foreign policy has proved to be disastrous. The isolationists were admittedly an odd coalition—some were genuine noninterventionists, while others merely wanted unfettered discretion to intervene unilaterally—but they provided a much needed critical analysis of the establishment's vision of collective security, with America as the "free world's" leader in a permanent world war.

One result of our bipartisan foreign policy has been a permanent American global role, particularly in the "containment" of communism through continual confrontations with the Soviets, even when our national security is not at stake. Containment required America to create a worldwide network of military commitments and bases. The flagship alliance, NATO, was sold as a temporary measure—Acheson assured Congress at the time that there would be no need for a permanent presence of American troops in Europe—but thirty-five years later 300,000 troops remain in place and new nuclear missiles are being deployed.

Other treaty tripwires for American military involvement are the Rio Treaty with twenty-two Latin American nations (including Nicaragua), the ANZUS alliance with Australia and New Zealand, and "Mutual Defense Treaties" with Japan, South Korea, and the Philippines. All told, we have pledged to defend forty-one nations, more than a fourth of all countries on earth.

So many foreign commitments could be maintained only by a peacetime garrison state. The United States has 360 major bases and 1240 other military installations scattered around the world, as well as 461,000 servicemen aground and 284,000 more afloat. This presence is supplemented by military aid to often brutal foreign regimes. In fact, we have aided one side or the other in half of the forty conflicts now raging across the planet.

Military spending has also continued to rise; even when the Soviet military was far behind that of the United States in the 1950s and 1960s, presidential campaigns were infused with fears of exaggerated Soviet threats and phantom missile gaps. And the arms buildup has required more than equipment. The draft lapsed at the end of World War II, but in 1948 Congress voted to institutionalize the most coercive power of government—forcing people to fight and die—in peacetime. It took a quarter of a century to get rid of that rite of manhood, but today calls for bringing back conscription are increasing.

However, perhaps the most important legacy of bipartisan foreign policy has been the elimination of the distinction between peacetime and wartime. Since World War II the United States has not been in a single official, or declared, war, but more than 100,000 servicemen have died in combat in Korea, Lebanon, Vietnam, the Dominican Republic, Cambodia, and Grenada. American agents have conducted covert operations involving assassination attempts and quasi-military campaigns against governments and rebel movements.

Support for this permanent state of war has unfortunately been bipartisan. Even the War Powers Resolution, adopted over a presidential veto, has done little to limit foreign interventionism. Former Assistant Secretary of State Hodding Carter III observes that the resolution "has largely served as an after-the-fact vehicle for Congress to give assent to actions it lacked the will to oppose in meaningful ways when it mattered."

Bipartisanship may have brought us consistency, but it has not brought us peace or security. Taft once said that "the purpose of an opposition is to oppose." It is time for politicians of both parties to stop hiding behind the illusion of bipartisanship and start opposing America's permanent state of war.

# When to Intervene?

## 156. Using Force Abroad

*January 10, 1985*

Secretary of Defense Caspar Weinberger and Secretary of State George P. Shultz seem to agree on virtually nothing. The question of when to use military force abroad is no exception.

Shultz, the Reagan administration's most vocal advocate of the hopeless Marine mission in Lebanon, first took to the public podium last spring, complaining that military muscle, not diplomatic efforts, led to the administration's failure. He also argued that the United States should be prepared to make pre-emptive strikes and retaliatory attacks against terrorists, even if U.S. troops and foreign civilians would end up as casualties.

This fall Shultz returned to his anti-terrorist theme, declaring that the public must give its approval "before the fact" for military action, lest the United States become "the Hamlet of nations, worrying endlessly over whether and how to respond."

But Weinberger, supported by Vice President George Bush, urged caution. "We're not going to go out and bomb innocent civilians or something of that nature," said Bush.

In November Weinberger went before the National Press Club to declare that U.S. forces should be committed "only when other means have failed or have no prospect of success."

Weinberger set out six preconditions for military intervention: that the interest protected be vital, the administration's intention be to win, the political and military objectives be clearly defined, the relationship between forces committed and goals be continually reassessed, support of Congress and the public be expected and the use of troops be a last resort.

A month later, Shultz—the two longtime Reagan aides are too polite to mention each other directly—told the convocation crowd at Yeshiva University in New York that readiness to dispatch U.S. forces was "the burden of statesmanship" even when public support was not guaranteed.

"Our greatest challenge," Shultz argued, "is to learn to use our power when it can do good, when it can further the cause of freedom and enhance international security and stability."

Shultz is right on one point. Though public support is probably necessary before the United States gets involved in an extended conflict—otherwise any sacrifice would be in vain—the government should not have to conduct a referendum on every international move. Every administration has a duty at times to lead, not follow, public opinion.

However, elsewhere Weinberger has staked out the higher ground. For Shultz's "great challenge" has rarely, if ever, been met. U.S. wars against Mexico and Spain in the 1800s, for example, were imperialistic land grabs, nothing more, despite the high-sounding rhetoric.

World War I saw the United States fight on the side of czarist Russia; the resulting post-war settlement, embodied in the Versailles Treaty, was almost guaranteed to break down into another, even bloodier, global conflict. U.S. intervention in World War II helped replace one vicious totalitarian power, Nazi Germany, with an equally totalitarian and even more vicious one, the Soviet Union.

As for Lebanon, an erudite man like George Shultz should have recognized that a couple thousand Marines could not bring peace to a part of the world that has been rent by bitter sectarian hatreds for centuries.

It is perhaps recognition of U.S. failure to fund the formula of fighting for freedom and stability that has caused Weinberger to draw back, ever so slightly, from the global alliance network that underlies the Reagan administration's military buildup.

"Recent history," Weinberger opined, "has proven that we cannot assume unilaterally the role of the world's defender."

State Department aides reportedly have complained that Weinberger has offered the Soviets free rein in the Middle East, Southeast Asia and Central America. But to spell out, for U.S. citizens and the world, clear limitations on the use of force overseas is not equivalent to surrendering to the Soviet Union. Instead, it is to simply redefine the interests for which young Americans should be expected to die, and the circumstances under which they should be committed to protect those interests.

In short—and even Weinberger hasn't yet acknowledged that this is where his position logically leads—the United States should not try to guarantee the security of the more than 40 nations with which it currently has defense commitments. Nor should it extend a nuclear umbrella over the rest of Europe, threatening a nuclear Armageddon if NATO and the Warsaw Pact ever collide.

The most important questions to be asked before using force abroad are whether our vital interests are at stake and whether military action is absolutely necessary to protect them. If the answer to either is no, the "burden of statesmanship," as Shultz put it, requires U.S. military abstinence, not participation.

## 157. The Legacy of Vietnam

*April 18, 1985*

Ten years ago a U.S. campaign "for democracy" that cost 58,000 lives and billions of dollars finally came to an end. The Khmer Rouge captured Phnom Penh, Cambodia, on April 17, 1975; Saigon, Vietnam, fell 13 days later.

The legacy of that war has become a partisan issue. Liberals intone the word "Vietnam" to warn of the perils of intervention in Central America. Conservatives, still celebrating America's triumph over tiny Grenada, argue that the Vietnam conflict proves we must fight to win.

Ironically, both sides are more wrong than right. At the time, for example, many on the left seemed to think not so much that the United States should stay out of the war as that we should support the other side. North Vietnam, the Jane Fondas of the world said, was really a nice place.

It is hard to understand how even then anyone could think of communists as humanitarians—just consider Josef Stalin's reign of terror, North Korea's airtight police state, and the island gulag named Cuba. But the experience in Indochina now makes such a belief impossible.

In Cambodia, Pol Pot and his crazed murderers unleashed a holocaust not unlike that of World War II. The northern conquerors in Vietnam were not quite so brutal: most opponents simply ended up in "re-education camps." State control now is total and emanates from Hanoi; southern revolutionary leaders, like Truong Nhu Tang, a former high-ranking National Liberation Front official who defected in 1979, found themselves out of power. The northerners, Nhu says, acted "almost as if they believed that they were the conquerors and we the vanquished."

Indeed, our Vietnam experience demonstrates the validity of the much-maligned distinction between authoritarian and totalitarian regimes. South Vietnam was governed by a corrupt and often brutal elite, but there were functioning opposition parties and papers; today such bourgeois freedoms are non-existent. As for Cambodia, the misdeeds of astrology-led Gen. Lon Nol and his aides were nothing compared with the butchery perpetrated by the Khmer Rouge.

In fact, some war opponents, like American Enterprise Institute scholar Michael Novak, appalled by the bloody result of communist misrule, now believe U.S. involvement was proper. And Richard Nixon, the man responsible for prosecuting the war after 1969, has just written his view of the war's legacy. In *No More Vietnams,* published by Arbor House, Nixon argues that the war was moral and winnable, and that it proved force could and should be used against communist insurgencies. Indeed, while the United States sat by, having lost its will to use the military—the "Vietnam syndrome," if you will—Nixon says the Soviet Union and its proxies "licked their chops and gobbled up South Yemen, Ethiopia, Angola, Mozambique, Afghanistan and Nicaragua."

Many conservatives share this view: a more efficient application of force could have won the war and military intervention remains a proper tool for use in Nicaragua and elsewhere.

Yet as evil as are the communist regimes that took power in 1975, their brutality does not justify the war retrospectively. Much happens in the world that we disapprove of, and even are horrified by. But that does not mean it is our duty to try to right every wrong.

The Soviet Union, for example, has been an international slaughterhouse for nearly 70 years; should we invade it? (In fact, the Western powers did so in the aftermath of World War I, and failed to overthrow the Bolshevik regime.)

Or how about the darling regimes of the right?

Gen. Augusto Pinochet rules with an iron fist in Chile; how about a paratroop drop tomorrow in Santiago to liberate the country?

And South Africa's system of apartheid is a scandal. But presumably it's nothing that a little invasion couldn't solve.

The point is, these are not our fights. Moreover, there often is little the United States can do.

In Ethiopia a group of ruthless military officers seized control from a doddering old emperor; Nicaragua's Somoza dynasty fell to the Sandinistas in a revolution that was supported by every segment of society. Must the United States protect every petty tyrant from overthrow? As for the Afghanistan tragedy, should we go to war with the Soviets in response?

In today's uncertain and dangerous world the use of force eventually may become necessary to protect our nation. But Vietnam proved that military intervention is costly—in terms of lives, money, international prestige and domestic unity—and still may fail. It certainly should not be undertaken lightly.

The world would be a better place had Vietnam and Cambodia not fallen, but tens of thousands of Americans and millions of Indochinese would be even better off—that is, alive—had we never gotten involved. This is the real lesson of the sad events of a decade ago.

## 158. Fewer Guns for Fewer Commitments

*May 29, 1986*

The president is upset. In his view, the budget passed by the House is "totally unacceptable," especially the $285 billion in spending authority for the military, $35 billion less than Mr. Reagan asked for.

In fact, the House number is in large measure a bargaining chip for negotiations with the Senate and president. Most observers expect Congress to eventually agree on an amount close to the $301 billion approved by the Senate.

Still, complains Defense Secretary Caspar Weinberger, refusing to accept the administration budget will "destroy the recent and impressive momentum we have made in rearming America."

Actually, refusing to fill the Pentagon's entire wish list will not irreversibly undermine America's national security. Congress will not even be "cutting" defense; it will only be reducing President Reagan's proposed 11.5 percent increase. The administration will have more money to spend, just not as much as it wants.

Indeed, if Congress simply keeps real spending constant, it will have locked in the huge increases in military outlays previously pushed by President Reagan. In 1980 budget authority for defense was $145.7 billion; this year it is $286.1 billion, nearly twice as much.

Even these numbers underestimate Mr. Reagan's long-term impact on military spending, for the administration has successfully pressured Congress to approve weapons programs that will require steady spending increases in the future.

Commented OMB Director David Stockman before he left office last year, "There is a certain inevitability to it all. The major systems have been launched, mission and policy objectives have been approved, the force structure of our armed forces has been raised, so there are not a lot of things that can give way. Congress and the Defense Department are really fighting on the margin."

Nevertheless, the administration has done a better job defining the issues than have congressional Democrats. Weinberger, for instance, is quite right in arguing that military spending should be set according to the external threat facing us, not the size of the deficit. For if the nation is not successfully defended, then the deficit will be the least of our concerns.

However, just how serious is the threat to America?

According to CIA estimates, which are the subject of some contention,

Soviet military spending outpaced that of the United States by roughly $420 billion during the 1970s. But adjusting the figures to account for statistical vagaries, the Soviet forces diverted against China, and NATO/Warsaw Pact outlays, actually place the West $740 billion ahead of the Eastern bloc.

Moreover, while the CIA estimates that real Soviet expenditures climbed 2 percent annually between 1979 and 1984, average American outlays increased three times as fast during that same period. Though the Soviets lead the United States in numerous areas, the United States has substantial strengths as well.

More important is the fact that this country is allied with the world's leading economic powers and does not maintain a long, hostile border with the most populous nation on Earth. If America's forces are over-matched, it is only because they are expected to guarantee the security of Europe, East Asia, the Middle East and Latin America.

The question, then, that must be asked is: are all these commitments necessary?

President Reagan, not surprisingly, says yes and wants more money to pay for America's global role.

But the Democratic opposition, while equally happy to play the role of international policeman, doesn't want to spend enough to do the job well. Their approach, unfortunately, is even more irresponsible and dangerous than President Reagan's.

The defense budget should be cut—and cut sharply. But to do so America must start dropping its commitments to some of the 40-odd nations around the world that the United States has pledged to protect.

For instance, in April Weinberger visited Seoul, South Korea. U.S. troops, he said, would remain in that nation "as long as the people of Korea want and need that presence."

But the South has a population twice that of the North, and a gross national product five times as large. The regime in Seoul may want the United States to stay involved—a free ride is a free ride—but it surely doesn't need American support.

Tough questions also should be asked of our defense subsidies for other countries, such as Japan and Europe, which have the wherewithal to defend themselves.

Congress's budget may be "totally unacceptable" given the president's global defense strategy, but it is really his strategy which is wrong. We can safely spend far less on guns; all we have to do is start using our guns to defend the United States, not the rest of the world.

# 159. What Next for NATO? Get the Superpowers Out of Europe

*April 1989*

The Western alliance, which celebrates its 40th anniversary this year, is in disarray. The fissures among its members were growing even before Mikhail Gorbachev's accession to power in the Soviet Union. But now the Soviet "great communicator," who used a speech to the United Nations in December to announce unilateral troop reductions in Eastern Europe, is threatening to emasculate NATO.

Observes foreign policy analyst Christopher Layne, "Gorbachev has been able to manipulate Western European perceptions of the Soviet threat and in so doing undermine NATO's cohesion and support for nuclear force modernization and conventional military buildup." In fact, a recent poll in West Germany, the front-line state most at risk, found the 75 percent of respondents didn't believe the Soviets pose a threat to their nation; people ranked defense spending last among the 17 listed budget priorities.

Not that the formal collapse of NATO is imminent. But the alliance is increasingly incapable of responding to the Soviet challenge. "We are continually allowing ourselves to be caught off guard and put on the defensive," says Layne. Unless the United States develops its own initiatives for reducing continental military tensions, NATO threatens to become an expensive but militarily ineffective alliance torn by constant squabbling.

There is an alternative. Washington should immediately press for unrestricted arms reduction talks to build on Gorbachev's latest proposal. By advocating mutual superpower disengagement, the United States should indicate its willingness to fundamentally transform the European military landscape. That goal is ambitious, but nevertheless worth pursuing. "Gorbachev has given us virtually everything we've wanted," says Hudson Institute analyst Jeffrey Record, including elimination of the SS-20 missiles, withdrawal from Afghanistan, and pullbacks in Central Europe. So "maybe he's prepared to give us more."

Four decades ago, Europe was still digging out of the rubble left by six years of total war. Stalin's Red Army quickly subjugated the states it had "liberated." The only thing that blocked Moscow from imposing its rule on Western Europe was America's threat to intervene. But no one believed that Europe would not one day recover and thereafter be able to look after its own affairs. In fact, Secretary of State Dean Acheson told Congress that American troops were to be stationed in Europe only temporarily, to act as a shield until Europe was able to stand on its own.

But a crutch once relied on is not easily abandoned. Even as Britain and France rebuilt their economies and West Germany regained its sovereignty, U.S. forces remained. And NATO chose to respond to Soviet conventional superiority with the threat of massive nuclear retaliation. As long as the United States maintained an overwhelming nuclear advantage, extended deterrence was viable. But during the 1960s and 1970s, as the United States lost that decisive superiority, the threat of a nuclear response to a conventional attack lost credibility.

In fact, in 1983 former Defense Secretary Robert McNamara revealed that he had advised both Presidents John Kennedy and Lyndon Johnson not to initiate the use of nuclear weapons to save Europe. And today, while the possibility that Washington would ignite a global nuclear war in response to a Warsaw Pact invasion may have some deterrent effect on the Soviet Union, the Europeans would be foolish to assume that an American president would commit national suicide, sacrificing dozens of U.S. cities to prevent the Soviet flag from flying over Bonn and Paris.

As a result of its reliance on the nuclear threat, NATO has been left with an apparent conventional inferiority that the Pentagon has used incessantly to justify increased U.S. military spending. In reality, the gap—expressed in such hideous ratios as 1.4 to 1 in troops, 1.5 to 1 helicopters, 2 to 1 in combat aircraft, 3.1 to 1 in tanks, and 3.1 to 1 in artillery—has always looked worse on paper than it really is on the field. The West possesses better-trained soldiers and more-advanced equipment; its units are more combat ready, and it has roughly as many reservists as the Warsaw Pact. NATO's decentralized command structure would operate better in fluid combat situations. And the Eastern European states are dubious allies at best; since World War II the Soviets have had to crush outright rebellions in East Germany and Hungary, forcibly suppress reform in Czechoslovakia, and threaten an invasion of Poland.

Moreover, in recent years NATO has been outspending the Warsaw Pact and upgrading its forces (largely as a result of U.S. efforts). Charles Price, America's ambassador to Great Britain, commented in 1988 that "the alliance has reached a level of preparedness not seen in years." It may not match the Soviets man for man, but it doesn't have to. NATO need only maintain a sufficient force to deter aggression, and there seems little doubt that the alliance now does so. Observes one NATO planner, "the conventional structure is presently enough to persuade Moscow that an attack would bring costs far beyond any perceived political gains."

To assuage any doubts that NATO does indeed possess such a deterrent capability, the member states could easily augment their forces. The Western nations spend less than half as much per capita as does the Eastern Bloc, and the problem is not the United States. On almost every measure the Europeans' performance is simply dreadful. West Germany, for instance, spends barely 3.0 percent of its GNP on defense, half the U.S. level. While the United States devoted $1,164 per capita to defense in 1986, Germany spent $454. (Some NATO defenders note that Germany has conscription while the United States does not. But it is not clear that the $454 therefore understates Germany's defense spending; studies indicate that reintroducing a draft in the United States would actually *hike* costs.) Britain, France, and Norway contributed slightly more; everyone else spent less. Since roughly half the U.S. defense budget goes for NATO, American citizens are spending more per person that the Europeans to simply defend Europe.

Were the Europeans to take the Warsaw Pact seriously, they could easily overwhelm the East: NATO's collective GNP is two-and-a-half times that of the Warsaw Pact and its population is 50 percent greater. Even without the United States the Europeans exceed the entire Soviet alliance economically and nearly equal it in population. Moreover, Europe faces no other continental threat, while the Soviet Union has to maintain significant forces on its border with China.

Whatever Europe's capabilities, however, it does not currently appear to have the will to do more. The West German high command, for instance, has warned the Kohl government that without added resources the army will be able to support only 6 of the planned 12 divisions by the end of the century. And even Kohl's conservative government seems unlikely to back a major military buildup when three out of four citizens believe the Soviets constitute no threat. Not that Germany is alone in its apparent indifference to defense. Spain forced the United States to close its Torrejon air base and move a wing of F-16s. Greece equally intent on reducing America's military presence, though elections this summer could result in a new, more pro-American government.

For years European states could get away with this sort of irresponsible behavior because Uncle Sam was still there to defend them—with nuclear weapons, if necessary. Now that the intermediate warheads have disappeared from Europe as part of the INF agreement, however, America's promise to use strategic nukes appears less serious and the Warsaw Pact's conventional edge looks more threatening. Since Washington is unlikely to substantially increase military spending, any effort to upgrade NATO's forces will have to come from the Europeans themselves.

Gorbachev, however, may have saved NATO a lot of money. Though his U.N. speech was clearly aimed at making diplomatic points and putting the incoming Bush administration on the defensive, Gorbachev's initiative was, first and foremost, a major military retreat. If the Soviet leader did not propose to unilaterally disarm, his plan was nevertheless "good news," says the Hudson Institute's Jeffrey Record. "On the basis of what he said, and I think we can rely on him to carry out his program, it is a fairly substantial reduction. It is more than military tokenism."

Gorbachev pledged to: reduce total Soviet manpower by 500,000 and tank inventories by 10,000; disband 6 Soviet tank divisions (along with their short-range nuclear weapons, said foreign minister Eduard Shevardnadze in January); withdraw from East Germany, Czechoslovakia, and Hungary 50,000 soldiers, 8,500 "artillery systems," 5,000 tanks, and 800 combat aircraft; and pull out an unspecified number of assault-landing and river-crossing units from the same three front-line states. The overall manpower reduction may be the least significant, since total Soviet forces are estimated to number 5.2 million, of which some 1.5 million are in noncombatant labor units. But, observes Record, "if you look at what he's cutting where, it substantially reduces the Soviet capacity to do the one thing that NATO has most feared for years—launch a surprise attack."

For instance, withdrawing 10,000 tanks will unequivocally degrade the Soviet Union's offensive capability. Of course, Moscow may demobilize the oldest tanks, of Korean War vintage, but their age has never stopped the Pentagon from including them in the military balance figures in order to show NATO's need for more money. Moreover, in January Gorbachev said that half the tanks to be withdrawn would be "the most modern ones." Says Anthony Cordesman, a Washington, D.C.-based military analyst, "no matter how you slice it, Gorbachev can't make these tank cuts in these areas without seriously affecting their offensive capability."

While leaving the Soviets with clear numerical superiority, the artillery and aircraft reductions, too, will reduce the edge that would be useful, and probably necessary, in any attempt to overwhelm the West. Disbanding 6 of the 16 Soviet tank divisions in Eastern Europe may be even more important, since NATO has always feared a blitzkrieg through Germany's central plains.

But perhaps most significant of all is Gorbachev's pledge to reduce the Soviet's assault forces. Though less glamorous than tank divisions, these units would be at the forefront of any invasion. Admits one NATO official, "this certainly helps stability by reducing the chances of a bolt-from-the blue attack." Even Christopher Donnelly, head of Soviet Studies Research at Great Britain's Sandhurst Military Academy, and a Gorbachev skeptic, acknowledges that a major cutback in this area "could make a lot of difference in their ability to attack."

CIA Director William Webster made a similar point in December. Though the withdrawal would eliminate only part of the Warsaw Pact's military edge, he said, "they will substantially reduce the ability . . . to launch a surprise, short-warning attack." In sum, as a dramatic change in past Soviet policy, Gorbachev's plan should be used to initiate efforts to substantially reduce military spending in both West and East and to eventually eliminate America's role in defending Europe.

In response, Washington should push for large-scale, bilateral troop cuts during the ongoing Negotiations on Conventional Armed Forces (CAFE). Those talks essentially succeed 16 years of fruitless discussions under the rubric of the Mutual Balanced Force Reduction negotiations, which drowned in the minutiae of arms control and were insufficiently far-reaching. If NATO again presses for narrow reductions, CAFE will likely suffer the same fate.

Instead of fighting over "cuts in this or that," argues David Calleo, director of European Studies at the Johns Hopkins School of Advanced International Studies, our approach should be to decide "what we want for the final security arrangement that will make us all feel and be more secure." Given Europe's ability to stand on its own, that goal should be the complete withdrawal of superpower military forces from the continent. Layne, for instance, suggests that the Bush administration propose removing all U.S. and Soviet nuclear and conventional forces from Central Europe (East and West Germany, Czechoslovakia, Hungary, and Poland), demobilizing significant portions of the conventional troops, and pledging not to be the first to reintroduce units in the region. Such a plan, argues Layne, would "wrest the diplomatic initiative from Moscow, casting America as the champion of pan-European aspirations for an end to the continent's artificial division." It would also guarantee the security of both the West and the Soviet Union, since the Eastern European states would pose no threat to West Germany or its neighbors, while operating as a buffer for Moscow.

Of course, the USSR might reject mutual disengagement, since withdrawal would reduce the Politburo's influence in Eastern Europe. Yet Gorbachev has already measurably loosened Moscow's reins over the satellite states, and his planned troop reductions are clearly "driven by domestic economic concerns," says Record, a factor that is likely to grow ever more important. Anyway, we will never know whether such a program is viable unless we propose it. And it is a no-lose proposition: should the Soviets reject mutual disengagement, they would be blamed for the continued superpower militarization of Europe.

If the continent-wide proposal initially fails, Moscow might agree to more-limited cuts. Last year, for instance, Soviet and Czechoslovakian officials suggested creating a "depletion zone" in the central front, with fewer offensive weapons. In 1987 Poland's Wojciech Jaruzelski proposed reducing battlefield nuclear weapons with "the greatest strength and strike precision, which could be used for a sudden attack." Since Gorbachev's initiative includes cuts in assault forces and forward tank divisions, further progress in this area seems possible. And partial withdrawals today could lead to a full pullout tomorrow.

Even with a complete superpower disengagement, Europe would, of course, have to possess some defense capability, "unless the Soviet state collapses, the chances of which seem remote," says Calleo, "Europe will need a military balance to live in reasonable comfort next to the USSR." But Europeans themselves should increasingly provide those forces. Irrespective of Moscow's reaction to a proposal for mutual disengagement, part two of a new U.S. defense strategy should be the steady Europeanization of NATO.

The process has already begun. Germany and France plan to create a joint brigade, and Bonn has suggested establishing an air cavalry division made up of Belgian, British, Dutch, and German troops; more such steps should be encouraged. So, too, should ongoing efforts to make the Western European Union, established in 1948 to encourage cooperative defense efforts among the Europeans, into a more potent organization.

Simple burden-sharing—getting the Europeans to spend more—is not the goal, however. In late December Deputy Defense Secretary William Taft argued that even if the other NATO states do more, the United States must maintain present expenditure levels. "Our view—and we have been emphatic about this throughout the discussion—is that the United States needs to do at least as much as it is doing, that it can afford to do what it is doing."

This argument only "proves the public choice economic theory," says Ted Galen Carpenter, director of foreign policy studies at the Cato Institute. "These people are out to protect their bureaucratic interest. They don't recognize that changes in the world necessitate changes in military posture; they're just adjusting their justification for the status quo."

After all, Europe has the capability to defend itself. Were the wealthier NATO states simply to spend as much per capita as does the United States, the alliance would move steadily toward parity with the Warsaw Pact. They don't because they can rely on American aid. "Permanent troop establishments abroad," warned Dwight Eisenhower 26 years ago, will "discourage the development of the necessary military strength Western Europeans countries should provide for themselves."

What conceivable justification is there for the United States to impose nearly triple the defense burden on its citizens as does Germany, which faces the greatest invasion threat? Bonn argues that mere statistical measurements undervalue its contribution, which includes the fact that it hosts the bulk of NATO's forces and suffers from constant maneuvers and training missions. However, 245,000 American troops are not stationed in that nation because Bonn selflessly agreed to accept units otherwise destined for, say, Luxembourg. The forces are there to protect Germany. Since that nation derives the most direct benefits from the alliance, it should, in turn, spend the most proportionally on defense.

Indeed, a process of Europeanization would fulfill the original intent of the Western alliance. America's involvement in NATO was supposed to be merely temporary, until the Europeans had recovered. For example, Eisenhower, NATO's first supreme commander, wrote in 1951 that the United States should "establish clear limits" regarding how long America would station troops in Europe. Even Harry Truman, who pushed the treaty through a skeptical Senate, would undoubtedly be shocked to learn that Washington was still subsidizing its wealthy friends. The policy simply doesn't make sense.

Further, only a reduction in America's commitments can bring defense spending into line with reality. Though the Reagan administration undertook a $2-trillion military build-up, that still wasn't enough money to enable Uncle Sam to play world policeman. With U.S. military spending coming down in real terms, force totals have to fall as well. Former Defense Secretary Frank Carlucci warned last year that unless the Pentagon continued to receive real increases of 2 percent a year, cuts would have to be made in "deployable battle groups and some force structure overseas." Europeanizing NATO would make such reductions painless. And while moderate alliance critics such as Calleo support a continued, if smaller, American presence in Europe, there is no reason for the United States to ultimately maintain any military forces on that continent: the Europeans are able to eventually take responsibility for their own defenses.

Some analysts fear that though Europe could defend itself, it won't. The result of an American withdrawal would then be the "Findlandization" of Washington's closest international friends. Yet the Europeans have battled each other for centuries to defend their independence; their experience reflects what Layne calls "the historical tendency of states to balance power centers rather than join a bandwagon." The Europeans are especially unlikely to accede to domination by a power that is visibly decaying. If anything, it is Eastern Europe that seems to be moving toward the Finland model, with greater national autonomy and a growing Soviet reluctance to meddle in internal disputes. (After Gorbachev's U.N. speech, Hungary and East Germany announced that they were reducing their military budgets; Poland, too, is considering military cutbacks.)

In any case, the unlikely prospect of Europe's Finlandization is not worth keeping U.S. troops in Europe and, by extension, threatening to go to war. Finland maintains an independent, democratic, and capitalist system. It avoids offending the Soviets, but that hardly threatens the United States. If Europe's internal dynamics are such that the NATO states would go neutral without an American troop presence, then we should consider ourselves lucky to have discovered our allies' faithlessness in peacetime rather than during a war. If Western Europe, with its independent heritage, strong democratic institutions, and successful market-oriented economies, is unwilling to undertake the relatively modest steps necessary to bolster its defenses after a U.S. pullout, then it is unlikely to hold together in a full-scale war.

As NATO approaches its 40th anniversary, the international marriage partners are suffering from differences that are fast becoming irreconcilable. Where countries disagree over the potential threat as well as the proper response, a strategic divorce is inevitable. And, in contrast to 1949, Europe now has the wherewithal to defend itself; the reliance of numerous advanced industrial states on the United States for their protection has turned them into international welfare queens of the worst sort, profiting from their indolence while sniping at their benefactor.

Gorbachev's unilateral troop withdrawal program comes at a particularly propitious time. But the opportunity will be wasted if the West simply presses for some additional cuts in a few weapon and troop totals. Instead, Washington should push for total, mutual superpower disengagement, a program that would provide enormous economic benefits for both the United States and the Soviet Union while sharply reducing the risk of war in Europe. Such an agreement may seem unlikely, but two years ago no one would have predicted Gorbachev's latest initiative, Moscow's interest in troop reductions in East Asia, the INF agreement, the Soviet withdrawal from Afghanistan, or Moscow's sharp reduction in naval spending. Today it appears the more far-reaching the proposal, the greater its likelihood of success.

In any case, the United States should begin turning over Europe's security to the Europeans, allowing those who benefit most from that continent's defense to foot the bill and call the shots. The world has changed over the last 40 years; politics as usual will no longer suffice. President Bush, observes former National Security Adviser Robert McFarlane, will need "enormous vision and political skill to preside over the alliance at a time when its members are going to be very fractious." Bush can demonstrate that vision and skill by reducing America's military role in Europe and elsewhere around the world.

# 160. Cut South Korea's Umbilical Cord

*March 31, 1988*

Although South Korea has been shaken by allegations of financial misconduct by the brother of former President Chun Doo Hwan, the nation's transition to democracy is proving to be smoother than many people expected. Key opposition leaders have reconciled themselves to the ruling party victory in the presidential election late last year.

Nevertheless, President Roh Tae Woo faces several challenges, including earning the support of the nearly two-thirds of the electorate that voted against him, deciding whether to release some 1,000 political prisoners and addressing the concerns of labor and the military.

If any of these issues cause the move toward democracy to stall, Washington will likely be blamed, fairly or not. The United States should disengage itself from Seoul's political and military decisions. It can start by withdrawing the 40,000 American troops based there—military protection that Seoul no longer needs.

The United States has been tied to Seoul through a mutual defense treaty since 1954. Today, the American soldiers act as a tripwire that insures American involvement in any future war. The Reagan Administration treats this commitment, which costs the United States as much as $23 billion annually, as irrevocable. But South Korea is now capable of defending itself and the agreement should be adjusted to reflect that.

At the end of the Korean War, South Korea was helpless. It had lost one million people and more than half of its industrial capacity. Per capita income was a bare $134 a year. But 35 years have passed, and per capita income is now $2,300, nearly three times that in North Korea.

Moreover, the gap between North and South is growing. Since 1970, North Korea's economy has been stagnant while South Korea's economy has expanded by 8 percent annually, and by 12 percent last year. North Korea's gross national product is less than one-fifth that of the South.

Pyongyang has a larger military because, like most Communist regimes, it invested a disproportionate share of its resources in its military. But since the mid-1970's Seoul has outspent its antagonist. Last year, the South Korean Defense Minister, Lee Ki Baik, said his country would reach military parity with the North within three years. Indeed, the South, which could not even produce rifles a little more than a decade ago, is now manufacturing sophisticated aircraft and missiles.

Over the long term, Pyongyang will lose its edge. The Rand Corporation estimates that the North would have to devote 36 to 42 percent of its G.N.P.—more than twice the current share—to the military in order to match the South's annual expenditure.

Another important change since the Korean War is the reduced likelihood of Chinese or Soviet involvement in any future conflict. China appears to place a high priority on the peninsula's stability and has indicated it would not support a North Korean invasion of the South, with which Beijing has forged a variety of political, economic and cultural ties.

The Soviet attitude toward the North is more equivocal, but there is no evidence that Moscow wants Pyongyang to start a war or that it would play an active role in one.

Japan, which is ready to surpass the Soviet Union as the world's second ranking economic power, is capable of playing a major role in the defense of East Asia. Japan already provides foreign aid to Seoul. It could also provide military assistance, thereby restoring any safety lost by removing United States troops.

American disengagement would not be risk free, yet no foreign policy is without cost. For decades we have risked a bloody new war, spent billions of dollars annually and backed a succession of unpopular military rulers, all to subsidize the defense of a wealthy trading partner that could protect itself. The real question is not should South Korea be defended, but who should pay for it?

As circumstances change, so should our foreign military commitments. With the apparent emergence of a stable democracy in South Korea, it is imperative that we begin pulling American forces out of the peninsula, and eventually removing Seoul from the American defense safety net.

## 161. Reagan's Senseless Persian Gulf War

*May 4, 1988*

Defense Secretary Frank Carlucci criticized congressional proposals that the U.S. strike at Iran's Kharg Island oil facilities because doing so would undermine America's neutral stance. "We're not at war with Iran," he said. "Our policy is to bring an end to the Iran-Iraq war."

But administration protestations about its innocent intentions are growing increasingly tiresome. The United States has, for example, regularly provided Iraq with intelligence on Iranian troop movements.

Moreover, while the administration has been attacking Iranian installations, it was Iraq, not Iran, that initiated the "tanker war" that brought the United States into the Gulf. In fact, Iraq has shot up more foreign vessels, including a U.S. warship last year, than has Iran.

And now the administration plans on extending naval protection to neutral ships under assault, even if they are not American-flag vessels. That really means guarding tankers carrying oil from Iraq and its allies. Is it any wonder, then, that Iran is convinced that the United States assisted Iraq in carrying out its assault on the Fao Peninsula in mid-April?

While that charge is, as far as we know, at least, false, the administration is slowly but surely turning America into a belligerent in the Iran-Iraq conflict.

True, the Navy's extended garrison duty is supposed to ensure free Gulf passage. But until U.S. ships arrived last year, the tanker war was limited to Iran and Iraq occasionally attacking vessels carrying each other's oil, depending on the ebb and flow of the overall conflict. Gulf traffic never stopped: in fact, despite increased insurance premiums, oil supplies rose and prices collapsed.

However, the Great Satan's arrival in the Persian Gulf waved the proverbial red flag at Iran. While U.S. convoys ensured the safety of the 11 Kuwaiti tankers reflagged as American vessels, Iran intensified its attack on other nation's ships, many of which are owned by American firms. In fact, there have been nearly twice as many assaults on oil tankers in the time since the Navy arrived in the Gulf as during the previous year.

Moreover, while Iran has been cautious in taking on the United States directly—relying instead on mines, like the one that almost sank the U.S. frigate in mid-April—it has felt no similar reluctance in attacking Iraq's Arab friends. After the latest American strikes, Iran fired at oil facilities in Kuwait and the emirate of Sharjah and shot up tankers owned by Saudi Arabia and the United Arab Emirates.

In fact, as a result of the latest round of fighting, oil prices rose to their highest levels of the year and Gulf traffic stopped for a time. "No sane operators are moving ships at this juncture," observed an Arab fleet manager. The United States even halted its convoys. In short, American involvement has made the Gulf more, not less, dangerous.

The only other reason for U.S. forces to be in the region is to tilt the military balance against Iran. In effect, the administration is attempting to stop Iran's attacks on Iraq's oil trade while ignoring Iraq's assaults on Iranian vessels. The United States wants an open Gulf—except for Iran.

The administration's antipathy toward Iran is understandable. But we shouldn't forget that the U.S. was a long-time supporter of the Shah, a brutal thug about whom most Iranians do not have fond memories.

Anyway, Iraq is no international virgin. It may not have seized an American embassy, but it did start the war with Iran. Iraq also has used chemical weapons against Iranian forces and Kurdish rebels, initiated missile and air assaults on Iranian cities, and attacked neutral shipping.

It is true that an Iranian victory might be more dangerous than either a continued stalemate or an Iraqi success. But the tanker war is but a minor sidelight to a massive land war which has so far cost most than 1 million lives. Unless the administration is willing to support Iraqi ground forces, the United States can have at best a marginal impact on the conflict.

While that sort of direct intervention is inconceivable, the status quo, too, is unacceptable. American lives continue to be at risk; the region continues to be unnecessarily unsettled; and the Iranians continue to have an incentive to strike out at the U.S., whether in the Gulf or through terrorist action elsewhere.

It's time to bring the Navy home. If the administration seriously wants to help end the Iran-Iraq war, it should pull out our forces. For just as a few thousand Marines could not bring peace to Lebanon, a couple dozen ships cannot solve the problems of the Persian Gulf. American involvement is only making a bad situation worse.

## 162. Break Relations with South Africa

*February 27, 1987*

Moralism triumphed over pragmatism when Congress imposed economic sanctions on South Africa last fall. For many critics of the regime, the actual impact of sanctions seemed less important than the moral satisfaction they derived from expressing their distaste for apartheid. But there is now a growing realization—expressed only in whispers by supporters of sanctions—that Congress's action has been, at best, ineffective.

And a recently released report commissioned by the Southern African Catholic Bishops' Conference goes even further, concluding that the trade and investment restrictions have backfired: "The whole sanctions issue has consolidated the Government in its retreat from meaningful and, indeed, any reform."

President P.W. Botha reportedly has exploited the American legislation to foster resentment against the international community and build support for his party in upcoming parliamentary elections.

That does not mean that sanctions have had no effect. Yet the effect has been perverse. Just as the legislation's opponents predicted, the greatest impact has been felt by the black community.

"There is no doubt," the conference report said, "that sanctions are and will become very hurtful to the economic and therefore the social fabric of the country." For that reason, most blacks, in contrast to their leadership, apparently oppose sanctions.

Since sanctions are both strengthening apartheid and impoverishing the black majority—and no one has presented any contrary evidence—Congress must reconsider the issue.

No politician likes to admit he made a mistake, but if our goal is to help black South Africans and not just to feel righteous, then we have to acknowledge, as one observer recently put it, "the only people who can be cheered by events in South Africa" are those who hope economic chaos will foster a bloody revolution. Is that what we really want? If not, sanctions must be lifted.

But simply re-establishing trade links would appear to reward the Botha Government for its intransigence. And it would be especially hard for those who last year argued that economic sanctions were imperative to now reverse themselves, at least without offering a substitute.

The answer is to strike at the South African Government—which, after all, is the institution that created and enforces apartheid. We should break diplomatic relations, severing all official ties between the two countries.

Allied states should be encouraged to do likewise. This would discomfit South African Government officials by making their nation a complete diplomatic pariah without burdening the oppressed black underclass. Sending South Africa's ambassador home would also show the black majority that America does not support the Botha regime and is doing all it can to end apartheid. Indeed, there is little else we could do, having tried both economic and diplomatic sanctions.

Of course, breaking official ties would not itself end apartheid. But as the failure of economic sanctions has proved that short of launching a military invasion the United States cannot force white South Africans—especially Afrikaner-speaking whites, who control Parliament—to cede control of the country to blacks. Closing both nations' embassies, however, would reinforce South Africa's sense of international isolation without throwing blacks out of work.

Some people might see a break in relations as inconsistent. After all, the governments of the Soviet Union and a host of other states are more repressive and less legitimate than South Africa's. In the case of the Soviet Union and many other countries, however, such sanctions would almost certainly have no effect; by contrast, a "friendly" country like South Africa is far more likely to be concerned about its relations with the West and embarrassed by any disruption in those relations.

Such a move would also send an overdue message to South Africa's blacks, who may be confused about where we stand. America needs to make no special effort to convince the Polish people that we do not support the policies of their leader, Gen. Wojciech Jaruzelski. Yet we cannot be equally certain that most South African blacks understand that

America opposes apartheid and the vicious police state that their nation has become.

In any event, imposing diplomatic sanctions against South Africa, as against, say, Poland or the Soviet Union, would be desirable if only because it offers a way out of the present conundrum: how to drop a manifestly counterproductive policy, economic sanctions, without giving the Botha Government a significant political victory.

There is no easy answer to the problem of South Africa, but the economic cutoff evidently is not one. Indeed, if we are hoping for a nonviolent transformation of South Africa into a democratic, capitalist and pluralistic society, then we should drop the trade and investment restrictions that can only push that nation closer to a bloody revolution.

The United States' real quarrel lies not with the South African people but with their Government, which will never be truly legitimate as long as it is based on apartheid. So let's use the one form of sanctions that we've yet to try—diplomatic—and send the South African ambassador home. Then we will know that we have done all we can, without hurting the South Africans who most need our help.

# Leaving the Third World Alone

## 163. Forging a Policy of Benign Detachment

*February 13, 1986*

A corrupt, brutal dictator faces widespread popular unrest. A longtime U.S. ally, he turns to this country for support. But official Washington hesitates, fearing a disastrous upheaval whatever it does.

This scenario is an all too familiar one. Nicaragua's ruling Somoza dynasty collapsed in 1979 before a coalition including Marxist theorists and conservative businessmen. The same year a fanatical Moslem revolt toppled the Peacock throne held by Muhammad Reza Shah Pahlevi for more than a quarter century.

Today the venal autocrats out or on their way out include former President-for-life Jean-Claude Duvalier of Haiti and faltering President-for-decades Ferdinand Marcos of the Philippines.

In both cases the United States is tied to repressive regimes of the past. For instance, Haiti annually receives tens of millions of dollars in foreign aid and President Kennedy even sent a ship full of Marines to sit off Haiti's coast when Francois "Papa Doc" Duvalier's hold on power seemed threatened in 1963.

American involvement in the Philippines dates back to 1899, when Spain ceded the islands as part of the settlement of the Spanish-American War. In return for access to Subic Bay and Clark Air Field the United States poured nearly $4.6 billion into the Philippines between 1945 and 1983. In recent years up to one-third of U.S. payments have been in the form of military aid, strengthening Marcos' hold on power.

How to maintain continued friendly relations with both countries has policy-makers puzzled.

Duvalier did not survive the recent round of protests in his desperately poor nation. And despite Marcos' apparent fraudulent election win, he has demonstrated no willingness to adopt the reforms necessary to satisfy an increasingly alienated urban population or to pacify a growing communist insurgency in rural areas.

Most of the answers proposed by both left and right are to increase U.S. intervention. Either stand by the incumbent leadership or encourage its overthrow.

But it would be far better to adopt a posture of what Cato Institute foreign policy analyst Ted Galen Carpenter calls "benign detachment." Let the United States pursue cordial economic and diplomatic relations with Third World states of left and right; American dollars would be used neither to prop up friendly autocrats nor undermine hostile totalitarians.

Of course, we would prefer that other nations follow our lead. But American intervention abroad does as much harm as it does good: Supporting brutal oligarchies is hardly the most persuasive way to sell democracy and capitalism.

Indeed, it is U.S. intervention that pushes so many nations, and guerrilla movements, closer to the Soviet Union. Third World revolutionaries might not look to the United States as a model in any case, but reflexive American support for any thug who calls himself an anti-communist causes them to treat this country as an enemy.

Hostility from regimes as diverse as Iran's Ayatollah and Nicaragua's Sandinistas, for example, is a predictable outgrowth of years of bungled meddling in those nation's internal affairs. In contrast, writes S. Neil MacFarlane, "the Soviet Union has been widely perceived in the Third World to be a friend of national liberation."

Despite the Third World's natural affinity for the Soviet Union, however, MacFarlane's detailed look at foreign independence movements in "Superpower Rivalry and Third World Radicalism" (Johns Hopkins Press) concludes that the Soviet edge is not overwhelming—at least when the United States does not intervene promiscuously in favor of decaying dictatorships.

The practical evidence of Third World pragmatism is clear: Marxist Angola leases offshore lands to U.S. oil companies, while a host of other leftist regimes around the world are edging toward the West as their economies implode. The key factor is U.S. non-involvement in the countries' internal political struggles.

America cannot isolate itself from an interdependent world. But this nation can pursue a policy of non-intervention, encouraging peaceful economic and cultural ties while eschewing political and military meddling.

Without our support, some repressive, reactionary "pro-western" states, such as the Philippines, might fall, but even with U.S. intervention the existing governments may collapse. And any succeeding regime would likely pursue friendly relations with this nation, as long as the United States had not tried to block the transfer of power.

Both Haiti and the Philippines provide America with an opportunity to demonstrate that it is neither a reflexive opponent of indigenous change in other nations, nor the patron saint of corrupt autocracies. Let us leave the fate of dictators like Duvalier and Marcos up to the people whom they oppress; only then can America's foreign policy both attain success and maintain honor.

## 164. Learning the Limits of Intervention

*June 22, 1988*

Bungling seems to come naturally to the Reagan administration.

After spending months trying to oust Panama's strongman, Manuel Noriega, Washington only managed to wreck that nation's economy while leaving Noriega more firmly entrenched than before.

Negotiations have broken down, but the administration refuses to give up. President Reagan now says he won't let Noriega's supporters visit the United States.

"Let them do their shopping somewhere else," says one White House aide.

The Panamanian had looked like an easy target. A corrupt autocrat who is hated by his country's large middle class, Noriega was long on the CIA payroll. So Washington thought that all it had to do was give him a gentle shove.

But the administration has learned the limits of U.S. power. The world simply does not revolve around America's every whim.

Noriega deserves to be deposed, of course. But there's no reason to single out Noriega. His sort of small-minded autocrat, whose brutality is only exceeded by his greed, is actually quite common around the world.

What Latin American nation has not had at least a dozen coups in its history? What African state is not ruled by a thug with military connections?

In fact, Noriega is pretty moderate by international standards. He has murdered an occasional political opponent, but the Mengistu regime in Ethiopia, for instance, has killed an estimated 100,000 people through its forced relocation program.

How about corruption? Noriega undoubtedly has stashed some loot in faraway bank accounts, but his ill-gotten gains are minuscule compared to those of Zaire's President Mobuto Sese Seko. Yet Mobuto, who recently visited Washington, remains a close American friend.

What about the drug connection? Two successive administrations tolerated Noriega's collaboration with drug smugglers; President Reagan became concerned only after Noriega's indictment made his activities impossible to ignore.

And Noriega's ouster would have little impact on the flow of drugs into
America. The elected government of Colombia, for instance, is officially
dedicated to eliminating drug production; however, payoffs are made,
public officials are assassinated, gun battles are staged, and the drugs
continue to flow.

Indeed, U.S. politicians who blame Noriega for drug use in America are
simply looking for a cop-out. Noriega is not responsible for the fact that
an estimated 90 million Americans have tried drugs; Noriega and drug
smugglers like him exist because 90 million Americans have used drugs.
Beating up on Noriega may score a few political points, but it is not a
serious attempt to solve the drug problem.

In any case, the administration's crusade in Panama was not only
misguided from the start; it was also doomed to fail. The Philippines and
Haiti proved that tottering autocrats can be overthrown, but unrelenting
domestic pressure is the key.

In the Philippines then-President Ferdinand Marcos tried to steal an
election, creating an avalanche of support for the opposition; even the
military, his last base of support, eventually split. In Haiti it was widespread civilian opposition and declining military support that led to Jean
Claude Duvalier's exile.

But neither factor is present in Panama. Noriega is unpopular among the
middle class and in the cities, but he retains significant support in the rural
areas. Moreover, the national guard, which benefits greatly from Noriega's
corrupt connections, has remained loyal to him.

And the administration's attempts to shake that support have proved
disastrous.

Economic sanctions have devastated the economy, harming the urban
population, which generally opposes Noriega, the most. Washington's
bellicose public demands that Noriega step aside have allowed the strongman to consolidate his rural backing by appealing to Panamanians' nation-
alistic pride.

In fact, decades worth of gringo interference in Latin American affairs
have also made Panama's neighbors leary of U.S. intervention. No one in
that region welcomes the specter of "Yanqui imperialism."

Washington's failure has caused a curious coalition of conservatives and
liberals to advocate the use of military force to remove Noriega. But such
a course would be bloody—Panama's military would likely fight—and

would give the United States a well-deserved reputation for heavy-handed hypocrisy.

Admittedly it's not easy to sit idly by while venal autocrats despoil poor nations around the globe. But the United States needs to learn the virtues of restraint. We can no longer act as the world's policeman: Noriega's future must be decided in Panama city, not in Washington.

## 165.  Good Riddance to Mozambique's Machel

*November 5, 1986*

Mozambique President Samora Machel was just one of the many petty dictators who dot the globe, but you wouldn't know it from the flood of laudatory laments over his recent death. Even Reagan administration officials, who regularly denounce communism around the world, expressed concern over losing a "voice of moderation."

Indeed, President Reagan met with Machel last year, calling him a "friend" and offering the Marxist government tens of millions of dollars annually in foreign aid to woo it away from the Soviet Union. The State Department also has proposed that the United States underwrite a $500 million transportation network between landlocked Zimbabwe and the Mozambican port of Beira.

Yet the Machel regime was far more accomplished at repression than is the government of neighboring South Africa. A one-party state, Mozambique has banned unions, forcibly collectivized villagers, and pressured the church.

Moreover, reports Freedom House, a New York-based human rights organization, in Mozambique: "All media are rigidly controlled. Rights of assembly and foreign travel do not exist. There are no private lawyers. Secret police are powerful; thousands are in re-education camps, and executions do occur."

With Machel's death, the government is likely to crack down even more on any domestic opposition. And a leading contender to head the FRE-LIMO Party, and thus to become Mozambique's president, is Marcelino Dos Santos, a pro-Soviet hard-liner.

Fortunately, Machel's death provides the United States with a convenient opportunity to reconsider its policy toward Mozambique, for our expensive attempt to buy the friendship of that nation's Marxist dictatorship has failed.

Indeed, if anything, U.S. aid has made the situation worse. American funds have helped prop up a government that is staggering to a well-earned collapse, both economically and militarily.

As is typical of the socialist states across Africa, Mozambique has mismanaged its economy and strangled its farmers. Though economic figures are hard to come by, that country's per capita income appears to be falling; the life expectancy of Mozambicans is among the dozen lowest in the world.

Military resistance to the government also is growing. RENAMO—the *Resistencia Nacional Mocambicana*—is a pro-Western group that now controls an estimated 80 percent of the countryside. In recent months RENAMO has cut the government's main transportation routes to the sea and isolated the nation's capital, Maputo.

Concern over the security of the Zimbabwe-Mozambique railway has caused Zimbabwe to send 15,000 troops to try to protect the line. And there has been talk of intervention by other African states to bolster the government.

While RENAMO leader Afonso Dhlakama has not received the same international attention as Angolan insurgent Jonas Savimbi, for instance, Dhlakama may be in a better position to actually take power. And while he probably would not create a Western-style, capitalist, democracy, he is unlikely to be as repressive as Machel.

Anti-apartheid activists dislike RENAMO for the same reason they attack Savimbi's UNITA—it receives aid from South Africa. But why is that worse than accepting assistance from the Soviet Union, probably the bloodiest regime in world history?

Mozambique, for instance, signed a Treaty of Friendship and Cooperation with the U.S.S.R. two years after Machel took power. The Soviets have supplied the Mozambique government with more than $1 billion worth of weapons and some 1,000 communist advisers currently serve in the country.

The fact that the regime has close relations with the U.S.S.R. does not, of course, warrant U.S. support for RENAMO. As sympathetic as is the RENAMO cause, this nation has no business promiscuously intervening in civil wars around the world that do not involve fundamental American interests.

But the United States should turn off the aid spigot to Mozambique. The administration certainly shouldn't press Congress for a half billion dollars to underwrite a system of brutal minority rule—in this case, blacks over blacks.

The increasing willingness of subject people to challenge communist as well as right-wing regimes around the world is a positive one. And in few places is the fight more important than in Mozambique.

Machel died the way he lived: violently. The stability he brought to his troubled nation was one of unceasing repression.

So it's good riddance to yet another aspiring Stalin. Machel's death offers the Mozambican people a new, if slender, hope of eventual freedom.

## 166. Preparing for a New Jungle War?

*March 30, 1988*

The administration has found yet another pretext for flexing American military muscle in a distant land.

President Reagan dispatched 3,200 soldiers to Honduras, doubling the U.S. military presence in that country, in response to Nicaragua's attack on Contra bases in its northern neighbor.

The troops, the president assures us, are merely meant as a symbol of U.S. support for Honduras. But what purpose does that symbol serve?

There is no evidence of a threat to Honduras' security. The Nicaraguan incursion is not the first time the Sandinistas have carried the war to the Honduran Contra camps.

Indeed, this practice is common in guerrilla wars. In 1970, for example, U.S. forces invaded Cambodia to hit North Vietnamese sanctuaries. Like other conflicts, the Central American war respects neither human life nor national borders.

Anyway, U.S. officials have long appeared to be more concerned than Honduran leaders about that nation's security. In 1986, for instance, the administration had to pressure President Jose Azcona to request emergency aid in the face of a similar Nicaraguan incursion. Honduras used barely 1 percent of the resulting $20 million in assistance to respond to Nicaragua's assault.

Similarly, Azcona's latest letter calling for help in repelling "the invading army" appears to have been written at America's insistence. Even Secretary of State George Shultz admits that the troop buildup was proposed by administration officials—"They've been twisting every arm they could," says one U.S. diplomat. And Honduras made virtually no military response to the border crossing.

Since Honduras is not in danger, the real purpose of the administration's military maneuvers is probably to intimidate Nicaragua by suggesting the possibility of American intervention. However, is the administration really willing to go to war to depose the Sandinistas?

Daniel Ortega and his associates are a bunch of thugs, but that hardly makes them unique in a world filled with petty despots. If the United States decided to truly fight to make the world safe for democracy, we would never be at peace. Anyway, freedom and democracy have always been minor considerations in American foreign policy; for decades this nation backed the venal Somoza autocracy that ruled Nicaragua.

The United States has security interests at stake in Central America, but they hardly warrant a military invasion. For instance, while Nicaragua's large military could threaten its neighbors, it doesn't appear to fear a direct attack. And none of them, other than El Salvador, faces a serious domestic insurgency.

Nicaragua could also provide the Soviet Union with access to forward air and naval facilities, which is presumably why the Soviets have been willing to subsidize Sandinista economic mismanagement. However, Cuba already provides the U.S.S.R. with a ready-made base in Latin America.

In any case, the way to meet this threat is to warn Nicaragua that if it creates large-scale military assets and forges a close military relationship with a hostile power, namely the U.S.S.R., the United States will not hesitate to pre-emptively take out any threatening military forces, whether troop concentrations, airfields or naval installations, in the event of war with the Soviets.

If the United States is not willing to invade Nicaragua, and 3,200 troops are obviously not enough to do the job, then making the threat is counterproductive. For Nicaragua's President Daniel Ortega has regularly used the spectre of American intervention to justify the Sandinistas' dictatorial powers and military buildup. Indeed, loyal Sandinistas have responded to his most recent warnings by digging air raid ditches and planting emergency vegetable patches.

And given U.S. saber rattling, it should come as no surprise that Ortega is believed by many of his countrymen. In fact, he has history on his side: America helped create the brutal Somoza dynasty and has intervened militarily in Nicaragua five times so far this century.

There is no good solution to Central America's wrenching political, economic and social problems. The world would certainly be a better place were the Sandinistas driven from power, but the Contras, even when funded by the United States, have never been close to achieving that goal. Unfortunately, short of embarking on a new jungle war, there is little that the United States can do.

Thus, the regional peace agreement proposed by Costa Rica's President Oscar Arias, though flawed, probably provides the best hope today for limiting regional subversion and protecting U.S. interests. President Reagan should work to support that effort—and bring home the troops from Honduras.

## 167. Good People, Bad Cause

*May 13, 1987*

The well-publicized death of Benjamin Linder in Nicaragua has brought home to America yet another bloody foreign war. Linder, an engineer, died in a Contra attack on a hydroelectric project.

Linder's death is a tragedy, of course. The loss is particularly painful because so few people are willing to risk their lives for what they believe.

Unfortunately, however, well-intentioned *internacionalistas* like Linder are hurting rather than helping the Nicaraguan people. For the Sandinista regime, supported by thousands of foreign volunteers, is controlled by the same sort of grasping, oppressive thugs who rule most poor Third World countries.

Not that the gullibility of American leftists should surprise anyone. After all, throughout this century leading intellectuals and activists in Western democracies have looked to communism to provide a new, worldly utopia.

In the 1930s, for instance, a steady stream of visitors made the pilgrimage to Moscow to view the Soviet experiment.

"I have seen the future, and it works," opined journalist Lincoln Steffens.

Revelations of mass murder, starvation and deprivation finally dimmed the luster of the Russian Revolution, but China provided a convenient substitute.

Alas, Mao, too, turned out to be a genocidal dictator. After he died, the Chinese Communist Party rejected his legacy and that country now is struggling with student protests for democracy.

North Vietnam was seen as a heroic example of Third World revolutionaries resisting U.S. imperialism. Since then even anti-war activists like Joan Baez have acknowledged the vast expanse of re-education camps.

A companion socialist paradise was thought to be Cuba. But today only the most unreconstructed Stalinist denies that Castro has turned his desperately poor nation into a stagnant island *gulag*.

So Nicaragua is just the latest in a seemingly endless pattern.

Not that Sandinista President Daniel Ortega is another Stalin or Mao. His modus operandi is more selective repression than mass murder. But that hardly justifies the more than 60,000 Americans who have spent weeks or months helping Ortega's ever more authoritarian government.

The Sandinistas, like all good revolutionaries, have seized control of the press. The TV is government-run; all radio stations are in Sandinista hands. The only opposition newspaper, *La Prensa,* was censored for years before being shut down in 1986.

The government has harassed Protestant evangelicals as well as the Catholic Church. The Catholic newspaper and its offices were confiscated in 1985; on Jan. 1, 1986, the church's radio station was closed.

The regime has promulgated a state of emergency and suspended the rights of assembly, free speech and travel. The government also has banned strikes.

Even the Interior Ministry acknowledges that Nicaraguan soldiers have killed, raped or injured dozens of civilians. The military has forcibly relocated some 80,000 peasants; in fact, the Sandinistas' brutal mistreatment of the Miskito Indians has fomented an insurgency unrelated to the Contras.

Finally, the regime holds an estimated 4,000 political prisoners—more than were incarcerated in former President Anastasio Somoza's jails at their fullest—and has harassed independent human rights groups.

The Nicaraguan Permanent Commission on Human Rights, which highlighted abuses under the previous Somoza regime, reports that during their first year alone the Sandinistas were potentially responsible for 520 "disappeared persons" and some 200 summary executions. In fact, defector Alvaro Baldizon Aviles, formerly the chief investigator of the Interior Ministry's Special Investigations Committee, reports that the Sandinistas have killed and tortured numerous political opponents.

That the Nicaraguan government is oppressive is not in itself justification for American intervention to topple the regime, of course: if so, the United States should be working to overthrow most governments around the world.

But even Linder's justifiable opposition to American aid for the Contras does not change the fact that he was supporting a ruthless, exploitative regime intent on communizing an unwilling society. Just as thousands of Western volunteers misguidedly supported savage governments in the Soviet Union, China, Vietnam and Cuba, Linder was unintentionally helping to subjugate the Nicaraguan people.

"For our dead, we swear to continue with the revolution," said Linder before he died. But his revolution, like every other communist upheaval this century, is devouring society's weakest and poorest. The greatest tragedy of Linder's death is that he died serving such a cause.

# The Terrorist Temptation

## 168. Reagan Takes on Libya—Sort Of

*March 1986*

Eleven days after the December attacks on the Rome and Vienna airports, perpetrated by a Palestinian terrorist group apparently supported by Libyan leader Muammar Qaddafi, President Reagan cut off all trade with Libya and ordered home the 1,000 or so Americans working in the North African nation. Reagan later froze Libyan assets in U.S. banks as a precaution against seizure of American assets by Qaddafi.

Yet Reagan's sanctions against what he denounced as an "outlaw state" only illustrate the limits of a superpower in the modern world. "Let terrorists be aware that when the rules of international behavior are violated, our policy will be one of swift and effective retribution," declared Reagan in 1981, after being elected president on a platform of toughness. However, Reagan, no less than Jimmy Carter, has relied on genteel diplomacy rather than force in dealing with Libya and other murderous states.

Over the years Libya has backed terrorists around the world, attacked American jets in international air space, invaded Chad, destabilized the Sudan, and threatened Egypt. The administration's response was some economic sanctions—particularly a boycott of Libyan oil—in 1982, and, three years later, after more Americans had been killed in various terrorist attacks than ever before, more economic restrictions. "Civilized nations cannot continue to tolerate, in the name of material gain and self-interest, the murder of innocents," says Reagan. But nothing the administration has done has eliminated terrorism or toppled Qaddafi.

Indeed, can anything be done? Emotionally, the answer is easy—just murder Qaddafi, suggests liberal Sen. Howard Metzenbaum (D.–Ohio)—but reality and morality, too, must be considered.

After all, Libya has attacked no American directly. Qaddafi is ultimately responsible for more than his share of human misery, but how is he different from, say, Syrian President Hafez al-Assad? Syria is equally guilty in promoting terror and even downed two U.S. planes in 1984, but the U.S. has taken no action against that nation.

More important, the Soviet government floats in a sea of blood that circles the globe. Yet Reagan has just concluded a chummy summit with Mikhail Gorbachev, reopening economic ties that had been severed after the invasion of Afghanistan. A consistent response to terrorism should place the U.S. at economic war with dozens of countries around the world.

However, such a program would almost certainly founder, as have the various embargoes, boycotts, and sundry other punitive actions against friends and adversaries over the years. The U.S. usually inflicts some economic harm on its target, though at prohibitive cost to our own people; the larger political objectives, however, rarely have been achieved, except in the case of small U.S. allies, such as Taiwan. Failure is almost certain when America stands alone, as it is doing in the case of Libya.

Do such economic strictures, even if ineffective, at least set an important moral standard by preventing Americans from trading with murderers? U.S. firms probably "shouldn't" buy oil from Libya, just as people "shouldn't" purchase goods from businesses controlled by the Mafia. However, in a free society the government best concerns itself with national policy, not personal morality—especially when public officials themselves exhibit so little understanding of such basic values. So where no fundamental national interest is advanced by government intervention, the state has no excuse for interfering with the right of consenting adults to engage in capitalist acts.

Anyway, the U.S. does not come to the terrorism issue with entirely clean hands. For America is supporting, dare I use the word, "terrorism" through its aid to the Nicaraguan contras. The guerrillas are probably less brutal than the Sandinista forces, and America's policy ends are certainly better than those of Libya, but we occupy only morally higher ground, not the moral high ground.

Of course, the U.S. is not limited to economic warfare. Warned Reagan when he announced the economic sanctions: "If these steps do not end Qaddafi's terrorism, I promise you that further steps will be taken."

Preemptively striking against terrorists may be a form of self-defense, and retaliation may substitute for the individualized punishment that we only so rarely are able to mete out. But here again, the constraints of being a superpower with global political—and transcendent moral—responsibilities weigh heavily. Large-scale military responses, such as the Israeli strike on Palestinian camps in Tunisia, kill innocents and directly spawn further rounds of terror, such as the December airport shootings.

Attacks limited to narrower objectives, such as kidnappings and assassinations, can more easily be confined to guilty parties, but they raise the specter of "state terror" directly carried out by the U.S. government. Even if a government "murder bureau" could be tightly controlled, would it be an appropriate policy tool for a democratic nation? Further, killing invites retaliation—there has been speculation about Cuban involvement in the assassination of President John F. Kennedy, for instance, as a response to repeated U.S. attempts to kill Fidel Castro. A downward spiral of assassinations would certainly have resulted had the U.S. attempted to murder other "deserving" candidates, such as the two greatest mass murderers of all time, Josef Stalin and Mao Tse-Tung.

Ronald Reagan, the "cowboy president," has shown remarkable restraint in the face of repeated terrorist assaults. And despite criticism from the political right for not taking more vigorous—that is, military action against terrorists and their patrons, Reagan has probably done as much as can be done, at least within the constraints of our own system.

Not that there is no effective response to terror: the Soviets reportedly won the release last year of three kidnapped diplomats in Beirut by capturing, torturing, and killing an innocent relative of the head of the extremist Islamic group holding the Soviets. But resorting to terror to stop terror would eventually transform this society into one not worth defending. And that is the dilemna faced by Ronald Reagan and the rest of us.

# Bombs Away

## 169. Two Cheers for SDI

*May 11, 1988*

As Ronald Reagan's influence wanes, his proposed Strategic Defense Initiative is coming under increasing attack. The Senate and House Armed Services committees, for instance, have sharply cut the administration's funding request, and the full House has voted to ban any tests that do not comply with a restrictive reading of the 1972 Antiballistic Missile Treaty.

But the growing opposition to Reagan's proposed space-based defense system only illustrates the need for more research and tests. For we will never know whether SDI can fulfill its promise unless we try to build it.

The objections to SDI are many. One is cost—some opponents argue that a fully deployed system could run a trillion dollars or more.

That number, however, based on an arbitrary guess by former Defense Secretary Harold Brown, seems far too high. Deployment of a first-stage system, for example, is likely to run between $120 billion and $150 billion over a period of years.

Costs would obviously increase as other features were later added to the system, but the total expense, even in the unlikely event that it ultimately hit $1 trillion, must be compared with the cost of a nuclear exchange. Protection from even the unlikely threat of nuclear annihilation is surely worth a lot of money.

Anyway, if costs do begin escalating so dramatically as to make SDI infeasible, then the program could be killed at that time. The unsubstantiated fear of crippling expenditures—initial criticisms of the program greatly overestimated the number of satellites that would be required, for instance—should not stop us from moving ahead to determine whether a space-based defensive system could be effective and affordable.

Of course, some analysts argue that SDI simply cannot work. A new study by Congress' Office of Technology Assessment concluded that it likely would "suffer a catastrophic failure."

But we really don't know what is possible. Many people scoffed at the thought of air and space travel. Though it would be enormously difficult to develop software capable of organizing a layered defensive system to destroy incoming missiles, the recent advances in computer technology have been enormous. To simply abandon the effort without even trying would be foolish, even reckless.

Objection number three is that no system can be leak-proof—that is, SDI cannot effectively protect every American from a full-scale attack. Yet does the impossibility of constructing a perfect defense mean that we should remain completely defenseless?

While SDI is not an utopian answer to the threat of nuclear war, surely we would be better off if fewer rather than more warheads landed in the America in a conflict. SDI may not obviate the need for sustained arms reductions, but it could save millions of lives, if not the lives of all Americans.

Moreover, even a limited system could prove invaluable if the Soviets accidentally launched a few missiles or an irrational small nuclear power decided to strike. This sort of "insurance system," in the words of former Reagan aide Martin Anderson, has been endorsed by Senate Armed Services Committee Chairman Sam Nunn, a Democratic skeptic of the administration's comprehensive plans.

Nor is SDI likely to militarize space or escalate the arms race with the Soviets. After all, Mikhail Gorbachev has admitted that the U.S.S.R. has its own Star Wars system under development. Shutting down the U.S. program might eventually leave this nation vulnerable to a Soviet attack.

Perhaps the only real risk in building SDI is that doing so would encourage U.S. officials to be even more promiscuous in guaranteeing the security of other lands. But this concern is not a fault of SDI, but of America's underlying strategy of extended deterrence. Especially as both France and Great Britain continue to expand their own nuclear forces, there is no need for the United States to risk the incineration of its cities to protect Paris and London.

In fact, SDI should be looked at as an instrument to make the United States strategically independent of its often feckless allies. "Secure in the knowledge that the American homeland would enjoy a degree of protection previously unavailable," argues Ted Carpenter, director of Foreign Policy Studies at the Cato Institute, "the United States would have the opportunity to forge a new, more flexible and unilateral defense strategy."

If thousands of years of bloody history have proved anything, it is that there is no utopian answer to the problem of war. And a space-based defense would not make nuclear weapons obsolete.

The threat of a nuclear holocaust is too serious to ignore, however.

Maybe SDI will turn out to be too expensive or too complex to deploy. Maybe—but maybe not. And we'll never know unless we try.

## 170. Ban Nuclear Tests

*November 7, 1985*

The Reagan administration is approaching the forthcoming U.S.-Soviet summit with all due seriousness, at least from a PR standpoint. However, far more is at stake than favorable press reviews: Both countries have an interest in peaceful, if not cordial, relations, a reduction in international tensions and meaningful arms control.

Therefore, President Reagan should use the summit to press for a permanent ban on nuclear testing. As the Washington, D.C.-based Center for Defense Information observes, "At a time when existing nuclear arms limitation agreements seem in danger of being abrogated—and prospects for new agreements are fading—an end to the explosive testing of nuclear weapons is the most significant and achievable arms control measure on the agenda today."

Since 1963, when atmospheric explosions were prohibited, the United States and the Soviet Union have been theoretically committed to reaching a comprehensive nuclear test ban. Yet both nations continue to explode 20 to 30 nuclear devices a year.

An agreement now may be attainable, however, because the Soviets are observing a unilateral moratorium that will run to the end of the year, and longer if the United States forgoes any new tests.

A permanent ban on new nuclear explosions is in our interest. First, it would slow the arms race by preventing the development of new nuclear weapons. Of particular concern, warns the CDI, are "the H-bomb pumped X-ray laser, directed plasma weapons and other more 'usable' and therefore more dangerous weapons that both sides would be better off without."

Second, a prohibition of new tests, says Sen. David Durenberger, R.-Minn., chairman of the Senate Select Committee on Intelligence, "would stop Soviet developments while preserving the technological edge the United States enjoys in their nuclear warheads." Indeed, a recent White House report acknowledged that with continued testing the Soviets may "develop efficient miniature warheads," with which they could "exploit fully" the possibility for increasing the number of warheads per ICBM.

Nevertheless, the administration peremptorily rejected the Soviet proposal for a joint moratorium. National Security Adviser Robert McFarlane calls it a "contrivance," proved by the fact that the Soviets have "accelerated the number of tests that they've had so they wouldn't need to test for the next five months or so."

But the facts don't support his claim. According to the internationally respected Swedish National Defense Research Institute, the Soviets have run seven tests this year, and the United States nine. This is "hardly a spurt in testing for the Soviet Union," notes CDI.

McFarlane also argues that a test ban would "prevent us from doing what they have already done," giving the Soviets an advantage in weapons development. However, the United States retains an overall technological lead, has already tested the MX and Trident II and could fit the "Midgetman" missile with an existing warhead. A moratorium would impede new weapons development, but by both parties.

A related argument is that tests are needed to maintain the reliability of America's nuclear arsenal. Not true: A group of experts, including Hans Bethe, Richard Garwin, and Norris Bradbury, recently wrote Congress that "in no case was the discovery of a reliability problem dependent on a nuclear test." Anyway, fear of diminished reliability also would affect both sides, making everyone more reluctant to initiate the use of nuclear weapons.

Finally, the administration has objected to a ban because of verification problems. This concern is not invalid—the Soviet regime is hardly distinguished by its honesty or openness—but can be overcome in practice.

The U.S. Atomic Energy Detection System comprises a network of seismographic stations in more than 35 countries, some of which border on the Soviet Union. All told, there are more than 1,000 stations capable of detecting underground nuclear tests operating worldwide.

Moreover, since the mid-1970s, recently testified Ralph Alewine, a scientist with the Defense Advance Research Projects Agency, "there have been some important changes" in our detection capabilities. Most experts estimate that the United States could identify explosions of under 1 kiloton, while cheating at even the 5-kiloton level would not permit new weapons development.

The administration should use the summit to commit the United States to a temporary test moratorium and to press Mikhail Gorbachev to begin negotiations on a permanent treaty. What if the Soviets are just posturing? We will tell only by testing them, and the resulting delay in conducting nuclear explosions would not endanger our security.

These days summits are far more pomp than circumstance. But by pressing for a permanent nuclear test ban, President Reagan could regain the PR initiative while genuinely enhancing the prospects for a more stable peace. It's an opportunity that none of us can afford to waste.

# A Cold Draft

## 171. Mercenary Morality

*October 19, 1987*

Support for conscription is on the rise, but the newest advocates of involuntary military service are Democratic politicians, not all of them especially hawkish, rather than war-hungry generals. The arguments they make are based on what they see as important social values, rather than in terms of military needs or efficiency. Senate Armed Services Committee Chairman Sam Nunn thinks the draft should never have been abandoned. South Carolina's Fritz Hollings regularly introduces legislation to reinstitute conscription. Former Virginia Governor Charles Robb and Representative David McCurdy, Democrat of Oklahoma, also favor a return to the draft. Even Senator Paul Simon, perhaps the most unabashed liberal among the Democratic presidential contenders, supports mandatory military service as part of a universal national service program.

This liberal enthusiasm for conscription comes at a time when the volunteer military's success is undisputed. Recruits today are better educated and score higher on Pentagon tests than do civilian youths. Discipline and morale are superior to that of the draft era. Military officers once led the chorus for a return to conscription, but now the Army chief of staff, Gen. John Wickham, says that today's soldiers "are the best in my 33 years of service. They'll fight, and they are as patriotic as you and I. They follow orders, and they die."

Long perceived to be soft on defense, some Democrats see the draft as a cheap way to appear pro-military. Others view the volunteer military as an unseemly affair that entrusts the common defense to "mercenaries." The system is also thought to be unrepresentative, allowing the rich and middle class to escape their civic duty. Simon complains, "We are relying excessively on the poor of this country."

These issues are more interesting than sterile debates over recruit quality backed by tables of Armed Forces Qualification Test (AFQT)

437

scores. But soldier competence relates to the basic purpose of a military—its ability to fight—in a way that "representativeness" and "civic obligation" do not. In fact, manipulating the armed services for ill-defined social objectives would make the military less able to do its job. The sort of military desired by most conscription advocates would be dumber, less well educated, and more poorly motivated.

But draft supporters really don't believe their rhetoric. While they wax eloquent over the citizenship obligation of young men, they fall strangely silent when it comes to the duty of women, 30-year-old investment bankers, and 50-year-old congressmen. National defense presumably benefits everyone, so why don't we all have an equal obligation to serve? Eighteen-year-old males aren't the only ones who can be cooks, mechanics, and support personnel.

In contrast, the volunteer military exacts a contribution for the common defense from everyone, but it does so in a way more consistent with this nation's basic principles. A volunteer military financed by a universal taxation—a far less intrusive and destructive form of coercion than conscription—spreads the defense obligation to every member of society. Indeed, the progressive income tax imposes the highest defense cost on those who, by one measure at least, have the most at stake. As Nicholas von Hoffman once put it, "Draft old men's money, not young men's bodies."

Is there still something wrong with relying on dirty mammon to hire soldiers? The question is bizarre on its face: America has never drafted its officer corps and career enlisted force. Even conscription advocates support increased compensation to help retain skilled service personnel. Can anyone seriously object to paying a living wage to combat grunts—some of whom qualified for food stamps in the late 1970s—when generals earn $72,500 a year? Yet the built-in logic of a draft army is that soldiers will be paid less than it would take to attract them in the free market. After all, if the pay is good enough to fill the ranks with volunteers, there will be no place to put the draftees.

A volunteer military relies on patriotism as well as cash to sign up new enlistees. Surveys consistently show that the desire to serve the country is among the most important reasons recruits join; enlistments actually rise after traumatic events such as the bombing of the Marine barracks in Lebanon. In contrast, the draft completely ignores people's patriotic feelings, relying instead on the threat of jail to meet recruiting quotas. Conscripts—or slaves, if volunteers can be called mercenaries—are pressed into service irrespective of their devotion to the nation. And if the choice is between mercenaries who want to be in the foxhole and slaves who don't, the decision shouldn't be hard to make. A volunteer military simply pays a decent wage to its members, ensuring that those who most want to defend their country don't have to accept food stamps to make ends meet.

Simon's criticism still remains, however. In relying on free choice to fill the military's ranks, are we making the poor and minorities carry the bulk of the defense burden for a society in which they share few of the benefits? In fact, we aren't. The All-Volunteer Force (AVF) is roughly representative of society as a whole. But even if the poor were grossly overrepresented in the military, how could that justify a draft to reorder things? After all, a draft will mean one of two things for those now serving in the military as volunteers. Either (a) they will still be serving, as volunteers or as draftees, only for less pay in either case; or (b) they will not be serving when, for more money, they would have chosen to do so. Replacing the AVF with a draft doesn't increase opportunities for the poor; it only eliminates one option they might otherwise wish to take.

Another problem: the military just doesn't need the services of every 18-year-old American male. The annual demand for roughly 334,000 new recruits could be met by taking about one out of every five. Lowering pay enough to eliminate anybody's wish to volunteer and then filling the entire quota through a draft lottery would make the armed services slightly dumber on average than they are now, but arguably more "representative." And yet four out of five youths would still escape this would-be mandatory patriotic duty.

Of course, the government could be "fair" by taking all 1.6 million 18-year-old males. Since draftees serve two-year terms, there'd be 3.2 million young men to keep busy. Some versions of the Democratic draft envision a broader kind of national service, where draftees could choose among soldiering, teaching, raking leaves, etc. But the cost of administering any such program would be phenomenal—all the while forcing both the draftees and the volunteers they replace to work at jobs they wouldn't choose, and for less money than they would otherwise get. And all to what end? To rejuggle slightly the racial and socioeconomic complexion of the first-term military force, which constitutes less than one-third of the military.

But the volunteer military is already broadly representative of mainstream America. Nearly all officers have a college degree and both career enlisted men and officers are solidly in the middle class. Even new recruits are better educated than the population they are defending. Last year 91 percent of Army first-termers were high school graduates—the best measure of likely service success—compared with only 75 percent of civilian youth. New enlistees are less likely than average to have attended college, but that results in large part from recruiting efforts that focus on 18-year-olds.

And, based on SAT scores, military recruits are generally as capable of attending college as civilian youths. The AFQT test provides even more impressive evidence on this point: last year the military accepted just four percent of military recruits scoring in the bottom two categories, even though nearly one-third of civilian youths fall into those two groups. Surveys have also found the socioeconomic backgrounds of military recruits and civilian young people to be similar. Their parents' educational attainments are remarkably close, and the occupations of recruits' families are only slightly more blue collar. In short, the best of middle America is choosing military service over college.

What about the overrepresentation of blacks? Last year 15 percent of the 18- to 24-year-old population was black, compared with 19 percent of new enlistees and 22 percent of Army first-termers. However, the black share of Army enlistments has been falling and is close to where it was when the volunteer military was inaugurated in 1973. Anyway, no one has demonstrated any harm from the high level of black enlistments—not to the military and certainly not to the black volunteers. After all, they're qualified and perform well. And to the extent that they've joined because they believe the military offers them an opportunity to succeed, they're right. Sociologist Charles Moskos observes, "Blacks occupy more management positions in the military than they do in business, education, journalism, government, or any other significant sector of American society."

Sometimes the new draft supporters even admit that one part of their thinking is that a draft will save a few billion in the cost of defense. Universal service, of course, far from saving money, would cost untold billions. Even a selective lottery might well end up costing money, even though pay-per-soldier could be dramatically lowered. Most service pay goes to careerists, retirees, and civilians, and therefore wouldn't be cut. Conscription raises training expenses since draftees serve shorter terms and re-enlist in fewer numbers. A recent Pentagon study figured a draft would cost as much as $2.5 billion more than today's AVF.

More to the point, even if a few billion could be saved, this wouldn't reduce the burden of defense so much as redistribute it—from the broad spectrum of American taxpayers onto the backs of a few 18-year-olds. What social values would truly be served by such an exercise?

## 172. America Has No Need for a New Draft

*June 14, 1987*

The U.S. military's All-Volunteer Force has been working—and working well—for 14 years, but arguments for a draft refuse to disappear. Indeed, many Democrats, including Sen. Sam Nunn (D-Ga.), chairman of the Senate Armed Services Committee and a potential presidential candidate, hope to use conscription as a cheap way of demonstrating "toughness" on defense.

Meanwhile, most Pentagon officials seem pleased with the volunteer force. The Army chief of staff, Gen. John A. Wickham Jr., says simply, "the volunteer system is working." A return to the draft, many officers fear, would reduce the quality of recruits and destroy public support for the military.

And they're right. The volunteer system will face future challenges but the fact that maintaining it will take work does not mean it should be abandoned. We should be wary of turning back to conscription, said a former Marine Corps officer, Lt. Col. David Evans, because "today the volunteer military has all the attributes of a truly professional standing military: quality, experience and stability."

That voluntarism has worked should come as no surprise, for in no other occupation, service or profession are people conscripted. The military is dangerous, of course, but that does not make it unique. Police are shot in the line of duty, firemen die fighting fires and steeplejacks fall off skyscrapers.

Indeed, America has always had a volunteer officer corps and career enlisted force, having relied on voluntarism to man the entire military for all but 38 years of the nation's history. It took a wrenching Civil War to inaugurate conscription in America and two world wars to institutionalize the practice.

Yet the political appeal of involuntary service never seems to fade. Perhaps the most fundamental attack on the volunteer force is on the grounds that it neglects the principle that citizenship carries burdens as well as benefits. The "privilege" of being an American, some argue, justifies requiring men to serve in the military.

Yet the political appeal of involuntary service never seems to fade. Perhaps the most fundamental attack on the volunteer force is on the grounds that it neglects the principle that citizenship carries burdens as well as benefits. The "privilege" of being an American, some argue, justifies requiring men to serve in the military.

This contention implies, however, that government is the grantor, rather than protector, of rights—fundamentally misconstruing the relationship between the individual and the state in a free society. It is a privilege to be an American in the sense that one is lucky to live in a country that respects individual liberty more than most others, not in the sense that the government is bestowing unearned freedom benefits on the citizenry.

Even if citizens do owe service to the state, why are only young men liable? Conscription disproportionately burdens 18-year-old men. In contrast, a volunteer military financed by universal taxation—a far less intrusive and destructive form of coercion than a draft—spreads the defense obligation throughout society.

Perhaps the most misleading objection to the All-Volunteer Force is that it is "too expensive." But a draft wouldn't lower federal costs. Roughly 90% of all spending on military compensation goes to careerists, civilians and retirees. If the Pentagon slashed recruit pay by one-third, outlays would fall a mere $2 billion; any savings would be offset by increased costs elsewhere. For example, conscripts serve shorter terms and re-enlist in lower numbers than do volunteers; increased turnover would increase both training expenses and re-enlistment pay scales. President Reagan's Military Manpower Task Force estimated that a return to conscription would probably hike federal outlays by $1 billion.

Does the military inadequately represent American society? Presidental contender Sen. Paul Simon (D-Ill.) has complained that "we are relying excessively on the poor of this country." Not so. The All-Volunteer Force is generally representative of society. In terms of education, 92% of all recruits and 91% of Army enlistees were high school graduates last year, compared with only 75% of the overall youth population. The draft army never did as well, even before Vietnam.

The socioeconomic composition of the volunteer force does not differ markedly from that of the rest of society. A research study found the educational attainment of the parents of army recruits to be much greater than that of full-time employed youth and virtually identical to that of all civilian young men, including college students. The occupational background of young servicemen's parents is only slightly more blue-collar than that of the same age group of civilians. Incomes are only marginally lower for recruits' families: a Rand Corp. report explicitly rejected the contention that the All-Volunteer Force was "an army of the poor."

Finally, although blacks are overrepresented among new enlistees—15% of the 18- to 24-year-old population is black, compared with 19% of new recruits and 22% of army first-termers—the black share of total army enlistments has dropped roughly 40% from 1979, when the volunteer force was experiencing its greatest recruiting difficulties. Black overrepresentation, regardless, has caused no problems: Blacks who volunteer are as well-qualified as their white comrades. A draft, by contrast, would make all blacks worse off—excluding some who wanted to join, paying less to those who were inducted and conscripting many who didn't want to serve.

In any case, people concerned about the "unrepresentativeness" of the military are unrealistic in turning to the draft. Even if the mirage of a "fair draft" were achievable, the small number of conscripts required would have little effect on the overall composition of the military. A draft that brought in roughly 100,000 of the 334,000 annual new personnel would ensnare only 5,000 to 10,000 upper-class youths. The impact of such a number on a nearly 2.1 million-man military would be minimal.

Discipline, too, is better under the volunteer system, with courts-martial, desertions and absences without leave far below their draft-era levels. Discharges are somewhat higher than in the conscription army, but that reflects the ability of the services to "fire" soldiers unsuited for military service rather than incarcerating them. Recruits now work hard to stay in rather than doing their best to get out.

Some proponents of a draft have voiced a fear that a voluntary military is more likely to be used for undemocratic purposes. But armies of conquest and coups have usually been conscript forces. The most effective way to prevent foreign adventures—like Vietnam—is to rely on a volunteer military that the people can shut down by simply refusing to join. A draft, by contrast, allows the government to call up additional soldiers even in the face of growing popular opposition.

Congress' most important task is to ensure that military pay stays comparable with civilian wages. Enlistments fell in the late 1970s because a recruit's base pay fell to 83% of the minimum wage—even less if the soldier worked more than 40 hours a week. "What do recruiters tell prospective enlistees?" complained Otto Hirr of the San Diego Council of the Navy League: "Join the service, get married and become eligible for food stamps?" Paying soldiers a living wage doesn't minimize the importance of patriotism. But there is no reason why soldiers who are prepared to risk their lives to defend their country should make less than supermarket clerks.

The volunteer military has not failed. And a draft would not enhance our national security. Most important, a draft would violate the fundamental principles of liberty that underlie our republic.

## 173.  It's Time to Drop Draft Registration

*July 23, 1987*

Jimmy Carter has been out of office for more than six years, but his legacy lives on. Gillam Kerley of Madison, Wis., has become the latest young man to be convicted for failing to register for the draft. And Mr. Kerley's sentence—a three-year prison term with a mandatory year before parole and a $10,000 fine—is the harshest yet.

This punishment is grossly disproportionate to the "crime" of publicly refusing to fill out a one page form. His sentence also highlights the Reagan Administration's scattershot enforcement policy. Though at least 450,000 young men annually commit the same crime as Mr. Kerley, fewer than two dozen have been prosecuted.

Mr. Carter proposed draft registration in early 1980 after the Soviet invasion of Afghanistan. Under the plan, 18 year old men must register for the draft, although they will not actually be drafted unless Congress approves conscription. While the official justification was to increase emergency readiness, the program's real purpose—which proved ineffective—was to show toughness in the face of Soviet aggression.

During the 1980 Presidential campaign, Mr. Reagan criticized the Carter program, arguing that registration "destroys the very values that our society is committed to defending." Once in office, however, he accepted the sign-up as his own, citing national security concerns. But the President was embarrassed when his manpower task force's report on registration was leaked to the press. The study showed not only that a postmobilization sign-up could bring in men almost as quickly as the current program, but also that the Pentagon's training camps would be filled to overflowing with volunteers and other military personnel even without peacetime registration.

In fact, Mr. Reagan maintained the program for the same reason that Mr. Carter created it—to demonstrate national resolve, this time after the Polish military's crackdown on Solidarity. Unfortunately, though, registration had no more impact on events in Poland than in Afghanistan.

Today, with prosecutions continuing, a program that was supposed to help free Polish Solidarity members has instead been used to jail young Americans. And a system intended to accelerate mobilization in the event of war has made both the defense establishment and the public complacent about a future conflict.

President Reagan should simply drop registration and end the persecution of vocal nonregistrants. But Pentagon planners like the illusion of security that the peacetime sign-up provides. Thus, a registration analogue of the All-Volunteer Force is needed, something that provides a sure source of emergency manpower but is consistent with America's tradition of individual liberty.

Consider a reserve volunteer force, a pool of untrained volunteers who would be subject to immediate call-up in a mobilization. Using the most pessimistic Pentagon estimates, 130,000 men would be needed for sufficient untrained manpower in the first two months after mobilization.

Reserve volunteers would sign up for a set term, during which they would enter the military only during a national emergency. Members would receive a modest financial stipend and would be invited to become part of the "military family" through involvement with the active forces, reserves and service associations.

Reserve volunteers would provide a better source of emergency manpower than does the current system. Members would automatically report when called up; because of exemption claims, Selective Service would have to issue 600,000 draft notices to assure 100,000 inductions.

Are there at least 130,000 young men ready to serve? Today's young people are patriotic; qualified recruits are flocking to the active duty forces. Moreover, draft registrations soared after the bombing of the Marine barracks in Lebanon and the Grenada invasion.

With some Democrats calling for a return to a peacetime draft, there would be no better way for the Administration to demonstrate its commitment to the volunteer military than to abolish registration. Let's raise America's entire armed forces in a manner consistent with our principles of freedom, which the military is sworn to uphold.

# War in Color

## 174. Journalists at War

*September 13, 1984*

Many Septembers ago the Army of the Potomac and the Army of Northern Virginia collided at the small Maryland town of Sharpsburg. Nearly 24,000 men fell on both sides, making that day in 1862 the single bloodiest in U.S. history.

A tactical draw, the battle ended Confederate Gen. Robert E. Lee's invasion of the North. But another milestone was set along the banks of the Antietam River: the emergence of war photojournalists.

Though a few military photos had been taken as far back as the Mexican-American War in 1846 and 1847, most were posed shots behind the lines. No photographer captured the real meaning of war until Sharpsburg.

The importance of reporting today's conflicts equally honestly and graphically is recognized by the newly released report of a joint military-press panel created after last fall's invasion of Grenada.

"The American people," the commission concluded, "must be informed about the United States' military operations."

Unfortunately, a year ago the Reagan administration thought otherwise and barred reporters from its island assault. Secretary of State George Shultz declared that the reporters were not "on our side."

Reed Irvin, the head of Accuracy in Media, said journalists wanted to "show the blood and gore of war on the television screens of millions of American homes," thereby "undermining the will of the American people to fight." Only by keeping the press out could the administration present its war as a glorious, nearly costless, triumph.

Though the Pentagon/press panel did not expressly evaluate the administration's censorship in Grenada, its chairman said that had the group's recommendations—advance preparation for media coverage and an established "pool" of reporters available to travel on short notice—been in place last October, "there might have been no need to create our panel."

447

No such commissions were operating 122 years ago when Alexander Gardner and James Gibson, who worked for the famous Matthew Brady studio, made their way to Sharpsburg, but none was needed. Gardner and Gibson simply rode into town and took nearly 100 photographs—a lengthy task at the time—including dozens of bloated and decaying corpses.

When the photos went on display they created a sensation. A New York Times reporter wrote: "We recognize the battlefield as a reality, but it stands as a remote one. . . . Mr. Brady has done something to bring home to us the terrible reality and earnestness of war. If he has not brought bodies and laid them in our dooryards and along streets, he has done something very like it."

It is for precisely the same reason that live, independent coverage of conflicts is so important today. Only by accurately seeing the results of war can the U.S. people make informed decisions regarding when their sons and husbands should fight and die.

Winston Churchill, for example, did not attempt to hide the reality of the German blitz from the British people in World War II; instead, he promised them "blood, sweat and tears." And they responded.

Of course, knowledge of the real costs of war may cause public support for remote kill-fests, like the Vietnam War, to flag. But the press does not create the death and destruction it reports; it only reflects the carnage that is there. Unfortunately, wars are bloody.

Thus, some conservatives, who realize that most Americans don't want to send young men off to fight and die in Nicaragua, El Salvador and similar spots around the globe, apparently hope to build support for global intervention by making people think that military action is cheap. Let the Pentagon roll the cameras and ignore the bodies; what the people don't know won't hurt them.

However, this tactic will not work. Despite initial public backing for the administration's self-serving censorship last fall, the U.S. people do want the truth. A 2-to-1 majority believe that a press pool should have accompanied U.S. troops to Grenada. And a more than 6-to-1 majority agree that "a basic freedom is the right to know about important events, especially where the lives of American fighting men are involved."

Many Septembers ago a couple of photographers in the town of Sharpsburg rendered the U.S. people an inestimable service by bringing the battlefield into everyone's home. After that no one could be ignorant of the terrible price of the conflict that had begun so gaily.

The press must continue to operate as the founders of our nation intended—freely, not obediently. For as biased, ignorant and obnoxious as journalists can be at times, government officials can be, and usually are, far worse.

The Reagan administration should emphasize close civilian review and implement the Pentagon/press panel's recommendations. Then we could be sure that the administration was "on our side."

# Disunited Nations

## 175. No Longer a Baby at Age 40

*October 24, 1985*

'Tis the season to be merry as the United Nations celebrates its 40th anniversary. Dozens of heads of state were expected to attend the official festivities on U.N. Day, Oct. 24.

Despite widespread and withering criticism of the United Nations in recent years, hope burns eternal.

Austrian Ambassador Thomas Klestil recently reaffirmed his nation's support for the international body: "Give it a chance," he said, for "the United Nations is only 40 years old."

And the United States seems prepared to give the world organization that chance. Secretary of State George P. Shultz called for rejuvenation of the United Nations in his address to the General Assembly. The administration is even opposing congressional efforts to cut the U.S. share of the U.N. budget—now 25 percent—even though the smallest 85 countries, a solid voting majority, contribute less than 2 percent of the international body's revenues.

A fundamental reappraisal of our involvement in the United Nations is called for.

The United Nations' most important failure is its inability to promote, let alone keep, world peace. As for the United Nations' extensive network of humanitarian programs, many have been drawn into fractious international disputes or merely duplicate the work of private agencies.

Some projects actually hurt their intended beneficiaries. The U.N. Disaster Relief Office, charges *The New Republic,* is "a cumbersome bureaucracy, which further delays the response to urgent requests, if it does anything at all."

There simply are few advances for peace, improvements in living standards, or increases in personal freedom and civil liberties anywhere that

451

can be cited as achievements on the part of the United Nations, even after 40 years.

Those inclined to be charitable nevertheless argue that the United Nations provides a harmless forum to "let off steam." However, more than idle chitchat is involved: by serving as a forum for persistent attacks on the values of political and economic freedom that underlie our system, the United Nations has become what Midge Decter terms "a center of agitation against the democratic order."

Under the control of the numerous developing nations, the United Nations has been actively promoting a comprehensive system of global management. The overriding U.N. goal is international control of natural, financial and information resources, as well as global regulation of economic and even cultural activities.

The United Nations and its alphabet-soup conglomeration of official and related specialized agencies not only provide an international forum for demands for wealth redistribution, but also help underwrite the development and spread of the redistributionist ideology. The highly paid professional staff essentially acts as union organizers for the Third World.

Virtually every U.N. agency has joined in the assault on the free world economic order: treaties have been drafted to place the oceans and space under U.N. jurisdiction, and similar proposals have been advanced concerning Antarctica, the airwaves and the geostationary orbit.

International taxation and "democratization" of independent financial institutions like the World Bank and International Monetary Fund have been urged; regulatory codes for businesses have been drafted. U.N. agencies also have proposed to confiscate private technology, license the world press and combat Western "cultural pollution."

The demands for international wealth redistribution suffuse virtually every U.N. activity. Even the 1982 Conference on the Global Environment was not spared discussion of the need for a new coercive international economic order.

The United States should continue to work with like-minded states to try to block the United Nations' multifaceted drive for global management. But this country shouldn't hesitate to reduce its financial contribution or withdraw entirely from U.N. agencies where the abuses are particularly egregious.

Indeed, that sort of decisive action by the Reagan administration blocked the Law of the Sea Treaty from taking effect and crippled the U.N. Educational, Scientific and Cultural Organization. The United States should stop paying for attacks on its economic and political values in other U.N. bodies, like the United Nations Conference on Trade and Development and the United Nations Industrial Development Organization, as well.

In firmly rejecting proposals for global management, the United States should show sensitivity to the problems of the Third World. But creating international regulatory systems that would further impoverish the peoples of developing nations would be no act of compassion.

In September Singapore's foreign minister, Suppiah Dhanabalan, told the General Assembly that the United Nations' prestige "is at an all-time low." He's right, and it's time to stop pretending that all the international body needs is one more chance. At age 40 the United Nations is neither a helpless infant nor a misguided juvenile delinquent; it's a hardened, career criminal.

## 176.  The Dangerous Side of the UN

*May 18, 1983*

The proliferation of United Nations conferences and organizations is revealing a harmful—even dangerous—side of the international body. A number of UN institutions are providing forums for Third World nations to promote their own totalitarian, domestic, economic, and political systems at the international level. These systems not only work to the detriment of the U.S. and other industrialized nations, they also help impoverish the people of the Third World.

Underlying most of these Third World efforts is the proposal for establishing a New International Economic Order (NIEO) under which Western technology, natural resources, and money would be transferred to the developing countries. The most recent campaign by proponents of a NIEO is the sustained drive to increase Western funding of the World Bank and International Monetary Fund and the loans those organizations make to Third World governments. Related to that is the demand, made by nations that abhor democracy at home, for "democratic" one-nation, one-vote control of international economic organizations.

A noteworthy example of NIEO proponents' handiwork is the Law of the Sea Treaty, a 175-page document signed by more than 100 countries last December. The treaty covers a wide range of subjects and provides few benefits to the U.S.—in its treatment of seabed mining, it is worse than no treaty at all.

The treaty is the cutting edge of the Third World's economic assault on the West, institutionalizing for the first time many of the principles of the NIEO. The treaty creates an International Seabed Authority (ISA) ruled by a one-nation, one-vote Assembly. Many of the ISA's goals and regulations would discourage development, and the ISA could order the transfer of private technology to itself for developing countries and would redistribute wealth to Third World nations. Also created by the treaty is The Enterprise, an organization to mine the seabed on behalf of the ISA. It would be subsidized by the West and would benefit from substantial discrimination against private miners.

Another treaty, based on precisely the same premise—that unowned resources are owned by the world's governments—has been ratified by five countries. The so-called Moon Treaty was approved by the UN General Assembly in 1980 and, if it had been generally accepted, would have similarly discouraged private space development. Even the Carter Administration declined to sign it.

The United Nations Conference on Trade and Development (UNCTAD), established as a permanent body, has promulgated the Code of Conduct for Liner Conferences, which, in mercantilist fashion, apportions shipping tonnage and regulates rates. UNCTAD is also working on a Code on Restrictive Business Practices, which is likely to discourage beneficial economic activity all over the globe.

Restrictions on business have come from several other U.N. organizations as well. These include the World Health Organization, which voted to ban advertising of infant formula and is currently working on a proposal to create an international agency to rule on drug quality; the United Nations Industrial Development Organization (UNIDO), which has development proposals to redistribute income and technology from the pharmaceutical industry to Third World governments; and the Commission on Transnational Corporations, which has developed working papers favoring state-owned enterprises and burdensome international regulation of private concerns. These perverse economic regulations would give Third World politicians more power, but make Third World peoples worse off.

The UN, led by the United Nations Educational, Scientific, and Cultural Organization (UNESCO), which has attempted to restrict the international press, is also promoting what it calls the New International Information Order. Efforts are underway to spread international control to the transmission of information as well.

All of these proposals for global management are based on the same myths that have resulted in manifold failures at the national level throughout the world—that voluntary exchange and cooperation are inferior to state planning and management. Another misconception holds that Third World nations are poor because of Western exploitation. In fact, the developing countries with the most open economic and political systems, and the greatest contact with the West, are also the most prosperous ones.

Thus, perhaps the greatest tragedy is that instead of freeing the peoples of the developing world from the very totalitarian systems—including economic suffocation and political oppression—that make them poor, this move toward global management would institutionalize these systems at an even higher level, further choking off economic and political development.

Support for an expensive failure is bad enough. But the U.S. certainly should not be subsidizing a dangerous one, which is what the UN has become.

## 177. America Turns Away the World of Refugees

*September 11, 1988*

When hundreds of thousands of Jews attempted to flee Europe as Adolf Hitler's Nazis took over Germany, America was a logical refuge. But the United States began closing its immigration door in 1939, accepting less than 40,000 European refugees. In mid-1940, admissions were cut in half, and in June, 1941, the same month Hitler inaugurated his bloody campaign against Slavic Jews, Congress passed the Russell Bill, cutting immigration quotas still further. Once America joined the war, the Franklin D. Roosevelt Administration admitted barely 21,000 European refugees, even as the Nazis were murdering millions of Jews.

A half-century later, desperate refugees flee Vietnam every day. In May, for instance, 110 people left the town of Ben Tre in a 35-foot boat; during their 37-day voyage 58 passengers died and the survivors reportedly resorted to cannibalism. They came across an American amphibious landing ship; the captain refused to take any on board. The refugees were ultimately rescued by Filipino fishermen, but they may now languish for years in camps awaiting a permanent home.

Indeed, the plight of Vietnamese "boat people" is becoming steadily more acute. The number of seaborne refugees is up 44% over last year and most Southeast Asian nations have grown tired of the exodus: They speak of "compassion fatigue."

Hong Kong plans to deport most new arrivals, while Malaysia warns that next year it will force refugees to set sail again. Singapore refuses to allow any boat people to land; Indonesia has begun turning away refugees. And the United Nations says that several hundred boat people died earlier this year when Thailand began enforcing a new policy of pushing refugee vessels back to sea.

One answer is for a nation created by immigrants, the United States, to open its borders.

Though the number of Vietnamese in camps throughout Southeast Asia, 54,000, seems large, America could easily accept them all tomorrow. In fact, America has admitted about 700,000 Vietnamese since 1975 and has not only survived, but prospered. The Vietnamese are reliant, industrious people, committed to the same values as the rest of us.

But just as Washington closed its eyes 50 year ago, U.S. officials today are unwilling to help Vietnamese fleeing their repressive homeland. The Administration has proposed reducing, by 6,000, the number of Vietnamese who can settle in America next year.

There is more than enough blame to go around. Congressmen, Immigration and Naturalization Service bureaucrats and State Department officials do nothing as human beings die daily. The excuse offered by opponents of expanded immigration is that boat people are "economic migrants," motivated by poverty. Indeed, Washington has long denied political asylum to refugees who supposedly were fleeing poverty rather than tyranny. The INS, for example, presumes that people leaving war-torn El Salvador seek economic enrichment rather than political freedom. But why does it matter whether a person fears starvation more than a death squad?

In a scathing opinion regarding the Administration's treatment of Salvadoran refugees, Federal District Court Judge David V. Kenyon recently observed that "the impressions of the INS agents and officials that Salvadorans come to the United States solely for economic gain reflect a lack of sensitivity and understanding, and derive from ignorance on the part of INS agents as to the complex motivations and situations of those who have fled El Salvador."

Between 40,000 and 50,000 people have so far died in that guerrilla war; there were more than 3,600 political murders and disappearances in 1985 and 1986 alone. A 1986 Massachusetts Institute of Technology study found that the number of Salvadorans seeking refuge in the United States rose as the level of political violence in their home country increased.

Yet the Administration has done its best to keep this country free of Salvadorans. From October through June, the INS granted asylum to just 78 of 2,683 Salvadoran applicants, an abysmal 3%. And the INS's abusive campaign against El Salvadoran refugees caused Kenyon, in April, to order the agency to cease its use of "threats, intimidation, deceit and misrepresentation to pressure detained Central Americans to return to their countries."

Washington is even stingy about escapees from the Soviet Union. With rising unrest in Armenia, the Administration has been accepting some 1,200 a month, up from 200 annually in the early 1980s. Now some State Department lawyers are complaining that these refugees—who are fleeing a state that for 70 years has suppressed individual liberty—have not been articulating "a well-founded fear of persecution," a requirement for a grant of asylum.

Sen. Alan K. Simpson (R-Wyo.) says "we must distinguish between the right to leave the Soviet Union and the right to enter the United States."

That certainly seems to be the INS philosophy. So far this year the agency has rejected more asylum requests than it has granted, 5,439 compared to 4,932, and is sitting on a backlog of 68,087. What justification is there for turning away even one Soviet or Pole or Nicaraguan or Ethiopain? All those governments maintain power by massively violating human rights; everyone, aside from the ruling elite, is persecuted.

The problem is that the INS requires an applicant to prove he reasonably believes he is likely to be singled out for persecution if he returns home. Thus, the more general the oppression, the more difficult to gain asylum. Indeed, one State Department official, charged with reviewing asylum requests, argues that people who are in "privileged" occupations and allowed to travel probably aren't persecuted.

What irony: The fact that you have the opportunity to defect makes it harder to do so; the only people with ironclad proof that they will be persecuted are those who already languish in the *gulag*.

Until 1980, people fleeing communist lands were almost always considered to be political refugees eligible for asylum; Congress changed the law to make it "fair" by requiring everyone to demonstrate a likelihood of personal persecution.

Unfortunately, standing up for foreign refugees has never been politically popular. Congressional xenophobes read the polls showing enormous popular resentment of refugees.

Yet there is no more worthy cause. Congress need only look to one of its own for an example of the importance of welcoming the poor and oppressed to America. The family of Sen. Rudy Boschwitz (R-Minn.) fled Germany in 1932, after his father was dismissed as a judge for being Jewish. They lived in Czechoslovakia, Switzerland, Holland and Great Britain before emigrating to the United States.

There is nothing America can do to resurrect the tens or even hundreds of thousands of would-be immigrants who perished after Washington refused to admit them. But we can avoid making the same mistake again. Today people are dying daily at crowded camps in Thailand and on overloaded boats in the South Pacific.

The richest nation on earth refuses to help, treating brave, resourceful people as a threat. With a world of refugees so desperately in need, this is the time to live up to our immigrant heritage—offering to share America's bountiful opportunities.

# 178. How Many Embassies Do We Need?

*September 2, 1987*

The U.S. Embassy in Austria fills a large building on Boltzmanngasse Street in the north of Vienna. The heavy steel doors are opened and closed by a security guard at the foot of the stairs; there is another door at the top, backed by a Marine guard in a separate enclosure.

The embassy is staffed by several hundred employees, including a high-profile ambassador; by all accounts they do a good job. But do we really need so many people in Austria, or in any other country, for that matter?

Last year the State Department spent $1.94 billion on administration alone. And in the age of terrorism, embassy security has become increasingly expensive.

Between 1980 and 1985 the State Department spent $966 million for new buildings and to upgrade old ones. Last year Congress appropriated $702 million for the same purpose; this year the department is spending another $340 million to protect U.S. facilities.

In fact, the administration has asked for a special security supplemental allotment of $.3 billion for salaries and $1 billion for building acquisition and maintenance as part of a multibillion-dollar program to fortify the compounds of American diplomats. The buildings are to include blast-resistant walls, spacious grounds and controlled entrances. The department argues that these steps are necessary to protect U.S. personnel.

However, the building program has been a fiscal disaster. The new chancery in Cairo was to cost $27 million; the total eventually will exceed $40 million. Roughly $3.6 million was spent on the ambassador's residence in the same city—nearly twice the estimated completion cost of $2 million—before the project was shelved because of poor workmanship.

Perhaps the most egregious disaster is the new U.S. Embassy in the Soviet Union. Hopelessly compromised by Soviet bugs, the building is six years behind schedule and more than $100 million over budget.

Concluded the House Appropriations Committee last year, "The appalling waste and mismanagement that have plagued so many [State Department] construction projects simply must stop."

But reform of departmental procedures is not enough. The more basic issue is whether we need the staff who are being housed and protected at such great expense.

In Fiji, for instance, the State Department first decided to build a new embassy residence for $1.7 million before eventually settling for an existing building costing $375,000.

The department also is spending $3.2 million for a new embassy in Guyana, a South American nation of 775,000 people. The new embassy for Belize will cost $33 million, nearly one-fourth of that nation's entire gross national product.

Why do we need an embassy in any of these countries? They may be very nice places to live, but it is hard to imagine anything of consequence coming out of our official relations with any of them. Such nations simply aren't important enough to warrant the cost.

Does a large embassy make sense in the Soviet Union? Yes—the issues that divide the two nations are many and complex and the diplomatic mission provides a cover for U.S. intelligence activities. But even in Moscow there is room for cuts: about 70 percent of the current staff represents agencies other than the State Department.

Embassies in even the smallest countries perform a number of functions, of course, like distributing visas to foreigners who want to visit the United States. But this nation is much more restrictive than European countries, like Austria, which allow anyone to enter. We could simply dispense with such unnecessary travel restrictions.

Closing down—or at least reducing—foreign missions also would reduce the amount of information sent to the State Department. But retired Foreign Service Officer John Krizay figures that the daily volume of embassy reports to the department exceeds by 250 to 300 times the volume of foreign reporting by *The New York Times*.

In fact, about half of mission reports have nothing to do with foreign policy. The State Department surely could get by without every one of the half-million reporting telegrams that annually pour in from embassies around the world.

While I was at the embassy in Vienna, I overheard one senior official dictating a memo decrying potential staff cutbacks.

"Essential embassy functions would be impaired," he warned.

Maybe so in his case. But an awful lot of the work conducted by U.S. diplomats overseas is anything but essential.

So it's time we followed the example of Uganda. While the United States is building a $30 million complex in that poor African country, Uganda is closing its embassy in Tokyo. The cost of living, the Ugandans have decided, is simply too high to justify staying around for the parties.

# Foreign Aid or Hindrance?

## 179. Cut Foreign Aid

*November 25, 1987*

Congress won't give the administration as much money as it wants, so, warns Secretary of State George Shultz, the world is coming to an end.

Says Shultz: "Much of what we have worked so hard to achieve over many years will wither. Our ability to act as a world leader engaged abroad as a force for progress, peace and human dignity will erode."

This would be a moving argument were there any evidence that foreign aid actually advances these goals. But after funneling nearly $400 billion over 40 years to almost every foreign nation, the United States has very little to show for its efforts.

Billions in development assistance year after year have had little discernible impact on Third World economic growth. America simply has created dozens of dependent client states.

Aid to subsidize foreign purchases of U.S. goods undoubtedly has enriched big American exporters—though at great taxpayer expense. But Third World borrowers often have ended up worse off, using cheap U.S. credit to finance the sort of money-losing, prestige industries that have resulted in an unendurable debt burden.

So-called security assistance now goes to more than 100 countries, including nations like Botswana, Jamaica, Bangladesh, Fiji and Luxembourg, which face no military threat. These funds may buy some influence with local regimes, but the long-term value of such outlays is largely nonexistent.

Indeed, in many cases foreign aid has been counterproductive, tying America to authoritarian regimes that subsequently were overthrown. Iran, Nicaragua and the Sudan, among others, were all recipients of large amounts of U.S. assistance before they moved away from American influence.

Anyway, Shultz is acting as if Congress were threatening to eliminate all

461

foreign outlays. But expenditures this year, roughly $13.2 billion, remain $4.8 billion above 1980 levels—a not insignificant 57 percent increase. That is more than enough money to fund programs that can demonstrate a genuine relationship to America's national interest.

What Shultz really is complaining about is that the high budget consensus that once backed growing foreign aid outlays, irrespective of their effectiveness, has collapsed. Now Congress and the administration have to make hard choices on how to divide a limited foreign aid pie, a painful experience for a Cabinet member used to having his demands for ever more cash rubber-stamped by Congress.

The hero in this saga is the much-maligned Gramm-Rudman-Hollings deficit bill.

No one took the legislation seriously even before the Supreme Court voided the bill's enforcement mechanism. Virtually everyone, including members of Congress, expected Capitol Hill to continue its spendthrift ways.

But Gramm-Rudman has placed surprising pressure on Capitol Hill to curb spending growth, especially for a program that middle-class America loathes: foreign aid.

In fact, foreign assistance never has been popular, especially with conservatives. But President Reagan treated the program as one of his favorites, upping outlays from $8.4 billion in 1980 to $15.5 billion in 1986, an 85 percent increase.

Though Reagan focused his attention on security assistance, more than doubling those expenditures, he hiked economic aid as well. Between 1980 and 1986 development outlays climbed from $3.6 billion to $5 billion.

But Gramm-Rudman brought an end to the administration's free-spending ways. Economic assistance peaked in 1985; 1986 was the high point for security assistance. Reagan requested a total of $15.9 billion for 1987, but Congress only approved $13.2 billion.

Nevertheless, the administration, predicting imminent doom if its request was denied, asked for a $2 billion increase in budget authority for 1988. Complained Rep. Mickey Edwards, R-Okla., to one State Department witness, "We need to get beyond the public statements about how our nation's ability to conduct foreign policy is in jeopardy because of the cuts in foreign aid. We really need to be facing reality."

Which is all to the good. Shultz continues to frantically lobby for more foreign aid money, not because it has proved effective in promoting Third World economic growth, ending hunger abroad, or containing communism, but because it functions as "walking-around money" for him to use to buy access to foreign dictators. That wouldn't be an appropriate use of Americans' money even if the budget were in surplus. It certainly is not justified given the continuing need for serious budget restraint.

The benefits of foreign aid have almost always been assumed rather than proved. We can thank Gramm-Rudman for forcing Congress to start paring away these perennially wasted billions.

## 180. Foreign Aid Prescriptions

*September 1986*

*Reagan's America should only help those who help themselves.*

In June the United Nations General Assembly adopted a resolution calling for a five-year infusion of $128 billion into Africa. One-third of that, naturally, is expected to be foreign aid from the West: African leaders promised to raise the rest, as well as to reform their own domestic policies to promote economic growth.

The willingness of struggling Third World nations to acknowledge the failure of their statist development strategies is a welcome step forward. But action, not just talk, is necessary before Africa can reverse its slide into economic oblivion. And billions more in aid from abroad will do little other than reduce the pressure on recipient governments to introduce reforms.

There is no clearer example of the failure of foreign aid than the tragedy in Ethiopia. That country's problem is not one of insufficient funds; Ethiopia collected more than $900 million in bilateral and multilateral assistance between 1979 and 1982. Nevertheless, Ethiopia is today the poorest nation on earth. The basic problem in Ethiopia, as elsewhere, is a totalitarian political and economic system that cannot meet its people's needs under any circumstances.

But no matter how powerful the evidence that international assistance programs are mostly useless, and often harmful, foreign aid remains one of the constants of the federal budget. The amount spent may decrease in the era of Gramm-Rudman, but the U.S. government will continue to spew forth a cornucopia of dollars to other lands. The practical question, then, is not how to cut assistance programs, but how to transform them into something that will promote economic progress abroad, in however attenuated a form.

Between 1946 and 1983 the U.S. contributed more than $131 billion in grants and loans for economic assistance alone; the Export-Import Bank and other federal agencies added another $55 billion in loans to that total.

Military aid during the same period topped $100 billion, and humanitarian assistance ran some $34 billion. In all, Americans have loaned or given away more than $320 billion since World War II.

American bilateral aid has been supplemented by nearly $173 billion from a dozen multilateral organizations over the same period. Since the U.S. is a member of most of these bodies, $40 billion or so of that assistance came from the U.S. The steady multi-billion dollar flow, moreover, is supplemented by nearly $1 trillion in lending by Western commercial banks and other institutions.

Almost two-thirds of this assistance is intended to promote economic development. In fact, its effect has been quite the opposite. By providing governments with bundles of extra cash, says British economist P.T. Bauer, international aid "accelerates and aggravates the disastrous politicization of life in the Third World." In societies where politics already dominates everything else, and where few alternative social and economic power structures exist, official foreign aid makes the government sector almost omnipotent. As a result, the brightest and most ambitious people in society are further channeled into the state sector, dampening any entrepreneurial possibilities.

Not surprisingly, the World Bank's 1983 World Development Report found that the degree of state interference was dramatically and inversely related to economic growth rates, as well as production and savings levels. Experience yields a similar conclusion: countries that maintain market-oriented policies, whether Hong Kong, Taiwan, Singapore, South Korea, the Ivory Coast, or Sri Lanka, have achieved relatively high levels of economic development, often in dramatic contrast to their neighbors, which rely on state direction of the economy.

In some cases, unfortunately, no reform can be expected—Ethiopia, for example—and the U.S. should thus cut off economic aid entirely. But in cases where countries, though authoritarian, are inclined to be pragmatic, a new, market-oriented foreign-assistance strategy may yield significant results. For any reforms to be successful, however, there has to be a fundamental change in the way policy-makers think about the foreign-aid issue.

For example, they should recognize budgetary reality: the new initiative should be implemented with existing funds and food stocks. There is always a surplus of ideas on how to spend more money—the Administration has pushed a special $500 million African Economic Policy Initiative, for instance. But U.S. taxpayers already contribute nearly $10 billion annually in economic assistance, surely enough to pursue an effective foreign-aid policy.

Congress also needs to give the Administration wider latitude in reprogramming existing funds—the bulk of development funding is currently set both by program area and country—and in using existing "sunk cost" resources, such as stockpiled crops and local currencies generated by the Food for Peace program, in innovative ways. Otherwise, congressional micromanagement will kill any prospect for genuine change.

Equally important, Administration appointees must support the new free-market assistance strategy. It is said that State Department and AID officials always oppose reductions in foreign assistance to a nation for one of two reasons: our bilateral relations with the aid recipient are getting better, or they are growing worse. The foreign policy leadership, above all the President, must be committed to overriding pervasive bureaucratic resistance if a new program is not to be stillborn.

If these conditions are met, can a market-oriented aid policy make a difference? Yes, though only if the program changes are fundamental and are pursued vigorously. AID under Reagan, for instance, has rhetorically committed itself to a market-oriented foreign-assistance strategy, making "economic policy reform" and "private sector participation" two of its major objectives. However, internal bureaucratic opposition, limited authority to cut off aid monies, and inadequate vision have greatly undercut the impact of the Administration's reforms.

Thus, a more far-reaching market initiative is needed, one that encourages both substantive change and a greater likelihood of practical success. One possible, fourfold approach would involve:

• *Conditioning Aid on Policy Reform.* Many foreign-aid recipients have a host of "parastatals"—government-owned enterprises—that lose money, draining away valuable capital and personnel from more productive economic sectors. Restrictions on prices and production skew the incentives of suppliers and the demand of consumers, distorting the whole economy. There are also perverse monetary, fiscal, and credit policies, contributing to widespread economic instability and stagnation. And foreign investment is actively discouraged by many developing countries.

To correct these disastrous policies, the United States must be willing to condition its aid on genuine policy reform, which also means that we must be willing to cut off recalcitrant regimes if such reform is not forthcoming. A number of Third World countries, such as Bangladesh, Morocco, and Ecuador, are already moving, albeit haltingly and usually only after exhausting all alternatives, in the direction of a freer market. Knowing that continued aid depended on additional economic reform would encourage regimes to continue and expand those changes.

Further, despite minimal authority to reshuffle assistance monies, AID has made "policy dialogue" one of its major goals and has had some success in convincing recipients of U.S. funds to reform their economic policies. The agency helped convince Bangladesh to reduce its role in the retailing of fertilizer, for instance. The overall effect has been small, but again the trend is positive. If the Administration possessed—and was willing to use—authority to reward and punish countries based on their domestic policies, more significant reforms should be possible.

• *Funneling Assistance Through the Indigenous Private Sector.* AID has made development of local enterprises another of its basic goals. Unfortunately, the portion of the budget devoted to the Private Enterprise Bureau is minuscule, and some of the agency's efforts have done more to subsidize U.S. firms and local governments than promote efficient local businesses.

With greater flexibility in the use of funds, however, there are ways to keep foreign aid out of the hands of local governments. In particular, assistance could be loaned directly to private individuals and businesses, either through AID directly, or through intermediaries, such as American Private Voluntary Organizations like CARE and Catholic Relief Services and indigenous private banks and credit unions. Dr. Carl Liedholm, a professor of economics at Michigan State University, reports that these sorts of credit programs have the greatest chance of success if they rely on working rather than fixed capital, use local institutions to screen borrowers, and make initial loans for small amounts and short periods to encourage repayment.

There's no reason why the U.S. cannot press the World Bank and other international financial institutions to direct more of their lending to private firms. The Asian Development Bank has begun a loan program for local firms without requiring local government participation, as it has in the past; the other regional development banks could do likewise.

Providing financing—at roughly market interest rates—to local enterprises would be particularly important in countries where the government monopolizes financial institutions and uses credit for domestic political ends. Creating private financial conduits for locally owned enterprises also is important because the majority of firms in Third World nations are small and rural-based, while the economic policies of their governments tend to favor larger industries located in urban areas.

The success of this approach, however, will be limited by two factors. One is that unless fundamental economic reforms are adopted, local businesses, even with new sources of capital, will not flourish. The other is that the amount of money available for distribution to private operators will be constrained by the size of the bribe necessary to convince local authorities to change their policies. Where regimes are fearful of any economic growth outside of their control, they may block private sector assistance even if government-to-government aid is contingent on accepting such a program.

• *Lending Food for Peace Monies to Local Enterprises.* The Food for Peace program generates significant amounts of funds which could easily be shifted to support a market-oriented strategy. Currently Title I of Public Law 480—which provided for about $985 million in aid last year—also allows the U.S. to sell food, on credit, to developing nations. Repayment, at interest rates of two to three percent, begins ten years after the loan is made; in the meantime, the recipient government must give the U.S. the equivalent amount in local currency. Those funds are usually left with the borrower as long as he pledges to undertake "self-help projects." Unfortunately, in the words of one Senate staffer, P.L. 480 recipients just "use the funds to hire more people for the central government."

The U.S. could better use these funds by lending to local businesses through financial intermediaries. The process would be similar to that proposed for general U.S. aid, except that to preclude any budget increase these funds would have to be repaid to the U.S. government beginning in ten years. Such a program shift would be quite practical: Senator Jesse Helms pushed through an amendment to the Farm Bill which designated ten percent of Title I funds a year for this purpose. Within a month of the measure's passage, cooperatives and Private Voluntary Organizations had already met to discuss methods of distributing the funds. American corporations, too, have indicated an interest in working with partner firms in developing countries to loan out P.L. 480 money.

• *Using Crop Surpluses as Inducements.* As of last fall the Commodity Credit Corporation possessed nearly $5.6 billion in crops purchased from farmers to help prop up domestic prices. That includes 2.1 billion pounds of dairy products, 407 million bushels of wheat, 225 million bushels of corn, 410 million pounds of rice, 112 million bushels of grain sorghum, and four million bushels of soybeans. These stockpiles are of no use to Americans, since the food cannot be released on the U.S. market except in limited distributions to the poor; indeed, the federal government spends hundreds of millions of dollars every year to process and store the surplus. These supplies could easily be used as another tool to reward Third World governments that initiated genuine policy reform, particularly in the area of agriculture.

AID and State need legislative authority to use the crops to encourage cooperation by recipient nations. A modest "Food for Progress" program, utilizing two to three percent of the corn, wheat, and sorghum reserves, and 25 percent of the rick stockpile, was developed within the Administration last year, but opposition from AID—which administers existing P.L.

480 programs and therefore favored the status quo for bureaucratic reasons—killed it.

Nevertheless, Helms and other Agriculture Committee members, like Rudy Boschwitz, included a modest version of this initiative in the Senate Farm Bill. The program would not be tied to yearly appropriations and would focus on promoting market-oriented agricultural policy reforms. Moreover, Food for Progress will actually save money: the Department of Agriculture estimates that the cost of processing and bagging food under the original Administration proposal would have run $43.3 million, less than half the $89.1 million cost of continuing to store the same supplies.

Most important, this approach, if expanded, will help recipients buffer the impact of policy reforms—including those adopted in response to the conditioning of other U.S. foreign assistance—on politically sensitive groups, particularly urban populations. Most Third World nations now control food prices to pacify consumers; Egyptian farmers are said to buy bread to feed their chickens because it is cheaper than unprocessed wheat. Extra crop shipments would allow countries to maintain modified subsidies of food prices, for example, while paying domestic farmers at market levels.

Distribution of the aid would have to be carefully controlled so as not to undercut demand for domestic foodstuffs; traditional Food for Peace shipments have damaged indigenous farmers in countries like Guatemala, Haiti, and India by driving down crop prices. But the availability of large stocks of wheat, corn, rice, and other products would be a powerful inducement for regimes to modify or abandon their most damaging economic controls. Countries would develop most quickly without any subsidies or economic distortions; but the political situation in most of them ensures that such state intervention will not disappear overnight. Surplus U.S. grains could help ease the transition.

In a perfect world there would be no government-to-government foreign aid, at least not for development purposes. But large-scale U.S. economic assistance is not going to disappear any time soon.

Therefore, if foreign aid is to have any beneficial impact, existing programs must be fundamentally restructured. First, aid levels should come down, not go up. The U.S. must not let pressure for increased appropriations obscure the real cause of global underdevelopment: Third World regimes that stifle economic incentives, confiscate personal earnings, discourage private investment, and terrorize their people.

Second, assistance should be carefully targeted, to reward countries that adopt growth-producing policies and to punish recipients that do not. Some countries may not be willing to cooperate with the U.S. at any price; cutting them off, even if they are the poorest of the poor, would be painful but necessary. For continuing to subsidize governments that knowingly wreck their economies, whether for political or ideological reasons, would be far crueler.

Other regimes, however, may be pragmatic or desperate enough to respond to the new American approach, making everyone better off, particularly the Third World peoples most in need. And that, at least, would make the annual foreign-aid bite a little less painful.

## 181. The Marshall Plan Myth

*June 3, 1987*

Forty years ago Secretary of State George Marshall gave a speech that changed history. At Harvard's commencement on June 5, 1947, Marshall proposed a massive economic aid program for Europe, later known as the "Marshall Plan."

The program soon passed into popular mythology, being viewed as the savior of Europe from both economic ruin and communist aggression.

Indeed, so powerful has the Marshall Plan legend become that hardly a month passes without someone proposing a similar initiative for one or another underdeveloped region of the globe.

But the problems of the Third World today bear little relationship to Europe's situation after World War II. That continent's industrial base was devastated, but its legal system, economic infrastructure and educational standards remained. Europe had to reconstruct what had been, not develop what never had been.

In contrast, massive new infusions of aid to deteriorating, statist economies in Africa or Latin America would promote more political graft and waste, not economic prosperity. Indeed, the Third World has amassed a $1 trillion debt even without the benefit of a "Marshall Plan." The problem is that these vast resources have been squandered.

But the more fundamental flaw in the call for a huge new foreign assistance program is that the success of the Marshall Plan is largely an illusion. Europe did indeed recover, but, contends University of California economist Tyler Cowen, it did so in spite of, not because of, U.S. assistance.

In fact, Cowen has debunked several myths surrounding the Marshall Plan, including the belief that U.S. aid spurred the European recovery.

First, despite all of the publicity surrounding the program, the Marshall Plan's transfers never exceeded 5 percent of the gross national product of the recipient nations. These funds were simply not enough to make a major difference.

More important, it was Nazi economic controls—maintained even after the European countries were liberated—rather than a cash shortage that originally hampered the continent's recovery.

"Rapid economic growth occurred only after the controls were lifted and sound economic policy established," observes Cowen. "This happened irrespective of the timing and extent of Marshall Plan aid."

Countries like Germany, Italy and France started to recover before the Marshall Plan took effect; Austria and Greece did not start to grow until aid was ending.

In Germany, for instance, the country's economic miracle began when economic director Ludwig Erhard eliminated price controls and other restrictions in July 1948, months before U.S. funds started flowing into the economy. Indeed, the Marshall Plan actually did not increase German resources; the aid funds were less than half of the 11 percent to 15 percent of GNP estimated to have been absorbed occupation costs. That is, Germany recovered while money was being siphoned out of its economy.

The experience in Belgium was similar. One month after its liberation in 1944, the government threw out the Nazis' statist economic policies. The nation then recovered faster than any other—years before the Marshall Plan had even been formulated.

Another Marshall Plan myth is that the U.S. aid program promoted market economic policies in Europe. But the program was administered by the same government that had greatly expanded public control of the American economy.

Thus, U.S. officials encouraged state planning in France and opposed Italian efforts to liberalize. Says Harry Bayard Price in his exhaustive study of the Marshall Plan, the aid program caused many European governments to expand "the apparatus for central supervision of their economies."

Another myth is that the Marshall Plan stimulated the American economy. While U.S. aid may have generated some export business, it did not make up for the $17 billion extracted from the domestic economy. Giving away money abroad in the hope that some of it ultimately will be spent at home is a losing proposition.

Legends die hard. And with the anniversary of Secretary Marshall's speech upon us, Americans are going to be hearing no end of tributes about his vision and farsightedness.

But the experience of the Marshall Plan, as well as a host of other foreign assistance programs, actually shows how little such transfers help other nations develop. It is sensible domestic economic policies, stable legal systems, and positive cultural attitudes that promote economic progress.

So the poor nations of the globe don't need a new "Marshall Plan." Instead, what they require is the good sense to follow the market-oriented domestic policies that really caused Europe to recover four decades ago.

## 182.  The Foreign Aid Panacea

*April 6, 1988*

The nation's capital is full of people who want to save the world. Unfortunately, however, they have yet to learn that good intentions are not enough.

The latest example of foolishness covered with a humanitarian gloss is the "Global Poverty Reduction Act," newly introduced by a bipartisan gaggle of congressmen. The legislation requires the president to develop an international plan that "would contribute measurably to eradicating the worst aspects of absolute poverty by the year 2000." As originally written, the bill would have ordered the president to do so without relying on measures to spur poor nations' economic growth.

The human tragedy of international underdevelopment is appalling, of course: 38,000 children die daily around the world from starvation and related diseases. Americans should do all that they can to help stem this human carnage. But more foreign aid—officials at the Agency for International Development (AID) figure the bill's cumulative price tag could run anywhere between $30 billion and $300 billion (depending on the specific policies adopted)—is simply not the answer.

Developing nations have not lacked for financial assistance. The United States alone has provided nearly $400 billion in grants and loans to poor nations over the last four decades and the Third World owes Western banks $1.2 trillion. The problem is that this bounty has been largely squandered.

And there is no reason to believe that new financial transfers would have any more beneficial an impact. Waste and abuse are endemic to autocratic governments dedicated more to their own survival than to the welfare of their citizens.

The only way to lift Third World people out of poverty, then, is to promote self-sustaining economic growth. While overall prosperity may not be sufficient to ensure that everyone receives enough food, health care and shelter, it is a necessary condition.

For example, only four of the 37 poorest countries have life expectancies at birth above 54 years; 26 of the 36 middle-income nations fall into that category. No high-income state has a life expectancy below 54 years.

This relationship should come as no surprise. Advanced medical treatment, larger meals and better schooling all arise naturally in a system where people are doing better economically.

True, a foreign donor can construct a clinic or school in a poor Third World country. But such projects are not sustainable unless the nation has achieved some minimal level of development.

For example, even as AID was building a new hospital in Cairo last year 21 others sat unfinished, some started as long ago as 1963. Even when such facilities are completed underdeveloped countries often cannot afford to staff them.

How can the U.S. spur Third World economic growth? Not through more foreign aid.

The world's poorest country, Ethiopia, collected $1.8 billion between 1982 and 1985. Yet masses of its people starve, largely because the brutal Communist dictatorship has collectivized the economy, including agriculture, and forcibly relocated much of its population.

India is the largest borrower from the World Bank and a foreign aid favorite: it ranks near the top of the world's poverty sweepstakes, with a per capita gross national product of $270. Tanzania, which has received more assistance per capita than any other nation, is only slightly better off with a per capita GNP of $290.

In short, there is no evidence that foreign financial transfers alone achieve anything.

But not all small foreign states are poor. Both Taiwan and South Korea have made dramatic progress in recent decades, far outstripping their ethnic neighbors, China and North Korea, respectively. Singapore and Hong Kong lack natural resources but have also performed spectacularly.

Thus, what is critical to the development process are sound domestic economic policies. Does a country welcome or discourage foreign investment, for instance?

Are farmers allowed to sell their crops at market prices? Is domestic capital wasted in huge, inefficient state enterprises? Do small entrepreneurs have access to credit? The answers to questions like these determine both whether a country will grow and whether its people will be fed and cared for.

No one can disagree with a goal of reducing or eliminating world poverty. We have a moral responsibility to care for those in need, both at home and abroad.

But the "Global Poverty Reduction Act" would throw good money after bad without addressing the fundamental causes of Third World suffering. The future of developing states ultimately lies in their, not America's, hands. And until those governments give their people the freedom necessary to survive and prosper, there is very little that Congress or the president can do to help.

# 183. Starving the Third World

*August 17, 1988*

The American people are nothing if not well-intentioned. Every year the United States sends between $1.5 billion and $2 billion worth of food to Third World countries.

Yet the so-called Food for Peace program, also known as P.L. 480, actually causes wide-spread hunger abroad. For every starving person who makes a meal with U.S. grain, there may be another who does not have food because P.L. 480 shipments have put local farmers out of business. Indeed, argues Washington analyst James Bovard, Food for Peace "has been one of the most harmful" foreign aid programs.

During the early 1950s crop surpluses began to accumulate due to the federal government's generous agricultural price support programs. To solve this embarrassing political problem, Congress created the Food for Peace program.

Enacted in 1954, P.L. 480 subsidizes food shipments to poorer nations. The program's prime objective has always been to unload the maximum amount of crops, not to promote agricultural self-sufficiency abroad.

The basic problem is simple: Consumers will not pay for what they can get for free. Dumping tons of free or cheap crops in small nations inevitably harms local farmers.

Were American aid limited to instances where a natural disaster had disrupted indigenous supplies, production disincentives would be less serious a concern, but just 14 percent of P.L. 480 shipments go to disaster areas; the rest provides an unending dole for Third World governments.

One of the early "beneficiaries" of P.L. 480 was India, where huge wheat shipments discouraged local production. Assistant Secretary of Agriculture George Dunlop admits that American food may have helped cause mass starvation.

Food for Peace shipments to Indonesia and Pakistan during the 1960s had similar consequences. According to the General Accounting Office, U.S. food aid "restricted agricultural growth by allowing the governments to (1) postpone essential agricultural reforms, (2) fail to give agricultural investment sufficient priority, and (3) maintain a pricing system which gave farmers an inadequate incentive to increase production."

Unfortunately, U.S. policymakers consistently ignored such evidence of the harm wreaked by P.L. 480 and continued to shovel food into poor nations. In 1976 shipments of wheat to Guatemala impoverished farmers who had just harvested a bountiful crop; three years later one development consultant reported that producers in Haiti do "not even bring their crops to market the week that [U.S. food] is being distributed since they are unable to get a fair price."

Nor has anything changed under the Reagan administration. In 1984 P.L. 480 rice shipments to Jamaica ruined local farmers. In the same year the United States helped Jamaica develop a food stamp program that serves half the population; complains University of Jamaica political scientist Carl Stone, "Our people are being subsidized to buy imported food when our farmers can't sell their produce."

And last year the Agency for International Development, which manages the P.L. 480 program, acknowledged that "nearly all" Food for Peace "deliveries to Somalia in 1985 and 1986 arrived at the worst possible time, the harvest months." The result? The "deliveries lowered farmers' prices thereby discouraging domestic production."

Where Third World people don't want the American food, Washington has forced it on them. In 1985 and 1986, for instance, U.S. officials conspired with Senegal to close local cracked rice markets to force the Senegalese people to eat the whole-grain rice shipped under P.L. 480.

Other abuses—well documented by Bovard in a new Heritage Foundation study—include the sale of U.S. food by Congo and Ethiopia to buy arms. Mauritus used P.L. 480 shipments to feed foreign toursts. Cape Verde requested American food aid even as it was selling donated wheat to other countries. And so on.

Congress has tried to reform the program from time to time, but no amount of tinkering will solve the most fundamental problem: Food for Peace is designed to dump crops, not advance Third World development. As such, the program is fatally flawed.

It's time for Congress to abolish P.L. 480. Domestic crop surpluses could be easily eliminated by killing the price support programs that cost taxpayers more than $20 billion annually.

And the problem of foreign hunger could best be left to private organizations, which represent neither the farm lobby nor foreign dictators. At most the United States should provide limited food shipments as temporary help after a natural disaster. Anything else, such as P.L. 480 today, will do more harm than good.

# 184. Mengistu's Policies Responsible for Famine

*April 12, 1986*

Few issues unite the American people as does fighting world hunger: individuals, private aid agencies, and the government contributed in excess of $1 billion for Ethiopia alone last year.

Yet even as the tragedy fades from the top of the news, warns Rep. Howard Wolpe (D.-Mich.), chairman of the House Foreign Affairs Subcommittee on Africa, the impression that the crisis has been resolved stems from "a false sense of optimism."

Indeed, the U.N. Office for Emergency Operations estimates that roughly one million metric tons of grain—as much as was donated in 1985—will be needed this year to meet the food needs of Ethiopians. Heroic relief efforts apparently have done nothing to solve the underlying crisis, with as many as six million Ethiopians still threatened with permanent harm or death.

Despite the Administration's vigorous response, criticism from abroad and at home has been unrelenting. Ethiopian officials rebuked Western donors for their "apathy" and "neglect" which caused the "current tragedy." Only slightly less obscene was the behavior of House Speaker Tip O'Neill, who in one instance pointed to television reports of starving African children and blamed the Administration for "allowing this to happen."

The calamity in Ethiopia and elsewhere demonstrates the appalling failure of foreign aid, but not due to inadequate spending. The U.S. has not been niggardly when it comes to food assistance; outlays under P.L. 480, or "Food for Peace," have grown under Reagan; in 1984 the U.S. provided roughly half of all food aid to Africa.

Nor is the problem of underdevelopment one of insufficient cash. Ethiopia received nearly $1 billion in aid between 1979 and 1982 alone. Yet that country is less able to cope with drought and famine now than it was in 1974, when 200,000 Ethiopians perished.

In fact, Ethiopia is the poorest country in the world. Its per capita food production has dropped sharply and its per capita GNP has stagnated; growth rates for both the agricultural and manufacturing sectors have steadily, and dramatically, fallen.

The consistent failure of massive infusions of money and food in developing nations should give supporters of foreign aid pause before they propose their perennial panacea: more. For countries like Ethiopia suffer so grievously for reasons other than just unfavorable weather and lack of arable land. Unfortunately, most Third World regimes knowingly adopt policies guaranteed to result in poverty, ill-health, and death for many of their people.

First, many governments, like Ethiopia's, simply do not value human life. For a time Mengistu refused to acknowledge the existence of a problem, and denied journalists and relief workers access to distressed areas.

The government also refused to buy food from abroad; when it finally decided to act, it had insufficient foreign reserves to make the purchases, having spent as much as $200 million celebrating its tenth anniversary in power. Then tons of U.S. food aid rotted on piers in port when Mengistu failed to release military trucks to transport the produce to the dying. Even today, grain sits in ships for months before it is unloaded, let alone transported inland.

The regime long refused to allow food aid to rebel-held areas. And Mengistu has used donated grain, powdered milk and butter to pay his troops, conserving cash for purchasing higher-priority items like bombs.

At the same time, reports the French humanitarian group, Medecins Sans Frontieres, the Ethiopian government is siphoning off Western aid to undertake a massive resettlement program that has killed an incredible 100,000 people: "International assistance is being used in such a way that it is killing more people than it is saving," says Dr. Claude Malhuret, a spokesman for the organization.

Second, many governments throughout the developing world have adopted economic policies that do not—indeed, which cannot—work.

In 1983, the World Bank estimated that ill-considered government intervention in the form of subsidies and price controls "alone may slow down GDP growth by as much as two percentage points a year."

Uneconomic state enterprises, bloated bureaucracies, stifling restrictions on indigenous private enterprise, and barriers to foreign investment also contribute to economic chaos, not growth. As long-term African correspondent Xan Smiley observed in the *Atlantic Monthly,* "It is mainly the fault of the Africans themselves that African economies have collapsed."

A decade ago Ethiopia, for instance, embarked on a grand Socialist experiment. Virtually every sector of the economy, including agriculture, was placed under close state control.

Large farms were nationalized, small farmers were moved under the Socialist Resettlement Program, and collective state farms were established. Peasants who continued to work their own fields were prohibited from hiring help. The results were the same as for socialized agriculture in Tanzania and the Soviet Union: huge losses and little production.

What should U.S. policy be, in light of the fact that many Third World leaders not only seem unconcerned about the well-being of their subjects, but also regularly disable their countries' economies? The usual response is simply more. More money, more food, more equipment, more everything. But what may superficially appear to be the most humane response is something quite different.

For one thing, food aid can have perverse long-term consequences. Over the years P.L. 480 food sales and donations have undercut domestic farmers in such nations as India, Haiti and Guatemala.

An audit conducted by the Agency for International Development of food shipments to Kenya and neighboring countries concluded that "the long-term feeding programs in the same areas for 10 years or more have great potential for food production and family planning disincentives." Former U.N. official Sudhir Sen has bluntly declared that "Food for Peace became a stumbling block to development."

Moreover, massive aid from abroad effectively subsidizes the very policies that are in large part responsible for mass starvation today. Regimes that keep food prices low to enrich powerful interest groups or collectivize their farmers to satisfy ideological whims are in effect rewarded when the U.S. ameliorates the disastrous, and foreseeable, consequences. In the case of Ethiopia, assistance simply covers the financial deficit left by the Mengistu government's anniversary celebration and huge military buildup, and helps the regime continue to fight its unceasing wars and resettle its hapless peasants.

Therefore, the U.S. should provide only limited amounts of emergency aid, and only for short periods of time. Further, the government should closely control the distribution of food and other products, and condition assistance on substantive reforms in the policies of recipient nations.

We must be sensitive to the many problems of underdevelopment—most obviously that of widespread starvation—and the pain that people all over the world continue to endure as their nations enter the industrial age. But shoveling more money abroad in a manner that does no good—or even causes harm—is not compassionate.

Though to not act vigorously might seem harsh, to act, thereby perpetuating the causes of Third World poverty, disease and hunger, would be far more cruel. The result of such a policy may be more dead today. But unless governments throughout the Third World dramatically change direction, there will be far more dead tomorrow.

## 185. Aid Money That Just Buys Guns

*June 14, 1988*

The Third United Nations Special Session on Disarmament is meeting in New York and the air is full of denunciations of the superpowers. But some of the Third World nations now staggering beneath billions of dollars of debt are equally guilty of excessive arms purchases. In fact, if these overburdened debtors are serious about devoting more money to economic investment and social welfare, they need only stop buying so many guns.

According to the Arms Control and Disarmament Agency, between 1980 and 1985 developing nations spent $924.6 billion on their militaries. Many of these nations faced no serious security threat; instead, the arms were meant for foreign aggression and domestic repression. Had Third World states cut this spending by one-third, they would have had an extra $58 billion in capital in 1985 alone, slightly more than enough to cover the annual interest on all LDC loans.

*Soviets' Role*

In fact, international aid largely serves to underwrite poor nations' prodigious appetites for weapons. The U.S. and a few other nations provide some assistance explicitly for military purposes, but America's $27.4 billion in "security aid" between 1980 and 1985, for instance, did not come close to covering even the Third World's bill for imported arms, $213 billion, during the same period. The Soviet arms role was larger, but not by terribly much.

Instead, payment was provided largely by the West's many generous economic and humanitarian programs, which channeled $239 billion to developing states from 1980 to 1985. The U.S. gave $44 billion in bilateral economic aid; other nations, principally the Europeans and Japan, contributed roughly $75 billion; and various international agencies allocated an additional $121 billion.

Year after year, foreign aid has in effect fueled a massive arms race in poor debtor countries. A longer view only enhances this picture. From 1970 to 1985, for example, military spending of developing countries grew about fourfold in current-dollar terms, about the same magnitude of increase as for total U.S. economic aid. U.S. security assistance in the period didn't even double in current dollars.

Of course, aid shuffles are not the intent of the nations and organizations that provide loans purportedly for dams, power plants or housing projects. But money is fungible. By underwriting specific development projects, Western donors and lenders free up domestic capital for military uses. Were the foreign aid—and commercial credit—not available, Third World governments would have to make far tougher choices before allocating so much of their limited resources to guns.

Though the relationship between aid inflows and weapons purchases is not a simple one, in a number of cases increased assistance has been matched by higher defense spending or arms imports. In Ethiopia, Ghana, India and Nepal, for instance, foreign-aid increases between 1982 and 1985 were generally matched by higher military spending.

Reductions in assistance during the same period were reflected by either falling overall military outlays or weapons imports in such countries as Burma, Chile, Congo, Ivory Coast, Jamaica, Jordan, Liberia, Mauritania, Nigeria, Paraguay, Somalia, Suriname, Tanzania, the Yemen Arab Republic and Zimbabwe. In Burundi and Haiti both aid and military expenditures remained relatively constant, while in Malaysia defense expenditures, arms imports and assistance all moved both up and down, roughly in concert.

Among the poor states that devote disproportionate shares of their gross national products to military purposes are Mozambique (38%), Egypt and Pakistan (both 28%), Ethiopia (more than 25%) and Laos and Zambia (about 20%).

This Western-subsidized arms race has been catastrophic for Third World peoples. A U.N. study of 54 developing nations concluded that in every case higher defense spending resulted in lower economic growth; each additional dollar in military outlays cut agricultural output 20 cents.

Consider Ethiopia, one of the world's poorest countries. The Communist government is determined both to suppress Eritrean separatists and maintain its tyrannical control, and therefore spent $1.6 billion on its military between 1982 and 1985. During the same period it collected $1.8 billion in Western assistance. (Due to Soviet generosity, the value of Ethiopia's weapons imports, $3.6 billion, actually exceeded its defense expenditures.)

There's also Zambia, a country that recently pledged to undertake domestic economic reform but then backed away almost immediately from its promises. Aid from abroad, at $1.6 billion between 1982 and 1985, more than covered Kenneth Kaunda's $700 million arms buildup.

Zimbabwe is moving steadily toward a one-party dictatorship while remaining a favorite of Western donors. Military outlays ran $1.3 billion from 1982 to 1985. Foreign assistance over the same period was nearly $1.5 billion.

The list goes on. From 1982 to 1985, Egypt spent $24.4 billion on its military and imported $6.9 billion of weapons. At the same time, it collected $12.3 billion in foreign aid. During the same period Pakistan spent $7.8 billion on defense and received $3.3 billion in assistance. Tiny Guyana got $139 million and its arms outlays were $96 million.

It is not easy to tie particular aid packages to individual arms sales, since they usually are arranged separately by different ministries. But the timing of some transactions seems more than coincidental. In the fall of

1981 India was simultaneously negotiating a $2 billion purchase of 150 Mirage jets from France and a $3.6 billion loan from the International Monetary Fund. (India ultimately bought only 40 French planes, turning to the Soviets for additional fighters.)

In fact, India, which has proclaimed a desire to eliminate poverty by the year 2000, is engaged in an unprecendented arms buildup. Military expenditures totaled $26.5 billion between 1982 and 1985 and annual outlays have since jumped 60%, to roughly $12 billion. India plans to acquire nuclear submarines, aircraft carriers, new battletanks and lightweight combat aircraft. Its weapons imports alone ran $9.2 billion from 1982 to 1985.

That such an impoverished nation, with a per-capita income of $270, wants to become a regional superpower might not be our concern were it using its own money to buy arms. But India has long been a favorite of the international aid community, collecting $8.8 billion between 1982 and 1985. Last year alone the World Bank lent India $2.8 billion, much of it from the "soft-loan window," while the U.S. provided $137.7 million in bilateral assistance. Funds also regularly flow from the Asian Development Bank, the U.N. Development Program, European donors, and Japan—the latter, in fact, is expected to provide India with $1 billion in easy credit this year. Yet every dollar of assistance effectively will go to India's military.

If 40 years of attempting to buy friendships and promote political and economic change abroad have proved anything, it is that the U.S. has little control over the actions of other nations. No amount of American jawboning will prevent sovereign countries from spending themselves into poverty in an effort to expand their militaries for political reasons.

But the U.S. can stop subsidizing the foreign arms buildup. In fact, the Agency for International Development has a legal responsibility to do so— the Foreign Assistance Act requires the president to take into account military expenditures by recipient governments before doling out funds. In the past, AID has routinely concluded that no country, even relatively unfriendly ones such as Zambia, should be barred from receiving assistance because of excessive arms expenditures. But the new AID administrator, Alan Woods, has made a point of linking uncontrolled military spending to underdevelopment. He should turn rhetoric into action by recommending the end of U.S. aid to dozens of nations that are essentially using American economic and humanitarian assistance for military purposes.

*Foreign Bailout*

Such a cutoff just might have an impact. Nigeria, for instance, allocated $5.8 billion for its military between 1982 and 1985, during which time it received $5.6 billion in Western aid. But Nigeria sharply cut its military expenditures in both 1984 and 1985 when Western assistance dropped. The same phenomenon was evident in the countries cited earlier.

France and West Germany now plan to forgive part of the debt of poorer African countries, but those debtors are largely responsible for their own plight. They should start cleaning up the mess themselves instead of looking for a foreign bailout. And their first step should be to slash unproductive weapons expenditures.

Until they do, the U.S. and other Western donors should refuse even to consider proposals for increased aid. For if Third World governments won't abandon their expensive militaristic programs, increased assistance, whether higher World Bank lending or additional U.S. support, will only subsidize more tanks and soldiers that will be used to terrorize domestic dissidents and neighboring nations alike.

## 186. U.S. Aid Is a Costly Disaster

*March 13, 1988*

Foreign assistance has been part of America's arsenal for overseas intervention since World War II. Between 1946 and 1986 the US contributed more than $370 billion in grants and loans to other nations. A number of US-financed multilateral agencies, such as the World Bank, spent another $239 billion during the same period.

Foreign aid spending has continued to increase in virtually every category despite the advent of the Reagan administration. In 1980, Jimmy Carter's last year in office, outlays ran $8.4 billion. In 1986, the total was $15.5 billion, an 85 percent increase. Under pressure to cut the deficit, Congress has begun paring administration requests, but outlays this year will remain well above the Carter-era levels.

US foreign aid falls into three broad, though related, categories: humanitarian, development, and security. Leading members of the foreign policy establishment seem to harbor few doubts about the efficacy of the different programs. Yet what evidence is there that they actually work? In 1983 even the Carlucci Commission admitted that it was not clear "that specific programs have been consistently effective with regard to any one objective." In fact, 40 years of experience indicates that few foreign aid programs do a good job of promoting their theoretical objectives, let alone America's overall interests.

The only apparent reason that grievous failure has been tolerated— indeed, rewarded with increased appropriations year after year—is because many US officials simply look at assistance as different forms of bribes to buy influence abroad. So long as the funds are thought to enhance the US ambassador's *entre* to foreign regimes, the State Department shows little concern over the programs' effectiveness in achieving their purported goals.

But what kind of access are we really buying? Much of the $14 billion spent in 1987 on foreign aid goes to either avowed adversaries of the US or hostile neutrals. This year, for example, the Reagan administration originally wanted to support 87 different countries that voted against the US in the United Nations at least two-thirds of the time. Another 13 would-be beneficiaries of US largesse opposed American interests at least half of the time.

Of course, UN votes may be an imperfect scale upon which to judge a country's friendship, but many aid beneficiaries are not friends of the US on any measure. Among the more egregious cases of American subsidies going to foreign adversaries:

• Angola. Bilateral aid to this Marxist nation has been low, but has continued to flow even as the US has assisted UNITA, the insurgent group. Since 1981 the US has given Angola $13 million in Food for Peace aid. Moreover, the Export-Import Bank has routinely subsidized Angolan purchases of American goods, underwriting $217.5 million worth of credit since 1980. Finally, during the last four years the African Development Bank, of which the US is a member, has pumped $80.2 million into the Angolan economy.

• People's Republic of China. It may be good politics to maintain friendly relations with the mainland, but that hardly justifies large-scale financial transfers to what remains a totalitarian state. The US provided China with $1.8 million during 1981 and 1982. Though Congress has since terminated bilateral aid, Export-Import Bank subsidies continue apace: last year the bank lent the PRC $37.1 million, on top of $65.4 million in 1986.

Even more significant has been international support for China. In November 1986, the PRC arranged a $484.1 million loan with the International Monetary Fund. Over the last three years China has also borrowed nearly $3.7 billion from the World Bank—more than $1.4 billion in 1987 alone. Finally, the United Nations Development Program (UNDP) has contributed $64.8 million to China since 1980.

• Ethiopia. This country's Communist government was largely responsible for the mass suffering caused by the drought in 1984 and 1985, yet America and other Western nations rushed in to provide the execrable Mengistu regime with $105.6 million between 1981 and 1987. Ethiopia has borrowed a total of $73.3 million from the Export-Import Bank since 1978.

Ethiopia has also been a major customer of the World Bank, collecting $324.5 million over the last three years alone. The African Development Bank has provided $227.8 million since 1979; the UNDP kicked in $55.6 million over the same period.

• Hungary. This Warsaw Pact nation does not currently receive direct US support, but it has borrowed $27 million from the Export-Import Bank in the past. In 1979 the Commodity Credit Corporation extended Hungary a $15.8 million loan. More important, Hungary regularly borrows from the World Bank—$833.7 million during the last three years.

• Laos. The Laos People's Democratic Republic, a nation that fell under Communist control along with Vietnam and Cambodia, borrowed $29.7 million from the World Bank in 1986 and 1987. During the past decade, Laos has also borrowed $60.4 million from the Asian Development Bank, of which the US is a member, and benefited from $41.9 million in assistance from the UNDP.

• Nicaragua. The Sandinistas long ago perverted the 1979 revolution that overthrew dictator Anastasio Somoza. Yet the US provided Nicaragua with $105 million in bilateral assistance in the early 1980s. At the same time, Nicaragua was borrowing $106.7 million from the World Bank and $140.1 million from the Inter-American Development Bank, which receives more than a third of its funds from the US. Though these lines of credit shut temporarily because of Nicaragua's default, the IDB recently released $11 million in prior disbursements that had been withheld. Also, the UNDP has funded $9.1 million worth of projects from 1980 to 1985 and other UN agencies contributed another $1.1 million to Nicaragua in 1986.

• Poland. Even as this Communist government was cracking down on the Solidarity labor union, the US was subsidizing the Jaruzelski regime. While aid tapered off after 1984—bilateral assistance totaled just $4.6 million during the last two years—from 1981 to 1984 Poland received $138.8 million, largely through the Food for Peace program. Moreover, Poland has been a customer of the Export-Import Bank in the past, accumulating almost $42.2 billion in loans and guarantees during the 1960s and 1970s. The UNDP has provided Poland $21.8 million in aid since 1953; Poland recently joined the World Bank and is now reportedly negotiating a $50 million loan from that institution.

• Romania. This thuggish regime, a desperately poor Stalinist holdover in Eastern Europe, received a $425,000 loan guarantee from the Export-Import Bank in 1986. Romania has been a major bank customer in the past, borrowing $267.8 million since 1962; during the same period Romania has also received $341.8 million in loans from other US agencies. Moreover, since 1962 Romania has borrowed $1.8 billion from the UNDP.

• Yugoslavia. Though this Communist nation has maintained a relatively independent national course, it has never done anything to warrant treatment as a close friend. Yet from 1981 to 1987 the US provided Yugoslavia with $550,000 in bilateral assistance. More important, the Export-Import Bank extended loan guarantees and insurance worth $159.1 million in 1986 and $83.6 million so far this year; between 1962 and 1986 Yugoslavia's credit from the Export-Import Bank came to $928 million. Over the years Yugoslavia has also received $187.8 in other US government loans, $38 million from the UNDP, and $4.7 billion from the World Bank—$504 million in the last three years alone.

Only slightly less disgraceful is American support for hostile neutral countries, nations that may not be formally arrayed against the US, but which nevertheless evince substantial animosity towards America. The US, it seems, believes in equal opportunity subsidies for all of its antagonists. Among the worse of these cases are Burma, Guyana, India, Tanzania, Mozambique, and Zimbabwe.

Indeed, Mozambique provides an example of the futility in attempting to use foreign aid to "wean" a self-proclaimed Marxist-Leninist regime away from the Soviet bloc. Mozambique has forged a close relationship with the USSR, is carrying on a brutal campaign against an anti-Communist insurgency, and ruthlessly suppresses human rights.

Nevertheless, the US has pumped more than $176 million into Mozambique since 1981—$85 million in 1987 alone. Mozambique borrowed $65 million over the last three years from World Bank. The Marxist state has also borrowed $109.8 million from the African development Bank since 1979 and received $40.1 million from the UNDP over the same period. Last June, Mozambique negotiated a $23.2 million loan from the International Monetary Fund.

Has this flood of Western money turned Mozambique away from the Soviets? That nation's president, Joaquim Chissano says his country will not reduce his reliance on Communist advisers or change his country's voting pattern in the U.N. Nor, he adds, should anyone "feel that we have doubts about the socialist vision."

At the end of World War II, America naively embarked on a crusade to reshape the world by creating several international organizations and distributing hundreds of billions in largesse abroad. Four decades of bitter experience has shown foreign aid to be largely a failure: The unending loans and grants have done far more to centralize Third World economies and strengthen brutal dictatorships than to promote economic development and political freedom.

But even more important, the use of American money to underwrite countries that routinely opposed US interests cannot be justified. With Gramm-Rudman putting increased pressure on all areas of the budget, there is no better time for Congress and the administration to reevaluate the foreign aid program, putting into effect some of the painful lessons about foreign assistance that they should have learned long ago.

## 187. Subsidizing Our Adversaries

*April 20, 1988*

Defending Europe against the Warsaw Pact will cost America anywhere between $114 billion and $171 billion this year. Nevertheless, neither budget pressures nor arms control agreements, promises President Reagan, will cause the United States to leave NATO.

Yet the very president who thinks nothing of spending $171 billion to protect Europe wants to subsidize one of the countries that supposedly threatens the continent's security. The administration is lobbying Congress to allow the Overseas Private Investment Corp., a federal agency, to underwrite American investment in Hungary.

OPIC was created in 1971 to "mobilize and facilitate the participation of United States private capital and skills in the economic and social development of less developed, friendly countries and areas." OPIC makes loans and loan guarantees to American firms; OPIC also provides political risk insurance to protect U.S. companies from losses caused by war or expropriation.

The agency now backs projects in some 100 countries. Subsidizing companies to invest in stable, prosperous states like Singapore, Korea, Taiwan and the Bahamas seems strange enough, but even more bizarre is OPIC's support for investors in communist Yugoslavia and China, as well as Marxist-leaning Mozambique.

At least none of these three countries is formally arrayed against the United States. But now OPIC wants to underwrite projects in Hungary, a Warsaw Pact member.

As always, the State Department believes it has good reasons for asking Congress to act against America's interest: The administration wants to wean Hungary away from the U.S.S.R. And Hungary says it hopes to expand its trade with the United States, which ran $560 million last year.

Does the administration really believe that a few dollars in federal aid can buy the friendship of a country occupied by Soviet troops? Of course we should encourage the Eastern Europeans to emancipate themselves from Soviet control. But we should also have no illusions about the likelihood of success.

In fact, Hungary, which owes $17.9 billion to Western creditors, has long benefited from the largess of American taxpayers. Over the past three years alone Hungary has borrowed $833 million from the World Bank; this year the communist nation is seeking another $350 million from the World Bank and the same amount from the International Monetary Fund.

The Export-Import Bank and Commodity Credit Corp., both federal agencies, have provided Hungary $43 million in credit in the past. Other Western governments, like Germany, have also proved eager to finance Hungary's failing collectivist economy.

There's no reason to add OPIC's backing to this long list. Indeed, it's hard to see how Hungary qualifies as the sort of "friendly" nation mentioned in the original authorizing legislation. If it really does, then who is NATO supposed to be protecting us from?

Unfortunately, Hungary represents only part of a concerted effort by the Soviet bloc to gain greater access to Western cash. Poland, too, has asked to be covered by OPIC. And President Reagan backed Poland's recent entry into the International Monetary Fund and World Bank.

Even worse, World Bank President Barber Conable, selected by this administration, favors Soviet membership in his organization, the leading international financial institution. Between 1980 and 1986 the World Bank funneled $8.9 billion to just four communist states: China, Hungary, Romania and Yugoslavia. What conceivable justification is there for letting the Soviets jump on this U.S.-funded gravy train?

Why the federal government even has an agency underwriting private investment abroad is a mystery. OPIC, which was originally capitalized by Congress, now makes money; if political risk insurance is really cost-effective, then the job could be left up to private firms.

If not, then the program should be killed, since it is not the taxpayers' responsibility to, for example, see that RJR Nabisco's assets are protected from nationalization by the Philippines. The federal dole for corporate America is already far too generous.

But even if OPIC stays in business, it shouldn't cover investments in every foreign country. Extending the program to a Warsaw Pact member would be a geopolitical bad joke.

Ronald Reagan has spent his entire political career talking tough about communism. But now he wants to subsidize America's adversaries.

Before it votes on the administration proposal, Congress should think about the thousands of Hungarian patriots who died fighting for freedom in the ill-fated uprising of 1956. There was then nothing the United States could do to help. Today, however, we can at least refuse to finance the evil system that killed so many.

## 188.  No More Aid for Mobuto

*January 21, 1987*

While President Reagan likes to pose as the great budget-cutter, he has his own pet boondoggles, particularly foreign aid. Outlays in this area have more than doubled since he took office.

Indeed, even as Reagan finalized his 1988 budget in December, he was promising more money to Zaire's President Mobutu Sese Seko. Mobutu—whose visit went almost unnoticed because of the Iranamok scandal—long has been a favorite of Western governments and already receives roughly $70 million a year from the United States.

But additional aid for Zaire can only be considered another bribe to reinforce Mobutu's loyalty to the West, since more money for debt relief, as Reagan termed it, simply will be wasted or stolen.

Zaire has one of the richest resource endowments of any nation, including large deposits of cobalt. But Mobutu, who took power in 1965, literally has destroyed his nation's economy.

The central African nation is the fifth poorest on the globe, with a per capita income of just $170 annually. Industrial production has fallen over the last decade; inflation ran 48.2 percent annually between 1973 and 1983.

This economic chaos was the inevitable result of Mobutu's policies. First, by all accounts Mobutu literally has looted his government's treasury and foreign aid receipts to become one of the world's richest men. His kleptocratic style of mismanagement has infected the entire government, making it impossible for entrepreneurs to operate, let alone flourish.

Second, Mobutu, despite his pro-Western political leanings, has operated as a doctrinaire socialist. For instance, he nationalized foreign firms, contending that Zairians could operate them more efficiently. Needless to say, the results of state ownership were catastrophic.

Mobutu's campaign for "authenticity" included decreeing that Zairians had to use African names; coats and ties were banned in favor of a Mao-type suit called an abakos.

The status of political freedom and civil liberties in Zaire is about what you'd expect with a capricious dictator who seeks to control his people's names: nil. The New York-based Freedom House reports that "prisoners of conscience are numerous, and execution and torture occur."

The only good news about Zaire is that Mobutu's policies have been so disastrous that even he acknowledges something has gone wrong. Mobutu no longer worries about his people's clothes and he turned to the International Monetary Fund in 1983 to help bail out the economy. With increased scrutiny from the IMF and other international organizations, Mobutu seems to have reduced official graft.

But there's still no reason for the United States to bail out Mobutu by pouring more money into the Zairian black hole. Let Mobutu clamp down on corruption and end state control of the economy. Then private investment—which currently totals roughly $200 million—will start flowing into the country.

And if Zaire can't meet its debt obligations, it can reschedule its loans, or default if necessary. It's not the U.S. taxpayers' responsibility to make good on bad Zairian paper.

Would Mobutu stay bought without more American aid? Maybe not, though he already has two decades invested in the West. Moreover, only Western business is capable of providing Zaire with the capital necessary to develop. The Soviets certainly have nothing to offer the impoverished central African nation.

In any case, one has to ask what we are doing to the Zairian people and our own freedom values in our attempt to buy a little strategic advantage. The world is a rough place, of course, and the Soviets accept few rules, but at some point the price of playing the game is just too high.

And it's not even clear that America's investment in Mobutu will pay off in the long run. U.S. support for corrupt authoritarians like Nicaragua's Somoza and the shah of Iran bought years of loyal service, but both pro-Western leaders were eventually overthrown by virulently anti-American movements. Thus, money that seemed well-spent just a few years ago now has to be written off as a complete loss.

So too could it be with Mobutu. Someday he may be overthrown and his successors may not be very enamored of a country that did so much to keep him in power.

One of the reasons the federal budget has risen 73 percent under Ronald Reagan is this administration's support for thuggish regimes like Mobutu's. Conservative politicians like to spend money; they just want to spend it on different things than do liberals.

But it is hard to think of a less worthy cause than debt relief for Zaire. It's time the United States stopped subsidizing the repression, statism and corruption that Mobutu has made endemic to Zairian life.

# Robbery at the International Development Banks

## 189. Throwing Good Money after Debt

*November 20, 1988*

A $1.2 trillion international debt overhangs the Third World, threatening the economic future of the world's poor and the fiscal solvency of the West's banks. A score of developing countries are behind on their interest payments.

Brazil, the world's largest debtor, again began repaying its loans only after receiving $5.2 billion in new credit, while number two borrower Mexico seems likely to back away from even its modest economic reforms with the leftist surge in the recent election.

Solving a problem involving scores of sovereign nations and hundreds of private financial institutions is no easy task. Almost everyone is looking to the World Bank for direction; indeed, shortly after taking office that institution's president, Barber Conable, declared that "the bank's role is to lead."

But the bank only sees the solution in terms of more money—and lots of it. The bank wants a $74.8 billion general capital increase, which would allow it to up its overall lending from $17.7 billion to roughly $24 billion a year by 1991. And the supposedly conservative Reagan administration has just pushed an initial $70 million contribution through Congress.

However, none of the bank's supporters have explained how piling new bad loans on top of old bad ones will end the debt crisis. In fact, runaway bank lending is part of the problem.

The World Bank—originally the International Bank for Reconstruction and Development, later supplemented by a soft-money affiliate, the International Development Association—was created to help reorder the global economic system after World War II. In its early years, the bank did not reflexively hike its lending, but Robert McNamara, appointed bank president in 1968, transformed the institution into an international extension of America's Great Society.

Between 1968 and 1981, when McNamara retired, lending jumped from $954 million to $12.3 billion, a nearly 13-fold increase. "We're like a Soviet factory," admitted one official at the time. "Our ability to influence projects in a way that makes sense is completely undermined."

With this flood of loans, the bank supported the very bloated state enterprises that have left dozens of Third World states on the brink of insolvency. The bank also shifted from investment projects, which, however flawed, had at least some relevance to the goal of promoting economic growth, to social welfare programs; McNamara "seemed almost obsessed with redistribution of income," reported *Forbes* magazine. The bank even underwrote brutal social engineering schemes, such as Julius Myerere's forced collectivization program in Tanzania.

Under McNamara's successors, A.W. Clausen and now Barber Conable, the institution's rhetoric has improved but its lending priorities remain virtually unchanged. First, bank staffers are still primarily concerned about increasing overall lending—up 43.7 percent between 1981 and 1987—irrespective of the quality of individual loans. An internal operations evaluation department (OED) audit last year conceded that "the bank's drive to reach lending targets" had resulted in "poor project performance." In fact, a detailed 1987 OED study of two decades worth of rural development programs found that 37 percent of them had failed.

Moreover, the bank continues to underwrite the very statist development strategies that have wrecked the economies of so many Third World countries. Last year, for instance, the bank committed $418.1 million to primarily state-controlled foreign industrial projects; in 1986, it loaned $821.1 million for the same purpose. Largely government-owned development finance companies (DFCs) collected an incredible $2.3 billion last year, even though bank audits have regularly found DFCs to be wasteful, poorly managed, and disinterested in economic reform.

Indeed, the bank is not unaware of the results of its own policies: in 1987 one internal report acknowledged that "foreign loans have reinforced the heavy public sector bias of African investments."

The bank has not just continued to support inefficient economic policies; it still underwrites draconian "development" plans. For instance, the bank subsidized, albeit indirectly, the Ethiopian resettlement program that humanitarian groups estimate has killed as many as 100,000 people.

In 1985, the Ethiopian government borrowed $30 million for "relief and rehabilitation services"; the money went to finance, among other things, the purchase of trucks, which were the primary means used by the government to forcibly relocate people. One bank employee called this "genocide with a human face."

In fact, for more than a decade the bank has been a willing accomplice in Ethiopia's agricultural collectivization program, which is largely responsible for that country's devastating famine; year after year, the bank has funded expensive rural projects while the government was systematically destroying the farm sector.

Finally, despite its claim to have a "central role in promoting growth-oriented adjustment programs," the bank has done more to hinder than to advance economic reform abroad. One problem is that even projects that theoretically support development often fail.

The 1987 OED study cited earlier is only one of many internal audits that have revealed poor performance by bank projects; a 1985 review found increasing cost overruns, growing completion delays, decreasing rates of returns, and rising numbers of failures. Project after project has suffered from fatal design and implementation problems.

True, the bank is now arguing that its increasing reliance on structural adjustment loans (SALs), which are tied to general policy reforms rather than to specific projects, justifies a general capital increase. Yet SALs are largely a fraud, a convenient tool to deliver more money faster to overburdened debtors and a public relations device to improve the bank's image.

In fact, the best that one study by two bank consultants could say about SALs was that the loans encouraged bank staff and borrowing nations to think about policy reform—a rather meager result for a program that now accounts for nearly one-fourth of bank lending. The report found that SALs had no measurable impact on the gross national products of borrowers.

But that should have come as no surprise since in practice SALs change few policies: "The SALs seemingly hard and all-encompassing conditionality is largely illusory," concluded the study. Unfortunately, bank officials want to lend money more than they want to promote reform, so they constantly push countries, even those that have breached past commitments, to accept new loans.

Sovereign states will change their domestic policies only when they believe they have to; they certainly will not act when they know the World Bank will loan them more money anyway. Thus, the only way to encourage economic reform abroad is to stop subsidizing foolish debtor behavior. Then poor nations will have no choice but to divest money-losing parasites, encourage foreign investment, and reduce political interference in their economies.

Until now Third World debtors have been treated like drunks who were handed a wad of five dollar bills and told to drink no more.

The World Bank should lead the way out of the international debt crisis—but by cutting, not increasing, lending. Even without a general capital increase the bank could continue lending indefinitely $17.5 billion a year, far too much for an institution that has yet to learn anything from its past failures.

Other Western nations may nevertheless choose to ignore the bank's dismal record and increase their capital contributions, but there's no reason for the United States to throw more good money after bad. Next year Congress should just say no.

## 190. Reagan's IDA Boondoggle

*March 11, 1987*

One of the earliest accomplishments of the Reagan administration was to interject a new realism into America's economic relations with poorer Third World states. The answer to international underdevelopment and poverty, argued U.S. officials, was not more foreign aid, but domestic reforms in statist economic policies.

The Treasury Department under Secretary James Baker is increasingly returning to its pre-Reagan giveaway tradition, however. The department has been negotiating hefty funding increases for a number of the multilateral development banks; most recently the United States agreed to a three-year, $12.4 billion "replenishment" of the International Development Association.

IDA is the so-called soft-lending window of the World Bank. It makes subsidized loans—essentially grants—to poorer nations, theoretically to promote economic development.

In 1979 President Jimmy Carter approved a $12 billion infusion for IDA, but Reagan's Treasury Department, then headed by Donald Regan, held the next replenishment to $9 billion.

Now the administration is pressing for a 38 percent increase in IDA's funding, however. And America, as usual, would be responsible for the largest share: $2.875 billion.

Of course, no one denies the seriousness of the economic problems facing developing states. But it should be obvious by now that giving more money to countries that have amassed a trillion-dollar debt will not contribute to international economic growth.

First, much of IDA funds go to creditworthy states that could borrow commercially and have no conceivable need for Western subsidies.

India, for instance, traditionally has accounted for 40 percent of IDA's loans. It collected $625 million from IDA last year and $4.262 billion over the last five years. Not surprisingly, India has used its access to cheap IDA credits to avoid borrowing privately and accepting foreign investment. China, too, is a major IDA recipient, receiving $450 million in 1986 alone. Yet it is now one of the largest foreign currency holders in the world and is a net creditor, lending more than it borrows.

Second, though half of IDA's future loans will be targeted to impoverished African states with non-existent credit ratings, there is no reason to believe these nations will use the funds effectively. Among past IDA beneficiaries are Ethiopia, Mozambique and Tanzania, whose collectivist economic and repressive political policies have guaranteed perpetual stagnation and poverty.

IDA's loans to Ethiopia, for instance, are inexplicable. It is difficult to image a nation that more needs to change its domestic practices, especially those governing agriculture—forced collectivization, confiscation of crop stockpiles, and so forth.

However, the regime of Mengistu Haile Mariam feels little pressure to abandon its counterproductive policies when Western nations so generously underwrite the Ethiopian economy. Since 1984 the East African country has borrowed $333 million for farm projects, fertilizer purchases, telecommunications services and electric power. Unfortunately, these loans have done more to help the government consolidate its control than to increase its people's living standards.

Thus, rhetoric from international bureaucrats about helping "the poorest developing countries" should not be allowed to obscure the dismal results of four decades of failed foreign aid projects.

Yet the Reagan administration nevertheless is preparing to throw a lot of good money after bad. So it is up to Congress to act, blocking America's IDA contribution.

Indeed, last fall the Senate Appropriations Committee warned "that increased funding for the IDA VIII replenishment is simply not possible. . . . Therefore, the committee would expect any new replenishment would not be greater than current levels."

And Congress should make good on its threat even after administration officials and foreign diplomats begin trooping to Capitol Hill to explain all the wonderful things IDA will accomplish. The legislators simply need to remember that good intentions are not enough.

For the cause of international development will not be served by forever subsidizing the counter-productive policies that have stifled economic growth throughout the Third World. Instead, progress will come only through the sort of tough-minded compassion that forces Third World states to come to grips with their own problems and to make the hard choices necessary to solve them.

And that means no more wasted foreign aid, through IDA or any other program.

## 191. Banking's International "Black Hole"

*May 13, 1987*

America's banks have been trying to slowly disengage from their essentially insolvent Third World borrowers, but the U.S. government continues to try to push the financial institutions deeper into the international debt quagmire.

The Federal Reserve and Treasury Department, for instance, long have pressured commercial banks to make new foreign loans, promising favorable regulatory treatment in return. Banks that refused to lend more, in contrast, risked greater federal scrutiny.

But rarely have government officials gone public with their threats. Until now.

Fed vice chairman Manuel Johnson has told a group of foreign central bankers that new lending by private banks is "disappointing." It is inappropriate, he complained, for the major banks "to retreat precipitously from international lending." Those that do so should be punished: "A method needs to be considered where banks that opt out of participating in new financing packages not receive the same collective benefits as those banks providing net new lending."

Yet it is government officials like Johnson, not the banks, who are being irresponsible.

Brazil, for instance, the world's largest debtor with $108 billion due, has suspended interest payments. As a result, profits at major banks like Manufacturers Hanover fell sharply during the first quarter of 1987.

Equador, too, has stopped repaying its debt—a more modest $8 billion—because an earthquake disrupted oil production. Peru, which owes $15 billion, has unilaterally cut its loan repayments.

Argentina owes $45 billion and its economy is faltering; the rate of inflation for January alone was 7.6 percent and is rising. And in Mexico, the world's No. 2 debtor, with $100 billion in foreign loans, prices are accelerating even faster than in Argentina.

Into debtors such as these Johnson wants the banks to pour more money.

Unfortunately, Johnson—usually one of the Fed's most thoughtful and market-oriented members—has fallen for the pernicious myth that more dollars can create economic growth. Yet developing states already have acquired a $1 trillion debt: the problem is a misuse, not lack, of resources. Of course, almost every borrower now promises to adopt growth-producing reforms. But little real progress has occurred.

Consider Mexico, an economic basket case that recently negotiated a new $7.7 billion commercial loan package. Bank resistance was intense, and appropriately so: even the World Bank has acknowledged privately that Mexico is "not creditworthy in terms of new voluntary lending." In fact, with old Mexican paper trading at barely 62 cents on the dollar in secondary markets, the latest loan package means the banks essentially have given away almost $3 billion.

And what will they get for their charity? Just requests for new loans when Mexico runs out of money again.

Even though its economy suffers from stultifying central government control, the Mexican regime so far has refused to initiate meaningful reforms because of domestic political pressure. "You must not push Mexico too far," warned one member of that nation's Chamber of Deputies.

True, the de la Madrid government has pledged anew to slash regulation, encourage foreign investment, and cut the budget deficit. But the regime has "reduced" the number of state enterprises by simply merging them together; the government's 1987 budget includes a 15 percent real increase in public sector spending.

And things will only get worse as the 1988 presidential election draws closer. Yet, warns Bernardo Ardavin, president of the Mexican Employers Confederation, "if we make the same mistakes again, we won't be able to repay our old or new debts."

Instead of pressing American banks to continue funding an international Ponzi scheme, where new loans are used to pay off old ones, Johnson and his regulatory colleagues should be urging banks to stop throwing good money after bad.

Existing loans need to be written down; interest payments should be rescheduled. Loan loss reserves must be increased and poor paper should be sold in secondary markets. Finally, banks should swap debt for equity investment in borrowing nations. A combination of these steps—based on a recognition that much of today's debt will never be repaid—has the greatest chance of resolving the crisis without dragging down America's banks.

The international debt party is over. Third World borrowers, like alcoholics, need to be told, "No more." Additional lending, however Johnson and his colleagues try to package it, will only make the crisis worse.

# Index

Abortion, 369–373
Abramson, Mark, 43, 44
Acheson, Dean, 395–396, 405
Adams, Brock, 191
Advertising: attorney, 287–289, 291–292; television, 27–28; tobacco, 341–343
Africa, 463, 475
Agency for International Development (AID), 77–79
Agricultural Act of 1956, 166–167
Agricultural Adjustment Act of 1933, 166
Agricultural subsidies, 79–81, 110–111, 116–117, 120–121, 129, 143–144, 167–172. *See also* Rural development
Agriculture industry: crisis in, 166–168, 178–179; dairy, 168–169; grain, 169–171; overview of U.S., 165–166; solution to problems in, 172–174
Airbag rule, 207
Airline deregulation, 212–213
Albers, Maxine, 241
Allen, Ted, 162–163
Aluminum Can Company of America, 257–258
American Airlines, 84
American colonies, 32–34
American Federation of State, County and Municipal Employees (AFSCME), 71–72
American Home Economics Association, 77–78
American Medical Association (AMA), 313–314
Amtrak, 191–192
Anderson, Martin, 49, 134, 329, 434
Andreas, Dwayne, 81, 179
Andrews, Mark, 317
Angola, 482
Animal rights, 372–373
Annunzio, Frank, 338
Antitrust laws, 257–259
Apartheid, 416–418

Appliance standards, 213–215
Arbatov, Georgi, 29, 30
Archer Daniels Midland, 167, 179
Ardavin, Bernardo, 495
Arms reduction, 405–412. *See also* Military spending
Art subsidies, 385–387
Artists' rights, 387–389
Aspen, Les, 94
Association of Community Organizations for Reform Now (ACORN), 75–77
Astrology, 67–68
Austin, Gilbert, 352
Automobile imports, 245–246
Azcona, Jose, 425

Baade, Robert, 391
Babbitt, Milton, 387
Baden, John, 240
Badham, Robert, 86
Baker, James, 95
Balanced budget, 135–137. *See also* Budget cuts
Baldridge, Malcolm, 99
Banfield, Edward, 386
Banking industry, 75–77, 217–219, 494–495
Barry, Marion S., Jr., 295, 296, 390
Bartlett, Bruce, 301
Bates, John, 291
Bauer, P. T., 464
Baxter, William, 257
Becker, Michael, 338
Beekeepers, 171, 175
Bell, Terrel, 209
Bellak, Alvin, 366
Bellamy, Edward, 17
Bennett, James, 69, 70
Bennett, William J., 209, 315
Benson, Arthur, 278
Bentsen, Lloyd, 243, 244
Berger, Raoul, 274
Bethe, Hans, 436

Biaggi, Mario, 219–220, 301, 387
Biden, Joseph, 279
Biden-Pell grants, 77–79
Bierne, Kenneth, 333
Bilingual education, 209
Bipartisan Budget Appeal, 81–82
Bipartisanship, 93–95, 395–397
Black Americans: in Congress, 359–360; in military, 440, 442; problems of, 357–359
Blackmun, Harry, 291
Block, William E., 98, 100
Blum, Jack, 89
Boesky, Ivan, 264
Boff, Leonardo, 34–36
Boggs, Danny, 229
Bolick, Clint, 223
Bonhoeffer, Dietrich, 4
Bonneville Power Administration (BPA), 189–190
Boorstin, Daniel J., 156–158
Booth, Heather, 73
Borden, Enid, 351–353
Borge, Tomas, 29, 30
Bork, Robert, 274–276, 278–280
Boschwitz, Rudy, 172, 457, 468
*Boston Herald,* 104–105
Botha, P. W., 416
Bovard, James, 237, 473
Boyd, John, 151–152
Bradbury, Norris, 436
Bradford, Charles, 243
Bradford, William, 32–33
Bradley, Joseph P., 285
Bradley, Tom, 360
Breaux, John, 148, 208
Brennan, William, 276, 342
Broadcast regulation, 219–221
Brown, Harold, 433
Brown, Jerry, 135
Brummond, David, 84
Buchanan, Patrick, 369
*Buckley vs. Valeo,* 46
Budget cuts: corporate, 81–83; in Reagan administration, 99–103. *See also* Balanced budget
Budget process: need to revise, 141–143; president's authority in, 137–139
Building codes, 323
Burdick, Quentin, 176–178
Burger, Warren, 272, 281
Burr, Richard, 366
Bush, George, 159: charity contributions of, 355; on child care, 306; in Lebanon, 399; potential impact of, 95, 97; presidential campaign of, 61–64

Business Roundtable, 89–92
Butler, Stuart, 188, 1333
Byrd, Robert, 45, 113–115, 212

Cable television, 221–223
Calleo, David, 409, 410
Cambodia, 401, 402
Campaign contributions, 45–48
Canaris, Wilhelm, 4
Capital punishment, 378–380
Capitalism, 36–40
Carlucci, Frank, 411, 414
Carner, William, 218
Carpenter, Ted Galen, 410, 420, 434
Carter, Hodding, III, 397
Carter, Jimmy, 29, 43, 181: on draft registration, 443–444; federal spending under, 126–127
Casein, 252–254
Castro, Fidel, 431
Cattle industry, 168–169
Censorship, 373–375, 447–449
Center for Excellence in Government, 43
Chaikin, Sol, 298
Charity contributions, 10, 354–356
Charren, Peggy, 27, 28
Child care, 306–308
Children's television programming, 27–28
Chiles, Lawton, 106
China, People's Republic of, 482: aid to, 482, 293; economic reform in, 30–32
Chisholm, Shirley, 126
Chissano, Joaquim, 484
Christfield, Cynthia, 376
Christian ethics, 36–40
Christian symbols, 20–22
Christo, Carlos (Brother Betto), 34–36
Churchill, Winston, 448
Chrysler Corp., 84, 120
Cigarette advertising, 341–343
Citizen/Labor Energy Coalition (CLEC), 72–75
Citizens Network for Foreign Affairs, 78
Civil Rights Act of 1964, 362
Civil Rights Restoration Act of 1987, 362–364
Clark, Russell, 276–278
Clarke, Dave, 380, 381
Clausen, A. W., 490
Clay, Henry, 57
Clean Water Act, 235, 236
Coal leases, 210–211
Coal scrubbers, 206–207
College financial assistance, 317–319
Commissaries, 188

Commission on Merchant Marine and Defense, 148
Community Development Block Grants, 144
Community Reinvestment Act (CRA), 73–75
Comparable worth, 365–367
Conable, Barber, 486, 490
Condominiums, 325–326
Congress, U.S.: abuses of, 104–107; appropriations procedures in, 13–14
Congressional elections, 57–59
Conservation, 232
Consortium for International Cooperation in Higher Education, 78
Constitution, U.S.: economic philosophy in, 136; effectiveness of, 11–13; First Amendment, 21, 374, 376–378
Constitutional convention, 136–137
Consumer fraud, 335–337
Conte, Silvio, 106, 175
Continuing Resolution (CD), 104, 114–115, 137, 138
Cooke, Jack Kent, 390
Copulos, Milton, 190, 230, 238
Corn products, 170
Corporate Average Fuel Economy (CAFE), 216–217
Costello, John, 78
Cost-of-living (COLA) adjustment, 346
Cotton farmers, 170–171
Cowen, Tyler, 469, 470
Crandall, Robert, 211, 216
Crane, Philip M., 193
Craswell, Richard, 325
Crawford, H. R., 337
Credit cards, 337–339
Creedon, John, 261
Crime, 380–381
Crutchfield, Edward, 77
Cuba, 29–30
Cullinan, Terrence, 18
Cuomo, Mario, 71
Cyclamates, 339–340

Dairy subsidies, 116–117, 168–169, 253–254
Dale, Edwin, 113, 346
Danforth, Douglas, 81–82
Danforth, John, 243
Darling, Karen, 184
Davis, Al, 15, 390
Davis-Bacon Act, 296, 299–300, 358
Day, William, 283
Death penalty, 378–380
Deaver, Michael, 46, 49

Decter, Midge, 452
Defense budget. See Military spending
Defense Intelligence Agency (DIA), 105
Del Ponte, Paul, 354
Delaney Clause, 208–209, 340, 341
DeLay, Tom, 161
Democratic Party, 71, 72
Denzau, Arthur, 251, 252
Depository Institutions Act of 1988, 75
Deregulation: airline, 212–213; natural gas, 72–75, 229–231
Deukmejian, George, 135
Dhanabalan, Suppiah, 453
Dhlakama, Afonso, 424
Diggs, Charles, 360
DiLorenzo, Thomas, 69, 70
Dingell, John, 57, 310
Discrimination: rent control and, 329; Supreme Court cases on, 360–362; women and, 364–365. See also Black Americans
District of Columbia government, 19–20
Dixon, Travis, 333
Dodd, Christopher, 306
Dole, Elizabeth, 207
Dole, Robert, 110–112, 179, 345, 349, 382
Donnelly, Christopher, 408
Douglas, William, 272
Dower, Susan, 351
Downey, Thomas, 386
Draft. See Military draft
Drexel Burnham Lambert, 263, 264
Drug war, 382–385, 422
Du Pont, Pete, 173, 316
Due diligence, 210–211
Dukakis, Michael, 61–64, 115, 159, 254–256, 306
Dunlap, George, 373
Durenberger, David, 435
Duvalier, Jean-Claude, 419, 422

Early, Joseph, 14, 106, 153
East, John, 271
Economic Development Administration (EDA), 152–154
Economic freedom, 31–32
Economic intolerance, 23–24
Education: bilingual, 209; conflict over teaching values, 8–10; financial assistance for higher, 317–319; present state of, 315–317. See also Public schools; Schools
Edwards, James, 97–99
Edwards, Mickey, 462
Efron, Edith, 209, 340
Egg King, 85–86

Ehrlich, Paul, 227
Eisenhower, Dwight D., 410, 411
El Salvadoran refugees, 7, 456
Elderly health care issues, 309–313
Elections: financing, 45–48; incumbents in
    Congressional, 57–59; presidential, 61–
    64
Eli Lilly & Co., 384–385
Ellig, Jerome, 391, 392
Embassies, U.S., 458–459
Employer-provided health insurance, 83–
    84
End Hunger Network, 78
Energy: appliance efficiency and, 213–215;
    development, 231–232; McClure's rec-
    ord on, 107–110; nuclear, 232–234. See
    also Natural gas: Oil industry
Energy Fuels Nuclear Inc., 239–240
Environmental issues: rangeland grazing,
    241–242; toxic waste, 237–238; water,
    235–237; wilderness preservation, 239–
    240
Erhard, Ludwig, 470
Ethiopia, 463, 472, 475–477, 479, 481–482,
    490–491, 493
Evans, Daniel, 190, 366
Evans, David, 441
Exclusionary rule, 283–285
Exon, James, 195
Export-Import Bank, 120, 125, 130, 132,
    143, 150–152

Falk, Joseph, 295
Falwell, Jerry, 65, 68
Family and Medical Leave Act of 1986,
    304–306
Farm Bill of 1985, 167, 168, 172
Farm Credit System, 165, 178, 217, 218
Farmers. See Agricultural subsidies
Farmers Home Administration (FmHA),
    79, 182
Farrow, Mia, 331
Fasi, Frank, 255
Favretto, Richard J., 290
Fazio, Vic, 198
Federal Aviation Administration, 213
Federal Coal Leasing Amendments Act,
    211
Federal Communications Commission
    (FCC), 27, 104, 105, 220–221
Federal Contracts Compliance Programs,
    209–210
Federal debt: consequences and solutions
    to, 139–141; growth in government and,
    162–163
Federal Deposit Insurance Corp., 217, 218

Federal Energy Regulatory Commission,
    230
Federal grants, 69–70
Federal spending, 133–135. See also
    Budget cuts; Subsidies
Federman, Irwin, 251
Femske, Bill, 326
Ferguson, Daniel, 242
Ferguson, Nancy, 242
Ferrara, Peter, 346, 348–349
Ferraro, Geraldine, 10, 71, 355
Fiori, Laurie, 346, 349–351
First Amendment rights, 21, 374, 376–378
Fitzgerald, Randall, 107
Foggan, Laura, 19
Foley, Thomas, 94
Food and Drug Administration, 339–341
Food for Peace (P.L. 480), 467, 468, 473–
    475, 477
Ford, Gerald, 61
Foreign aid: failures of, 463–465, 471–473,
    481–488; for food, 475–477; Food for
    Peace program, 467, 468, 473–475;
    Marshall Plan, 469–471; for military
    purposes, 477–481; need to cut, 461–
    463; questionable recipients of, 77–79;
    suggestions to improve, 465–469
Foreign investment in U.S., 254–256
Foreign policy, bipartisan, 395–397
Foster, Richard S., 346
Foster, Wendell, 358
Fowler, Mark, 221
Frank, Beryl, 145
Free enterprise, 83–84
Free trade restrictions: automobile, 245–
    246; casein, 252–254; problems regard-
    ing, 243–245, 336–337; semiconductor
    chips, 250–252; steel, 247–248; textile,
    249–250
Freeman, Harry, 43–44
Frieden, Bernard J., 323–324
Friedlander, Saul, 4
Friedman, Milton, 386
Fringe benefits, 302–304
Fuel Use Act, 229–230
Fumento, Michael, 179
Furman, Rosemary, 288–289

Gartside, John, 79
Garwin, Richard, 436
Gasohol, 179–180
Georgetown University, 19, 20
Georgine, Robert, 299
Gephardt, Richard, 115, 166, 243–246, 387
Gergen, David, 48
Gieringer, Dale, 202

Gilder, George, 251
Gingrich, Newt, 183
Giuliani, Rudolph, 263
Glasnost, 6
Glasser, Ira, 284
Global Poverty Reduction Act, 471, 472
Gold standard, 135
Goldfarb, Lewis, 290–291
Goldsby, Matthew John, 372
Goldwater, Barry, 29
Gonsalves, Joe, 116, 144, 167, 176
Goodkin, Sanford R., 322
Gorbachev, Mikhail, 405, 407–408, 412
Gore, Al, 115–117
Government management, 43–45
Government regulation: airline, 212–213;
    appliance standards, 213–215; banking,
    75–77, 217–219; broadcast, 219–221;
    excesses of, 201–204; list of unexcept-
    able, 204–211
Grace Commission, 188
Graham, John, 216
Graham, Robert, 289
Grain industry, 169–171
Gramm, Phil, 299, 300
Gramm-Rudman bill, 156, 158, 162, 462,
    463
Grant, Ralph, 359
Gray, Virginia, 298
Gray, William, 114
Greene, Jim, 340
Greenfield, Meg, 125, 133
Greenhalgh, Peter, 222
Greenspan, Alan, 347
Grenada, 447, 448
Greve, Michael, 361
Griffiths, Brian, 36–39
Grosz, Karoly, 6
Guccione, Bob, 373–374
Gun control, 380–381

Haas, Ellen, 167
Haig, Alexander, 51, 99
Haiti, 419, 421
Hamor, Ralph, 33–34
Hands Across America, 353–355
Hanlin, Russell, 184
Hansen, Jim, 202
Harkin, Tom, 73, 172–173, 354
Harrigan, Anthony, 244
Hartnett, Thomas, 58, 59
Hatfield, Mark, 190, 241, 356
Hawaii Housing Authority v. Midkiff, 269–
    270, 275–276
Hawkins, Augustus, 300–301
Hayek, F. A., 48

Hayes, Patrick, 386
Hayes, Shirley, 382
Head Start, 351–353
Health insurance, 83–84, 302–304
Heinz, John, 150
Helms, Jesse, 167, 467, 468
Higgs, Robert, 11–13
Hill & Knowlton, 183
Hirr, Otto, 443
Hitler, Adolf: persecution of Jews, 455;
    plot to assassinate, 4
Hollings, Ernest "Fritz," 105, 249, 286
Holocaust memorial, 6–7
Homework prohibition, 205–206, 297–298
Homosexual rights, 19–20, 367–368
Honduras, 425–426
Honey price support program, 171, 175
Hooks, Benjamin, 357, 358
Hoover, Herbert, 323
Hostile takeovers, 259–260
Housing: crisis in, 321–330; public, 332–
    334; rent control issues in, 23
Huber, Ernest, 16
Hudgins, Ed, 244
Humbert, Thomas, 333, 334
Hungary, 5–6, 483, 485–486
Hunger, 353–355, 375–477. See also Food
    for Peace program
Hurd, John, 114

Iacocca, Lee, 81, 84, 86–88, 92, 245
Idaho, 241, 242
Illinois v. Gates, 283, 285
Immigration, 455–457
Impeachment of federal jurists, 271
Importation. See trade restrictions
Incumbents, 57–59
India, 472, 479–480, 493
Individual retirement accounts (IRAs),
    348–350
Industrial homework prohibition, 205–206,
    297–298
Inouye, Daniel, 14, 105–106
Insider trading, 263–264
Interest groups: federal grants to, 69–70;
    religious, 65–67. See also individual in-
    terest groups
International Business Machines (IBM),
    257, 258
International Development Association
    (IDA), 489, 492–494
International Ladies' Garment Workers'
    Union (ILGWU), 297, 298
International Seabed Authority (ISA), 453–
    454
International Trade Commission, 253

Interstate Commerce Commission, 83
Intervention: in Honduras, 425–426; limits
  of, 421–423; in Third World, 419–421.
  *See also* Military intervention
Intolerance: as American heritage, 22–24;
  religious, 20–22
Iran, 414–416
Iraq, 414–416
Isray, Robert, 15, 16
Irvin, Reed, 447

Jackson, Henry, 94
Jackson, Jesse, 65, 115, 359
Jacob, John, 357
Jamestown Colony, 33–34
Japan: auto imports from, 245–246; semi-
  conductor industry in, 251–252
Jaruzelski, Wojciech, 409, 417
Jefferson, Thomas, 21, 69, 136
Jensen, Michael, 260
Jerusalem, 6, 8
Johnson, Manuel, 494–495
Jones Act, 148
Jordan, Hamilton, 54
Journalism, 447
Judicial accountability, 267–274
Judicial imperialism, 276–278

Kadar, Janos, 5
Kasselbaum, Nancy, 73, 111
Kates, Don, 381 \
Kaufman, Herbert M., 151
Kaus, Mickey, 273
Kemp, Jack, 333
Kennedy, Edward, 73, 83, 104–105, 279,
  300–301, 303, 363, 388, 389
Kennedy, John F., 61, 431
Kenyon, David V., 456
Keogh, James, 90–92
Kerley, Gillam, 443
Kildee, Dale, 306
Kirk, Andrew, 36–39
Kirkland, Lane, 243–244
Klestil, Thomas, 451
Kline, William, 249
Koch, Edward, 17, 295–296, 331, 382
Koch, June, 334
Kondratus, Anna, 353
Korea, 413–414
Kozinski, Alex, 330, 332
Kragen, Ken, 353
Krizay, John, 459

Lafferty, Dennis M., 391
Lamm, Richard, 311, 312
Lamp, Virginia, 306

Laos, 483
Lave, Lester, 216
Law of the Sea Treaty, 452, 453
Lawyers: advertising of, 287–289, 291–292;
  regulation of, 289–290; restrictions on
  competition of, 290–292; restrictions
  on supply of, 289–290
Layne, Christopher, 405, 409, 411
Leahy, Patrick, 166
Lebanon, 399, 400
Legal Services Corp. (LSC), 285–287
Lehman, John, 48
Lehman, William, 14
Lehnen, Edward H., 324
Leveraged buy-outs (LBOs), 261–263
Levine, Dennis, 264
Lewis, Drew, 97, 98
Liberation theology, 34–36
Library of Congress, 156–158
Libya, 429–430
Lillienstein, Maxwell, 377
Lindbeck, Sssar, 326, 330–331
Linder, Benjamin, 426–428
Line-item presidential veto, 134–135, 138
Lipson, Gerald, 107
Lobbies. *See* Interest groups
Lobbyists, 52
Local government, 162–163
Logsdon, John, 159
Lucas, George, 388
Lucy, William, 71
Lyng, Richard, 179

McCartney, Forrest, 158
McClaughry, John, 63, 321–322
McCleskey, Warren, 378
McCloskey, Pete, 17
McCloskey, Robert, 268
McClure, James, 14, 107–110, 115, 189,
  241, 242
McComic, R. Barry, 323
McCulloch, Rachel, 151
McCurdy, David, 437
McEntee, Gerald, 71–72
McFarlane, Robert, 412, 435–436
MacFarlane, S. Neil, 420
Machel, Samora, 423–425
McKean, John, 192, 194
McKenzie, Floretta, 9
McKenzie, Richard, 162
McNamara, Robert, 406, 489–490
McPherson, M. Peter, 79
Madison, James, 275, 280
Malthus, Thomas, 227, 228
Mann, July, 9
*Mapp v. Ohio,* 283, 284

Marcos, Ferdinand, 419–420, 422
Mariam, Mengistu Haile, 493
Maritime Administration (Marad), 147, 149
Maritime subsidies, 144, 147–149
Marketing loans, 172, 175–176
Marketing orders, 204–205
Markey, Edward, 387, 388
Marshall Plan, 469–471
Mass transit, 160–163
Maurice, Charles, 227
Maybury, Richard, 32
Maynard, Mike, 85, 86
Mazur, Jay, 297
Mead, Margaret, 17
Mecs, Imre, 6
Medicare, 309, 310
Meese, Ed, 49
Melcher, John, 175
Mencken, H. L., 166
Mengistu, 475–477
Mergers, 259–261
Metzenbaum, Howard, 128, 386, 429
Mexico, 495
Mikva, Abner, 279
Military aid, 477–481
Military draft: Carter on, 443–444; regis-
    tration, 205; support for, 437–438, 440–
    441; vs. voluntary military, 438–445
Military intervention: justification for, 401–
    402; and Persian Gulf War, 414–416;
    preconditions for, 399–401; and South
    Korea, 413–414. See also Intervention
Military operations censorship, 447–449
Military spending: cuts in, 101–102, 130,
    141–143, 403–412; nondefense related,
    128; rise in, 396–397; SDI, 433–435
Milken, Michael, 264
Miller, James, 13
Minimum wage, 23–24, 301–303
Minorities in Congress, 359–360. See also
    Black Americans
Missouri Plan, 272
Mobil, 82
Mobutu Sese Seko, 487–488
Moffett, Toby, 73
Mokhiber, Russell, 157
Mondale, Walter, 71, 72, 355
Moody, Jim, 183
Moon Treaty, 454
Moore, Stephen, 137, 138, 161
Moral rights, 387–389
Mosbacher, Robert, 347
Moseley, Phil, 346
Mozambique, 423–425, 484
Murdoch, Rupert, 104, 105

Muth, Richard, 325, 328
MX missile, 93–94

NAACP, 357, 358
Nader, Ralph, 221, 255
Nagy, Imre, 5
NASA, 158–160
Nathanson, Bernard N., 371
National Appliance Energy Conservation
    Act, 214
National Audubon Society, 232, 240
National Commission on Social Security
    Reform, 345–348
National Rural Electric Cooperative Asso-
    ciation, 106
National service, 17–18
NATO, 395, 396, 405–412
Natural gas, 72–75, 229–231
Natural Gas Policy Act, 229
Natural Gas Supply Association, 72, 73
Nazis, 7–8, 455
Nelson, Robert, 242
New York Post, 104, 105
Nicaragua, 425–428, 483
Nigeria, 480–481
Nilson, Spencer, 338
Nixon, Richard, 61, 402
Nobel, Josef S., 325
Nominal spending, 126
Noriega, Manuel, 421–423
North Korea, 413–414
Novak, Michael, 35–36, 401–402
Novak, William, 117
Nuclear power, 232–234
Nuclear testing ban, 435–436
Nunn, Sam, 434, 437, 441

Oakar, Mary Rose, 365, 366
Oakes, John, 240
O'Beirne, Kate Walsh, 351–353
Obey, David, 14, 120
O'Brien, Harold, 193
Occupational licensure, 296
O'Connor, Sandra Day, 270, 275, 279
Oil industry: prices, 225–227; production,
    231–232
Oliver, Charles, 250
Omnibus Reconsiliation Act of 1987, 114–
    115, 147
O'Neill, Thomas P. "Tip," 117–122, 141,
    179, 345, 475
Orange production, 183–185
Organization of Petroleum Exporting
    Countries (OPEC), 225–227
Original intent, 274–276, 278–279
Ortega, Daniel, 425–427

O'Steen, Van, 291
Outer Continental Shelf land, 231–232
Overseas Private Investment Corp (OPIC),
    485, 486
Owen, Bruce, 222
Ozar, Hatorah, 105

Packwood, Robert, 241
Palmer, Jeffrey, 327
Palmer, Tom, 388
Panama, 421–423
Parsons, Randall, 163
*Patterson vs. McLean Credit Union*, 360–
    361
Payment-in-kind (PIK) program, 169–170,
    172
Payne, Donald, 360
Pellachio, Anthony, 350
*Penthouse*, 373–374
People's Republic of China. *See* China,
    People's Republic of
Pepper, Claud, 309–311
Persian Gulf War, 414–416
Pertschuk, Michael, 211
Pescosolido, Carl, 184
Petersen, Donald, 245
Peterson, George, 323
Peterson, Peter G., 81
Philippines, 419, 421
Physicians, 313–314
Pickens, T. Boone, 259
Pickle, J. J., 118
Pierce, Samuel R., Jr., 97, 98, 332
Pinochet, Augusto, 402
Pirie, Madsen, 187
*Playboy*, 374
Plymouth Colony, 32–34
Poland, 483
Political action committees (PACs), 45–48
Pollution. *See* Environmental issues
Pornography, 373–378
Postal Service, 192–194
Potomac Institute, 17, 18
Powell, Adam Clayton, 360
Powell, Lewis, 378
Power, 48–55
Power Marketing Authorities (PMA), 188–
    190
Pozsgay, Imre, 6
Presidential debate, 61–62
Presidential election: 1988, 62–64; role of
    debate in, 61–62
Presidential veto, 134–135, 138
Price, Charles, 406
Prince, Harry Bayard, 470
Price Leontyne, 386

Price-Anderson Act, 232–234
Privatization, 187–189
Protectionism, 24, 243. *See* Free trade re-
    strictions
Pryba, Barbara, 376
Pryba, Dennis, 376
Pryor, David, 175
Public housing, 332–334
Public schools: failure to educate blacks,
    358; state of U.S., 315–317; teaching
    values in, 8–10. *See also* Education;
    Schools

Qaddafi, Muammar, 429, 430
Quayle, Dan, 254
Quigley, Joan, 67

Rabkin, Jeremy, 209–210
Racketeer Influenced and Corrupt Organi-
    zations Act (RICO), 375–378
Radio regulation, 219–221
Rahn, Richard, 347–348, 350
Rangeland, 241–242
Reagan, Nancy, 67
Reagan, Ronald: on abortion, 372; antigov-
    ernment rhetoric of, 43; budget control
    under, 178; on children's television reg-
    ulation, 27, 28; contribution to charities
    by, 10, 355; evangelical leaders and,
    67–68; failures regarding excesses in
    regulation, 204–211; on hunger, 354; on
    military draft, 444; on military spend-
    ing, 403, 404; in presidential debate, 61;
    record of, 95–97; restrictions of free-
    dom, 30; Supreme Court appointments
    of, 267, 269–270; on synthetic fuels
    projects, 97–99; on taxes, 196; on ter-
    rorism, 429–431; veto of Clean Water
    Act, 235
Reagan administration: budget cuts by,
    125–133; lack of change in, 99–103
Real spending, 126
Record, Jeffrey, 405, 408
Rector, Robert, 307
Regan, Donald, 67, 132
Regulatory process. *See* Government regu-
    lation
Rehnquist, William, 267, 280
Religious displays, 20–22
Religious lobbyists, 65–67
RENAMO (Resistencia Nacional Mocam-
    bicana), 424
Rent control, 23, 326–332
Rice farmers, 170
Rinaldo, Matthew, 263
Risk, personal, 25–27

Ritchie, Mark, 169
Robb, Charles, 162, 437
Robbie, Joe, 391–392
Robertson, Pat, 65
Robinson, A. Haeworth, 347
Rodino, Peter, 359, 360
*Roe v. Wade*, 268
Roger, Will, 46
Rollins, Edward, 45
Romania, 483
Rommel, Erwin, 4
Root, Elihu, 17
Ross, John, 169
Rostenkowski, Dan, 57, 114, 262, 310, 345
Rothschild, Ed, 73–75
Rowe, Jim, 48
Rudman, Warren, 286
*Runyon vs. McCrary*, 361–362
Rural development, 180–183. *See also* Agricultural subsidies; Agriculture industry
Rural Electrification Administration (REA), 180–181, 183, 190
Russell-Wood, Christopher, 139

Saccharin, 208–209, 339–341
St. Germain, Fernand, 58
Samuelson, Robert, 244
San Diego, California, 20–21
Sandinistas, 425–428
Saunders, Charles B., Jr., 317–318
Savimbi, Jonas, 424
Scalia, Antonin, 267, 280
Schaefer, William Donald, 15, 390, 391
Schaeffer, Frankly, 36, 39, 40
Schenkel, William M., 322
Schlafly, Phyllis, 221
Schmoke, Kurt, 383
Schnittker, John, 167
Scholl, Hans, 4
Scholl, Sophie, 4
Schools: judicial power over, 276–278; state of U.S., 315–317. *See also* Education; Public schools
Schwartzman, Jay, 27
Schweiker, Richard, 100
Schweitzer, Albert, 371
Scowcroft Commission, 93, 94
Sea-Land Corp., 147, 149
Search and seizure, 283–285
Seat belt laws, 25–27
Securities and Exchange Commission, 263, 264
Seiberling, John, 241
Seidman, William, 218
Seifert, Gerald, 147

Self, David A., 16, 390
Semiconductor chip industry, 250–252
Sen, Sudhir, 477
Senior, Nassau, 24
Sewage treatment, 236. *See also* Environmental issues
Shapiro, Irving, 89
Shapiro, Martin, 268
Sharkey, Andrew, 248
Sharpe, James, 359
Sherman Antitrust Act, 257, 258
Showers, Robert, 376
Shrontz, Frank, 81
Shultz, George P., 30, 399–401, 425, 447, 451, 461–462
Simon, Paul, 73, 437, 439, 442
Simpson, Alan K., 457
Skinner, Samuel, 215, 217
Small Business Administration (SBA), 143, 154–156
Smith, Adam, 100
Smith, Fred, 92, 217
Smith, Virginia, 318
Smithson, Charles, 227, 228
Social Security, 94, 311, 345–351
Solow, Robert, 261
South Africa, 416–418
South Korea, 413–414
Soviet Union: military spending by, 404; refugees from, 456–457; weapons development in, 434, 436
Speakes, Larry, 131
Spielberg, Steven, 388, 389
Spike (tebuthiuron), 384
Sports stadiums, 15–16, 389–392
Standby Petroleum Allocation Act (SPAA), 108
Starr, Roger, 326, 328
State government, 162–163
Steel imports, 247–248
Steffens, Lincoln, 427
Stennis, John, 106, 153
Stern, Marc, 362
Sternlieb, George, 322
Stevens, John Paul, 361
Stevens, Ted, 14
Stewart, David, 317, 319
Stockman, David, 98–103, 128, 130–131, 183, 208, 403
Strategic Defense Initiative (SDI), 433–435
Street vendors, 295–297
Stroup, Richard, 240
Struntz, Linda, 73
Subsidies, 24: agricultural, 79–81, 110–111, 116–117, 120–121, 129, 143–144, 167–172; art, 385–387; excesses in, 145–147,

162–163; foreign, 69–70; maritime, 144, 147–149
Sugar, 171, 207–208
Sunflower industry, 176–178
Sunkist, 183–185
Superfund, 237, 238
Supreme Court, U.S.: on abortion, 369, 371–372; Constitutional interpretation by, 342–343; on death penalty, 379–380; discrimination cases, 360–362; on pornography, 376, 378
Supreme Court justices: accountability and, 267–274; life tenure for, 280–282; original intent and, 274–276
Switzer, Barry, 263
Synar, Mike, 341, 342
Synthetic Fuels Corporation, 82, 112, 120
Synthetic fuels projects, 97–98

Taft, Robert, 395
Taft, William, 410
Taiwan, 31–32
Tanzania, 472
Taxes: battle over, 195–196; increases in, 102–103, 111; IRS instructions to explain, 198–200; progressive rate structure of, 112; withholding, 197–198
Taxis, 161
Tebuthiuron (Spike), 384
Television: cable, 221–223; commercials, 27–28; program regulation, 27–28
Tennessee Valley Authority, 181–182, 189
Terrorism, 429–431
Textile industry, 249–250
Thanksgiving, 32–34
Thomas, Franklin, 17
Tobacco advertising, 341–343
Tolchin, Martin, 255
Tolchin, Susan, 255
Totalitarian government, 3–4
Toxic waste, 237–238
Trade. *See* Free trade restrictions
Tramontozzi, Paul, 235
Transportation subsidies, 160–163
Travel restrictions, 29–30
Truman, Harry, 411
Truth-in-Taxing law, 198–200
Tucker, William, 331

Udall, Morris, 241, 242
Umoja Construction Co., 299–300
Unauthorized practice of law, 288–289
United Auto Workers (UAW), 245, 246
United Egg Producers, 85–86
United Nations, 451–455
U.S. Embassies, 458–459

Unruh, Jesse, 45
Urban Development Action Grants, 144, 163

Valencia oranges, 183–185
Value Added Tax (VAT), 238
Values, 8–10
Vandenberg, Arthur, 396
Vendors, street, 295–297
Veterans Administration, 188
Veto, presidential, 134–135, 138
Video games, 22, 23
Vietnam war, 401, 402
Vietnamese refugees, 455–456
Viguerie, Richard, 280
Voluntary Restraint Agreements (VRAs), 247, 248
Von Raab, William, 382
Von Stauffenberg, Claus, 4
Vote, right not to, 59–61

Wallace, George, 43
Wallenberg, Raoul, 8
Wallop, Malcolm, 241
Walsh, Richard, 248
War Powers Resolution, 397
Warner, John W., 390
Warren, Earl, 271, 272, 281
Warsaw Pact, 406, 407, 485–486
Water pollution, 235–237. *See also* Environmental issues
Watkins, Wes, 106
Wattenberg, Ben, 93, 94
Weaver, Paul, 89, 91, 92
Webber, Stephen, 305
Webster, William, 408
Weicker, Lowell, 106, 153
Weidenbaum, Murray, 201
Weinberger, Caspar, 97, 98, 399, 400, 403, 404
Weinstein, Bernard, 218
Welfare programs, 129
Wesslund, Debbie, 341
White House staff, 49–55
Whittaker, Bob, 73
Whitten, Jamie, 106, 153
Wicker, Tom, 284
Wickham, John A., Jr., 437, 441
Wilderness preservation, 239–240
Wilkey, Malcolm, 285
Wilson, Charles, 105
Wilson, T. A., 81, 150
Wilson, Zev, 105
Winans, R. Foster, 263–264
Winpisinger, William, 73, 74
Winston, Cliff, 212

Withholding tax, 197–198
Wolfe, Sidney, 341
Wolpe, Howard, 475
Women: comparable worth and, 365–367;
  discrimination against, 364–365
Woods, Alan, 480
Wooster, Martin Morse, 374
World Bank, 489–492
Wright, Jim, 57, 106, 112–113, 115, 118,
  154, 262
Wrobleski, Ann, 384

Yad VaShem, 7, 8
Yannello, Judith Ann, 339
Yorck, Peter, 4
Yugoslavia, 483–484

Zaelke, Durwood, 278
Zaire, 487–488
Zambia, 479, 480
Zimbabwe, 479
Zimny, Max, 206, 298
Zoning, 322